The Criminal Personality

Volume I: A Profile for Change

by

SAMUEL YOCHELSON, Ph.D., M.D.

and

STANTON E. SAMENOW, Ph.D.

JASON ARONSON INC.
Northvale, New Jersey
London

First softcover edition 1993

Copyright © 1976 Kathryn and John Yochelson

Library of Congress Catalog Number 75-13507

Yochelson, Samuel, 1906-77
      The criminal personality
      Includes bibliographies and index.
      1. Criminal psychology.   I. Samenow, Stanton E., 1941-   joint author.
      II. Title
[DNLM: 1. Criminal psychology. HV6080 Y54c]
HV6080.Y62   364.3
ISBN 1-56821-105-8 (softcover)

Manufactured in the United States of America. Jason Aronson Inc. offers books and cassettes. For information and catalog write to Jason Aronson Inc., 230 Livingston Street, Northvale, New Jersey 07647.

DEDICATED TO THE MEMORY OF

DR. WINFRED OVERHOLSER,
PHYSICIAN

Preface

THIS IS THE FIRST of three volumes entitled *The Criminal Personality*. It presents a detailed description of criminal thinking and action patterns. Our experience in deriving this material is described in the first chapter, entitled "The Reluctant Converts." It describes how we were persuaded by emerging facts to discard sociologic and psychologic theories of causation in favor of a careful probe into the criminal's thinking and action patterns. Basically we could establish no causal connection between the way the criminal thinks and acts and the circumstances of his life. Sociologic and psychologic explanations were abandoned, as well as the mental illness concept, because they stood in the way of an effective process of change. The use of such time-honored concepts has hardly altered the national crime picture.

Volume 2 will present new procedures for achieving change in the criminal in which choice and will (redefined) have been combined with an operational, phenomenologic approach. These procedures have produced gratifying results. Volume 3 will extend our findings and procedures to the drug-using criminal.

Criticism of concepts should be directed at the senior author. An indispensable contribution has been made by the junior author without whose grasp, ideas, dedication, and hard work these publications would not have been possible.

In this volume, the reader will search for social solutions. In our desire to present only the facts, we have carefully avoided social advocacy of any type. We are well aware that some readers who have biases and have made prejudgments will see these facts as confirming their own views. Those with other points of view will criticize the work as omitting considerations that they regard as crucial. Still others will wedge the facts presented into diverse preexisting prejudices. We appeal to the reader to approach these findings with an open mind and to grasp the content firmly before reaching his conclusions.

vii

Unless the reader understands how the term *criminal* is used in this volume, he is likely to misinterpret a great deal of the material presented. Currently, the trend in society is to avoid using the word "criminal." Juvenile delinquents are rarely called criminals. Adults arrested for white-collar crimes are often not viewed as criminals. Drug-users, though they break the law, are not regarded as criminals in most cases. Most people do not consider a person a criminal unless he has been convicted of a crime. In this volume, we use the term criminal far more broadly than this as we describe patterns of thought and action, the emphasis being upon the former. The patterns described in Chapters 4 through 7 all *ultimately* contribute to the final product—criminal acts by the hardcore people with whom we work. The reader will observe that some of the thinking patterns described here and called "criminal" are shared by responsible people. However, while in the criminal they eventuate in crime, they do not have that outcome in the responsible person (although they may contribute to his irresponsibility). For example, as we point out, the consequences of a lie told by a criminal and of a lie told by a noncriminal are very different. The same is true of anger, perfectionism, and all the other patterns described.

All the thinking patterns in the criminal included in this volume *must* be altered in the change process. Some of these same patterns in the noncriminal do not require such attention. Furthermore, in the process of change, by applying the term *"criminal* thinking patterns," we reinforce the fact that the man with whom we are working is indeed a criminal. This is essential because, no matter how many crimes he has committed, the criminal regards himself as a good person. We hope that as the reader becomes familiar with the material, he will better understand our use of the term criminal. The issue of "Who is a criminal?" is treated more extensively in the introduction to Chapter 4.

We should like to extend our appreciation to Thomas Gosselin for his collation of materials, to Norman Grossblatt for editing the entire manuscript, and to Sylvia Samenow for her helpful suggestions. We also thank Rhonda Atchinson and Doretha Vaughan, our typists.

CONTENTS

THE CRIMINAL PERSONALITY

Chapter 1

The Reluctant Converts

THIS CHAPTER IS ADDRESSED largely to issues of conceptual and procedural validity. Our work eludes the precise evaluation that is characteristic of the natural sciences and some of the social sciences, in which findings lend themselves to statistical treatment. Replication poses further problems, in that a given treatment cannot be administered to a subject more than once, and only time can reveal whether other investigators can use our procedures effectively and with comparable results. We describe here how we tried various approaches, discarded what failed to work, and developed and refined new concepts and techniques. Our end product is a systematic process that, under specified conditions, can achieve the single objective of helping a criminal to change himself into a totally responsible and constructive person.

The title of this chapter may seem to refer to criminals. It does not. We, the investigators, were reluctant to give up concepts and theories that had worked for us in treating noncriminals. We knew that psychotherapeutic work was fraught with additional difficulties when one worked with criminals, psychopaths, antisocial personalities, or whatever one wanted to call them. In fact, like many practitioners, we had elected to stay away from this particular group for the most part and to work with patients who wanted help and whom we thought we could help. When we decided to become involved with forensic psychiatric patients, we did not imagine that we would eventually have to discard all that we had practiced with noncriminals. If the criminals were reluctant to change (and they were), we too were reluctant to change. Nevertheless, we did.

When the senior investigator began this project in 1961, he realized that he knew very little about the criminal mind. From his reading and general knowledge, he knew that criminals were extremely refractory to current corrective and therapeutic measures and that the old approaches were not working. He had been overextended in private practice, with little time for the writing and reflection he desired. He wanted to work in a field of

1

investigation in which he might contribute something of importance to society. He viewed work in forensic psychiatry as an opportunity to "search," rather than "re-search." At the age of fifty-five, he gave up private practice for an opportunity to immerse himself completely in a "search" in a field that was new to him and that others had been unable to conquer.

In private practice, he had not worked with criminals—indeed, did not accept anyone who was obviously psychopathic for treatment. However, some of his patients, although basically neurotic, had psychopathic characteristics that were expressed in antisocial activity. At first, these patients were not regarded as psychopathic; rather, the psychopathic characteristics were viewed as symptomatic of neurotic conflict. As treatment went on and these patients failed to establish a positive transference, some of the psychopathic qualities became more evident; the therapeutic enterprise faltered; and either the patients quit treatment or there was mutual belief that further progress was so unlikely as to make termination of treatment the best course. In addition to this experience, the investigator assisted in making legal determinations of insanity for the courts of New York State operating under the M'Naghten rule. He spent six to ten hours with each of some twenty criminals. It was not very difficult to make a determination relative to the M'Naghten rule, because it was a matter only of whether the defendant knew the difference between right and wrong; great insight into the dynamics of his personality was not required. But the investigator began to understand that he was dealing with people very different from those whom he treated in a conventional office practice. He did not understand the criminals' patterns of thinking and acting, but he adopted a compassionate view that these people were the way they were because of deep-seated psychologic problems.

Having decided to leave private work and to dedicate himself to a new enterprise, the investigator was faced with the question of where to conduct his study. At the time, Saint Elizabeths Hospital in Washington, D. C., appeared ideal. In Washington, under the Durham rule, crime could be considered a product of mental illness. The investigator believed that he could work better in an institution in which criminals were treated therapeutically, rather than punitively. At Saint Elizabeths, patients would be readily accessible over long periods. In addition, this federal facility offered an opportunity for a multidisciplinary approach, especially with its access to laboratories, which most prisons could not offer. Furthermore, an understanding was worked out whereby the investigator would have no administrative authority over, or responsibility for, participants in his research, nor would the hospital ask him to testify in court. And Saint Elizabeths guaranteed him privileged communication, not only with respect to outsiders, but also within the hospital. No one would be privy to what happened within the investigator's office—not even members of the staff, doctors, or administrators.

From here on, the pronoun "we" is used, both as the editorial "we" and to refer to the project staff, inasmuch as both authors have been using the techniques in question as agents of change with the criminal. The junior author had known Dr. Yochelson for several years and had accepted his suggestions for a doctoral dissertation on the college dropout. The requirement for that dissertation was that Dr. Samenow approach the dropouts with the assumption that they were having problems that could be explained in conventional psychoanalytic and sociologic terms. Using procedures then being developed in Dr. Yochelson's work, the junior author obtained material that turned out to be more cogent from a descriptive point of view than that originally sought and obtained. This had a great impact on him. Despite being trained in an analytically oriented clinical psychology department and having had his own four-and-a-half year analysis, Dr. Samenow was shocked into the recognition that he would accomplish little by using conventional techniques in working with adolescent youths with behavior disorders. Indeed, at most he would achieve the kinds of unsatisfactory results that others around him (more seasoned than he) were obtaining. With initial reluctance, Dr. Samenow abandoned working with adolescents to join Dr. Yochelson. After reviewing nine years of Dr. Yochelson's work and being given an opportunity to work with criminals and to learn more about their thinking processes, Dr. Samenow experienced his conversion; later events confirmed its wisdom.

In our work with criminals, we were not restricted to those at Saint Elizabeths. But at the beginning, we selected participants who were immediately available—Saint Elizabeths patients who had been found "not guilty by reason of insanity" (NGBRI). To preclude involvement in adversary proceedings, which might have led subjects to withhold information, we accepted patients only after evaluation of their mental state. We did not want to be perceived as having anything to do with the evaluation process that would determine a man's fate (e.g., the kind and duration of a subject's confinement), because to be viewed as playing a role in such a determination would undoubtedly affect what an individual would tell us.

Of the sixteen criminals we approached initially, thirteen decided to accept our invitation to participate in a research and treatment effort. When the program became better known, more people asked to join than we could accommodate. We have broadened the base of participants to include patients being evaluated for determination of their mental condition at the time of a crime, as well as nonhospital subjects. The latter group has included criminals on parole and probation and people on the street who are active in crime but have not been arrested. In addition, we have interviewed adolescents, including youngsters performing poorly in school, college dropouts, and youths brought to community clinics because of anti-social behavior. We have interviewed family members, girlfriends, employers, and other people important in the lives of "our" criminals. And we have talked with people who have dealt with criminals in hospitals, correctional institutions, the military, and the community.

Our criminal patients have come from a wide range of backgrounds, with respect to socioeconomic status, religious preference, and domestic stability. Our subjects were of average intelligence, as determined by prior testing. We have worked with more blacks than whites, as would be expected in a city the majority of whose population is black. The age span of our group has been fifteen to fifty-five. We have worked with drug users and nonusers.

We began our work with the attitude that it was to be an open, diligent search for facts. We encountered things that we did not understand at the time, but we kept minutely detailed notes, which were a continuing source of methodologic change. We were not interested in diagnostic labels, having believed for years that such labels concealed more than they revealed. Our emphasis was to be on patients' underlying motivational factors that led to their committing crimes. We were actively interested in sociologic factors, as well as psychologic. In addition to the criminals' native habitat, we studied the milieu of Saint Elizabeths Hospital, their temporary habitat, to try to understand the relation between man and institution. Our major emphasis, however, was on the psychologic factors behind crime. We wanted to know what differentiated mentally ill criminals from nonmentally ill criminals and each of these from other segments of the psychiatric population.

Having medical facilities and consultants from Saint Elizabeths and other institutions at our disposal, we conducted a number of physical studies. Dr. William Sheldon, an authority in constitutional medicine well known for his "somatotyping," served as a consultant and analyzed constitutional factors (body structure) as they related to criminal behavior. With the assistance of Dr. Avery Sandberg of Roswell Park Memorial Institute in Buffalo, slides of chromosomes cultured from lymphocytes were examined. There were studies of fingerprints, palmprints, blood chemistry, steroid chemistry, and electroencephalograms. All these efforts were directed toward understanding the makeup of criminals and developing techniques for curing the mental illness that produced crime.* As it turned out, the results of these studies were either inconclusive or negative and are not presented in this work, although they may appear later in article form.

---

* We also used sodium amytal and later Valium with criminals who claimed amnesia, a procedure that we later realized was unnecessary.

EARLY WORK WITH INDIVIDUAL PATIENTS

HISTORY-TAKING

Our investigation proceeded on a one-to-one basis. To a criminal, seeing a doctor meant that he would get therapy. Our initial approach was to present an overview of our research program and to inform him that, in return for his participation, he would receive psychotherapeutic treatment in five sessions per week for approximately twenty weeks.

Our primary objective was a comprehensive understanding of the criminal's mind. We attempted first to get a detailed developmental history, to identify underlying unconscious motivating factors, which would enable us to help him. We tended to focus on the crime for which the man had been arrested. We expected to see three distinct personality profiles much like three disease syndromes, for sex, assault, and property crimes. Our view was that one kind of crime had little or no relation to another; we saw white-collar crimes as totally different from the crude criminality of mugging or rape. An exhaustive history was taken daily focusing on nine categories:

1. The immediate environment
2. The family—a study of each member as seen through the criminal's eyes
3. School patterns, grade by grade
4. Job patterns, including military service
5. Social patterns
6. Sex and marriage
7. Religious life
8. Physical health
9. Antisocial patterns, including experience in confinement

We guaranteed all participants privileged communication and informed them that we would have no administrative responsibility and thus would not be in a position to assist or impede their release. We also told them that any publications resulting from our research would conceal their identity.

We launched our study with no information about the participants, except which crimes they had been charged with. We wanted to begin afresh and avoid preconceptions. Accordingly, we informed the patients that we were not going to read their hospital records or discuss their cases with the hospital administrative staff. Typed interview notes were made available to each patient, and he had an opportunity to make additions or corrections if he so desired. In fact, we often dictated our notes in the subject's presence. In short, we embarked on the project with openness and good faith. We expected that operating this way and guaranteeing privileged communication would improve our chances of getting accurate histories and eliminate the patients' need to falsify and play games. In retrospect, it became clear that our procedures were critical in determining how much the patients would tell us. As they realized that we would not "snitch" or inform and that we were dedicated to learning and helping, they revealed more. As a consequence, what emerged was a great deal of material about crimes in addition to those with which the men were charged. For example, the child molester was also a gunman and the thief a rapist. We noted this, but did not pay special attention to it. We were not thinking of these men as hardened criminals, but as mentally ill patients.

We began our inquiry with the crimes with which the men were charged. The first six men we worked with had been charged with serious crimes and were admitted to Saint Elizabeths as NGBRI. Their crimes included homicide, rape, child molestation, and numerous other acts, violent and nonviolent. When we saw them, they had advanced to minimum security status and could come to our office, which was located in a separate building. We were viewing the material in psychodynamic (analytic) terms and were planning to use analytic procedures. However, not all cases were amenable to analytic therapeutic techniques. A few of the patients did use the couch, gave their free associations, and recalled dreams for analysis. Early memories were vivid and relatively easy to elicit from these men. However, we did not attempt to force square pegs into round holes. If a patient did not seem responsive to deep probing, we restricted ourselves to helping him cope better with present problems. In such a situation, we did not probe into intrapsychic conflicts by analytic procedures. Instead, we used interpretation derived from analytic theory to point out to the patient some aspects of his own psychology.

In the case of every patient, as major issues became delineated, a rather puzzling and somewhat frustrating phenomenon began to occur. The material seemed to "dry up," and the sessions grew less and less productive. The men grew impatient and pressed us as to how long therapy would take. They were applying for conditional release, and, as we were to find out, being released took precedence over everything else, although some thought they were truly being helped with lifelong problems. As their interest in our program dropped off, we concluded this phase of our work with these men. Only then did we decide to check other sources to find out all we could; we read their hospital charts and requested records from schools, legal agencies, and from others who had had contact with them.

We decided to continue our efforts and enlisted new participants on the same basis as before. With the experience of the first group behind us, we were in a position to be more self-critical. For example, we were dissatisfied with some of the stereotyped responses in which forensic patients constantly blamed others for their lot in life. So we probed more deeply and asked harder questions. With a change in approach, there was a change in the material obtained. For example, we learned that most of the men had hard-working, caring parents, who did their best to cope with troublemaking children. Some of our causal assumptions were being shaken a bit. We faithfully recorded everything, but our orientation remained: to get to the crime's "roots," which lay in familial and social factors.

PSYCHOANALYTIC TREATMENT TECHNIQUES

Surprisingly, some criminals recalled early events very readily. A few had rehearsed the material well and had used it with other therapists; others had not been treated analytically, but had amazingly rapid access to pertinent material. We used the couch to facilitate the recovery of memories and to lessen inhibitions in reporting. In addition to classic free association, we used image association. An image might be suggested by us as a starting point to set the scene for the criminal's elaboration. We would then ask for a description of the flow of images and accompanying feelings. Here is an excerpt from an imagery session with C,* a rapist:

> Today, we re-created the imagery of the last rape effort. He described seeing a woman on a bus, wearing a sheer blouse. He could see through the slip and bra that she was an ample-breasted woman, about 40. He described how he followed her to her second-floor room in a particular apartment. The images then went to a later night, when he successfully entered. His fantasies involved three significant items: fellatio on him, his striking her, and her striking him. In the fantasy, there was a shifting from one to the other. He described how he had a cold, determined feeling as he quietly climbed into the window of the living room and eventually entered the room of the woman, who was asleep. He pulled the gown up her thighs, getting about three-fourths of the way on one side when, still asleep, she turned over and he could get no further. This gave us our first image association of sucking her vagina. Then returning to reality: with the cover off her, he played with her breast through a not very sheer nightgown; he could not see the breast or the prominence of the nipple. But the image association carried us to the need to caress and kiss this structure. It was a need to have her accept the kissing and caressing. The image quickly gave way to a beating of this breast with hate. Associated with the hitting of the breast and the pure hate was a crying and saying "No, no," the meaning of the words not too clear, but implying some resistance.

> This gave rise to images of mother, with ample breasts, sitting on a chair, fully dressed. The associations that went along with this dealt

---

* Throughout this volume, criminals cited in examples will be identified simply as "C."

with a desire to put his head on her breast or have some other kind of contact. But this occurred in a situation in which she had been criticizing or berating him and in which he could not do what he wanted to do. The association between condemnation and the desire for this kind of activity was very clear. His mother is an extraordinarily young-looking person for her age, even now at 44, and she looks younger than this woman did at 40.

The return to reality came when the woman woke up. She yelled and then there was fear and anger—fear of detection and anger at her yelling—whereupon he clamped his hand over her mouth and warned her not to shout, and she agreed. From here on, she complied. Very promptly, he unzipped his pants and put his penis into her mouth. The image association at this point was that this was his mother sucking his penis and he was in the role of a little boy. The image was distant and small, but he had trouble getting rid of it. It stuck there, and with it came some kind of realization of the abnormality of the process—an abnormality that he did not quite carry over into the abnormality of the rape effort on this 40-year-old woman that he wanted to have do the same thing to him, and who happened to be the mother of somebody.

From such sessions, we were able to get into C's sexual desires toward his mother, her rejection of these desires, and his anger and hatred, which generalized to all women. Over and over, there was a connection of all other women with mother. We perceived C as a boy who had been angry and hurt by his mother's sexual restrictiveness. As a man, C continued to view himself as a boy with a small penis and expected to be rejected by other women as inadequate. He had to demonstrate that he was a man, not a little boy with an inferior penis. We viewed the rape effort as an attempt to prove that. In addition, by hurting a woman, he was unconsciously getting back at his restricting and rejecting mother. Finally, he would punish himself by being caught and thereby expiate his guilt over both his forbidden desires toward mother and his anger.

During our therapeutic work with C, we realized that he did not confine his antisocial activities to rape. He had also done much stealing and was a chronic liar. We believed that the stealing was tied to the same basic problem: his perceived rejection by mother. Stealing represented an attempt to regain love lost. Mother had been "forbidden," and now he turned to another forbidden source.

We thought C was improving as his rape thinking declined. This occurred, we believed, because he was gaining insight into the fact that the world was not as prohibitive as he had experienced it early in life. We turned our attention to other problems. His sexual sadism seemed to have been dealt with successfully, but he still had poor interpersonal relations. After 8 months of bringing out material about mother and linking it to the "rape problem," we focused on particular personality traits, such as C's egocentricity, inferiority feelings, and overscrupulousness. C then had less material to offer and requested a reduction from five sessions per week to one. At this time, he seemed not to be making much use of the material covered:

> The patient uses psychiatric explanation as an excuse to justify past behavior and a way of arousing agreement with him that he does not have any control over what he does. We have in him a problem in which he does not effectively utilize the information he obtained. Thus, he falls back on his inability to feel and think, and then falls back on the fact that standards set for him when he was a child were too severe. This is a misappropriation of the therapeutic procedure. When he is asked what he has gained from the session, he acts like a mental defective.

As the material "dried up" and C wanted to see us less, we learned that he had been involved for weeks in criminal activity, mostly petty. He had exposed his criminal thinking to us, but he had not decided to alter it and cease his criminal activity. A few months later, after severing his connection with us, C was again arrested for rape.

Our failure was obvious: C had treated our program as he had treated everyone else; he had played along with us, appearing to cooperate, but concealing what he thought would put him in an unfavorable light. Despite privileged communication, C concealed a great deal because he was afraid that, if it emerged, his conditional release would be imperiled. Again we saw that release was foremost, not change. This experience was valuable to us. We had penetrated to the "roots" of the problem, as we viewed it. But C's insight into the past clearly did not alter the criminal pattern at all. *In fact, insight had given him more material to excuse his behavior*. We believed that we had erred in not giving sufficient attention to the development of other patterns that were not directly related to the crime itself.

We had used analytic techniques with C, who was a white middle-class young adult. But our patient group included blacks and whites, well-to-do and poor, young and old, and we also used analytic techniques with another criminal, a black grade-school dropout. C sought treatment for child molesting, which was only one of a series of numerous arrestable activities, but the one that had resulted in some qualms of conscience on his part. We thought that resolving this problem might contribute to uncovering aspects of his personality development that were productive of other types of crimes. As C lay on the couch, we got the standard material—castration anxiety, a fear of and repulsion toward the adult vagina, and so forth. He had never experienced sexual satisfaction with an adult because he was afraid that he would not live up to an adult's expectations. In every adult sexual experience, he was certain he would fail, and he always wanted to hide his nude body, especially his penis. He feared that he was physically insufficient and that a woman would be dissatisfied and reject him. In this mental state, he often experienced premature ejaculation. But C had no such problem when his partner was a child. He regarded a child as pure and undefiled. With such a person, he was in control and did not fear being rejected. As we probed into C's past, we elicited feelings of unworthiness that he experienced with his mother, who constantly told him he was a bad boy. Throughout his life, feelings of inadequacy and inferiority persisted. Mother was the first and most important woman in his life whom he could not satisfy. From this, we went into his anger toward inviolable figures—i.e., first mother and then young girls, whom he would molest in a displacement of a conflict over mother. He wanted from young girls what he never got from his mother: uncritical acceptance. A nine-year-old girl was a "pure" figure who would not be critical of his sexual performance, because she herself was not experienced. This would give him something of a buildup.

The outcome of treatment was that C did stop the child molesting.* But he was already predisposed to do this, and it turned out to be well within his control. Nevertheless, the patient persisted in crime, committing armed robbery, homosexual prostitution, rape, and other acts of violence. Thus, the insight gained had had no effect on other criminal patterns, and we saw again that getting to the early "roots" is insufficient for change. In fact, it could be counterproductive; some of the men used what occurred in their early lives to justify present conduct. They were "good patients," in that we fairly easily uncovered incestuous desires, castration anxiety, feelings of inferiority, and so forth. But we were having little, if any, impact on the way they were functioning in their daily living.

NONANALYTIC TREATMENT TECHNIQUES

Several patients did not seem suited for the analytic process. One of these was declared NGBRI in the homicide of his child. We saw him as having the intelligence and psychiatric sophistication both to contribute to our program and to profit personally by it.

We probed into the homicide, about which C claimed amnesia. He maintained that his girlfriend, the mother of the child, rejected him, that he took the child home, and that he remembered nothing thereafter. C had been

---

* We attributed the elimination of child molestation to the insight the patient gained via psychoanalytic techniques. Later work with this man revealed that "insight" was not responsible for the success, but rather the fact that he applied choice, will, and deterrence to a pattern that offended him.

particularly fond of the child; in fact, he was closer to her than anyone else. He stated that he did not recall anything that happened until he found himself in restraints at a hospital. Actually, he had stabbed his daughter with a knife, thrown her out of a window, and jumped out the window after her. We had C lie on the couch to try to reconstruct what had occurred. In addition, we used sodium amytal. He was then able to remember everything except the knife incision. We worked with C for about eight months trying to piece together the crime and the contributing psychologic factors.

C was not responsive to the kind of probing we were doing. Consequently, we focused on specific problems of daily living, in addition to examining the details of the crime. He spoke of how people were trying to injure him and how they were out to get him. He carried a gun to deal with these threats. We believed that this man had a paranoid psychosis. He progressed to the point where, although the paranoid thinking continued, he began to regard it as something that could get him into trouble if he acted on it precipitously. C also drank excessively in order to be more effective sexually and to relieve headaches, gastrointestinal distress, and other symptoms. As C drew near conditional release, the management of his drinking and the regulation of his "abnormal thoughts" were the focuses of our therapeutic efforts.

It was not until several years later that we got a completely different view of C. In 1966, when we saw him once again, we had learned a great deal about the criminal mind. What we had regarded as a "paranoid condition" was not that at all. This man had been a chronic violator and thus was suspicious of others for good reason. People were in fact in pursuit of him, because he had committed many crimes. His being on guard was realistic. There was a time when we saw C in a transitory psychotic state. At that time, however, he was not at all interested in criminal activity. Rather, he was in touch with God and harmless to society. In our focus on paranoid ideation, drinking, and reconstruction of a crime, we had failed to see the many criminal patterns of thought and action that had been operative during all his life.

CRIMINALS IN A GROUP

During our history-taking, we found that the criminals spent much time complaining angrily about conditions in the hospital. We tried to push this aside at the time, on the grounds that the intensity of this dissatisfaction was simply an expression of their basic problem of adjustment. However, we could not truly disregard it, because their incessant discontent interfered with history-taking and constituted a barrier to treatment. Therefore, we decided to form a group of twelve men (who were being treated individually) with the purpose of providing an outlet for "gripes" that were impeding the individual treatment. We made their reactions to the hospital and to each other the objects of study. A four-hour session was held once a week for twelve weeks. Each session was devoted to a different topic: nurses, attendants, doctors, the clergy, each of the hospital programs. For example, a meeting began this way:

> "What are the group's feelings about nurses and attendants? I don't know whether you want to take this as a combined category, or would you like to take it separately? Do you have feelings on this matter?"

Topics ranged over nearly every aspect of the hospital affecting the care of these patients, from the discussion of their legal status under the Durham rule to an evaluation of particular programs and personnel. Names were kept out, so that issues would be the focus.

During the interchange about the implementation of the Durham rule and its meaning to criminals, some of these men stated that they were not "sick" and that their criminal acts were calculated and deliberate. It turned out that eleven of the twelve group members had schemed and feigned mental illness to get into the hospital and avoid being found guilty. As soon as they were admitted to Saint Elizabeths, they disliked the idea of being sentenced indefinitely to a place they regarded as a prison and began scheming to get out.

> "I succeeded in getting rid of a 30-year prison term. I gave no thought at all to the indefinite feature of the Durham decision that could keep me here indefinitely until they felt that I was ready to leave. I gave no thought to that when I first arrived. Then I hated the indefinite feature of it. I felt that if I had to continue on the same basis and the position that I've been in the first 22 months, that I would lay very carefully a plan to elope and stay away from the hospital."

Several sessions were devoted to the "hospital or prison" theme. The point of view expressed was that Saint Elizabeths Hospital functions as both, depending on the situation.

In short, complaints were made whenever a criminal did not have his wishes satisfied. Almost never was there any consideration of the staff's point of view. Our position was that the poor living conditions, punitive policies, and caliber of the staff interfered with change, rather than promoting it. We did not totally subscribe to a criminal's version—that he was a victim of his environment and that others were wholly to blame for his difficulties. We inquired as to his role in creating the problems about which he complained. However, we did believe that locking a patient up for an infraction had a "corrosive effect" on treatment. We thought that some administrative attitudes and policies were inciting the patients to violate. We believed that the focus should be on exploration of the reasons behind violations and that understanding, rather than punishment, was necessary to change ideas and feelings.

Because these men realized that we sympathized with some of their grievances, they saw us as being basically "on their side." If one were to read our notes from this period, he would see a basis for that perception:

> "The boys, who really did nothing seriously wrong, were pretty much treated with suspicion and skepticism. To Doctor R's mind, these boys, though found NGBRI, were still prisoners. This was an obviously incorrect statement, but I assume that he meant that they were "criminals." So they had been branded."

We did not know it, but these "boys" who had done "nothing seriously wrong" were still violating both inside and outside the hospital. We did not consider them "criminals," and we were critical of those who did.

We were perceived by the patients as permissive. They viewed Behavioral Studies, where the group met, as a "freedom house," in the sense of a place of understanding, with less restraint and surveillance. The patients regarded us as sincere, hardworking, truthful, and friendly. In fact, they favorably contrasted our dedication with that of other staff members at Saint Elizabeths of whom they were sharply critical. They viewed our program as being separate from the hospital; one of them stated that it was so different that it could as well be "on the moon." They had been accustomed to doctors' being nearly inaccessible, and sometimes had gone for weeks or even months at a time without having any doctor talk to them. Our program was unlike anything else they had been offered at Saint Elizabeths. They credited the group with giving them insight, closeness, and concern for other people. The man quoted above as complaining about the "indefinite feature" of the Durham rule changed his tune, allegedly owing to the impact of the therapy.

> "My feelings now since the twentieth of March, when I became associated with this group, is that the indefinite feature is the only logical thing I can expect, because no doctor can say that on the thirty-first of December you will be well enough to leave. This is an impossibility. I may regress. I may improve so fast that I'll be released on June 30. The indefinite feature here I feel is for my own good."

This was a complete turnabout from his previous statement. We believed that these patients were sincere and that they were expressing positive attitudes toward the group largely because of our stance toward them. We accepted the forensic patients as human beings and did not view them as "criminals." We did not criticize them for their past, but put our trust in them for the present and were concerned about their future.

In addition to the group meeting, each of these patients was receiving individual treatment either from us or from two capable psychiatric residents whom we supervised. We believed that the patients were improving as a result of insight from an intensive, high-quality treatment effort. Our criterion of improvement was that they did not appear to be "acting out illegally." In fact, they were doing well enough to have bright prospects for release. We were so pleased with their apparent sincerity and the changes that were occurring that we contacted the Big Brothers organization to sponsor these men on the outside. However, people in the organization were skeptical and declined. Perhaps they saw something in our "changing men" that we did not.

Because the patients perceived us as somewhat sympathetic to their needs, they asked us to do things for them. Despite our having said that we would take no administrative role, they pressured us to intercede for special privileges. For example, they all wanted to be on one ward isolated from those who were not of the "Yochelson group." When they did not get what they wanted, they had one additional complaint against their ward doctors.

It was not long before we began to see that what was ostensibly a therapy group was really operating as a gang. The men were functioning in the hospital much as they had in society, limited only by some institutional restraints and not always by these. Some had known each other from early in their hospitalization; when they were all in the group, they became a special group of "Yochelson people." Having developed this relationship, they began operating in crime together. Several collaborated in an elaborate check-writing scheme. Some cooperated in stealing and fencing the proceeds. The group banded together to avoid entanglements with the administration. They would take care of a drunk member, end fighting, help each other with money, and generally cover up for one another. They withheld information, because they did not want to "snitch" or inform on each other. Their loyalty to the group and to us was expressed in frankly criminal terms. They thought that we and our program were to be protected at any cost. This meant that, if they found that anyone was causing us difficulty, they would avenge the wrong. For example, they were eager to know who dented one of our car fenders, so that they could pay him back. The group pressure to help individual members and the investigator was strong. But there was never a thought about helping one another avoid criminal behavior. Their version of "helping" was to bail one another out of trouble by conning, intimidation, violation, and cover stories. Criminality was viewed as "wrong" only if it entailed too much risk. When these men were held accountable for violations, they would offer as justification the material from our group meetings about the shortcomings of the hospital. During this period, our relationship with many members of the hospital staff became strained. The ward and administrative personnel were unhappy about our adherence to privileged communication. They resented our singling out some men for special treatment and then not letting the staff know what we were doing. The claim of "special treatment" was accurate, to the extent that our patients were receiving a lot of attention compared with most forensic patients, who received no individual therapy. The hospital staff accused us of having pets for whom we were seeking special privileges. Some thought we were harboring criminals and perhaps were even criminals ourselves. These charges were based on a belief of some that we knew about the violations of our group members but were covering up for them. In fact, we did not know of the offenses being committed. Contempt for us rose when some staff members saw that we who were reputed to be so knowledgeable had been fooled. They watched criminals return to the ward from their meetings with us, praise our work, but continue to violate.

We finally recognized that our individual and group therapies were not instrumental in achieving change. In our individual work, our objective had been to get to the "root" of problems. We probed parental attitudes, sibling rivalries, rebellion against authority, and environmental influences. In the group work, we had tried to help patients deal effectively with the institution. We had failed in both. As new material emerged, we noted it, but it took time to conceptualize what we were learning and to make use of it. For example, criminals said that they had schemed to get into the hospital to beat a charge. They also contended that they knew their crimes were "wrong" from society's standpoint, but at the time they committed the crimes, the crimes were "right" in their own minds. None of this material made much sensse to us as we heard it. We regarded these men as mentally ill patients, not "criminals." We perceived their lying, scheming, and other patterns as symptoms of an underlying mental condition for which they needed therapy. We recognized that procedures that we had used successfully with noncriminals were not effective with the forensic group. Our patients were interested primarily in getting out, rather than in change. In fact, there was nothing even approaching a commitment to change. We had to find a new way.

NINETY-DAY MEN

We decided to turn our attention to people who had been arrested and were awaiting psychiatric evaluation. We wanted to see whether we could elicit from those awaiting adjudication the same type of material that had been gathered from the group judged NGBRI. Five days a week for three months, we interviewed individually thirteen criminals sent to the hospital by the courts for a ninety-day period of observation and evaluation. Participation in our study was voluntary; only one man declined our invitation. The men were told that this was a research investigation into their backgrounds, their mental makeup, and their problems. We had no role in deciding their status with the courts. We guaranteed privileged communication, informing them that their records would be kept under lock and key in a different building. We said that, on their request, we would release the material to them or their attorneys. The participants were told that what they might get out of this was a better understanding of themselves.

Our reputation for not informing was spreading. Because at that time no staff doctor was permitted to interview forensic patients for evaluation until the last month of their three-month stay, the men welcomed the attention of someone interested. Our many hours of interviews with them were in stark contrast to what they experienced as neglect or indifference by young, uninformed residents. These conditions were conducive to a criminal's revealing to us a tremendous amount of material that would have been incriminating without privileged communication. Because they disclosed so much so freely, the thought of having us testify in their behalf never arose. As we began, we did not look at any information in their personal files. For the record, we simply placed in their hospital charts the following statement of our purpose:

> "I began a series of interviews with [C] during his 90-day commitment for determination of competency and criminal responsibility. It is my intention to interview him an hour each day, five days a week for the purpose of deriving material relevant to our research program. We are not interested in the matter of diagnosis, rather the dynamics of the criminal pattern."

As we began this series of meetings with the ninety-day men, we had had twenty months of experience in interviewing forensic patients, and thus we were approaching them with what we thought was considerably more knowledge. It should be noted that we continued to treat NGBRI patients individually and in groups.

Slowly, we began to modify our view that criminals were products of early deprivation, whether emotional or socioeconomic. In the light of the data we were gathering, it was increasingly difficult to adhere to this point of view. We were finding the same patterns among ghetto-raised blacks and suburb-raised whites. White or black, rich or poor, college graduate or grade-school dropout—none of these variables seemed to be causal. Not only did we have men from a number of different environments, but we learned that even within a given family there could be two children whose paths in life were totally different.

In each facet of life, we were focusing increasingly on what the subject did, rather than on what he claimed was done to him. When a criminal* blamed school for his failure, we asked him about his study habits and attitudes.

> Education did not mean anything to C. It wouldn't guarantee him money, which was the important thing. There was no thinking along the lines of education's being useful for professions. And in an interesting way, he tried to put the blame on factors outside himself. There was the line, "My family didn't help me in my lessons." Actually, C did not want any help and was making no efforts of his own. As a matter of fact, he was much brighter than his brother David, who was rather slow, but David was a hard worker and was persistent.

Basically, school had nothing of interest to offer these people. School did not reject them; rather, they rejected school. The same was true of jobs. Work, like school, was for "suckers." Unless it offered a man a buildup in some way or gave him an aura of responsibility, he saw no purpose in work.

Sometimes, they blamed their friends for being bad influences on them. But in case after case, these men, as youngsters, had sought out others who shared their desire to do the forbidden. They were not "enticed" into crime, but rather looked for what they wanted. In fact, even as young children, these people had wandered blocks from home to seek out others who wanted "action."

We became more and more skeptical of the self-serving stories in which a criminal justified what he did, usually by casting blame on others. Now we sought to establish how these people dealt with life, whatever the circumstances. We were interested in the conditions of their lives, but more interested in how they met those conditions. To be sure, we had not abandoned our orientation of looking for roots and causes. As early experiences emerged, whether oedipal or anything else, we noted them. However, we were now more interested in eliciting new information. Chapter 3, on the criminal's way of life, will present the bulk of that new information.

During our interviews, we discovered an extensive pattern of criminal activity to be characteristic of these men. Antisocial activity began when they were very young, some as early as the age of four. As we pursued sex,

---

* Although we are using the term "criminal" here to refer to these men, we were not designating them as such at the time. Actually, because the 90-day men had not been found NGBRI, they were not yet "patients," and so cannot be referred to in this way.

property, and assault violations, we uncovered a great deal of material that these men had never revealed to anyone. Each participant in the study had committed literally thousands of crimes, but had been apprehended very few times. From very early in life, the patterns grew and grew.

> C was involved in just about everything from an early age. The stealing pattern began at 4, when he took toys that weren't his, and then he began taking nickels and dimes from his grandmother's purse. When he was 8, the breaking and entering began. This continued for some time, with stealing money and major items, such as cameras, jewelry, radios, and so forth. From this time on, he was breaking into automobiles. Around age 8, he decided to hang another youngster by putting a noose around his neck. He threw the end of the noose over a stick and kicked the can out from under the child, but the stick broke and the child fell to the ground. About 9 years of age, C was becoming pretty convinced that crime was the best way of life. At age 11, he organized and headed a protection racket with 9 other boys. They managed to get 450 students in the school to contribute a dollar a week. At age 12, he was fencing stolen goods. Also at about this time, he became a member of a gang and soon became one of its leaders. At ages 16 and 17, he was very much involved in the gang fighting and had his own gun. C was a war council chief, directing other members of the gang in their fights with zip guns, chains, and knives.

All this occurred before the age of eighteen. A history of theft, assault, and sexual violation was elicited in almost every case. (All that was missing here was the sexual material, which C practically refused to allow us to pursue.) Almost without exception, the participants in our study either were involved in sexual activity very early or had a great deal of sexual thinking.

Our experience in eliciting this material ran the gamut from concealment to florid exaggeration by the criminals. At first, some perceived us as government agents sent to acquire information. Because we used a room in the maximum security building for interviewing, they suspected that we might have some connection with the hospital administration, which could imperil their status. Thus, there was considerable lying by omission. Then, when they revealed information later, they attributed the earlier failure to disclose to poor memory. In some cases, we had the opposite problem. Some would exaggerate what they did to build themselves up and found it exciting to describe their criminal activities in minute detail. Because they wanted to be adjudged NGBRI, the more sordid or bizarre they could make a crime sound, the greater the likelihood, they thought, that others would view them as insane.

As they got to know us better and as we understood more about them, we were able to overcome some of these obstacles. Word began to get around that we could be trusted, that we were not part of the administration. We were spending tremendous amounts of time and energy with these people, attempting to be thorough and detailed. We were straightforward, letting the patients know that we knew they were chronic violators. The fact that we were beginning to tell them some things about themselves, rather than ask them open-ended questions, helped reduce the lying. Word started to be passed along: "You can't con Dr. Yochelson." Of course, this was not true—we could be conned. But our reputation for integrity and knowledge helped eliminate some of the game-playing.

In our interviews, we saw contradictions within a given criminal's thinking and action. He appeared both fearless and fearful, grandiose and meek, independent and parasitic, sentimental and brutal, suggestible and rigid. In addition, his attitudes toward his own criminal activities were puzzling. Occasionally, these men viewed what they had done with disgust, but this disgust did not last long enough to deter them from a repetition. More commonly, a criminal took the position that he was justified in what he did. These men, who had been in crime all their lives, regarded themselves as good people. Astoundingly, to a man they told us that they had never viewed themselves as criminals. A crime was an offense that someone else committed. Although what they did was against the law, they believed that it was right for them at the time. Such a psychology was totally baffling to us.

During our interviews with the ninety-day men, we were interested in learning how their minds worked from the time the thought of a crime occurred until after the execution of the crime. We paid considerable attention to the mental mechanism whereby a criminal was able to rid himself of concerns of conscience and fears of apprehension. It was through this "shutoff mechanism," as we called it, that a man could change from sentimental to brutal. During our discussions of "idea through execution" thinking, we learned that some criminals heard a voice just before committing a crime. As they described this phenomenon, it was clear that it was not a manifestation of psychosis. Rather, it was an internal conscience deterrent, which a criminal could choose to heed or disregard. He did not think he was being directed by outside forces.

We were approaching the view that criminals were very much in control of their actions. To execute what were sometimes elaborate schemes, they had to be "in contact with reality." The rare criminal who was having a psychotic episode was either too confused or uninterested in crime. An active criminal, however, had a steady stream of criminal ideas from which he had to choose, partly on the basis of feasibility. Thus, his act was the product of deliberation. We began to realize that so-called crimes of passion were not really sudden, impulsive acts, but had already been deterred many times. Clearly, a criminal was not a victim of impulses or compulsions—he made choices. For example, if he were about to commit a crime, but realized that the chances of getting caught were high, he had the self-control to postpone the act. It was when he was accountable to others that he used the excuses that he thought would get him off the hook. We began to study the psychology of accountability by which he did this. At the time, however, we still regarded criminals as mentally ill, and, while recognizing that they made choices, we called these "sick choices."

Some of these ninety-day men were drug users. Thus, we had the opportunity to study the effects of drugs on mental processes. We learned that some criminals use drugs to "shut off" fear, so that they have the "heart" or courage to commit a crime. That is, there are some criminals who cannot hold up a bank, commit a rape, or break and enter without a drug to reduce fear. Drugs made them feel "ten feet tall" for whatever activity they wanted. With an optimal heroin dose, a man might be King Kong sexually. On too high a dose, he would lose interest in sex altogether. In Volume 3, we go into detail about the effects of drugs on thinking processes and behavior.

Expanding on the information we obtained in the first group, when we discussed the Durham rule, we concentrated upon the criminals' tactics in seeking admission to a hospital in order to avoid serving long sentences in prison. We gathered a great amount of information about the fraudulent character of their current efforts to be admitted to the hospital. We found out that these men were indoctrinated by other prisoners in jail, by their lawyers, and by other patients once they were in the hospital. Although they did not consider themselves mentally ill, they adopted strategies to convince the staff that they were. They malingered on the ward, acted "crazy," faked responses on psychologic tests, and so forth. We found out that these men had little interest in getting "help" with respect to changing life patterns. Receiving "help," from a criminal's perspective, meant only one thing: assistance in getting into the hospital.

In summary, the time spent interviewing the ninety-day men was fruitful. We were getting material from criminals in jeopardy that we could not have gathered from patients adjudged NGBRI. In our position as researchers, we held communication as privileged and did not participate in administrative decisions affecting the criminals. We established ourselves with forensic patients as committed to our work and intensely interested in learning. All these factors were helpful in eliciting a great deal of information that added to our knowledge of the criminal mind. We continued to modify some ideas, discard others altogether, and find new subjects for inquiry.

While interviewing the ninety-day men we were confronting them with material developed in our work with NGBRI patients. Not only were we confirming what we found, but we were also discovering new patterns. We then cross-checked the new information with the NGBRI patients. When we did this, even more material came forth from that group. In other words, we were finding that the same features of the criminal mind were present in men in jeopardy of going to prison and those already adjudged NGBRI. After nine months of this process, we were conducting a more effective inquiry; our knowledge was greater and our techniques better.

THE STUDY OF CRIMINAL TRAITS IN A TREATMENT GROUP

Time did not permit us to offer individual psychotherapy to all who requested it. Thus, we decided to have a two-hour group meeting each week in one of the maximum security facilities of the forensic division. This arrangement continued for about a year. All group members had had some earlier contact with us and wanted to participate for various reasons. We had made an impact as dedicated investigators by offering patients many hours of attention with privileged communication. As part-time workers in maximum security, we were more accessible than most full-time ward doctors. Some clung to the idea that they could use us on their behalf, despite our stipulation that this would not occur. Another reason for their interest was that, in previous contacts with us, these men had found the discussions interesting, and they were curious as to what would come up now. Some hoped that evidence of their desire for therapy would demonstrate their seriousness of purpose in wanting to change and facilitate their getting out; the fact that they were seeing a therapist might be interpreted by the staff as a constructive effort. Still another factor was that the group sessions occupied those who otherwise would sit idly on the ward.

This time we stated that this was not to be a gripe session. We were even more emphatic about our separation from the administration, underscoring that we would not go to bat for a criminal's privileges or change in status and would not bail him out of difficulty. No matter how many times we reiterated this, it did not stop these men from thinking that they could exploit us for such purposes. We also made it clear by our format that we were going to direct the discussions, rather than leave them open-ended and thereby invite complaints, personal vendettas against others, and so on. Despite these ground rules, the complaining continued. Finding us understanding of many of their grievances, the patients continued to pour out their discontent. However, this time we imposed limits. We pointed out that the criminals were using their dissatisfactions to disown personal responsibility for their behavior. We did not want to sit in judgment and arbitrate grievances. Rather, we began to turn things around and ask how the criminals were creating their own difficulties.

Our major focus in this group was on character traits.* First, these traits had to be identified. Then we would assist the criminal in gaining insight into the connection between their criminal behavior and these traits. We believed that such insight would be attended by the elimination of criminal behavior.

We continued to view these criminals as "sick," but began to phrase it a little differently. It was the maladaptive underlying traits that were "sick." What impressed us was that each of these traits was present in every patient, without exception. For example, one striking feature was their fearfulness, which they tried to conceal from others. These men had the same fears as the noncriminal, but they were greater in number and intensity. Whereas a noncriminal overcomes many of his childhood fears, they persisted into a criminal's adult life. The list of fears centered about darkness, height, water, closed space, and bodily injury. In addition they were terrified of physical injury and pain. Some let their teeth rot, rather than face the drill of a dentist, which might have prevented further decay. The greatest fear of these criminals was that others would see some weakness in them. They were hypersensitive to what was said to them and reacted very angrily when "put down." Another kind of fear in what appeared to be conscienceless men involved the "conscience fears." They would not engage in acts that offended them. Some would never victimize a child or an older person, for example. Some could break and enter, but tried to avoid physical injury to anyone. Although conscience fears were present, their deterrent power was weak. Through the shutoff mechanism, a criminal could rid himself of conscience and any other fear that might stand in the way of what he wanted to do. To be sure, not all criminals had the same fears. But fearfulness as a trait was present in every one of them.

Another trait present in all was the inclination to view oneself as worthless. These criminals, who thirsted for power and who appeared grandiose, sometimes experienced the feeling that they were "nothings." These "zero feelings," as we termed them, were present very early in life. Though intelligent, good-looking, and talented, these men often viewed themselves as stupid, ugly, and total failures. A devalued concept of the self seemed to give rise to an overvalued concept of the self. At this time, we viewed one state as compensatory for the other. We thought that the enormity of a crime

---

* We should point out to the reader that the terms used in this chapter reflect the language that we actually used in the group. In other words, in the group meetings we spoke of "character traits," a term that we later changed. This material is broadly conceptualized and expanded in Chapter 4.

might be in direct proportion to the magnitude of the feeling of being a nothing.

During all our work with the criminals, we had to contend with the trait of lying. To these men, lying was nearly as essential—indeed, automatic—as breathing. An interesting thing happened when we discussed lying or any other trait. These very concrete thinkers latched on to the trait under scrutiny as being the key to change. They might think, for example, that, if only they told the truth, this would ensure total change everywhere. They failed to relate lying to all the other traits. Of course, in discussions of individual traits, we were fractionating the personality for teaching purposes. The criminals lacked the perspective to see that this was being done to reintegrate a whole person without the "sick traits." A further problem was that, as the group members discussed the traits, each participant could spot it in the others, without being convinced that it applied to him. He viewed himself as different from all the rest. This led us to realize that every criminal regarded himself as totally unique and that his sense of superiority was enhanced by this sense of uniqueness.

As we dealt with men who were liars and who cloaked themselves in secrecy, we saw that we were dealing with people who were very suspicious of others. Our early notes referred to the "paranoid" quality of the criminals. As we reexamined this concept over time, we recognized that, unlike those of true paranoids, the suspicions of these men were grounded in fact. The responsible world *was* hostile toward them and *did* want to apprehend them. For self-preservation, a criminal had to be on guard and suspicious. Realizing this, we dropped the term "paranoid." It simply did not apply.

In a general way, we have described only a few of the traits we were studying. We noted dozens of characteristics, some of which we did not understand until later. During this period, we did more than stick a label on behavior and term it a "trait." For example, it did not take much study to see that the criminals were liars; in fact, they were known for this. However, we began to explore the various lying patterns—the forms that lying took and under what conditions.

A very important attribute that we studied intensively was what we had previously designated as the "shutoff mechanism." The process of pushing fears away from conscious consideration appeared to be more rapid than repression. We thought that it might be an hysterical phenomenon, almost an amnesic or dissociative reaction. We considered the shutoff mechanism to be a critical psychologic defense that needed much further study. We realized that such a mechanism posed a formidable obstacle to the change process. With it, a criminal could shut off anything said at a meeting. This meant responsibility, too, could be shut off. We found that, after discussing a given trait throughout a two-hour meeting, a criminal might not recall at the next session even what the topic had been, much less have initiated any change.

Related to the shutoff mechanism were successive changes in mental state. A man might go on a crime spree, but then turn around and be a crusader against crime. In a few cases, we observed truly psychotic conditions in which a criminal believed that he was God's chosen messenger to wage the battle of good and evil. We had a strong hunch that these "cycles," as we called them, resulted from a physiologic process. We thought that perhaps adverse circumstances triggered them, but we recognized that the cycles often seemed to be independent of circumstances. Some left the hospital and appeared to be doing well, but then seemed suddenly to explode into criminal patterns. These cycles puzzled us and were to remain phenomena for further investigation.

Throughout all our contacts thus far with the criminals, we continued to be struck by their refusal to view themselves as criminals and their finding the very word *criminal* offensive when applied to them. The patients continued to spot and condemn criminality in others, but they believed that they were decent people. This led us to rethink our use of the term "criminal" and led to our conceptualizing a continuum of criminality. At first, we thought that a person's place on the continuum was determined by the scope and frequency of involvement in criminal activity. But we knew that the commission of even one serious crime was indicative of the presence of the "sick traits" that we had been studying.

As we oriented ourselves to a study of traits, we were shifting the focus from *why* things are as they are to a descriptive dissection of *who* the criminal is. That is, we cared more about the fabric of mind and less about cause.

At this point, we had much detailed information about criminals and their traits, but we did not know what to do with it. We were striving to make our concepts operational. We had been better at establishing facts than at achieving change. At first, we thought that we could capitalize on some specific criminal traits that could be rechanneled in the direction of responsibility. For example, we thought that a criminal's alertness and perceptiveness in perpetually scanning the environment could be applied to self-examination. We also believed that a criminal's abundant energy could be harnessed toward change. We had worked on giving a criminal insight into his traits, but this was no more effective than insights about his early experiences. After being exposed to our point of view, he agreed with us about the presence of these characteristics, and in fact was quick to point them out in other group members. He expected us to see this as evidence of change in him, and we did. Only later did we realize how naive we had been. What the men were doing was building themselves up and scoring points, often by knocking others down. They did not relate traits to behavior. They talked about their lying, controlling others, thirsting for power, and so forth, but did nothing to change. The overriding objective remained: to get out of the hospital. Even more discouraging was their use of these character traits as excuses for their behavior. It was as though they were saying: "That's the way I am. What can you expect?" We evaluated this period of our work as a time of fact-finding within the context of a therapeutic effort. However, in addition to describing the criminals, we were seeking results from a process of change. Clearly, we needed to reevaluate and revise our therapy format and procedures.

SEEKING INFORMATION FROM OUTSIDE SOURCES

At all stages of our work, we were seeking additional information from relatives, friends, employers, or any other significant figures in our criminals' lives who were willing to talk with us. In 1964, a social worker who joined our staff and another hospital social worker did some interviewing and counseling of families.

We soon ran into a problem: Blood is thicker than truth. That is, honest people covered up for their criminal kin; they condemned the criminal's behavior, but they protected him. The social histories that the social workers obtained proved to be of little value. Mothers had a tendency to present distorted views as they clung to idealized pictures of their offspring. They insisted that their sons were "good at heart," but that they had had "bad breaks." In some cases, the information was sparse, because a criminal's family had been kept in the dark and did not know the extent of the criminality. Even more surprising to us was that otherwise responsible people assisted the criminals in violations during confinement. For example, they took a criminal off the grounds without permission or failed to cooperate with the hospital in the event of an elopement.

Another problem was a criminal telling his family, friends, and others that we did not want to see them. In more than one case, a relative refused to cooperate with us, because he had been intimidated by a criminal who feared that something unfavorable would be revealed. In a few cases, a relative or acquaintance refused to talk with us, because he himself had been in crime and did not want to be questioned, even if it were not about himself. All these obstacles impeded us in obtaining information.

We believed that social workers could help families in their interpersonal relations. At the time, we thought that a criminal would have fewer problems if his family would straighten out. Our social workers wanted to be useful—to them, that meant doing things for both patient and family. They saw their mission as assuming a supportive role to help family members maintain self-esteem in difficult situations. We found, instead, that a focus on personal deficiencies would have been more constructive than merely shoring up qualities that were potential assets.

The social workers were sometimes exploited by families that made requests—asking to be taken places, for example. In a sample of the type of contact being made at the time,

> Mrs. M [a social worker] thought that she had made a little bit of progress with Mrs. G, in that the latter talked a little more freely about the problems of her children, particularly about David and his toilet training. Mrs. G asked Mrs. M to get a copy of "Dr. Spock" for her, because she had lost her own copy. She also asked Mrs. M to help her cut out slipcovers.

During the meeting, there was no reference to any of the criminal's behavior, except that he had not been drinking lately. Most of the talk dealt with problems of running the household, but there was no constructive discussion of budgeting or of anything else immediately relevant to improving the home situation.

As we evaluated social worker contacts, we recognized that it was important to use a direct approach with families, much as we had with criminals. Rather than offering "support" to family members, it was important to spell out problems and deficiencies, so that constructive action could be taken. Eventually, we used some of the techniques we had used with the criminals. Without detailing specific violations, we told a family what we knew about the character of its criminal relative. This helped to eliminate some of the concealment and attempts at denial and generally opened up discussion.

From time to time, we talked with family members who were at wit's end in dealing with a criminal who was totally refractory to change. Their dilemma was that they were continually being exploited, but were at a loss as to what to do in handling a criminal sibling or child. For such a person, to give up all hope and refuse assistance to a relative who appeared incorrigible was to assume the burden of violating one's own concept of loyalty and duty to family. At times, we realized that, for the family members concerned, it was better for them to use their energy, time, and money in trying to help the criminal than to live with the belief that they had betrayed their own consciences by refusing assistance.

ESTABLISHING INDIVIDUAL RESPONSIBILITY: THE ELIMINATION OF SOCIAL AND PSYCHOLOGIC EXCUSES

We came to Saint Elizabeths Hospital with many years of experience in group psychotherapy with noncriminals. During our group work with criminals, we had held sessions to assist in history-taking, to serve as forums for complaints, and to discuss traits. After these experiences, from which we were primarily learning, we decided to make treatment our major objective. We knew that groups were practical in terms of time and economy, offering greater service to a greater number of patients. In a group, issues raised by individual members would be applicable to all. Members could learn from each other. In addition, an analysis of resistance would be easier, in that a criminal would be confronted by his peers, and not only by an "authority." We decided to form a new group that would meet five days a week for two and a half hours each time, with individual sessions being offered to patients as necessary or on request. This was the first time we included people with whom we had no separate, individual contact; accessory individual sessions were held only when crises arose.

The group was a mixture in almost every possible way. Some patients promoted the group among fellow patients. Some men we had known from earlier contacts; others we were seeing for the first time. Some were drug users; others spurned drugs. All but three were hospital patients adjudged NGBRI. Two were civilly committed patients who also had a history of criminal offenses. One other member was a criminal on probation who did not regard himself as mentally ill. Some participants came out of curiosity; others believed that they might somehow score points with the administration by showing an interest in "therapy," and of course there were some who seemed remorseful about things they had done and the way they had lived and sincere in wanting to change.

This section covers the period from the spring of 1964 to the fall of 1965. During this time, the group changed its composition, as new people entered and some dropped out. Some remained in the group for its entire lifetime.

We established new guidelines, of which the most important was that the group members were to know that we did not regard them as mentally ill. Our operating within a mental-illness framework, whatever form it had taken, had resulted only in an illusion of accomplishment. Finding what we thought were the root causes of a man's criminality had not resulted in the elimination of criminal patterns. In our study of the ninety-day men, we had come to realize that these men did not regard themselves as "mentally ill." They were "sick" only for the purpose of getting admitted to the hospital and avoiding jail. Once admitted, they were eager to get out and sought to convince the authorities that they had recovered. Now we recognized the element of choice in criminal behavior. These men had control over what they did. The concept of "choice," rather than "illness," was essential in emphasizing personal responsibility. If we operated from the premise that a criminal was sick, a victim of mental illness, then we could not consider him responsible, and it would be up to someone else to cure him of his sickness. What an absurdity—to have a man await a cure of an illness he did not believe he had! Not only did we eliminate the concepts of "mental illness" and "sick choices," but we also discarded the word *therapist*, for two reasons. First, a therapist is one who administers therapy for an illness; if one is not ill, he does not need a therapist. Second, to a criminal, "therapist" means a person who can be easily influenced and led.

We had avoided calling our patients "criminals" because we had believed that we were dealing with mentally ill people. No longer did we hesitate to use this term. However, our definition of "criminality" was not contingent on arrestability or on the seriousness of an offense. We had been establishing that a criminal act was the end product of specific thinking processes and personality characteristics; thus, with our concept of a continuum the term "criminal" was broadened to encompass a wide range of thinking processes, as well as criminal acts.

The permissive attitude that we had taken earlier had not worked. These men had approved of us as therapists and even thrown parties for us out of appreciation and affection. But the most significant testimonial was not forthcoming—a change in their criminal patterns of thought and action. Now, we were changing our approach. We did not court the criminals' favor or appear at all sympathetic. We believed that their evasion could be broken down only by vigorous invasion of the inner man. We were uncertain as to how these men would react to an intense, direct approach; perhaps they would become upset and discouraged and leave the group. But our other methods had led to failure, and we had nothing to lose. We were convinced that we had to be firm, consistent, and evocative without being provocative. We had to afflict the comfortable, rather than comfort the afflicted. Of course, this shift from relative permissiveness to firmness did not occur overnight, but was gradual.

The changes in procedure gave us access to new material. In turn, the new material led to still further changes in procedure. For example, when we dispensed with mental illness and established personal responsibility, much of what the criminals had told us earlier became open to a far different interpretation. Instead of being viewed as the exploited, they were the exploiters. Instead of suffering from past traumas, they were the ones who had traumatized others. Instead of focusing on what others had done to them, we examined what they had done to others. Instead of subscribing to post facto justification, we were pursuing current thinking.

We still had not completely abandoned psychoanalytic formulations, but we were emphasizing them less. Occasionally, we reverted to analytic theory, almost by habit. Sometimes, we had to admit retrospectively that we had done so for the satisfaction of tying observations into neat packages that made events comprehensible. Our notes of September 4, 1964, indicate well our attitude on this matter at the time.

> C asked the question that permitted me to take over. He stated that the thing that had bothered him most was how he got this way. At this point, I presented very briefly the psychoanalytic point of view of the oedipal and castration problems. C fits into this beautifully, and one can point out, if one wished to, that the oedipal problem existed in him, that the castration anxiety was great, that it produced within him a terrible fear of weakness, and that he has had to prove his power, which he could do only in sexual violence and other kinds of crime. Now, we asked whether this kind of knowledge would be sufficient to achieve an objective. One might ask whether C is different from others having oedipal and castration problems. The answer is that he is not different. This is regarded as universal. How, then, does C differ? It is precisely this difference that we are interested in. Can we get it through conventional psychoanalytic concepts? The answer that I gave was that, as far as I knew, we could not.

Analytic concepts were insufficient as explanation, and analytic techniques were unsatisfactory in producing change. The reenacting and analyzing of a parent-child relation that an analysis of transference entails would have been counterproductive. We realized that it would only reinforce a criminal's blame of others and his victim position. We had taken that path earlier and had seen "insight" become "incite," as a criminal, in righteous indignation, railed against others so as to absolve himself of responsibility.

Nevertheless, our objective was to clarify earlier concepts and to probe further, to improve our understanding of the fabric of the criminal mind. To this end, we initiated thematic discussions, so that each member of the group would examine how he had dealt with various aspects of life. Then we elaborated on the need for patterns of thought and action to change. We had regular three-hour meetings about family, work, school, social patterns, and women. It was hard to maintain continuity, because we were often confronted with day-to-day crises. For example, our men still were violating and receiving restrictions. Our approach was not to come to their aid or preach, but to help them learn. Many themes evolved from a single incident that could be generalized to other situations. Here is where we tried to teach these concrete thinkers to think conceptually. We discussed control, sexual competence, suggestibility, and so on. These discussions brought out new characteristics and thinking errors. They also enabled us to study their tactics and decision-making, as well as their thinking before, during, and after a crime. These studies continued for the next several years, as we gathered what was to be the substantive material of Chapters 4 through 8.

We found the criminals' compartmentalization of life almost beyond comprehension. We have referred to the simultaneous presence of extreme sentimentality and extreme brutality within a given man. What seemed paradoxical to us did not seem so to the criminals. From our point of view, a criminal was living in a state of anarchy. From his point of view, he was not. Although he was not psychotic, he appeared to be creating his own reality. Yet he was oriented, his memory was intact, and he was intelligent and shrewd in his dealings with the world. His different reality did not make him psychotic. We were learning that, from a criminal's view of *his* reality, it was we (the noncriminals) who were stupid, crazy, or both. We began to recognize that, to understand what constitutes reality for a criminal, we would have to know his premises of life, his desires, his experiences. Once we discarded "mental illness" as a factor, we began to understand more about a criminal's reality. The concept of mental illness had been the greatest barrier to acquiring this fundamental knowledge.

Recognizing that our understanding of criminal characteristics was far from complete, we made what use we could of our observations. Their sentimentality was so striking that we thought that we could make an inroad with the criminals by appealing to the "good" in them, and somehow dipping into this well of sentimentality. There is a part of a criminal that is "noble"— a part that he himself often cannot tolerate. We were thinking in terms of an "index of reachability" based on how strong the sentimentality was. We considered drug-users to be more reachable, because, in our experience, they seemed to show more sentimentality than non–drug-users. We knew that criminals had consciences, but we also saw them fail to function. We thought that we could make conscience operable by appealing to sentimentality.

As we looked into the operation of conscience, we spent some time in considering guilt. Some men who earlier had psychotherapy talked about guilt related to oedipal desires. It is true that many of these men had had not only incestuous desires, but also some actual incestuous experiences. To the extent that this was true, they may have had some basis for talking about guilt. However, their insight into the basis of their guilt did not seem to keep them from harming others. Thus, we tended to disregard the significance of such insight in these men who mugged, raped, and murdered. Instead of trying to alleviate a feeling of guilt in the criminals, we wanted to increase it. If a criminal experienced any guilt about his criminality, it apparently did not stay with him long; and he could turn it, like other deterrents, off. Instead of viewing guilt as disabling, as it may be in noncriminals, we stressed the benefits of guilt and encouraged the criminals to keep in mind the many injurious things that they had done to others.

We learned that many of the psychiatric concepts and techniques that we had found effective with noncriminals were not applicable to criminals. Their depressions, anxieties, and tensions were different phenomena. We were dealing with a different breed of person, so different was the mental makeup.

The criminals also used language differently, so we became students of semantics. Sometimes, we thought we grasped what a criminal was saying, and later found out that he had meant something quite different. He had a different frame of reference. If he said he was "lonely," it did not refer to a lack of companionship—he knew nothing of companionship based on a community of interest and experiences. "Lonely" meant having no one to control and exploit. In addition, much of our descriptive terminology was inadequate or meaningless when applied to criminals. Saying that a man was "manipulative" reflected his effect on us more than it indicated how his mind worked; the criminals did not view themselves as manipulative, but we thought that we were being manipulated by their tactics. Furthermore, we began to understand the criminals' view that society was manipulating them, which in some cases was true. Our words did not contribute to an understanding of the world *as the criminals viewed it*. Psychiatric parlance was also inadequate when applied to this population. For example, we could have termed many of the criminals' traits "defenses," but using the word so broadly would have rendered it meaningless. Superimposing a traditional theoretical framework hindered our understanding of the people with whom we were dealing. Although we sought to understand the criminals' language, we did not adopt it ourselves. We did not have to say, "Where did you get the bread?" for them to see that we were referring to money.

We encountered the problem others have had of establishing an open channel of communication. Although we were maintaining privileged communication, the criminals still did not disclose fully. The channel was closed by self-serving stories and rationalizations in which they were either victors or victims. Sometimes a criminal lied merely for the pleasure of putting one over on us. On other occasions, we thought the channel was open when it was not. It was common for a criminal to disclose a small part of the truth and give us the impression that he was telling everything. When he informed on others, we thought that this breaking of the criminal code of "no snitching" was an advance; instead of opening the channel, what he was doing by informing was building himself up and improving his image. Similarly, we thought that full disclosure was occurring when he confessed to crimes and violations; this, too, was often done solely for impact. He was feeding us what he thought we wanted, and the reporting was usually shot through with distortion and minimization.

Another major impediment was the criminals' insistence that change be brought about by their own rules; our program was to be a "do it yourself" procedure. Basically, each of them wanted to control us and convince us of his point of view. The group resembled a football team in which each member considered himself the quarterback. Every criminal wanted to be the big shot and determine what would happen. He confronted others, but responded angrily when he was confronted. When we firmly opposed his point of view, he accused us of being "inflexible" and disregarded what he did not want to hear. Thus, what we thought had been absorbed was not implemented. In fact, it sometimes seemed as though the criminals had not been present at the preceding meetings. The criminals shut us out just as they turned off deterrents so that they could execute crimes. The mechanism was the same. In fact, it operated so rapidly that we termed it a "cutoff": With almost surgical knifelike precision, a criminal in an instant would turn from tears to ice. He could pray devoutly at 9:00, and be involved in a holdup at 10:00. He could participate avidly in a group discussion on anger and show considerable insight, and assault someone an hour later.

These men were not only fighting change, but asserting that they were incapable of it. They did not necessarily blame others for this; they knew that we would not accept it. Instead, they declared simply that "I can't do it." Exploring what this meant, we found that "I can't" signified that they were not putting sufficient effort into living responsibly. Behind this was a refusal: "I won't" or "I don't want to." There was no issue of "can't" in terms of capacity to change. After all, these were men who in their criminal lives rarely said "I can't" to anything. However, they were now whining "I can't" with respect to having to give up their criminal excitement.

With increased knowledge, we began to tell the criminals immediately that we knew how their minds worked and what their tactics were. We were no longer fishermen, dangling our lines in the water, casting about to catch something. Instead, we knew exactly where the fish were and went to hook them. Thus, we were able to extract more information and reduce the criminals' game-playing. They found our candor refreshing, something they had not previously experienced. Consequently, they believed that, inasmuch as we knew so much to begin with, there was less point to their trying to put on a front and hide things.

We had come to believe that these men had to be "won" early in our contact with them, or they would be "lost." We controlled the interviews and did not wait for a criminal to bring things out or to direct the conversation. Our men had to recognize that we were knowledgeable and firm. We assumed the initiative to bring out important material, probing beyond surface reports. We disallowed the criminals' numerous excuses, their blaming of others, and the victim stance in its various forms. One of our notes gives the flavor of how we responded to a criminal's presentation of himself as a victim:

"He began by saying that his wife told him that he has never been able to develop a true, sound, and trusting relationship with anybody. The way he explained this was to go back to his mother and himself, because, when he was a little boy and he came to her, she was sometimes too busy and pushed him away.
The rest of this session was a "victim" or "crybaby" session, in which he told us the weary tale, the broken record of his misfortunes in his early life. At this point, I stated that, if he didn't get the attention from his mother, did she teach him to lie? Did she teach him to con women for money? Did she teach him to shoot and kill a woman he scarcely knew and seriously injure her escort? Did she furnish him with a model of infidelity? I asked him whether I was dealing with an 8-year-old boy or with a 28-year-old man."

Here, we "knew" the victim stance and were prepared to meet it. Every such obstacle introduced by a criminal said something about the kind of person he was. We encountered the same obstacle in many forms. For example, if a criminal did not tell us he was a victim of environmental circumstances, he said he was a victim of his own character structure, but put it in terms of "feelings." A man might try to explain away his violations by saying that he had been depressed, tense, or upset. He also used his feelings as an excuse not to change. Here, again, we took a firm position. We told the men that sitting around waiting for feelings to change was futile. Feelings do not change in a vacuum, but as a result of thinking processes. Emerging was the beginning of a concept (developed later) that feelings were on epiphenomenon of thought. They could be changed by substituting different thinking processes.

We had found that the thinking that gave rise to feelings was the most important unit for dissection. If thinking processes changed, feelings would change. Whatever the tactics, we showed the error in thinking, in much the same manner as when we met the countless permutations of the victim stance. This reduced the obstacles. One consequence was that the same men who had provided us originally with self-serving stories when we had taken histories now volunteered to review that material and correct it. In some cases, if one were to compare the two accounts, he would not know they were from the same man.

We were still not making the progress we desired. Just as we thought some of our people were doing well, things started going awry. Some criminals showed old behavior patterns precisely when they were about to advance in status, such as by obtaining ground privileges or a conditional release. When a man gained more privileges, he had less supervision, and thus a greater arena for "action." Then he began to stay away from the group, or, if he came, to attend in body only. He told us that there was nothing more to learn and that he did not need us, because he was ready to handle things on his own. All the "insights" that we thought he had gained seemed to vanish. The familiar patterns at first took a nonarrestable form, such as lying, irresponsible handling of money, and exploitation of women. Soon, they were reflected in more serious offenses: elopements, coming to group meetings on drugs or intoxicated, and engaging in a variety of criminal activities both on and off the grounds.

The failures were disappointing, but they prompted us to reexamine our idea and techniques. Clearly, we had placed too much faith in the efficacy of talk. To a considerable extent, we had been judging a criminal's progress by his verbalization. Here was the treachery in relying too much on the value of insight; it was not the insight of psychoanalysis, but the insight into characteristics. As used by a criminal, the whole insight procedure was itself a "criminal enterprise." A criminal assented and conned just as he had done with others in the past. He used psychiatric formulations as excuses. One criminal commented tersely: "If I didn't have enough excuses for crime before I had psychiatry, psychiatry gave me more." The end product of insight therapy was a criminal with psychiatric sophistication. He was still a criminal. Thus, we heard our terms and concepts coming back to us as a defense of indefensible patterns.

We did not totally discount the value of insight or self-understanding. Indeed, we recognized that it was necessary, but only as a part of the change process. In addition, a criminal needed to be educated about the responsible world, which was so foreign to him. So we began to stress our role as teachers, rather than therapists. We knew that words alone were insufficient to accomplish change. New knowledge had to be implemented. Old patterns had to be destroyed, and new habits established. We had worked out only a broad outline of what this process of change entailed. We had no foolproof system by which to evaluate the extent of change. We did list some specific indicators:

1. Less complaining
2. Less assuming of the victim or victor stance in reporting
3. Dissociating oneself from criminal cohorts
4. Less using of street slang
5. Adopting more of a help-seeking attitude—e.g., spontaneously bringing in problems and raising questions in a self-critical fashion
6. Eliminating violations

We had made significant changes since 1961. We had abandoned the search for causes, discarded mental illness as a factor in criminality, thrown out psychologic and sociologic excuses, and assumed a firm, directive stance based on a considerable body of knowledge about the criminal mind. We knew the characteristics of the population with which we were dealing, so we knew what had to be changed. We ourselves had changed from "therapists" who were easily led around to "agents of change" who were much more knowledgeable about what had to be accomplished. We now recognized that a radical change had to occur and had to culminate in a totally new way of life. This was stated by us in a dictation, describing our view of the scope of the change process.

> "As I consider the challenge that a criminal provides us, I am convinced that there is no helping these people unless there is a "metamorphosis." "Change" is not a sufficiently descriptive term for the degree of overhauling that is necessary. The overhauling, the tearing down and rebuilding of the engine is absolutely essential. I don't like to say this. It's hard, it's tedious, and there will be tremendous practical problems in achieving this objective. But what has to be done has to be done. I wish there were shortcuts, but I can see none. Perhaps there will be shortcuts in the future. If basic character structure is not dealt with, even when criminal operations are not intended or there have been some barriers against it, the defects of the character produce dilemmas that, in turn, ultimately make for crime."

Our task now was to develop the substance of a program, so that we could achieve a "metamorphosis."

TOWARD A PROGRAM FOR TOTAL CHANGE

"CONVERSION"

With the more effective techniques we were developing, it was easier to make inroads. When we appeared on the wards, forensic patients approached us. This was not simply a case of their wanting to overcome us or to manage us, but we were continuing to gain a reputation for our different approach, as well as for our knowledge and dedication. These men were curious about us and wanted to understand more about themselves through us. We often encountered men who were serious about change and who joined our program enthusiastically. However, they soon balked at living in a vacuum of no excitement. To them it was meaningless. We had to deal with their boredom, anger, and desires for power, which in time evolved into a resumption of criminal activities. Some of our participants got fed up and dropped out.

Despite these difficulties, we were beginning to see some results. Some of our men were altering their ways of thinking and behaving. A decline in violations gave us some indication that we were on the right track. But we put more and more stock in a change in thinking patterns, rather than in a reduction in violations. We knew that without the former, the latter would be short-lived.

As early as the summer of 1964, we had the idea that a "conversion" to a whole new lifestyle was required. By 1965, we knew more of what this would entail: a total destruction of a criminal's personality, including much of what he considered the "good" parts. Converting involved a "surrender" to a responsible agent of change. It would not be a conversion in the religious sense, in which a person is persuaded to embrace a faith. We recognized that it was futile to exhort a man to commit himself to a way of life that he did not know anything about. To decide whether he truly wanted to change, a criminal first required information. Because he could not be converted to something amorphous, our task was to define what this conversion entailed.

A statement of intention to change was sufficient at the start. Whether a sincere intention would become a matter of conviction could not be predicted. We told a criminal who wanted to change that change had to be for its own sake, and not to satisfy someone else. To make a beginning, the criminal had to be fed up with himself. Working in our favor was the fact that all these men had experienced transient phases of disgust with their own criminality. At times they had secretly envied a noncriminal sibling or some other responsible person. In addition, they had had the idea of "going straight" after a final "big score" in crime.

A criminal is most vulnerable to change when he is locked up or is about to face a period of confinement, when his options in life are considerably reduced and he is more likely to reflect on his past. We approached the criminals who appeared to be in a phase of self-disgust. We tried to show them what their lives had been, while beginning to educate them as to what their lives would be if they changed. We reminded them of the three options open to a criminal: crime, suicide, and change. It was clearly up to them. We knew that we could not persuade them to make a particular choice, but we could help to clarify the issues.

THE MENTAL PROCESSES OF RESPONSIBILITY

Our stance had gradually been changing from an amoral one to an emphasis on moral living, in very strong terms. Now it was on responsibility. But *responsibility* was an overused word, which could mean both everything and nothing. When the criminals used the word, it was either to denote being accountable (responsible) for a crime or to denote some very concrete act, such as paying a bill. We sought to broaden the meaning of responsibility, so that it could be taught and then implemented as a *set of mental processes*.

To that end, we met with another group of patients, some old and some new, for several hours a week during a three-month period to formulate the evolving principles of responsible thinking and action. We examined current life problems in detail and applied concepts to their solution that could be generalized beyond concrete incidents. At these meetings, we formulated what we called "tools for responsible thinking and action," a set of concepts that were to form the foundation of a new set of thinking processes. We were teaching criminals concepts that were second nature to a responsible schoolchild, but totally new to them. Effort, trust, interdependence, responsible initiatives, a time perspective, consideration of injury to others, and responsible decision-making were among the topics. If implemented, these thinking patterns of responsibility would be incompatible with old patterns and in time would replace them. In this work, we were functioning more and more as teachers and less as traditional psychiatrists.

Education, however, was insufficient to ensure a commitment to change. It took implementation of what was learned. And that meant living without former pleasures and excitement while encountering a host of new problems. In short, the criminals would have to be prisoners of this program in order to be free. We found that, although they grasped our concepts, there was a sizable gap between education and implementation. The criminals' knowledge of the "tools" or mental processes of responsibility turned out to be largely academic. Just as they had cut off deterrents in order to violate, they now cut off the new material. Thus, the "tools" did not serve a deterrent function. We held a series of "postmortem" discussions about which "tool" should have been used and how a situation should have been handled.

The idea that the "tools" would be a "first aid kit" or an emergency set of deterrents was a misconception on our part. Recognizing that we were being too didactic, we instituted a procedural change. We endeavored to present the same material more within the context of real-life situations, so that there would be greater opportunity for implementation.

It was common for a criminal to expect us somehow to do the job for him. He wanted guarantees and expected miracles. He waited for others to "motivate" him. He waited for his feelings to change or until he got interested in doing something. Of course, all his life he had operated on this basis. What had interested him were the activities that gave him a "charge"—and these were usually irresponsible. He was not "interested" in school, so he did little studying and was truant. He did not "feel like" working, so he stayed away or drifted from job to job. We recognized that, if habituation depended on a criminal's waiting for a change in feelings, all efforts were doomed, because he would continue to feel little enthusiasm for activities that he had scorned. Any effort to arrive at what *caused* him to feel as he did only vindicated his refusal to take initiatives in responsible ways. We had found out earlier that "reasons" are used by criminal for justification. But "feelings," "interest," and "motivation," which are important considerations in most psychotherapeutic work, were irrelevant in our work with criminals. In fact, we were observing that, as criminals changed, a change in motivation, interest, and feelings eventually followed. Insight occurred as a consequence of change.

THE REQUIREMENT OF TOTAL IMPLEMENTATION

We knew that the effort had to be total. A "crack in the door," even the slightest violation, inevitably opened the door further, to irresponsibility and eventually crime. It was mandatory for a criminal to go from one extreme in life to the other—from total irresponsibility to impeccably responsible functioning. This requirement was a considerable departure from our stance of a few years earlier, when we viewed minor infractions as unimportant. Our new position called for a total alteration in thinking, as well as in action. In line with this 100 percent requirement, we warned the criminals that the work of change was never done and that they could never rest on what had been achieved. Crimelessness without other change was an impossible objective. A criminal had to become something, not just live in a vacuum. What he had to become was a person who acted and *thought* responsibly. We regarded complacency as a particularly dangerous state of mind. We decided that we ought not to compliment these people on improvements, but instead to focus constantly on corrections to be made, no matter how much progress there seemed to have been. The criminals developed an understanding that their position was similar to that of alcoholics. A "crack in the door" would spell destruction for either. Thus, "once an alcoholic, always an alcoholic" we changed to "once a criminal, always a criminal"; the criminals should never regard the job as completed. Just as a committed member of Alcoholics Anonymous never considers himself an *ex*-alcoholic, neither should a criminal view himself as an *ex*-criminal.

As we worked with the criminals, we had problems dealing with their frequently changing mental states. We spoke earlier of the criminals' passing through "cycles," or fluctuations in mental states and attitudes. At first, we believed that a criminal maintained a homeostasis through crime. We then began to see that there were a number of "alternating states," each of which seemed to be a homeostasis. For some, there were periods of near "monasticism," in which they were crime-free. Some had infrequent, but genuine, psychotic episodes, during which they were not at all interested in criminal activity. Psychosis seemed to be a backlash of conscience in which a criminal became preoccupied with religious ideas, in the broad sense. Another of the alternating states became apparent as we saw criminals strive for power along socially approved lines; some would be zealots in social change. However, the appeal of such movements was in the opportunity for self-aggrandizement, far more than in the cause itself. This "criminal equivalent," as we termed it, was a homeostasis for some in which they remained nonarrestable at least for a brief period. Another alternating state was despair and suicidal thinking. The antidote to this was a return to crime, in which a criminal could become "somebody," rather than no one. Suicide actually occurred in only one case. These "alternating states" lasted longer than the momentary changes of mind that we called "fragmentation." A psychosis or monastic period might last for months. The elimination of fragmentation and the creation of a new, stable homeostasis of responsibility were major challenges.

The issue of meaning was paramount in the development of our program. Even as children, the criminals had found the expectations of the responsible world to be meaningless. What others considered the "good things in life" seemed empty—financial security, a challenging job, a comfortable place to live, loyal friends. Such a life had no impact! Nevertheless, the criminals were not satisfied with the life they had chosen, at least when we reached them. They had rejected responsible living before, and now it came to symbolize nirvana, a problemless existence. Instead of finding responsible living to be without problems, they encountered one new problem after another. Some reacted like caged animals when unrealistic expectations went unfulfilled. The struggle was hard as they renounced "achievements" in crime but achieved nothing solid in the responsible world. Out of self-pity, some reverted to "I can't." There were rushes of criminal thinking and, in some cases, violation. We called on the criminals to live with their fears, endure discomfort, take the world as they found it, and make the best of it, rather than demand a different world. One does not derive satisfaction in the responsible world from sitting passively. It is achieved through an active process. The process itself is more meaningful than the accomplishment. Once one has accomplished something, he moves on to something else. For a criminal, this would mean that life would be "meaningful" only as he achieved things responsibly and developed self-respect and the respect of others.

We had abandoned analytic formulations and interpretations and rejected psychologic and sociologic excuses. Now, we emphasized choice and will —a man's ability to make of life what he desires. Our tasks were to help a criminal destroy old patterns and to educate him so that he would choose to be responsible and be able to implement that choice.

Drug-users constituted a special problem. We became increasingly aware of the manner in which drugs affected mental processes. We knew that some criminals were using drugs to give them the "heart" or courage to do what they wanted to do but were afraid to do. We studied the role of drugs not only before but also during and after a crime. We had thought that the drug-users would be easier to reach, because their fear and sensitivity were greater than those of non–drug-users.

> "Drug-users are easier to get to, because deterrents last longer, and when you have them without drugs, you can work with them more effectively."

We saw the non–drug-using criminals as harder to get to, because they could at will cut off deterring factors, including us. As we worked with the users, we began to realize that they were in fact the more difficult ones. More than the nonusing criminals, the users lacked courage to take responsible initiatives and make the required effort. Drugs always offered a rapid and effective way of achieving the desired mental state of being "ten feet tall" and simultaneously dispelling the tedium of responsible living.*

PHENOMENOLOGIC REPORTING

Our problem was to find the most effective means to bring out all of a criminal's thinking, so that correctives could be offered. In 1966, we came up with an idea that was to evolve into an important new procedure.

> "I have often thought that a very good discipline would be to have a subject report every thought, every idea that travels through his mind, like a "stream of consciousness," to try to get him to bring things out. The reason for this suggestion, in which I am not too serious, is that there is a divergence between the criminal mind and the noncriminal mind as to the nature of a "problem." In the noncriminal mind, a problem is a situation that should be worked out to achieve the best possible results for all concerned. A criminal's idea of a "problem" is not having his

---

* In Volume 3, we shall describe the methodologic problems encountered with drug-users.

desires achieved. One of our great obstacles is the closed channel. We must put these people into a position where we can have a profitable transaction with them, or else it is hopeless. I believe that this is a matter of education and indoctrination, because we are talking about something so foreign to them that we cannot assume that they are aware of the things that are self-evident to anybody else who seeks such help. This applies not only to psychiatrists, but to anybody or everybody who deals with them on any level. The transaction is worthless unless a channel can be established and kept open."

The idea that was "not too serious" at the time became the procedure of choice. Our objective was to get the entire spectrum of a criminal's thinking without limiting the data. We could then examine his mental processes without bias, interpretation, or prejudgments. To accomplish this phenomenologic reporting, we had to train him to observe his own thinking. Phenomenologic reporting was the total disclosure called for by our open-channel requirement. No longer did we accept "Nothing much happened" or "There wasn't anything important since yesterday." We knew that a mind was constantly active, even if the person had remained in bed all day. With more material, we refined old concepts and formulated new ones, with respect to both the components of the criminal mind and the requirements for change. Our way of instructing them to monitor their thinking was to use the analogy of a mythical closed-circuit, soundtrack television camera recording all thoughts and actions over twenty-four hours every day.

Phenomenologic reporting, an intense probe of a criminal's stream of thinking throughout the day, gave us the substance of how he thought. It laid open thinking errors and exposed the tactics used with us and in life outside our office. The thinking, from idea through execution, that accompanies criminal activity was more readily observed. In other words, through the phenomenologic report, we obtained a microcosm of a criminal's functioning everywhere in life.

With more feedback from the criminals, we were better able to examine our functioning as agents of change. For example, we were increasingly aware of the multiplicity of tactics the criminals used to close the channel, but we also recognized that we might be doing things that put obstacles in the way of change. We called for the criminals to be self-critical, and we too had to be self-critical.

Of course, teaching the criminals a new style of reporting hardly ensured a wide-open channel. When a man did not want to subject his thinking to critical evaluation, he simply closed the channel. For example, the presentation of oneself as victor or victim was still a problem. The men wanted us to think they were doing well. Some became very optimistic, believing after

a short while that they "had it made" and orienting their reports in terms
of the things they were doing well. For example, one of the men had persistent criminal thinking for months before he set a fire, but he wanted to
preserve his good image with us and therefore did not tell us about this
thinking. Some men were eager participants and grasped the material quickly,
but had little real interest in changing.

> I then turned to what he was doing with me. And he made a couple
> of very interesting points. One was that, while he was sitting here, at
> a time when he was trying to get out [of the hospital] but couldn't,
> he was cutting me off. Or we were developing some themes, [and] he was
> thinking of his "business," which was criminal activity. The second
> thing he did was to come here at times and be very straightforward in
> what he said, much of which was true. Generally, he didn't enjoy being
> here, and he closed the channel and did not express this. What he did
> enjoy was reporting habits, mental attitudes, and tricks of the other
> criminals. He got a bang out of it. He told others that he was my
> assistant, that he was helping me out. There was no thought about his
> being helped. This idea of his helping me out he expressed to other peo-
> ple. When I came up in a discussion, he said that he was gaining here a
> better vocabulary. Or he pointed out that he was gaining more knowl-
> edge about the criminal mind. This led others to believe that Yochelson
> was making him a slicker criminal. And, of course, it built him up.
> The sum and substance of this is that, when he came here (and he often
> enjoyed it), he got himself into a temporary mood, which was cut off
> when he got out of here. He always used and exploited us in terms of
> his association with us. So he was using me in a couple of ways—first,
> to boast about his affiliation with me, and second, to get out. At no
> time did he ever tell any criminal that I was his therapist in the sense
> of producing change or that our objective was to change a criminal to
> a noncriminal.

We had to contend with such self-satisfied, smug performances, in which a
criminal sat in our office day after day and participated, but thought that
he was doing us a favor. He believed he was a special person in a special
program, and this in itself he regarded as a badge of distinction.

Another problem was that some wanted to change just enough to have
the best of two worlds. In a sense, they wanted to be better criminals. They
thought that understanding themselves and their fallibilities would make
them more careful and thus more successful in crime. In addition, they
sought the good name that attends responsible living, which would be a
cover for crime. That is, a man might look good by living with his family,
holding a job, saving money, and generally having the trappings of responsibility. But, if one were to examine in detail how the criminal was thinking
and acting, he would find old patterns operative, although more effectively

concealed. The desire to look good while operating according to old patterns, thus getting the best of two worlds, indicated to us that we were short of achieving "conversion." Clearly, the criminals still wanted their excitement.

Once these men decided that they were entitled to some excitement on the side, they took matters into their own hands. The channel was closed, and they kept criminal thinking to themselves. Some contended that they could attain the program objectives in their own way and that they did not have to meet the 100-percent responsibility requirement. They had decided that they had changed enough. Particularly when a criminal received greater freedom, with more privileges, he became cocky and certain that he could go his own way. Every man we dealt with committed some violation at such a point. We redoubled our efforts to deal with this indication that change was insufficient. We knew that, even if violations were deterred, the deterrence would be only temporary unless the criminal thinking patterns were altered. In cases where violations continued to occur and where there was little effort at implementation, we believed that it was time to terminate our contact. However, as things worked out, in all cases, termination was the criminal's decision as a result of the pressures of the program, and not a decision by us. We even took back men who had quit, so that we could gain further knowledge, and also because we found that further progress was sometimes possible.

THE GENERAL FORMAT

Throughout this period, we were seeking confirmatory data and refining our concepts. In search of further understanding, we had spot interviews with criminals who were not in our program. We developed a format for use with a criminal whom we might see only a few times. We did not ask open-ended questions, but from the beginning told him what we knew about how his mind operated. Our opening statement might last a half-hour before the criminal had his turn to speak. We established our competence and knowledgeability from the outset. The criminal realized, as he put it, that we had "peeped his hole card"—we knew who he was. This eliminated some of the early game-playing and minimized diversionary tactics. We controlled the interview totally. We spent three to twenty hours with each such person, to check out current concepts and to look for new ones.

We also followed the criminals in our program for up to twelve years after they left the hospitals. We were dissatisfied with the extent of their change. So we provided them with our newest concepts, developed after they left the intensive part of the program. Through our continuing contacts, we helped them to deal more effectively with the outside world. Never having budgeted money, never having had a nonexploitative relationship with a woman, and so forth, they were much like stumbling children who had a lot to learn from experience.

In examining the trends of our work during this period, we could say the following: We had abandoned traditional techniques, especially the search for causes. We had at first exhorted and tried to persuade a criminal that change was in his best interest, then dropped that approach. We came to recognize that a criminal needed two types of education: self-understanding and knowledge about the outside world. We insisted on conversion as an indication that a criminal meant business, and was not just giving lip service to change. However, we could not produce a conversion as a result of our direct effort to convert by education; there was a gap between education and implementation. We learned that conversion is achieved as an *end product* of the way a person lives, not as a starting point. The most important education had to take place outside the office, in life itself. Talk was not a valid indicator of conversion. Now we knew that we were on the right track, because, after nine years, despite many failures, we were seeing some success.

RECENT WORK

REFINING CONCEPTS AND PROCEDURES

Since 1970 we have continued to interview men sent to Saint Elizabeths for determination of competency. In addition, patients who have been declared NGBRI and have heard about us have sought us out. Most of the criminals from Saint Elizabeths who have participated in our program have done so mainly as outpatients. Furthermore, we have begun work with four men on probation and with several who are full-fledged criminals, but have never been arrested. We have continued to refine and formalize our concepts, preparing to communicate them to others in published form. The snowballing process of getting more material with each change in procedure has continued. As our people altered their thinking and became responsible, concepts that had been fuzzy became sharp. With a clearer idea of what we were dealing with, we modified procedures. Occasionally, we came upon new findings or enlarged our understanding of a phenomenon already under study. For example, we advanced in our understanding of criminal equivalents and gave special attention to these as they occurred in the military, politics, and social activism. We formulated the concept of still another mental state, which we designated the "limbo state." We came upon this as a result of our follow-ups of mostly older criminals who had elected not to change. These men were not living responsibly, but neither were they engaging in major violations, because of their strong fear of apprehension. There was still plenty of criminal thinking and also crimes of a more minor nature, such as petty theft, cheating the welfare department, and gambling. Our further delineation of the criminal's mental states helped to clarify our concept of a continuum of criminality.

During these years, we have achieved a better understanding of how a criminal views existence. It is important that the reader understand at the outset what it took us a long time to recognize. Most descriptions of criminals are from the standpoint of a responsible person. In viewing a criminal this way, one is imposing a frame of reference that does not fit. For years, we had been observing what we thought were contradictions in the criminal personality. Once we began to view criminals from the standpoint of *their* premises, we understood that they were consistent in their thinking. We had been introducing obstacles by mixing the criminals' premises with ours, their thinking processes with ours. The results were paradoxes. Once we understood what we were dealing with, there was nothing paradoxical. Criminals have a system of thought that has premises that are erroneous from our point of view, but that has an internal consistency and logic of its own. This new way of looking at criminals was important, because it made procedural changes possible. No longer were we attacking one system by using the premises of another. We were much more effective when, in approaching a man for the first time, we could show that we understood his view of life, rather than disputing it.

Of continuing importance to us has been the study of the hospital milieu. Of course, we had the criminals' evaluation of hospital programs. Now we have interviewed those in charge of various divisions of forensic psychiatry. We have observed psychodrama and attended therapeutic community sessions and ward meetings. We have talked with heads of activity programs. We have compared official hospital records on these patients with our own material and found tremendous differences. We have learned more about how wards are run and about the personalities of the staff. We have obtained more information from our subjects who were well along in the change process. We put more faith in what they said than we did in the views of unchanged criminals or in the views of staff members who had vested interests.

A NEW SELECTION PROCESS

During these years, we were establishing a new selection process. We interviewed criminals from one to as many as twenty times in our screening. The "you know I know" approach became more sophisticated and yielded even more information in initial contacts. The "television camera" idea was impressive. The feedback to our initial approach was positive, although the criminals often did not like what they heard about themselves.

> C stated that our first approach to him was one by which he was totally shocked. Here, we were called "conceited asses" and "opinionated." Then, when we were telling him things about himself that had not come out earlier in our first couple of meetings, he stated, "You were telling me things about me and reading my mind." He understood that we had a lot of facts to back up our statements, because they were so valid not only in themselves, but in his own experience (as a counselor to delinquents) with people like himself. The third phase of his reaction was to recognize, "He knows more than I do." And then the fourth stage was his acknowledgment that we could be very valuable to him, and he wanted to see us again.

As agents of change, we needed some kind of external leverage to use with the criminals. We knew that we could not expect to change any criminal just off the street. A man was more likely to be disposed to a program for change if he were faced with prison as an alternative. Thus, we worked with the criminals who came to us initially as a condition of probation. Of course, we could not rely solely on external deterrents to do the job; eventually, an internal commitment had to be made. In obtaining such a commitment, it was important to bring out and sustain a man's disgust with himself. We attempted to indicate to him just how rotten a person he was. We were outspoken in our condemnation of his way of life. This was a far cry from our refusal in 1961 to take a moral stance. Now, we voiced our contempt while at the same time indicating our willingness to work with him. In addition to bringing out a criminal's disgust with himself, we have had another important objective: to assist him in understanding the type of life he would lead if he became a responsible person. We gave him an overview of the hard work, self-discipline, and endurance that would be necessary. Obviously, all this was just words. The criminal had never experienced what we were describing, so the best we could hope for was some sort of verbal understanding. To show that total change was possible, we sometimes asked others who were far advanced in the program to describe their experiences. This often impressed a new candidate, who would think, "If he can do it, so can I." Some men did not want any part of the life we sketched. As one put it, "I'd rather rule in hell than serve in heaven." He would have chosen to be a big shot among criminals, even in jail, rather than a responsible person. To him, responsibility meant ordinariness, which was being a "nothing." Those who shared this point of view either rejected our approach or slowly faded out. Others chose responsibility over the other two options—crime and suicide. They believed that our program might be the best opportunity to exercise their choice.

We did not assume the position of taking a man as he first presented himself to us. Instead, we screened prospective participants. We assessed his degree of self-disgust and carefully observed the quality of his receptivity. Rarely did we exclude a criminal. Instead, he might decline by himself, once he understood something of our approach and understood the strict demands of the program. We gained from these selection interviews, no matter what the criminals decided, because they gave us an opportunity to test our concepts and techniques. We did not use the group format in the initial contacts. We believed then and now that groups have tremendous potential for working with criminals, but only after the initial interviews. If one starts out with a group, there are so many obstacles that the change agent is unduly hindered in making the most effective presentation. He has to contend too much with the "gang" operations described earlier in this chapter.

Much to our satisfaction, many criminals selected themselves out in the initial phase of our contacts with them. We had no problem in getting them to see how criminal they were. The difficulty was that, once they were presented with a perspective of the stringent requirements for change, they did not want to accept the discipline to achieve something that they were unsure they wanted to begin with. It became clear that only a minority of criminals would choose to participate. We were pleased when a criminal decided early whether or not to exclude himself. It was most economical for us when a criminal did this. (Some candidates did not drop out until later, after much more had been invested in them.) The more that poor risks can be weeded out, the greater the savings in time, financial resources, and energy. We wound up with the confidence that, if a criminal adhered to the program's requirements, it was impossible *not* to achieve basic change.

STAGES IN CHANGE

During the last few years, we have spent more time in developing techniques for change than in learning about mental processes. In Volume 2, we describe in detail the procedures that we initiated and refined. Making the phenomenologic approach operative and productive was a major outcome of our efforts. Toward the end of 1972, we formalized the stages of participation in the program. After the selection process a criminal was to join a group that would meet fifteen hours each week for a year. Then we saw him individually for follow-up less frequently, accommodating the time of our sessions to his working schedule.

At the same time, we decided not to work with criminals while they were patients at Saint Elizabeths Hospital. We constantly had to cope with personal antagonism by those in administrative positions at John Howard. Working with patients in the hospital created obstacles in addition to those offered by the criminals. In the hospital, there were a wide variety of points of view and ways of operating, depending on the doctor in charge. Within a given building, the whole gamut of approaches and philosophies of treatment could be found. The inconsistencies were glaring. A prison would have had a more uniform and coherent approach. Another problem attached to treating criminals in the hospital was that the arenas for change were insufficient. A criminal needed to be in society under close supervision, so that he could have experiences with a family, a job, and friends, in order to implement new patterns. Living day after day among criminals at Saint Elizabeths was too limiting after a few months in our program. Responding to these difficulties, we outlined what we envisioned as an effective treatment institution. Volume 2 includes a proposal for such an establishment.

We indicated that earlier we had been didactic in teaching criminals how to function responsibly. Now we were moving away from this. We were presenting concepts in the context of life situations, where they would be more operational. As a criminal presented his phenomenologic report, we gave microscopic attention to thoughts, as well as actions. We selected a seemingly insignificant incident and generalized from it to comparable situations, and then to a view of life. Thus, we began with the concrete, proceeded to the general, and wound up with the abstract. As problems were dealt with, we extended the range of considerations and options in decision-making. There were no more "tools" as abstract ideas; now, this material was blended into our analysis of a criminal's daily report.

In 1972, we began to survey the literature to determine how our work contrasted with current thinking and practice. As our historical chapter in Volume 2 indicates, we paid considerable attention to themes that existentialists addressed themselves to, including will, choice, meaning, and personal responsibility. We emphasized that criminals are not victims. We told a criminal that we had the tools at hand to assure him that, if he implemented the program, he could build a meaningful life. This required a choice and the implementation of the choice. No longer did we tell a criminal that he would suffer and that the program would be hard. Rather, we asserted that, if the choice to be responsible were firmly made, the implementation of the program would be easy. The choice would be firm if the criminal viewed the program as a lifeline.

Our program demanded impeccable functioning. We knew that even the most complete phenomenologic report was worthless unless a criminal implemented what he was learning. Some of our men wasted hundreds of hours in reporting, but did not shut the door tight on crime. If the criminals did not go with us 100 percent, then the transactions in the office would be far less useful, because we would be occupied with confessionals and "post-mortems." The door had to be shut on violation. Violation was to be distinguished from mistakes. As these men began to function in a way that was new to them, we expected some trial and error. But the mistakes made would be due to inexperience with responsibility, and not to criminal thinking. In the past, we had guided and advised the criminals in their decisions. We stopped doing that. A decision itself was less important than the fact that it was responsibly arrived at. If the decision itself were in error, the criminal could learn from his mistake. Again, we emphasized the necessary change in thinking, not only in action, because an undeterred criminal thought constituted a danger.

A condition for participation in the program was that we have access to information from outside sources, such as family members. To rely solely on an unchanged criminal's evaluation of himself was unwise. Thus, we made it clear that we expected to talk with people important in the criminal's life. With those people, we used a modified form of "you know I know," so that they would place confidence in our knowledgeability. In all outside contacts, we adhered to privileged communication.

There was a marked alteration in our attitude toward a criminal's changes of mind or ulterior motives in joining the program. Our attitude was that it was the criminal's life; he must make the choice. If *he* made the choice to change and would implement in that direction, we would assist him. If he chose to score points or build himself up, we would find out in time. The failure would be his, not ours; it was the criminal and not the agent of change who would pay the price.

What we have arrived at is a format that begins with a criminal's detailed twenty-four hour phenomenologic report. We examine the contents of mind (thinking processes and thinking substance) without editing or psychologizing. Concomitant feelings are expressed, but not worked with. Criminal thinking is exposed, only to have it opposed and destroyed by rationality and logic. A sophisticated set of deterrents is used to eliminate criminal thinking and irresponsibility. Anything even suggestive of irresponsibility is attacked; we want to remove the seeds of irresponsibility so that the weed of crime will not grow. In addition, the criminal learns a new set of thinking processes as correctives to his thinking errors. The decision-making process is carefully discussed, and decisions are arrived at with consideration of even the smallest details. There is a careful evaluation of money and the criminal's thinking relative to expenditure. Implementation of what is learned in the office is required, so that at the next meeting we can evaluate further what correctives are needed. The program emphasizes that self-disgust be maintained and that fear serve as a cornerstone and guide to responsible living. In developing procedures for change, we formulated an operational concept of will, related mainly to endurance. With this format, we ourselves were surprised at the efficacy of our procedures in the rapid elimination of criminal thinking and its replacement by responsible thinking and action.

FOLLOW-UP

Our extensive follow-ups of nearly all our criminals sensitized us to the notorious lack of thorough follow-up in other studies. We have followed some of our people for more than ten years. Many criminals with whom we had contact earlier initiated calls or visits. We maintained correspondence with the criminals whom we had known, but who were now in confinement in various parts of the country. That even our dropouts and our brief contacts kept in touch can be explained in several ways. Some wanted to brag about how they were doing without us. But in most a different factor was operating. We had shown these men a knowledgeability, a dedication, and an approach that they had not encountered elsewhere. Most had confided in us to a greater extent than they had in anyone else. A kind of lingering sentimentality seemed to be operating. This was expressed in letters, Christmas cards, calls, and personal visits. The positive results are in the form of a dozen men who are functioning impeccably. Others who have examined them have found the degree of change to be almost unbelievable. As investigators, we never dropped available people, because we could always learn from them. Thus, we no longer invoked "conditions of termination." Some men who entered the program dropped out after a brief "honeymoon" period. A few tried to change on their own, failed, and returned to the program. We kept track of some who dropped out and never returned. We also heard about many with whom we had had brief contact, but who never joined the program. In every case that we were able to follow, the criminals who went their own way returned to crime.

We continued to observe and seek information from other sources. We spent some time in studying drugs and criminal behavior in the military. We conducted a small study at Fort Carson, Colorado, and offered some guidelines to the Department of Defense on drug policy. We studied criminal patterns in early adolescence in working with teenagers in a therapy group at a family service agency. We attended professional conferences as observers and interviewed other experts in corrections. And, for the last three years, there has been a continuing intensive literature review, the products of which are the historical surveys in each of these volumes.

We have presented a story of a "search," rather than a "re-search." The present chapter deals with our difficulties in "converting" criminals. But the major emphasis has been on the even greater problems in "converting" ourselves. We persisted in applying concepts and techniques that we had used successfully with noncriminals. It took us a long time to see that we were dealing with a very different population, for whom tried and esteemed procedures would not work. Only very gradually did we lead sacred cows to pasture and slaughter them. It was out of frustration and failure that we reluctantly discarded what did not produce results. We were truly "reluctant converts." Out of the mountains of data before us evolved a body of knowledge that we struggled to utilize in practice. Now, we, the former reluctant converts, are presenting this material to others, who we hope are not so reluctant to receive it, but are instead ready to use something that works and to improve on it.

We do not necessarily assert that the way we have gone about this study is a model for others. We hope that we have offered an encouraging illustration to those who want to pioneer new approaches. A search like this requires both idealism and realism. It also demands that one who seeks to produce change in others be self-critical and change himself.

THE THEMES OF VOLUME ONE

Right from the first day of our work, long narrative notes were dictated, usually in the presence of the criminal, and transcribed. The group and individual sessions lasted between one and three hours. This documentation —some 300,000 pages of it—clearly reveals our thinking, from naïveté to sophistication and from failure to success. Our problem was how to present this material lucidly for effective conceptual grasp. We decided to present the structure of the criminal mind in the first volume, the change process based on this structure in the second, and the special problem of the criminal drug-user in a third.

Chapter 3, "The Criminal's Way of Life," describes the criminal's functioning in his environment. This account of how he operates at home, in the neighborhood, at school, at work, in the military, and on the streets is based on material recalled and reconstructed by him (before, during, and after change) and by others in his life (family, friends, employers, etc.). The most important concept that emerges from this evaluation is that the search for causation, primarily sociologic and psychologic is futile. From the standpoint of society, correction or attempted correction of such causative factors has failed. For the criminal, sociologic and psychologic factors serve as acceptable excuses.

Abandoning the search for causation and deciding not to work with feelings, we probed the criminal's patterns of thought and action. For clearer presentation, we abstracted and developed these in five successive chapters. Each thinking pattern is part of a totality; and each pattern is interrelated with the others, so the substance of each chapter is interrelated with that of the other chapters. The order of presentation or length of development of each component does not reflect a primary or secondary significance of the material.

Chapter 4, "Criminal Thinking Patterns," comes closest to what others might call "character traits." We develop sixteen features that are not found exclusively in criminals. The criminal expression of these features must be replaced by responsible thinking patterns. The topics discussed are energy, fear, the "zero state," anger, pride, the power thrust, sentimentality, religion, concrete thinking, fragmentation, uniqueness, perfectionism, suggestibility, the loner, sexuality, and lying. Each of these is redefined on the basis of our data.

Grouped in Chapter 5, "Automatic Errors of Thinking," are thinking patterns so automatic that they may even escape notice. Although observed by others, these thinking errors have been tagged mainly as labels that are then used by others to justify the futility of change in the criminal. These automatic errors are the closed channel (lack of disclosure, receptivity, and self-criticism), the "I can't" defense to requirements of responsibility, assumption of a victim stance, a lack of time perspective, failure to put oneself in another's position, failure to consider injury to others, failure to assume obligation, failure to assume responsible initiatives, an unrealistic sense of ownership, fear of fear, lack of trust, refusal to be dependent, lack of interest in responsible performance, pretentiousness, failure to make an effort or endure adversity, and poor decision-making in responsible living. Not only did we probe these thinking errors more deeply, but we have redefined them as well. It is striking that, although these automatic errors draw notice mainly with reference to a grossly "criminal" situation, they actually play a role in all that the criminal does. Automatic thinking errors occurring even in nonarrestable situations inevitably lead to the arrestable in the extreme criminal and to irresponsibility in both the criminal and the noncriminal.

In Chapter 6, "From Idea through Execution," we describe the thinking errors that most directly result in the commission of a crime. This chapter is based on our work with criminals who, with a guarantee of privileged communication, told us of crimes that they were planning to commit, were in the process of committing, or had committed. Little recognition is given to the fact that so many ideas of crimes occur to the criminal that he can implement no more than a tiny fraction of them. The role of choice is pronounced in the process by which he selects from among all these ideas. Our discussion of how ideas are eliminated involves consideration of deterrents. That the criminal responds to external fears, primarily the fear of getting caught, has been well established. We call these "external deterrents." However, there are also deterrent forces from within, such as sentimentality and the criminal's good opinion of himself. These "internal deterrents" are defined here. A decision to commit a crime calls for elimination from the mind of deterrent considerations. This occurs via a process of corrosion and what we call "cutoff" because of its rapid, total operation. A decision to commit a crime is immediately accompanied by an inordinate optimism, which we call "superoptimism." In Chapter 6, we also describe the criminal's pursuit of the "big score" and his deferment of responsible behavior. We discuss the criminal's thinking and action after the crime, both during the "celebration" and when he is caught. There is a discussion of his accountability reasoning, including the idea that getting caught is itself an injustice. The whole concept of "impulse" as it relates to crime is reexamined.

The criminal's thinking patterns operate everywhere; they are not restricted to crime. It is remarkable that the criminal often derives as great an impact from his activities during nonarrestable phases as he does from crime. Some criminals hold respected positions in society, which they exploit in their own self-serving ways. They pursue power for its own sake, but do it in ways that are acceptable to society (or, at least, avoid breaking any laws). Some criminals go through a "limbo" phase, during which criminal activity is held in check, because of an intense fear of getting caught or because the criminal is older and not able to get around as well. We describe how he finds his excitement in this phase. In the monastic state, the criminal views himself as purer than pure, cleaner than clean, holier than holy. There is power in purity. In suicidal states, the criminal is too good for this mundane world. The power component in this phase is described. In a nontoxic psychosis, the criminal occupies a station as lofty as the highest forces in the universe. Although totally nonarrestable, the power feature in psychosis is striking. Chapter 7, "Nonarrestable Phases in the Criminal," describes criminal equivalents, the limbo state, monasticism, suicide, and psychosis.

From the beginning, the criminal, when confronted, uses many of his criminal thinking patterns to substantiate his belief that he is not a criminal. If he is apprehended, he tries to exonerate himself in whatever way he can. If the evidence against him is strong, he still tries to absolve himself of blame. To do this, he uses tactics that are basically similar to those used in the crime itself. He puts the examiner and thereby society on the defensive. Chapter 8, "Tactics Obstructing Effective Transactions," presents a detailed description of nineteen specific tactics used—feeding the examiner what the criminal thinks he wants to hear, calculated vagueness, minimization, distortion, generalizing a point to absurdity, and so forth. The chapter ends with a discussion of a formidable obstacle to any transaction, namely, the semantic problem. An agent of change and a criminal often use the same words to mean different things. We provide specific illustrations of this. Chapter 9, "The Work in Perspective," offers a short statement that orients the reader to our change process, which is fully developed in Volume 2.

Chapter 2

History of the Concept of the Criminal Personality

SOME NINETEENTH-CENTURY TRENDS

THE CLASSICAL SCHOOL of criminology, represented by Bentham in England (1748-1832) and Beccaria in Italy (1738-1794), reflected the "eye for an eye" principle of the Old Testament. It held sway during the eighteenth and nineteenth centuries, with the classicists defining crime strictly in terms of existing criminal law. They emphasized the nature of a crime, the consequences to its victims, and the efficacy of punishment as a deterrent. The guiding conception of man was that he had the ability to think, choose, and act appropriately. Classicists believed that people knew what constituted trespassing on others' rights and that, before acting, they should consider the effect of their behavior on others. Therefore, anyone who broke a law did so willfully, putting self-gratification ahead of the rights of others. Punishment was proportional to the nature and severity of the crime, without regard for the criminal's motive.

In the nineteenth century, both in Europe and in the United States, the study of criminals began. It emanated directly from considerations of law, and the pioneers in "criminology" were lawyers, academicians, and magistrates. The early focuses were the judicial process, police functions, enforcement, and the management of criminals in prison.

A new trend began in the nineteenth century, as Europeans attempted to put crime detection and the whole approach to criminals on a scientific basis. This represented what has been called the "positivist" movement.

> Virtually every element of value in contemporary criminological knowledge owes its formulation to that very remarkable school of Italian criminologists who took pride in describing themselves as the "positivists" and who, in contradistinction to the "classicists" . . . regarded criminal law as a changing social institution and crime as a product of individual disposition and environmental forces (Radzinowicz, 1961, p. 3).

55

Law school faculties were broadened to include a variety of disciplines. For example, Franz von Liszt (1851-1919) in Austria and Germany challenged the retributive emphasis in the criminal code and brought auxiliary disciplines into criminology. The law was beginning to view criminality, at least in part, as a social phenomenon. In the Netherlands, there was a comparable movement culminating in institutes at Utrecht (1934) and Leiden (1936). An objective was to gain pertinent knowledge from fields other than the law. Utrecht's institute was connected with a psychiatric observation clinic having a staff of psychologists, psychiatrists, social workers, and nurses; the emphasis there was on diagnosis and prognosis.

Hans Gross (1847-1915), an Austrian lawyer, is considered one of the outstanding pioneers in the science of crime investigation. He produced treatises on physics, psychology, medicine, and science and in 1912 opened a Criminalistic Institute at the University of Graz. Criminalistics was a special police science calling for the collaboration of specialists in different fields. The Graz institute attracted the interest of criminologists and criminal lawyers from all over the world. Gross helped to make crime detection scientific. A similar movement was developing in France and Italy.

Meanwhile, there was an increasing tendency to question whether criminals were indeed responsible for their behavior. Medical science became an arbiter of the relation between alleged mental illness and responsibility for an illegal act. In 1835, Dr. James Prichard gave wide popularity in England to the concept of "moral insanity." According to the 1843 M'Naghten rule, responsibility was to be determined on the basis of whether a person could tell the difference between right and wrong. An 1870 New Hampshire rule stated that an accused was not criminally responsible if his unlawful act was the product of mental disease. This was the forerunner of the 1954 Durham decision of the U.S. Court of Appeals of the District of Columbia, which established that a person was not criminally responsible if his illegal act could be shown to be the product of a mental disease or defect. After fifteen years of experience with Durham, that court moved to adopt the Brawner decision, which espoused an insanity test proposed by the American Law Institute (ALI). Under the ALI ruling (cited by Bazelon, Oct. 12, 1973), a person was not responsible for an illegal act if at the time "as a result of mental disease or defect he [lacked] substantial capacity either to appreciate the wrongfulness of his conduct or to conform his conduct to the requirements of the law." As Judge Bazelon (Oct. 12, 1973) put it, the approach was adopted in the hope that juries would receive information from a wide variety of sources.

Thus, since the nineteenth century, there has been movement away from strictly legal considerations to an attempt to understand the causes of crime.

The remainder of this chapter is a review of the major controversies of crime causation and criminal personality. We shall not discuss our own findings and techniques here; this review is intended to stand by itself as a source of historical information. When the reader has become familiar with our point of view, he will understand how it differs radically from other schools of thought and practice.

THE ORGANIC CONTROVERSY

In the search for etiology, the positivist school in the nineteenth century relied heavily on the biologic sciences as well as the social sciences. Most influential in this orientation was Cesare Lombroso (1836-1909), an Italian physician, who believed that some men were born criminals and were at the mercy of unalterable genetic factors. He saw such persons as biologic anomalies—nothing could be done to change them, and they remained savages in a civilized world. The anomaly was viewed as possibly due to atavism, a throwback to earlier stages in man's development, or to degeneracy, the product of diseased ancestral stock. Lombroso conducted thousands of postmortem studies of criminals, paying special attention to skulls, in which he claimed to observe numerous primitive and pathologic characteristics. He described the reciprocal relation of the individual in society: nature makes the raw materials, and society provides the circumstances, which may call forth anomalies that in turn further affect the structure of society.

Early in the twentieth century, a British investigator, Charles Goring, attempted to discredit Lombroso's work on methodologic grounds. His study emphasizing statistical precision did in fact raise significant questions about Lombroso's work. For example, the incidence of the physical traits noted by Lombroso was as high among English university students as among convicts. Goring and others believed that criminality did have a hereditary base, but they stressed mental deficiency.

The idea of some kind of constitutional inferiority in criminals has never disappeared. In 1939, Hooton reported results of a survey of 17,077 white American prisoners to determine whether any of their physical characteristics were related to their crimes. He studied a great variety of physical features—eyebrow thickness, moles and freckles, etc.—and found that criminals are "inferior to civilians in nearly all of their bodily measurements." He refuted Lombroso's claim about atavism or degeneracy, but he stated that there was a "general constitutional inferiority," irrespective of the nature of the crime. Hooton's view was that the poorer and weaker specimens tended to be selected for antisocial careers. Like Lombroso, he believed that criminals are products of "the impact of environment upon low grade human organisms"

(p. 309). Hooton viewed criminals as despicable and hopeless: "the dregs of every population draught, pure or mixed, are poured into the prison sinks" (p. 306). He called for complete segregation in an "aseptic society" of the types that were already present and for "the ruthless elimination of inferior types."

Hooton too was criticized. Sutherland (cited by Barnes and Teeters, 1944, p. 166) stated that Hooton's sample of noncriminals was too small and unrepresentative to be a satisfactory control group. Sutherland also pointed out the lack of evidence to prove that physical inferiority is inherited and that physical deviation is not the same as physical inferiority. As for cause and effect, Sutherland perceived a more general problem in Hooton's work: Hooton explained inferiority in terms of criminality and criminality in terms of inferiority, using one condition to explain the other.

An age-old attempt to match body types with temperaments has continued into the mid-twentieth century. The most noteworthy systematic work is that of Sheldon (1942, 1949, 1954), who believed that personality is reflected in observable bodily features, which are hereditary. Sheldon correlated body type with temperament. He viewed temperament as expressive of and elaborating original constitutional endowment and saw most criminals as mesomorphs and therefore destined to follow a criminal path. The Gluecks (1950) compared 500 delinquent boys with 500 nondelinquents from similar neighborhoods and also found that the delinquents were mesomorphs. Lindzey (in Lindzey et al., 1973), reviewing several studies on the issue, pointed out that, although one cannot set up a causal connection between mesomorphy and crime, there is a strong and consistent relation between the two that warrants further investigation. Studies continue to appear that purport to demonstrate the interrelation of physical (constitutional) features and criminality (Nielsen and Tsuboi, 1970; Cortes and Gatti, 1972).

Investigators have long studied families in a search for a possible hereditary basis for criminality. In 1877, Dugdale published his analysis of the Jukes, in which he described a vast amount of criminality among the blood relations of an extended family. Dugdale concluded that heredity determines physical and mental "capacity" (p. 65), but that environment determines the use to which that capacity is put. In 1930, Lange published his frequently cited study of thirteen pairs of monozygotic twins and seventeen pairs of dizygotic twins. In ten pairs of monozygotic but only two pairs of dizygotic twins, both twins were sentenced for crimes. Lange concluded:

> Even allowing for all necessary reservations . . . these facts show quite definitely that under our present social conditions, heredity does play a role of paramount importance in making the criminal; certainly a far greater role than many are prepared to admit (p. 210).

From time to time, studies have been reported of the incidence of criminality among criminals' offspring who are adopted by others. Newkirk (1957), Crowe (1972), and Schulsinger (1972) presented data that would support the contention that genetic factors at least predispose offspring of criminals to develop a criminal personality, even if they are removed from their parents when young.

With sociologic and psychologic factors appearing to be inconclusive with respect to causation of criminality, it is perhaps understandable that attention has turned to genetic considerations. It has been said (e.g., Eysenck, 1970) that prevailing cultural attitudes sometimes constitute a barrier to inquiry and understanding, especially when it comes to the issue of the role of biologic factors in shaping personality.

> Biological theories of crime have never been well received by American criminologists. Tappan said that the little attention given—except in a negative and critical way—was in large part due to the "strongly environmentalist orientation of the sociological criminologists and because of the preoccupation of the dynamic psychiatrists with their postulated processes of psychogenesis." To this may be added the all-pervading impact of the American image in sociology and psychology. Sociologically, life was epitomized in a conception of success in which initiative, opportunity and chance played the main role (Lopez-Rey, 1970, p. 135).

Some writers, although citing no specific hereditary mechanism involved in criminality, nevertheless believe that at least a partial explanation lies in genetics (Henderson, 1939; Karpman, 1961; Trasler, 1962; Eysenck, 1970). Rosenthal (1972) cited a number of specific biologic factors that he believed to be associated with criminality. Among the list of "genetically influenced variables" were electroencephalographic differences, low intelligence quotient, mesomorphy, a possible role of an XXY (not XYY) factor, sexual disturbance, hyperactivity, and tendencies toward psychosis and alcoholism. We shall consider some of these in the following discussion.

Only recently have scientists had a specific clue to a genetic abnormality. Until they fastened onto the XYY chromosome, the speculation was mostly general. McWhirter (1969), in a note to *Science*, observed of boys with the XYY anomaly:

> Characteristically, the home environments of criminal XYY boys are flawless and their behavior is "mystifying." ... It is not improbable that genes (at present "invisible") conferring a raised probability of criminal behavior will be discovered as geneticists increasingly refine population statistics and electrophoretic or other methods of analysis (p. 1117).

Both positive and negative findings have been reported in studies of XYY groups. Jarvik et al. (1973) surveyed chromosome studies conducted by others. They reported that the total frequency of XYY's in the criminal population was fifteen times that found in newborn males and normal adults and almost three times that found in mental patients. They commented that the data of these studies "provide strong presumptive evidence for an association between criminal behavior and the extra Y chromosome" (p. 679). A significantly higher risk of criminality among those with the "XYY syndrome" was reported by Nielsen and Henriksen (1972) in a study of 151 males admitted to Danish youth prisons and by Razavi (*The San Juan Star*, 1/4/70) in a study of sexual offenders.

However, a 1969 National Institute of Mental Health conference (*APA Monitor*, 12/70) reported that no causal link had been demonstrated between chromosomal patterns and antisocial behavior. The investigators called for more thorough study, urging that "prevalence data be gathered among newborns in the population at large." Montagu (in Karlins and Andrews, 1972) has said that, although genes appear to influence behavior, it is still possible to modify the environment in the hope of keeping predispositions latent; in other words, there is not the finality of outcome that some people may fear.

Investigators who have studied criminals have been puzzled by their seeming lack of impulse control and their failure to learn from experience. Eysenck (1970) maintained that there is an "innate predisposition to form weak and fleeting conditioned responses" (p. 187). He believed that an organic condition, possibly localized within the brain, might play an important role. Thompson viewed the psychopathic personality as the product of "psychogenic factors working upon a previously injured brain" (1953, p. 37), but later stated his frustration with psychogenic factors and emphasized the role of brain pathology:

> Data are now available which establish certain points. Analyses of these patients, carried out over a lifetime (that of the patient and the analyst), have revealed no provoking psychogenic causes. In many cases the patient and the analyst (therapist) lived out old ages and died from exhaustion and in confusion; the patient unimproved, the analyst bored and neurotic from frustration. It is needless to state that over 60 per cent of all psychopaths . . . show gross neuropathological signs. It is needless to state that the histories of psychopaths reveal brain disease in 75 percent of cases (depending on how thoroughly the medical history is taken, if taken at all). It is needless to state that countless individuals were non-psychotic persons until a brain injury or disease took its toll and that then, forevermore they became psychopaths (Thompson, 1961, p. 737).

Many other investigators have published findings and opinions advancing the idea that criminal behavior may be caused by brain damage or dysfunction. In their 1973 textbook of abnormal psychology, White and Watt stated:

> It is at least a legitimate hypothesis that some subtle inadequacy of cerebral tissue might underlie the psychopath's inability to be governed by the standards and restraints of society (p. 331).

Winkler and Kove (1962) have contended that an organic brain lesion is the "agent which conditions the individual to react with aggressive behavior to environmental pressures" (p. 329). Pontius (1972) has hypothesized that a frontal lobe dysfunction due to a "developmental lag (and/or neuropathological deficit)" (p. 303) is the basis for some forms of juvenile delinquency. She believed that this was responsible for "a genuine, neurologically based loss of mastery over one's actions."

A tie-in has been suggested between violence and epilepsy. Rubin (1964) noted that Schafer's psychologic testing of Jack Ruby revealed organic brain damage with possible psychomotor epilepsy. Gunn and Bonn (1971) found no correlation between epilepsy and violence in a group of criminals. Climent (1972) contrasted violent emergency-room patients with a control group of nonviolent patients. He found that "severe head injury, judged by unconsciousness," is not associated with later violence in adults. Lidberg's (1971) findings were in a different direction: Among his group of 439 Swedish criminals there was a greater incidence of concussion than among a normal population of Swedish military conscripts. He also found a significant correlation between concussion and a "tendency to criminal violence." The above studies are indicative of what one can find in the literature—both sides of the issue are supported.

One line of inquiry to diagnose and determine the impact of brain dysfunction has been the study of electroencephalograms (EEG's). EEG studies of psychopaths and criminals appeared often in the literature in the 1950s and 1960s, less often after 1967. In 1942, Hill and Watterson contended that an abnormal EEG was indicative of a serious problem.

> One can have little doubt that an abnormal E.E.G. constitutes for its possessor a handicap in the business of biological adaptation, failure of which may show itself, as in our present series, in undesirable asocial behaviour (p. 65).

The authors speculated that "cortical immaturity" might be a contributing factor in criminality. Twenty-seven years later, Williams (1969) maintained that a "major factor" in "pathological persistent aggression" is a "disturbance of cerebral physiology" (p. 519). The EEG has been used as a diagnostic tool to assess such factors. Various percentages of abnormal EEG's have been reported in the criminal population. Ellingson (1954) reported that the literature showed EEG abnormality in 47 to 58 percent of psychopaths studied. Also reporting around 50 percent abnormality were Silverman (1943), Hill and Pond (1952), and Arthurs and Cahoon (1964). Citing figures between 50 and 80 percent were Brill et al. (1942), Stafford-Clark and Taylor (1949), Glaser (1963), and Williams (1969). Brown and Solomon (1942) discovered EEG abnormality running around 80 percent or higher in their sample.

One can also find in the literature evidence that EEG abnormality is not particularly characteristic of this group: Gibbs et al. (1945), Simon et al. (1946), Gibbs and Gibbs (1964), Loomis (1965), and Loomis et al. (1967). As one might expect, studies reporting no significant relation between EEG abnormality and criminality are fewer than those reporting positive findings. In general, investigators tend to publish "negative results" less frequently. There have been several criticisms of EEG research. Kennard (1956), Glaser (1963), and Mensh (1965) have pointed out that the diversity of findings in EEG studies is often due to inconsistency in terminology and diagnostic criteria. Mark and Ervin (1970) mentioned this and other problems:

> The diversity of results in studies mentioned above illustrates the extreme variability in EEG techniques, definition of criminal behavior and interpretation, use of control groups, and correction of data for age (p. 136).

A survey of the literature shows a decrease in interest in this line of investigation. There have been very few reports in the 1970s of American studies of EEG abnormality and criminality. It appears that, in the light of the types of criticism made by Mark and Ervin, other approaches have appeared to be more promising. Such institutions as St. Elizabeths Hospital in Washington, D.C., which used to administer EEG's routinely, now do so only rarely, when it is warranted by a specific incident in a patient's life.

Some investigators have tried to pinpoint exactly what is going on physiologically in the brain that might contribute to criminal behavior. Delgado (1970) found that outbursts of violence could be elicited by electrically stimulating the right amygdala. Other scientists (Schwade and Geiger, 1956; Mark and Ervin, 1970) have implicated the limbic system, in particular the amygdala, as the "seat" of violence. This line of investigation has led to new procedures for treatment, such as amygdalectomy. Many questions have arisen about brain circuitry.

> The individuals with the impulsive aggressive dyscontrol syndrome are on a continuum in regard to the frequency of their violent outbursts

and the amount of provocation required to elicit such outbursts. . . . It is . . . reasonable to assume that circuits for angry and aggressive behavior are built into all men's brains and, in some men, they are more easily fired or more difficult to suppress than in others (Moyer, in Eleftheriou and Scott, 1971, p. 233).

Some scientists have believed that events occur in the brain that require a criminal to seek excitement. His stimulation-seeking pathology is viewed by Quay (1965) as a manifestation of an "inordinate need for increases of changes in the pattern of stimulation" (p. 181). Quay maintained that psychopaths require greater sensory input to produce "efficient and subjectively pleasurable cortical functioning" (p. 181). The rapid adaptation to stimuli causes a need for rapid and intense variation in stimuli; without this variation, a psychopath finds himself deprived of stimulation, which is an unpleasant state. Zuckerman et al. (1972) made the same observation of what he called the "sensation seeker." In thinking along these lines, Quay and others have raised a question of a constitutional pattern of reactivity peculiar to psychopaths. Goldman (1972) reported a neurologic finding that he believed was related to a sociopath's requiring so much stimulation: a "diminished function of the catecholamine-secreting nerve endings, including those involved with sensory receptors" (p. 17). Where neurons do not develop normally and where they develop normally but later "regress or degenerate," a person's perception of incoming information is altered and he "accumulates a store of faulty learned responses." Goldman went on to say that, in "reaction to a perceived diminution of sensory input," the person would "seek stimulation in an attempt to optimize his input" (p. 17).

Hare (1970) has studied the functioning of the autonomic system in psychopaths to attempt to understand their underresponse to emotionally charged situations. The question at issue is whether the autonomic correlates of emotional experiences are reduced or absent among psychopaths. In laboratory studies, Hare found the following:

> During periods of relative quiescence psychopathic subjects tend to be hypoactive on several indices of autonomic activity, including resting level of skin conductance and autonomic variability ("spontaneous" fluctuations in electrodermal and cardiac activity). Although these findings must be interpreted with caution, they are at least consistent with most clinical statements about the psychopath's general lack of anxiety, guilt, and emotional "tension" (p. 57).

Some investigators have thought that malfunctioning endocrine glands contribute to criminal behavior. Research along these lines was conducted mostly in the 1930s. Schlapp and Smith (cited in Barnes and Teeters, 1943,

p. 169) referred to the criminal's "chemically disturbed bodily mechanism." However, Barnes and Teeters (1943) noted that many criminals have normally functioning glands and many law-abiding people suffer from glandular aberrations. Molitch (1937) reported an endocrine disorder incidence of 25 percent among boys' home inmates showing behavior problems. However, there was no unique pattern of behavior in members of the group that would distinguish it from other inmates. A more recent study (Moyer in Eleftheriou and Scott, 1971) cited evidence that the "sensitivity of aggression circuits," which are in part hereditary, is influenced by neonatal endocrine changes (p. 249). Ziporyn (in *Medical World News*, 11/23/73), the Chicago psychiatrist who examined Richard Speck, has stressed endocrine sources of violence. He observed that 62 percent of violent crimes committed by women occurred within a week before the beginning of their menstrual periods. He attributed this to a decrease in circulating progesterone. He also stated that the high homicide proclivity in some young men may be due to a high testosterone concentration. Rada (1974), citing studies that support this finding, stated that new efforts in the field of psychoendocrinology are opening new areas for investigation.

In this overview of research efforts, it is inevitable that some kinds of investigation have been omitted. For example, there have been attempts to determine whether there is a relation between some diseases and criminality. Rosanoff (1944) looked into the incidence of rheumatic heart disease among criminal psychopaths, but found no positive correlation. Some researchers have studied the role of low blood sugar. Rodale (1968) contended that psychiatrists should consider the "dining room as a factor in the cause of juvenile delinquency" (p. 76). Maintaining that a low blood sugar content plays an important role in contributing to crime, Rodale claimed that many children are eating themselves into delinquency. He largely exonerated criminals from culpability when he said that

> we can only blame the official attitude that overlooks malnutrition as the most important cause of juvenile and adult delinquency (p. 38).

Rodale stated that the delinquency problem should be attacked "in the cooking pots of the home" (p. 181). Rodale was not alone in claiming a relation between blood sugar and crime. Trotter (1973), an ethnographer, observed that

> as long ago as 1947 researchers suggested that there might be a relationship between glucose levels and aggressivity (p. 77).

He said that hypoglycemia may be the basis for hyperaggressivity. Another organic factor is lack of facial attractiveness. Cavior and Howard (1973) cited two studies which they conducted supporting the hypothesis that delinquents are less attractive facially than nondelinquents. The authors believed that this finding tended to support the idea that a lack of facial attractiveness "may play a contributory role in the development of antisocial behavior" (p. 209). This is allegedly due to the different ways in which adults respond to attractive and unattractive youngsters. Finally, Pokorny et al. (1973) described an attempt to confirm what two other studies had found—higher concentrations of neutralizing antibodies to herpes simplex virus in psychopaths. Pokorny's team found no convincing "serologic evidence" to support this.

The search for organic causative factors continues. Even those who have supported other theories do not rule out the organic. The psychoanalyst Lindner (1946) stated that disease could be a contributing factor, to the extent to which it impairs ego functioning. He also conceded a remote possibility that there may be a predisposition toward "forbidden or extravagant behavior" (p. 110). Glover (1960), also of analytic persuasion, stated that he believed constitutional factors to be responsible for irritability, excitability, strength of aggressive impulses, and reactions of intolerance to frustration. At this stage of knowledge about criminals, few people are willing totally to exclude organic considerations as causal. A perspective often encountered is that "congenital factors produce vulnerabilities, not inevitabilities" (Wattenberg, 1973, p. 84). Jeffery (1972, p. 4) believed that the coming decades will see a "major revolution in criminology," as biologic aspects of behavior come to be better understood.

Related to the organic controversy has been the issue of criminals' "natural" intelligence. That is, criminality has been associated with physical inferiority, but also with feeblemindedness. Goring's work in 1913 (cited by Hooton, 1939, p. 18) on English convicts showed a high association of criminality and "defective" intelligence. In 1912, Goddard tested imprisoned delinquents with his own translation of Binet's then limited tests. Having found 50 percent of the subjects to be feebleminded, he asserted dogmatically that mental deficiency was the chief cause of antisocial behavior. Goddard believed that intelligence was determined by genetic factors and was not subject to the influence of environment (cited by Caplan in Quay, 1965). However, Healy and Bronner (1936) found no difference in intelligence between 4,000 delinquents and a control group. Perhaps a turning point in this controversy was Tulchin's far-reaching 1939 study of more than 10,000 Illinois prisoners. He found that the distribution of intelligence was the same among the prisoner group and among a group of noncriminals drafted into the Army.

Some later investigators found delinquents to be particularly bright. Eissler, writing in 1949, stated that "the proficient delinquent has a keen, alert mind."

A New York study of gangs (New York City Youth Board, 1960) pointed out that delinquents are quick to despair of school, but "quick to learn and question in areas that are real to them" (p. 56). Warburton (1965), in talking with thirty-eight prisoners who were among the toughest at a prison, observed that "another shock, evident at the first coffee break, was the high order of intelligence of many of the subjects" (p. 135). West (1967), a sociologist, observed that "modern delinquents are not conspicuously duller than their social peers" (p. 111). Cleckley (1964), in his comprehensive volume on psychopaths, stated that psychometrics shows this group to be of superior intelligence.

The controversy over the relation of intelligence and crime is far from settled. The idea of mental deficiency still has some currency. A pilot presidential study (*The Washington Post*, 10/7/64) showed that 40 percent of the 200,000 United States convicts are morons or of borderline intelligence. The study pointed out that, although the average intelligence quotient in the general population is 100, the average for convicts is 95. Then, of course, there is the furor over whether intelligence tests really measure intelligence.

THE SOCIOLOGIC CONTROVERSY

SOCIOLOGIC FACTORS AS CAUSATIVE IN CRIMINALITY

The idea that criminal behavior is a response to adverse social situations has its origins in the Industrial Revolution, when the style of life changed drastically for many people. (This idea and organic causation are not mutually exclusive.) It places the causes of crime mostly outside the individual, rather than within. Right into the 1970s, sociology has been at the center of most discussions regarding the causes of crime. The conditions cited may be very specific, such as the adverse influence of poverty or broken homes, or they may be more general, as when people indict a "sick society" as causative of crime.

The positivist school of the nineteenth century sought to establish social responsibility, rather than criminal liability. Ferri (1856-1929), an Italian lawyer and a student of Lombroso, was considered a leading spokesman of the positivists. He and others of this group denied the concept of free will and moral responsibility and called for the end of punishment. They believed that society must make man responsible. Ferri was primarily a legal reformer with interests in social and legal consequences of crime. However, Marxian ideology also influenced him, and he stressed economic factors as contributing to crime. Bonger, a Dutch law student and sociologist, took the position that the roots of crime were in an unjust economic system. At the time of his death, in 1929, Ferri believed that crime "is the result of biological, physical and social conditions" (in De Quiros, 1967, p. 21). Today's concerns are with the same issues, but with a content appropriate to the time and place.

To illuminate further the sociologic aspects of crime, some investigators began assembling vast bodies of statistics. Statistics have been gathered to relate almost anything to crime, including geography, climate, season, and time of day; and efforts in this direction continued well into the second quarter of the twentieth century. In 1939, Hooton published a vast work with hundreds of pages of statistical data related to sociologic variables and constitutional measurements. He attempted to correlate education, vocation, marital status, and economic status with crime. His results were scattered (e.g., first-degree murderers have a "large excess of illiterates"). Most important in all this work was its failure to shed any light on causation. Social scientists and the educated public became increasingly wary of the uses to which statistics were put. Both the mass media and the researchers began to warn against concluding causation from correlation. For example, Hirschi and Selvin (1967) devoted an entire book to appraising the methods used in research on delinquency. They pointed out a number of flaws in research design and analysis, one being that investigators sometimes conclude that two phenomena are causally related simply because both are related to a third variable.

Sociologists believed that it is difficult to define who a criminal is. They argued that there are differences as to what constitutes criminality not only between societies but even within a single society. George Bernard Shaw was quoted as saying that "you go to jail if you steal a loaf of bread, but you go to Parliament if you steal a railroad." The social circumstance into which one was born could determine whether one is prosecuted as a criminal.

It has been contended that antisocial activities are often adaptive responses to environmental pressures (Dumpson, 1952)—that, encouraged by those around him, a person learns behavior that is commonplace and allows him to "fit in."

> Behavior that is called delinquent sometimes results from an entirely normal process of psychological development (White and Watt, 1973, p. 315).

In other words, a criminal is branded as a criminal by society at large, whereas he has done only what is required of him to adapt to his own environment.

Closely related to this is the "contagion" theory of crime, the time-honored idea that a man is influenced by the company he keeps. Tarde (1843-1904), a French lawyer, criticized Lombroso and minimized physical causes and emphasized social origin. Tarde believed that imitation is the instigating force for crime. He argued that crime starts as a fashion and becomes custom, spreading from the high strata of society to the lower. Sutherland (1961) expressed the same idea in his theory of "differential association." He maintained that people are "initiated into crime" (p. 253) by others.

> The hypothesis of differential association is that criminal behavior is learned in association with those who define such behavior favorably and in isolation from those who define it unfavorably, and that a person in an appropriate situation engages in such criminal behavior if, and only if, the weight of the favorable definitions exceeds the weight of the unfavorable definitions (p. 234).

The modern view of the contagion theory is that people are pressured to try things to prove themselves worthy of belonging and to avoid being rejected. The modern formulation is that youngsters learn their "wrong ways" owing to "peer pressure" to conform. The contagion theory has been extended to prisons, which have been described as "factories of crime." The argument is that, by being exposed to other criminals, an offender learns new tricks of the trade and becomes more confirmed in his antisocial attitudes. This is still a current point of view (Rothenberg, 1971). The contagion theory advanced by Tarde in the nineteenth century has assumed new forms, but still has considerable impact. For example, recent articles and even an entire book (R. E. Clark, 1972) on "reference group theory" and delinquency have been published.

Investigators have stated that crime is found disproportionately in the "soul-searing conditions" of the city slums, where there is social, cultural, and economic deprivation (Warburton, 1965, p. 130). A causal connection between crime and adverse social conditions has been taken for granted in many quarters. Schmideberg (1971) stated that "we all know that the horrible social conditions in the ghettos, and/or bad family life are major causes of delinquency" (p. 28). Official reports and the mass media have focused on slums, poverty, joblessness, and racial discrimination as giving rise to hopelessness, despair, futility, and rage.

> It is inescapable that juvenile delinquency is directly related to conditions bred by poverty (Report of the Atlanta Commission on Crime and Juvenile Delinquency in President's Commission on Law Enforcement and Administration of Justice, 1967, p. 57).

Notable among these reports is the Department of Labor ("Moynihan") report of 1965 on the Negro family. It documented the "tangle of pathology" (pp. 29 ff.) of the Negro family and, after citing the "incredible mistreatment" of the Negro in the United States, stated that one predictable result of "poverty, failure and isolation" is a "disastrous delinquency and crime rate" (p. 38).

The 1967 report by the President's Commission on Law Enforcement and Administration of Justice summed up the deprivation argument:

> From arrest records, probation reports, and prison statistics a "portrait" of the offender emerges that progressively highlights the disadvantaged character of his life. The offender at the end of the road in prison is likely to be a member of the lowest social and economic groups in the country, poorly educated and perhaps unemployed, unmarried, reared in a broken home, and to have a prior criminal record (p. 44).

"Deprivation" has become a relative term as people increasingly have come to realize that crime is not totally endemic to the ghetto, but is also committed by those who live in environments of cultural and economic advantage. The 1967 report of the President's Commission also noted that "crime flourishes in conditions of affluence" (p. 17). In the 1960s and 1970s, the papers have contained many articles about suburban crime. Even in places that were envisioned as crime-free, the problem emerged (*The Washington Post*, 7/16/72: "Reston at 7 Years: New Town Loses Its Innocence"). Cavan (1962) pointed out that discussions of middle-class delinquency are mainly speculative and that there had been little organized research on the subject.

Some people began to wonder whether the "hidden delinquency" of the suburbs that was just coming to light was the tip of an iceberg. Loth (1967) pointed out that enforcement patterns in the suburbs have been different from those in the city. Many crimes do not result in arrests, and many arrests end in dropped charges. Hence, from figures alone, it would be impossible to get an accurate index of crime in these areas.

> Although it is a common assumption that (affluent) families produce fewer delinquents than poor families, it is an assumption that cannot possibly be proved because accurate records on affluent delinquency have never existed (Lelyveld, 1964, p. 108).

Investigators became interested in forces in suburban living that might contribute to crime. Middle-class life, with its upward striving, competition, and premium on material goods, was assailed for its sterility. The whole style of living in the suburbs was under attack and "deprivation" was used to refer to conditions other than economic poverty. Papanek (1961) spoke of the "deprivation of challenge" that comes with overabundance (p. 216). A study (in Freeman and Savastano, 1970, p. 264) by the Probation Department of Nassau County, N.Y., referred to "social and emotional deprivation" of middle-class youngsters. Some of the conditions of life to which many

Americans aspired were also seen as productive of crime. Even the relative economic security of middle-class life was considered contributory.

"Neglect" became a relative term. Those who studied or treated juvenile delinquency were on the lookout for "delinquency" on the part of the parents. When a youngster got into trouble, the parents were considered morally responsible. Parents were even held responsible by law for their offspring's misconduct. Gladstone (1955) pointed out that most states have such laws, although they are infrequently enforced. Almost every approach to child-rearing was viewed in terms of possible neglect. "Permissiveness" was attacked repeatedly, on the grounds that failure to set limits would lead to youthful delinquency, although authoritarianism had long been under attack as stifling development and resulting in withdrawn or rebellious children. "Democratic" approaches to child-rearing have been evaluated as producing mixed results. Mussen et al. (1963, p. 296) described a 1948 study by Baldwin of the behavior patterns of sixty-seven nursery-school pupils. Those from homes evaluated as "democratic" were generally active, competitive, outgoing, and curious, but they also ranked high in aggressiveness, cruelty, and disobedience. Studies indicate that almost any home climate can produce angry youngsters. Sears et al. (1958) stated that children who show "aggressive outbursts" often are from homes in which

> the mother has a relatively tolerant (or careless!) attitude toward such behavior, or where she administers severe punishment for it, *or both* (italics added, p. 358).

Individual social classes have been critically characterized and perhaps stereotyped for particular practices in child-rearing. For example, Kvaraceus (1966) asserted that delinquency is one outcome of the middle-class "perfectionist-compulsive syndrome." Parents were also blamed generally for setting poor examples—being inadequate models.

> Does the child lie and cheat? Well, maybe that is because he heard Daddy talk at dinner about a new gimmick to cheat the government out of some income tax dollars (Wyden, 1962).

In addition to the home, other social institutions came under fire. Schools were a popular target (Clinard, 1963; Burke and Simons, 1965).

> The high degree of correlation between delinquency and failure in school is more than accidental (President's Commission on Law Enforcement and the Administration of Justice, 1967, p. 71).

School was seen as a destroyer of self-esteem, particularly of pupils from the lower socioeconomic classes. Friedenberg (1962) described these students as "helpless in the meshes of middle class administrative procedure." A more basic criticism has been that schools have a way of reinforcing failure and ultimately tend to exclude some students from the mainstream of society. That is, once a student is regarded by others as a failure, his self-esteem plummets and he forms a concept of himself as a failure. The failure experiences snowball until the child gives up. Denied the opportunity to succeed in school, the youngster tries to succeed as a delinquent (Liddle, in HEW, 1963). Havighurst (in HEW, 1963) described boys of below-average intelligence from lower-class homes who acquire a history of failure and misbehavior at school. As a consequence of school failure, they seek "illegitimate ways of getting the symbols of adulthood" or they find "substitute thrills" (p. 31). They "seek certain gratifications that make their failure to grow up more tolerable" (p. 29). This can take the form of stealing, sex, fighting, or drinking.

Curricula have come under fire as not "relevant" to these students. Kvaraceus (1966) maintained that by failing to deal with real life problems, the high school "lulls the adolescent into a stupor or drives him in his resentment to overt aggression in the delinquency pattern" (p. 123). Criticism of impersonality and irrelevancy in curriculum has extended to the college level. In the 1960s, large universities were viewed by some as impersonal "multiversities" specializing in the "knowledge industry." Bigness was seen as dehumanizing the learning process and, in its own way, contributing to crime.

> Education is the magic carpet over the hurdles that make the dropout the shutout in our society. But, even at this most distinguished of universities [Berkeley], bigness robs many students of individual dignity or purpose. This feeling helps explain the spread of drug addiction and senseless crime among many well-to-do youngsters (Raskin, in Lipset et al., 1965, p. 431).

The communication media also came under attack. In *Seduction of the Innocent* (1972), Wertham described comic books as "primers for crime." Comics were seen to pose such a potential danger that the Senate Subcommittee on Juvenile Delinquency held hearings on them. Television was investigated by Congress because of serious questions about the effects of watching television for hours at a time. In 1969, the National Commission on the Causes and Prevention of Violence (in Van Dyke, 1970) found that "violence on television encourages violent forms of behavior" (p. 48). Parents and educators were increasingly concerned about the prevalence of violence in programming and its influence on the country's youngsters. Wertham (1972) extended his criticism of comics to television: "Television has taken the worst out of comic books, from sadism to Superman" (p. 381). Social scientists began to study the effects of television on behavior. After interviewing 689 mothers and 522 fathers, Eron (1963) concluded that "definite relationships are established between TV viewing habits and aggressive behavior in real life" (p. 195). Motion pictures were subject to similar criticism.

> There is no question that the motion picture often presents a version of our culture emphasizing wealth, materialism, and immoral conduct, both criminal and sexual, which as far as juveniles are considered, furnishes them with approved models conducive to delinquency (Clinard, 1963, p. 180).

Newspapers were criticized for highlighting crime, giving excessive coverage, and providing vicarious emotional thrills, as well as providing criminals with prestige by publicity. Advertising was faulted for conveying false values, making people dissatisfied with what they had so that they might resort to illegal means to get what they lacked.

> The cumulative impact of advertising is to nurture a disposition both to engage in and succumb to fraudulent practices and appeals . . . in all institutional realms and at all social levels of our society (Schur, 1969, p. 169).

Pornography has also been blamed for an increase in crime (DeRiver, 1956, p. 269). In a study of 100 teenage inmates of the Cook County Jail, Haines (1955, p. 198) concluded that pornography (as well as television and movies) plays a "distinct role in the creation of anti-social behavior in susceptible teenagers." In 1970, the Presidential Commission on Pornography (*The Evening Star*, 8/6/70) set out to determine whether there was a significant relation between exposure to obscene materials and sex crimes. Despite findings that indicated no strong correlation, some people remained convinced that there was indeed a relation between the two.

Even the church has been charged with contributing to crime, in that it does not practice the values that it preaches and is concerned more about ritual and money than about spiritual values. In 1942, Taft cited a different criticism of the religious establishment. Some people had held that by resisting the ideas of determinism the church was itself being a factor in the causation of crime.

As times change, almost any social issue can be related to crime. People have stated that the immorality of modern warfare can only have a corrosive impact on values in the United States. Entry into Vietnam was seen as undermining the moral fabric of the United States in that it legitimized violence as a solution for settling differences between men. The fact that we live constantly under the shadow of nuclear destruction has been seen as contributing to crime.

> Young people had worked hard against the bomb. They had been snubbed. They were not likely to work again, except in the interests of their own sensationalism. . . . We could . . . live for sensation, as the hipsters and the teds had, but we could do it deliberately, like for sex, rather than love, for speed rather than safety, for kicks . . . (Nuttall, 1968, p. 118).

The scope of forces seen as contributing to crime became more global as people began to speak about the "sick society." Goldenberg (1973) maintained that the concept of juvenile delinquency as an "instance of individual pathology is both unhelpful and untenable" (p. 455). Instead, he pointed to forces outside the individual that bespeak just how bad off society is:

> Juvenile delinquency occurs when the adolescent's needs are unrecognized by the greater society, unmet by social institutions, purposefully distorted by lingering economic, racial, sexual, and generational legacies, and/or psychologically denied by those powerful and entrenched interests whose sense of control would be threatened or compromised by their realization (p.454). . . . We can no longer accept the practices of our socializing and rehabilitating agencies with unquestioning faith . . . (p. 455).

Social scientists who are looking for fundamental malignant social processes have found the concept of "anomie" useful. It was advanced late in the nineteenth century by Emile Durkheim, a French philosopher and sociologist, who saw crime as resulting when there was no criterion of value in society, where cohesive forces were lacking and each man was a law unto himself. This milieu was seen as productive of antisocial disorder and crime. The concept of anomie was extended by sociologist Robert Merton (1968), who maintained that a breakdown in the culture occurs when there is "an acute disjunction between cultural norms and goals and the socially structured capacities of members of the group to act in accord with them" (p. 216). In essence, this means that when people cannot attain what they want through legitimate means, one "adaptive response" is to resort to rebellion, which may take the form of crime. Jeffery (1959) emphasized the role of anomie in his "integrated theory of crime":

> The sociopath appears to be a product of anomie, social alienation in modern society (p. 543). . . . Modern urban society is characterized by a decrease in social cohesion. Crime is a product of any social force which decreases the cohesiveness of a group (p. 552).

Jeffery pointed out that crime is highest in areas of social alienation and anomie, in which social cohesion is minimal. In such locations, old group ties have been broken, and new group ties have not yet been formed.

To some it may seem that alienation from the mainstream of society is a recent mood or psychologic state. However, during the nineteenth century, Dostoevsky wrote, in *Crime and Punishment*, that Raskolnikov was "absorbed in himself" and had "withdrawn from the world completely." The alienated Raskolnikov was a murderer. Contemporary writers have been describing how alienated youths also withdraw from the mainstream, although, to be sure, not all turn to crime. In the vein of Merton and others who wrote about anomie, Keniston (1965) analyzed the process by which some college students make "an explicit rejection" of what they perceive as the dominant values and norms of society. Goodman (1960) described both the "beat" movement and delinquency as alternatives chosen in preference to the "standard culture":

> It is immensely admirable that the Beat Generation has contrived a pattern of culture that, turning against the standard culture, costs very little and gives livelier satisfaction.... Much of it is handmade, not canned (p. 65). . . . The delinquent fatalism is the feeling of no chance in the past, no prospect for the future, no recourse in the present; whence the drive to disaster (p. 211).

Some sociologists (e.g., Goffman, 1959) have pointed out that strains in people's roles can alienate them from themselves, their friends and family, or the rest of society. Writers have commented that people do not always choose the roles in which they find themselves, but rather that some roles are forced on them. Quinney (in Geis, 1968), focusing on particular strains within occupations, contended that white-collar crime may be a "normal response" (p. 216) to one's particular location within the occupation.

Social scientists and others have published numerous books and papers on alienating forces in American life. The forces named have been both very specific, such as technology, and more global, such as "the sick society." Former Attorney General Ramsey Clark (1970) has made a sweeping indictment of American society by maintaining that America's "national character and condition . . . create capabilities for crime" (p. 37). What often follows a presentation of adverse social conditions is the contention that crime is a "natural" response by those who are the real victims.

> [The] system and its mores are death to the spirit, and any rebellious group will naturally raise a contrasting banner (Goodman, 1960, p. 241).

Fearey (1954) has stated the environmental argument in the extreme. He said that, "As a car does not choose to be made, so a human being does not choose to be born" (p. 24). He contended that man is "as passive to his creation and development, and hence as unaccountable for his actions, as an inanimate machine" (p. 24). According to Fearey, man is victim of both heredity and environment. Even his "soul" was placed in him by an external "Creator."

LIMITATIONS OF THE SOCIOLOGIC APPROACH

For decades, there has been recurrent criticism of those who focus on aspects of the environment as primary causative factors of criminality. During the twentieth century, sociologic influences have been emphasized more at some times than at others; for example, during the 1960s, when there was considerable social upheaval, a tremendous stress was placed on social factors.

As early as 1915, people both in and outside the field of sociology observed that different people react to the same environment differently.

> Poverty, and crowded houses, and so on, by themselves alone, are not productive of criminalism. . . . The knowledge that 60 per cent of all repeaters come from bad homes does not prove that any particular repeaters come from bad homes, nor does it prove that a bad home in any given case produced the delinquency. There should be evaluation of the personal traits of a bad young man from a bad home, as well as a bad young man from a good home (Healy, 1915, pp. 284, 285).

Observers have pointed out that even in deteriorated "ghetto" areas, only the minority are criminal. Taft (1942) cited Cyril Burt, who said: "If the majority of delinquents are needy, the majority of the needy do not become delinquent" (p. 175). Many have pointed out that sociology does not explain why only a minority of children who lived in ghetto areas have police records. Jeffery (1959) criticized Sutherland's "differential association" theory on this and other grounds:

1. The theory does not explain the origin of criminality, since criminality has to exist before it can be learned by someone else. Why the first criminal act?
2. The theory does not explain crimes of passion or accident.
3. The theory does not explain crimes by those with no prior contact with criminals or criminal attitudes.
4. It does not explain the case of the non-criminal living in a criminal environment.
5. The theory does not differentiate between criminal and non-criminal behavior, since both types of behavior can be learned. A person can become a dentist or a Catholic as a result of differential association.

6. It does not take into account the psychological factor referred to as motivation or "differential response pattern."
7. The theory does not account for the differential rate of crime associated with age, sex, urban areas, and minority groups. . . . Why are criminal patterns concentrated in certain groups and not in others (p. 537)?

Thus the theory that a man becomes a criminal because of the company he keeps is broadly challenged. Matza (1964), a sociologist, observed that, whether it be the family, the school, or any other institution of the community, the overwhelming influence is in the direction of being a responsible person. He emphasized will and a decision to be delinquent, rather than "compulsion" or inevitability. Even Reckless and Dinitz (1972), who have a strong sociologic orientation, have spoken of "an inner containing factor" (p. 48) that some youngsters lack, thus making them "more susceptible to the pressures and pulls of life in the inner city." It seems that this factor is critical in determining the outcome, given the situation of two individuals having to cope with equally unfavorable environments.

In 1935, Alexander and Healy pointed out that a person may be a criminal under even the most favorable conditions. Although crime statistics may have underestimated the incidence of crime in the more privileged neighborhoods, public attention eventually became focused on that sector. Socioeconomic deprivation was an insufficient explanation, in that much crime was coming to light in stable, affluent neighborhoods. Even before this awareness dawned, instances of "white-collar crime" were notorious. People who were well off financially were embezzling, cheating, and bribing; crime was by no means restricted to the destitute. Loth (1967) summarized what people know on a common-sense basis, but were tending to lose sight of:

> Fortunately neither in the slums nor the suburbs do most people succumb; criminals are still a minority problem in both (p. 19).

As mentioned earlier, some writers have believed that crime is rooted in the economic system. There has been a tendency to think that the incidence of crime is greater during "bad times." Addressing himself to that point, J. L. Robertson, a Federal Reserve Board governor (*The Washington Post,* 9/22/70), stated that crime is not rooted in economic conditions and that crime rates had soared in recent years as economic prosperity had increased. He went on to observe that an increasing amount of violent crime had been committed by young people from affluent families.

The communication media have come under strong attack especially in the second quarter of this century. Both observational and experimental studies have been conducted to try to determine the effects of cinema, television, and newspapers on crime. Although the studies have not been uniform in their conclusions, the indications are that cause-and-effect connections have not been conclusively demonstrated. In fact, the findings point to a lack of causal relation. Even a Surgeon General's report (Public Health Service, 1971) that linked criminal behavior with watching violence on television added the qualification that watching television programs *can* result in aggressive behavior, but does not necessarily have that effect upon *all* children. It was further stated that television contributes to violence *only* in children who already have such tendencies. Picking up on this point, Berkowitz (1971) attributed aggressive and sexual activities to the makeup of the individual, rather than linking such behavior causally to environmental stimuli.

> For what they are worth, several investigations indicate that aggressive youngsters tend to prefer violent television programs: given the opportunity, they generally like to watch people fighting and beating up each others . . . Sexually more active persons might seek out sexual stimuli, In both cases, people want to look at the kinds of activities that give them a particular "charge," activities that were rewarding to them in the past (Berkowitz, 1971, p. 22).

Values of a "sick society" have also been cited as contributing to crime. However, what sociologist Schur (1969) stated was increasingly obvious to all—"the very same values promote law violation and law-abidingness" (p. 186). Keniston (1965) indicated that his alienated students had exercised free choice to reject what others accepted. He declared that alienation is a "matter of choice" and that the same circumstances of life in modern America are reacted to very differently. Even Jeffery (1959), who based his theory of crime largely on the anomie produced by a lack of social cohesion, stated that

> whether the behavior resulting from social alienation is criminal or not depends upon (a) the individual's reaction to the alienation, and (b) the reaction of society to the behavior in terms of legal control of such behavior (p. 552).

In the first part of that statement, Jeffery appears to recognize the "choice" factor.

Of course, some notions of causation of crime have come from statements by criminals themselves. Arieti (1967) observed that the psychopath sometimes uses environmental factors to excuse his antisocial behavior (p. 255). Articles about criminals and their backgrounds have tended to emphasize the environmental influences, but, to some extent, this was a result of what the criminals themselves said, as well as of current opinion. The communication media gave wide circulation to this line of thought.

The issue sharpened into whether the adverse conditions or the people who committed the acts are responsible (see, e.g., *The Washington Post*, 2/9/72). Some commentators lamented the tendency to romanticize and exaggerate the role of social factors and to exempt people from responsibility on the grounds that they were conditioned by their society or were reacting to society. In fact, Coombs, a black professor of literature at New York University, said that to excuse criminals on the basis of social injustice was to take a step backward and give license to crime. Instead of blaming society, he called for the assumption of individual responsibility and for constructive measures to improve conditions.

> No matter how discriminatory life is, one's problems cannot be resolved by a stiletto in somebody's chest. And we can stop finding excuses for criminality and not allow it to mask itself by any other name. We must find the truths in such old commonsensical propositions that nothing lasting is won without sacrifice and that even if discrimination ended tomorrow, there would be no shortcuts to achievement. . . . We can no longer excuse crime because of society's inequities. . . . We stand menaced by our kith and kin (in *The Washington Post*, 12/3/72).

The idea that crime is committed by blacks to avenge social or political injustice was countered by Carl Lawrence, president of the New York City chapter of the National Association for the Advancement of Colored People (*The Washington Post*, 5/28/73).

> The average young black is not that sophisticated. Those who commit crimes are out to get something for nothing, and they're doing the same thing to black people. They jump on whites for another reason: they feel they won't be identified because whites think all blacks look alike.

Perhaps the most telling attack on the sociologic approach to the causation of crime may be made by assessing the results of society's subscribing to it. Many socially constructive projects designed to eradicate causes of crime have had little success. In the literature review of Volume 2, we shall describe these programs and their results.

People began to recognize that former explanations of crime causation were inadequate. Sykes (1971) spoke of a "new kind of crime" that failed to fit "much of the theorizing of criminology in the past" (p. 596). It had been assumed that the criminal wanted what everyone else did—money and prestige. As Sykes observed, however, this formula was no longer applicable. Instead, "there is a strong possibility that crime as sport may be on the increase" (p. 595). Others stated that crimes were being committed for the thrill of it. But they thought they were obliged to explain this phenomenon, and, in attempting to get away from the sociologic perspective, many fell back on it for lack of anything better. For example, Loth (1967) observed that suburban youngsters commit crimes for "kicks," but then he returned to the argument that pressures of suburban living are responsible. Matza (1964), who had stated that a youth gravitates toward infraction and is not impelled, went on to say that youngsters are victims of "shared misunderstandings" and "miscues of the environment," and that they see themselves as "effect rather than cause." Some investigators paid lip service to the importance of probing the personal characteristics of the individual, but, lacking information on this, they also reverted to the sociologic approach. For example, the President's Commission (1967) stated that to identify and treat personality traits of offenders is another approach to the crime problem. This was on page 17, but the remaining 291 pages failed to consider personal characteristics at all. Similarly, the report of the President's Commission on Crime in the District of Columbia (1966) acknowledged that there are "emotional, intellectual and physical factors," but again stressed environmental conditions, despite the recognition that most people who are exposed to these conditions "mature into law-abiding, constructive members of the community" (p. 795). In the absence of knowledge, people fell back on what they believed, even if they were uncomfortable with it. The D.C. crime report stated that "the precise mechanism by which environmental conditions contribute to criminal behavior cannot be stated with certainty" (p. 796).

Some people in the field became discouraged and declared that looking for causes in terms of sociologic influences was futile. Even in 1940, Reckless took the position that seeking causative factors may be an endless or impossible task, unlikely to yield conclusive results (p. 255). Some writers say simply that a multitude of factors cause crime, and so they call for a "biopsychosocial approach" (e.g., Cortes and Gatti, 1972). MacIver (1966) believed that focusing on causation was futile: "To ask why any delinquency occurs is like asking why human nature is what it is" (p. 41).

THE PSYCHOANALYTIC CONTROVERSY

PSYCHOANALYTIC THEORY APPLIED TO CRIMINALS

The most far-reaching event in psychiatry during the first half of the twentieth century was the demonstration of the continuity of mental life and the impact of early experiences on later development. An adult was to be understood and treated in relation to the child he had been. The importance of unconscious motives as a dynamic influence on present thought and action was recognized. The emphasis was placed on *why* a person does what he does and *why* he thinks the way he thinks. The reasons generally were not part of the person's conscious awareness. This approach to mental disorders was considered an advance over the search for biologic or hereditary defects, which lacked conclusive or convincing results.

Freud himself had very little to say about criminals. In an article (1915) entitled "Some Character Types Met with in Psycho-analytic Work," Freud (1946) addressed himself to "criminality from a sense of guilt" (pp. 318 ff.). His thesis was that everyone bears the burden of oedipal guilt, which is largely unconscious. Freud stated that children are often naughty to provoke punishment, which assuages this guilt. In "The Ego and the Id" (1961), Freud stated that

> it was a surprise to find that an increase in this Ucs. sense of guilt can turn people into criminals. But it is undoubtedly a fact. In many criminals, especially youthful ones, it is possible to detect a very powerful sense of guilt which existed before the crime, and is therefore not its result but its motive. It is as if it was a relief to be able to fasten this unconscious sense of guilt on to something real and immediate (p. 52).

In his article (1906) entitled "Psychoanalysis and the Ascertaining of Truth in the Courts of Law," Freud (1948) distinguished between the hysteric, who acts guilty and is not, and the criminal, who is in fact guilty and secretive because he has committed a crime.

> With the neurotic, the secret is hidden from his own consciousness; with the criminal, it is hidden only from you (p. 21).

Freud did not advocate psychoanalysis as a treatment modality for delinquent children. In his preface (1959, p. 100) to Aichhorn's work, *Wayward Youth,* Freud pointed out that both criminal and juvenile delinquents have not developed the psychic structures and the particular attitude necessary for analytic therapy, and he urged that "something other than analysis" be used. Although very few criminals have undergone an orthodox psychoanalysis, investigators use analytic concepts in their psychologic studies and formulations of what criminals are like and how to deal with them.

Freud's "unconscious sense of guilt" concept was latched onto and stressed for decades. Glover (1960) referred to this concept as "the key to all problems of delinquency" (p. 302). This approach leads to the idea that crime results from a need to assert one's sexuality and to compensate for a precarious sexual identity (Lewis and Yarnell, 1951; Freeman and Savastano, 1970). Those of analytic persuasion believe that the need to be punished for unresolved oedipal guilt is an important causal factor in criminal behavior.

They point out that occasionally a criminal takes such foolish risks that he appears to be trying to be caught. They also cite the self-neglect, the injury, and the self-defeating behavior in confinement as testimony to a need to be punished. The desire for self-punishment, or criminality out of a sense of guilt, is widely referred to and forms the basis of understanding by many therapists working with this population.

From a case analysis:

> . . . Rick Anderson may represent the "criminal out of a sense of guilt," whose unconscious self-condemnation motivated punishable behavior. Guilt over incestuous behavior was profound and led to massive repression of the superego (conscience) with the appearance of apparently guilt-free psychopathic behavior. However, the underlying punitive vengeance of the conscience broke through. The "senseless" shootings of strangers, unaccompanied by conscious emotion, can be seen as a defense against and a displacement of strong, murderous impulses toward the wife-mother figure and the child who represented living proof of incest. . . . Rick's case demonstrates how seemingly senseless attacks can at least be understood (Solomon, in Daniels et al., 1970, p. 372).

Glover (1960) explained criminal acts partially in terms of the mental mechanism of projection of guilt. He stated that criminals unconsciously project on the environment their need to be punished. That is, instead of deserving punishment themselves, they become the punishers. Delinquent acts are "punishments" they inflict.

In the psychodynamic view of man, crime has been viewed as a "symptom" of underlying conflict. Criminals are viewed as victims of largely unconscious processes. Because their acts are not subject to conscious control, criminals are viewed as not being susceptible to influence by punishment. Karl Menninger (1968) took the position that punishment of a man for behavior that is unconsciously motivated and that he cannot help is itself a crime.

Franz Alexander, a disciple of Freud, was among the pioneers in applying analytic interpretations to criminal behavior. He and Staub (1931) stated that criminality is part of man's nature. The difference between a criminal and a "normal" person is that the normal person controls his criminal drives and finds socially acceptable outlets for them, whereas the criminal does not. The first "crime" that every human being inevitably commits is the violation of the prescription for cleanliness. The authors stated that,

> as a prototype of certain refractory criminals who persist in their spiteful rejection of social demands, one can imagine a baby sitting on its little chamber pot persistently rejecting any demands coming from the outside; it sits in this sovereign position and feels superior to the grownups (p. 38).

The anal character traits were thus seen in their exaggerated form as contributing to or at least prototypic of a number of antisocial characteristics. Alexander and Staub were then faced with the question of why the "unconscious criminal fantasy" is expressed as a symptom in a neurotic but as a "motor expression in the form of criminal acts" in other people. It was argued that, inasmuch as all people have criminal ideas, it is the relative strengths of id, ego, and superego that are the critical factors. Where the id dominates the ego, drives that are unacceptable to the ego break through and overwhelm the latter, resulting in a criminal act. In "compulsion," the ego remains intact, but lacks inhibitory power over the id. The ego can be "won over" to carry out crimes by means of "special mechanisms which loosen the ego from the influence of the inhibitory superego." The ego-superego conflicts are related to a seeking of suffering for the purpose of moral relief, which could occur on a neurotic or psychotic basis. Alexander and Staub (p. 82) stated that a criminal who is held accountable lies, because he has to invent reasons for committing crimes. The true reasons are not known; they are unconscious. The cure, then, is to discover the reasons for committing crimes, to make the unconscious conscious.

Alexander and Staub contrasted neurotic criminals with normal ones. They characterized the latter as belonging to "a sort of caste that has a certain ideology all its own." Such people are psychically healthy, but socially abnormal. The authors maintained that unconscious processes brought about a conflict-free acceptance of crime by the ego. Alexander and Staub described a continuum of participation by the ego, ranging from criminality only in fantasy to the commission of a criminal act. Others of analytic orientation also saw that not all criminals are neurotic (e.g., Yarvis, 1972). Writing in 1946, Lindner described what he termed the "criminotic":

> The criminotic lives in another world, a special community with interests and ambitions different from those of the rest of us. He even has a unique argot. In a very basic sense, he does not live in the real world (p. 331).

Writers and others working in mental health continue to use analytic language, but sometimes with a different emphasis to describe a very perplexing type of human being. For example, Redl and Wineman (1951) spoke of "hypertrophically" developed ego functions (p. 141) "applied in the service of the wrong goal." Analytic concepts and terminology continue to be widely applied to criminals, because they afford the most unified and comprehensive system to account for human behavior.

Investigators of criminal behavior, using psychoanalytic concepts, turned from the organic and the environmental to a study of the individual's psychic organization of experience. In 1936, Healy and Bronner wrote *New Light on Delinquency and Its Treatment*. The "new light" was the individual psychologic approach. The authors sought especially to understand why siblings do not all become delinquent, even if one does. They focused on the impact of family dynamics on an individual, and they saw delinquency as a response to "deeply felt emotional discomfort." That is, delinquent behavior permits compensation for frustration, flight from an unpleasant situation, or bolstering of the ego. The "new light" in 1936 consisted of investigation based on these and other concepts of individual psychology.

Researchers set out to determine whether Freud's concepts could be validated outside the clinical setting. Hundreds of studies were undertaken to validate, supplement, and criticize the all-encompassing theoretical framework of psychoanalysis.

Child-rearing practices in particular were investigated in a variety of research designs ranging from simple observation to carefully controlled laboratory experiments. Bowlby (1953), in *Child Care and the Growth of Love*, cited the detrimental effects of maternal "deprivation" on young children:

> During the late 1930's, at least six independent workers were struck by the frequency with which children who committed numerous delinquencies, who seemed to have no feelings for anyone and were very difficult to treat, were found to have grossly disturbed relationships with their mothers in their early years. Persistent stealing, violence, egotism, and sexual misdemeanours were among their less pleasant characteristics (p. 33).

Bowlby repeatedly stated that prolonged separation of a child from his mother or mother-substitute during the first five years of life "stands foremost" among the causes of delinquent character development (p. 38). Bowlby's was one of many studies of the impact of maternal deprivation. Other writers pointed out that overattentive and controlling mothers were just as harmful. "Smother love" came in for its share of attack (Riley, 1971; Binstock, 1973). Fathers have been given relatively less attention, although some studies have emphasized that inadequacies in fulfilling paternal, rather than maternal, roles predispose males to delinquency (Andry, 1960; Newman and Denman, 1970/71; Cortes and Gatti, 1972). Those who address themselves to this issue observe that physical *or* emotional absence of a father can have serious adverse consequences. Numerous studies have related child-rearing practices to the development of aggression in children. Bandura and Walters (1959) studied adolescent aggression. The focus was on maladaptive or pathologic parental behavior that contributes to the development of aggressive patterns. The authors maintained that aggression is a learned response to frustrating situations, and that aggression is reinforced as it proves successful in overcoming frustration. In this study, it was clear that aggressive behavior was regarded as symptomatic of frustration and conflict related to dependency. The authors indicated that retrospective accounts by parents supported the hypothesis that "parental rejection and lack of nurturance are determinants of aggression" (p. 69). Whiting and Child (1953) studied child-rearing practices, but undertook a cross-cultural perspective, comparing societies with respect to the degree of indulgence and severity in their child-rearing practices. The expression of aggression was seen as closely tied to cultural norms.

Analytic formulations did not necessarily exclude the effect of environment. There was room to consider the interaction of psychic and environmental events. For example, response to environmental stress was related to "ego strength." If a person had a "weak ego," he would be more vulnerable to environmental forces. Blackman et al. (1963), writing about the "sudden murderer," stated that an "insignificant insult" from the social environment could lead "inadequate, oversensitive and overdoubting" people to "an explosion of aggressive feelings, culminating in murder" (p. 294). This is one example of coalescence of social and psychologic influences in producing criminal activity. Glover (1960) pointed out that a person's unconscious reactions to the conditions around him also need to be taken into account.

Practitioners treating patients who "acted out" antisocially were also prolific on the subject of delinquency. There has been a flood of clinically oriented papers based on analytic concepts. Johnson and Burke (1955, p. 565) stated that "the specific stimulus for a child's antisocial behavior is the unconscious, or less often conscious, sanction from a parent." Johnson and Szurek (1952, p. 332) contended that parents give "tacit but unwitting approval" to their children's delinquent behavior. Unwitting parental prompting causes acting out, with the consequence that the parent vicariously enjoys his child's delinquency:

> The superego lacuna of the child has always been traceable to a specific parental permission. Our thesis is not *post hoc ergo propter hoc*. The enmeshing interplay of parent and child in the affected area bespeaks more than a fortuitous time sequence (pp. 341, 342).

This theme is the subject of an entire book by Reiner and Kaufman (1959), *Character Disorders in Parents of Delinquents*. The view that parents unconsciously foster delinquent behavior has gained increasing acceptance, to the point where for some it is a guiding concept in treating criminals. They see a child as the victim of conscious or unconscious parental expectations (e.g., Mailloux and Lavallee, 1962).

To cite the many scholarly investigations and clinical reports that use psychoanalytic concepts to describe criminals would be beyond the scope of this review. We have tried merely to sketch the type of work along analytic lines that has been going on since the 1930s.

LIMITATIONS OF THE PSYCHOANALYTIC APPROACH

The psychoanalytic school has been regarded by many as the most comprehensive conceptualization of man's psychologic processes. However, it has been argued that the entire psychoanalytic system is reductionistic; it rests on too few concepts. As Conn (1973) put it, "the couch had become a Procrustean bed" (p. 36). It has been argued that a system that attempts to explain all mental life in terms of only a few concepts is too limited. Unresolved oedipal conflicts have been viewed as critical factors in the etiology of homosexuality, reading disability, alienation, delinquent behavior, and a variety of other pathologic behavior patterns. Clearly, the absence or passivity of a boy's father does not in itself determine the path that the boy will follow (Peterson and Becker, in Quay, 1965).

The point is that cause and effect from a single factor, such as father absence, cannot be so easily predicted. The few key concepts in psychoanalysis can be used to explain anything. The practitioner may become trapped within his theoretical framework to the extent that he does not open his mind to disparate information. Cleckley (1964) cautioned, in particular, the therapist who works with criminals. He indicated how a criminal can learn the therapist's system and feed it back to him. Citing a specific case, Cleckley noted that "anything the examiner chose to seek was readily produced by the patient and elaborated with marvelous conviction" (p. 446). Glasser (1965) regarded this as a pitfall even with noncriminals. If one were to obtain data this way, the integrity of the data would be open to serious question. In fact, Reckless (1940) asserted that psychoanalytic explanations transcend "the realms of visible proof and validation" when they "fabricate the complexities of motivations, conflicts and mechanisms" (p. 216).

It has been argued that psychoanalysis adds little to descriptive psychology. One might arrive at a number of possible causes in theory, but still be at a loss to understand the fabric of the individual being treated.

> Psychoanalysis shows an amazing disregard for the material contents of mental states and of their phenomenological peculiarities. The theory is really interested only in genesis. The only question it asks and desires to answer is where some mental fact had its origin. The particular nature of the mental state is of no importance (Allers, 1940, p. 251).

Another criticism of psychoanalysis is that it ignores individual choice and personal responsibility. Man is seen as subject to inner psychic forces, unknown to him. In the following statement by Lindner (1946), the individual is viewed as a victim of the unconscious and of the environment.

> The prevailing economy acts to precipitate crime by confronting individuals with problems which are evocative of dormant infantile situations (p. 245).

Mowrer (1964, p. 201) addressed himself pithily to this issue of individual responsibility by quoting a "psychiatric folksong":

> At three I had a feeling of ambivalence toward my
>   brothers
> And so it follows naturally I poisoned all my
>   lovers.
> And now I'm happy, I have learned the lesson this
>   has taught:
> That everything I do that's wrong is *someone else's*
>   *fault.*

Some professionals in the mental health disciplines have begun to doubt whether it is possible to establish causation by probing into early experience. Glasser (1965) stated, "Knowledge of cause has nothing to do with therapy" (p. 53). Accordingly, he stated his conviction that even if one discovers unconscious motives, such knowledge does not help a patient change. In fact Glasser viewed a concern with causation as counter-productive, in that it tends to absolve a person of responsibility. Schmideberg (1960) pointed out that interpretations are likely to be used by offenders to justify their crimes. Some experts have become convinced that it is not even necessary to ask the question, "Why?"

> The search for the causes of an event or a situation has a great deal of appeal to the scientist and usually absorbs the greatest part of his intellectual energies. The scientist justifies this effort by pointing out that when you know *why* certain phenomena occur or why certain events take place you are then in a position either to make the events take place at will or prevent their occurrence. As legitimate and commendable as such a scientific intention might be, it leads very quickly to simplistic and misleading answers when it is applied to as complex phenomena as those present in human personality development. . . . Thus to ask the why of an event in which an infinite number of possible variables take a part may be intriguing and exciting, but carries the awesome risk of leading to simplistic and, at times, disastrous answers (Des Lauriers, 1972, pp. 46, 47).

Perhaps most important of all is the criticism that some tenets of psychoanalytic theory cannot be confirmed by empirical observations of criminals.

> It strikes me as a quaint fantasy to assume without real evidence that they unconsciously go to such pains to obtain punishment and win redemption for unknown sins when they plainly and glibly ignore responsibility for every known misdemeanor and felony and pride themselves in evading penalties (Cleckley, 1964, p. 249).

Cleckley and others, including some analytically oriented practitioners (Schmideberg, 1960; Karpman, 1961), have questioned one of Freud's earliest and most basic ideas about criminals, namely, that they commit offenses out of an unconscious sense of guilt and seek punishment to assuage guilt. Cleckley contended that criminals attain some of the major gratification of their lives by "flouting the basic principles of justice" (p. 250) and, in doing so, take pains to avoid apprehension and punishment.

Observations by others, including nonprofessionals, have also failed to confirm some of the psychoanalytic formulations.

> Certainly the suburbanites are not driven to steal by the proverbial forces stronger than themselves, an explanation they often offer. . . . They really can restrain themselves when they think someone may be watching (Loth, 1967, p. 120).

Loth advanced the idea that crime is not a matter of impulse or compulsion. Parents and those in regular contact with criminal youngsters repeatedly have experiences that fail to confirm some of the things the professionals are telling them. For example, some parents had been told that the delinquent activity of their offspring was a "cry for help," that the youngsters wanted to be caught. On a television program, several of the frustrated parents reported that they heard cries for help only when their children asked them to cover for them when it came to accountability with the law.

Professionals and lay people who evaluate the effectiveness of systems designed to reduce crime by observing the results are increasingly dissatisfied with psychoanalysis. Indeed, as a rule, analysts rarely treat criminals. Analytic techniques are not "reaching" and changing this population.

> Psychiatrists who happen to see delinquent cases in their practice or in an out-patient department remark on the impossibility of treating them on account of their unreliability and unresponsiveness (Friedlander, 1947, pp. 222, 223).

Most approaches have been hybrids of the analytic and something else. Some investigators find themselves ensnared by analytic concepts and fall back on them, at least in their thinking, if not in practice. They set out to chart new courses, but, lacking sufficient knowledge of criminals, they return to the familiar, which usually entails a search for causes. Understandably, investigators resort to what they know, what they have been trained in—i.e., the established and most comprehensive theory of the mind—even if it does not work.

Campbell (1971) pointed out that Freud wrote no books or articles on crime or on criminals *per se.*

> Perhaps the most disastrous effects of these [Freudian] ideas has been on our courts and penology, and for this we have to place responsibility squarely on those medical advisors to our courts and penal institutions. Most of these advisors are of the Freudian persuasion.... [Freud] did not seek to apply his theories and discoveries to the field of crime. The attempt to apply his theories to the criminal mind is altogether the extension by his followers (p.. 33, 34).

But it is not our purpose here to decide whether practitioners have been "responsible" in applying analytic concepts to criminals.

Recently, the "directionality" of causal thinking within the analytic system is being challenged by empirical studies. Some writers have described how a child actively shapes his environment, rather than being passively shaped by it.* Bell (1968) has reinterpreted studies of socialization to show how a cogent case can be made for stressing the effects of children on parents, rather than vice versa. Buss and Plomin (1975) have discussed the importance of inherited temperaments. These temperaments, although originally independent of the environment, affect it. A ten-year study cited in *Psychiatric Progress* (12/65) has pointed out that an individual's "intrinsic temperament" affects the environment, as well as being affected by it. At issue is direction: is a child molded or does he do the molding? Kagan (1971) has described a "delicate ballet" between mother and child. The mother's behavior is "guided by her motives . . . but it is also under the direct control of her child" (p. 18). The youngster is seen as "structuring his environment" (p. 193) and having an impact on it, instead of being "buffeted by instinctual energy and the socializing actions of the environment" (p. 192). Schaffer and Emerson (1964) over a decade ago also noted how parents' behavior is shaped by their children. The continuity hypothesis of

---

* A sizable literature argues that children are "lively educators" (Bell, 1971, p. 71) of parents and that, beginning as neonates, they have a profound effect on the way the world responds to them (see, e.g., Chess et al., 1959; Birns, 1965; Korner, 1965, 1971; Harper, 1971; Yarrow et al., 1971; Bell and Ainsworth, 1972; Lewis and Rosenblum, 1974).

cognitive development is seriously questioned by such studies, as is the schema of the inevitable conflicts of the psychosexual stages.

It might also be noted that Freud (1948) himself stated that the sequence of events that produced a particular result might have had a different outcome. He was aware of the problem of *post hoc, ergo propter hoc* explanations.

> So long as we trace the development [of a mental process] from its final stage backwards, the connection appears continuous, and we feel we have gained an insight which is completely satisfactory or even exhaustive. But if we proceed the reverse way, if we start from the premises inferred from the analysis and try to follow these up to the final result, then we no longer get the impression of an inevitable sequence of events which could not be otherwise determined. We notice at once that there might have been another result, and that we might have been just as well able to understand and explain the latter (p. 226).

Chess et al. (1960) and many other investigators have found retrospective data insufficient for understanding the processes of human development. Naturalistic studies and longitudinal investigations are putting psychoanalytic concepts to the test. It now appears that the belief that analytic concepts do not lend themselves to proof or disproof is itself being disproved.

THE PSYCHOPATHIC PERSONALITY

The term "psychopath" was first used in the late nineteenth century, when "psychopathic inferiority" referred to patients with severe behavior disorders.* Since then, the term "psychopath" has had wide circulation. In 1915, Kraepelin listed seven types of psychopath. He viewed these people as personality failures whose development was hindered by unfavorable hereditary influences and "early inhibition." In a 1931 work still widely quoted, Kahn devoted an entire volume to describing psychopathic types, but used the term "psychopathic" to cover a much broader spectrum of abnormality than the term now denotes. Schneider (1958) listed ten types of psychopath, but used the designation with reference to a persistent personality disorder, and not to antisocial behavior. Cason (1943) indicated how broadly the word has been used: In 139 summaries of writing on psychopaths, he found 202 different words and phrases that were considered basically synonymous with "psychopath" and "psychopathic." Perhaps the most thorough description of psychopaths is to be found in Cleckley's book, *The Mask of Sanity*,

---

* Some of this material is derived from Cleckley's review of "Psychopathic States," in S. Arieti (ed.), *American Handbook of Psychiatry*. Vol. I (1959), pp. 569–571.

which has been published in four editions from 1941 to 1964. We shall refer often to this volume.

In 1952, the term "sociopathic personality disturbance" (p. 38) appeared under "personality disorders" in the *Diagnostic and Statistical Manual* of the American Psychiatric Association (APA). This label was discarded by the APA in 1968 in favor of separate diagnostic entities, such as "antisocial personality," "dyssocial personality," and other terms for various behavior disorders of childhood and adolescence.

Despite changes in official terminology, there has been considerable agreement on how to describe these people whose irresponsibility and antisocial attitudes are so well known. Hare (1970) cited a study by Gray and Hutchison (1964, pp. 9, 10) in which Canadian psychiatrists were surveyed as to their view of psychopaths. Of 677 who responded to a questionnaire, about 90 percent said that "psychopathic personality" is a meaningful concept. They considered the following features to be the most prominent in the diagnosis of the psychopath:

1. does not profit from experience;
2. lacks a sense of responsibility;
3. is unable to form meaningful relationships;
4. lacks control over impulses;
5. lacks moral sense;
6. is chronically or recurrently antisocial;
7. fails to have punishment alter behavior;
8. is emotionally immature;
9. is unable to experience guilt; and
10. is self-centered.

The most common observation is that psychopaths are unreliable and generally irresponsible. They are failures from society's point of view for this reason. They are sensation seekers (Eysenck and Eysenck, 1973) who do not respect the laws, manners, or mores of society. Their irresponsibility becomes apparent everywhere, the better one knows them. Even actions that appear responsible are often means to self-serving ends (Karpman, 1961).

The second most widely cited characteristic—a component of the first— is the insincerity and untruthfulness of psychopaths. Cleckley summed it up graphically when he said that "during the most solemn perjuries he has no difficulty at all in looking anyone tranquilly in the eyes" (p. 370). A psychopath's lying is so pervasive that some observers have characterized him as being "unable" to tell the truth.

It has been said that psychopathy represents a failure of maturation of the personality.

It corresponds in terms of personality development to a failure to emerge from the explosive period of early infantile development. The psychopath has not matured emotionally beyond the age of four or five; has not, in fact, reached the latency period (Stafford-Clark, 1964, p. 59).

A psychopath's failure to learn from experience, either his own or that of others, is another hallmark (Henderson, 1939, p. 129; Redl and Wineman, 1951, p. 126). Observers have been so struck by this that they refer to an "inability" to learn from experience (Darling, 1945).

A psychopath is viewed as a person who requires immediate gratification. He lives in the present and fails to follow any life plan (Freyhan, 1955; Yablonsky, 1963; Arieti, 1967). He is restless, lacks perseverance, and therefore fails to "sustain constructive activity" (Hill, 1961-2, p. 227). His enthusiasm may run high initially, but it evaporates (Freyhan, 1955), and he goes on to "seek out the daring, the prohibited or reckless act."

Psychopaths have often been cited for their egocentricity, lack of empathy, and downright callousness toward others. Gambino (1969) observed that their "ability" to feel emotion is stunted or bizarre." They are described as being "unable to love or take the role of another person" (Cameron, 1963, p. 658). Undoubtedly related to this is what Offer et al. (1972) referred to as seeing the world in "black and white" terms (p. 350), which precludes a realistic assessment of others' needs and desires. Eissler (1950) spoke of psychopaths as having an "incapacity" for love or trust (p. 99). With the "incapacity" for love goes a poorly integrated sex life. Despite their heterosexual experience which, as Offer et al. (1972) pointed out, is "significantly more and earlier" (p. 350) than that of normal adolescents—sex has little meaning for them. It is a relatively impersonal act divorced from caring about a partner.

> The woman is degraded to a physiological tool and is never perceived in her totality as a human being with her own personality. . . . His partner becomes important only as a tool by which he can gratify his own ego needs (Eissler, 1949, p. 12).

Hill (1961-2) pointed out that, among people of this type, "happy marriages are unknown" (p. 227). Characteristically, a psychopath uses people and shows little, if any, remorse or shame (Freyhan, 1955; Cameron, 1963). The adjectives "greedy" and "manipulative" are often applied to psychopaths (e.g., Eissler, 1949); as Dumpson (1952, p. 317) put it, they are "little men in quest of power and adventure."

Another well-agreed-on characteristic of psychopaths is that they fault others when held accountable for some infraction or violation. They are masters at rationalizing, which often takes the form of casting blame. As

White and Watt (1973, p. 326) put it, a psychopath "readily gives a plausible excuse for everything that has occurred."

Psychopaths are described as people with numerous, rapidly changing moods. Suicidal thinking in psychopaths has been cited by many writers (Kahn, 1931; Henderson, 1939; Hill, 1961-2; Cleckley, 1964; West, 1965). But they emerge from pessimism to buoyancy by setting out on yet another "adventure."

Descriptions of psychopaths have contained some recognition of qualities perceived as assets. For example, Henderson (1939) and Winthrop (1965) pointed out the talents and creativity of this group. News features often include accounts of artistic skills and creative expression by those who might well be diagnosed "psychopathic." Also commonly mentioned is the average or superior intelligence of psychopaths (e.g., Cameron, 1963; Cleckley, 1964).

Some characteristics of psychopaths have also been found in other groups, whose members are not labeled "psychopathic." Personality sketches of assassins have highlighted features also attributed to psychopaths (e.g., Ellis and Gullo, 1971; *The Washington Post*, 5/21/72). Another group showing the same characteristics are the alienated, disaffected youthful dropouts from society so widely written about in the late 1960s and early 1970s. The chart below shows a commonality of personality factors between psychopaths and *some* dropouts.

ALIENATED YOUTHS (*social "dropouts"*)	PSYCHOPATHS (*Freyhan's 1955 characterization*)
I. Untruthfulness e.g., with parents: "I will not let them know what I do. . . . What they don't know won't hurt them" (Halleck, 1967, p. 644)	I. Untruthfulness e.g., "lying to gain immediate advantages [is among] the stock-in-trade of the assault upon the family" (p. 25) e.g., "their promises prove to be meaningless" (p. 27)
II. Restlessness, easily bored e.g., "drifts from experience to experience" (Halleck, p. 643) e.g., can't get interested in school, etc. (Cervantes, 1965)	II. Restlessness, easily bored e.g., "repetitious desire for change, for new scenery, new people, or something exciting" (p. 19) e.g., "restless, unable to concentrate in school" (p. 18)
III. Lack of time perspective A. "Cult of the present" (Keniston, 1965, p. 180) B. "Collapse of future time perspective" (Hirsch et al., undated) C. Rejection of the past (Halleck, 1967, p. 642) D. Death theme (Keniston, 1965) e.g., "washed up by 25" (Halleck, p. 642)	III. Lack of time perspective A. "Live from one day to the next" (p. 21) B. "Often there is no specific goal" (p. 17)

IV. Exaggerations in moods, attitudes, work patterns, including pessimism, suicidal thoughts.
e.g., "a tendency towards sudden severe depression often accompanied by attempts at suicide" (Halleck, p. 643)

IV. Exaggerations in moods, attitudes
e.g., "since affective fluctuations are not only of the crescendo-decrescendo variety but also change abruptly, we have personalities who are impulsive and explosive" (p. 8)
e.g., "spells of dramatic despair" (p. 9)

V. Unsatisfactory sexual performance
A. Impotence, premature ejaculation, inability to ejaculate
B. Promiscuity with little gratification (Halleck, p. 644)

V. Unsatisfactory sexual performance
e.g., "sexual intercourse is a matter-of-fact business. . . . No problem of emotional sharing or obligation [is] involved" (p. 26)

VI. Antisocial activities
(little attention to this; usually seen as "symptomatic" of other problems; nevertheless, noted by Keniston, 1965)

VI. Antisocial activities
(wide variety included in Freyhan's discussion)

VII. Talented, bright
e.g., Berkeley Free Speech Movement participants—"strong intellectual orientation" (Heist, 1965)
e.g., in intellectual discussions—"Arguing is a characterological necessity" (Keniston, 1965, p. 95)

VII. Talented, bright
e.g., "intelligence . . . *not* impaired" (p. 19)
e.g., "Psychopaths with artistic talent or creative ability often start out with a promising piece of work which may show elements of brilliancy" (p. 21)

Psychopaths, assassins, and disaffected dropouts have rarely been termed "criminal" or "delinquent" in the psychiatric literature, although many commit crimes. On occasion, however, a writer in the psychiatric field will do so.

> To put it bluntly, the hippie herd of Haight-Ashbury consists essentially of college-age delinquents. The whole scene is a glorification of delinquent irresponsibility. There can be no question about the delinquency. It is illegal to beg, it is a felony to seduce and sexually exploit minors. Possession of illicit drugs is punishable by imprisonment. To cohabit inindiscriminately, to ignore sanitary codes and housing regulations are breaches of the law (Ball and Surawicz, 1968, pp. 67, 68).

Mental health professionals tend to avoid the term "criminal." Fenichel (1945) pointed out that "criminality is not a psychological concept" (p. 505). He and others prefer to leave this term in the domain of the legal profession. Some writers consider the mental operations of psychopaths and criminals to be different and thus do not think the two terms should be used interchangeably. They contend that the issue of awareness or intent is critical:

> [Criminals] have embarked upon a way of life, often through accident, which brings them profit as an illegal industry. But if they recognize what they are doing, and the risks they run, they cannot be classified as sociopathic personalities (Cameron, 1963, p. 658).

The distinction is that a criminal has been characterized as purposeful in his activities, whereas a psychopath is more a creature of impulse. Cleckley believed that the ends that a criminal pursues are more understandable than those of a psychopath. He stated that a psychopath seems to jeopardize himself more for what is trivial and does not "utilize his gains" (p. 277) as the criminal does. He maintained that a "typical psychopath" is a less serious offender, not committing murder or other offenses calling for major prison sentences. Cleckley said that a criminal spares himself but harms others, whereas a psychopath only incidentally causes injury and sorrow while putting himself in a position that the ordinary man or criminal would be ashamed of.

Clearly, it is difficult to maintain the distinction between criminal and psychopath. Karpman (1961) viewed a "primary psychopath" as an asocial person who has "never become a member of society" (p. 636) and who commits any crime to get what he wants. This seems to fit more the definition of a criminal, in that purpose is implied. Although Cameron (1963) has maintained that the criminal is the more calculating of the two, he agreed that "it is hard to distinguish sometimes between the sociopathic antisocial personality and the criminal" (p. 659). Some writers do not find making a distinction clinically useful. Schmideberg (1949) merged "criminal" and "psychopath." In "The Analytic Treatment of Major Criminals," she said: "Psychiatrically this group consists mainly of psychopaths, some of them borderline psychotics or even psychotics." Eissler (1949) did not use the term "psychopath," but instead wrote about treating "delinquents." Freyhan (1955) has said that many delinquents are psychopathic. Yablonsky (1963) described a "new type of criminal," whom he also termed a "new breed of sociopathic offender" (p. 54). And so it goes, there being no clearcut distinction between groups that share so many personality attributes.

Even within the category of "psychopath," there have been distinctions. Trasler (1973, pp. 70, 90) stated that a distinction between primary psychopaths who lack the ability to acquire social avoidance responses and neurotic psychopaths may be useful. Hill (1961-2, p. 231) differentiated between primary and secondary psychopathy: The former is an abnormal state based on developmental factors, which may include hereditary and various environmental aspects; the latter is a change in character that follows a specific "cerebral illness, trauma or psychosis."

Whittet (1968), citing Macaulay, said of a psychopath that "his intellect is that most unfortunate of all states, too disordered for liberty and not sufficiently disordered for Bedlam." Observers agree that psychopaths' life-style is very different from that of most people. Lindner (1946) coined the term "criminotic" to refer to a person who does not live in the "real world" and "who has different allegiances and loyalties." It seems to be agreed that psychopaths fall into a no-man's-land with respect to psychiatric classification.

> The symptomatology of these cases is difficult to classify. Most author-ities list various classifications and describe each of the classifications without giving any symptomatology of the psychopath *per se*. . . . A fair cross section of the various opinions might be stated thus: Symptoms of psychopathic personality are stereotyped deviation in the moral, social, sexual and emotional components of the personality, without intellectual impairment, psychosis or neurosis, and lacking more than insight or the ability to profit from experience. . . . It seems safe to state that the disease is of lifelong duration in almost all cases (Darling, 1945, p. 125).

> When we come to psychopathy, we are confronted with the most striking situation in the entire field of psychiatry. Whereas in all other instances, we deal with illnesses that have their etiology, however obscure, with a fairly definite pathology, incubation period and course of disease, symptomatology, treatment, prognosis, a resolution or an end, no such situation obtains with psychopathy. Its etiology has so far remained undiscovered. . . . Treatment is nil. . . . Its course is life-long . . . and its prognosis is in accord with its life course. Psychopathy, therefore, is, in a sense, more of a defect than a disease (Karpman, 1961, p. 643).

The thinking has been that psychopathy is a disorder, but not a psychotic one. Psychopaths do not suffer from thinking disorders or bear other signs of psychotic disturbance. Those speaking from an analytic perspective be-lieve that psychopaths have egos that either are undeveloped or function "in the wrong way." Redl and Wineman (1951, p. 156) said that the ego of delinquents has "played a trick on them," in that they are "hypertrophic-ally" developed, but in the service of the wrong goals. That is, a delinquent does learn, and he does have values, but in areas other than what society requires (Eissler, 1950, p. 113). Clinicians observing and working with psy-chopaths have realized that, although they may have some neurotic character-istics, they are not basically neurotic in makeup. This is because they lack the anxiety of autoplastic disorders, their life patterns are fundamentally different from those of the neurotic, and they are not motivated for change. Furthermore, professionals using analytic techniques have noted that psycho-paths do not establish the transference so necessary to effective treatment, as neurotics do.

Kiger (in Rossi and Filstead, 1973, pp. 286, 287) has commented on the "paradoxical traits" of psychopaths, which are so puzzling to an observer. He pointed out that a psychopath may be both untruthful and extremely frank, cruel and yet sympathetic, indolent and industrious, and impulsive and restrained and show both "callous indifference" and "sensitive chivalry." Kiger stated that often those who interpret psychologic tests state their findings as "gross psychosis." Some clinicians (e.g., Glover, 1960) have viewed the pathology of psychopathy as being closest nosologically to psychosis.

> Despite the psychopath's lack of academic symptoms characteristic of those disorders traditionally classified with psychosis, he often seems to belong more with that group than with any other (Cleckley, 1964, p. 423).

Kalina (1964) stated that "virtually all criminotics are either schizophrenics or schizoid" (p. 2). For some observers, it is simply a matter of their perception that no person is in a "normal state of mind" when he commits a crime, especially a murder (Glueck, cited by Weihofen, 1960, p. 524). Cleckley (1964) believed that pragmatically, in terms of disposition, it would be best to say that the criminal is psychotic:

> If . . . it is necessary to say that he is psychotic in order to make attempts at treatment or urgently needed supervision possible for him, the most serious objections are primarily theoretical. Perhaps our traditional definitions of psychosis can stand alteration better than these disordered patients and those about them can stand the present farcical and sometimes tragic methods of handling their problems (p. 423).

The legal profession has been baffled by the diagnostic issue. Judge Bazelon (Jan. 19, 1974) asked why a defendant may be characterized by an institutional expert as an "anti-social personality with no mental disorder" and by a private psychiatrist (appointed at the request of the accused) as schizophrenic and thus "with a mental disorder." Bazelon is critical of the labels because they are used to conceal, rather than reveal, information.

PSYCHOLOGIC TESTS AND THE STUDY OF CRIMINALS

The psychopathic personality seems to be a character type that everyone can describe at least in a general sense from everyday encounters. But identifying people with such a personality and probing their inner makeup by formal procedures presents a challenge to both the designers of the procedures and the psychologists who administer them.

Roy Schafer (1948) has developed what is widely regarded as the most complete and systematic schema for interpreting and diagnosing mental conditions by psychologic tests. Interpretation of test responses results in a characterization of a person's thinking and functioning. Schafer's description of the "psychopathic character disorder" corresponds to the characteristics discussed in the preceding section of this chapter. Diagnostically, the term is meant to apply to people with the following features:

1. a long history of coming into conflict with legal or social rules or both;
2. blandness with respect to antisocial acts and to the absence of an over-all life pattern . . .;
3. a general lack of time-perspective;
4. minimal capacity for delay of impulses;
5. a superficially ingratiating, over-polite, and deferent manner of relating to other persons.

The chief personality features to be sought out are weak integrative ability and underlying primitiveness of thinking, blandness, ostentatious over-compliance covering a basic callousness and inability to empathize with others, impulsiveness, fabulizing and preoccupation with anti-social behavior (Schafer, 1948, pp. 53, 54).

Schafer shows psychopathic response patterns on a battery of psychologic tests: the Wechsler-Bellevue Scale, Sorting Test, Rorschach Test, Word Association Test, and Thematic Apperception Test (TAT). An example of a pattern is that, traditionally, psychopaths score on the Bellevue Scale a performance intelligence quotient (PIQ) superior to their verbal intelligence quotient (VIQ). He discusses other characteristics of their responses, such as poor form level on the Rorschach and, on the TAT, stories of holdups or other illegal acts or idyllic stories with the idea of "virtue is its own reward." In other words, the tester carefully develops a characterization based on patterns of scores and interpretation of content.

Much controversy surrounds the usefulness of psychologic tests. Research literature abounds with studies of the validity and reliability of nearly all such tests in use. What one concludes depends both on what he happens to read and on his own experience. We raise here only a very few issues as examples of questions suggested by some of the studies related to the assessment of the psychopathic personality. An example of the type of inconsistency encountered is the observation that a psychopath's PIQ is higher than his VIQ. Wechsler (1958) stated:

The most outstanding single feature of the sociopath's test profile is his systematic high score on the Performance as compared to the Verbal part of the Scale (p. 176).

This finding is supported by some studies (eg., Glueck and Glueck, 1950, p. 204; Fisher, 1961) and contradicted by others (e.g., Gurvitz, 1950; Kahn,

1968). Manne et al. (1962) have given some thought to the discrepancy in findings of such studies. One problem, they maintained, is that different investigators have been studying different kinds of subjects under the same diagnostic label. In other words, there is a problem in selecting criteria. These investigators also found a significant PIQ-VIQ difference among 193 "defective delinquents" at the Patuxent Institution in Maryland, where the mean full-scale IQ was 90.52. This team suggested two possible reasons for the higher PIQ. One is that a delinquent may do poorly on verbal tasks because he "brings to the exam a tradition of not talking" (p. 76) and thus would do worse on tests that he thinks may be more self-revealing. The other is that the PIQ-VIQ difference may reflect cultural factors, rather than personality or diagnostic features; in other words, anyone from a lower socioeconomic group might show this. There is an abundance of literature dealing with the issue of "cultural bias" in IQ tests. An additional factor cited as explanatory of the difference is that delinquent youngsters and criminals do worse on tests that tap school learning because they have rejected school for so long. This was the thinking of Richardson and Surko (1956) who studied scores on the Wechsler Intelligence Scale for Children (WISC) of 105 court-referral children. They found that these youngsters scored lowest on tests involving linguistic or symbolic abilities that are developed in school.

Psychopaths are often unresponsive to instruments that call for fantasy expression (Silver, 1963). Their stories on the TAT are often short and unexpressive. Criminal themes may be represented in the stories (Hirsch, 1970, p. 635), but generally this is unusual, and the investigator has to look at what appear to be "underlying problems" (Tomkins, 1947). In addition, some test protocols are constricted because the subject is concealing. Patterns of malingering, lying, and distortion have been treated in considerable detail in the psychologic test literature. It is well known that test responses can be faked. In fact, some tests, such as the Minnesota Multiphasic Personality Inventory (MMPI), have "lie scales" built in, presumably to take this factor into account. Observations have been made as to how adept criminals are as they use mental tests for their own ends. One man, in an effort to learn what psychiatrists expected, reportedly memorized twenty-eight different tests while in confinement (*The New York Times*, 11/11/73).

As to the Rorschach Test, disagreement exists as to whether summary scores are useful in differential diagnosis. Knopf (1956) found that these scores do not differentiate among neurotics, schizophrenics, and psychopaths. Rader (1957) examined aggressive content in the protocols of thirty-eight prison inmates. He found that "mutilation content was significantly positively related to aggressive behavior" (p. 305). However, the relation was not strong enough for "precise individual prediction."

On the MMPI, a scale has been derived from persons referred to as "psychopathic deviates." Contributing to this scale—the Pd Scale (Good and Brantner, 1961)—is an array of items related to social maladjustment, family difficulties, paranoid trends, absence of strongly pleasant experiences, and depression. There have been attempts to use other standard instruments (e.g., Megargee 1972) and to devise new ones (Hartman, 1967; Howell et al., 1971) to identify or study psychopaths, delinquents, and criminals. It is beyond the scope of this chapter to review the many assessment devices that have been developed. However, it might be noted that psychologic tests are usually interpreted within the theoretical framework of the examiner. Hammer (1954) and Hammer and Glueck (1955) formulated hypotheses along psychoanalytic lines for their work with projective tests that they administered to sex offenders. "Truncated" points of "Gestalt figures," "elongated objects" in projective drawings, and omission of areas that "carry sexual implications" were all seen to point to "intense castration anxiety."

The view that psychopathy is not a readily identifiable clinical entity has led some investigators to conclude that it is a "wastebasket of psychiatric classification" (Beck, 1937, p. 4). Those who share this view contend that is is futile to try to arrive at a diagnosis of a group that does not exist as a separate diagnostic entity. The same argument has been applied to the use of the terms *delinquent* and *criminal*.

> There is no basis for the assumption that, so far as personality makeup is concerned, juvenile delinquents are a homogeneous group (Schmidl, 1947, p. 157).

> There is no unit delinquent character; personality differences are probably as great among criminals as general intellectual ones. Therefore, we cannot expect any clear-cut "signs" to disclose themselves (Walters, 1953, p. 445).

Jacks (1962) has criticized the practice of transferring in an uncritical manner psychologic procedures useful in one setting to other settings. He admonished practitioners that the use in prison of instruments developed for the school or mental hospital "violates one of the fundamental tenets of good psychological practice" (p. 36). Jacks went on to state that the results of such a practice may be irrelevant to the problems at hand. Consequently, he called for either restandardizing tests or developing new ones.

PREDICTION AND FOLLOW-UP

Society is interested in two types of prediction that are related to the crime problem: predicting who will be a criminal, and predicting which criminals will continue to be criminals. We shall address ourselves to both these questions. The central problem in both cases is the determination of who is a criminal. The chief criterion of criminality is apprehension. However, in light of the fact that many offenses go undetected, arrest statistics are an insufficient criterion. Caplan (in Quay, 1965) warned that making the absence of an official arrest record the criterion for inclusion in a control sample is unsatisfactory.

> While official records may be indicative of delinquent acts among children who are known delinquents, the absence of such records apparently does not mean that confidence can be placed in a corresponding absence of unlawful behavior among unadjudicated children (p. 120).

Unfortunately, the question of who is a criminal or whether a criminal will repeat his patterns is not answered accurately by statistics. Crime statistics have been in disrepute for a long time (e.g., Healy and Bronner, 1928). The President's Commission (1967) pointed out that the rate of forcible rapes was more than $3\frac{1}{2}$ times the rate reported in the F.B.I.'s "Uniform Crime Reports," and the rates of larcenies over $50 and aggravated assaults, 2 times the reported rates (p. 21). The commission pointed out that even this assessment is probably an underestimate. A study by the Law Enforcement Assistance Administration and the Census Bureau (*The Washington Post,* 4/15/74) disclosed a crime rate up to 5 times as high as police figures show for some cities. Former Attorney General Ramsey Clark (1970) observed that millions of serious crimes remain unreported every year; he stated that "tens of millions of lesser crimes," such as petty larcenies, are not counted in official statistics. Wattenberg (1973) has compared entries of juvenile offenses on police logbooks with the official reports that finally are issued. He stated that "it is not unusual to find that two-thirds or more of the juvenile offenders known to the police have been handled unofficially, 'warned or released'" (p. 374).

Writing in *The New Republic,* Goldfarb (1969) pointed out that statistics are unreliable because of differential patterns of law enforcement. He contended that, in American society, wealth and social position have often been the deciding factors in whether a person is charged and convicted:

> Typical juvenile crimes like vandalism, truancy, illicit sexual relations are often repaired privately by upper and middle-income families; but not among the poor. . . . The point is: in the classes of offenses committed by rich and poor *equally,* it is rarely the rich who end up behind bars (p. 17).

Loth (1967), as well as Goldfarb, cited differential enforcement rates between blacks and whites and between different areas of a city. Then, too, for many reasons, charges are not pressed, as in the case of a rape victim who does not want to face the ordeal and embarrassment of testifying in court. Many persons who are arrested manage to avoid further prosecution, and then the arrest is erased from the official record.

Crime statistics sometimes become a political football (Weis and Milakovich, 1974), varying with the zeal of enforcement agencies and the public image they want to convey. If a police force really wishes to convince others that it is doing its job, crime statistics fall, showing that the police are effectively deterring crime. If an enforcement agency wants to show that it needs more men and money, a crime explosion may be reported.

Who's On First with the Crime Figures?

Remember that crime in Washington is a national political issue. And like everything else topical, the subject's up for grabs. Everybody has his own instant analysis every month when the District police release the latest installment in crime statistics.

The only trouble is that the numbers can fit just about anybody's theory (*The Evening Star*, 3/6/71).

Deceit need not be intentional, although sometimes it is. Rather, the different ways of reporting may be the relevant variable. Opinions differ on the question of whether the crime rate is higher now than at other times in history. Papanek (1961) shed this perspective on the matter, at least with respect to juvenile crime:

Juvenile delinquency is as old as mankind. When Cain slew Abel and when Jacob's sons sold their brother Joseph to the Egyptians, the percentage of juvenile delinquency in relation to the total population may well have been higher than the horrifying figures we read today (p. 212).

But one often reads not only of the rising number of incidents of crime, but of a rising crime rate. In short, there is widespread agreement that, if one seeks an accurate portrayal of the dimensions of the crime problem in America, statistics are not a valid source.

Similarly, when one is trying to discern whether a criminal is continuing his criminal career, recidivism records, because they are also arrest records, have the same shortcomings. One might argue that these would be more accurate because of parole or probation supervision, but it has become evident that in the 6 days and 23 hours per week in which a man is not sitting before the authority to whom he reports, he may commit and then conceal numerous violations. Although rearrest records are not accurate, it has long been apparent that recidivism has been and still is high. In their 1937 report, the

Gluecks pointed out that nearly 80 percent of juvenile delinquents continued to be delinquent 5 years after expiration of their sentences (p. 7). A *New York Times* survey (5/20/68) showed that 80 percent of the muggers arrested in New York City had been arrested previously—40 percent of them 5 times or more. In a 30-year longitudinal study of 524 problem children, Robins (1966) found that 75 percent of the men and 40 percent of the women originally referred for juvenile antisocial behavior had been arrested as adults (for nontraffic offenses) (p. 46). Even if incomplete, the statistics have nevertheless shown that the same people are arrested repeatedly. New York City Police Commissioner Howard Leary told *The New York Times* (5/20/68) that

> our problem as police officers is that we arrest the same person again and again for robbery, we arrest the same person again and again for burglary, we arrest the same person again and again for pushing narcotics.

This raises the question of whether there are some who "grow out of" antisocial activity. The Gluecks stated that 60 percent of their juvenile delinquents were criminals at the age of 29. Robins found that 61 percent of the group earlier diagnosed as sociopathic were still seriously antisocial at the age of 44 (p. 296). One does not know the actual number of crimes committed, because the arrest records form the basis of reporting. Even if these people were no longer violating, one would want to know the conditions. Did they change internally, or were there strong external deterrents, such as close supervision? Statistics cannot provide the answers.

Attempts to probe beyond official crime statistics have met with two crippling obstacles: difficulty in finding the subjects and difficulty in obtaining truthful information. In following up her group, Robins consulted both relatives and official records. She found that 25 percent of her subjects had reported fewer arrests than those which were a matter of public record and that 20 percent had understated the time they spent in jail (p. 271). With such concealment of information, there was no way to determine the number of violations for which this group had not been apprehended. In addition, Robins found that 43 percent underreported aliases (p. 269), and so it was not possible to determine how many offenses were committed under different names. The essential point here is that the criterion of "number of arrests" will reveal only a tiny fraction of crimes.

Perhaps the most well-known longitudinal study of criminals is that of the Gluecks. These investigators (1950) arrived at a "social prediction scale," in which five factors, dealing exclusively with the home environment, predicted whether a person would be criminal: discipline by the father, supervision by the mother, affection of the father, affection of the mother, and cohesiveness of the family (p. 261). Craig and Glick (1963) used the Gluecks' social prediction scale and found that it was inaccurate and overpredicted delinquency in the group "having a little less or a little more than an even chance of becoming delinquent" (p. 257). In 1966, the Gluecks proposed to identify future delinquents at the age of two or three. The Glueck's statistical interpretations have been criticized by Hirschi and Selvin (1967), who found that the investigators consistently failed to distinguish between factors that preceded delinquency and factors that may have resulted from delinquent acts or institutionalization.

Psychoanalysts have maintained that their approach goes into such depth that it allows one to generalize some useful predictions.

> If we can uncover a person's early psychological motivations and their influence upon his character and personality structure, we are able not only to construct a meaningful picture of the forces shaping his present and past behavior, but also to predict some significant trends of his possible future behavior (Abrahamsen, 1970, p. 131).

Unfortunately, most of the "uncovering" occurs after the fact. For example, Abrahamsen offered a postmortem account of the life of Lee Harvey Oswald, assassin of President Kennedy. As we pointed out earlier, retrospective analyses have a way of being fitted to the theory that is being used to account for the criminal act itself. This has been the contention of critics who have disparaged the interpretations of events and men's lives from a psychoanalytic perspective.

Attempts have been made to use the MMPI to formulate a "delinquency proneness scale." There was little success in this endeavor.

> We have satisfied ourselves that we could not find a single dimension, measurable with available items, which could be effectively used as a delinquency proneness scale. The personality patterns of the delinquency-prone adolescent are diverse, not monotonic (Hathaway and Monachesi, 1963, p. 90).

It should also be noted that the MMPI has been used to identify recidivists. Mack (1969) met with failure in this endeavor, as did Smith and Lanyon (1968), who tried to predict probation violators by MMPI profile. The latter stated that "the MMPI failed completely as a predictive device."

It seems that the best predictor of criminal behavior is criminal behavior —it is a better index than any predictive measure devised so far by social scientists. Kvaraceus (1966, p. 107) found teacher behavior ratings to be a promising means of identifying "future norm-violators." In her 30-year study, Robins concluded that the best single predictor of sociopathic personality was the degree of juvenile antisocial behavior. The variety of the behavior, the number of episodes, and the seriousness of the behavior were important. The greatest area of agreement seems to be simply that "nothing predicts behavior like behavior" (Kvaraceus, 1961, p. 434). No sophisticated reliable predictive devices have been developed.

SUMMARY

We have described various paths trod in the study of one of society's oldest and most serious problems—criminality. Studies undertaken from a legalistic point of view have been directed toward protecting society, rather than changing the criminal. Detection, enforcement, management of prisoners, and judicial processes have been among the chief concerns of this approach.

We have discussed the views of those who have emphasized the organic and genetic aspects of criminality. These have ranged from Lombroso's nineteenth century "born criminal" to current investigations of the XYY chromosome. Theories of intellectual deficits in criminals have been contradicted by studies showing that most criminals are of at least average intelligence. Man's state of knowledge is such that he simply does not know which aspects of personality have an inherited basis.

Sociologic explanations have been unsatisfactory on various grounds. The idea that a man becomes a criminal because he is corrupted by his environment has proved to be too facile an explanation. Most family and community influences weigh in the direction of responsibility. Careful observers have noted how a criminal gravitates to others like himself, rather than being "made" into a criminal by them. "Deprivation" of one sort or another has been used to explain many pathologic outcomes, including criminality. Some investigators have noted, however, that criminals come from the entire range of backgrounds. Their siblings and peers who live in similar surroundings have for the most part chosen a life of responsibility. Alienation is a distressing phenomenon in American life, but people deal with it differently. Many of the disenchanted struggle to change what they are disaffected with, rather than seek a criminal "solution." Evaluation of the effect of mass media has yielded conflicting findings. Obviously, many millions of Americans watch violence and crime, but do not become violent themselves unless there is already such a predisposition. In response to sociologic theories of criminality, various social programs have been developed. (As we shall point out in Volume 2, it is distressingly clear that attempts to improve the environment have had little impact on crime.) The issue that still must be faced squarely is how much a criminal is a victimizer, rather than a victim—a molder of his environment, rather than a mere product of that mold. It is evident to some that, for change to occur, the focus must be on a person's reaction to his environment, rather than on what the environment has "done" to him. Healy put it well in 1915:

> The makeup of the personality is the largest part of the story. . . . Poverty, and crowded houses and so on by themselves alone are not productive of criminalism. . . . A public playground is no incentive toward good conduct unless better mental activities and better mental content are fostered there. . . . All problems connected with bad environmental conditions should be carefully viewed in the light of mental life (p. 284).

Psychoanalysis has been seen by many as the most comprehensive theory of personality development. Analytic theory and techniques have produced change in noncriminals, but not in criminals. Those who view criminals in psychoanalytic perspective are forcing data to fit an existing theoretical framework. Those who write of such mental phenomena as a criminal's "unconscious desire for punishment" show little familiarity with how criminals operate or with their basic premises of life. In Volume 2, we shall discuss at length the most important disqualifier of psychoanalysis—that psychoanalytic procedures have not been successful in changing criminals. In the preceding chapter on methodology, we described how we ourselves used analytic concepts and techniques and failed.

The psychopathic personality, with its variants (sociopath, dyssocial personality, etc.), has been termed a "wastebasket" category, because it seems to describe so much and yet is of so little practical value. That is, some characteristics of psychopaths are readily identifiable, but most clinicians and professionals in corrections have found that describing a person's traits may be little more than labeling. What is missing is a thorough dissection of mental processes. For example, there is a consensus that psychopaths or criminals are liars. This is readily observable, but not very useful. We shall go beyond the identification of the trait of lying to examine specific patterns and the purposes to which they are directed. It could properly be said that we go into the phenomenology of lying in an operational manner.

Attempts to predict who will be a criminal or which criminals will be recidivists have been unsuccessful. To a great extent, this is because not enough is known about how the criminal mind works. Logically, it is nearly impossible to predict what a person will do when one does not fully understand the thinking processes of that person. We shall spell out these thinking processes in sufficient detail to permit those who work with criminals to arrive at more informed statements and predictions.

Our predecessors have tried the approaches described in this chapter. They have all been necessary in the evolution of knowledge. This survey of the literature was undertaken only *after* we had been working in this field for close to a dozen years. In our own training and practice, we went through what others did in considering sociologic factors, the influence of early experience, and so forth. A historical survey *before* a search for answers often has a stultifying effect on one's initiatives, because a careful study of the literature can lead one to accept something as established or proved when it really demands further inquiry.

Our work is yet another step in the process of coming to terms with a pressing social problem. Although it is by no means the final answer, we hope that it will advance man's understanding of how the criminal mind operates and of what is required for change. As this is written, we are continuing to acquire information and to refine concepts so as to be more effective in our work. We anticipate that others will pick up where we leave off.

BIBLIOGRAPHY

Abrahamsen, David. *Our Violent Society*. New York: Funk and Wagnalls, 1970.

Alexander, Franz, and Healy, William. *Roots of Crime*. New York: Alfred A. Knopf, 1935.

Alexander, Franz, and Staub, Hugo. *The Criminal, the Judge, and the Public*. New York: Macmillan, 1931.

Allers, Rudolf. *The Successful Error: A Critical Study of Freudian Psychoanalysis*. New York: Sheed and Ward, 1940.

American Psychiatric Association. *Diagnostic and Statistical Manual—Mental Disorders*. Washington, D. C.: American Psychiatric Association, 1952.

American Psychiatric Association. *Diagnostic and Statistical Manual of Mental Disorder*. Washington, D. C.: American Psychiatric Association, 1968.

Andry, Robert G. *Delinquency and Parental Pathology*. Springfield, Ill.: Charles C Thomas, 1960.

Arieti, Silvano. *The Intrapsychic Self*. New York: Basic Books, 1967.

Arthurs, R. G. S., and Cahoon, E. B. "A Clinical and Electroencephalographic Survey of Psychopathic Personality," *American Journal of Psychiatry*, 1964, 120, 875-877.

Ball, John C., and Surawicz, Frida G. "A Trip to San Francisco's 'Hippieland': Glorification of Delinquency and Irresponsibility," *International Journal of Offender Therapy*, 1968, 12, 63-70.

Bandura, Albert, and Walters, Richard H. *Adolescent Aggression: A Study of the Influence of Child-Training Practices and Family Interrelationships*. New York: Ronald Press, 1959.

Barnes, Harry E., and Teeters, Negley K. *New Horizons in Criminology*. New York: Prentice-Hall, 1943.

Bazelon, David L. "Institutional Psychiatry—'The Self Inflicted Wound?'" Conference on Mental Health and the Law at Catholic University, Washington, D. C., January 19, 1974 (reprint of talk).

Bazelon, David L. "Is the Adversary Process Essential to Due Process in Psychiatry?" Joint Meeting of the Cleveland Bar Association and the Cleveland Psychiatric Society, October 12, 1973 (reprint of talk).

Beck, Samuel. *Introduction to the Rorschach Method*. Research Monograph No.

1 of the American Orthopsychiatric Association. Menasha, Wis.: George Banta, 1937.

Bell, Richard Q. "A Reinterpretation of the Direction of Effects in Studies of Socialization," *Psychological Review*, 1968, 75, 81-95.

Bell, Richard Q. "Stimulus Control of Parent or Caretaker Behavior by Offspring," *Developmental Psychology*, 1971, 4, 63-72.

Bell, Silvia M., and Ainsworth, Mary. "Infant Crying and Maternal Responsiveness," *Child Development*, 1972, 43, 1171-1190.

Berkowitz, Leonard. "Sex and Violence: We Can't Have It Both Ways," *Psychology Today*, December 1971, 5, 14-23.

Binstock, Jeanne. "Requiem for Momism," *Intellectual Digest*, January 1973, 3, 72-73.

Birns, Beverly. "Individual Differences in Human Neonates' Responses to Stimulation," *Child Development*, 1965, 36, 249-256.

Blackman, Nathan et al. "The Sudden Murderer," *Archives of General Psychiatry*, 1963, 8, 289-294.

Bowlby, John. *Child Care and the Growth of Love*. Baltimore: Penguin, 1953.

Brill, Norman Q. et al. "Electroencephalographic Studies in Delinquent Behavior Problem Children," *American Journal of Psychiatry*, 1942, 98, 494-498.

Brown, W. T., and Solomon, C. I. "Delinquency and the Electroencephalograph," *American Journal of Psychiatry*, 1942, 98, 499-503.

Burke, Nelson S., and Simons, Alfred E. "Factors Which Precipitate Dropouts and Delinquency," *Federal Probation*, March 1965, 29, 28-32.

Buss, Arnold H., and Plomin, Robert. *A Temperamental Theory of Personality Development*. New York: Wiley, 1975.

Cameron, Norman. *Personality Development and Psychopathology*. Boston: Houghton Mifflin, 1963.

Campbell, Horace E. "Freud in the American Scene," *Rocky Mountain Medical Journal*, June 1971, 68, 33-36.

Caplan, Nathan S. "Intellectual Functioning," in Quay, Herbert. *Juvenile Delinquency*. Princeton: Van Nostrand, 1965, 100-139.

Cason, Hulsey. "The Psychopath and the Psychopathic," *Journal of Criminal Psychopathology*, 1943, 4, 522-527.

"Cause for Alarm," Book review of *Report from Engine Co. 82* by Dennis Smith. Reviewed by William McPherson in *The Washington Post*, February 9, 1972.

Cavan, Ruth S. *Juvenile Delinquency*. Philadelphia: Lippincott, 1962.

Cavior, Norman, and Howard, L. R. "Facial Attractiveness and Juvenile Delinquency Among Black and White Offenders," *Journal of Abnormal Child Psychology*, 1973, 1, 202-213.

Cervantes, Lucius F. *The Dropout*. Ann Arbor, Mich.: University of Michigan Press, 1965.

Chess, Stella et al. "Characteristics of the Individual Child's Behavioral Responses to the Environment," *American Journal of Orthopsychiatry*, 1959, 29, 791-802.

Chess, Stella et al. "Implications of a Longitudinal Study of Child Development for Child Psychiatry," *American Journal of Psychiatry*, 1960, 117, 434-441.

"Chromosomes May Be Crime Factor," *San Juan Star*, January 4, 1970.

Clark, Ramsey. *Crime in America*. New York: Simon and Schuster, 1970.

Clark, Robert E. *Reference Group Theory and Delinquency*. New York: Behavioral Publications, 1972.

Cleckley, Hervey M. "Psychopathic States," in Arieti, S. (Ed.), *American Handbook of Psychiatry*. Vol. 1. New York: Basic Books, 1959, 567-588.

Cleckley, Hervey M. *The Mask of Sanity*. (4th edit.) St. Louis: C. V. Mosby, 1964.

Climent, Carlos E. "Historical Data in the Evaluation of Violent Subjects," *Archives of General Psychiatry*, 1972, 27, 621-624.

Clinard, Marshall B. *Sociology of Deviant Behavior*. New York: Holt, Rinehart and Winston, 1963.

Conn, Jacob H. "The Rise and Decline of Psychoanalysis," *Psychiatric Opinion*, 1973, 10, 34-38.

Coombs, Orde. "It's Blacks Who Must Stop Crime," *The Washington Post*, December 3, 1972.

Cortes, Juan B., and Gatti, Florence M. *Delinquency and Crime: A Biopsychosocial Approach*. New York and London: Seminar Press, 1972.

Craig, Maude M., and Glick, Selma J. "Ten Years' Experience with the Glueck Social Prediction Table," *Crime and Delinquency*, 1963, 9, 249-261.

Crowe, Raymond R. "The Adopted Offspring of Women Criminal Offenders," *Archives of General Psychiatry*, 1972, 27, 600-603.

Darling, Harry F. "Definition of Psychopathic Personality," *Journal of Nervous and Mental Diseases*, 1945, 101, 121-126.

"Debate Set Off by Mass Killing," *The New York Times*, November 11, 1973.

Delgado, Jose M. R. "ESB," *Psychology Today*, May 1970, 3, 49-53.

De Quiros, C. Bernaldo. *Modern Theories of Criminality*. New York: Agathon Press, 1967.

DeRiver, J. Paul. *The Sexual Criminal: A Psychoanalytical Study*. Springfield, Ill.: Charles C Thomas, 1956.

Des Lauriers, Austin M. "What Has Happened to Gene," *Forum* (of the Devereux Foundation), 1972, 7, 46-49.

Dugdale, Robert L. *The Jukes: A Study in Crime, Pauperism, Disease and Heredity*. New York: G. P. Putnam's Sons, 1877.

Dumpson, James R. "Gang and Narcotic Problems of Teen-Age Youth," *American Journal of Psychotherapy*, 1952, 6, 312-346.

Eissler, K. R. "Ego-Psychological Implications of the Psychoanalytic Treatment of Delinquents," *The Psychoanalytic Study of the Child*. Vol 5. New York: International Universities Press, 1950, 97-121.

Eissler, K. R. "Some Problems of Delinquency," in Eissler, K. R. (Ed.), *Searchlights on Delinquency*. New York: International Universities Press, 1949, 3-25.

Ellingson, R. J. "The Incidence of EEG Abnormality Among Patients with Mental Disorders of Apparently Nonorganic Origin," *American Journal of Psychiatry*, 1954, 111, 263-275.

Ellis, Albert, and Gullo, John. *Murder and Assassination*. New York: Lyle Stuart, 1971.

Ernst, Franklin H., and Keating, William C., Jr. "Psychiatric Treatment of the California Felon," *American Journal of Psychiatry*, 1964, 120, 974-979.

Eron, Leonard D. "Relationship of TV Viewing Habits and Aggressive Behavior in Children," *Journal of Abnormal and Social Psychology*, 1963, 67, 193-196.

Eysenck, Hans J. *Crime and Personality*. London: Paladin, 1970.

Eysenck, Sybil B. G., and Eysenck, Hans J. "The Personality of Female Prisoners," *British Journal of Psychiatry*, 1973, 122, 693-698.

"Fear of Muggers Looms Large in Public Concern Over Crime," *The New York Times*, May 20, 1968.

"Fear Seen Disproportionate to Crime," *The Washington Post*, May 28, 1973.

Fearey, Robert A. "Concept of Responsibility," *Journal of Criminal Law, Criminology and Police Science*, 1954, 45, 21-28.

"Fed Officer Rejects Crime Root Theory," *The Washington Post*, September 22, 1970.

Fenichel, Otto. *The Psychoanalytic Theory of Neurosis*. New York: W. W. Norton. 1945.

Fisher, G. M. "Discrepancy in Verbal and Performance IQ in Adolescent Sociopaths," *Journal of Clinical Psychology*, 1961, 17, 60.

Freeman, Beatrice, and Savastano, G. "The Affluent Youthful Offender," *Crime and Delinquency*, 1970, 16, 264-272.

Freud, S. "Preface to Aichhorn's *Wayward Youth*," in *The Complete Psychological Works of Sigmund Freud*. Vol. 19. London: Hogarth, 1961, 273-275.

Freud, S. "Psycho-analysis and the Ascertaining of Truth in Courts of Law," in *Collected Papers*. Vol. 2. London: Hogarth, 1948, 13-24.

Freud, S. "Some Character-Types Met with in Psycho-analytic Work," in *Collected Papers*. Vol. 4. London: Hogarth, 1946, 318-344.

Freud, S. "The Ego and the Id," in *The Complete Psychological Works of Sigmund Freud*. Vol. 19. London: Hogarth, 1961, 12-68.

Freud, S. "The Psychogenesis of a Case of Homosexuality in a Woman," in *Collected Papers*. Vol. 2. London: Hogarth, 1948, 202-231.

Freyhan, Fritz A. "Psychopathic Personalities," *Oxford Loose Leaf Medicine*. New York: Oxford University Press, 1955, 239-256.

Friedenberg, Edgar Z. *The Vanishing Adolescent*. New York: Dell, 1962.

Friedlander, Kate. *The Psycho-analytical Approach to Juvenile Delinquency*. New York: International Universities Press, 1947.

Gambino, Richard. "Crime and Punishment—Toward a Policy for Our Time," *The Ethical Forum*, 1969, 12, 1-18.

Gibbs, A. et al. "Electroencephalographic Study of Criminals," *American Journal of Psychiatry*, 1945, 102, 294-300.

Gibbs, Frederic A., and Gibbs, E. L. "Psychiatric Disorders," in *Atlas of Electroencephalography*. Vol. 3. Reading, Mass.: Addison-Wesley, 1964.

Gladstone, Irving A. "Spare the Rod and Spoil the Parent," *Federal Probation*, June 1955, 19, 37-41.

Glaser, Gilbert H. (Ed.). *EEG and Behavior*. New York: Basic Books, 1963.

Glasser, William. *Reality Therapy*. New York: Harper and Row, 1965.

Glover, Edward. *The Roots of Crime*. New York: International Universities Press, 1960.

Glueck, Eleanor T. "Identification of Potential Delinquents at 2-3 Years of Age," *International Journal of Social Psychiatry*, 1966, 12, 5-16.

Glueck, Sheldon, and Glueck, Eleanor. *Later Criminal Careers*. New York: The Commonwealth Fund, 1937.

Glueck, Sheldon, and Glueck, Eleanor. *Unraveling Juvenile Delinquency*. New York: The Commonwealth Fund, 1950.

Goffman, Erving. *The Presentation of Self in Everyday Life*. New York: Doubleday Anchor, 1959.

Goldenberg, I. Ira. "An Alternative Definition and Conception of Juvenile Delinquency: Implications for Planning," *Professional Psychology*, 1973, 4, 454-461.

Goldfarb, Ronald. "Prison: The National Poorhouse," *The New Republic*, November 1, 1969, 161, 15-17.

Goldman, Harold. "Sociopathy and Diseases of Arousal: Psychopharmacology, Treatment and Prevention," in *Proceedings: Crime Prevention through Environmental Design Workshop*. Ohio State University, July 19-23, 1972.

Good, Patricia, and Brantner, John. *The Physician's Guide to the MMPI.* Minneapolis: University of Minnesota Press, 1961.

Goodman, Paul. *Growing Up Absurd.* New York: Vintage, 1960.

Gunn, John, and Bonn, John. "Criminality and Violence in Epileptic Prisoners," *British Journal of Psychiatry,* 1971, 118, 337-343.

Gurvitz, Milton S. "The Wechsler-Bellevue Test and the Diagnosis of Psychopathic Personality," *Journal of Clinical Psychology,* 1950, 6, 397-401.

Haines, William H. "Juvenile Delinquency and Television," *The Journal of Social Therapy,* 1955, 1, 192-198.

Halleck, Seymour L. *Psychiatry and the Dilemmas of Crime.* New York: Harper and Row, 1967.

Hammer, Emanuel F. "A Comparison of H-T-P's of Rapists and Pedophiles," *Journal of Projective Techniques,* 1954, 18, 346-354.

Hammer, Emanuel, and Glueck, Bernard C., Jr. "Psychodynamic Patterns in the Sex Offender," in *Proceedings* of the American Psychopathological Association's 43rd Annual Meeting, 1955, 157-168.

Hare, Robert D. *Psychopathy: Theory and Research.* New York: Wiley, 1970.

Harper, Lawrence V. "The Young as a Source of Stimuli Controlling Caretaker Behavior," *Developmental Psychology,* 1971, 4, 73-88.

Hartman, Robert S. *The Hartman Value Inventory.* Boston: Miller Associates, 1967.

Hathaway, Starke R., and Monachesi, Elio D. *Adolescent Personality and Behavior.* Minneapolis: University of Minnesota Press, 1963.

Havighurst, Robert J. "Research on the School Work-Study Program in the Prevention of Juvenile Delinquency," in United States Dept. of Health, Education and Welfare. *Role of the School in Prevention of Juvenile Delinquency,* 1963, 27-45.

Healy, William. *The Individual Delinquent.* Boston: Little, Brown, 1915.

Healy, William, and Broner, August F. *Delinquents and Criminals.* New York: Macmillan, 1928.

Healy, William, and Bronner, August F. *New Light on Delinquency and Its Treatment.* New Haven: Yale University Press, 1936.

Heist, Paul. "Intellect and Commitment: The Faces of Discontent," edited version of article in *Order and Freedom on the Campus.* Western Interstate Commission for Higher Education and the Center for the Study of Higher Education, 1965.

Henderson, D. K. *Psychopathic States.* New York: W. W. Norton, 1939.

Henderson, David. "Psychopathic States," *British Journal of Delinquency,* 1951, 2, 84-87.

Hill, Denis. "Character and Personality in Relation to Criminal Responsibility," *Medicine, Science and the Law,* 1961-62, 2, 221-232.

Hill, Denis, and Pond, D. A. "Reflections on One Hundred Capital Cases Submitted to Electroencephalography," *Journal of Mental Science,* 1952, 98, 23-43.

Hill, Denis, and Watterson, Donald. "Electro-encephalographic Studies of Psychopathic Personalities," *Journal of Neurology and Psychiatry,* 1942, 5, 47-65.

Hirsch, Ernest A. *The Troubled Adolescent As He Emerges on Psychological Tests.* New York: International Universities Press, 1970.

Hirsch, Steven et al. "Psycho-social Issues in Talented College Drop-outs" (Draft).

Hirschi, Travis, and Selvin, Hanan C. *Delinquency Research.* New York: Free Press, 1967.

Hooton, Earnest A. *Crime and the Man.* Cambridge, Mass.: Harvard University Press, 1939.

Hooton, Earnest A. *The American Criminal.* Vol. 1. Cambridge, Mass.: Harvard University Press, 1939.

Howell, Robert J. et al. *Bipolar Psychological Inventory.* Orem, Utah: Psychological Research Associates, 1971.

Jacks, Irving. "Psychological Testing in Institutional Rehabilitation Centers," *Crime and Delinquency,* 1962, 8, 34-39.

Jarvik, Lissy F. et al. "Human Aggression and the Extra Y Chromosome: Fact or Fantasy?" *American Psychologist,* 1973, 28, 674-683.

Jeffery, C. R. "Environmental Design and the Prevention of Behavioral Disorders and Criminality," in *Proceedings: Crime Prevention through Environmental Design Workshop* at Ohio State University, July 19-23, 1972.

Jeffery, Clarence R. "An Integrated Theory of Crime and Criminal Behavior," *Journal of Criminal Law, Criminology and Police Science,* 1959, 49, 533-552.

Johnson, Adelaide, and Burke, Edmund C. "Parental Permissiveness and Fostering in Child Rearing and Their Relationship to Juvenile Delinquency," *Proceedings of the Staff Meetings of the Mayo Clinic,* 1955, 30, 557-565.

Johnson, Adelaide M., and Szurek, S. A. "The Genesis of Antisocial Acting Out in Children and Adults," *Psychoanalytic Quarterly,* 1952, 21, 323-343.

Kagan, Jerome. *Change and Continuity in Infancy.* New York: Wiley, 1971.

Kahn, Eugen. *Psychopathic Personalities.* New Haven: Yale University Press, 1931.

Kahn, Marvin W. "Superior Performance IQ of Murderers as a Function of Overt Act of Diagnosis," *Journal of Social Psychology,* 1968, 76, 113-116.

Kalina, Roger K. "Diazepam: Its Role in a Prison Setting," *Diseases of the Nervous System,* 1964, 25, 101-107.

Karpman, Ben. "The Structure of Neuroses: With Special Differentials between Neurosis, Psychosis, Homosexuality, Alcoholism, Psychopathy and Criminality." *Archives of Criminal Psychodynamics,* 1961, 4, 599-646.

Keniston, Kenneth. *The Uncommitted.* New York: Harcourt, Brace and World, 1965.

Kennard, Margaret A. "The Electroencephalogram and Disorders of Behavior," *Journal of Nervous and Mental Diseases,* 1956, 124, 103-124.

Kiger, Roger S. "Treating the Psychopathic Patient in a Therapeutic Community," in Rossi, Jean J. and Filstead, William J. Ceds.). *The Therapeutic Community.* New York: Behavioral Publications, 1973.

Knopf, Irwin J. "Rorschach Summary Scores in Differential Diagnosis," *Journal of Consulting Psychology,* 1956, 20, 99-104.

Korner, Anneliese F. "Individual Differences at Birth: Implications for Early Experience and Later Development," *American Journal of Orthopsychiatry,* 1971, 41, 608-619.

Korner, Anneliese F. "Mother-Child Interaction: One- or Two-Way Street," *Social Work,* 1965, 10, 47-51.

Kvaraceus, William C. *Dynamics of Delinquency.* Columbus: Charles E. Merrill, 1966.

Kvaraceus, William C. "Forecasting Delinquency: A Three Year Experiment," *Exceptional Children,* 1961, 27, 429-435.

Lange, Johannes. *Crime and Destiny.* New York: Charles Boni, 1930.

Lelyveld, Joseph. "The Paradoxical Case of the Affluent Delinquent," *The New York Times Magazine,* October 4, 1964, 13 & 106-110.

Lewis, Michael, and Rosenblum, Leonard A. (Eds.). *The Effect of the Infant on Its Caregiver.* New York: Wiley, 1974.

Lewis, Nolan D., and Yarnell, Helen. *Pathological Firesetting (Pyromania)*. New York: Nervous and Mental Disease Monographs, 1951.

Lidberg, L. "Frequency of Concussion and Type of Criminality," *Acta Psychiatrica Scandinavica*, 1971, 47, 452-461.

Liddle, Gordon P. "Existing and Projected Research on Reading in Relationship to Juvenile Delinquency," in United States Dept. of Health Education and Welfare. *Role of the School in Prevention of Juvenile Delinquency*, 1963, 46-68.

Lindner, Robert M. *Stone Walls and Men*. New York: Odyssey Press, 1946.

Lindzey, Gardner. "Morphology and Behavior," in Lindzey, Gardner et al. (Eds.), *Theories of Personality: Primary Sources and Research*. New York: Wiley, 1973.

Loomis, S. D. "EEG Abnormalities as a Correlate of Behavior in Adolescent Male Delinquents," *American Journal of Psychiatry*, 1965, 121, 1003-1006.

Loomis, S. D. et al. "Prediction of EEG Abnormalities in Adolescent Delinquents," *Archives of General Psychiatry*, 1967, 17, 494-497.

Lopez-Rey, Manuel. *Crime: An Analytical Appraisal*. New York: Praeger, 1970.

Loth, David. *Crime in the Suburbs*. New York: Morrow, 1967.

MacIver, Robert M. *The Prevention and Control of Delinquency*. New York Atherton Press, 1966.

Mack, James L. "The MMPI and Recidivism," *Journal of Abnormal Psychology*, 1969, 74, 612-614.

Mailloux, Noel, and Lavallee, C. "The Genesis and Meaning of 'Antisocial' Conduct," *Contributions à l'Etude des Sciences de l'Homme*, 1962, 5, 158-167.

Manne, Sigmund H. et al. "Differences Between Performance IQ and Verbal IQ in a Severely Sociopathic Population," *Journal of Clinical Psychology*, 1962, 18, 73-77.

Mark, Vernon H., and Ervin, Frank R. *Violence and the Brain*. New York: Harper and Row, 1970.

Matza, David. *Delinquency and Drift*. New York: Wiley, 1964.

McWhirter, Kennedy. "XYY Chromosome and Criminal Acts," *Science*, 1969, 164, 1117.

Megargee, Edwin I. *The California Psychological Inventory Handbook*. San Francisco: Jossey-Bass, 1972.

Menninger, Karl. *The Crime of Punishment*. New York: Viking Press, 1968.

Mensh, Ivan D. "Psychopathic Condition, Addictions and Sexual Deviation," in Wolman, Benjamin (Ed.), *Handbook of Clinical Psychology*. New York: McGraw-Hill, 1965, 1058-1081.

Merton, Robert K. *Social Theory and Social Structure*. New York: Free Press, 1968.

Molitch, M. D. "Endocrine Disturbances in Behavior Problems," *American Journal of Psychiatry*, 1937, 93, 1176-1180.

Montagu, Ashley. "Chromosomes and Crime," in Karlins, Marvin, and Andrews, Lewis M. (Eds.), *Man Controlled: Readings in the Psychology of Behavior Control*. New York: Free Press, 1972, 191-204.

"Most Crime Found Unreported," *The Washington Post*, April 15, 1974.

Mowrer, O. Hobart. "Does Psychoanalysis Encourage Sociopathy and Paranoia?" In Mowrer, O. Hobart, *The New Group Therapy*. New York: Van Nostrand, 1964, 181-214.

Moyer, K. E. "A Preliminary Physiological Model of Aggressive Behavior," in Eleftheriou, Basil E., and Scott, John P. (Eds.), *The Physiology of Aggression and Defeat*. New York: Plenum Press, 1971, 223-265.

Mussen, Paul Henry et al. *Child Development and Personality.* (2nd edit.) New York: Harper and Row, 1963.

Newkirk, P. R. "Psychopathic Traits are Inheritable," *Diseases of the Nervous System,* 1957, 18, 52-54.

Newman, Gustave, and Denman, Sidney B. "Felony and Paternal Deprivation: A Socio-psychiatric View," *International Journal of Social Psychiatry,* 1970/71, 18, 65-72.

New York City Youth Board. *Reaching the Fighting Gang.* New York: New York City Youth Board, 1960.

Nielsen, J., and Henriksen, F. "Incidence of Chromosome Aberrations among Males in a Danish Youth Prison," *Acta Psychiatrica Scandinavica,* 1972, 48, 87-102.

Nielsen, Johannes, and Tsuboi, Takayuki. "Correlation between Stature, Character Disorder and Criminality," *British Journal of Psychiatry,* 1970, 116, 145-150.

"Nixon Panel Says Obscenity Doesn't Cause Sex Crimes," *The Evening Star,* August 6, 1970.

"No Definite Link Found Between XYY and Crime," *APA Monitor,* 1, December 1970, p. 5.

Nuttall, Jeff. *Bomb Culture.* New York: Delacorte Press, 1968.

Offer, Daniel et al. "Delinquent and Normal Adolescents," *Comprehensive Psychiatry,* 1972, 13, 347-355.

Papanek, Ernst. "Some Factors in the Treatment of Juvenile Delinquency," *International Journal of Social Psychiatry,* 1961, 7, 212-221.

Peterson, Donald R., and Becker, Wesley C. "Family Interaction and Delinquency," in Quay, Herbert C. (Ed.), *Juvenile Delinquency.* Princeton: Van Nostrand, 1965, 63-99.

Pokorney, Alex et al. "Depression, Psychopathy, and Herpesvirus Type I Antibodies," *Archives of General Psychiatry,* 1973, 29, 820-822.

Pontius, Anneliese. "Neurological Aspects in Some Type of Delinquency Especially Among Juveniles," *Adolescence,* 1972, 7, 289-308.

"Portrait of a Presidential Assassin: White, Short, Weak-Sighted Loner," *The Washington Post,* May 21, 1972.

President's Commission on Crime in the District of Columbia. *Report.* Washington, D. C.: Government Printing Office, 1966.

President's Commission on Law Enforcement and the Administration of Justice. *The Challenge of Crime in a Free Society.* Washington, D. C.: Government Printing Office, 1967.

Quay, Herbert C. "Psychopathic Personality as Pathological Stimulation-Seeking," *American Journal of Psychiatry,* 1965, 122, 180-183.

Quinney, Richard. "Occupational Structure and Criminal Behavior," in Geis, Gilbert (Ed.), *White-Collar Criminal: The Offender in Business and the Professions.* New York: Atherton Press, 1968, 210-218.

Rada, Richard T. "Alcoholism and Forcible Rape," *American Journal of Psychiatry* (prepublication copy, 1974).

Rader, Gordon E. "The Prediction of Overt Aggressive Verbal Behavior from Rorschach Content," *Journal of Projective Techniques,* 1957, 21, 294-306.

Radzinowicz, Leon. *In Search of Criminality.* Cambridge, Mass.: Harvard University Press, 1961.

Raskin, A. H. "The Berkeley Affair: Mr. Kerr vs. Mr. Savio and Co.," in Lipset, S. M., and Wolin, S. S. (eds.), *The Berkeley Student Revolt.* New York: Anchor, 1965, 420-431.

Reckless, Walter C. *Criminal Behavior.* New York: McGraw-Hill, 1940.

Reckless, Walter C., and Dinitz, Simon. *The Prevention of Juvenile Delinquency*. Columbus: Ohio State University Press, 1972.

Redl, Fritz, and Wineman, David. *Children Who Hate*. Glencoe, Illinois: Free Press, 1951.

Reiner, Beatrice S., and Kaufman, Irving. *Character Disorders in Parents of Delinquents*. New York: Family Service Association of America, 1959.

Renshaw, Domeena C. *The Hyperactive Child*. Chicago: Nelson-Hall, 1974.

"Reston at 7 Years: New Town Loses Its Innocence," *The Washington Post, Post*, July 16, 1972.

Richardson, Helen, and Surko, Elise. "WISC Scores and Status in Reading and Arithmetic of Delinquent Children," *Journal of Genetic Psychology*, 1956, 89, 251-262.

Riley, David. "Runaways and Then There Were Thousands," *The Washingtonian*, November 1971, 7, 64ff.

Robins, Lee N. *Deviant Children Grown Up*. Baltimore: Williams and Wilkins, 1966.

Rodale, J. I. *Natural Health, Sugar and the Criminal Mind*. New York: Pyramid, 1968.

"Role of Temperament Is Stressed in Childhood Behavior Disorders," *Psychiatric Progress*, December 1965, p. 3.

Rosanoff, Aaron J. "Incidence of Rheumatic Heart Disease among Criminal Psychopaths," *American Journal of Psychiatry*, 1944, 100, 708.

Rosenthal, David. "Heredity in Criminality," Reprint of Address to American Association for the Advancement of Science, December 27, 1972.

Rothenberg, David. "Prison Is a Real Education," *The National Observer*, December 3, 1971.

Rubin, Zick. "Yale Psychologist Finds Ruby's Brain Damaged," *Yale News and Review*, February 15, 1964, 2, 2-3.

Schafer, Roy. *The Clinical Application of Psychological Tests*. New York: International Universities Press, 1948.

Schaffer, H. R., and Emerson, Peggy E. "Patterns of Response to Physical Contact in Early Human Development," *Journal of Child Psychology and Psychiatry*, 1964, 5, 1-13.

Schmideberg, Melitta. "Promiscuous and Rootless Girls," *International Journal of Offender Therapy* (London), 1971, 15, 28-33.

Schmideberg, Melitta. "Psychiatric Study and Psychotherapeutic Study of Criminals," in Masserman, Jules, and Moreno, J. L. (Eds.), *Progress in Psychotherapy*. Vol. 5. New York: Grune and Stratton, 1960, 156-160.

Schmideberg, Melitta. "The Analytic Treatment of Major Criminals: Therapeutic Results and Technical Problems," in Eissler, K. R. (Ed.), *Searchlights on Delinquency*. New York: International Universities Press, 1949, 174-189.

Schmidl, Fritz. "The Rorschach Test in Juvenile Delinquency Research," *American Journal of Orthopsychiatry*, 1947, 17, 151-160.

Schneider, Kurt. *Psychopathic Personalities*. Springfield, Ill.: Charles C Thomas, 1958.

Schulsinger, Fini. "Psychopathy: Heredity and Environment," *International Journal of Mental Health*, 1972, 1, 190-206.

Schur, Edwin M. *Our Criminal Society*. Englewood Cliffs, N. J.: Prentice-Hall, 1969.

Schwade, Edward, and Geiger, Sara G. "Abnormal Electroencephalographic Findings in Severe Behavior Disorders," *Diseases of the Nervous System*, 1956, 17, 307-317.

Sears, Robert R. et al. "The Socialization of Aggression," in Maccoby, Eleanor

E. et al. (Eds.), *Readings in Social Psychology*. (3rd edit.) New York: Holt, Rinehart and Winston, 1958, 350-359.

Sheldon, William. *Atlas of Men*. New York: Harper and Brothers, 1954.

Sheldon, William. *The Varieties of Temperament: A Psychology of Constitutional Differences*. New York: Harper and Row, 1942.

Sheldon, William et al. *Varieties of Delinquent Youth: An Introduction to Constitutional Psychiatry*. New York: Harper and Brothers, 1949.

Silver, Albert W. "TAT and MMPI Psychopath Deviant Scale Differences between Delinquent and Nondelinquent Adolescents," *Journal of Consulting Psychology*, 1963, 27, 370.

Silverman, Daniel. "Clinical and Electroencephalographic Studies on Psychopaths," *Archives of Neurology and Psychiatry*, 1943, 50, 18-33.

Simon, B. et al. "Cerebral Dysrhythmia and Psychopathic Personality," *Archives of Neurology and Psychiatry*, 1946, 56, 677-685.

Smith, James, and Lanyon, Richard I. "Prediction and Juvenile Probation Offenders," *Journal of Consulting and Clinical Psychology*, 1968, 32, 54-58.

Solomon, George F. "Case Studies of Violence," in Daniels, David N. et al. (Eds.), *Violence and the Struggle for Existence*. Boston: Little-Brown, 1970, 367-391.

Stafford-Clark, David, and Taylor, F. H. "Clinical and Electro-encephalographic Studies of Prisoners Charged with Murder," *Journal of Neurology, Neurosurgery and Psychiatry*, 1949, 12, 323-330.

Stafford-Clark, David. *Psychiatry for Students*. New York: Grune and Stratton, 1964.

"Study of Convict Intelligence Levels Destroys Myth About Criminal Mind," *The Washington Post*, October 7, 1964.

Sutherland, Edwin H. *White Collar Crime*. New York: Holt, Rinehart and Winston, 1961.

Sykes, Gresham M. "New Crimes for Old," *American Scholar*, 1971, 40, 592-598.

Taft, Donald R. *Criminology*. (2nd edit.) New York: Macmillan, 1942.

"The Mind of a Murderer," *Medical World News*, November 23, 1973, 14, 39-45.

Thompson, George N. "Psychopath," *Archives of Criminal Psychodynamics*, 1961, 4, 736-748.

Thompson, George N. *The Psychopathic Delinquent and Criminal*. Springfield, Ill.: Charles C Thomas, 1953.

Tomkins, Silvan S. *The Thematic Apperception Test*. New York: Grune and Stratton, 1947.

Trasler, Gordon. "Criminal Behaviour," in Eysenck, H. J., *Handbook of Abnormal Psychology*. (2nd edit.) San Diego: Robert R. Knapp, 1973, 67-96.

Trasler, Gordon. *The Explanation of Criminality*. London: Routledge and Kegan Paul, 1962.

Trotter, Robert J. "Aggression: A Way of Life for the Qolla," *Science News*, 1973, 103, 76-77.

Tulchin, Simon H. *Intelligence and Crime*. Chicago: University of Chicago Press, 1939.

U.S. Dept. of Labor. Office of Policy Planning and Research. *The Negro Family*. Washington, D. C.: Government Printing Office, 1965.

U.S. Public Health Service. Surgeon General's Scientific Advisory Committee on Television and Social Behavior. *Television and Growing Up: The Impact of Televised Violence*. Washington, D. C.: Dept. of Health, Education and Welfare, 1972.

Van Dyke, Henry Thomas. *Juvenile Delinquency*. Boston: Ginn, 1970.

Walters, Richard H. "A Preliminary Analysis of the Rorschach Records of

Fifty Prison Inmates," *Journal of Projective Techniques*, 1953, 17, 437-446.

Warburton, F. W. "Observations on a Sample of Psychopathic American Criminals," *Behaviour Research and Therapy*, 1965, 3, 129-135.

Wattenberg, William W. *The Adolescent Years*. (2nd edit.) New York: Harcourt Brace Jovanovich, 1973.

Wechsler, David. *The Measurement and Appraisal of Adult Intelligence*. (4th edit.) Baltimore: Williams and Wilkins, 1958.

Weihofen, Henry. "Treatment of Insane Prisoners," *Law Forum* (University of Illinois), 1960, 524-532.

Weis, Kurt, and Milakovich, Michael E. "Political Misuses of Crime Rates," *Society*, July/August, 1974, 11, 27-33.

Wertham, Frederic. *Seduction of the Innocent*. Port Washington, N. Y.: Kennikat Press, 1972.

West, Donald J. *Murder Followed by Suicide*. Cambridge, Mass.: Harvard University Press, 1965.

West, Donald J. *The Young Offender*. New York: International Universities Press, 1967.

White, Robert W., and Watt, Norman F. *The Abnormal Personality*. (4th edit.) New York: Ronald Press, 1973.

Whiting, John W. M., and Child, Irvin L. *Child Training and Personality*. New Haven: Yale University Press, 1953.

Whittet, Martin W. "Medico-Legal Considerations of the A9 Murder," *British Journal of Medical Psychology*, 1968, 41, 125-138.

"Who's on First with the Crime Figures? Not Jerry Wilson," *The Evening Star*, March 6, 1971.

Williams, Denis. "Neural Factors Related to Habitual Aggression," *Brain*, 1969, 92, 503-520.

Winkler, Guenther E., and Kove, Sally S. "The Implications of Electroencephalographic Abnormalities in Homicide Cases," *Journal of Neuropsychiatry*, 1962, 3, 322-330.

Winthrop, H. "Creativity in the Criminal," *Journal of Social Psychology*, 1965, 65, 41-58.

Wyden, Peter. "The Button-Down Delinquents," *New York Herald Tribune*, September 25, 1962, p. 38 (from book by the same title published by Doubleday, 1962).

Yablonsky, Lewis. "The Research Frontier: The *New* Criminal: A Report on the 'Hip' Killer," *Saturday Review*, February 2, 1963, 54-56.

Yarrow, Marian R. et al. "Child Effects on Adult Behavior," *Developmental Psychology*, 1971, 5, 300-311.

Yarvis, Richard M. "A Classification of Criminal Offenders Through Use of Current Psychoanalytic Concepts," *Psychoanalytic Review*, 1972, 59, 549-563.

Zuckerman, Marvin et al. "What Is the Sensation?" *Journal of Consulting and Clinical Psychology*, 1972, 39, 308-321.

Chapter 3

The Criminal's Way of Life

THIS CHAPTER PRESENTS a detailed, comprehensive picture of how a criminal lives, including how he interacts with his family, his peers, his teachers, and his superiors at work and in military service. We describe a criminal's physical attributes, sexual life, marital patterns, antisocial behavior, and confinement experience. In Chapter 1, we indicated that history-taking with a criminal is laden with pitfalls. The information given is unreliable; he conceals much, and what he reveals is edited to suit his own purposes. His story is self-serving, in that he tells the people in authority what he thinks they want to hear. Most criminals are cognizant of society's current way of thinking; even those who are untutored quickly pick up the prevailing views. They use life's adversities, sociologic or psychologic, to justify their criminal activity. In a setting where confessions are valued, a criminal may describe crimes that he has never committed. He may brag of his conquests and accomplishments in crime, to make himself more of a criminal than he is. Much of what a criminal tells an examiner has been repeated so often that he half-believes it himself. As pointed out in Chapter 1, we have been no different from other investigators in initially accepting some of the self-serving stories. The criminals told us what they thought we wanted to hear, and, owing to the conditions under which we were interviewing them (privileged communication), we had no reason to think that they would lie to us.

The reader may well wonder how we can now be so certain of the accuracy of the material in this and the remaining chapters when its source is criminals who are notoriously untruthful. The development of new techniques has permitted us to document life stories that have greater validity. We recorded early self-serving accounts, but we have been able to correct and update them, because, as a criminal progresses in the program for change, he has less and less need to justify what he does and he presents us with a different picture. Our changing people have reviewed and revised what they told us earlier. We have also talked with family members, many of whom were at first instructed by the criminal to lie. We took information from criminals who were changing and from their families and presented it to totally unchanged criminals. In part, we did this to establish the validity of that material.

Improved techniques enabled us to confirm material more quickly and then derive additional, more accurate information about thinking and action patterns. This additional information was confirmed by the same procedures, making for a snowballing process over a fourteen-year period. What we found in one group of criminals we confirmed with the next, constantly adding to our knowledge. We present here only material that has been validated over the years. Whatever was uncertain or equivocal was discarded. The actual techniques that were used with the criminal before, during, and after change will be presented in Volume 2.

As of May 1, 1975, our sample numbered 240. Of these, 162 are hard-core adult criminals. Another 59 from 13 to 21 years old can be considered hard-core, in that criminal patterns of thinking are present and violations have been numerous over a period of years; these 59 subjects we interviewed and evaluated or worked with briefly in community clinics. We interviewed thirteen others only a few times; these are adults and teenagers who showed less extensive criminality in both thought and action and who participated purely as research subjects and were not in our program for change. Finally, we have interviewed six children under thirteen whose parents asked us for an evaluation because they were worried about their offsprings' behavior, which pointed the way to more serious future difficulties. The breakdown of time spent with the total sample over a period of fourteen years is as follows:

1,000 hours or more	17*
500-1000 hours	7
100-500 hours	23
50-100 hours	28
10-50 hours	72
less than 10 hours	93

Our sample has been male, except for three cases. However, in working with criminals over many years, we have acquired a great deal of information about the women in their lives. Not all this has been secondhand. We have interviewed wives and girlfriends, many of whom showed the same criminal patterns of thinking and action. Our few scattered references to female criminals reflect these contacts with them, as well as the information from our male sample.

The reader may reflect that some observations made about the criminal are also true of some noncriminals. For example, we point out that the

---

* In about a dozen cases, we spent more than 5,000 hours per person.

criminal as a child plays one parent off against the other in an attempt to achieve an objective. Although a responsible child may well take advantage of and even create parental differences of opinion, he does not have a prevailing attitude of "divide and conquer," which is part of an exploitative pattern in a criminal. Discrete observations about a criminal as a youngster must be viewed within the larger context of a set of *patterns* that are different in kind and degree from those of responsible children. In Chapter 4, we shall elaborate on the issue of "Who is a criminal?" as we discuss the continuum of criminality.

The reader may be bothered by the term "criminal child" used throughout this chapter. It is true that parents, teachers, and others had considered the youngsters described here as having "behavior problems" or as "going through a phase"—but not as criminals. We use the term "criminal child" not only for fluidity in writing (rather than saying each time "the criminal as a child"), but also because it is evident that the patterns that these youngsters showed early in life were similar to those which were evident in their adult lives as hard-core criminals.

We believe that those who know little about criminals will be surprised by much of the material presented here, such as the scope and frequency of criminality beyond what is in official records, as indeed we were when we realized how different things are from how they seem. Many of our men had committed hundreds, even thousands of crimes before they became known to the community as "first offenders." Those who have encountered some of the phenomena described here but have not recognized them as characteristic of criminals will be more fully informed. For those who have been working with criminals, this chapter will confirm what they already know, supplement it, and place it into a more complete perspective.

FAMILY

Except in the earliest phases, our techniques of interviewing have excluded formal history-taking. Although we have detailed information on patterns of thinking and action that began in childhood, we lack precise biographic details on the parents of some of the criminals. Thus, as we discuss the families, we speak in terms of patterns. We know, for example, whether a home was stable. We have some indication of the characteristics of the people who resided in the home and constituted the family unit. Indeed, we were able to interview some of these individuals.

Over half the criminals come from stable families in which the parents have lived together, have raised the children, and have experienced the usual tensions in living. Like other researchers, we have also found broken homes, poverty, and other truly adverse circumstances. However, as we probed beyond the fact that a home was broken, we found that the breaking of the home in some cases helped to stabilize life for the children, because what remained was a cohesive concerned family unit; for if the father left, mother, grandparents, uncles, and aunts still remained. In fact, every home we looked into had some stabilizing influence, with caring, responsible people stepping in to assume parental roles. When called to account, however, the criminals have attributed their violating patterns to the tensions of family life, exaggerating them or citing them out of context.

> C's mother died when he was 8 years old. Apparently, his father was unable to take care of him, so he went to live with older sisters. He describes the relationship with one of the sisters with whom he spent considerable time as warm and comfortable, with emotional and material needs being met. To be sure, the sisters differed in how they brought up the children, but in all cases the upbringing was in the direction of honesty, morality, and assisting them so that they could improve their lot in life. C became a criminal, but the other youngsters whom the sisters raised did not all follow that path.

> C's father was a substantial drinker and was unfaithful and abusive to his wife, who was also unstable. Practically from birth, C lived with his grandmother and grandfather. Grandpa gave C almost everything he could, even though he was under financial pressure. C wanted a bike, candy, and toys, and Grandpa saw that he got them. There was always food in the house, even during the lean times, when Grandpa had to borrow money. His grandfather was the kind of man who never whipped the children; when somebody else, like an aunt did so, he would interfere. C's grandmother, although nervous, was a very hard worker and extremely religious.

These two examples are representative of what occurred in broken homes. Even when the child had to leave his home, someone who was responsible tried to care for him and provide for him, even if it required personal sacrifice.

Many of the criminals, when children, rejected the people who attempted to show them affection and stabilize their homes.

> C's father had married an irresponsible woman, who, with little warning, took off, abandoning her husband and three children, including C. Custody of the children was awarded to the father. After a few years, the father married a woman who was fond of the children and treated them as her own. However, being more responsible in her supervision of the children than the biologic mother, this woman ran into opposition from C, who was used to doing whatever he wanted. When the stepmother set some limits in a kindly manner, C became abusive and

threatening. He resented having to be accountable for his whereabouts. The stepmother, very upset, sought counseling with C, who saw the "problem" as lying entirely with her.

This case is an example of how criminals when children resented anyone who tried to limit their freedom. Both biologic parents and surrogate had a difficult time if they tried to restrict a criminal child's activities.

Some criminals came from homes of severe poverty and deprivation. What is striking is the sacrifices made by hard-working parents who struggled to surmount considerable adversity.

C's father never brought home a paycheck. In fact, he could be counted on for nothing. Mother furnished the support, financial and otherwise. She had been a high-school dropout because of her pregnancy. She looked after the children in a virtually fatherless home. Mother began working as a domestic and in a laundry. She also took some correspondence courses, which qualified her for a high-school diploma. For more than 20 years, she worked for the government, rising to a supervisory position. Her life was characterized by conscientious work in government, keeping a good home going, paying the bills, and eventually earning enough to buy a house. She devoted her time and energy to improving herself and taking care of her family. She was a regular church-goer, honest, thoroughly dependable, and reliable, and well regarded by everyone. Even though the children had to be put into day-care centers, Mother was with them every night.

This mother, of the highest caliber and greatest devotion, continued to function in this way and assumed even greater responsibilities later when she cared for her criminal son's six children. In homes of hardship, this pattern is more the rule than the exception: a mother or parent substitute who is honest and reliable makes a selfless effort to improve the lot of her children.

The important fact here is that one cannot predict from an evaluation of early circumstances how a child will turn out. Even in the few homes in which both parents were irresponsible, not all the offspring became criminals. The leading concept of this section is that circumstances do not determine children's lives. Within single families, whether stable or unstable, affluent or poor, the children have differed widely. Some children have become responsible adults despite adverse environmental influences, and some who came from what would be considered the most favorable backgrounds have become criminals. (We are using the terms "responsible" and "irresponsible" rather broadly. A responsible parent or child is one who is basically moral, fulfilling obligations and functioning within the law. An irresponsible person is one who generally lacks these qualities.) Following are some actual examples of the possible parental combinations that we encountered.

RESPONSIBLE MOTHER-RESPONSIBLE FATHER

Father: Owner of flourishing garment business that collapsed during Depression, then owner of tailor shop in which he worked long days; an observant Jew, for whom mother kept a kosher home. Family wealthy until Depression; then living standard dropped; financial needs of family adequately met.

Mother: Devoted wife and mother; did not work; stayed home and looked after house and children.

Subject: Spent nearly all his years from age 19 to 35 in jail.

Sister: Eight years older; very bright, always at top of her class; happily married; working as bookkeeper and secretary; responsible.

Brother: Six years older; no criminal offenses; some marital difficulties, resulting in divorce; basically responsible.

RESPONSIBLE MOTHER–IRRESPONSIBLE FATHER

Father: Criminal; narcotics-user; jail sentence.

Mother: Separated from husband while he was in jail; common-law relationship with responsible man who helped family; employed as hotel clerk; faithful in work and well-liked; handled money carefully at home; good housekeeper.

Subject: In many kinds of crime, including assault and child molestation.

Sisters: One unstable. One very stable; hard-working; responsible.

Brothers: Two in crime.

IRRESPONSIBLE MOTHER-RESPONSIBLE FATHER

Father: Self-educated; skilled mechanic steadily employed; got along well socially; respected member of community; interested in family; always trying to do the best he could; one offense of whiskey-running, for which he spent 6 months in jail.

Mother: Drinker; assaulted husband with knife and other objects; arrested for drunk and disorderly conduct several times.

Subject: Long criminal history from childhood, including stealing, fighting, etc.

Sisters: Four irresponsible. Three responsible.

Brothers: One irresponsible. One responsible.

IRRESPONSIBLE MOTHER-IRRESPONSIBLE FATHER
(ONLY INSTANCE)

Children lived with grandparents almost from birth.

Subject: Drug-user; assault, larceny, etc.

Brother: Two years younger; steady worker; never in trouble with the law; thoroughly disapproves of criminal brother.

These are sketchy accounts, but they indicate that outcomes differ despite similarities in environment. However, when criminals account to others for violations, they seek exoneration by claiming to be victims of their environment. They may cite the broken home, the drinking father, and so forth, without mentioning any of the mitigating factors that helped to stabilize their homes. Nor will they mention that a brother or sister confronted by the same problems managed to surmount them.

GRANDPARENTS

The criminal knows little about family origins or history. Such matters were never of interest to him. We managed to gain only some sketchy recollections from him. Visiting relatives was burdensome, unless there was a promise of something exciting. In his youth, he spent time with his grandparents if it meant less supervision or somehow a "better deal" than he had with his parents. Looking back, men who had spent time with their grandparents were sentimental in their reflections. The grandparents of the criminals were from a variety of social stations; one was a slave who became a farmer (and through hard work managed to send two of his three daughters to college), and two were socially prominent. Nearly all lived by a strict moral code, being ambitious, honest, hard-working people to whom family was of primary importance. Whether sharecroppers or lawyers, most of them tried to improve their lot in life and provide for their children.

MOTHER

The criminals' mothers ranged from a poor farmer's daughter to the daughter of a socially prominent family. Many grew up under conditions of hardship that precluded adequate education. Some married before they were twenty. Some had no formal education; a few had received master's degrees. For the most part, the mothers had stable and dependable employment patterns, with jobs ranging from domestic work to partnership in business. With few exceptions, the mothers were responsible. Many were strongly religious and frequent church-goers. Nearly all placed a premium on duty to family and willingly sacrificed for their children when it was necessary. There were exceptions to this pattern. Two of the men in our study never knew their mothers and were brought up in orphanages. Another was adopted in infancy by a schoolteacher and her husband, who was a government worker with a Ph.D. Two others were adopted by professional people. In only a minority of cases were the mothers heavy drinkers and unfaithful in marriage. Only a few were involved in serious crime.

When a criminal initially described his mother to an interviewer, he generally presented her in an unfavorable light, citing what she "did" to him and what she failed to do for him. In these accounts, the definition of a bad mother was one who failed to do everything the criminal wanted. When one later hears the same person described by a changed criminal, it is as though he had two different mothers.

> C described his mother as a "mean" person, functioning as a bootlegger in the black area of a southern town. He stated that she was too strict to be physically affectionate, and he could not feel close to her. He described himself as having grown increasingly bitter toward her and having gradually separated himself from her, until, at age 15, he left home.

> We later met C's mother, a warm, caring woman with whom C had reestablished contact, both for his own benefit and so that his children could know their grandmother. Now that he was well along in the change process, C told us it was the "bad things" that he did from early childhood that caused her to be restraining and punitive. With no father in the home, she did the best she could to take care of the children, but C was more than she could handle. As far as the bootlegging went, C said that he had exaggerated it. To be sure, it was against the law; but at the time and place, it fit the mores of the community. She was basically honest in all interpersonal transactions and was extremely concerned about and devoted to her children.

Such radically different depictions of the same person are typical. The most critical aspect of these accounts is that the criminal makes himself the victim of unreasonable, punitive parents, never describing what he did to evoke the restraints or punishments.

Not all criminals describe their mothers consistently in negative fashion. What the criminal says depends on whom he is talking to and his current frame of mind. Most criminals at some time speak sentimentally of what good people their mothers were. But whether a mother was an angel or a devil depends on the circumstances in which the criminal finds himself. We obtain a far more balanced perspective when the criminal is not justifying what he has done, but is concerned with viewing his life realistically.

FATHER

Father can also be friend or foe, depending on whom the criminal talks to and what he wishes to establish. When we tried to obtain facts about fathers that had no bearing on the criminals themselves, information was sparse. The criminals knew very little about their fathers' backgrounds, occupations, attitudes, or interests. One might be tempted to speculate that the fathers of these men were passive, weak, or uninterested. This was usually not the case. Instead, it was the criminal who was uninterested in his parents. As youngsters, the criminal children were outsiders to family life. Rather than being rejected by their parents, the parents were rejected by them. These youngsters chose a way of life that they wanted to keep secret from their parents. They rejected the family and often declined to participate in its activities, which they found dull. Even a father who clearly favored his son and wanted to spend time with him was spurned, because the criminal was interested in other things.

The fathers of our criminals came from a great variety of educational, occupational, and social backgrounds. Educationally, the range was fourth-grade dropout to Ph.D. By occupation, they included a farmer, a sheet-metal worker, and a college instructor. Most of the fathers were stable, responsible, hardworking men. They strove to improve themselves and provide a decent life for their families.

> C's father received only a sixth-grade education. Despite this, he was a very alert and bright man. C stated that his father could get along intellectually as well as college graduates. His father began work on a farm as a sharecropper right after he got married and after 16 years owned his own farm. His father built a home and always had enough money to feed and clothe the family. Although there were money deficits at times, his credit was good, because he always paid his bills. This man was a Sunday-school teacher and deacon in church and attended services regularly. Basically, C's father lived a life of hard work, honesty, and loyalty to family and church. He maintained good social relationships with people, although he was not an inordinate socializer.

This was the type of father most of our criminals had. The details are different for each, but the characterization as responsible obtains for most. Even the few who were criminals were averse to their children's pursuing the same path. Criminal fathers wanted their children to be good citizens and often were very strict. Most were attentive to what their children did. In addition, the mother or someone else close to the family stepped in and tried to steer the child in a responsible direction. Clearly, parents' personalities and behavior are not all-determining.

SIBLINGS

Most of the brothers and sisters of the criminals in our group are responsible. They have not all achieved highly, but they have functioned quite differently in life from their criminal siblings. Our findings confirm what other studies have noted: that the several offspring from one family may follow very different paths. The communication media have helped to make this a well-known fact. *Time* Magazine (4/24/72), for example, in a story on the Mafia pointed out that only four of twenty-seven fourth-generation Italian-Americans in one Mafia family, are connected with organized crime. Of the remaining twenty-three, one is a university professor and all the rest are doctors, lawyers, and legitimate businessmen. So has it been with the families we have studied, most members of which have been and are responsible. We can cite a criminal whose sister worked her way through college and is now happily married and a criminal whose brother owns a computer programming company. This is not to say that the criterion of responsibility is career advancement; some of our criminals have also reached positions of authority and prestige. What is important here is that most of the siblings are conscientious, loyal workers, and concerned parents and members of the community who have carved out lives within the boundaries of society's laws, manners, and mores.

These responsible siblings try to guide their criminal brothers and sisters in the direction of more responsible behavior. They often help their criminal siblings out with money and other resources. In many instances, they take a protective attitude and cover for a criminal when he violates. They may not turn him in when he is a fugitive. Throughout their lives, they attempt to advise, exhort, and persuade the criminal siblings to reform.

The criminal has a spectrum of attitudes toward his noncriminal siblings. The attitude varies from time to time, between the extremes of strong sentimentality and bitter hatred. On the one hand, the criminal views his responsible brother's or sister's way of life as "square" or "stupid." On the other hand, there are moments when he envies the sibling for his achievements and for the freedom he enjoys in living responsibly. This occasional envy is usually well concealed, rarely finding its way into verbal expression. The criminal may physically abuse a sibling. If his brother will not lend him his car or give him money, he may turn on his brother and beat him up. Or he may be crassly exploitative.

> Ron shielded and protected his criminal brother, C, in every imaginable way. Although not wealthy, through the years Ron spent over $12,000 to bail C out of difficulties. He would cover forged checks that were signed in their father's name. C used Ron time and again. Ron responded as a member of the family who wanted to help, trying to convince C to change. He would not have done the things he did for anyone but a family member.

Here a brother acted in accord with his conscience and idea of family loyalty. The criminal took advantage of it.

The criminal distorts his relationship to his siblings when he talks to others. He may say that a brother or sister got more attention, despite the fact that he compelled more attention by the things he did and may, indeed, have been the favorite child initially. Of course, in some instances, the siblings did receive greater attention, if the parents had to protect them from the criminal youngster.

Later in life, the criminal stays away from his siblings, just as he avoids close relationships with all who have chosen to be responsible. However, the criminal is quick to return to a brother or sister when he wants something for himself.

There is still another dimension to the relationship of the criminal with his siblings. Although exploitative and vicious, he is at times sentimental toward them and goes out of his way to assist them. We have seen criminals who think that they are their sisters' guardians, to the extent that they will assault anyone who insults a sister. Yet when siblings refuse to be exploited, the criminal discards his protective stance and calls them unfair, inhuman, and disloyal.

Seven of our criminals had older siblings who were delinquent, and the criminals admired and emulated them. Particularly at the ages of five, six, and seven, they tagged along, seeking to be "in" on things. They rarely succeeded because the older siblings did not want them along. The younger criminal then used his own resources to find others who wanted to do the forbidden. Invariably, if a criminal has a younger sibling who is delinquent, the criminal is self-righteous and reprimands his parents for not being firmer.

C was amazed to learn from his mother that his two younger brothers, with three other boys, had broken into a store and stolen $80 worth of locks. When his mother told him this, he scolded her for not disciplining his brothers more. She cried when he did this.

The criminal enjoys informing on a younger brother or sister for even the slightest infraction. This takes the focus off him.

THE CRIMINAL CHILD AS DIFFERENT

An important commonality among most family members is that they live responsibly. Where there is parental irresponsibility, some children seem determined to be responsible, despite it.

C and Mary had a criminal father. C followed the same path. In contrast, Mary saw her objective in life as being different from her father. She utilized her contempt for what she saw as a stimulus to function differently. The result was that C wound up behind bars, and Mary is responsible and has worked hard in government, gaining several promotions.

From a very early age, the criminal-to-be is observed by his parents as "different." His behavior is extreme, either swinging from being an "angel" at five or six to a "hellion" by ten or alternating between the two right along. His energy never seems to be depleted, and he is chronically restless, irritable, and dissatisfied. He seems never to outgrow the period of the brief attention span. He has to have things his way; he will not take "no" for an answer.

> C needed a pair of sneakers and wanted a specific type. When his mother bought him another brand, he asked whether he could have them returned for the brand he originally wanted. She said that he would have to wait until these wore out. C promptly cut the soles and heels out of those she had just bought. They were then paper thin and quickly wore out, thus allowing him to achieve his objective.

The criminal child seems not to do anything right around the house. His parents constantly tell him to "put your mind on what you are doing," because he has his mind on things far more exciting than the task at hand. Mowing the lawn cannot compete with thoughts about "hanging around with the guys" at the nearest shopping mall and doing some shoplifting! The endless reply to his parents' reprimands is "I forgot." He forgets what his parents told him five minutes earlier, forgets what the teacher told him, forgets what the class did in Sunday school. This is not a learning or memory problem. His mind is on exciting things, and his interests are centered on the forbidden. He does not consider himself obliged to fulfill the mundane requirements of school and home. He thinks others should fall into line with whatever he wants to do. Rather than being appreciative when a parent or someone else gives him something or does him a favor, he generally takes it for granted and expects more the next time. Doing chores, coming in on time for dinner, keeping appointments, running an errand—the criminal child often reacts to these as though they are serious impositions. He uses any excuse at hand to put off what he is required to do. He usually does what he wants to when he wants to and is remarkably insensitive to others' needs and desires.

The criminal child is distressingly different in still another way. His parents find that, unlike most children, he shies away from affection, neither giving it nor receiving it. As one mother sadly said in describing her son as a young child, "He didn't need me." The adult criminal might say that his parents did not love him and that is why he turned out as he did. Actually, he rejected the love that was offered, viewing it as "sissy" or "weak."

There is a mantle of secrecy surrounding the criminal child. Parents slowly begin to sense that they do not know their own youngster. They are uneasy, especially those having another child, with whom they can compare him. The secret life is established early. Lying is a major ingredient. The child says he is going one place, but goes another. His accounts of what he does are vague and superficial. He is hard to pin down, with lies of omission being far more frequent than lies of commission. He may even lie when there is seemingly no point to it—for example, saying he is going to the A & P, when he knows he is going to the Grand Union. What seems to matter to him is getting away with things.

The criminal child sets himself apart. He does not confide in his family, and he conceals ideas and emotional reactions. Because he lies so often and engages in forbidden activity, he is ever distrustful and suspicious of other family members. This keeping to himself is a self-imposed isolation. He simply does not want other members of the family to be privy to what he is doing. This may take the extreme form of the child's virtually refusing to participate in any family affairs. When he goes to a function with his family, it is likely to be grudgingly. The family may be having fun, but inevitably the criminal child does something to spoil it. At a picnic, he shoves other children. He is the one who plays with the barbecue fire. In playing ball, he starts a fight over an umpire's call. If he attends a family activity or a school function because he is required to, he wanders off, and others do not know where he is. When he is older, he refuses to go at all.

With so much lying, sneaking, and concealment, there is clearly a "communication gap" in a home with a criminal child. Usually, the parents are faulted for not understanding the younger generation. But it is the child himself who imposes the secrecy and sets himself apart. He wants to keep his activities secret, so that others will not interfere with him. There is indeed a communication breakdown, but the child has been the determining factor. Sometimes, he pulls away entirely and gives his family the "silent treatment" for months at a time, erecting a barrier that his parents cannot penetrate and becoming even more of a stranger and a mystery to his own family. His more customary mode of operating, however, is to go through the motions of doing what is expected, so that his family will have less reason for suspicion; communication is at best superficial, because the parents think they know more than they do. When the parents become aware that their child has been leading a secret life, it is usually they who frantically search for ways to "restore" communication, which either never existed or existed only when the child was much younger. But the parents cannot establish communication that the criminal child does not want. Of course, if the criminal youngster wants something from his parents, he "communicates" quite well.

The criminal child gets his way in one fashion or another. Sometimes it is through secrecy and slickness. Perhaps even more frequently, he engages in constant battles with his parents, wearing them down until they capitulate. The youngster makes a contest out of anything, no matter how minor. He looks for a victory in a dispute about whether he will clean up his room, hang up a wet towel, take out the trash, or be in at a specified hour. Winning the fight overrides the significance of the issue at hand. It results in attrition of parental morale; eventually, his parents decide to ignore certain behavior. Another technique the child utilizes to get his way is to be "legalistic." He makes so many requests and contests so many things that the parents cannot keep track of them. Inevitably, the child will catch mother or father in a contradiction. In doing this, he may play one off against the other. His memory is adequate, when it comes to reminding a parent of something said earlier. A favorite tactic is to dredge up something said long before and apply it in a different context. It is practically impossible for his parents to avoid being tripped up by his maneuvers. When the criminal child is blocked from doing as he wants, he tries to circumvent the barrier.

> When C was 7 years old, he wanted to take a girl to the movies, but his family thought it improper. He went to the corner store and informed the man, with whom the family had credit, that his mother told him to borrow a dollar. With this, he took the girl at 4:30 in the afternoon. It was a double feature, and they got out at 8:30 p.m., only to meet both families waiting outside.

When the parents tighten up their restrictions, the criminal child has to be more ingenious and more careful, or else he becomes sullen, angry, or withdrawn.

The criminal child turns on "being good" when it suits his purpose. We have seen more than one set of parents become more hopeful when there was harmony in the house or on a family outing. Some of their fears and pessimism melt away as they point out that "he was so good while we were all in New York; really, we had no trouble at all." Then they are chagrined when they recognize that the reason they had such a good time was that they did everything the youngster wanted and thus avoided any altercations. It is not long until the old patterns are resumed, the first time the parents say "no." When a criminal child seeks a specific privilege or wants his parents to get him something, he can be endearing.

> C had created continual turmoil in the family by his neglect of chores, his sullen and sometimes antagonistic attitude toward participating in

family activities, and his activities in the community, which included stealing and threatening a girl with a knife. His parents, at a loss as to what to do, took him to a counseling agency. As Christmas approached, C told the counselor he would be "good." For 5 weeks, he did his chores, maintained a pleasant, cooperative attitude around the house, and did not get into trouble. He presented his parents with a list of more than $100 worth of gifts, which he wanted them to purchase. A week after Christmas, he resumed old patterns.

This illustration contains all the essentials of a "con job." Many parents will do almost anything, if they think it is for the good of the child and will contribute to family harmony. They pay for special schools, counseling, gifts, and so on, all to no avail. The criminal child exploits this and "blackmails" his parents to give him what he wants. They know that life will be miserable for them if they do not accommodate their child.

The basic stance of the criminal is that he wants to hold on to the comforts of home, as well as do the things he wants to do. The criminal child expects his family to meet his needs. Rarely does he consider anyone else's rights. He thinks that he should be able to do as he wants, but that others should be limited in interfering with him. He plays with a sibling's toys and breaks them, but he beats up a brother whom he finds using something of his without his explicit consent. He invades the privacy of others, but becomes furious when anyone asks him what he is doing. Emotional blackmail is an effective way for the youngster to get what he wants. His presence in the house becomes negotiable. His parents, already alarmed at his estrangement from them, may be fearful of his running away. Only a small minority actually leave the house. However, the criminal may keep running away a live issue to frighten his family into doing what he wants. A more menacing type of coercion occurs when the criminal warns his parents, "If you don't——, you'll be sorry," with an implied threat of retaliation in the form of violation.

C wanted an air rifle, but his family thought it was dangerous. His attitude was that, if they would not give it to him, he would steal $5. After all, it would be "their fault" for not giving it to him. The only way to avoid the theft would be for his parents to give him what he wanted.

The tactics may become extreme, as in the case of the youngster who threatens suicide and inflicts some superficial cuts on himself. When the criminal youngster creates some "emergency," he does his utmost to see that his parents are embarrassed and faulted. For example, if the neighbors find that he is using the family house for drinking, drugs, and sex in the parents' absence, it is seen as a case of parental neglect or permissiveness.

The criminal youngster engages in crimes against his family—unauthorized use of the family car, stealing money from mother's purse, misusing parental charge accounts, keeping weapons in the house. The list is endless, but the worst crimes are those which cannot be measured in dollars and cents. The broken hearts and disrupted lives are the most costly of all. His violations frighten his parents, so they curtail their own activities to stay home and supervise him. He does not hesitate to misrepresent his parents and give them a bad name in the community. Because of his conduct, the entire family lives with constant stress and uncertainty. These patterns at home are a microcosm of the child's functioning everywhere. Within them are contained all the essentials of a street crime, as will be seen later.

HOW THE CRIMINAL CHILD EXPLOITS HIS PARENTS' METHODS OF DEALING WITH HIM

Studies of child-rearing practices describe three basic attitudes—authoritarian, permissive, and democratic. A parent either is a severe disciplinarian, does not set limits, or allows his child to develop without excessive intrusion or interference. When a criminal child is apprehended, his parents are faulted, no matter which approach they have taken. The parents may be accused of being too punitive if they are "authoritarian," too indulgent ("spoiling") if they are "permissive," and indifferent or ignoring if they are "democratic." If there is variation from one pattern to another, the parents are called "unstable" or "inconsistent."

Supported by current views of child development, most people see parents as almost totally responsible for shaping a child's early behavior patterns and outlook. However, as our literature review showed, recent studies have documented the child's profound influence on parental behavior, beginning early in infancy. This confirms what we learned early in our investigation. By his own behavior, a criminal child virtually compels new attitudes and behavior on the part of his parents. Rarely does a family adopt an inflexible attitude toward child-rearing from the time the child is born. In attempting to deal with a child who is restless, rejects affection, and is difficult to please, parents often take approaches that they do not anticipate. A parent who vows never to be as punitive with his children as his strict parents were with him may, to his dismay, find himself being severe in an attempt to restrain the activities of his own child. The child has provoked the parent into behavior that the former then calls harmful and "unfair." As to "inconsistency," the criminal child does succeed often in creating differences in families. If one parent says "no," he tries the other, misrepresenting or omitting what the first said. The criminal child may throw a united set of parents into such uncertainty that they shift from one approach to another, in trying to cope with problems at hand.

From a psychiatric standpoint, children are traditionally regarded as the bearers of "family pathology." Consequently, a child's parents are usually called on to participate in a program in which often they become more of a focus than the child. It is assumed that the parents have caused the child to be the way he is.

> Doug and Carol were called in to participate in a therapeutic community where their daughter, C, was an inpatient, owing to her delinquent behavior and a wrist-cutting episode. The mere fact that her parents were coming for "treatment" gave C further ground for her contention that nothing was wrong with her. She insisted that it was her parents who needed to change. The parents had had a stable, happy marriage and had provided well for their two adopted daughters (the other one was responsible and well-adjusted). Doug and Carol were put through a virtual inquisition to determine what there was about them and their marriage that might have led to C's delinquency. It was implied that the parents still unconsciously resented having had to adopt and were bitter about not being able to have children of their own. And so it went, with the therapists determined to ferret out the "cause" of C's delinquency.

The format of counseling such as this is commonly directed toward an examination of what the parents have "done." The therapist or counselor usually subscribes to the child's version without focusing on what the child has done to the parents to lead them to act as they did. The criminal youngster gains another forum to use the tactics he has used at home and everywhere else. He may say that he wants treatment, but it eventually becomes clear that all he wants is to find in the therapist an ally against his parents. The youngster "uses" the therapist to change his parents, so that they will be "fairer"—which means less restrictive. A frequent outcome of such proceedings is that the parents are raked over the coals and the criminal youngster convinces the therapist that his parents are mentally disturbed. This in part exonerates him and gives him greater license for crime.

In some communities, criminal youngsters have friends who are also visiting psychotherapists or counselors. These children get together and compare notes, bragging among themselves about how they are "fooling the shrink." They go to psychotherapy sessions under protest, but, once there, they exploit the situation, just as they do all others. They enjoy "putting one over" and then laughing about it with friends. The possibilities for total chaos are especially great if one therapist treats the youngster and another treats the parents.

> Mr. and Mrs. Morton were seeing one therapist, and their daughter, C, another. C was telling her own doctor how inconsistent her parents were. The therapist who was seeing Mr. and Mrs. Morton found them to be unusually consistent and sound in their handling of a very taxing situation. He knew that his colleague would not treat C, unless he continued to see the parents, but he did not know what to "treat" the parents for. When he asked C's therapist what would be a productive issue for the parents, the answer was "consistency." This advice was based on C's self-serving version of her parents. Seeing no alternative to having their daughter treated, the parents continued to be counseled. They were increasingly irritated at spending time and money for therapy that they did not need and money for their daughter's treatment, which was not resulting in her changing.

With good intentions on all sides, except that of the "patient," added strains were imposed on an already stressful situation. Such is the array of difficulties that frequently exist in parent-child psychotherapy arrangements.

COUNTERMEASURES BY PARENTS

Although parents may notice differences among their children, by no means do they regard their wayward child as "delinquent" or "criminal." There is instead a tendency to hope for the best, to pass things off as youthful mischief or adolescent rebellion, and to think that the child will grow out of it. This may result only in irresponsibility, but most do commit alarming infractions. Then the parents react with disbelief, despair, or anger.

Sometimes, in an attempt to look at their child benignly, parents find themselves embracing views that the youngster advances, but that they themselves never held. Consider the conservative mother who suddenly declares her support for the legalization of marijuana, or the businessman father who becomes an apologist for "revolutionaries." A parent may also adopt a new position to keep a line of communication open. This may be part of a larger process in which the parents are deceiving themselves about their child's delinquency. They may be defensively avoiding facing the seriousness of the problem, because facing it will be "proof" to them that they have failed as parents. Some parents search their souls and flagellate themselves as the culprits responsible for their youngster's plight. These parents may spend years in this desperate attempt to understand how they failed to measure up as fathers and mothers.

A minority remain confident in themselves and hold a firm line that "what is right is right," placing responsibility squarely on the child's shoulders.

Most parents waver between blaming themselves and trying to give the youngster more freedom, on the one hand, and blaming the child and tightening up, on the other. Stricter discipline may deter the child for a while; but, for the chronic violator, it is just an incitement to be more careful, so as not to get caught. When such a youngster is caught and punished, he maintains a stiff upper lip to show that he can "take it."

Numerous other countermeasures are resorted to. Some families believe that a change in environment is warranted, so they move or transfer the child to a different school. Some seek professional help for their children and themselves privately or at community agencies. Even when the situation worsens to the extent that the child commits a serious offense, most parents do not reject their child. They may believe that it is time for the youngster to face the legal consequences, but this is not usually out of harshness toward the child.

> Mr. Gray had had more than 11 years of trouble with his now 20-year-old son, C. The straw that broke the camel's back was C's arrest on three counts—reckless driving, hit-and-run, and intoxication. Having taken C to counselors and therapists on and off since the boy was 9, Mr. Gray now thought it would be unwise to help the boy get off the hook. Although he did not believe that jail would change his son's character, he did hope that "a taste of the inside" might bring the boy to a point where he would seriously consider what he was doing with his life.

This father had pursued every conceivable route to help his son and had run out of alternatives.

Even after a child has been caught doing something very serious, his parents may go to great lengths to protect him from having a police record. For their own flesh and blood they may do things that they believe should never be done for other offenders. This includes lying or hiding the youth from the authorities. It entails a payoff to someone in the community to forget about the matter or expunge the record. The latter objective is in line with a current social movement in some areas. In short, parents who are not themselves criminal view their children from the standpoint of parental duty to assist and protect them. They do not see their own children as "criminal."

If a child is ultimately confined, most parents maintain contact and do everything possible to assist him. This includes such sacrifices as extra employment to pay for legal or psychiatric services. The family door is usually open even to one who has strayed and caused so much worry and misery. Very few parents, usually those with many responsibilities and large families, fail to continue frequent contact, but still the door is left open, and the child will be welcomed back to the family fold.

Over more than a dozen years of working with criminals and their families, the prevailing pattern we have seen is that parents destroy or are destroyed in their efforts to salvage a criminal child. Other members of the family are continually exploited, and resources are channeled into efforts to help the criminal and facilitate his changing. All this could be considered a great waste, except for one important factor: As one distraught mother said, "I have to live with myself." The parent may be faced with a hopeless case, but to do anything less than to help is to violate his own conscience. So he tries to retrieve his child and redeem him, never totally giving up.

NEIGHBORHOOD AND FRIENDSHIPS

In Chapter 2, we noted the traditional belief that a person can become corrupted by the company he keeps. Indeed, one of the questions on the Wechsler Adult Intelligence Scale (one of the two most widely used individual IQ tests) deals with this very issue:

Comprehension

#4 Why should we keep away from bad company (p. 36)?

(Full credit answer). Any response containing the idea that a person is changed for the worse, corrupted or improperly influenced by bad company (p. 55).

Social scientists have emphasized the influence of various "subcultures" on the individual. The youth subculture has received extensive attention in the mass communication media, as well as in the psychology literature. The delinquent subculture is seen as having a pernicious influence on young people. The President's Commission on Law Enforcement and Administration of Justice (1967) pointed out how young people, especially slum-dwellers, are "exposed to the example of the successful career criminal as a person of prestige in the community" (p. 67). Accounts of ghetto life commonly emphasize how difficult it is not to follow such people, who "did everything." Yet, many an observer has noted that most children who grow up in areas of high delinquency do not become delinquent. In other words, the delinquent subculture does not appeal to them and they have as little to do with it as possible. Actually, people choose the company they keep. The criminal child gravitates to others like him. He goes to the people whom he wants to get to know, rather than being sought out and corrupted.

Even in the most blighted neighborhoods, children are exposed to responsible influences in some form—parents, siblings, close relatives, friends, school, or church. The greater community is organized along responsible lines. Most children, even in ghettos, grow up to be responsible, not criminal. Most struggle to overcome the adversities of their environment. We interviewed the responsible brother of a tough criminal known as "the gorilla." The family grew up in a rough neighborhood, but the brother did not respond favorably to the delinquent groups around him. As a consequence, he was picked on a few times and beaten up. But he never entered into a criminal act. When we asked him why, he replied simply, "I wasn't interested." Instead, he went on to become a cadet in training for police work. The criminals with whom we have worked have mentioned children in their neighborhoods who did not become criminals, but functioned responsibly, continued their education, launched careers, and had stable, rewarding family and social relationships.

The criminal youngster knows responsible children, but rejects their way of life. To play the games and share their interests is dull and "sissy," as they see it. Early in life, the criminal child associates with those who always seem to be telling adults that "there's nothing to do." This statement simultaneously rejects the conventional and justifies the forbidden. If one looks at the play of the criminal child, one is struck by how he goes beyond what most youngsters do to make things sufficiently exciting for himself.

When the criminal child rides his bike, it is not for a leisurely recreational ride, but to race and perform feats that others do not. He often rides his bike where he is not supposed to and in violation of the laws. If the criminal youngster is on a team in sports, he insists on being the captain and telling others what to do. He wants to be the number one man; he has no sense of teamwork. At the swimming pool, the criminal child exceeds the bounds of recreation or friendly competition.

> C always played in the deep end, regarding the more shallow water as the territory of the "sissies." He was not one of the kids who would stay out of the water for long or lie around and get a tan. Instead, he would play "shark," a form of tag in the deep end that involved tagging other youngsters and pulling them under water. This often got quite rough. He would race, not swim. When he dived off the board, it was with the intention of getting others on the side wet.

At an amusement park, the criminal child drives the bumping cars with a vengeance, angling for headon collisions when possible. When he plays a "board" game, he ignores the directions, but later refers to them when it benefits him, and then sulks or quits if he is losing. His play usually pushes beyond what is acceptable or permissible and nearly always beyond what is considered sportsmanlike.

The criminal child's interests and hobbies are not sustained, but the things that attract him even for a while provide "kicks." Throughout his life, he has strong interests in powerful people, powerful machines, and powerful natural phenomena. Some criminal youngsters play with chemistry sets to cause explosions. Some acquire BB guns while young and then graduate to pistols and rifles.

> C had gone out on a farm at the age of 8 and shot at cows with a BB gun. At 14, he bought a 0.22-caliber rifle. He stated: "It's just a challenge, shooting at something that's alive. We go out and shoot gulls. It's illegal. It's something to shoot at. If you hit them in the wing, it just goes right through and never bothers them. It's target practice. We shoot frogs, snakes, anything that moves around." At age 20, he was saving $80 for a "hard-to-find" brand of pistol.

Go-carts, minibikes, motorcycles, and fast cars are important to many criminal youths.

> "I used to have a red convertible. That was the time the compacts were first coming out with big engines. When I started driving it, I got four tickets in three months, 11 points or something like that. One time, I was racing this guy; but his car was so much faster than mine, I quit. [In another car later] I did 75 with that [in a residential area]. That put me at 13 points, so I lost my license."

One criminal gave his image of himself as cyclist:

> "I believe I was sort of a threat to [a psychiatrist neighbor's] sexual pose. I was always riding around in a black jacket, and there were always girls upstairs. He was just completely terrorized—just incensed."

A large part of what the criminal youngster considers "fun" constitutes violation. Throwing rocks at street lights or eggs at houses, putting sand in gas tanks, and other acts of vandalism are his idea of a "good time." These acts are often committed against people whom the youngster does not know. They are done for the thrill of it, and not for retaliation. The criminal child seeks out other children who want the excitement of the forbidden. In some neighborhoods, he may not have to search very far; in others, he may have to roam some distance from his own block. One of our men recalled that, as a child, he went from the far northwest corner of his city to the far southeast, where he could find other youngsters who shared his interests. Some criminals live in places remote from the "delinquent subculture" of suburbs or cities. Not having companions to engage in crime with, they are their own agents.

> Living on a remote military base abroad, C was in crime on his own. Undetected, he stole magazines and books, squirt guns, models, paint, and many other items. Then he started going into other students' lockers, and the crime patterns expanded.

Even children who live in rural areas, where there is less opportunity for crime, avail themselves of whatever chances there are. They steal farm produce, rob country stores, vandalize property.

> "I remember stealing some peanuts from my father's barn. At 10 or 11, some friends and I stole some grapes from a neighbor's store more than once. It was a 'lark.' In the eleventh grade, I sent for some books from bookclubs, knowing that I couldn't pay for them. I filled a room with books."

Never satisfied with his own age group, the criminal child usually turns to older youngsters. He envies them, because in his view they have more "fun." The fun is not ordinary recreation or entertainment, but rather the excitement of doing forbidden things that other children his own age are reluctant to do. The criminal is open to these other youths, almost to the point of gullibility. He is *not* induced to commit crimes. Rather, he strives to be admitted—in fact, he passes tests to be accepted. If he is not successful in joining the older youngsters, he can swallow this by telling himself, "They're older than I am anyway." But he is usually persistent enough to gain acceptance. He will do practically anything to belong, including spending time in deliberate rehearsal to make the proper impression.

> C envied the "wild boys." He would go to his room and speak the language they spoke, generously laced with profanity. When he came out to the streets, intending to use their language, he lapsed into his usual silence. He was very envious of these boys and in time became practiced enough to be accepted by them.

The criminal child emulates the others in dress, language, and violating pattern. To show that he has "nerve" or "heart," he breaks rules everywhere and engages in delinquent activity. He is an eager student in the ways of violation. He has an energy, resourcefulness, and quickness of mind that are rarely put to use in school. To prove himself worthy of the criminal group, the youngster takes risks and goes to great lengths to demonstrate that he is not "chicken," even though he is fearful. The test may be high-speed driving, jumping from high places, running across the street in front of a car, or keeping his hand on a hot stove or burning his arm with a cigarette to show that he can stand pain.

As he gains increasing acceptance from the criminal group, both parties benefit. An experienced criminal does not teach others to be criminal. However, a newcomer does learn criminal tactics as he is used by older associates. The younger criminal's stature is enhanced by being "accepted" by the older group. In turn, those who already belong acquire an eager student to do some of the "dirty work" and take some of the risks. They also get a kick out of managing someone else.

Furthermore, there are exceptional cases in which a youngster is intimidated into participating in violation, such as a child who lives in an area where criminals congregate, but who does not want to have anything to do with them. Of those who are subjected to harassment, only a few join the criminal element in some of its activities and crime does not become the pattern of their lives.

> Most of Elliot's crime was in concert with C. Elliot was very frightened, because C told him he would beat him up if he did not participate. For several years, Elliot went around with C, but even then refused to do some things, because they did not appeal to him and he was afraid. In return for cooperating with C, Elliot was offered protection from some of the other rough kids in the neighborhood. When C became less of a factor in Elliot's life, he stopped engaging in these activities. He took no initiatives of his own in a criminal direction.

Had Elliot been more inclined toward criminal behavior he would not have needed C for a criminal foray, but would have been active before C entered the picture. When Elliot was not intimidated, he did not violate. (In fact, he later moved out of the area and was a responsible person.)

Once he has established himself in the criminal ranks, the criminal youngster scorns the noncriminal all the more. He makes a clear distinction between the strong and the weak, having "heart" and being "chicken," "lame," or "sissy." The criminal youngster is proud to be with the criminal group. He has less and less in common with peers who are responsible and truthful.

Now, he learns to ferret out others' weaknesses and exploit them if he needs to. Even his sense of humor is based on building himself up by tearing others down. He takes pleasure at others' distress or embarrassment and can be very cruel. He pokes at any little thing that downgrades others, to build himself up. He laughs at a person's dress, speech, or physical attributes. What is funny to most of his noncriminal peers is not funny to him. He finds it humorous to do something that is blatantly destructive and watch the reactions of his victims.

> When C was 15 or 16 years old, he began searching out places where couples "parked." He would come to a site where a man and woman were having intercourse in an automobile. He would station himself where he could see them, yet remain unseen by them. Having a rifle, he would wait until the lovemaking commenced, and then he would shoot at the windshield or headlights. Sometimes the woman was entirely undressed, and sometimes the man was also undressed. After he shot the rifle, he would shout to frighten them even more. His greatest pleas-

ure was in seeing the man get angry. He would enjoy running away, especially when pursued by one of the parties. There was no interest whatsoever in whether the woman or man was naked. It was the running and the anger that were most exciting.

C was an ambulance driver. His idea of fun was to place artificial feces in a hospital entranceway. He enjoyed watching people assiduously avoid walking into the feces. He did this repeatedly and in particular relished seeing funeral-home personnel edge around these. When people at the hospital became aware that the feces were not real, C put his own feces in the doorway. He roared with laughter when hospital personnel tried to pick them up or walked into them and found out they were real.

The criminal is a social dropout early in life. He does not like the "sissy" games of the other kids in the neighborhood. He disdains conventional groups and organized activities. He might join because his parents insist, or because he does not realize that there are rules and requirements. Boy Scouts, church groups, and school clubs usually do not give him the charge he wants, and in time he will probably drop out. When he attends a function, it is successful to the extent that it is exciting or provides him with a buildup. A fifteen-year-old attended a weekend encampment of the Civil Air Patrol from which he returned enthusiastic because of the highly exciting nature of the activities:

A lieutenant took the group out to a camp area with a shelter. Most of the first day they spent shooting a 0.22 rifle and pistol. Everything the boys did was a contest. C bragged that he stayed up until midnight, later than the others. When the group got ice cream, it was exciting to see who got the biggest cup, who scooped out the most, and who got left out because it was all gone. The next night, C and his cousin decided, would be "hell night"; they would beat up everybody. But the others vetoed this. Instead, they walked the streets in the area, playing hide and seek with the lieutenant. The youngsters would hide in ditches, pop out and blind the lieutenant with a flashlight, and then race him back to the shelter. The next day, all were up early and enjoyed handcuffing each other with their leader's handcuffs. Then, the group decided to toss a blanket over the lieutenant's head and in fact pulled him off a bench. At this point, he sprayed mace at them.

C did not join the Civil Air Patrol, despite this exciting encampment. He learned that the group required attendance at meetings and other responsibilities and had rules that C did not want to obey; the initial luster wore off quickly.

The criminal child may participate in some conventional activities for a while. He does this, however, not to be part of a team and not for fun or friendship, but because he desires to be a big shot. If he can run an organization, he may remain a member. He may stay in the school safety patrol, if he is captain and can tell others what to do. But he will soon tire of being an ordinary street-corner patrol boy.

Participation in organized activities also provides an appearance of respectability, which makes violation easier. He is less likely to be viewed as an offender if he is part of the student government, is on an athletic team, or is a member of the Boy Scouts. Because of his energy, intelligence, and resourcefulness, he is likely to perform far better than the average student while becoming a big shot. But his interest wanes, and he eventually drops out. He rarely quits abruptly.

The criminal child appears to be unsociable, because he rejects being friends with responsible children, who are in the majority. His enjoyment of other children depends on opportunities to violate with them. But he generally does not retain the same associates, even within the criminal group. He lacks stable relationships and deep friendships. Liaisons that do continue are based on mutual exploitation, although the criminal does not view it that way.

The criminal does maintain associations (which are mostly superficial) with responsible people. He may have a sentimental attachment to some, such as a person who is close to the family or who is working for a noble cause. But more often than not, he maintains the contacts for his personal use. He is likely to display weakness and ignorance, to get others to do things that he does not want to do himself. Basically, people are to the criminal what money in the bank is to a responsible person. The criminal wants them available to draw on. Even being seen in the company of a respected person builds him up.

Many criminals do not know how to act with responsible people, because they have never learned the rudiments of social behavior. It was observed at a reformatory that many youthful offenders did not know how to use knives and forks properly. With regard to politeness, the criminal usually does the proper thing if he thinks it will put him in someone's good graces. The criminal is rarely respectful of a responsible person who is older and more experienced than he. When a criminal says, "Yes, sir," it may be to ingratiate himself as part of a "conning" effort, rather than a sign of courtesy or genuine respect; or it may be a rejection with ill-concealed contempt.

Although the conforming world may view the criminal child as "different," in the sense of being apart, he is actually highly gregarious, energetic, and has rapport with children who share his interests. When the criminal child is seeking admission to the ranks of the delinquents, he is somewhat secretive, because he is trying to show that he is unfraid. He does not want others to know about the fears and sentimentalities within him, and he may appear quiet.

But he may become a socializer as he frequents the bars, poolrooms, street corners, restaurants, homes, and apartments where criminals hang out. In time, he comes to believe himself to be a "big man," although this may not be objectively verifiable. In the primary grades, he may try to live up to this image of himself by stealing or misappropriating money, then treating other youngsters to ice cream. It may be shown in his use of street language. He seeks unceasingly to establish himself as a powerful figure among the criminal group. He will eventually swagger, boasting of his deeds and exploits and earning a name for himself. He may do this by the way he dresses.

> At 16, C belonged to a "club" of four friends who were all spending huge sums of money, some of which was stolen, on clothes to impress each other and the girls. At this age, C had 32 pairs of shoes, including a $215 custom-made sharkskin pair, 25 suits, 20 sport jackets, nine hats, and large quantities of slacks, sweaters, shirts, and coats.

Of course, not all criminals disport themselves flamboyantly. Some prefer relative obscurity and go about their "business" in a more subdued manner. Relying on themselves, they are very secretive and move about silently and stealthily. Flashing money, dressing nattily, and "talking big" to impress others is not their style. They are isolated even with regard to the criminal group, at least until they "need" something. Then they are not at all hesitant to approach others.

What we have tried to show in this section is that crime does not come to or force itself on a child. It is not the neighborhood or the "bad company" that makes him "bad." Rather, a child decides very early whom he wants to be with and what kind of life he wants to lead. He makes choices all along the way, and criminal patterns are identifiable by the age of about ten.

SCHOOL

EARLY YEARS

The criminal has no concept of "education," and it is rare for him to derive any benefit appropriate to what a school purports to offer.

Many criminal youngsters perform satisfactorily until the fourth grade, although some have problems before then. They have able minds and learn quickly if they choose to.

> When C was three years old, his mother began teaching him to read, and he soon read proficiently. There were many books around the house, because mother was a schoolteacher. At the age of 5, he was reading saga poetry and memorizing large sections of it. Everyone began to see

that he was precocious. C did not live up to his early promise. As an adult, he appeared almost illiterate and was almost totally unable to spell.

When the criminal is about nine, competing interests arise, and school is subordinated to them. The degree to which this is visible is in part a function of the strictness of the particular school. Among our criminals, those who went to parochial schools stated that they had disliked those schools because their discipline was more severe and it was harder to get away with things. Some who transferred to public school observed that they took advantage of the much greater freedom.

> At the end of the seventh grade, C prevailed on his mother to allow him to shift from a parochial to a public school. In the former, the discipline by the nuns was firm. The usual pattern was a slap on the hands with a ruler and a whipping for more serious infractions. On entering public school, C found virtually no discipline. From then on, he was in constant difficulty. Things got so bad that the family, knowing there was a major problem, withdrew C and sent him to a military school, where he conformed to the military training but was uninterested in the curriculum and used all sorts of devices to get away with things. At the end of the eleventh grade, he left school, never to return.

Whether in public or parochial school, it is around the age of ten that the criminal child begins to be recognized as a problem. He is restless and inattentive, misses assignments, disobeys teachers, and tries to draw other youngsters into mischief. Truancy may be sporadic, with the child wandering off from school or faking illness in order to stay home.

> "You really had to be sick in my family to stay home and miss a day of school, but I concocted to do that. I used to hold a thermometer next to a light that was by my bed and regulate the temperature on the thermometer. I prolonged going back to school; I made like I was sick."

The criminal child may also be tardy often or leave school early, simply walking out of class.

Such a youngster may try increasingly to control all that goes on in the classroom. He pulls the girls' hair, acts as class clown, interrupts lessons, and is insolent to teachers, deliberately arguing with them and challenging them. He may seek to establish himself as a "tough kid." He engages so much of his teacher's attention that he is often the one whom the teacher selects to send on errands to get him out of the room. The criminal child may be sneaky, rather than obstreperous. He may not be viewed as a "behavior problem," but, unknown to the teacher, gets away with a lot on the sly.

It is natural for pupils to compare teachers, but the criminal does this in a somewhat different way from his noncriminal peers. To him, a "good teacher" is one who assigns little work and is lax about discipline. As one youngster put it, a "nice teacher" is one who "is on our side." A good teacher allows gum-chewing, sitting next to friends, and talking in class. A good teacher frivolously entertains the class (an inordinate amount of time), takes the children on many trips, grants frequent play periods, and permits time-wasting. A bad teacher insists that work be completed and maintains high academic and disciplinary standards.

The criminal youngster does not evaluate a teacher (or anyone else) with anything approaching open-mindedness. He makes up his mind how others should act before he knows them. This he does everywhere. He decides how a person will function. If things do not turn out as he had decided, it is the other person who has erred. For example, if he decides that his teacher is a "pushover" for an "A" and then does little work and gets a "C," it is the teacher who is to be faulted, not he. If he decides that his teacher is gullible and then is caught in a lie about why he was absent from school, he is indignant toward the teacher for not responding as expected.

THE DROPOFF IN JUNIOR AND SENIOR HIGH SCHOOL

By the time he gets to junior high school, the violating patterns of the criminal youngster are likely to be obvious, although he may behave well at school and seek his excitement elsewhere, especially if the school is strict about disciplinary infractions. This section focuses on what we call the "dropoff" in junior and senior high school. A dropoff is a person who occupies a seat in school, but has no constructive purpose in being there. Academic or vocational education is irrelevant to what he wants out of life. He perceives the formal educational enterprise as fruitless. He views serious students with contempt. He believes that he is superior to the common herd, which plods along completing daily assignments, studying for tests, and doing homework. The criminal child considers himself above the others, because he does things that others would not do and refuses to do what is required of him. The dropoff is basically the same as the dropout, except that he is present, whereas the dropout has already withdrawn from school.

The criminal youngster believes that he is brighter than most and that his native ability exceeds that of his classmates. He thinks he can become anything if he will only set his mind to it; to become a doctor, an astronaut, the president of a corporation, or anything else awaits only his decision. With this certainty of mind, he does not consider it incumbent on him to prove anything to anyone—at least, not by working hard.

"If I know that I can accomplish something, then it doesn't bother me that I don't accomplish it. I just don't feel that I should put in the time to be a master at something."

He thinks it is beneath him to pore over books at home, as the others do.

C's pattern was to arrive at school and risk being unprepared, hoping the teacher would not call on him. He might then dash through the assignment hurriedly as class began. If he got a "C" or a "B," he considered himself far superior to the student who struggled with the assignment and earned a top grade. His triumph was that he could get a passing grade with little or no work. To have had to study would mean to him that he was not the brilliant person he believed himself to be.

The criminal child believes that things should come to him naturally; if they do not, it is the teacher's fault. Even when he is doing poorly academically, he knows that it is a matter of not caring, rather than ineptitude or inability. In fact, he does not regard himself as a poor student at all. He believes that he knows a great deal and is capable of knowing anything and everything if he so desires.

He does not ask questions in school, unless it is to show off or embarrass the teacher. To do so would be to show ignorance, which would be incompatible with his "know-it-all" attitude. He may actually prefer to remain unnoticed. If he does not call attention to himself, it is easier to get away with things. Unprepared and uninterested, the criminal child wants to avoid having to recite in front of his classmates. He may try to get out of reading aloud, answering questions, working at the blackboard, or giving an oral report.

C rarely volunteered, and his teacher knew that this was because he was unprepared. She would ask him to come to the front of the room and try to work out a problem, to determine what he did know. This was not designed to be punitive, but was an attempt to instruct. C reacted to this with outrage. He became mortified and angry at his conspicuousness, despite the fact that he was responsible for it. After an episode of this sort, he might do some work for a while; but this soon petered out, and he resumed the old pattern.

Seeing the difficulties such youngsters have, teachers wonder why they do not ask questions when they do not understand something. What the teachers fail to recognize is that the criminal is not interested in what they have to offer. He will not ask questions to acquire information that he regards as useless. Furthermore, he is reluctant to ask questions because he does not want to appear ignorant in anyone's eyes.

The criminal child may at times become very much interested in the work and undertake assignments with vigor. *When he works*, he may be a perfectionist. He strives to do the best and to be the best: "If I can't do something well, I would just as soon not do it at all." When he attacks an assignment, his expectations are high. He wants to do a perfect job instantly. This kind of child wants the masterpiece completed almost before he begins a first draft. It is insulting to have to be bothered with preliminary details, such as outlining and compiling a bibliography; if he cannot complete a task instantly, it is not worth bothering with at all. His work habits are such that he does not make a sustained effort even in activities that initially capture his interest. As in so many other activities, there may be an initial rush of enthusiasm, but then a quick falling off.

While in school, the criminal youngster wants to call the shots, rather than perform on someone else's terms. Grading is sometimes offensive to him; he believes that his work is topflight and that others should recognize it. If he receives a poor evaluation of his work, he finds fault with the grader. Even when something of interest is assigned, he has little enthusiasm for the task, because it has been assigned, rather than freely chosen. If the criminal child decides he is not "interested" in something, he either refuses to do it or puts forth a token effort to placate the teacher. He reserves for himself the right to determine what is important. If an activity does not appeal to him, it is not worth doing at all.

The attitudes and work habits we have described might lead one to think that these dropoffs are academic failures. Actually, most are bright enough to get by; in some instances, they do relatively well. They learn all the shortcuts. They rarely take home any work, but do it in class when they should be attending to other things. A minority of these children may even appear to be model students, achieving academic records of some distinction. Those who become known as "good students" make things easier for themselves, in that they are less likely to be suspected of being violators. In a sense, they use school as a cover for their less savory activities. However, the majority have at best spotty academic records. They may earn an "A" in something for which they have a natural aptitude, which makes it easy for them. Such an "A" does not reflect a teacher's indulgent act. Poor grades are earned in courses that require drill, intensive study, and review, and the criminal youth tries to bypass courses requiring this kind of discipline. He elects general mathematics, rather than algebra. Foreign languages are a particular stumbling block for him. If he can avoid them, he does. If required to study a language, he does poorly, because he refuses to do the necessary memorization, drill, and review.

Despite spotty or failing records, most schools promote these youngsters, for a variety of reasons. In many cases, the school recognizes the criminal's capability and promotes him on the basis of intelligence rather than performance. Some criminals manage to con the system by ingratiating themselves with teacher after teacher. They graduate from high school, but cannot do seventh-grade work. Many educators believe that putting a child in a grade that he is too old and too big for increases his emotional maladjustment and adds more barriers to learning. Hence, some schools promote children who can barely read and write and offer remedial work later, if at all. In school systems subject to great mobility and change, standards for promotion often are lowered. The criminal child is aware of promotional policies and takes advantage of them. If he is reasonably bright and is attending a school with a large number of educationally handicapped, disadvantaged youngsters, he may be able to coast along, doing minimal work, and earn above-average grades. Of course, he may then criticize the school for not stimulating him and for wasting his time when really he had little interest in an education in the first place.

Many analyses of delinquent youths' school careers mention intellectual deficiency, dyslexia, and other learning disabilities. The criminal may not score very high on intelligence tests, which rely considerably on previous school learning, but he is quick to learn the things of importance to him. He may appear slow, or even "retarded," in school, but he is alert and shrewd when it comes to learning in the street. The trap into which some educators fall is to confuse a failure to learn that is due to lack of interest with a failure to learn that is due to an intellectual deficiency or organic impairment. If a child does not see any point in learning to read, he will be a poor reader. His illiteracy will be a consequence of choices he has made, and not a result of a lack of ability or a mental deficit.

The criminal youngster is far more interested in things outside the academic curriculum. He takes advantage of opportunities at school to create excitement. He dares to do what others will not and thus feels bigger, older, and more important. Some of these junior and senior high-school youngsters become major problems to teachers and other students, at times bringing the educational process to a standstill. It takes only a few of them in one classroom to destroy efforts to instruct the others. These youths seek each other out and can institute a reign of terror in school. They steal from teachers and other students and take school equipment. They establish protection, extortion, and confidence rackets.

C organized a protection racket in the sixth grade. Nine boys got 450 other students in the school to contribute a dollar a week, for which they were "protected" against being beaten up. If a fellow did not contribute, he was attacked.

C became known at school as an inexpensive source of tapedecks, stereos, and other sought-after items. He sold goods that he procured during break-and-entry forays. C delivered some of the goods, but pocketed money for some articles, in which case the intended student customer had little recourse.

Vandalism also offers excitement. The young criminals break into buildings, destroy equipment, at a cost of millions of dollars a year. Schools have had to curtail athletic and musical programs for a whole year because of the theft and destruction of equipment and instruments. Sometimes, acts of vandalism are directed against a particular person, such as a teacher.

C and a friend poured 10 pounds of sand into the gas tank of a teacher's car. They then "hot-wired" it and ground the pistons out, poured tar over the interior, and splashed egg all over the outside. They then broke into an area that contained explosives. With 15 sticks of dynamite, they blew up the teacher's sailboat at a dock adjacent to his home.

Some criminal youngsters look for fights alone or in a group. If they do not actually start one, they do all they can to provoke someone else into taking the first swing.

As he grows older, the criminal youngster uses school as an arena for the conquest of girls. He seeks to win the admiration of others by his sexual activities—profane talk, obscene gestures, solicitations, and the pursuit of girls to see "how far they can go." If the opportunity presents itself, sexual activity will occur on the school grounds. The teen-aged criminal gives young, attractive female teachers an especially difficult time, directing sexually tinged remarks and gestures their way. As he sits in the classroom, his mind races with fantasies of sexual power, only a minuscule portion of which is ever implemented at school. Thinking about sex is far more absorbing than thinking about equations on a blackboard.

In addition to property damage, assault, and sexual offenses, the infractions of school rules are too numerous to detail. Truancy is common, especially in schools that do not take roll or whose staff is lax in enforcing discipline. If a youngster is caught and has to account to his parents or others, he says that "everyone does it," "the teacher really didn't mind," etc. When he is in class, there is little integrity to his work. Plagiarism is common. Sometimes, he gets answers from a noncriminal child by intimidation or force. He may copy answers from the back of the book, missing a few to make it look as though he did the work himself. During a test, he uses many devices for cheating, being more resourceful in this than he is with respect to school-work itself.

Most of the excitement at school occurs in the criminal's own mind. No matter how much of a hellion he is, he thinks of far more violations than he ever commits. Absorbed in his own thoughts, he is inattentive to classroom lessons. A favorite response when he is called on is that he did not understand what the teacher said. He may put down the teacher for not being clear in explaining even simple things. He thereby gains the upper hand, as he makes the teacher attempt to clarify. To an observer, the criminal appears to be slow to catch the drift of an academic discussion. But he may enter into the middle of a conversation with friends and be very quick to pick up the gist of what is being said and add to it.

Some criminal youngsters do not implement violating thinking at school. If strong penalties are attached to various offenses, they divert their activities to a less perilous arena. If a child violates in a very strict school, he may be in a lot of trouble quickly. If he exhausts the patience of the school personnel, he may be suspended. He would then have to contend with his parents and the many others in the community who will be keeping an eye on him. Rather than put himself in a position where others will keep him under tight surveillance, he avoids trouble at school. Nevertheless, there are a few criminal youngsters who regard a tightening in the school's disciplinary measures as a greater challenge to overcome, and they are not deterred.

WHY THE CRIMINAL YOUTH REMAINS IN SCHOOL

Most American families recognize the critical role of education as a determinant of a person's position in society. The pressures of society favor staying in school to get a better job and live a better life. In the case of a criminal, this requirement asks a person to get an education that he does not care about in order to prepare him for a job he cares even less about. It is not the concern over future employment that keeps him in; it is family pressures. In most families, it is taken for granted that, just as the adult goes to work, so the child goes to school. Whether a youth attends school is not a matter for debate. Thus, when a youngster is doing poorly in school, and especially when he talks of leaving school, it precipitates a family crisis. This is true at all socioeconomic levels. Ghetto families are often even more insistent that their offspring continue to attend school, so that they can take advantage of opportunities that their parents did not have. For the criminal child (as well as for the noncriminal), it is generally *easier* to stay in school. If a youngster leaves school, he is expected to assume responsibilities, such as a job. Because he is relatively bright and can get by in school with minimal effort, the criminal youngster often realizes that he has a "good thing going" and stays where he is. Certainly, most prefer school to working, which they would have to do as an alternative to satisfy others.

At school, the criminal can find or stir up excitement if he so chooses. He turns the educational institution into his arena. He may even join school organizations that he disdains, if he sees in them something that will build him up in the eyes of his peers. To some criminal youngsters, being in the limelight is very important. They seek positions of influence and recognition. They are rarely committed to benefiting an organization itself; their purpose is self-aggrandizement, being the "big shot."

By remaining in school, a criminal can play both sides of the street. School can be a cover: if a child does well, he is less likely to be suspected of violating; and if he gets into trouble elsewhere, he may be forgiven more rapidly if he is a student in good standing. Society uses school performance as the leading indicator of how a child is functioning, just as job performance later indicates responsibility and stability. In fact, there is such emphasis on just being in school that much irresponsibility elsewhere is overlooked. The criminal youngster is aware of this and makes the most of it. He satisfies others and thus is allowed more room to do what he wants.

THE SCHOOL'S RESPONSE TO THE CRIMINAL CHILD

Criminal children—energetic, restless, bright, capable, but performing poorly—are a source of tremendous concern to the school. Although we are using the term "criminal children," it is important to recognize that the school does not regard them as "criminal." Rather, they are viewed as maladjusted youngsters whose maladjustment is due to a variety of conditions of life. If a child is from an impoverished home, the school may offer him breakfast. If he is from a broken home, the teachers may try to give him additional emotional support. The school makes allowances and tries to help. There is usually no recognition of an inherent character problem.

In the early years, the school attempts to reach the pupil's parents and notify them of his problems in the classroom. If a teacher sends a note home via the child, it probably never reaches its destination. If the teacher personally contacts the parents, the criminal child tries to enlist his parents on his side, faulting the school and disclaiming personal responsibility. Many parents understand the teacher's problem only too well, but are at a loss as to how to help; they have their own difficulties with the child at home. The school may recommend transfer of the youngster to another classroom or placement in a special school. This fails to remedy the situation. At best, it enables a particular teacher or school to be rid of the child. Shifting schools does not induce a change in the youngster's attitude.

The school may insist that the child make up missed work. If a great deal of work has been left undone, the child may be retained, but this is unusual.

Suspension or expulsion for behavioral problems is uncommon, because the community believes that the school should deal with these children and that they should not be on the streets. In short, the prevailing attitude is usually a sympathetic one, in which educators believe that it is up to the school to find some way to "motivate" a pupil who is performing poorly. Thus, the school tries to cope with a child with whom no one else has been able to deal effectively. Administrators and teachers may try to reach the youngster at his level and in his language. One measure has been to hold group rap sessions, in an attempt to offer students a chance to express themselves and adults a chance to show their concern. Counselors and mental-health professionals also try to help. The criminal knows which school personnel are sympathetic and which are "hardliners." He recruits the former to bail him out of difficulty and avoids the latter. He may appeal for a change of teacher or ask that someone at the school talk to his parents to get them off his back.

Teachers go out of their way to befriend these children, whom they see as having such great potential. Often, they think they are having a positive influence, only to have a criminal child lose interest somewhere along the line, exploit them for favors, and ultimately break away. Even the "personal touch" does not succeed.

THE COLLEGE DROPOFF AND DROPOUT

Of the criminals who go to college, many find it tougher academically, depending on the institution's standards. Many enroll only because it is expected of them. As one young man put it, "I didn't even think about it. It just happened, more than being a rational decision." Once there, they find school unfulfilling. Some of those who go to college away from home are supported by their parents; thus, it is regarded as a "free ride," with parents shelling out money on request. Many criminal young adults come to college well recommended by their high schools—e.g.,

> "A most outstanding individual, excellent personal discipline, articulate, well-read, well-balanced, fine manners and control of self."

Occasionally, the high-school records contain less positive, and more revealing, comments by people who perhaps know the student better—e.g.,

> "At too young an age he has acquired a cynical chip-on-the-shoulder attitude with which he is so busy reforming society, that he neglects to invest the necessary time for studies. He needs to be reminded of the realities of the disciplines associated with survival and success in contemporary life."

> "He runs with questionable characters."

Not long after the freshman criminal arrives at college, discontent sets in. If he resides in a dormitory, he is dissatisfied with conditions there. He dislikes living with "Joe College" students and stands apart, contemptuous of them. Instead, he seeks out others like him.

> At a well-known exclusive private college, C found 14 other fellows who used drugs heavily and engaged in various violations. Only one of this group graduated on time; 11 were expelled. C did not have any "straight" friends at the college. Of the more than 400 students, he selected these to associate with. None of these young men was ever arrested.

In most sectors of college life, there is a discrepancy between what the criminal wants and what the university expects. The criminal resents having to be accountable to anyone about anything. He complains bitterly about the regimentation in the dormitories. Academically, he expects to receive good grades with little effort, as he did in high school; instead he is likely to meet stiffer requirements. He balks at much of the work, claiming that it is "boring" and "irrelevant."

Earlier patterns persist: the youth seeks shortcuts and elects the easiest courses. Many criminal students major in the humanities and social sciences, where requirements are often more flexible than those of other fields and which permit students opportunities to work independently. In some institutions, they can virtually design their own majors.

> "It is almost possible to major in revolution. There are enough specific courses offered in sociology and history and political science and philosophy to have enough credits to consider yourself a major in revolution."

Just as in high school, those who find courses that they like still refuse to do the work. The interest turns into a conflict. As one student said: "Reading something on my own was another story. As far as putting out for someone else, my hangups would start to come out."

College academic records are usually more spotty than those in high school, where the competition is less keen. Furthermore, colleges are less likely to hand out passing grades when a student is failing. In fact, the policy of some is to weed out early those who do not belong in college at all. For many criminals in college, the days of being automatically passed end, but their attitude toward grades remains scornful. The solution for most is to do enough to get by and then do what they want on the side. If they thought life was easy before, it is even easier now; there are no parents around to tell them what to do, and supervision at college is minimal or nonexistent.

"It was fairly easy living here [at college]. I could sleep in the morning because I didn't have any morning classes, and the routine wasn't hard to meet."

For the most part, they can cut classes without penalty. They try to con teachers into granting them extensions or "incompletes," or they ask to be excused from assignments altogether. One student persuaded an instructor to give him an "A" in a course, with the promise that some time within the next year he would write the required paper. He never wrote it. Some are able to obtain medical excuses from the student health service so that they can postpone work. Some are very calculating in the way they "use the system" for their own purposes. Some members of our group knew that, as long as they remained in school, they could avoid the draft (through student deferments), jobs, and possible unpleasant confrontations with their parents. One described the university as a "place to hide, nice and safe and secure."

Despite this sheltered life, the criminal is increasingly restless. He may look for excitement in campus activities, as he did in high school, by promoting himself in organizations. He may join activist groups. Often the cause being advanced is less important than the role the criminal can play. He may be at the forefront of protests, violent and nonviolent, sometimes as strategist, sometimes as activist. Eventually, the pressures of academic life might become greater than he wants to tolerate. If he blatantly ignores college requirements or performs poorly, the faculty and administration eventually hold him accountable. When the itch for excitement becomes strong and he is bored, he may begin to have psychosomatic symptoms. Once he finally decides to leave, the restlessness, physical symptoms, and inner discontent diminish markedly.

Most institutions try to be helpful and understanding. Accordingly, students are offered numerous "second chances," and some are referred to counselors and therapists. The institutions are reluctant to expel on either academic or behavioral grounds, unless a student is openly antagonistic and makes trouble. Those who leave voluntarily usually do so with the assurance that the door remains open for readmission. These criminals tell the dean that they have to "find" themselves or discover what they are interested in, and the institution's records reflects this.

"I [have] the impression his decision is not impulsive, and perhaps represents some careful consideration. He is in a state of confusion about what life is all about" (note by a college dean).

The patterns of the dropout and dropoff are not mutually exclusive. All criminals who are dropouts are initially dropoffs. In the lower grades, it is more difficult to leave school, if for no reason other than that the law in most states requires attendance until the age of sixteen. All criminals are dropoffs, but do not necessarily elect to drop out.

Since the 1960s, schools at all levels have been reflective about their role in society and self-critical of their programs and teaching techniques. To repeat, the designation "criminal" is ours, based on numerous "autopsies" of the failures in society who show criminal patterns of thinking and action. However, the schools and colleges do not think in these terms. Instead, educators see bright youngsters who are "maladjusted" and not living up to their potential. This results in much soul-searching on the part of faculties and administrations as to what they are doing wrong or not doing. To interest and retain these students, they often conclude that changes in the system are necessary. But innovations in curriculum and special programs do not change the criminal youngsters. The criminal will not involve himself in something that he views as meaningless, and some criminals have acknowledged to us that the only courses that might have interested them, especially during the junior-high-school years, would have been those in picking pockets, safecracking, and so forth.

When the criminal child is held accountable for violations at school or in the community, he is apt to use the educational institution's self-criticism as ammunition against it. Taking his cue from society, he blames the school, saying that it does not "motivate" him, that the teachers are arbitrary, the curriculum irrelevant, and that the values being imposed are alien to him. He decries the rules and "regimentation" and insists that his creativity is being stifled. The more sophisticated the criminal, the more he can couch all this in acceptable terms of educational philosophy.

Society keeps trying to educate the criminal long after his school days are over. In confinement, he is again offered educational opportunities; indeed, in programs throughout the country, criminals earn high-school equivalency diplomas while confined. Society believes that one constructive step toward changing the criminal is to educate him. If the criminal foresees that this will help him to achieve an earlier release, he may go along with the program offered. But his interest is less in the education and more in the overriding objective of getting out, although, to be sure, some do become interested in the subject matter.

> In prison, C taught himself grammar. Then he became further absorbed in language and taught himself French and Latin. He also studied algebra and trigonometry.

This criminal became enamored of the subject matter and studied diligently. He wanted this education so as to be regarded among the elite. He did not value the material so much for its own worth. A mastery of these subjects did set him apart in prison from his fellow inmates, but it did not alter his criminal patterns. After being released from prison, C committed many more crimes and was finally apprehended for rape.

WORK

Most descriptions of how the criminal functions contain the statement that he is "unable" to hold a job.

> In their ordinary lives they are *unable* to adapt to the work conditions provided for them and fail to co-operate or to show any sense of loyalty to the organization in which they may be working. . . . These . . . are the disaffected work people who are inclined to be agitators and stirrers-up of trouble and constitute the wastage turnover in any industrial organization. Henderson, 1951, p. 85, italics ours).

As one examines the work patterns of criminals, one does see frequent shifting of jobs and some periods of no employment. In fact, some criminals in their early twenties have never worked at all. However, this is not due to a lack of ability or talent. Most of the criminals with whom we have worked are intelligent and capable; some have exceptional aptitudes that would be vocational assets. By and large, they are quick to learn without formal training. Some are skilled in the arts, and most are good with their hands. In general, when they work, they are productive. The key phrase is "when they work," because their work patterns are often erratic.

Among criminal youngsters, the question, "What do you want to be when you grow up?" elicits remarkably uniform answers. Most select occupations that they perceive as exciting and adventurous—fireman, FBI agent, policeman, combat hero, pilot, race-car driver. The criminal child thinks that in these jobs he would play dramatic roles. The clergyman also has great power.

> C thought about being a Baptist preacher, delivering a message to a huge crowd outside the Pope's residence. He would be on the balcony, and the congregants would kneel before him. He went so far as to rehearse what he would say to the masses.

Some criminal youngsters have visions of being wealthy executives who give orders from behind large desks in plush offices. Most, even as they become young adults, do not have a concept of a "career" or lifework. Whatever the choice of occupation, they think mainly in terms of instantly becoming outstanding successes. There is no consideration of long-range goals and the intermediate steps required to attain them.

Most criminal youngsters who want to avoid working full time remain in school.

"Since I wasn't about to work anyhow, it was easier to go to school. I couldn't even imagine myself working. Work all your life and what do you have? A dull, boring routine."

Some drift in and out of part-time jobs, working on a newspaper route or in a store, an amusement park, a restaurant, a gas station, or wherever else anyone will hire them. They work until they tire of what they are doing, and then they move on.

From adolescence into young adulthood, C worked a total of 15 months out of 7 years. He worked 7½ months in an amusement park, 2 months in a second-hand store, 4 months in a restaurant, and a month delivering papers. The rest of the time, he drifted around, devoting increasing attention to crime.

Some of these youngsters steal from the places where they work or in some way cheat employers or customers. In the course of performing their duties, criminal youngsters often exploit other children in the neighborhood, getting them to work for them and offering little or nothing in return.

To understand the orientation of the adult criminal toward work, one must view different attitudes as lying along a continuum. The same person has a variety of attitudes toward work that are in flux. It is helpful to discuss five stances separately: scorning work and refusing to get a job, unless virtually forced to, as exemplified by one of our people who worked a total of sixteen months between the ages of seventeen and thirty-three; half-heartedly holding a job and maintaining a facade of working; working with the clear intention of using the job for criminal activities; being interested in a chosen field, but trying to control others with or without personal aggrandizement, rather than valuing the work itself, although perhaps staying in a job for a long time; and being very restrained in the work situation and keeping the thrust for power and criminality mostly outside the job. The first four of these attitudes toward work are not mutually exclusive and may be held by the same person at different times; the "longtime good-worker" pattern is much rarer, and in time it may come to an end.

THE INFREQUENT WORKER

We look first at the criminal who most of the time has no serious interest in working. He firmly believes that work gets one nowhere. He would consider himself a "sucker" if he worked, because there are better ways to get what he wants. It would be absurd to spend eight hours a day doing what is dull and meaningless. He views work as degrading, because it is accompanied by a loss of autonomy; to follow a routine set by someone else is offensive, and he would resent having to abide by rules that he had no part in establishing. Even taking advice is demeaning. Most important, the criminal has more exciting things to occupy him. Certainly, he does not need to work for the money—more money may pass through his hands in a few months of crime than he would earn in years of salary. Indeed, crime is his "job."

A criminal who views work in this way may hold a job, but only because that is easier than subjecting himself to the suspicions and pressures of others if he does not work. All his life, the criminal has been told to work by parents, relatives, teachers, law enforcement authorities, and some psychiatrists. Society assesses a person's stability in part by his work performance. Those who loaf and live off others are viewed unfavorably, and their activities are more subject to public scrutiny. People in some segments of society believe that work will make a man honest if he is inclined otherwise. Thus, the criminal may work to satisfy outside demands. Work, like school, helps to make him appear respectable and provides a cover for criminal activities.

There are times when a criminal who is ordinarily emphatic in his rejection of work sincerely wants to work. This occurs when he is fed up with himself and wants to be a decent person; he then equates work with "decency" and may work diligently for a week or two. Anyone who sees him during this period regards him as a good worker. However, the pro-work state of mind is not sustained.

The criminal may also work because he is required to do so as a condition for probation, parole, or unconditional release. If faced with a stipulation that he must work, he accepts any job, no matter how menial, knowing that he does not intend to remain at it. He will stay employed as long as he has to account to an authority.

> To satisfy a probation requirement, C worked for 4 months dispensing food at a restaurant. He worked 9 hours a day, with most of the busy periods being a lunchtime and during coffee breaks in nearby offices. He earned $37.50 per week plus tips, all the food he wanted, and uniforms. He was stealing on the side, and could make far more in 2 hours than he made at the restaurant in several days. Some of the money that he was making on this job went toward the purchase of tools that he later used for safecracking and breaking and entering. As soon as he was off probation, he quit the job and returned to full-time crime.

THE WORK FACADE

The criminal, not being eager to work, does not approach looking for a job very seriously. There is little long-range thinking about opportunities to develop himself and advance. He prefers enlisting others in setting him up in a job to canvassing the job market himself. It is fairly simple to visit an agency, submit an application, and await news of an opening. If he has a criminal record that is known to the agency, getting a job may be even easier, because the personnel may be impressed by his intention to reform and be doubly eager to assist him. Many of the people who work at such bureaus try to assess a criminal's interests and abilities. Of course, the criminal probably knows already where his talents and interests lie and does not need tests to tell him. The problem is that he does not want to harness his aptitudes to a job or job training. He is antiwork and wants to set the conditions of employment for himself. Thus, the whole testing-counseling process is usually futile.

If he decides that he does want a job, he can get one, because he has the wherewithal to present himself convincingly, often without having to reveal anything of his past. When a job becomes available, the criminal uses various excuses to refuse it if it does not suit him exactly. He may claim to have a physical disability when he does not, or he may say that the work is too heavy and he is not strong enough. He may state later that he could not find the place where the interview was to be conducted. He may oversleep or claim not to have transportation. He may say that there is no point even in looking, because his record will be held against him. Many criminals turn down job offers, on the grounds that they are qualified for something better.

> C stated, "I won't do any work I don't like to do. Nobody has a right to tell me what I have to do." C did not want work that was all physical. Washing dishes was beneath him. Janitorial work he regarded as all right only for Negroes. He did not want to be an usher, because people would give him a "hard time." He was a busboy for a while, but did not like the "crazy waiters" who told him to hurry. He did not want to work where bosses would tell him what to do. He offered various excuses, such as "nervousness," others' giving him orders, fatigue, and boredom. He made it clear that he would work only if he were threatened with rehospitalization in maximum security.

That is, he made it clear to *us;* the excuses he gave to the hospital staff. This criminal, who was being so selective, did not have job skills or even know how to read or write. But he systematically ruled out jobs appropriate for him at the time. It is interesting that criminals sometimes say that they cannot get jobs because of their illiteracy, thus turning illiteracy into an advantage, in that it automatically excludes them from consideration for some jobs.

Once the criminal is hired, he usually cares so little about what he is doing and is so unaccustomed to fact-finding that he neglects to learn the conditions of his employment. He neglects to ask about working hours, date of first paycheck, frequency of payment, sick leave, and fringe benefits. He may not even know how much he is supposed to be paid. All he knows is that he has a job.

Although the criminal may maintain a facade at work, he is unpredictable in performance. We have seen men rise from trainee, for example, to top salesman within 2 months. After functioning responsibly for a while, they steal money from the cash register and quit a week later. Some people view this chain of events as evidence of a "drive to fail." However, the fact is that doing well and rising in position are not sufficiently gratifying to keep them interested. The criminal finds even the most ideal working conditions unsatisfactory. No matter what his training and skills, he considers himself better than the job.

> C worked as a janitor. He came to work dressed like a prosperous businessman in a gray flannel suit, arriving ahead of everyone else. When he worked, he hid himself in a somewhat remote area for which he was responsible. He had to join the group for a weekly meeting after hours. When he did this, he was neatly dressed. When several workers wanted to give him a ride downtown, he would not take it, because they were dressed in dirty clothes and their cars were shabby. Instead, he took a cab. He described the job as intolerable, because he believed he was "better" than they. However, when he looked at himself in a janitor's uniform, he believed he was "nothing." In another job as a janitor, he came to work in minister's garb, with a turned-around collar.

> In one of C's jobs, he was situated high in a skyscraper, overlooking the city. He looked down at the "squirming ants"—the way he conceived of average workers. When he came downstairs and mixed with them, he got a feeling of panic when he realized that he was one of them.

To this man, being an ordinary worker was equivalent to being nothing at all.

One part of work that the criminal dislikes is taking orders. At no time in his life does he want to be subordinate. He dislikes even having to call his supervisor "Mr." or by any other title. Finding himself less than top man, the criminal tries to outsmart the person who in fact is the top man. But he rarely challenges that person directly. Instead, he cons, lies, and develops gimmicks, thinking that he is outwitting his superior. Occasionally, he is not so subtle and resorts to sarcasm or substandard performance—in short, anything to undermine the boss and assert his own "authority."

The criminal who maintains the work facade leaves work early without authorization, arrives late, and is absent illegitimately. The slightest ache or pain is used as a reason for not going to work. Rather than worry about whether he is satisfying job requirements, he insists that his job conform to his requirements. Although the criminal may invite criticism by his behavior, he is very sensitive about being taken to task. For example, rather than go to work late and be reprimanded, he may not go at all that day. When he is held accountable for deficiencies at work, he has a repertoire of responses in which he blames the job or other people: the job is not stimulating, or it offers no opportunity to be "creative." If the boss is angry at him for being late in getting a task done, he then asserts that the job is intolerable because of the pressures of an unreasonable, temperamental boss. Injustice is a common theme as he tries to explain away his poor work and his irresponsibility. Eventually, he quits his job abruptly and without notice; one day, he simply does not show up for work, and no one ever learns why.

The overriding purpose of having a job in the first place is to make the criminal look respectable to others. A man who has a good job is fulfilling the expectations of the community. Being known as a steady, competent worker enhances his status and makes it easier to get away with things while not on the job.

> C always used his job at the bank as a cover for crime. He appeared for work as a teller promptly and well-dressed. He had no interest in the work, but it was undemanding. The only pleasure he derived from it was the thought that he was conning society and throwing others off the track. C had access to the bank's books and money and thought of victimizing the bank, but decided that the risks were too great. He knew that suspicion would be directed toward him; anyone could look up his record and find that he had a criminal background. So he left the bank's funds untouched, but used his respectable position as a cover for crime outside.

Besides looking respectable, in the community, the criminal can make contacts on his job that may be important to him later. It always helps to have reputable people as character references. In some cases, what the criminal learns about his co-workers may assist him in setting up a crime against them. He comes to know where they live, what they own, when their homes are most accessible, and so forth. To make his schedule compatible with criminal activities, he works odd hours, taking midnight shifts or weekends. He may even earn the praises of his employer for being so "flexible" and assuming duties at times when others might not.

CRIME ON THE JOB

The criminal who seeks to use his job itself for criminal purposes is selective. He has to find an opportunity to implement criminal operations right on the job. He may seek employment that is compatible with his criminal interests. For example, one criminal who was a breaking-and-entering man set himself up in business as a locksmith. He not only had the facilities for making keys, but was in a position to acquire knowledge of potential targets. He used the keys to scout places to rob later. However, in the actual burglaries, he broke in, because he thought that, otherwise, as the keymaker or lock repairman, he might be traced. One criminal worked as an ice cream truck driver. While doing this, he molested over 1,000 young girls in a year. To stay above suspicion, he hired young boys to go on the truck with him.

It has been widely observed that "inside jobs" account for most losses to business firms. An article in the *Wall Street Journal* of February 5, 1970, pointed out that bringing one culprit after another into the spotlight could permanently damage a firm; a customer may take his business elsewhere, if he finds out that employees are stealing and that as a consequence he has to pay more for what he buys. The criminal does not steal on the job to get needed money or objects, nor because he is angry toward his employer, although, if apprehended, he may say this to others. Rather, it is the thrill of doing it and getting away with it that is important. The theft of one suit has a greater impact on the criminal than being a high-commission salesman in men's clothing. The criminal has little use for much of what he steals and may give the proceeds away.

The nature of the job itself may be crooked, entailing misrepresentation and outright deception.

> At the age of 15, C met a man who told him of the excitement and adventure of travel that could be his through selling magazines. Money was the alluring item with nothing being said about the method of selling. C described his first day as a trainee, when he saw sales of $8, $12, and $16 in rapid succession within the first three solicitations. This convinced him. The pitch was to play on people's sympathies with various kinds of fraudulent stories. With the salesman showing C's crippled leg (he was partially crippled) and scars and expressing his yearning for an education, C could get a customer to identify with him, as though C were his own child. The first day, C got $50 worth of business, $12.50 of which was his to keep. In a short time, he became manager of the enterprise, pocketing 25% of the front money. C then redistributed the money in such a way that he never filed a tax report. Both the accounting and the sales pitches were fraudulent. At 19, C was making enough money to live in the best hotels, frequent the finest restaurants, own a car, and still have $100 a week in pocket money. In time, he picked up

27 handicapped people to work for him. As he continued this operation, there were troubles all along the way. One of the boys was charged with rape. C had accumulated $6,000 and had to part with it all to get the boy out. The investigation entailed extensive unfavorable publicity for the whole enterprise. Things became even more difficult: magazine publishing companies passed tighter regulations prohibiting the exploitation of infirmities by any of their agents. C disregarded this and changed his name. He retained the same handicapped employees, but listed them under different names, so that even his own company thought he was employing people who were not handicapped.

This is an example of employment that is in itself a criminal operation.

Assaults also occur on the job. When the criminal does not get his own way in a matter of great importance to him or is surprised in the course of a violation, he may be dangerous. This occurred in the magazine racket described above: C, with gun in hand, pursued a man who had claimed that one of the representatives was immoral. There are many other types of violations, including the use of drugs and alcohol on the premises. To enumerate the specific types of crimes on record would be to compile a catalog of little value. But it is important to point out that, although so much crime is committed on the job, very few of the criminals are apprehended. A criminal may work for a company for years, violating its policies, misrepresenting it, and defrauding it without ever being detected.

An employer who knows that an employee is violating may not want to confront him with this knowledge or prosecute. One reason is to avoid unpleasantness and embarrassment to the company. Some concerns write off inside theft as a business loss.

The manager of a large furniture company recognized that his employees did some stealing of the merchandise and some items from the places where the furniture was delivered. He realized that the wages he was willing to pay and the nature of the work made it likely that he would get a particular type of employee. His force of workers included drifters who were irresponsible. The manager knew that, unless he set up an extensive security system, he could do little to put a stop to the stealing. It was a matter of weighing costs and being realistic about the nature of the people he was likely to attract.

When a man is first discovered violating, an employer may overlook it, especially if the employee has a good record with the firm. In addition, employers tend to be compassionate and do not want to embarrass a man and his family. When company officials realize that a man is a chronic violator, they may suggest that he resign, rather than fire him. When a man is fired, it is because the company can replace him and recognizes that he would do more harm than good if he stayed. It also happens that a criminal is apprehended for a crime outside the job and is forced to leave. Thus, the offenses at work may be detected only much later, or perhaps not at all.

Some criminals become involved in their work. However, their view of the job is colored by the expectation that they will be extraordinary and make outstanding achievements quickly. The criminal who considers being a lawyer thinks about being a dramatic courtroom prosecutor with a Perry Mason flair. If he wants to be a physician, it is one who makes dramatic lifesaving operations. If he thinks along business lines, he sees himself as a corporate executive who deals in high finance. The criminal with genuine humanitarian interests thinks of being a great benefactor who achieves virtual immortality. The criminal who assumes a position with instantaneous success in mind does not hesitate to take shortcuts or use unethical tactics. His orientation is toward recognition and power. To achieve them, he tolerates some humdrum work, but he expects his star to rise quickly, and when it does not, he is ready to dispense with the routine.

The criminal's idea of accomplishment emphasizes less the substance of the work to be done and more his elevation to a high station. He begins work enthusiastically, showing energy and drive. The nature of the work itself intrigues him. With serious application to the job, he is viewed by others as capable and committed. Consequently, it does not take long for his employer to offer him additional training and opportunities to ascend the promotional ladder. Now the criminal is in a position to go far if he immerses himself in the work and sticks with it. But he expects to be an overnight success and does not want to start at the bottom and work up. He resents having to do work that he considers beneath him. He believes that he knows more than his superiors and resents being told what to do by people whom he views as his inferiors. The attitude of being "above" the work leads to numerous difficulties. With a know-it-all attitude, the criminal becomes complacent, bored, and restless. Then, anyone can be a target for the expression of his dissatisfaction. Given this state of mind, interpersonal difficulties are inevitable. The criminal claims that he is not being promoted fast enough, that he does not gain sufficient recognition, that he is discriminated against and exploited, and so forth. He may quit before anyone can fire him, or he may stay on, enjoying the battles he has triggered. He may even push an employer to the point where firing is the only solution. Thus, he throws away what many people would consider a good opportunity. As one young criminal commented, "I have wasted more opportunities than many people ever have."

Some criminals stay at a job for a considerable period and are promoted rapidly. But their appetites are insatiable, and when they do move up, it is never fast enough to suit them. They desire higher positions and more authority than they have. They are chronic malcontents, who believe that they are indispensable to their organizations and should be recognized as such. Their behavior on the job effects this self-appraisal. Many are pretentious and presumptuous in their demands upon others. No matter how long the criminal remains at a job, he does not function responsibly. The following account of one person's work habits is typical with respect to *patterns*.

> C worked for a government organization as a planning consultant. He had plenty of problems of his own that were not well concealed at work, including the use of heroin. But on the job, he acted like the one who would solve the problems of others—both vocational and personal. He built himself up as an expert on everything. He often disregarded directives from his supervisor, believing he knew better what needed to be done. He "counseled" others on their personal problems during working hours. In particular, Becky, his secretary, took up a lot of time. Her husband had abandoned her and their child. Becky looked to C for advice, and C saw himself in her husband. This "work relationship" entailed taking her to lunch and buying her drinks. Becky phoned late at night about her husband's drug use, thefts, and so forth. Business hours were appropriated for further discussion.

> C was often late to work. When he arrived, he engaged in his "counseling" and other conversations not related to work. On some days, he went out to meet his drug connection. He kept a set of "works" in his desk drawer. Countless hours were wasted at extended lunches and on the phone. C's tolerant employer was aware of some of these patterns. However, C was a bright man with considerable potential. He also was participating in an outside program to change. Finally, the employer's patience wore out, and he was prepared to dismiss C.

> Rather than allow himself to be fired, C moved to another job. Through his "gift of gab," he was offered a job with a drug treatment agency. While working there, C was invited to a retreat and impressed others by his polished appearance and speech. Consequently, he was selected for a permanent position and appeared on television as a "rehabilitated addict." The fact is that all that time C was an arrestable showpiece. While serving as a model of a cured man, he was "chipping" heroin (using it occasionally) and using marijuana and considerable amounts of alcohol.

This criminal had created his own arena for power right on the job. Even if the criminal runs his own business, the same patterns prevail. He makes poor decisions, because he does not seek facts. He fails to screen employees and often hires those who are irresponsible. He himself gradually loses interest and delegates authority to others; before long, the business falters. If something unexpected and exciting occurs, the criminal may be reenergized with respect to business.

> C was running a family-owned carryout shop. He had reached the point where some days he did not show up for work at all. The business was barely limping along. One day, some delinquent youngsters were hanging around the parking lot, creating a general nuisance and disturbing business. They were bothering merchants, calling them names, and threatening passersby. C came rushing out of his shop with a gun and chased them away. The prospect of another encounter with these youngsters stimulated C to such an extent that for the next 2 weeks, he arrived promptly at work and put in a full day.

What contributed to this man's surge of interest and participation had no relation to the business. It should be noted that he had fancied himself "making it big" in real estate and that, when this dream collapsed, he went for a long time without working until moving into the carryout business, which his family offered him.

THE CRIMINAL AS A "GOOD WORKER"

Occasionally in a character profile of an arrested criminal, one is surprised to read that he was a good worker. The phrase "a good worker" when applied to the criminal has several meanings, depending on whom one talks to. A criminal who is seen industriously working at a construction site may confirm this notion. But the designation is based on what one sees at the time and not on the truth of the situation, which might be that this is the criminal's sixth job in two years. A man may be regarded as a good worker on the grounds that he fulfills an employer's expectations. The requirements may be minimal, such as simply showing up for work. However, they may be more substantial, and then it depends on what the employer knows. The criminal may be violating, but not detected. The good worker may be one whose criminal activities occur entirely outside his job. His good-worker image helps to keep him above suspicion.

> C was a teletypist in the service. He regarded the work as exciting and important. People depended on him: messages had to get through promptly, or others would be in danger. For the 12 years he spent on the job, he arrived at work early, performed well, and got along excellently with his superiors. C was known for adapting well to change. He was also a competent supervisor of other personnel. C looked forward to 20 years of service with the military after which he would become a teletypist in a civilian capacity with the government, receiving the security that comes with government service. He seemed to have his

future charted. However, overriding criminal interests on the outside surfaced. Among his offenses were child molestation, which had been occurring right along but was unknown to others. C was discharged from the military.

For twelve years, C was viewed as a good worker, and in fact he was. Those who knew him were shocked when they learned that this seemingly responsible man had molested children. In short, the criminal may actually perform very well on the job, and it is to his advantage to do so, because it enhances his status in the community and makes it easier for him to violate and escape detection.

WORK IN CONFINEMENT

When the criminal is confined, the same attitudes and patterns are present as those already mentioned. Even when extensive job-training programs are available, some scorn these and refuse to participate. The criminal offers a host of his usual excuses for not working. For some, it is a matter of pride not to work, especially on the institution's terms. This is simply an extension of the same attitude held outside confinement. Despite the near certainty of a penalty for not working, some criminals stand firm, refusing to do what they consider degrading.

Others persist in maintaining a facade, deciding to "go along with the program" and accepting almost any conditions to expedite getting out. Some have brief periods of sincerity, but very few are committed to their assignments. A proof of the lack of commitment is that, when these criminals achieve the ends they seek—the unconditional release or parole—the work performance declines, and they quit.

C was conditionally released with the requirement that he work. He was quickly able to get a job on a construction site. Knowing that he was coming up for an unconditional release, he continued to work at that job until the release went through. As soon as it did, he quit, got drunk, went back into crime, and committed an armed robbery.

The probation or parole officer usually wants to see pay slips as tangible evidence that the criminal is working. However, patterns of irresponsibility on and off the job remain unknown to him. Because of the large case load such officers have, supervision is often erratic and evidence of work, if anything, is all that is required.

When the criminal does have an assignment in confinement, he may use the job for criminal purposes, just as he did on the outside. In places of less security, this is easier than in a penitentiary. At Saint Elizabeths Hospital, criminals have had sexual relations with employees and patients on the way to and from their work assignments. They have stolen from their job locations. In short, they have engaged in a wide array of violations, including commission of crimes while off the grounds.

Some criminals take whatever job assignments they are given and try to be big shots on the job. They attempt to take over, giving orders and telling people who have been there longer how things should be done. Characteristically, irresponsibility and violation occur at these "industrial therapy" assignments. There are criminals who take genuine pride in a narrowly defined area of work; for example, they may be skilled at some craft or other artistic endeavor. However, their interest and commitment rarely endure. Whatever the purpose of the work in confinement is, whether it is just to keep the criminal busy or to rehabilitate him, the job does not succeed in changing the personality of the man from criminal to noncriminal.

THE CRIMINAL AND HIS MONEY

The criminal does not value money in the way the responsible person does. Financial security, advantages to the family, and even material comfort itself are not important. Naturally, there is no concept of money management; it would be absurd to manage what one does not value. As we have mentioned, the criminal is likely not to know how much his paycheck is supposed to be. He does not anticipate future requirements, and thus budgeting is a foreign practice. Bills are paid at his convenience, if at all.

Money is valued only as an index of his success in crime and as a symbol of a chance to play the big shot and extend his criminality. Most criminals have expensive tastes and great pretensions. Some spend large sums on women, clothes, and big cars. A criminal may want a lot of money just to "flash" at others and impress them. We have encountered those who set money on fire. Many derive a greater charge from giving money away than from spending it. They may do this for sheer impact. But it might also be to achieve a sentimental objective, such as sending money to someone needy. The criminal disposes of a great deal of money acquired illicitly. He may tell others that he desperately needs funds to fulfill obligations to his sick mother or for child support. If one follows the money, it becomes apparent that the mother or child receives very little of it when it is most needed. No matter how much money the criminal makes legitimately or how much passes through his hands illegitimately, he will have nothing to show for it.

In more than a dozen years, we have yet to find one case of a criminal's failing to get a job if he tried. To be sure, he may receive some rejections, but eventually he gets hired. This may be attributed in part to the mobility of workers in some occupations. In fact, we have seen criminals obtain security-guard positions without inquiry into their backgrounds and previous work records. A full confession by a criminal of his past often results in an employer's bending over backward to accommodate him.

MILITARY LIFE

The patterns that the criminal shows at home, school, and work also appear everywhere else. The military is no exception. Most criminals do not visualize themselves as enlisting in the service. However, some envy the man in uniform and glamorize his life. They do not see themselves as ordinary servicemen, but invariably as fighter pilots, members of special forces, paratroopers, commandos, and the like.

Criminal children may occupy themselves for hours at a time playing with toy soldiers.

> C owned 300 toy soldiers. He spent most of his time outside school alone, because few youngsters would have anything to do with him. C spent hours each day in arranging these men for battle. When school was out, he spent up to 8 hours in deploying various combinations of soldiers in war. He said: "There is no friend like a toy soldier."

Not only do these youngsters stage battles with toy soldiers, but they avidly play war games around the neighborhood. The fantasies of being a heroic military man continue for some time, depending on the child. For some, they are vivid up to the age of 10; then, as the youngsters follow a violating way of life and their interests carry them elsewhere, the fantasies recede. Others continue to aspire to be military heroes and plan to enter the service. This group did not worry about the draft; rather, they enlisted or were willingly drafted. Some falsified their ages in their eagerness to enlist. We know of boys who enlisted successfully when they were as young as fifteen and who served for years without being found out. In the process of enlisting, they concealed their criminality.

Before the end of the draft, most criminals tried to avoid military service altogether. Their tactics were numerous, including failing to register with the Selective Service System, moving around without notification of change of address, and fleeing the country. Some refused to cooperate in any way with the Selective Service System.

> "I am running from the draft—may have to leave the country."

> "I've worked with an antidraft group since I refused induction in January. The guys in our house are all noncooperators or A.W.O.L."

> "Did you get my letters from prison?"

These excerpts are from a series of letters written to us by one young man who roamed around the country stealing, selling drugs, and keeping on the move so that it took a long time for the authorities to catch up with him.

By malingering, some criminals managed to persuade doctors to write notes certifying physical disability when there was none. Some criminals at college tried to convince counselors and student health personnel that they were suffering from psychologic disorders that rendered them unfit for service. This was usually schemed well in advance; the criminals sought "help" before the issue of induction was too immediate. Thus, they established for themselves a clinical record of psychopathology. After seeing the mental health worker for a while, they asked him to write the draft board a letter. Criminals not in school did the same thing at clinics in their own communities.

There were some who did not bother to see a professional, but decided that they themselves would convince the draft board of their unfitness to serve. When they reported for the physical examination they made the most of any malady right on the spot, or they faked mental illness. In the latter pursuit, many were rather sophisticated. On the basis of their study of books, they mimicked the behavior and postures of a disordered person. Some used drugs before the examination to help achieve the desired effect. Others disqualified themselves as bed-wetters, conscientious objectors, or homosexuals. The few who already had police records were eager to disclose a history of serious offenses and were exempted, because the armed services at that time did not want to take known troublemakers.

Most of the criminals who decided to enlist had been in trouble at home, at school, and in the community. They were keeping "bad company" and engaging in delinquent activities, although very few had police records. Adults close to them and agents of social institutions encouraged these youths to go into the service, in the hope that a stint in the military would change them.

> At the age of 16, C and another fellow stole a car and were driving around late at night. The other boy started honking the horn loudly as they passed a mining camp. This aroused the police, who gave chase. C slammed down the accelerator and, while going around a curve, wrecked the car. C was apprehended, charged with car theft, and confined. The court appointed a lawyer for C and then stated that the record would be destroyed if C would join the Marines.

Here, C was erroneously viewed as a "first offender," because he had no previous record. At that time, the Marines would not have wanted a known criminal.

With the end of the draft, the services have established enlistment quotas.

It appears that, in the effort to fill these quotas, standards for acceptance have not been as stringent as before. A probation officer said that a young man with three breaking-and-entering charges could enlist with no difficulty. He commented: "They're even taking Jack the Ripper these days."

Some criminals who enlist are viewed as especially bright and capable. They are sent to school, given special training, and promoted rapidly to officer status. The three essential ingredients for promotion are intelligence, toughness, and loyalty. Criminals may have considerable authority and make important decisions. One with whom we worked was an officer who, as a comptroller, handled $3 million a month, all the while writing fraudulent checks. Another rose to the rank of major and instructed officers in ethical standards while, unknown to others, he was in massive crime. Those who become officers thrive on the power they have over others.

> "I chewed them out left and right and gave them a couple of verbal lashings. I'm a pretty tough, demanding sort."

> "They took advantage of the freedom they had, and so I decided to pull them back together and spend a lot of nights there being mean and started yelling a little bit. I had to get their respect and make them scared as hell of me."

They are often overly zealous in the exercise of their authority. We have found this to be true especially of criminals who serve as guards or military police.

> C was given considerable training in judo, karate, and marksmanship. He did well, rising rapidly to the rank of corporal, and was then assigned to guard the stockade prisoners. Things went smoothly for a while; he was firm, but polite. However, on one occasion when he took three men out, two ran in opposite directions. He told them to stop, then fired a shot into the air. When they kept going, he killed one and fatally wounded the other. After this incident, C was confined to his barracks to await a court-martial. After a long trial, he was declared not guilty. Actually, C had been in crime right along, especially larceny. However, he had not been apprehended for anything until this incident.

The criminal, whether enlistee or draftee, is contemptuous of the routines and procedures of military life. The obvious discontent is exemplified by the sarcasm of the following statement:

> "I could tell you what I think of the Army, but I'll spare you the obscenities. I like going to bed at night and detest getting up at, shudder, five o'clock. Really, the Army wouldn't be so bad if they didn't have the many meaningless tradition-bound procedures and regulations, and if the NCO's were not NCO's (No Chance Outside). Most of the things

that get me are a result of plain old inconsideration. But what the hell, I'm only a Pfc."

It is true that many soldiers think this way, but not all react like the criminal. The criminal often balks at requirements and regulations. As he did at school and at work, he intensely dislikes having to do what others require. He contests doing even the smallest things, because he views himself as above having to take orders from someone whom he scorns. As in civilian life, he wants to be the top man. However, deterrents in the military are usually so strong that the criminal rarely defies his superiors openly.

He does, however, look for adventure and excitement wherever he can find them; sometimes this is right on the job—even the toughness of basic training may be taken as a personal challenge.

> "Up until this time, I hadn't had a great deal of physical involvement in anything. In the Army, if I was up on the stand and they mocked me because maybe I was a little bit red in the face from the tenth pushup, then I might do ten more and get even redder in the face."

Some of these men get a charge out of learning combat skills, such as demolition, camouflage, setting booby traps, and riflery. They volunteer for dangerous patrols and take risks that many others wish to avoid. One man described his "undiluted enjoyment" of combat pilot assignments that were very perilous.

Some enjoy the killing in which they engage as combat soldiers.

> C, a former Marine captain, stated that, for a man to be an effective Marine, he must get "kicks" out of violence. C cited a statement by a seargeant who said, "Captain, murder is fun, isn't it?" and meant it. C observed that criminals make the best fighters. The Marines may have trouble with them on the post, but in combat they are very effective. C indicated that he himself was an adventure-seeker. He said that, despite his Catholicism, he got a real charge out of killing. He pointed out that nobody considers whether the killing is necessary to achieve a particular objective. In fact, the authorities turn their backs when the unnecessary killing of civilians comes to light. But those who engage in it have a full battery of justifications after the fact—the pride of the Corps, saving our way of life, the things the enemy has done, and so on.

This perspective on killing, related in 1966, came stunningly to the public's attention five years later.

Excitement from the missions of duty does not entirely satisfy the criminal; and some never even have the opportunity to go into combat. Although they may appear bland, compliant, and rather ordinary while on the base, they seek adventure outside their duty stations, trying not to jeopardize their standing on the post. Their criminality covers the entire spectrum—thefts, fights, and sexual forays. The sexual adventures consist of more than simply finding a willing partner for the night; coercion, extortion, blackmail, rape, and robbery all occur frequently.

> C and some other soldiers went out gang-raping Korean women. On one occasion, C was at a bar and was interested in a particular woman. When another man started to show some interest in her, C invited the man into an alley for a fight. In a rage, he beat the other fellow to a pulp, kicked him with heavy boots, and hurt him so badly that he was on the critical list. This was reported to the company commander, who let the incident drop with a reprimand to C.

> C started robbing homosexuals when he was in the service at the age of 19. During the week, he visited gay bars, made solicitations, and then went to the fellows' apartments. Once there, he would say he had to leave, turn around, and say he had forgotten something. When the victim asked what it was he forgot, he took out his gun and said, "The money, sucker." He took whatever he wanted, avoiding violence when possible. C operated by himself most of the time. Occasionally, he joined three other Marines to go out robbing homosexuals. C indicated that about 12 or 15 other Marines in the company were doing the same thing.

Many criminals violate while on duty, but are careful to cover their tracks. With respect to property, almost anything that is not tied down or too heavy to move is a potential target for theft, whether it be money, supplies, ammunition, or drugs in the medical quarters. Another type of offense is the misappropriation of property, such as vehicles, for private use. Criminals who occupy positions of authority may misuse their offices by buying and selling influence, as in the case of the person described below, who sold honorable discharges. The *patterns* described here are typical, although some of the particular violations may sound unusual.

> A couple of days after C arrived at the induction station, he went A.W.O.L. for a week. This was ignored and overlooked. C had not wanted to be a soldier, but was drafted. He most certainly did not want to fight overseas in the Korean War. Consequently, he deliberately shot so wildly when he was out on the rifle range that he was deemed a menace and was removed from the range. He was appointed company clerk because of his typing skills. In this capacity, he was relatively independent, not having to account for his time.

> In the course of his duties, C saw a trap door in the post exchange where he could enter before closing time, seclude himself, and spend the night. He walked off before the store opened with money, watches, and other

small items that he could pocket. He acquired a considerable sum of money and much merchandise and was never detected. He decided to show another fellow how to do this. However, his compatriot double-crossed him by going a night earlier; he waited where he should not have, came crashing down, and was apprehended. The other fellow was suspected of all the larceny that the authorities knew was occurring but had not been able to pin down. Fortunately for C, the other man did not inform.

As C went back and forth between the base and the town, he transported and sold heroin. Along the way, there was stealing and peeping in windows at women. In all this, he was perfectly safe and never held accountable.

Through some arrangements by his father in Washington, C was sent to camp for further training, although he was not a first sergeant. When he returned, he was given a secretarial function in which he had to fill out forms relative to types of discharges. On the pretext of not wanting to run to the commander every time one of these papers had to be signed, he had the Commander sign many of them in advance. He then reaped a fortune by selling honorable discharges to people who had in fact been censured for bad conduct and dishonorably discharged. This was never detected, but it stopped when, during a general shakedown, the authorities found the signed forms in his footlocker.

Concurrently with the sale of discharges, C was stealing from practically every place on the base. He bought a sports car and dealt more heavily in drug traffic of all sorts, even running drugs out of Mexico. C still was not suspected of anything irregular. As a reward for his good service, he was to be moved to a higher, more sensitive spot. For this, a security clearance was mandatory. He filled out the appropriate forms, listing three references, and was awaiting his clearance when the person who delivered the mail informed him that it was his habit to open all messages arriving in certain kinds of envelopes. He revealed to C that he, C, was regarded as a security risk. This had nothing to do with his criminality. Rather, one of his references had a relative who was regarded as a Communist (this incident occurred in the 1950s).

C was permitted to go home on furlough at about this time. On his return, he was told that a returning Korean veteran had preference and had elected the job for which C was slated. C knew that this was a brushoff because of the security question. Knowing of C's interest in cars, his superiors suggested a motor-pool assignment. C refused, choosing instead the mess hall. This request was granted. There, in league with the chief cook, he entered into organized thievery: they removed large amounts of supplies and sold them in a nearby store. He was also assigned to prepare the officers' breakfast. C urinated in the food, put dirt in it, and contaminated it as much as he could while making sure that it was presentable, so that he would not be detected. Concurrently, his participation in drug traffic was growing. He claimed that he was supplying 120 of the 192 men on the post with drugs.

Scarcely a day occurred during which C was not involved in some criminal activity—theft, drug sales, peeping, malfeasance of duties, and so forth. Interestingly, he did not permit even FBI surveillance to restrain him from his illicit activities; this added to the excitement and induced him to be even slicker.

Ultimately, C's term in the service expired, and he was honorably discharged. Not long after leaving the military, he contracted tuberculosis, established it as a service-connected disability, and reaped lifelong benefits.

This is a graphic example of a criminal's continuing a successful "career" in crime while a soldier. Most of that criminal's activities were conducted by stealth. However, in recent years, criminality on military bases has been more and more in the open, and the authorities have had considerable trouble contending with it. Conditions have been so bad that Major John T. Sherwood (*The Washington Post*, 9/13/71) was quoted as saying that one of the biggest problems was how to protect a soldier in his own barracks:

> "Crimes of violence, such as robbery, are at an all-time high and climbing," said Major John T. Sherwood Jr., staff judge advocate at the Nuremberg Trial Center. . . . "I'd just hate to live in the barracks. The guy who just wants to be let alone isn't being let alone."

Incidents of "fragging," which is an assault with an explosive, were climbing as the war itself was winding up. With bored criminals on bases in non-combat zones, a host of problems arose, including assault, gang warfare, theft, extortion, and almost every other kind of crime.

There are, in addition, all types of infractions of service regulations and neglect of duty, such as overstaying passes, returning late, leaving early, or going A.W.O.L.

> After payday, C decided simply to go home and show off his uniform. The idea of punishment for going A.W.O.L. did not deter him, because he knew that all that would happen was that he would get a 7-day restriction. So he left for 10 days. On his return, he was restricted and given some of the "dirty" details. He then figured that going A.W.O.L. again would not make much difference. So he went A.W.O.L. a second time. On his return, he was under closer supervision and was assigned more of the unpleasant details. After a third A.W.O.L., it began to dawn on him that he could be court-martialed. In the course of these A.W.O.L.'s, there was crime. Eventually, he received a general court-martial with a dishonorable discharge and 6 months of hard labor. During the hard labor, he became fed up. He cut his arm, hoping to get the attention of the neuropsychiatric unit. However, to his disappointment, he was treated and returned to duty.

The responses of superiors to violations by their subordinates vary. Just as an employer may overlook violations to retain a good worker, so the military has a high threshold of tolerance to enable it to keep good fighting men. Little may be said if a man steals from a company other than his own. However, a thief caught within his own company may be dealt with more severely. Even then, if a man is valuable to the unit, little may come of the infraction other than advice not to do it again. In some situations, the man may even be referred to the psychiatrist on base and the problem quietly taken care of. This is especially likely if the behavior is regarded as clearly "deviant."

> While in the service, C was very active in crime, including rape and robbery. He was successful in his ventures and remained undetected for a long time. When he was finally apprehended, it was for voyeurism. This being a misdemeanor, C was released and told that the incident would be reported to the authorities on base. He was also advised to see a psychiatrist. He did so, and this ended the problem, as far as his unit was concerned. The matter was handled delicately, because the NCO was a friend of his. The police report got buried in a safe, with no one except his CO and his NCO having access to it.

Violations, especially if considered to be "first offenses," are often disregarded if there has been "good behavior" in other areas. In some cases, a man is allowed to resign from the service, rather than have proceedings taken against him. Relatively few offenses reach the point of court-martial. A small number incur penalties, such as confinement in the stockade or military prison, reduction in rank, forfeiture of pay, or dismissal. Only a handful of the criminals we have dealt with have been discharged dishonorably.*

In order to get discharged honorably from service, some malinger—pretending to be ill or injured.

> C was in the Navy for 94 days. He did not like the basic training, because he found the commanding officer very strict and the whole system too rigid. During this training, he decided to get out of the service. He was told that if he ate sweets exclusively and heavily for several days and then complained about a kidney ailment, he would find his way out of the service. C also wet his bed at night deliberately and finally got admitted to a military hospital for 3 weeks. He was discharged as medically unsuitable.

We have seen men who got honorable discharges and 100 percent disability pensions for alleged mental illnesses, although they had not served overseas

---

* Our sources for the observations as to how offenses are dealt with are criminals and military officers.

in combat. One criminal committed a rape while in the service and was discharged with a diagnosis of "anxiety state"; he thereafter received full disability payments.

When these men return to civilian life, they make the most of their having been in the military. Although they committed crimes while in the service, they gain a mantle of respectability or nobility for having served. Some use their service experiences and knowledge for self-aggrandizement. A striking example of this is a man who stole naval uniforms after leaving the service, read up on the service rating that he pretended to have, and used the uniform to further his criminal enterprises.

> Dressed in a stolen uniform, C was welcome in many places. He wore civilian clothes at night to avoid the shore patrol, but during the day he wore the naval uniform. He went to a tailor shop, told the tailor that he was on 30-day leave, and got a job for a while. He soon found out that the tailor was a homosexual; when he gave the tailor sexual gratification, he was provided with all sorts of clothes and money and was generally well taken care of. He used the uniform to gain ready access to places where other sailors were and embarked on a career of homosexual prostitution. In Los Angeles, he was arrested and sentenced to 6 months in jail for wearing a uniform illegally.

Some of these men, now in civilian life, who do not want to work engineer admission to hospitals for one condition or another and are awarded non-service-connected disability pensions.

Those criminals who served in the military all report expansion of their criminal careers on discharge. The hopes of parents and community that the service would "straighten them out" are dashed. At best, service life had enough restraints to deter some temporarily from more serious acts. But what the military could not achieve was the changing of a violator into a responsible citizen. Violations were only more difficult to get away with, and the criminal had to be sneakier or much more brazen, depending on circumstances. Once the criminal returns to civilian life, the restraints are fewer, and violations increase. In every situation, the criminal patterns continue and expand. In a highly publicized case, a soldier who had killed 100 of the enemy and had won five Bronze Stars and two Purple Hearts was arrested soon after his return to his home town.

THE RISE AND FALL OF MIKE SHARP

> "Over there I was a big man with all my medals. I was really somebody. But here, back in my own home town, I was a nothing. A real, great, big nobody. . . ."

> Six months after his discharge . . . wearing his fatigue shirt and armed with an M1 carbine, he crawled over the terrain of a dark cemetery and up to a gas station. . . . Then, with a quick rush—he'd learned the value of surprise in warfare—he dashed into the station and at gunpoint robbed three attendants of $57. The next afternoon he was arrested (*Parade* [*The Washington Post*], 5/17/70, p. 4).

Mike Sharp was later arrested for arson and was sentenced to 2-15 years in prison. What happened to Sharp is routine for every one of our men. They do not all get caught and make the newspapers, but the pattern is the same.

SEXUALITY

The criminal is popularly depicted as highly sexual. This section tries to place the popular observation in perspective and separate fact from myth. It shows that, compared with the noncriminal, the criminal is indeed deeply involved in sexual activities at a very early age, but that, rather than having an excessively strong sexual drive, the criminal uses sexuality simply as one more area of life in which to strive for power.

Material about early sexual experiences is easily recalled by the criminal. Probative efforts are not necessary to ferret out latent dream content and other unconscious material, whereas it might take hundreds of hours to elicit comparable material from a noncriminal. Consequently, we have an abundance of data about the criminal's sexual patterns beginning early in childhood.

CHILDHOOD

As early as the age of three, the criminal child shows inordinate curiosity about sexual matters. Interest lies first in the most available people—females or males in his own home or in those of friends. He peeks through cracks in doors and peers through keyholes to catch glimpses of mother, sister, or a friend's mother or sister as she dresses, bathes, or uses the toilet. He is very resourceful in these attempts at peeping. He may enter his mother's room at a well-timed moment, ostensibly to retrieve something left there. In his probing and spying, he is likely to become cognizant of his parents' sexual lives.

> At the age of 5, C saw his parents having intercourse. Later, he stood outside a window watching his mother with another man. Then he broke in, interrupting the event. When his mother whipped him for this or for some other reason, he did not feel too bad about it, because during the whipping he ran his hand up between her legs or in some way managed to feel parts of her body. This heightened his curiosity and excitement.

Incestuous experiences are easily recalled by the criminal. Of course, fantasies far outnumber actual experiences. Both the fantasies and actual experiences sometimes occur when the criminal youngster gets into bed with his mother and attempt to explore her body. Sexual episodes with siblings are much more common. It is the criminal youngster who initiates the activity, although in telling others about what happened he divest himself of responsibility, making himself the innocent party who was seduced or coerced. In fact, if approached by others, he is afforded an opportunity for what he has long been desiring.

The criminal engages extensively in sexual fantasy and daydreaming that involves almost anyone with whom he has contact—parents, siblings, teachers, and playmates. A number of the fantasies that are feasible are implemented. The very young criminal, not yet pubescent, makes advances indiscriminately, anywhere he has the opportunity. One child was apprehended by the police when he was seven for pulling up a woman's dress. Playing doctor may take a rather advanced form.

> Under the guise of playing doctor, 6-year-old C "examined" some girls his own age, but preferred those 2 or 3 years older. In doing this, he attempted to penetrate the girl's vagina, but with little success. He had a doctor kit at the time and explored, kissed, and touched the vaginas of the girls he played with.

He also played a form of house that involved undressing, clambering onto a bed, and considerable sexual play, some of which culminated in attempts at intercourse. He initiated sexual activity wherever he was, if circumstances were favorable.

> When C was in the hospital, he made a grab for a nurse's breast. Apparently, she rather liked this, and the episode progressed, with the two of them fondling each other. In the course of time, the nurse's breasts and abdomen were exposed, and he was able to feel around her legs and thighs and even her vagina. This pattern with older women continued; when in the company of one, he somehow managed to sit in her lap and play with her breasts or somehow look up her dress.

Other youngsters in the neighborhood or at school are the most readily available partners.

> Ever since he could remember, and this was back to the age of 5, C attempted to insert his penis into a girl's vagina. At that age, his aunt did not allow him to go to school alone. A girl some 3 years older accompanied him to school, and they had sexual play most mornings before school. C also described how he played house with some of the other

kids. One of the boys, as the father, had intercourse with a girl in front of others. A rag doll served as the baby.

Who or what the partner is often makes no difference. Older women, prostitutes, other boys, animals—virtually anyone can be a target. Consequently, there is always the prospect of disease. Indeed, among our group, gonorrhea had been contracted as early as the age of ten. Voyeuristic and exhibitionistic patterns also develop early.

> Tremendously curious about sex, 7-year-old C lifted girls' dresses. He wanted to look at any female he could. So he went to the YWCA, where he and some other boys peaked through a hole in a window shade and observed whatever they could. This was stimulating and erection-producing.

Among criminals of higher socioeconomic status, the incidence of sexual activities is somewhat lower and they occur later, because in their milieu such behavior is not well tolerated and greater penalties are attached to it.

What is significant is not the incidents themselves, but the fact that these youngsters are interested in and attempt intercourse in the primary grades, when the sensuality of the experience is minimal. What is at work is less a matter of sexual drive than of a "drive" toward sexual activity. We have pointed out how the criminal child wants to be bigger and older. Here, in the likely absence of sensuality and orgasm, is another way in which the criminal child seeks to be more important. Sexual conquest is an achievement that provides buildup to himself and to others. Sometimes, the partner is not willing. The coercion pattern may begin very early.

> Whereas C could have sexual play with a girl almost any time, he developed a preference for forcing a girl into sex. With some other boys, he planned how to go about this. Generally, they chose an area near the school. Naturally, the girl would be afraid and might put up a struggle. Then, one of the fellows would hold her arms down and another her legs, and the other fellow would enter, with each of them having a turn.

Incidents of this type occur at a time of life when no orgasm is possible. There is far more excitement in coercion than if the girl agrees and willingly submits. The approach may not be physical coercion, but rather a kind of blackmail. One ten-year-old threatened girls that, unless they had intercourse with him, he would spread the word that they had in fact done so.

Not all criminal youngsters are this active sexually, even though the desire is present. Some stop short of attempting intercourse, because they fear that they will not be able to perform adequately. (Of course, many have inaccurate ideas and standards by which they judge themselves.) Some want to avoid the risk of being caught. They know that others are likely to tell on them. Masturbation begins early. The attendant fantasies are peopled by those with whom they have contact, including older women.

> When C was in reform school, he was excited by a secretary's exposure of her legs and thighs as she got out of her car. Some of the boys openly masturbated when they saw this. But most of the masturbation was private. In secret C evoked the image of this girl. The fantasies focused on her thighs, with occasional thinking about having intercourse with her. But orgasm would come when the thighs were prominent. This occurred when C was about 12.

Some, for the time being, seek excitement in activities other than sexual. However, in none of these youngsters is there a "latent period" in which sexual interests are relatively dormant. Even if the activity is limited, their sexual fantasy is more abundant and more criminal in content than that of the noncriminal. As one examines the fantasy lives of these youngsters, the content covers a broad spectrum of criminal activity including intercourse, homosexuality, coercion, and almost anything else. Some of these youngsters get hold of pornography as a further stimulant to an already very active mind.

ADOLESCENCE

Even in elementary school the criminal wanted to have a girl friend; it was more of an issue to him than to most of his classmates. As a teen-ager, he must be able to speak of "my girl." He regards some girls as an "easy make"; to get others, he has to work harder. All this may sound standard for adolescence. But what distinguishes the criminal adolescent from his noncriminal peers is how he operates. When a girl is "hard to get," she constitutes more of a challenge to him. He cons and misrepresents himself, believing that any girl will eventually "deliver." He has little respect or restraint. He gets a great charge out of boasting about his attempts at conquest. As one thirteen-year-old commented, "Talk is the closest thing to doing it." Each criminal adolescent has his own criteria of physical attractiveness. More than most noncriminal youngsters, criminals seek out a variety of partners, with a minority staying with one girl, and even then only briefly. Often the attraction is to a considerably older girl. If a youth finds one that is readily available sexually, he keeps her "on a string" as he continues other pursuits. The criminal adolescent and adult view a female not as a person, but as a body. It is the breast, buttocks, or thighs, and not the personality, that the criminal considers in his quest. Sex occurs through every conceivable route, with each criminal having his preferences for some practices and distaste for others. Who the partner is may not matter at all. Even an animal may be fair game.

Adolescent masturbation fantasies involve sex with almost anyone conceivable.

> C stole panties from anyone who was staying at his house—mother, aunts, and so on. He secretly hung them up in his room, looked at them while imagining that they were on someone, and masturbated. Or he put them in his bed and masturbated as though a girl were wearing them. This was more pleasurable if they were soiled and had an odor about them. He then discarded them. In each instance, he used them once and then threw them away.

The fantasies often have elements of voyeurism, exhibitionism, and rape. One man, for example, thought about viewing nude girls, exhibiting himself, tying up a naked girl, coercing her to do as he wished, and thrusting her out for public view and humiliation. Coercion often provides a special stimulation, if fantasying conventional sex is not sufficiently exciting.

> C knew that, if he wanted to masturbate and create a fantasy using a conventional situation, he could not get an erection. It was necessary for him to imagine mutilating a female, tearing her vagina apart, and ripping her breasts for him even to get an erection.

In this case, such fantasy occurred not only in masturbation, but also when he actually had a sexual experience with a consenting partner. This is a common phenomenon in many criminals who are impotent or frankly uninterested unless force is involved.

Some criminal adolescents masturbate very seldom, owing to fears of bodily injury or diminished reproductive capacity. Some masturbate rarely, because they scorn the practice, believing it to be a sign of weakness. In their view, only those who cannot find a partner have to resort to it. They do not view masturbation as "wrong," but consider themselves "less of a man" if they engage in it.

An activity that may begin at any age is the making of obscene phone calls. An anonymous call to an unknown party can be a childhood prank, as when a youngster calls up and says, "Is your refrigerator running? Well, you better catch it." But what we are talking about extends far beyond that. Some of these youths make a habit of dialing at random and looking for a sexual response. One criminal continued this practice for so many years that it ruined his promising career and jeopardized his marriage.

The criminal adolescent may increase his homosexual participation. Initially, when he engages in an episode with an adult, it enhances his self-image: in his mind, he is sexually managing an older person. With a peer or someone younger, he is in a position of even greater domination. Although they may frequently engage in homosexual experiences, most criminal adolescents are not homosexually oriented as a lifetime preference. Indeed, only three criminals in our group are exclusively homosexual. During adolescence, the criminal may learn that homosexuality is profitable. He may be offered money by an older person. Eager to try something new, he complies. The following account exemplifies the development of a homosexual prostitution pattern.

> C's first homosexual experience for money occurred one evening when he was hitchhiking. He was afraid of the person; but when he was offered money, he immediately realized that it was an easy way of getting it without having to work. Thereafter, if he needed money, he knew that he could get it this way. Support from his family ceased when he was 14, and he resorted to this practice as a way of life. At first, he felt some trepidation, but this faded quickly, as he became more and more adept at exploiting his partners. His fear that he might actually end up being a homosexual did not deter him. By the age of 16, he was having three or four experiences a week. He went to Florida, where he received up to $30 a night. Soon, he knew the professionals in the community who were homosexual. He sought out those who had money and status. He struck up a relationship with a minister, who gave him money, clothes, and whatever else he wanted. For 2 years, he had a homosexual relationship with a highly placed government official. This man was willing to pay $25-40 per night, and C met him several times a month.

Thus, a fourteen-year-old's hitchhiking incident evolved into a way of living. The homosexuality itself was not the crime—rather, it was the exploitation that was criminal. Many criminals use homosexuality as a way of gaining entrée into circles where they have good setups for crimes. The homosexual practices go hand in hand with blackmail, theft, and assault. In other words, homosexuality itself is not the issue. The sexual activity is far less important to the criminal than the events surrounding it—payment, coercion, and so forth.

The criminal adolescent develops a modus operandi for all desired types of sexual activity. His pattern for sex is similar to that for other crimes. He studies a potential partner, just as he studies a store that he plans to break into. Some are brazen in their approach to women, just as they may boldly enter a store and hold it up. But lies, conning, and flattery usually play a part, making sex more exciting than a consenting affair would be. Some go after seemingly helpless girls. One criminal judged as "insecure" any girl seen biting her fingernails; in his estimation, he had a greater chance of "making" her. Many "play it cool." They find out about a girl's availability from a third party. Then they go to places that she frequents, but do not give overt indications of interest. Engineering a situation so that a potential partner will come to them provides an even greater buildup than if they had made a direct approach and succeeded. It enhances their view of themselves as "studs." A few try to lure their partners by exhibiting themselves.

> C went where he knew homosexuals congregated and assumed such a position that his genital region was prominent. At the beach, he wore swimming trunks that were too small, the purpose being to attract attention to his crotch. He went to a beach frequented by homosexuals and got an erection by seeing an attractive girl or a man's buttocks. No matter where he was, if he were looking for a partner, he dressed so that his penis and testicles were prominent. The general idea was for him to be approached, rather than to do the approaching. Thus, he "advertised" his availability.

Now that the criminal is older, tougher, and braver, coercion is more common among those so disposed than it was before.

> At 15, C participated in gang rapes. Being the best dressed and most verbal, he approached a woman coming out of, say, a beer joint and convinced her to take a ride with him and his friends. Then they rode to a deserted area and had a gang rape. Age did not matter too much. They took whomever they could get. Because C was the initiator, he was first. C did this a half-dozen times or so, and then there was little pleasure in it. The novelty wore off. So he went on to operate by himself.

There may be one girl toward whom a criminal adolescent shows exaggerated admiration and respect. He may select for himself in thought or action a girl whom he considers untouchable. He puts her on a pedestal and enshrines her for her purity. Whether it is so or not, she is his girl. Thinking this builds up his opinion of himself. In reality, nothing enduring ever comes of this one-sided "relationship."

ADULTHOOD

It might appear that the criminal is truly a sexual giant, inasmuch as he is sexually active very early and with great frequency. As a youngster, he gains a crude, rudimentary sex education in the street. But, even as adults, many criminals still lack basic information and most adult criminals are not very competent sexually. They may have trouble getting an erection or have difficulty in maintaining it.

> "This thing with girls—I was very frightened. I am torn between sitting around and worrying about it and going out and doing something to see

what happens, because I am so immobilized by the whole problem. It is just the same problem, not being able to have a decent relationship on account of various fears and trepidations. At one point, I ended up in bed with a beautiful girl and wasn't able to do anything. It was too ridiculous for me to get any standard reaction out of it. So I was just sort of sitting there, which distressed her; and she didn't talk to me after that."

This fellow was scared both to try and not to try to demonstrate his sexual prowess. As he viewed it, the experience was a calamity. Most criminals report frequent premature ejaculations, sometimes within a minute or two after insertion. One criminal referred to his sexual response as being like a "jack rabbit."

With such problems, these men derive little pleasure from the sex act itself. In fact, intercourse is a struggle. For example, one man pointed out that he had set up as his criterion of success eliciting two orgasms from his partner before he would ejaculate. Sex often became an ordeal to "prove" himself. If the girl had two orgasms within five minutes, that was the end of it; and if it took two hours, he would struggle for two hours to accomplish this objective. Some criminals regard intercourse as disgusting while they are in the midst of it. Once it is over, they get away as quickly as possible. Such a person does not want to spend the night with his partner, but will have intercourse and leave. A few criminals give up trying with physically mature women. They seek out inexperienced children, who are not able to evaluate the adequacy of their sexual performance.

Some criminals are competent in their sexual performance. But they are rarely satisfied, because their idea of "competence" is to be a sexual colossus.

To an observer, the criminal's stance toward all women appears paradoxical. On the one hand, there are outpourings of sentimentality; on the other, unrelenting exploitation. A criminal writes poems to his loved one, and then turns around and defiles her. The criminal has shifting states of mind toward a given woman, just as he does toward his parents, teachers, employers, and everyone else. It is true that he may have a streak of idealism about women; he may express a desire for a woman who is pure and a virgin. And he goes through phases in which he wants to settle down and have a home life and all that goes with it. However, his sentimentality and ideals do not guide his conduct.

Common-law relationships are frequent in the criminal's adult life. Marriages occur as a result of a variety of circumstances. When the criminal is pressured by a woman from whom he wants something, marriage may be the only way to get it. When it is convenient or necessary to maintain a respectable front, the criminal will step to the altar. He may also get married to enhance his own image, if he can find a woman whom he can show off. He may be able to win over a virgin only by a promise of marriage.

> From early adolescence, C pursued virgins with special intensity. Anyone with whom he became "involved" had to be absolutely pure. (He would beat up any fellow who was a threat to the virginity of his sisters.) It took a pursuit of a year and a pledge of marriage for C to have sex with Carol, who was a virgin. He claimed to "respect" her virginity, which meant that he took it as a personal challenge. A few months after the wedding, C began losing interest and disappeared for days at a time. Things went this way for 4 or 5 months, and then Carol left.

Once C had made his conquest, there was nothing more in it for him. For him and for other criminals, marriage is an opportunity to use another person. In some instances, the criminal plans a marriage and breakup in advance, with the intention of bilking his partner for all she is worth. One man courted his prospective bride for two months, married her, and then left her after three months, taking the thousands of dollars she had saved over the years while working as a schoolteacher. The criminal may stop short of marriage, but lead a woman on with the expectation that a wedding will occur. This results in pregnancies and broken hearts. All his life the criminal has wanted to get as much as he can while giving as little as possible. The criminal acts as though a woman belongs to him and has no rights of her own. From early adolescence, he views a girl or woman as someone to be used to satisfy himself. As far as he is concerned, a girl is a "piece of ass," "pussy," or some other term referring to her in the language of the street as a sex object. Tenderness and consideration are absent. Romance is either faked or short-lived. Companionship and friendship are not what the criminal seeks.

The criminal views a woman solely in terms of what she will do for him. He requires that she operate strictly on his terms, no matter how much she is degraded.

> C was dissatisfied with his girl friend's sexual performance. He decided that she should go to bars, pick up men, have sex with them, and learn to have an orgasm. Then, warmed up, she should come back to him, and they would have sex.

The criminal must be the "one and only" person on whom a woman expends time, money, and affection. He will accept second place to no one.

Although he insists on a woman's fidelity, the criminal is himself unfaithful, often being very open about it. A married criminal may have extramarital affairs, sometimes with the frequency of sexuality before marriage. He does not get the excitement that he wants out of the sex that is available with

his wife. In more than a dozen years of working with criminals, we have yet
to encounter one who was a faithful husband.

> C impregnated a 17-year-old girl. Her family pressured his family, which
> in turn pressured him into marrying her. The families had known each
> other a long time; to avoid difficulties, the two did marry. Only a month
> after the wedding, C began having sex with other girls. They lived out
> in the country, and C drove five girls into town. At various times, he
> managed to have sex with all five. In addition to sex four times a week
> with his wife, he was also having it several times a week this way.

Some criminals commit rape, although they can get all the sex they want
in their marriages, or from their girl friends. In fact, they sometimes molest
children or rape just after prolonged sexual activity.

A woman who joins ranks with a criminal is pursuing a lost cause if she
expects fidelity and devotion. Whether girl friend or wife, such a woman is
in for a series of unpleasant surprises, as she discovers the waywardness
of the criminal.

> I have just returned from a party where as I was holding C's coat, the
> enclosed letter fell out. Well, of course, I read it.
>
> I was most upset. Of all times—when we are supposedly getting along
> fine—I [had] finally made the commitment to marriage and I have
> been trying my damndest—dieting with the help of my doctors and
> taking thyroid. I have become so to speak a new woman. The thyroid
> has been a great help.
>
> Now to this letter. It is almost verbatim of the letters he once wrote to
> me—the letter he wrote to Stacey, or to Nancy or to Sandy or to Judy.
> Every woman seems to be "the woman."
>
> I was almost distraught and I left the party and came home. I was
> quite close to something desperate but instead I called my boss to come
> and talk to me. He did. He says that this is C's pattern at the parties
> they have been to together. That C thinks he is the great lover, that
> all white women desire him which Nick says is not true. Nick says that
> C tried to make out with these women. . . . Am I to disbelieve all the
> things he has told me in the past few weeks? . . . It seems like the very
> things he used to love me for he now hates. . . . I guess all the passion
> he showed to me in the last couple of weeks was meant for someone
> else. . . . God I hope it's not too late (letter from a distraught wife to
> Dr. Yochelson).

The criminal goes to extremes to have his way. If he is caught in a lie
or encounters resistance, he threatens or becomes violent. This extends to
the rape of his own wife.

C had his wife so intimidated that she lived in constant fear of him. When C wanted a particular form of sexual activity, although she was opposed to it, she did not dare resist. Thus, she was forced into acts of sodomy against her will.

The criminal also uses emotional blackmail, such as the threat of suicide or stealing, if he does not get what he wants. He toys with a woman's emotional security by threatening her with desertion and divorce if things do not go as he wants.

When a male criminal and a woman of criminal temperament get together, each person is in the relationship for himself and cares little about the other's desires. Sex, money, or almost anything else may be the medium of exchange —but not warmth or tenderness. Each person believes he is getting a good deal and is in the driver's seat. When one party comes to realize that he is in fact being exploited, trouble arises, usually ending in a stormy breakup. In these relationships, sexuality often occurs concurrently with larceny and assault. We give two examples of the kind of relationship that occurs when two people of criminal makeup live together.

Roy and Joan

Joan was 22 and the mother of two children. Promiscuous and indiscriminate in her choice of men, she had lived with one man after another. Roy was attracted to her as someone who was very sexy. For 3 weeks, he went out with her, without so much as touching her. Being aggressive, Joan challenged him to have sex and said he was a "faggot" if he would not. Roy took her to a motel for their first sexual episode. Soon, they were living together. Joan had a long history of delinquency and found Roy's life of crime exciting. However, she was extremely possessive. If Roy even turned his head in the direction in which another woman was walking, Joan was likely to explode in anger. She was a heavy user of alcohol and barbiturates. At home, she went into tremendous tantrums in which she attacked Roy with razors and knives, threw bottles, pulled his hair, scratched him, and so on. This was a lifelong pattern, which in part accounted for her failure to remain with any one man for long.

Joan's greatest asset to Roy was that, with the help of drugs, she was intensely passionate and gave him quite a sexual buildup. She admired his penis and praised his sexual performance. This relationship went on for 18 months with a couple of breakups, after which they reunited. In the course of this, there were many fights. Roy recalled one time beating her up, throwing her down a dirt hill, and being afraid that he had killed her. Joan was extremely dictatorial, stopping at nothing to have her way. Both were in crime. Joan got sex from Roy, as well as money and excitement from his way of life. Roy believed that he was a good influence on Joan and that he could help her reform. Even after he recognized what kind of person she was and separated from her, he remained in contact.

That was one of the more tempestuous relationships. In the following one, two people tried to manage each other, but with less violent tactics.

Bob and Paula

Bob was chronically dissatisfied with life at home with his wife and two young children. He had left home before for one-night stands and for one prolonged affair out of town. This over, he met Paula, an employee where he worked.

Paula represented herself to be a part-time law student with well-to-do parents who were paying most of her living and school expenses. She lived rather opulently for a girl with a meager income of her own, occupying an apartment in a luxury building and driving about in a Jaguar, which she said her father bought for her. It was into this ready-made situation that Bob moved, baggage and all. Paula provided him with free bed and board, transportation to work, and more sex than he ever wanted.

Life quickly became a battle between two people each of whom wanted his own way. Bob resented Paula's having the upper hand, because she was providing all the benefits for him. Minor differences led to major arguments. They fought over whether to go for a walk or a drive. Paula left to walk, and Bob, furious, came after her in the car and made a scene. In their life together, Paula alluded to other men. The references grew more and more frequent. Paula finally indicated that she was considering going to New York for a week with a former lover who had been having dinner with her while Bob was working two evenings a week. The conflicts increased. Bob still did not have the keys to Paula's apartment. Sometimes, Paula was not home and failed to leave an "admit slip" at the desk. On some nights, Bob had to wait until late to get into the apartment, all the while imagining where she had been. It was a relationship of secrecy and nonaccountability.

As far as Paula was concerned, Bob belonged to her and to no other. She tried to hold him accountable for his time. Finally, Bob got fed up and decided to leave. Not wanting to let him have the last word, Paula informed him that a girl friend would be coming to stay and that he would have to move. Bob left to find a room.

But the affair was not over. Bob's wife appeared at work and introduced herself to Paula. Extremely vindictive, she threatened to tell the company manager everything and left. Despite all this, Paula once again made overtures to Bob, telling him how much she loved him and inviting him to return. Then Paula dropped the bomb, telling Bob that she was pregnant and wanted to have the baby. Ten days later, when Bob was on the verge of moving back with her, Paula told him that she had had a tubal pregnancy and had gone to a doctor to have it "scraped out."

The moving back was a matter of convenience and economic necessity; Bob could not pay for a place of his own and support his wife and children. But things were as stormy as ever. Paula was moody, changing from warmth and pleasantness to iciness and anger. The pitched battles continued. One Sunday, the water tap was running, and Paula commanded him to turn it off. Bob responded: "Who do you think you are? No one tells me what to do or orders me around that way." Paula replied: "You don't own me." This type of incident was common.

Throughout, sex continued daily. Bob was now viewing himself as a "stud" performing sex as an obligation. He counted that, of 60 days, there were only 4 on which they did not have sex. On some days, there were as many as five episodes.

Paula kept showing her true colors. She admitted that the pregnancy was a lie. Soon, she was fired for messing up a filing system. People at work discovered she had never earned even a bachelor's degree. She started going out at night, not saying where she was going. She would say that she was not feeling well and shortly thereafter go out for the entire evening.

After several more months of this, Bob moved back with his own family. This still did not terminate the relationship with Paula. He continued to see her, and she pursued him, imploring him to return. Seeing that she was not succeeding and determined to have the last word, Paula phoned Bob, informing him that she had ingested 36 Darvon tablets.

Paula survived, and Bob managed to extricate himself from the relationship. Neither of them was active in crime during this period, but their criminal temperaments precluded an enduring relationship.*

A woman who recognizes the criminal patterns of the man she goes with may have a number of reasons for selecting him. She may be fascinated by his criminality and find his way of life exciting. In fact, she may participate in the crimes as an accomplice or act as a cover, in which case the two form a partnership in violation. But this is where the idea of partnership ends, in that their domestic life is not a team effort: each party demands his own way, each lies to and cheats the other to get his way, and a strong clash of wills often results in assault.

A noncriminal woman may be attracted to a criminal because she perceives him to be a strong person and one who will treat her well. Although she knows of his crimes, she is not dissuaded. She believes that he is basically good and considers herself a potential reformer. She views him as having many favorable qualities. There is much that is engaging in a bright, shrewd

---

* Before their relationship, Bob had been in crime. Paula had many criminal personality features, but we do not know if she had been actively in crime; nor do we know what happened to her after the relationship with Bob ended.

criminal who is talented and has a fund of knowledge in some subjects. Such a woman hopes that marriage can settle and change him—if she gives him what he wants and provides a good home, he will have no reason to continue in crime. The criminal may convince himself that this is what he needs. Thus, the two of them may enter into marriage with high expectations. Before long, she starts to realize that nothing she does is successful in changing lifetime patterns and, as she sees more and more the intractability of her husband's criminality, must decide whether to continue. Nearly all regard the marriage contract as serious, if not sacred. Most women stay on, heartened every time there is even the slightest evidence of change. Some remain because they do not think they could attract another husband. Older women, in particular, prefer to hang on, rather than be lonely. Such a situation is the following.

Robert and Harriet

Robert asked Dr. Yochelson to support his bid to marry Harriet, a responsible woman who owned and managed a secretarial school. Dr. Yochelson refused to endorse the idea and told Harriet that there was much she should understand about her prospective husband's background. In an interview with the couple, Dr. Yochelson traced out Robert's criminal patterns without going into details of the individual crimes. He pointed out that the criminal does not know what love is.

Robert contended that the fact that he had brought out the truth meant that he was now honest. Dr. Yochelson pointed out that here the truth was the best "con" of all to persuade Harriet to go through with the marriage.

All this made little impression on Harriet; she was infatuated with Robert, who had changed her lonely way of living and been kind to her. They got married. Soon after the wedding, things that made Harriet question the wisdom of her decision began to happen.

First, she did not know what he did all day. Then, she began to be bothered by strangers appearing around her office. The police phoned her and said she had stolen equipment in the office. She found checks written in her name that were clearly stolen from the office. There were serious thefts in the building that housed her business. In addition, Harriet had been giving Robert a lot of spending money, but she never knew where it went. In short order, her reserves were depleted.

She then discovered that he was using drugs and writing his own prescriptions under a false name. He was arrested and detained for this. Harriet rushed to the rescue and posted a $500 bond.

Despite his taking her money, fleecing her office account, disappearing from the house, taking drugs, and storing stolen property in their apartment, all that really mattered to Harriet was that he was "so sweet" to her. She had never regarded him as even capable of the crimes that he said he had committed before their marriage. She maintained that he lacked the "brain power" to do these things and that even she could outthink him. She attested to his inherent goodness by citing an incident in which he burst into tears and had a prolonged grief reaction at the death of a pet kitten.

Finally, enough was happening that she decided if he did not stop using drugs by the end of the year, she would leave him. She put her foot down with respect to his associates; she declared that she would not tolerate having those criminals around her office. Harriet also refused to make good any more of his bad checks.

The relationship is very different if the woman does not know of the man's criminality and learns of it only later. She, too, may have been attracted initially by his charm, brightness, talents, and gestures of affection and appreciation. She believes that she can straighten him out by capitalizing on his assets and potential. The criminal usually has lied to her about himself, in that he has failed to reveal anything about his criminal life. In fact, he might deliberately misrepresent himself (as did one man who posed as a preacher and won the hearts of many women). He leads women on by their anticipation of marriage and a family. Marriage occurs, and of course the wife tries to see only the good. She deliberately overlooks flaws and signs that not all is well, and makes excuses to others and herself for her husband. In time, she becomes blind to what the criminal does. In fact, she even creates favorable features that do not exist. But such a woman cannot deceive herself indefinitely and eventually has to face reality. After much vacillation, she arrives at a firm position and leaves. When his marriage breaks up, the criminal is reluctant to sever the tie completely. He does not want to abandon someone that he can use; indeed, if his wife is also a criminal, they will continue the relationship, even though living separately. The relationship of Tony and Barb is a case in which a criminal married a basically responsible woman.

Tony and Barb

Tony met Barb, a very beautiful girl, and took her out several nights in a row. They went dancing and had a good time with very little physical play. Because they were getting along so well, Tony began operating on her for sex. She would not have sex without a promise of marriage. Tony built himself up as being a decent guy who just got out of the Coast Guard. He totally concealed his antisocial patterns and represented himself as never having had sexual intercourse. Sexual activity ensued and resulted in pregnancy before marriage. Barb had been charmed and sexually gratified.

Early in their married life, the couple had a vigorous sex life. Tony continually increased the activity, trying every conceivable route, including anilingus, as he sought more and more excitement. Barb, who was a devoted, steady woman, very much in love with her husband, did everything to oblige him. Occasionally, she objected in a good-humored way, but to no avail. What she did not realize at the time was that the sex had nothing to do with "love."

This sexual pattern was insufficient for Tony. He went to get sex wherever he could. When his wife was at her parents', he brought a deaf mute to the apartment to have sex. It was important to him to know whether he pleased her; so he asked. She responded with a gratifying statement to him, writing on a note card, "100%."

Tony's crime patterns of all kinds resumed—passing checks, gambling, stealing, and so forth. Barb remained faithful and hopeful that he would reform. She posted bond when he was arrested and forgave him. She hung on, blinding herself to what was happening. Once, she went to the police station when he was arrested, bawled out the police for holding him improperly, and threatened to inform her treasury-agent brother if they physically mistreated him.

No matter how much she did for him, Tony treated her like dirt. If she went to an office party, he railed at her. Suspicion, jealousy, and all sorts of accusations poured forth. When Tony received another prison sentence, Barb was shocked and hysterical to the point of fainting. Nevertheless, while he was in prison, she visited him regularly and wrote him 30-page letters. Barb did everything she could to promote the relationship. However, Tony began ignoring her and then berating her and making accusations. Finally, Barb decided that she had had enough and started divorce proceedings. Tony blocked her in this, and when he left prison, he tried to get her to return. But she was now afraid of him and would not be in a room alone with him.

There was a long separation, with Tony being heavily in crime and being involved with many different women on an exploitative basis. Confined again for one of his crimes, he had moments of acute self-disgust as he thought of all that he had done to harm the best woman in his life. This attitude was not sustained: Tony resumed his old patterns, was arrested for homicide, and was sentenced to life imprisonment.

THE CRIMINAL AS A FATHER

The criminal fathers children out of wedlock and within marriage. He says that he loves his children, and indeed he does—at times. But as with everything else, his attitudes shift and his caring is not sustained and translated into action. Consequently, he neglects, abuses, and exploits his offspring. They may be exposed to all kinds of horrors, not the least of which is visiting their father behind bars. As he does others in his life, the criminal uses his children for his own purpose. The mere fact that he is a "family man" and is seen with his children enhances the facade of responsibility that he strives to maintain. Children are handy: they are helpful in recruiting sympathy for a confined criminal, who requests passes allegedly to see them or presses his case to get out so that he can go to work to support them. In short, having children is an asset to his conning.

The criminal may use his children in more blatant ways.

> C's daughter was a little more than a year old. She liked to run toward people. When the two of them were out on a nice afternoon, and she ran in the direction of what C called a "hag," he called her back. If she ran toward a woman to whom he was attracted, he let her go and used her approach as his entrée.

This practice was perhaps not injurious to the child. Much more harmful were his absences from home, his beating the child when he was in a bad mood, and his affairs with women.

The criminal loves his children and is sentimental about them at times. However, he does little to make his caring count. When his marriage breaks up, he may hotly contest arrangements for custody or visitation. Then, he fails to pay child support and to show up when his children are looking forward to seeing him. From time to time, he has twinges of conscience about his children, which he resolves by appearing suddenly with gifts. Not one of our men has been a consistent father figure, available to offer guidance, support, and affection. Another significant aspect of the criminal's family relationship is his bragging about his offspring's responsible accomplishments and aspirations. If his own child is irresponsible, he is harsh and punishes the child. He lectures his youngsters about what they are in for if they follow a criminal course in life.

SEXUALITY IN CONFINEMENT

In confinement, the patterns are similar to those outside confinement. Sexual release itself is not the objective; if it were, the criminal would be content with masturbation. In prison, the purpose of sex is to establish oneself in a position of dominance. In lessened-security setups, such as in a hospital, the criminal will find anyone who is available, whether it is another criminal, a psychotic patient, or someone else. There is an even greater challenge to establish a sexual liaison with a staff member. The criminal can have a hold over such a person and use him to advance his quest for privileges. As on the outside, what counts in confinement is what the criminal can gain for himself, using sex merely as a means to an end.

The married criminal continues his association with his wife while confined. He still acts as proprietor and owner, demanding that his wife (or girlfriend) do as he says, bring him whatever he wants, and of course remain faithful. All the old patterns are followed, through whatever means of communication is allowed. There has been much publicity of the "rampant homosexuality" in prison. We can judge only from the experience of our men who have served time in numerous institutions. They report that, although their preference is still for a female, they take whoever is available.

> Between the ages of 20 and 24, C was out of confinement less than 6 months. In confinement, he had two methods of release. The first was masturbation, which he allowed himself only infrequently. His other practice bothered him a great deal, at least for a while. He did not want to be identified with the homosexuals in prison. But many were eager for it, including some young prisoners. They would perform oral or anal sex very readily. C participated in this a half-dozen times, when he was highly aroused. Under these circumstances, he imagined that the man was a woman; this permitted faster ejaculation. He was not romantically disposed toward any of his partners; he found it repulsive. He adapted his fantasies about women to fit the homosexual. There was no feeling of femininity, nor a desire to be identified with the others who engaged readily in such activity.

Sex itself is not so important. What is important is establishing one's position and going about getting what one wants.

> In jail, C met a homosexual whom he described as a "real queen." He provided C with all kinds of services, cleaning up his living area, doing his laundry, and waiting on him hand and foot. In return, there was a daily sexual episode. The relationship ended when C's "servant" showed his fickleness and turned to someone else. This was more than C could stand, and he threatened the man—but to little avail, because the man got himself transferred to another dormitory. C did not regard himself as a homosexual. Everyone in the jail knew about the couple, because the "queen" talked. But this did not bother C; everyone was so afraid of him and his "friends" that they did not dare say anything.

In an overwhelming fraction of the cases, homosexual incidents occur because the criminal desires the activity. In fact, many of our men have told us that there were opportunities in reform school, youth centers, prisons, and hospitals, but that they refused to participate and were left alone. Some turned down offers of money or material things. We have encountered only one case of a criminal's being intimidated or coerced into homosexuality.

RELIGION

All but one of the criminals in our series were exposed to religion while growing up. In the families of most of these men, a parent, other relative, close friend, or someone else with the child's interest at heart believed that church was good for him. Many of our criminals are black and from Baptist and fundamentalist backgrounds. Many have mothers who are ardent church-goers and devout believers and fathers who are less observant. However, our investigations have extended beyond criminals confined at Saint Elizabeths Hospital and so have included a full range of religious denominations. As youngsters, nearly all our criminals had religious schooling. For some, it was intensive. A Jewish boy who attended Hebrew school for one and a half hours each day (after public school) for six years was a top student, excelled in Jewish studies and Hebrew, and wanted to be a rabbi. Some were educated in Catholic parochial schools from kindergarten through college, and a few had some seminary instruction. Whatever the denomination, most of our criminals had attended church services and had some religious education.

The criminal child's attitudes toward religion span a continuum. Most of our people embraced religion when they were young and tried to be very "good" children. Some indifferently accepted their parents' efforts at religious education; they had little religious fervor, but complied with their parents' wishes. A few wanted no part of religion whatsoever; they never saw religion as having anything to do with them.

Fears played a strong role in the religious beliefs of many. Images of God and the devil and of life after death were often vivid.

> C thought of God as being very tall with black skin, white hair, red eyes, and a tremendous voice. He believed that God might punish people by striking them with serious illness, such as tuberculosis. C retained these ideas until he was 18.

> C viewed the devil as dressed in red, with horns, a tail, and red eyes. He believed that a violation of the Ten Commandments would put one into the hands of the devil to be punished by permanent burning.

> C learned about religion from his grandmother, who offered a funda-mentalist Methodist approach. In her home, there was to be no liquor, cigarettes, or profane talk. Grandma told C some Bible stories and warned him about the possibility of hell after death. With respect to heaven, a glorious picture was constructed in his mind. However, hell was populated by devils garbed in white. The sinner was chained close to a fire, and these devils would beat him. At the age of 5 or 6, C believed that he might go to hell for a single transgression.

Some of these youngsters were afraid to go to bed at night, because they feared they would not wake up, but instead find themselves in an inferno. To those who had no belief in an afterlife, the dread of punishment here on earth was just as great. God might cripple or otherwise afflict a sinner even during his mortal life. With such terrible possibilities, the criminal child,

well aware of his own desires, believed that he must try to be extra good.
To these children, being "good" meant impeccable conduct.

Those who refrained from doing the forbidden for a long period of their
childhood were a small fraction of our total criminal group. Within the family
constellation and in the neighborhood, these children tried to outshine all
the others in being good. Indeed, some appeared so tied to home that they
were regarded as "momma's boys." They wanted to abide by the letter of
God's law, so as to be truly children of God. They did not take wrongdoing
in stride, as other children did. During this phase, if they told even the
smallest lie, it would prey on their minds, and they would agonize over it
for days.

A number of criminals in our study at some point aspired to be clergymen.
In childhood, they imagined themselves preaching before congregations. These
youngsters became active in church, and some became altar boys and choir
members. One boy was asked to assume some teaching duties when he was
only fourteen years old.

Rather than object to the strictness of some of the churches they belonged
to, these men have preferred a firm approach. Some converted to Catholicism
when they were children, because it offered stringent standards and guidelines
for living. This occurred as early as the age of ten.

> C's parents were very religious. His father was a deacon in the Methodist
> Church, and his mother was a devout Baptist. As a youngster, C went
> to the Baptist church with his mother and then saw people violating the
> message of the scriptural passages referred to in the sermon. So he began
> to attend Mass with a friend on Sunday mornings and developed an
> interest in Catholicism. At the age of 10, owing to family problems,
> C went to live with his grandmother, with whom he spent much time
> in discussing the merits of Catholicism. He obtained her permission to
> begin taking instruction. C was an avid student and, although behind
> the class initially, he progressed rapidly and surpassed most of the other
> students. After about a month, he knew most of the responses and
> prayers of the Latin missal by heart. He recalled several reasons for his
> desire to convert:
>
> 1. He viewed Protestant churches as phony, particularly with respect
>   to promoting harmony between the races.
>
> 2. There were organized social functions, facilities were available, and
>   it was easier to mix in Catholic churches.
>
> 3. Catholic homes appeared to be more unified.
>
> But perhaps the most important reason was that C was aware that this
> conduct was increasingly being regarded as unsuitable: "I felt that the
> strictness of Catholic rules governing such conduct, the compulsory
> nature of the duties, and the fact that Catholicism is so much harder to

live up to would bring about the controlling factors that would deter my conduct, which others disliked." On first joining the Church, C led a crime-free life. He prayed often—before meals and in the evenings— fulfilled obligatory duties, attended Mass regularly, and was exceedingly scrupulous in his behavior.

In some cases admiration for a person of another faith provided the impetus for conversion.

C was very impressed by his sister's attraction to Catholicism and attributed her "straightening out" to her conversion. He became curious about Catholicism and asked many questions about the practices and rituals. He got answers in terms that an 11-year-old boy could grasp. He became more and more absorbed in it and was eventually baptized. At this time, he was very scrupulous in his daily life, arriving at Mass early in the morning. He felt good about life—went to dances, socialized, etc. He enjoyed a sense of freedom most when he sat in church alone and felt a kind of closeness to God. He was helped along in his religious pursuits by a strong friendship with the priest.

In neither case did a religious conversion provide a lasting deterrent to crime.

These attempts to maintain a behavioral extreme are unrealistic. At some time between the ages of seven and ten, such children, who have been so good, begin a gradual turnaround. At this point in life, the itch for excitement is especially strong, and the criminal child seeks to establish himself as bigger and older than he is. As pointed out earlier, it is at this time that sexual curiosity and experimentation intensify. These youngsters either are beginning to do the forbidden and getting away with it or have been violating with impunity right along. The incompatibility between purity and the forbidden things they want to do is not a problem to them. When they are in church, they are in church; when they are doing the forbidden, they are doing the forbidden. One has no bearing on the other in their thinking.* Most retain their religious beliefs, but begin to stray from them.

C had an orthodox training in the Irish Catholic Church. He learned his catechism and had very vivid ideas about hell and heaven. He believed that God knew everything that went on. The Church provided a way of coming to terms with his transgressions through confession and communion. C knew that sex, lying, stealing, disobedience to parents, and so on were sinful. He feared that he might be committed to the burning fires of hell for eternity. He said his prayers nightly. If he passed a church, he crossed himself; if he passed one without realizing it, he

---

* The criminal child does fear punishment, but he is able to push this fear out of his mind by a mental process (which we call "cutoff") to be described in Chapter 6.

returned to it and then crossed himself. He believed that he was born in sin and had to redeem himself. For example, after sex play with his sister, he could not bring himself to confess to the priest, but said prayers 30 or 40 times to inform God that he was penitent. He was having quite a struggle to be the holy child he wanted to be. He might be sitting on a step and want a bicycle belonging to another child who was passing by; this was coveting, and he would try to push the thought aside, because he knew he should not covet. In the meantime, his violating patterns were expanding, and his conscience became less potent a deterrent. From time to time, however, he still fulfilled church duties, especially if his mother were checking or if he had to bring back tangible evidence of attendance at a church function. If he could sneak away from church, all the better.

This is fairly typical. The criminal youngster may conform outwardly, but with less inner devotion. It is important to emphasize that the criminal does not rebel against the church and in fact may seek out a strict faith and adhere almost slavishly to its ritual. It is more a matter of competing excitements than disdain for religion itself that leads to the progressive moving away.

What puzzles parents especially is that their criminal child may appear to lose interest in religion, but still show occasional enthusiasm. Actually, unknown to them, the enthusiasm may be for something other than religion. For example, one family that showed strong religious leadership in the Jewish community had an adolescent son who refused to go to temple, fried bacon in his parents' kosher home, and stated repeatedly that being Jewish had no meaning for him. Yet, when the family held the annual Passover Seder dinner, he eagerly assumed leadership of the Seder. His parents remarked on the beautiful job he had done. Only a short time later, he was back to deriding Judaism and claimed that he had his own religion based on the teachings of two rock music stars. His parents did not understand that it was not the Seder ritual that meant so much to him, but rather holding the seat of authority to run the Passover meal.

Naturally, the clergy and lay religious leaders who see the early involvement of these youngsters try very hard to keep them interested in the church. These efforts are usually to little avail; by this time, what the criminal child wants overrides whatever he might get out of church. The strong, primitive childhood fears of God and devil recede in the face of desires to do the forbidden.

When parents, teachers, clergy, and members of the congregation question the criminal youngster about his disenchantment with the church, he has many justifications. These often are the very same reasons that the noncriminal offers when he is dissatisfied with religion. However, the noncriminal abandons religion out of intellectual conviction or for emotional reasons, not because he prefers to be in crime. The criminal youngster quickly picks up the same reasons commonly given by noncriminals for leaving the church: he maintains that there is no point in worshipping a God who is so unjust; he offers "evidence" that God does not exist, pointing to the suffering and inhumanity of mankind; he indicts the clergy, using any human foible that makes a minister appear less saintly as grounds for dismissing him and religion altogether; or he cites undesirable policies and meaningless practices in explaining his disenchantment with the church.

> As a youngster, C was told that the Sunday offering would get to God. He did not have money to donate, but his mother managed to give a small amount regularly. C became increasingly skeptical that this money ever got to God. In addition, he could not believe that the money was being used for a very good purpose. He and his family were living in terrible poverty. To him, it was farcical to be giving money to God, who would never get it, while their own luck never improved and they remained impoverished.

Whether C really thought this or it was something he told others after he dropped out of the church is not clear; what is clear is that his violating patterns were growing and the importance of the church was receding at the time. The criminal youth may point to congregants who fail to practice what they say they believe and conclude that the church serves no constructive function.

The criminal does not, however, completely abandon religion. He retains a residual, although perhaps amorphous, idea of God and may still be religiously observant in his own way. There is a compartmentalization; religion is separated from the rest of life. The criminal may pray for forgiveness of his sins at bedtime while contemplating the next day's crime. A nomadic criminal went around the country committing crimes, but always carried his Bible with him. Another, who was brought up in a religious home and who as an adult expounded on immorality in government, himself stole a Bible. We have known men to commit a crime on Saturday night, serve Mass at the altar the next morning, and then commit more crimes. Catholicism appeals to many of these men because it offers an opportunity to confess and be absolved.

> Every 3 months or so, C prepared for the precommunion service. He made a list of all his sins, generally 3 or 4 days before communion. He was very careful in compiling this list, being sure to include everything that *he* thought was a sin. For a few days after communion, he adhered rigidly to his determination to live honestly. However, he invariably gave this up and returned to his former ways.

Confession allows the criminal more inner and outer freedom. Having unburdened himself, he is freer to go about doing the things he wants with a lightened conscience.

Despite their criminality, many criminals sporadically return to religion and prayer. Some hang on to their own ideas of God, but do not find any organized religion acceptable. Nevertheless, they may drop into a church, where they are moved by the music and the beauty of the service. Some make up their own prayers, but do not go to church.

> C prayed to God when he was in jeopardy, but also when he was in no particular danger. He might call on God to keep him out of trouble. At times, he entered a church, lit a candle, and prayed. In a 12-hour stretch, there might be crime, prayer, and then crime in sequence. Often, he stayed away from church because he felt unworthy of being there.

> C, who viewed himself generally as an agnostic, admitted that he prayed when in a tight spot. He might begin his prayer with "if there is a God" and then continue the prayer, so that, in case there were a God, he would get his help. Of course, he never let others know that he prayed.

Some criminals are outwardly derisive of religion, but pray in private. They regard it as a sign of weakness to acknowledge their religiosity.

The criminal sometimes is fed up with life as he has lived it, and he prays for redemption. He may seek a miracle from God that will result in a radical change in him without his having to do anything. During these relatively monastic periods, the criminal reads religious tracts and becomes a serious student of philosophy and theology. He may go from one church to another, looking for inspiration. Young criminals may forsake the more orthodox or traditional faiths in favor of more mystically oriented sects. Some of our men have become interested in Far Eastern religions. One gave up eating meat for a while because of its link to violence—the killing of an animal. At times like these, there may be dramatic religious conversions, which inevitably turn out to be short-lived.

The criminal may become devoutly religious during periods of sentimentality—for example, on the death of his mother or the birth of his baby. One man went to work to earn money to pay for his mother's funeral, rather than use the proceeds of his crimes. The criminal sometimes prays for those who are less fortunate and tries to help the needy. At various points in his life, both as a child and as an adult, the criminal may go to church in response to family pressures and to maintain a respectable front.

> As an adolescent, C would pretend to go to church to please his mother, who was very religious. Each Sunday morning, he left his home and went to a bar. At the proper time, he returned and said he had been

at church. Sometimes, he went to a church function, so that he could bring back some evidence of his attendance.

Going to church can serve many functions at once. It has become almost a legend that many members of the Mafia attend church regularly. Some are so "devout" that they have chapels in their homes. They try to maintain a good relationship with God, both so that they can go to heaven and so that they can call on him for help here on earth. Many of their wives are devout, and the men respond to their desire for religious observance. Mafia members may make generous donations to the church, thus trying to achieve good standing in the congregation and community. Anticipating their own demise, these men often arrange for the most elaborate funerals; they would not consider being buried without a full church ceremony.

In confinement, the criminal may once again return to religion.

> When C was 26 years old and in prison, a priest befriended him. In the course of their meetings, C experienced a serenity and understanding that were new and agreeable. This evolved into his being baptized and becoming a devout Catholic. Catholicism offered him an opportunity to seek relief in communion, confession, and absolution. C believed that the state of his soul would be far better than in previous days.

Conversions to Catholicism in confinement are not unusual. Catholicism is often the most active religious denomination in institutions, with its clergy offering extensive services and programs and holding considerable influence. Furthermore, Catholicism provides the criminal with concrete things to do to redeem himself, which most other religions do not. In confinement, where he is face to face with his failure in life—failure even at being a successful criminal—he may enter a prolonged monastic state. The following is part of a letter written by a criminal sentenced to seven concurrent life sentences for a number of homicides.

> "Dear Bob [the criminal's brother]"
>
> " . . . Now I am a lamb of God. My eyes have been opened and I see the world for what it is and its days are numbered. If the people don't stop and get right with God, they will surely wish they had. For I am no longer afraid for myself because I have placed myself in the hands of God, and he is with me each and every day. I am now the head of the Bible Class. This change in me is so wonderful for I know the Lord is truly my shepherd. So my dear brother, Bob, I know how you feel and what you will do. If I can save just one man here to help him go as a better man than when he came, I will be happy. Read Romans 13. . . . Every day it is not easy to find faith. Trust in God now, and give thanks to him each day. One of my prayers is:

'Hail and bless the hour and moment in which the son of God was born of the most pure Virgin Mary. At midnight in Bethlehem, in piercing cold. . . . My God, hear my prayer and grant my desires, through the merit of our Saviour, Jesus Christ and of his Blessed Mother. Amen.'

"The prayer is up on my way along with the one you sent me. The chapter I read today is 5 Chapter Thessalonians. My Psalm tonight will be 119. Bob, my dear brother, I love you as my brother and friend. It is through you I have found peace and joy of finding the Lord Jesus Christ. In him I have found peace of mind and love for my fellow man. . . . May God bless you and your family. Give my love to all. Love and Peace."

We know of numerous criminals who have had life close in on them when they were behind bars and once again become religious. When they were released, they turned their back on religion.

A criminal may attempt to "score points" by participating in programs offered by the clergy. This is different from the sincere, transient religious states. It is a case of a criminal's effort to ingratiate himself with the clergy, who he knows may be able to help him out. Conversions occur out of expediency. One Irish Catholic converted to Judaism while in prison, to cultivate a relationship with the dedicated and influential rabbi and thereby work his way out of San Quentin. Phony confessions are made, because they are interpreted as evidence of change. The criminal does everything he can to impress others with his sincerity and to indicate that he is changing. In the process, he may make an errand boy out of a clergyman, by enlisting his help in getting privileges and by asking for things that will make his own life more comfortable. For example, the criminal may ask his minister to make a call for him, to bring him cigarettes, or to mail a letter. Most important, he wants the cleryman to use influence to help get him out of the institution.

In an institution with a sizable black population, the Black Muslim movement may be a strong force in the lives of some prisoners. The criminal in confinement may be attracted by the ways of living a good life that he believes this sect promotes. Like other criminals, these men often embrace the faith with little knowledge of its teachings, being aware only of specific practices, such as avoidance of pork, alcohol, and drugs. Most do not study in depth the writings of Mohammed or learn the philosophic and theologic premises of the movement. Those who do study rarely implement what they learn. However, being a Black Muslim does serve a protective function: the weaker prisoners are assured of protection by the stronger. It also provides a way to procure material things, because members will do favors for one

another. Even the observance of rituals and practices fades, once the criminal
is released from confinement.

> C and Bob (another criminal) were discussing their participation in the
> Black Muslim movement. They pointed out that, when a fellow gets in
> prison for the first time, he is frightened and wants protection. The
> Black Muslims form a community within the larger prison community
> and offer this protection. C and Bob acknowledged that, in the real
> practice of the faith, crime is out. In fact, the moral code is very strict.
> Bob pointed out that, in his first exposure to the group, he was stripped
> of the arms he was bearing in church itself. Both men balked at the
> moral teachings of the Black Muslims. What appealed to Bob was the
> militant drive for recognition of the black man. He stated that he did
> not know much about the religion itself and indeed had never been very
> interested in it. Rather, he had divorced himself from ethical concerns.
> To him, religion had been a convenience. In the past, when it had been
> convenient for him to be a Catholic, he was a Catholic. Furthermore,
> he alleged that there had been quite a bit of drug use and every kind
> of crime imaginable among the Black Muslims he had dealt with.

Other criminals to whom we have talked have made similar statements about
their contacts with Black Muslims. One effect of the behavior we have
discussed is that criminal elements have done much to discredit the Black
Muslim movement.

In summary, many criminals belong to a church, believe in God, and pray.
This is regarded as paradoxical by others, because it contrasts so sharply with
criminals' violating patterns. However, the conversions and religious practices,
although they may be sincere, are not sustained. The form is there with no
substance. This has often been regarded as the failure of religion to reach
these people. Religion can do much to add a dimension to the life of a noncriminal, but it does not make a responsible man out of a criminal.

HEALTH

Medical history, family reports, and hospital records indicate that the
criminals with whom we have dealt have been very healthy. Other than the
usual childhood ailments, they have had few serious diseases. Only two had
significant physical defects, one who had had polio as a child and one who
was afflicted with severe allergies. As youngsters, they were good-looking,
energetic, and vigorous.

However, most of them as children downgraded their physical condition
and appearance in numerous ways, placing themselves below other children
in the neighborhood. Their images of themselves were almost totally self-
deceptions. One young man remarked how ugly and puny he had been as

a child, but a snapshot taken of him at the age of nine with a group of other children showed him to be a well-built, handsome youngster. As adults some have continued to believe that they are quite ugly; one said that the word *ugly* did not sufficiently describe him, but that he was "oogly," which meant really unsightly. This too was far from the truth, in that women found him quite appealing and attractive.

The criminal's dissatisfactions with his body include almost any physical feature. In describing his unsuitable body proportions, a man might complain that his head was too long, too large, or poorly shaped. One young man stated that he wore his hair long to disguise what he considered unattractive features of his head.

> "I am very vain because I think I look better with long hair. I have a very high forehead, and my shape is sort of funny. I have to wear a certain length of hair. I probably feel more sure of myself than if I don't have it."

Complaints about facial features are numerous—the face is too fat, the lips too protruding, and so forth. One man often turned his head in such a way as to make his nose less prominent; he also cut or shaved his hair so as to make his forehead look larger. Some grow beards, moustaches, or goatees to conceal blemishes or otherwise improve their appearance. Dissatisfaction with body build is exceedingly frequent. Even as strong, attractive youngsters, many regard themselves as weak and scrawny.

> C remembered that at the age of 5 he regarded himself as weak and puny. He thought he was so skinny that perhaps he had some rare malformation of the ribs, which he referred to as being "chicken-breasted." From that time on, he did everything possible to hide his chest. He would not go swimming and was reluctant to shower in the presence of others. Even as an adult in confinement, he was more fully clothed than others, although it was hot and uncomfortable.

This was the self-image of a man who was actually rather handsome. One youngster almost always wore shirts with sleeves, because he thought his arms were too thin. Another source of dissatisfaction is coordination, some of these youngsters believing themselves to be ungainly and awkward. Unhappiness about skin appearance was also common. Overreaction to acne was typical; criminal adolescents were overly embarrassed and ashamed about a few pimples. Some black criminals were self-conscious about skin color. Black self-hatred was quite evident, especially in those who grew up before the present social consciousness about racial equality.

C stated that as a child he regarded himself as definitely inferior, because he was black. He remembered that he wanted to be white, and in fact he used a commercial product that he was told would whiten the skin if it were applied during the winter.

One of C's brothers was much lighter than he. Two other brothers were the same shade, and all his sisters but one were lighter. But C thought that he was much darker than any of the youngsters around. When he played, if there were any kind of argument, he would be called "blackie" or "smokey." (As a matter of fact, some of the blacks did not allow their light-colored children to play with the darker-skinned youngsters.) C believed that he was an outcast because of the general ugliness of all his features, but he was most conscious of skin color.

Undoubtedly, social circumstances did in part give rise to these concerns. This was true among blacks who were noncriminal, as well as criminal. We mention it here only because it was just one more feature about himself with which the criminal youngster was displeased.

Among the aspects of physical endowment that distressed the criminals, one of the most prevalent was penis size. Many of these men believed that they were underendowed. Consequently, they were fearful of being seen undressed in showers or locker rooms. Some went to considerable trouble to disrobe where others would not see them. More than one has tried to enlarge his penis by such practices as masturbating or attaching the penis to a string and then to a brick to stretch it. One man inserted cotton into a condom to make his penis look larger.

FEARS

Most young children, but criminal youngsters in particular, want to be stronger, bigger, and older than they are. However, as the criminal makes his way in the world and seeks to establish himself, he must contend with extreme fears. His parents may remember that early in his life the criminal child had more fears than the other children; he was the one who needed the night light the longest; he was the least tolerant of pain and the most afraid of the doctor. Criminal children fear thunder, lightning, water, heights, goblins—almost anything.

The fear of physical injury is particularly strong. Many are afraid to do things that other youngsters do naturally in play. They are afraid that they will fall or in some way get hurt. Many are so fearful of water that they never learn to swim. Fear of injury prevents them from becoming involved in athletics. It is not unusual for a criminal youth who likes to play a particular sport to be afraid to do so, because he might get hit by the ball or injured by another player. High on the list of fears is a dread of being hurt in a fight.

Criminal children, being creatures of extremes, deal with their fears in one of two ways. For example, some avoid swimming and do not go near the water; one man failed to receive his college diploma after completing four years of study only because he did not pass the swimming requirement, and another dreamed of joining the navy, but because he never overcame a fear of drowning in deep water, he was unable to do so. Other criminal youngsters fly in the face of their fears. They try to match the feats of others and so may plunge in and attempt to swim long distances and play rough games. Similarly, when it comes to fighting, some avoid a fight at any cost even if it means running and appearing "chicken." Others may be inclined to run, but in time manage to eliminate the fear. These are the ones who eventually enjoy fighting. Although the fear is initially strong, running away is so deflating to the youngster's self-image that he decides instead to stand fast and try to hold his own. The fear is replaced by a desire to win and dominate. In time, the youngster reaches the point where he is eager to fight and seeks occasions to do so. The fear, rather than serving as a deterrent, might function as an incitement to fight and prove himself.

> Right up to adolescence, C maintained an image of himself as being skinny and weak. His brother was stockier than he, as were many of the other boys. C was afraid to fight, because he might be injured. Confronted with the awareness that he was smaller and fearful, he tried to prove that he was strong and fearless. At first, he did this verbally. He was the "wise guy," the one with the "chip on his shoulder," the bully. This did not satisfy him, and he decided to prove his power physically. The turning point came when he was about 12 and was challenged to a fight by a youngster well-known for fighting. At this time, C had a broken arm. But even with the arm out of commission, he was able to subdue the other fellow. With this triumph, his confidence grew, and the use of "muscle" became more frequent.

Many criminal youngsters are preoccupied with building up their bodies. C, in the example above, walked around breathing deeply, believing that inflating his lungs by inhaling a lot of air would expand his chest. Others lift weights.

> When C was 13, he weighed 98 pounds and was rather frail. He took up weight-lifting. He set a target of lifting 200 pounds, a goal that he surpassed. His major concern was that his muscles be visible to others.

Such youngsters may walk around in sleeveless T-shirts or sweatshirts and display the muscles in their arms. The objective is not a good physique itself.

Being strong and tough means something to the criminal, in that he can throw his weight around and intimidate others. Some also learn specialized fighting techniques. Karate and judo are taught for self-defense, but the criminal may use them offensively. The physical-fitness tasks that require discipline and drill are often dropped when the initial enthusiasm wears off. Of course, there are criminals who scorn such pursuits, because they consider themselves "above" fighting. They deal with the world with different tactics —usually slickness, rather than muscle.

The criminal acts like an infant in the face of disease and pain. To suffer seems to be a personal affront to him and lessens his idea of himself as all-powerful. He also fears pain and disease, because they incapacitate him for crime, which requires sharpness, agility, and energy. Attitudes toward illness, like attitudes toward fear, assume extreme forms. Either the criminal is overly concerned and nearly convinced that he is going to perish, or he neglects his condition entirely.

Some criminals become so concerned about a common cold that they are positive they have contracted pneumonia. Some believe that their bodies cannot stand any strain, infection, or illness and that somehow their systems lack the recuperative function that others have.

> Coming in from washing cars in the sun, C saw that a flush had appeared on his cheeks. Having read about the "butterfly pattern" of lupus erythematosus, he was alarmed. Although he did not remember the name of the disease, C frequently checked his skin for signs of it.

To those who are so worried about physical well-being, health fads are attractive. They may eat "health foods" or consume large quantities of vitamins. If the criminal is seriously ill or injured, he is likely to become so preoccupied with his condition that his criminal thinking becomes quiescent.

The opposite reaction is to pay so little attention to one's health that a cold hangs on and does evolve into something more serious.

> "I have had a cold off and on now, never really recovering for about a month. It just ambled all over my body. Sinus congestion had pushed out my eyes. I was in constant pain for about 3 days. My muscles were sore."

Most criminals fear going to a doctor, because the doctor might find something wrong with them and subject them to pain.

> C's gums were bleeding. Immediately, he thought of leukemia. On another occasion some months later, he saw blood in his urine. Panicked, he phoned his wife to have her make an appointment with the doctor. C stayed up all that night, worrying. Yet he failed to keep the appoint-

ment with the doctor, for fear of finding out that something was seriously wrong. Also, he did not want to experience any further pain, which might come from examination or treatment. By the time he finally went, the diagnosis was a fairly advanced kidney infection.

The criminal is not likely to admit that he is afraid of a disease, the doctor, or pain, because he considers it a sign of "weakness" to do so. A visit to a doctor also constitutes a risk that the doctor may restrict his activity. As a result, he may omit going to the doctor altogether. Similarly, the criminal will avoid the dentist, fearing the pain of the drill more than the deterioration and eventual loss of his teeth.

C neglected his teeth and very early in life began to lose them. His defective teeth bothered him and were disfiguring. He could do nothing about the problem, except practice holding his upper lip so as to cover the bad teeth. However, this gave him a smile that he thought looked effeminate. Eventually, he got an upper denture and then a lower one.

Most criminals have psychosomatic ailments, their list of symptoms covering almost the whole body from head to foot. There are tension states, with headaches, gastrointestinal upset, and fatigue. Insomnia is a common complaint, a great deal of it attributable to the criminal's lying awake "boiling and scheming," as one put it; then he complains that he cannot sleep. He may experience dizziness, blurred vision, palpitations, and breathlessness to the point where he is convinced that he is having a heart attack. The psychosomatic symptoms are much less frequent when the criminal is actively in crime. It is when he is deterred or restrains himself that they plague him the most. A bored criminal is more likely to be psychosomatic than one who is "in the action." When the criminal is confined, there are numerous reports at sick call of reactions that are psychosomatic in origin.

In confinement, C began to feel as though he were passing out. He thought he was losing control of himself. His vision was poor, his muscles quivered, and his breathing was labored. He believed that he was ticketed for death in the form of a heart attack, ulcers, brain tumor, cancer, or syphilis of the brain. Examination showed that it was all "nerves."

The criminal can use any ailment to enlist people's sympathy and exploit them. As a youngster, he may exaggerate the extent of an illness to miss school. When there was a military draft, he may have sought exemption from military service by magnifying a minor physical ailment into a serious disability. We have mentioned how one man used a slight limp to get customers to subscribe to magazines in a fraudulent operation. The criminal often uses the slightest sign of illness as an excuse for not showing up for work. He may even decline to work at all, on the basis of an alleged disability, and claim that he is owed compensation because of it. When the criminal is hospitalized for legitimate reasons, he is likely to capitalize on his condition and seek special attention and favors, including sexual liaisons with female staff members. He is also likely to use the hospital as an arena for criminality. We know that the people we have worked with have committed property offenses against staff members, other patients, and hospital facilities. In short, although the criminal fears illness and is a coward when it comes to suffering, he is fully prepared to use any ailment in his own behalf.

The criminal expects to die young. As a child, he is unusually preoccupied with death and how he will die. The concern is present very early in life. Some write their own epitaphs and identify a specific age beyond which they will not live.

> At the age of 17, C had realized that because he was in crime, his life could be ended very abruptly. He decided that his epitaph would be just his name and "BYE." He believed this to be much more dignified than some of the epitaphs written by other criminals he knew, one of which was profane.

Some go so far as to think about the conditions of burial.

> C indicated his desire for cremation, because he did not want to be eaten by animals, such as foxes and field rats, that work their way in and destroy the bodies.

> C believed that he would die before the age of 30. At 15, when a cousin of his had cancer, he was sure that he had cancer. There had always been the idea that death would come early. He believed that his body could not withstand any serious infection or illness. Even as a youngster, he thought of death and preferred cremation. There was a disagreeableness about "rotting in the grave."

Criminals who are in good health live with the thought that death is imminent. Many of them anticipate the specific cause of death, whether it be in crime or from a terminal disease. Nocturnal dreams and daydreams often have death themes.

> "One of the things I daydream a lot about is death, thinking about dying in different ways. At times, I am terribly afraid that I will die before I get to be old, that I will just die earlier than most people. It is kind of scary when you think about a person dying and that means they do nothing for ever and ever. I mean, it is just kind of weird. Death can be a very scary subject."

Of course, death is frightening to most people. But, the criminal thinks about it repeatedly from childhood on. It is as though each breath may be his last. Some criminals develop superstitions about death and walk blocks out of their way to avoid a hospital, cemetery, or funeral parlor.

The outstanding aspect of the criminal's reaction to illness, disability, and death is the extremes to which he goes. Strong, energetic healthy men are as fearful of these adversities as many severely neurotic noncriminals. The way in which the criminal reacts to his fears is different. Unlike the noncriminal, he can rid himself of some fears abruptly, so that they do not stand in the way of something he wants to do.

ANTISOCIAL PATTERNS

The youngsters described throughout this chapter grew up to be hard-core criminals. From early childhood on, they were violating; but they were remarkably successful in concealing their activities. A small number of criminal children whom we have described as being very "good" did not become serious violators until they were about ten years old and then were skillful in getting away with things, so others still regarded them as "good kids." Even those who were brazenly irresponsible were usually given the benefit of the doubt and viewed as "mischievous" or "going through a stage," but not as "delinquents." The purpose of this section is to view these children's lives through the lens of an imaginary television soundtrack camera, following them 24 hours a day. If the parents and teachers of these youngsters were to watch such a videotape, they would be astonished at the number and diversity of violations that they would see. A person watching such a tape would see only what a criminal does, and never know the magnitude of the criminal thinking that does not get translated into action. The following account of what the viewer would see is supplemented with some additional material about the criminal's thinking.

CHILDHOOD

The criminal child operates alone, with an accomplice, or in a group. He is eager to gain acceptance by older delinquents and to learn from them. The criminals with whom we have dealt have each committed hundreds of crimes before the age of fifteen. The public is increasingly aware that many crimes are being committed by juveniles. According to F.B.I. statistics (*The Washington Post*, 7/2/72), children under 15 committed 17,283 *known* major crimes in the United States in 1970.

Early in life, the criminal shows considerable ingenuity in doing the forbidden. He uses the kind of cleverness shown by a young boy who steals watermelons and floats them down a creek so that he does not have to carry them, or a child who cons his "friend" out of a cherished possession. For every forbidden act carried out, hundreds of ideas occur but are not implemented. We group the violating patterns into three types: those involving property, assault, and sex.

The theft pattern usually begins with the criminal's stealing money from people at home.

> At the age of 5, C began taking nickels and dimes from his grandmother's purse. He did not take all the money, because he figured she would not miss a nickel or dime, but would miss all the change if it were gone. He bought ice cream with the money. His grandmother would have given him the money, but ice cream bought with a stolen nickel was more delicious than that bought with a nickel freely given.

Some of these early thefts involve more than loose change. One youngster stole a $20 bill and, not knowing what to do with it, buried it. Another recalled his stealing as a young boy from his father.

> "Today, for the first time, I really looked at that little kid reaching into his father's change pocket, getting a quarter, and hiding it under the rug. This was the father who was devoting his life to the little boy who was stealing from him. And, as has been the pattern of my conduct all along, I rapidly escalated from the change pocket to the wallet. It wasn't long before Dad found that $10 was missing from his billfold. I had taken it and hidden it under the rug in the living room. I have long since forgotten the specific thing I wanted it for, but I can remember, as with the quarter stolen before, the sneaky anticipation of waiting for Dad, home from a hard day's work, to settle down at the kitchen table so that I would be sure I would be unobserved. I can remember going into the living room, where Dad hung up his coat when he came home from work; the furtive glances toward the hallway, to make sure neither Dad nor my brother was coming in; and the quick, sickening feeling in the pit of my stomach as I reached into his pants pocket, took out the wallet, grabbed the bill, and shoved it under the carpet. I got the wallet into the pants pocket pretty much as it was and, with relief, walked back into the kitchen and faced my father with a polite, friendly smile on my face."

Thefts also take place outside the home—at construction sites, railroad yards, or wherever the criminal goes. At school, he steals items belonging to other youngsters and to teachers. One boy enjoyed stealing the teacher's lunch, not because he needed food, but just as a joke. The criminal child sometimes extorts money and property from other pupils. In some schools, students are "shaken down" for their lunch money in return for "protection" from being beaten up. Bicycles are often stolen and resold. Young criminals steal parts from bicycles or from stores to dress up their own, because they want to have the best bike around. Some youngsters con others out of money and possessions. They become adept at cards, dice, and other forms of gambling early in life. They also "borrow" money with no intention of repaying it. Shoplifting—the "five-finger discount"—begins very early. Whether the criminal needs them or not, he takes items ranging from candy bars to major appliances and gives away more than he keeps.

Vandalism is another property offense. Automobiles are favorite targets— young criminals pour sand into gas tanks, break windows, steal from glove compartments, cut seats, deflate and slash tires, and snap off radio antennas. Nationally, repairs of school buildings and school equipment cost millions of dollars a year. Windows are shattered, buildings entered, and lockers opened. Classrooms are broken into, and equipment is stolen or damaged. Some youngsters roam about the streets breaking up anything in their paths. They hurl rocks at lights, toss eggs against houses, tear up yards, and destroy almost everything in sight. Breaking and entering also occur in the early years.

> In the third grade, C began breaking and entering. He quickly learned that the police were investigating these incidents. Not only did C get a charge out of the entry, the theft, and the fencing of stolen items, but the biggest charge of all was eluding the police. Sometimes he saw them following him and then went into abandoned houses, where there was nothing to steal, thus frustrating them in their pursuit of the suspect.

Almost any crime pattern imaginable may have its inception early in life. For example, one man had set fifty fires by the time he was nineteen. He set his first one at the age of five and a half.

Like the theft pattern, the assault pattern appears early. Even if there are few or no instances of fighting, thinking along this line is present. When anyone puts a criminal child down, the assault thinking begins automatically.

> When C's parents were angry at him for not doing the few chores that he was assigned, C thought about using his father's paddle as a weapon and smashing each parent over the head with it. In several instances, he was so angry at his mother that he wanted to kill her. He frequently thought about beating his mother and father to death.

C's assault was deterred by thoughts of what would happen to him if he actually struck either parent. Some are deterred from fighting by their strong fears of bodily injury.But others do attack people physically from the time they are two or three years old. It often starts in the home with a sibling whom the criminal child pushes around.

> "I used to play with [my brother]. He would have to play whatever games I ordered him to play or get beaten up. We used to duel with wooden sticks, box, wrestle, and, as we would play, I would hurt him deliberately—twist his arm, punch him extra hard. And when he occasionally rebelled against this treatment, when he would strike out blindly against his tormentor, then I would really beat him hard. He was too much smaller to really fight back and when I finally broke his resistance, I would slap him across the face for fighting back. This wasn't once; this was many, many times over a period of years, until the kid ran away from me every chance he could get. I got pleasure from the deliberate extra hurts, the twists, the slaps, the pummelings I used to inflict. It got so bad that Dad discovered [my brother's] bruises one day and really gave me a licking—and I remember how I tried to lie and crawl my way out of it. [My brother] went through hell. He was tormented every day by a vicious, sadistic bully."

Some of the activities of these youngsters are truly sadistic, whether inflicted on other human beings or on animals.

> Around the age of 7, C decided to hang a child by putting a noose around his neck. He threw the rope over a stick and kicked the can from under the boy. However, the stick broke, and the child fell to the ground. Retrospectively, C stated that he would have been perfectly content to watch the child die.

> At the age of 8, C used to kill birds as they fed in the barnyard. During this time, he also killed other animals. He chased rats into dark corners and hit them with a stick until they were dead. He took shots at pigeons while they were in flight or perched on the barn roof. He enjoyed drowning cats and watching the bubbles float to the top. He reported that he used to fight with a groundhog and enjoyed watching the animal gnash its teeth and fight back. He then struck the groundhog on the head until its eyes popped out.

Some young criminals combine assault and theft, as in the protection rackets already mentioned. Some carry knives with them and are not averse to brandishing them to intimidate other children.

> C's interest in knives began when he was 6. This fascination grew when his widowed mother went around with a man who collected guns and knives. C began carrying a knife on his person. It soon became known that he was ready to use it. Once, he was fighting a bigger fellow, who hit him over the head. Although wobbly, C slashed him over and over on the chest and abdomen. His reputation spread as a knife-wielding tough who did not care whom he cut or how many times.

Sexual activity, too, begins early, the criminal aspects being conning, misrepresentation, and coercion. This is described elsewhere in this chapter.

In addition to property, assault, and sex violating patterns before adolescence, some use drugs and alcohol. Our main discussion of this will be in Volume 3, which will deal exclusively with drugs. For illustration, we note here only the case of a twelve-year-old boy who was involved in the "liquor trade."

> Around the age of 12, C had a friend whose well-to-do father received good liquor for presents. Unused, the liquor began to accumulate in the cellar. C got his friend to steal 30 bottles. The two of them sold this liquor and were never detected. On one occasion, they had to bury a bottle that they could not dispose of. However, unknown to his friend, C later dug up the bottle and sold it. Throughout this venture, C took advantage of the other boy. He received $3 or $4 per bottle for a total of close to $100. Of this, he gave his friend a dollar here and there, keeping the bulk of it for himself. He stopped this activity because his friend was getting scared. However, he remembered that the father of a boy at the other end of town sold liquor. So C began again, this time stealing it by the caseload, for which he found outlets.

Most young criminals are far more eager students in the "school" of the streets than they are in the classroom. These energetic youngsters are ready for "action" at all times, not restricting themselves to any one modus operandi (M.O.) or particular kind of violation. Some do develop an aversion to a specific type of crime. For example, some criminal children will not hurt an animal, and others will not use their fists, preferring conning to muscle. However, nearly all are "players"—i.e., there are very few things in which they will not participate. As their violating patterns grow and go undetected, these youngsters become increasingly confident that they will not get caught. Simultaneously, their contempt mounts for the responsible people whom they continue to deceive.

Most criminal youngsters are highly interested in law enforcement. They spend many hours with books, comics, television, and movies that have lots of criminal action. They play variations of cops and robbers. They like and admire the policeman as long as he does not interfere with them. The police officer is the "biggest man" in the world, with his badge, uniform, nightstick, and gun. Many criminal children consider becoming policemen when they grow up. Others who do not want to be policemen desire to become what they see as more powerful enforcement officers, such as F.B.I. agents or members of the Secret Service.

Usually, the criminal youngster is caught for violating, whether by his family, the school, or the police. If he is caught, the challenge is to escape or mitigate punishment. To this end, he conceals the truth by shading, distorting, omitting, or plain lying. For example, if his parent asks where he got extra money, he may reply that he earned it by doing a favor or chore for someone. If telling the truth will absolve him, he will not hesitate to open up. Then he will promise, "I won't do it again." In these early years, he learns what will work best to help him out of a jam. When he is first apprehended by the police, in all probability he will be warned and released if the official records show him to be a "first offender" and if the crime is not too serious. Possibly, he will simply be given a lecture by the officer and his parents will be informed. From his own experience and that of others, the child learns to size up the police to determine what tactics to use.

> By the age of 10, C had picked up tips from other youngsters about how to act with a policeman. He learned to tell the officer that he had his constitutional rights and that he did not have to answer any questions. Furthermore, he made it clear that he knew that it was incumbent on the police to furnish proof. The ultimate triumph would be to frustrate the officer in his quest for evidence so that the charge would be dropped.

The reader should bear in mind that all this youthful criminality occurs despite the fact that forces in the environment are predominantly anticrime. That is, family, school, church, and most of the criminal's peers are potentially responsible influences. However, the criminal in childhood and adolescence rejects these and goes in search of excitements that are forbidden. In other words, his way of life runs counter to the mainstream of life in his environment.

ADOLESCENCE

By the time they were sixteen, the criminals in our study were full-fledged criminals. Property offenses continue in adolescence, but with more complex and ingenious schemes. Thefts can occur anywhere, including rural areas, where there is less opportunity. Geographic location does not matter; wherever he is, the criminal makes his own opportunities. Crops, farm buildings, country stores, and houses are all potential targets. Even graveyards are vulnerable.

> C belonged to a group of boys called the Bluebells. They selected tombs that were family vaults of a much earlier era. It was easy to break open the door of a vault with a crowbar and get into a coffin. The odor of disintegrated bodies did not bother these youths at all. From the cadavers they took whatever there was, such as rings, necklaces, and other valuables.

Breaking-and-entering patterns may expand with the acquisition of knowledge about safecracking and lock-picking. Although car theft occurred as early as the age of nine among our criminals, it was more frequent later. Check-forging and the theft and misuse of credit cards are new activities for some. Those who have made their way by conning are sharpening their skills and adding new ones.

Sixteen-year-old C was adept at deceiving others. Small wonder that he was skilled at magic, card tricks, and gambling. Characteristically, he conned someone into betting with him. The two sat down for a game of blackjack. Although he knew he could win, C wanted to give his opponent the impression that C was not a very good player. As C put it, "Though I knew I would win, I wanted to make him think that he would." Early in their playing, C purposely lost. As the other fellow did well, he suggested to C that they play for money. Agreeing to this, C still allowed his opponent to win. Then, when C believed that the other player was nearly bursting with confidence, he pulled out his own "bag of tricks" and cleaned the other fellow out of all the money he had with him.

In time, the criminal learns new M.O.'s and can carry off schemes like a "Murphy": he promises to procure a woman for a potential customer; he takes the man's money and gives him a fictitious address or sends him to the woman, but no one is there; then the criminal disappears with the cash. To catalogue all the types of property offenses would require many pages. Suffice it to say that earlier patterns expand and increase in frequency during adolescence. Crimes that were only ideas before are now translated into action.

The criminal youth gradually becomes confident of his ability to get away with things. So he becomes bolder, more daring in what he attempts. Excitement mounts with each stage of the scheming, as well as during the actual commission of the crime.

"I would set the fire at night and on a Sunday. The reason for this is:

1. At night, it is very hard to see smoke.
2. At night, there is more of a chance to get away, and also it is a lot safer to break into a place at night.
3. On Sunday night, all the stores are closed, and there would not be a lot of people around.
4. There would be very few cars going by on ——— Street, and there would be no one in the alley.

I would break into the door in the back of the store. Then I would go down into the basement and set my fire in the southwest corner of the store. But before the day of the fire, I would turn in a false alarm and see how long it took the fire department to get there.

On the night of the fire, I would go to the movies, about a half-block up [from where he would set the fire]. When I got into the theater, I

> would go out the back door. I would go and break into the place and set the fire. Then I would come back to the movie and wait until the movie was over. Then I would go out and see what was going on. And then I don't know what I would do. It is hard to say. I may go out and set some more fires or go and get some coffee as if nothing happened at all."

The final triumph occurs when the criminal walks out and surveys the scene very calmly, "as if nothing had happened at all."

Assault patterns also expand during the teen-age years. These youngsters are now bigger, more daring, and more able mentally to eliminate the fear of injury in order to prove themselves. Some play the role of hero in trying to rescue a person under attack. In doing so, they function as attackers themselves.

> C used to come and break up fights. When he saw another youngster being beaten up, he dramatically came to the rescue. Playing the role of the savior, he might assault the attacker viciously. In one situation, he struck someone sharply on the head with a rock.

In behaving this way, the criminal still preserves a good image of himself, much as does the Robin Hood who steals and gives away the proceeds. In the 1960s and 1970s, firearms have been added to the arsenal of other weapons most notably used by teen-age gangs—tire chains, brass knuckles, zip guns, and knives. Assaults include muggings, yokings, and "rolling" of drunks and homosexuals. This may be done by criminals acting alone or in gangs. Present reports indicate a resurgence in teen-age gang activity.

In addition to early sexual patterns, new patterns that may have been incubating in the idea stage may now be acted on. There is a wide variety of activities—rape, child molestation, homosexual prostitution, voyeurism, exhibitionism, collaboration with prostitutes—and any of these may be combined with blackmail, assault, and robbery. The following is an account of the unfolding of a criminal's sexual patterns from the age of six.

> The earliest incident C recalled was at the age of 6; while he was in a movie, a man sat next to him and rubbed his genitals, which he enjoyed very much. The man bought him popcorn and promised him toys. Nothing further occurred, because C never saw the man again.

> From 6 to 10, there was mutual masturbation with other boys and competition in urinating the farthest. Interest in girls came early. At about the age of 10, he was stealing things and giving them to girls in order to make headway sexually with them. He tried to entice them to undress in his presence. At 10, when he was babysitting, he rubbed and looked at the vagina of a 3-year-old girl. At 14, he first inserted his

penis into a girl. At this time, there was enormous mental activity related to sex.

Running away from home, he took advantage of every opportunity for sex. There was considerable mutual masturbation with other boys, At 17, he allowed himself to be picked up and have fellatio performed. This began a pattern of every conceivable form of homosexual activity. Exploiting the partner for money and material luxuries was a standard part of the operation.

In the military service, he continued both homosexual and heterosexual experiences. He got out of service by establishing that he was a homosexual. Released after 7 months in the military, he easily located willing female partners and had intercourse with some 200 different girls in a short period. At this time, he was experiencing problems with premature ejaculation and "counted sheep" to prolong the experience. Between 19 and 24, there were close to 500 incidents of voyeurism accompanied by masturbation. At the same time, he was involved in homosexual prostitution.

He was often coercive and sadistic toward women. He enjoyed arousing a girl anally, inserting his penis, and then hearing her cry out in pain. In one of these situations, he locked a girl up and tried to rape her, because she would not do everything he wanted. When she was released, she called the police. C got out of this by claiming that she was a consenting partner. There were situations like the following: he had a friend call and make a date with a girl whom he knew but to whom he was not especially attracted physically; he watched the two have intercourse, and then he chased her around with a knife and then threatened her with a gun to submit to him; he got a big kick out of scaring her, but never did have sex with her.

C left the area in which he had been living and wandered about the country. Wherever he journeyed, there was peeping, intimidation, sadism, rape, and homosexual activity for material gain. Sometimes he snared a girl and threatened her with a razor, tied her up, told her to fight, and then talked her out of reporting him by begging forgiveness. Then after she agreed to forgive him, he did the same things all over. Use of knives was frequent. Masturbating on a girl was another practice. Interspersed with all this was conventional sex with a willing partner.

The sexual act was secondary to the excitement of the chase, the coercion, and the exploitation. But all of it was an expression of a criminal personality that began to show itself very early and expanded rapidly during the teen-age years.

Although the criminal adolescent is involved in a multitude of violations, parents still may be totally unaware of what their child is doing, especially because he manages to keep up a good front at home and at school.

Fifteen-year-old C was brought to a psychiatrist when his parents learned that he had stabbed the family cat and they found a diary he was keeping that chronicled some of his antisocial attitudes and activity. Guaranteed privileged communication, C revealed that he had been engaged in hundreds of violations, none of which his parents knew about.

He and a group of others went to stores for a stealing binge, "just for kicks." They pilfered some items and then sold them to other youngsters. Some evenings, when they were bored, they went out ripping open trash cans and dumping them and committing other acts of vandalism which included putting hydrochloric acid into the gas tank of a car. C had been involved in fights constantly; it was his standard way of reacting to people when they did not do what he wanted. On two occasions, he tried to kill people by throwing heavy objects down on them from a tree fort. In addition to all this, there had been heavy use of marijuana and some use of amphetamines and L.S.D.

C's parents were not informed of the details of these activities, and of course C had no intention of telling them. When the psychiatrist recommended institutionalization, the parents were shocked. They pointed out that he had high grades, could be "nice" to people, played an instrument, and had not gotten into any trouble before. Refusing to believe that their son could be in the kind of serious trouble implied by the psychiatrist, they decided to terminate the meetings.

It is common for parents to go by what they see at home and by a school report card. But they have no way of knowing what is really going on outside, unless they start playing detective.

We shall continue to emphasize that criminality is not simply a function of getting caught for an illegal act. Not only are far more crimes committed that go undetected and unreported, but also thousands of criminal ideas occur to the criminal that he does not implement, some because they are so extreme as to be infeasible. The criminal youngster's mind is filled with these ideas day in and day out. At fourteen, one of our most mild-mannered men was fantasying being a syndicate killer who would be so clever that he would make his victim appear to be a suicide. Another, at eight, thought recurrently of enclosing himself in a bunker with thick cement walls, calling the police, and then mowing down as many as he could from his impenetrable fortress. The fantasies are not only of illegal activities; they also include acts in which the criminal is a hero, a famous man, or the director of a large enterprise. The arsonist referred to before fantasied himself rushing to the scene of a large fire, where, as chief, he would direct the fire fighting.

It is from these many fantasies that actual criminal acts evolve. As the criminal grows older, the patterns become more complex and more sophisticated and take in new kinds of crime. The criminal is never satisfied with a triumph for very long. There is an ever-increasing stream of criminal fantasy, talk, and action. Although each man may have a preferred M.O. and favor some crimes over others, his criminal *thinking* is likely to embrace all kinds of crime. We shall say much more about the spectrum of criminal thinking and action in Chapter 6, where we shall present a running account of how the criminal functions.

INCIDENCE OF CRIME

Each of the men with whom we have worked admits to having committed enough crimes to spend over 1,500 years in jail if he were convicted for all of them. If we were to calculate the total number of crimes committed by all the men with whom we have worked, it would be astronomic. However, this is not represented in crime statistics. As we pointed out in Chapter 2, it is impossible to get accurate statistics even under the best possible conditions. Most criminals succeed at their enterprises. The preceding material in this chapter indicates that from early childhood the criminals in our study have committed thousands of offenses that are undetected or, if·detected, ignored. If one were to judge by official police records, he would be totally misled about the extent of criminal activity. To indicate the huge number of crimes committed by a single person, we present a tally of the criminal acts of three people with whom we have worked.

C-1

PROPERTY CRIMES

Stealing beginning at age 5; at 7, stealing such things as knife at school, tobacco from father, and toy guns

Organized a gang of thieves at age 9

Engaging in fraudulent practices at carnival at age 13

Had a "contract" to procure wine for other adolescents at age 13

Fraudulent magazine sales

Participated in arranging and carrying out illegal abortions

Fraudulent television repair service

Misrepresented self as foreign diplomat to get illegal supplies of heroin

Stole $4,000 worth of clothes and embezzled $3,000 cash in 18 days while working for a clothing store

Illegally wrote and cashed checks for $75-100 daily for 3 years, or about $25,000-30,000 per year

Stole check cashing and writing equipment and in 2½ days cashed $7,500 worth

Bank swindle using illegal and fraudulent securities involving $24,000

Stole negotiable securities, using these to get loan of $3,800

Impersonating a physician—writing fraudulent prescriptions, using some of these to obtain drugs, which he used himself or sold illegally

Extensive buying and selling of drugs
Theft of equipment from wife's place of business
Writing bad checks on wife's business account
Organized phony promotional and consulting firm

ASSAULT

At least three serious cases:
   One man shot fatally
   One man pistol-whipped
   One man made paraplegic by C's deliberately running him down with a car

SEXUAL CRIMES

Numerous cases of carnal knowledge with underage girls
Procuring for government officials
Pimping at 15 for a madam from whom he received money and sex

---

C-2

PROPERTY CRIMES

Arson at age 6
Stealing from parents
Stealing food for self while working in delicatessen
Working at appliance place, rebuilding machines with used parts (against
   company policy) and stealing and selling new parts
Theft of clothing and supplies in military
Shoplifting—thousands of incidents
Housebreaking—thousands of incidents
Selling stolen goods—thousands of incidents
Breaking and entering drugstores
Illegally procuring drugs from pharmacists
Daily drug violations—procuring, use, sales over many years—uncountable
   incidents
Theft of driving licenses for use as identification to write and cash bad checks
In the hospital, stealing drugs in liquid form and substituting water, which
   was given to patient in critical condition
Selling stolen property while in confinement

SEXUAL

Pimping
Carnal knowledge of minors

We calculated that C-1, in his 31 years, had committed more than 64,000
crimes. He was apprehended and convicted no more than seven times. Three

of those times he did not have to serve a term in prison, instead beating the charge and going to Saint Elizabeths. C-2 committed more than 200,000 crimes in his 40-odd years. In 1970, he paid $1.50 to obtain a copy of his official police record. Because he had gone to a hospital for treatment, rather than to a prison, for the one offense for which he was caught, it was stamped "No criminal record." These calculations are based on approximations of the numbers of individual offenses. They are undoubtedly underestimates, in that a criminal does not recall every theft and all the other illegal acts. We can cite many comparable figures from the histories of others with whom we have worked. One man committed approximately 300 rapes before being arrested and charged with rape. Another snatched about 500 purses in one year, more than one a day; he was not arrested for any of these. Another molested about 1,000 children per year when he was between 17 and 22, for a total of at least 5,000 acts, and was apprehended for only one.*

The cases just noted provide better accounts of crime in adult life than in childhood or adolescence. C-3 was a younger man who took the time to write down for us a year-by-year tally up to the age of twenty.

C-3

4th-5th years
—stealing from grocery stores
—stealing from farms
—stealing of money "every chance I had"

6th-7th years
—50 thefts from grocery stores
—25 thefts from cars
— 1 housebreaking
—25 thefts from drugstores

8th-9th years
—50 thefts from grocery stores
—25 thefts from drugstores
—20 thefts from clothing stores
—20 thefts from department stores
—10 breaking-and-entering crimes
—25 breaking into soft-drink machines

---

* By "5,000 acts," we are not necessarily referring to intercourse with a minor. This figure includes taking a variety of sexual liberties, often falling short of intercourse. The criminal had taken a job as an ice cream truck driver mainly in order to have easy access to children.

10th year
—10 thefts from drugstores
— 3 thefts of money from church
—20 thefts from students at school

11th-12th years
—started using barbiturates
—10 breaking-and-entering crimes (other than homes)
—15 housebreakings
—25 thefts from clothing stores
—50 thefts from department stores
— 4 thefts of tires from gas stations

12th-13th years
—continuing use of barbiturates and other drugs
— 6 breaking-and-entering crimes
— 8 housebreakings
—10 thefts from department stores
— 2 thefts of money from church

14th year
—continuing drug use
— 15 thefts from record shops
— 1 breaking-and-entering with vandalism (a school)
— 25 thefts from students at school
— 50 thefts from department stores
—100 breaking into newsstands, soft-drink machines, and pay phones
— 1 breaking into sealed state shipment of liquor
— 2 car thefts
— 2 breaking-and-entering with robbery (warehouses)
— 30 breaking-and-entering crimes

15th-16th years
—continuing use of drugs
—started carrying unloaded gun ("illegal possession")
—25 safecrackings
—15 warehouse thefts
—15 clothing-store thefts
—20 furniture- and appliance-store thefts
—75 breaking-and-entering crimes
—15 housebreakings

17th-18th years (on active duty in army)
— 35 thefts of drugs
— 35 selling of drugs in small amounts
—100 incidents of drug use
— 10 breaking-and-entering crimes
— 2 blackmail of homosexuals

19th-20th years
The following patterns continued:
—drug use
—carrying a gun
—safecracking
—breaking-and-entering (warehouses, stores, homes)
—blackmail of homosexuals
—car thefts
Also: homosexual prostitution, passing bad checks

One can note the expanding patterns, in terms of both types and frequency of crime.* With respect to C-1, C-2, and C-3, we have covered only the frankly arrestable crimes. There was also continued exploitation of people and other massive irresponsibility.

We could show comparable figures for each of our people. Some have committed hundreds of thousands of crimes and have *never* been arrested. Most have been apprehended only a few times. Our cases include even those who committed homicides and had never been caught. When a criminal gets caught for the first time, he is a "first offender" from an enforcement standpoint. Actually, of course, he has been in daily crime for years and was simply unfortunate enough (from his standpoint) to get caught this time. There is no way that crime statistics can approach accuracy, so long as there are crimes that no one even knows about. Even when a criminal is arrested, the crime may not be included in statistics. Most juveniles, for example, are released to their parents, unless a major crime has been committed, and there is now a movement to expunge all criminal records before the age of sixteen. On some occasions, charges are dropped because a victim does not want to press the case, for reasons noted earlier. Some criminals beat a charge on the grounds of "mental illness," and so the arrest does not show up on police records.

CONFINEMENT

A great deal of our experience has been with the criminals at Saint Elizabeths Hospital. A few criminals in our group had been sent there directly from other federal institutions, and nearly all had been incarcerated at some time before hospitalization. We found that the basic patterns of thinking and behavior are similar in hospital and in prison. Indeed, confine-

---

* The numbers C-3 provided were his estimates. Again the issue of credibility of such accounts may arise in the reader's mind. In Chapter 1, we offered an overview of our methods by which we elicited information. The details will appear in Volume 2.

ment is simply one more arena for expression of the criminal personality. Basically, the tactics are also the same in hospital and prison. In jail, the criminal hopes to have a sentence of definite length reduced by parole. In a hospital, the sentence is indefinite and can be reduced by conditional release or eliminated entirely by unconditional release directly from maximum security. The objective in each institution is to get out as soon as possible. The only real difference is that a criminal who is faced with a serious charge is initially eager to get into the hospital to avoid prison. Most criminals who come to Saint Elizabeths reside in Washington, D.C., and they are likely to learn about the setup well before ever being there, for example, during incarceration in the D.C. Jail. As soon as a criminal is admitted to the hospital, he uses previously learned techniques to get out. Other than the relative desirability of admission, the major differences between prison and hospital are the better living conditions and the purported offering of rehabilitation at the hospital. The hospital environment is also generally far more lenient than a prison, although the current trend is for prisons to become more permissive than they had been traditionally.

When the criminal is caught and charged, he does not think he will be convicted. The odds appear to be on his side. For example, in 1971, the New York City Police Department made 94,042 felony arrests. Only 552 of those arrested came to trial (cited in Buckley, 1972), and one would have to assume that not all of them were convicted. The criminal is optimistic about getting out on bail right away, and just as optimistic about beating the charge altogether in the long run. Initially, the idea is not to be confined before trial. Thus, the criminal tries to get out on bond. Over the last few years, bail procedures have been liberalized; in some places, those without money do not have to post collateral. The criminal may be released on personal recognizance. Those who are considered "first offenders" may be released into the custody of a third party such as the representative of a halfway house or even a family member. It is possible for a criminal to be out on several bonds simultaneously. To ensure further bonds and avoid retaliation, the criminal wants to be sure that the bondsman gets paid. He may make payment himself, or he may borrow money from family or friends. In situations where a criminal borrows, he seldom repays the lender. When he does, it may be with the proceeds of his first crime. Even though charges are pending, he may not be deterred; while out on bond, the criminal usually is active in crime. We have records of people who have been in crime a half-hour after their release from the precinct station.

Once he is incarcerated and is awaiting trial, the criminal goes through a variety of states of mind. Usually, he is angry and reacts with a sense of outrage and indignation. He views even being caught as an injustice. Some criminals become contrite and even prayerful, but most direct their mental energy toward avoiding a prison sentence. The lawbreaker now becomes a student of the law, searching for loopholes. In this pursuit, he seeks assistance from anyone—family, girl friend, wife, friends, lawyers. He may become a legal researcher, studying in the prison law library to which he is constitutionally entitled. He becomes a "jailhouse lawyer" for himself and also assists others, usually for pay, thereby building himself up and obligating fellow prisoners. He lies to his own lawyer as he does to everyone else. He complains that his lawyer does not understand him and does not see him enough. Either or both may be true, but the lawyer is criticized, no matter how conscientious he is, whenever things are not going as the criminal wants. In addition, the criminal may write to people of influence in order to seek a redress of grievances.

"MENTAL ILLNESS"

The criminal does not like the prospect of being adjudged mentally ill; but if his crime is serious enough and conviction is likely, he would rather go to a hospital than spend a long time in prison. He has been told by other criminals and by his attorney that his stay would be comparatively brief, and he concludes, "Why serve a ten-year prison term when I can get out of the hospital in a much shorter time?" The more serious the charge, the more likely the criminal is to consider pleading insanity.

The criminal may have been told by family, friends, and others who know him that his deviant acts are "sick." People sometimes reason that a man who rapes, robs, and commits other violations has to be "sick." In a not unusual incident, a woman took her twenty-year-old son to a psychiatrist, because she thought that he must have been "crazy" to steal a car. Every day, one hears the words *sick* and *crazy* applied to behavior that people do not understand. The criminal is usually insulted if others say or imply that he is mentally ill. It is an affront to be considered a "nut." However, he may have heard the term "sick" applied to him so often that he half believes that he does have a mental disorder.

> "The only reason that I spoke somewhat freely is that in a way I knew that being found 'not guilty by reason of insanity' was the only way that I could escape going to jail for a long period of time. When asked if I thought I was sick, I answered, 'I must be. Why would I do the things I do if I'm not?' "

In some instances, a criminal may plan in advance to use mental illness as a defense if he gets caught. He knows that others already regard his behavior as deviant, if not bizarre. So he can use this to help him establish a "history" of mental illness. He may go so far as to sign himself into a hospital voluntarily to establish that he has a mental condition. This officially gives him a "previous history of mental illness," which can be of use later. Another possibility is to enter a hospital after arrest and demand a mental evaluation, thereby stalling judicial proceedings. Not only do criminals read law books, but they also learn about mental illness. Besides consulting books, they ferret out information from other criminals, who readily offer advice.

> C was locked up in a cell with Al, another prisoner, also in for rape, who had previously been at Saint Elizabeths Hospital. When the lawyer talked with C, he made it clear that C was in serious trouble, having been indicted for four rapes. Al read the indictment and talked to C about it, advising him to try to get admitted to Saint Elizabeths. Otherwise, C might receive up to a 50-year prison sentence. Al pointed out that C might get out of the hospital in 5 years. C, who was reluctant to plead insanity, finally realized that this was the path to take.

The criminal is counseled by other criminals and sometimes by lawyers on exactly how to act. He may have members of his family, who already view him as sick, petition the court. He then puts on his act, simulating mental illness. This may occur at any time—on apprehension, in court before the judge, or in jail.

The malingering may be crude or subtle and sophisticated. For example, a prisoner may feign an attempt at suicide. But, in any case, if such behavior occurs before trial, the judge has little choice but to send the defendant to a hospital.

> C had six counts lodged against him. While in jail, he was allowed access to law books and discovered that, if found guilty for the six counts, he could wind up in prison for up to 52 years. Besides, it would be Lorton Penitentiary, and his impression of Lorton was distinctly unfavorable. Under these circumstances, his confidence about getting by with a minimal sentence began to fade. C had earlier rejected his lawyer's urging to plead insanity because he did not want to be considered insane. But when the outlook seemed bleak, C changed his mind. He then decided to put on an act. During his trial, he made a weak and abortive attempt to hang himself. The lawyers submitted the appropriate papers, and he was sent to D.C. General Hospital. There, he tore up a painting he had done, remained by himself, slept behind his bed, paced the floor, and took a double dose of sleeping pills. The outcome was that he was found incompetent and was sent from D.C. General to Saint Elizabeths Hospital.

These suicidal gestures are just that—calculated gestures. They are to be distinguished from the very few cases of serious suicide attempts in confinement. Of course, it is often difficult for the staff of an institution to distinguish what is serious from what is not. When this occurs in an institution for juveniles, it has to be taken gravely.

> "It is my understanding that he went AWOL and was returned the same day. So far as I can determine, his reason for going AWOL was an effort to see his mother. He was placed in isolation. On the 23rd of ———, he was found hanging by his sheet. Exact or specific data about this is unavailable to me at this present moment. There are some indications that this was a genuine suicidal attempt, and no suicidal maneuver in a child of this age [16] can be considered lightly even under the most extreme theatrical conditions" (Psychiatrist in a state training school).

Juveniles, too, learn that it is advantageous to be regarded as "sick," and they fake suicide attempts and symptoms of mental disorder.

The catalog of tactics to establish mental illness is virtually endless. The crudest involve acting "crazy" without attempting to simulate a specific diagnostic syndrome. A criminal may pace back and forth, "see" visions, "hear" voices, and generally pretend to be out of touch with reality. Then he earns a psychotic diagnosis. He may convince others that he is "schizoid" by keeping to himself and not relating to others. Some claim amnesia for the events of a crime. Others establish evidence of a paranoid psychosis, claiming that people have been spying on them, poisoning their food, or in some way trying to "get" them. Some fake epileptic seizures and try to establish evidence of an organic disorder. To this end, criminals have taken drugs before electroencephalography, in order to alter the results.

We must emphasize that not one of the hospital records of people with whom we have worked contains a valid account of what has really occurred. Institutional records of which we have copies all contain the lies and self-serving stories that the criminals have fed to their examiners in attempting to be adjudged mentally ill. The following contrasts the version of events the criminal gave us with what he told the hospital.

> C had been arrested for the armed robbery of the Sunday collection plate at a church. Because he did this in the midst of the service, before 500 congregants, he knew that the evidence was there to convict him. In the precinct cell, he wasted no time in trying to appear mentally ill. He attempted to seem disorganized, taking off his coat and throwing it on the floor, tearing his shirt off, taking off the rest of his clothes, and sitting on the floor naked. Bond was set at $3,500 for robbery and $300 for possession of the gun. However, the bondsman would not agree to have him released, because he was from out of state, and a number of unsolved robberies had occurred about the same time. Al-

though he showed signs of mental illness in the precinct cell, C acted normal in jail, once he figured that he would only be there for a day or two. When he realized that he was going to be confined indefinitely, he put to full use his knowledge gained from a course in abnormal psychology and from working on a V.A. hospital psychiatric ward.

He walked the length of the dormitory with a blank stare, not looking at anyone, and with a gait that was bent, awkward, and contorted. He took a sheet to the bathroom, took his clothes off, wrapped himself in the sheet, and sat in the corner staring and drooling. A jail attendant realized that there was something wrong when the staff could not even get his name from him. Later, he was taken on a stretcher to the infirmary. At this time he started to tremble and mumble that he was Jesus Christ. He figured that, if they saw this, they might believe that he robbed the church owing to his being mixed up about religion. As the doctor was checking him, C heard the word "catatonic." This gave direction to his efforts from then on. C was given medication and was strapped down. When unfettered, he did what he retrospectively called "some silly things." He refused to eat and screamed that the food was poisoned. When the doctor gave him an intravenous injection, it hurt, and he responded to the pain of the needle. The doctor then suspected that he was all right, because catatonics characteristically do not respond to pain in this way. But, because of all his other bizarre behavior, it was not believed that he was feigning. C resumed the mumbling, awkward gait, and so on, and he did not eat.

On the day he went to court, C realized that he must make his act convincing. In the clothes room, he made no effort to dress, acted confused, and appeared not to know what to do. He let an attendant move his arm, but he would hold the arm in position and would not move. He allowed the attendant to dress him, but did not communicate. When he did not respond to the lawyer, the lawyer was also convinced. In court, he said nothing, remained rigid, and stared into space during the hearing. There was quick agreement that he should be remanded to Saint Elizabeths Hospital.

At the hospital, he continued the act, giving his name as Jesus Christ. He continued his posturing, but only when observed. He had a private room and went around saying little to anyone. He would sit in a corner for a time immobile and then suddenly race to a water fountain as though his life depended on it. When an attendant was going to inject medication, C became hysterical at the sight of the needle and claimed that others were out to kill him. Therefore he got large doses of medicine orally. C said later that this period of not eating was difficult, because the Thorazine had increased his appetite.

C's sister visited every Saturday and knew what he was doing, but she played along. They would sit in a corner of the room, and she would tell an attendant that they were talking, but that her brother failed to make sense. One day, when C was watching a football game, he strained his neck to look at a pretty female attendant. He was observed, and the attendant claimed that C had been putting on an act. C got scared and began to wonder whether he had been convincing. When he saw the doctor, he hobbled, drooled, stared, and was unresponsive. Then his medication was increased to a sizable dose of Trilafon.

At his staff conference, C continued with the act. After the court declared him incompetent, an observant attendant commented, "You can straighten out, now that you have made it." C then tried to convince everyone that he was improving rapidly. But his show had been too good, and he had outslicked himself. The staff still thought of him as quite sick. Frustrated by this, C eloped from the hospital and was gone for 2 months. Finally, he was returned to the hospital. C went so far as to write the doctor a letter detailing how he had malingered. When this was brought up in the group meeting, it was doubted that he could feign such a condition for so long. In fact, the letter claiming that he had faked everything was interpreted as still further evidence of mental disorder.

C's account of the hospital's view of him is verified in the official hospital record. When admitted, he was described as "mute and manifesting waxy flexibility." At the screening conference, he was seen as "withdrawn" and with "considerable delusions," such as thinking that he was being poisoned by the people around him. After his elopement and return, C was evaluated as follows:

"He is completely oriented and without delusions or hallucinations. . . . In view of his marked improvement, we are going to recommend him as competent to stand trial. . . . His intellectual status seems to be restored to levels prior to his onset of psychotic behavior.

Diagnosis: 295.24 Schizophrenia, catatonic type, withdrawn.
Recommendation: The patient is competent to stand trial.
Condition on Discharge: Recovered."

In the examination, the criminal does more of the examining than the examiner. The objective is to find out what will best fit into the interviewer's theory of mental illness and respond accordingly. (We shall describe this process further in Chapter 8.) The attempt to fake mental illness does not always succeed. Malingering is occasionally overdone to the point that it is obvious to even the most casual observer.

In addition to the Saint Elizabeths files, we have records from other hospitals to which prisoners are sent by the courts for psychiatric evaluation. The task of the staff is to arrive at a diagnosis. While interviewing a patient, an examiner often encounters contradictions in behavior patterns and thinking that may seem foreign or illogical to him. What is not understood is likely to be labeled "psychotic." Even if the doctor cannot identify the psychotic process involved, he suspects that it is there. "Chronic undifferentiated schizophrenia" is a widely used diagnosis. It conveys that there is something wrong with the patient, but it is so vague that one does not know what it is. Sometimes, a criminal earns a psychotic diagnosis by displaying the symptoms convincingly. But he may be labeled schizophrenic, because the examiner does not know what else to call him.

Most institutional personnel do their best to evaluate and make a reasonable disposition of each case. They look to interviews, staff observations, and physical, psychologic, and psychiatric examinations to shed some light on the makeup of an inmate.

> "Unfortunately, there was no clear information given as to the reason for his commitment. . . . Nothing is known of his home, or any court record or of his past health. [C] himself, because of personality problems and possibly because of intellectual limitations, cannot give any significantly clear information about any of these areas. Consequently, no reliable evaluation and recommendations can be made for this boy, except as dealing with the immediate present situation, and even there the recommendations and evaluation are considerably hampered. . . . As seen by me today, his true affect is under considerable repression. . . . I think his judgment can be considered minimally adequate. Intellect appears to be retarded and/or undeveloped."

The staff was frustrated by this youngster's failure to respond. In trying to explain the boy's behavior, the new diagnostic consideration of mental deficiency was introduced.

Some criminals become very knowledgeable about the construction and interpretation of widely used psychologic tests. They attempt to figure out what is necessary to convince an examiner of something and then "feed" him accordingly. When a criminal wants to be admitted to a hospital, he is ready to show "pathology" on a test. When he wants to be released, he tries to convince the doctor that he is without mental disorder and withholds responses that he thinks might be interpreted as signs of mental illness. Attempts to beat the tests can be crude; for example, a man who wants to appear sexually deviant may give florid sexual responses on a Rorschach test, and then withhold all such responses when he wants to be released. Or a criminal may take great pains in the way he approaches psychologic tests, orchestrating his responses to produce a technically perfect case for mental illness.

> C had read a lot about tests, including Schafer's *The Clinical Application of Psychological Tests*.* He had also read psychiatric textbooks, so

---

* Shafer, Roy. *The Clinical Application of Psychological Tests.* New York: International Universities Press, 1948.

he was informed as to the characteristics of schizophrenic thought and behavior. His efforts during testing were directed toward establishing a schizophrenic condition. His IQ score of 80 on the Wechsler Adult Intelligence Scale was interpreted as lowered owing to mental illness. C performed erratically on several subtests. On Digit Symbol, he paused in the middle, ran off the page, and appeared confused and hostile—all this was designed to show that he falls apart under stress. This was the pattern on other IQ subtests; he would begin to do something in the correct way, show confusion, and then withdraw or otherwise perform erratically. On the Word Association Test, he responded quickly and illogically. For example, if the examiner said "chair," he would respond "ice cream." Another pattern was not to respond at all or to drift off and ask the examiner an irrelevant question, such as whether the watch he was wearing was a microphone. C pointed out that each examining situation is different, and that he cased out the examiner thoroughly. As C put it, "If they can't find it, they will invent it. You just play along and wait for an opening. When they start fishing, then you give them what they are looking for. You let them hook themselves." He stated that the less one tries to convince the examiner that he is crazy, the better off he is. If the criminal makes too many "way-out statements," malingering will be suspected. C's pattern was to maintain a facade of competence and to show psychotic behavior only occasionally.

C indicated that the examiner's initial impression is crucial. Consequently, he would appear unkempt, reluctant to enter the room, and hesitant to sit down and then would ask the examiner for identification. If he wanted to appear more withdrawn and slowed down, he might take pills before the meeting. If the examiner were suspicious and aggressive, he would not act aggressively psychotic. He stated that, if one trades verbal blows with a doctor, the doctor will realize that the person is in contact. Thus, attempts at malingering will be discovered, or at least suspect. Instead, one becomes cooperative, apathetic, withdrawn, and bland. In other words, he does not attempt to look psychotic—"You do not convince the examiner you are crazy; rather, the examiner must convince himself."

On the Draw-a-Person Test, C would draw a stick figure and place it in a peculiar position on the paper. He would omit a few details, such as hands or feet. He might dress the figure strangely or have it hold a knife or gun. He would draw things that could be interpreted symbolically, such as a tree trunk with a hole in the middle. On the Thematic Apperception Test, he would show problems in concentration by not following instructions. He would fail to tell a story and instead give only a cursory description of the picture. If the examiner pushed him for a story, he might refer to a radio program or something unrelated to the card: "I would give them a trip to Disneyland." Depending on his mood, he might tell a long, drawn-out story.

C knew that the Bender Gestalt is a test for brain damage, and he would usually copy the designs normally. He stated that it would be too blatant if he started messing up what is essentially a simple copying task. Again, it would depend on his perception of the examiner. He could always resort to copying the figures inaccurately, stopping in the middle of the picture, and placing it oddly on a page.

On the Rorschach test, C might give a straight record of popular responses, but do so with schizophrenic mannerisms. He knew the importance of reaction times and some of the criteria for diagnosing thought disorder in schizophrenia. There were other things that he might do: ignore the card and say that it looked like an ink blot; see animals, insects, and bugs; give movement responses; not respond to color, thereby showing "color shock"; pick out a small segment of the blot; respond to the white part; give bizarre answers; block entirely; or show a flight of ideas. For example, he might articulate a percept, such as "Mickey Mantle hitting a home run," and then deny that he saw it. With inquiry on the Rorschach test, he would indicate confusion, withdraw, appear apathetic and uninterested, and sigh a few times.

C made a study of the Minnesota Multiphasic Personality Inventory (MMPI) and knew about the validity checks. He said that he would give close to normal answers, but respond to some questions bizarrely. On Sentence Completion, he might alter his handwriting, as by starting with small letters and getting larger, use neologisms, make a letter backwards, show withdrawal behavior, and do whatever else was necessary to show the examiner that he was not in touch with reality.

Unquestionably, C's attempts at subterfuge were successful. He amassed a series of schizophrenic diagnoses.

Examination brings out underlying paranoid attitudes. From time to time he has experienced hallucinations and delusional ideas. There have been episodes of detachment from reality, and feelings of confusion. About a year ago while in court he slashed his arm when a judge refused to examine a cookie that the patient felt was poisoned. . . . At times he has been suspicious of his lawyers, has experienced grandiose ideas and persecution. Insight is superficial and limited and judgment impaired. . . . I have reviewed the report of psychological examination submitted by Dr. A as well as reports of prior examination sent to me by (C's) counsel. . . . Although much of his behavior appears to be typical of the personality disorder, I believe that the underlying illness is more serious and indicative of a longstanding chronic schizophrenic process. He has poor control of his impulses, and when not in a limited or structured environment he is likely to break out in explosive or antisocial acts. Anger, hostility and frustration are intense. For these reasons he must be considered potentially aggressive and dangerous. It is my opinion that he is suffering from a major illness, i.e. schizophrenia, and that he lacks substantial capacity to tell right from wrong, to appreciate the wrongfulness of his conduct and of conforming his conduct to the requirements of the law. Furthermore, it is my opinion that this condition exists now and did exist at the time of the offense for which he is presently charged (from a psychologic report).

We have studied at length more than 100 patients of Saint Elizabeths Hospital who have been adjudicated "not guilty by reason of insanity." From *our frame of reference,* their diagnoses do not stand up.

THE ATTEMPT TO GET OUT—"POINT-SCORING"

Once a criminal is confined, his objective is to move from maximal to minimum security and finally gain his release. Just as in crime, each criminal has his M.O. and personal style. He predicates what he does on his assessment of the personnel. "Point-scoring" refers to the criminal's appearing to cooperate with the institution and thereby exploiting the system for his own purposes. The criminal tries to impress the staff with his sincerity about reforming by appearing to go along with the program. In their efforts to obtain release, most criminals will eventually follow this course. However, some are obstinate and want to get out on their own terms. They refuse to subordinate themselves to the system, and they consider it demeaning to engage in point-scoring behavior.

Through point-scoring, the criminal conveys to others that he is now functioning within the expectations of society. Thus, he may participate in furthering his education and earn a high-school equivalency diploma through a General Education Development (G.E.D.) program. He attends group therapy, sports, occupational therapy, and church and engages in activities that are designed to foster adjustment to the outside world. Some participate out of sincerity to change, but this is usually short-lived. Sometimes, a criminal discovers something that allows him to develop a talent and spend time agreeably. But most of the activities he scorns. Although he does not want what most of the programs offer, the criminal will participate, at least sporadically, to keep the staff favorably disposed toward him.

The accomplishments of prisoners in institutional programs are often impressive to the outside world. They earn diplomas, tutor others, show leadership in activities run by civic clubs, and create items of artistic merit. Some seek out particularly the activities in which they think they can gain recognition for leadership. It is common, once a criminal is stationed at a work assignment or in a position of some responsibility, for him to try to run the place. Of course, not all criminals want to be bothered with leadership. Those who abstain from leadership consider the activities as less deserving of their time and energy. They may also use the leaders to get what they want, but they do not want the burden of heading an activity themselves. One need only note the large numbers of criminals who decline to run for office in prisoner governments and therapeutic communities. They refuse to volunteer to do what they scorn, unless they believe that there are truly some big gains to be realized. Instead, token participation gets them what they want. However, it does not result in change.

The man who cons is almost always suspected of point-scoring, but not so the man regarded as a "muscleman." When he cooperates, he is often deemed to have changed the most dramatically.

> At the age of 19, C had been in at least three prisons for a variety of offenses. He had been hard to manage in every place, but, on transfer to a fourth institution, he decided to cooperate. This cooperation prompted the staff to consider releasing him on parole.

From a staff report:

> "In spite of the unfavorable response to the institutional programs at ————, [C] has compiled a very favorable record at this institution. He has maintained a clear conduct record here; at initial classification, he was assigned to the Food Service Department and has remained on that assignment to date, consistently earning "very good" and "outstanding" monthly work reports. In April, he was assigned to Vocational Training: Cooking, and after an average start made outstanding progress. He has made frequent use of the library facilities here. . . . Though previously associated and affiliated with unstable inmates [at the other institutions], he quickly disassociated himself from this type of inmate shortly after arrival here. He has always conducted himself in a quiet and gentlemanly manner and has gained the respect of both inmates and staff."

Not long after this favorable report, C was paroled. Two months later, he was arrested for drunkeness, and nine months later, on three charges of assault with a deadly weapon. The string of crimes continued and eventually included a homicide. His "outstanding" work and "gentlemanly" conduct had not altered or reflected his criminal patterns.

OTHER EXPRESSIONS OF CRIMINALITY

Very few prisoners are content with a point-scoring existence. Their minds are racing with criminal thinking, even while they appear to the staff to be lethargic and uncommunicative. Furthermore, the criminal in confinement seeks to establish himself, just as he does on the street. He requires excitement, and point-scoring is concurrent with other thrusts for power. A videotape of twenty-four hours of confinement would show scores of little incidents in which the criminal stirs up excitement.

> C would bait others into some kind of argument and ultimately achieve a victory. For example, he used wire to tie together the shoelaces of a

sleeping man so that it would be very difficult to unravel. The man awoke and started hurling accusations at someone other than C. There was a lot of shouting back and forth, while C stood there thoroughly enjoying being a witness to the commotion he had caused. Had the act been attributed to C, he might have gotten an even greater kick out of it. His pattern was to bait people, have them fall for it, and then verbally master them in an argument. The victory was his, because he had the last word. Then he would pursue it even further and score points with the staff by saying that he was improved, inasmuch as in the past he would have killed the person.

In other words, the criminal takes a disturbance he created and, in recounting it, makes himself look good to the staff. Such incidents occur day after day in confinement. It may be a dispute in a card game, an argument over what television program to watch, a contest over who got in line for lunch first, etc.

The number one activity in confinement is talk, and getting out is the topic uppermost in everyone's mind. There are many discussions with each other about how to deal with the staff, what legal measures to take, how to behave on the ward, and so forth. On one ward at Saint Elizabeths, nightly "seminars," as they were called, were held to discuss how to work one's way out of maximum security. There is also speculation about elopements and murmurings about breakouts. Comparatively few of these materialize, but when they do, they provide endless rounds of conversation for days.

There is also a lot of boasting about past crimes. The criminal acts as he does on the street, exaggerating the number of his offenses, the amount of the proceeds, and the slickness or force he has used. In fact, it is characteristic for him to boast of crimes he has never committed. He often attributes to himself crimes that others whom he admires have gotten away with. Criminals who have been less inclined to use physical force may make up stories in order to gain acceptance by the tougher elements. Men who are afraid to fight may speak of guns that they never had and fights in which they never raised a fist.

> In prison, C got himself known as a dangerous man. He told the other prisoners how he had knifed someone. In fact, C threatened one man in prison with his fist, which was extremely unusual for him. By such talk and action, he established himself as a man with whom others should not fool. He was accepted by the criminals who he believed would otherwise pose a threat to him.

The criminal is reluctant to part with his secrets, and there is much lying by omission. He glories in letting out hints of what he has done, but avoids making firm statements. Establishing an image is paramount.

Another common topic is sex. Criminals share information on where to find available women on the outside and how to conquer them. They boast about females whom they have never "had" and exaggerate the details of encounters that actually took place. There is tremendous excitement in recounting the details of sexual activity. They also scheme sexual activity in confinement.

In still another part of the daily repartee, the criminal holds forth on various topics. He builds himself up as a source of information on almost any topic. Little of his point of view is based on substantive knowledge. For him, however, the actual issue is less important than his promoting himself as an expert. In fact, he may take opposing sides of the same issue at different times.

Prison does not make a man criminal—i.e., he already has criminal thinking patterns—but prison does offer education in criminal M.O.'s. One man referred to the Lorton Youth Center as "the young pimp school." In prisons and hospitals criminal behavior is not imposed on the criminal; rather, he must seek out whatever it is that he wants. Others are not out there teaching and coaching unless they are asked, and even then they are mainly boasting, because, for the most part, they want to keep their secrets to themselves. The criminal does have the opportunity to learn new M.O.'s. A man who is on his way to the penitentiary, especially a younger criminal, may actually look forward to receiving the "education" that is available. Once he arrives, he finds willing teachers—although their mentors may not tell them everything. There are also some criminals who stay to themselves, believing that they already know what they need to know and that they are above the constant chattering, bantering, and bickering.

Violating patterns do not cease simply because a criminal is locked up. In fact, with greater restraints, there is even more of a challenge to attempt the forbidden. Youngsters who are confined in reformatories, detention centers, and receiving homes are involved in sex, property, and assault crimes just as they were on the street. They may steal from the institution, as well as from other inmates. The extortion that took place on school grounds now occurs in prison. Assaults occur when two individuals or groups insist on having their own way. Homosexuality for privilege and profit, sex with girls in coed institutions, and use of alcohol and drugs all occur in juvenile centers. The youngsters learn more about how to avoid punishment than they knew before. It is in these places that self-mutilation and playing crazy begin, as routes to more advantageous treatment. As a result of such behavior, some prisoners avoid severe punishment and may be moved to hospital-like settings within the institutions. Escape is often more feasible from these institutions.

In jails and other maximum-security institutions, the adult criminal creates opportunities for violation. The newspapers have carried many accounts of what goes on in these places. Stealing from one another is routine. If a man sets anything of value down and leaves it, it is unlikely to be there a few minutes later. Prisoners working in the prison industries or in hospital jobs steal from the institution and from each other. Fights are commonplace when there is a group of people, each of whom is determined to have his own way. Physical attack and homicide are part of the law of this jungle.

Sexual activity is also widespread. It occurs with other criminals, with staff members if feasible, and with patients on the grounds (in the case of a hospital). Considerable attention has been given to the matter of coercive homosexual practices. We have found that many criminals who claim that their first experience was in confinement actually had previous experience or wanted such activity earlier but were too timid to seek it out. Some are bisexual and had a homosexual history long before confinement. A criminal may be fearful of homosexuality, but still secretly desire it. Once the act is accomplished, the fears are dispelled and he is the one in pursuit. The point is that a person who claims that he was intimidated may have wanted it, but there are different methods of operating. A criminal may not actively seek out a partner, and he may be unresponsive to someone's blunt approach. But, he may encourage others to play up to him and to seduce an already willing partner. If a person wanted no part of homosexual activity and were coerced by a group, lasting psychologic scars could result. This has been reported often in the press, but we have encountered only one case of coercion in the fourteen years of our work.

In institutions in which medication is prescribed, criminals may exchange pills "for kicks."* This is especially frequent in adolescent and young-adult settings, where inmates indiscriminately take almost anything into their bodies that they think will provide a thrill. On one ward, the criminals split table-tennis balls in half and sniffed them, claiming that one could get "high" from a chemical ingredient in them. In some settings, the staff may collude in bringing in drugs, alcohol, escape tools, and other contraband.

When things do not go the way the criminal wants, he is quick to criticize and blame others. Staff and administration are always popular whipping boys. The criminal erupts with righteous indignation whenever anyone interferes with him. He complains about not getting what he deserves and charges that others are being treated preferentially. Some criminals resort to bullying, intimidation, and force. They may threaten violence if they are prohibited from doing what they want. This can upset a ward, cell block, or dormitory. The criminal may threaten to go over the heads of the staff to more influential people and in doing so jeopardize the jobs of those who thwart

---

* This subject will be treated in depth in Volume 3.

him. Threats of revenge after leaving confinement are not uncommon. Of course, before acting, the criminal knows the institution and personnel well enough to use the most appropriate tactics.

> C believed that, if he directly physically assaulted prison personnel, they would beat him up and possibly even kill him. This idea was based on events in C's place of confinement. Consequently, C slashed into his own body to convince others that he was "crazy." Simultaneously, he destroyed property and attacked other people. Because the prison staff saw his attempt as "self-destruction," they regarded him as mentally ill and did not retaliate. Instead, arrangements were made for him in a psychiatric wing. C provided confirmatory evidence of his "insanity" and largely controlled the others.

The authorities may tolerate a wider latitude of behavior when they believe that a prisoner is mentally ill. C received psychiatric treatment owing to the actions mentioned above, but he sometimes outdid himself. In one prison, he was admitted to the psychiatric division, but was so unmanageable that he was returned to the cellblock.

When a criminal violates or is taken to task for the infraction of a rule, if he gives an explanation that appears to be based on insight, the penalty may be light or dispensed with altogether. The criminal is fairly certain before his violation how he will be dealt with later. This is true mostly in mental hospital settings. Often, just the right word is sufficient. For example, if he goes off the hospital grounds and acknowledges that he was "acting out" his anxiety or claims that he wanted to get caught, he may be praised, rather than penalized. Such insight is viewed as evidence of change. Serious offenses—such as destruction of property, beating up other prisoners, and assaulting staff members—do sometimes result in punishment. It may be placement in the "hole" in a prison or in seclusion at a hospital. The criminal knows beforehand that he runs this risk by behaving in such fashion. Although he knows that he is going to "solitary" at his own invitation, he starts screaming about the injustice of it even before he gets there. This attitude toward punishment has persisted since childhood, when the criminal violated, was punished, and then complained of being mistreated. Of course, the criminal tries to weasel out of punishment by his usual tactics—lying, distorting facts, blaming others, and so forth. If all else fails, then he maintains a stiff upper lip and shows everyone that he can take it. He serves his time and then either returns to old patterns, perhaps being more careful so as not to get caught, or decides that he can accomplish more by changing his stance and scoring points.

In some institutions, a clique or competing cliques representing a small number of inmates succeed in assuming control. A major criticism of prison conditions is that the inmates are at the mercy of the most aggressive people. In some situations, the "crime leaders" have such a grip on prison life that they have the power to determine who lives and who dies (*The Evening Star and The Washington Daily News*, 12/14/72). They reign through a system of favors, payoffs, and intimidation. In such settings, the staff is often too fearful to counter the steady erosion of its authority. The staff may be afraid to enforce discipline, particularly if there is violence. Administrators may take the position that catering to those who are violent will lead them to calm down. This notion usually turns out to be in error, because the criminal views greater freedom as license. Guards and administrators are sometimes at odds with respect to disciplinary policy. For example, some guards at the (Washington) D.C. Jail charged in 1973 that they had less authority than the prison inmates (*Washington Star News*, 8/16/73). The criminal exploits any division within the staff ranks and presses his cause further. This, in turn, permits ringleaders to gain even more authority, and additional violent incidents often ensue. When concessions are won from the administration, the leaders of the reform movement often do not want any part of the responsibility of actually working to implement the reforms. Many hospitals have trouble contending with criminals whom they consider agitators and try to send them elsewhere as soon as possible, rather than have wards disrupted.

THE "CRIMINAL CODE"

Popular lore has it that criminals adhere to a code of not informing on one another. The "code" is a myth, in that it is contingent on what is going to happen to the criminal in question. As one put it, "Every man has his price." Generally speaking, if a criminal can escape punishment or reduce its severity he will not hesitate to tell what he knows. He may turn state's evidence in return for immunity. If he is already confined and is facing a long sentence, informing on another criminal is not likely to get him anywhere and may result in his antagonizing fellow inmates. However, he may "snitch" to gain a privilege or as a means of retaliation. The criminal code amounts to what one man termed, "Fuck everybody else but me." In an interesting phenomenon that occurs regularly, if one criminal informs on another and the two meet later in confinement, they are likely to greet each other as buddies. This is in line with the criminal's great changeability and tendency to do whatever suits his purpose at the time.

STATES OF MIND

In confinement, as well as outside, the criminal's mental equilibrium shifts frequently. Periods of self-disgust occur when a confined criminal comes face to face with the fact that he has accomplished little in his life. Confinement itself attests to his failure even as a criminal. In such a state of mind, he may consider suicide. But the criminal rarely reaches the point of committing suicide; like other states of mind, this one does not last. He may get as far as writing his own epitaph, but he fears death more than he fears living. Thus, he emerges from a dejected, angry state into another frame of mind. He may return to violation. Or he may pray, meditate, and read philosophic or religious tracts to try to find answers; he may even try to bring religion to his fellow inmates.

Throughout the criminal's confinement, there are times when his sentimentality is visible. This may be seen in how he decorates his room. One man wrote to his girl friend about such a a project:

> "I'm getting along pretty good, and my old room has been plastered and painted, and I have put up 19 pictures of animals, landscapes, birds and children all over the walls. They look nice because I have them spaced evenly."

In confinement, the criminal may draw and paint, turn out handicrafts, listen to music, or play an instrument. To be sure, he has lots of time to reflect on life. He may express his thoughts in writing that he publishes in the prison paper or submits to an outside publication. He reserves the more revealing, personal sentiments to himself, because he does not want to look "weak" or like a "sissy." The criminal may be especially expressive of his hopes for a new life in his letters to a girl friend.

> "As I see it now, as time goes by, no matter what happens to you or to me, there will be a day when we are finally together and then we won't have nothing to worry about except how to make up for the time we are apart, to build a life together that will endure any trial or test of our love for each other. . . . I will take care of you in every way. . . . Everything is going to work out for us."

Isolated from society, the criminal may appreciate others in a new way, at least temporarily. He may pour out his thoughts in verse:

LOVE

There are all forms of Love
    In the world, as you know,
In the heavens above
    And the earth here below;
But they can't compare
    To the love you show for me,
Even when I've been unfair
    And did many things inconsiderately.

Yours is the love that my soul inspires;
    It is shown in oh so many ways.
It is the reason behind all my desires
    To do only those things that will elicit your praise.

I have known the love of many women
    And the pleasure that it brings,
But all their loves can never rend
    The joy of which my heart sings.
So what can I tell you,
    Really, what can I say?
Just thank you, my darling,
    For loving me in your own special way!

This state of mind is transient, as later events bear out when the criminal hurts the very people whom he professes to love.

Some prisoners write essays, letters, and verses on social problems:

EUPHONY OF SOCIETY '66 (The Lyndon Rock)

O wondrous leader of the pandemonium race
How many will die to save your face?
You bombed Hanoi-Haiphong while the ghettos burned
All pleas for peace you have spurned.
Dead soldiers, toasted people, hate in a flood
What will quench your thirst for blood?
How many will die to propagate
A decadent image that so many hate?
Leader of the Great Society, you have star-billing.
Your name is well known; you can stop the killing.
You have the fame and power you so desperately craved.
You're No. One in this farce depraved.
How your ego swells when the cameras click.
You're the epitome of what makes this world so sick.
You can't solve the problems in your own backyard.
Where is the well-being you project so hard?
In Asia you are the wolf in the guise of a lamb.
Regain your honor—get out of Viet Nam.

The author of this antiviolence poem was himself a very violent criminal. Such writings express attitudes that are sincerely held at the moment of authorship. However, even during the periods of such writing, criminals do become violent, depending on circumstances.

At the same time that the criminal is utilizing his talents, he may also be impressing institutional authorities. For example, he may truly enjoy doing a painting. The staff members may think that this shows a "good" facet of the criminal and commended him for it. Some prisons have art shows and even put the work up for sale. The high degree of performance and sentiments expressed, however, do not preclude concurrent or subsequent criminal activity.

The criminal may experience psychosomatic discomfort during confinement: gastrointestinal distress, headaches, and so forth. Many will not seek treatment for this, because they view it as a sign of weakness even to mention the symptoms or because they fear that the doctor will find something seriously wrong with them. However, they may use their symptoms to their own advantage, if it helps them to avoid responsibilities that they find particularly odious; if a criminal is regarded as ill, fewer demands may be made on him. A criminal may even fake illness to make things easier on himself. The following is an account of a prison doctor who describes the inmate's use of prison medical facilities as "the epitome of a copout."

> One can often acquire a single room (perhaps air-conditioned) by pretending to be ill. In this aseptic environment, a healthy appetite can be satisfied by walking only a few steps to the food carts, rather than waiting interminably in the prison cafeteria. As hospital patients are not required to do any work, they are free to while away the days in endless conversations, in lethargic states before the television set, or engrossed in weathered paperbacks by Zane Grey or Frank Slaughter (West, 1971, p. 107).

Psychotic episodes also occur in confinement, although infrequently. Confinement psychoses often have a religious content: the criminal considers himself to be in touch with God or believes that he is a personal agent of God. Of course, if the criminal is psychotic, he is not competent to stand trial. Those who observe the criminal in a postarrest psychosis may erroneously conclude that he was in the same condition at the time of the crime. Quite different from this type of psychosis, of course, are the toxic psychoses due to extensive use of drugs or alcohol. The criminal's nonarrestable phases, which include psychosis, are discussed in Chapter 7.

RELEASE

From his very first day of confinement, the criminal has believed that he should be released. Every day spent in prison he has regarded as an injustice. When he is approaching a hearing or conference about his release, he believes that his getting out is assured—it is as good as accomplished. If the decision is not what he wants, an outburst of angry, righteous indignation ensues, and the criminal contends that his rights have been violated.

Nearly every criminal knows that, over a span of time, he is likely to return to crime; at least, he never forecloses the possibility. While in confinement, the criminal who may be on the threshold of release may be scheming crimes that he plans to commit once he is released. In fact, we have known of criminals setting up crimes right from the hospital, to be committed on the street. In transient states of mind, the criminal is sincere in expressing the belief that he will live responsibly. But it is not an enduring conviction.

When the criminal is paroled or granted a conditional release, some conditions are usually specified, such as holding a job and reporting to an officer regularly. Parole officers usually have heavy caseloads, and supervision is therefore perfunctory. For the most part, the criminal will satisfy minimal requirements. He continues to "go along with the program," as he did in confinement; this keeps others satisfied that he is progressing. He dutifully shows up for appointments and brings his payslips to indicate that he is working. If he is to have psychotherapy, he tries to select a therapist who is sympathetic to his point of view, particularly one who believes that circumstances are more to blame for criminal behavior than the criminal. If the criminal is not working, he claims that employers will not hire him because of their reluctance to have "ex-cons" work for them, or he says that a disability of some sort disqualifies him. Even if the criminal does not appear for probation meetings for weeks at a time, he may not be tracked down by the busy officer. Some officers have known that the criminal is violating; but, rather than try to pursue him, they hope that the criminal will straighten out. Also, there are fewer problems in bringing him in if they wait for the criminal to be arrested. Some criminals even try to use the parole or probation officer as a character reference, on the basis of a belief that the officer is satisfied with their performance. The officer usually has good things to say about the criminal based on the impression that the criminal has conveyed to him. Of course, what the criminal has conveyed has been full of lies of omission and distortions.*

Most important about the postconfinement period is that old patterns of criminal thought and action continue and expand. There may be some self-restraint for a while, because the memory of confinement is still fresh. In time, however, the criminal wants greater excitement and commits crimes. The same people are arrested again, often for the same type of crime and sometimes for altogether different crimes. The official recidivism statistics do not give an accurate picture, because the criminal is apprehended for far fewer crimes than he commits.

In recent years, there has been growing support in some areas for having criminals reside in halfway houses, rather than releasing them directly from

---

* Our source for this information is not only criminals, but also probation and parole officers.

jail. The guiding principle is that a man can be helped to adjust to society better by a transitional process than by an abrupt release. In a pioneering Washington, D.C., program conceived in 1970, the convicted young felon was allowed to go directly to a halfway house and bypass jail entirely. This was acclaimed by the mayor (*The Evening Star*, 12/29/70) as "one of the greatest breakthroughs in corrections management I know of." The effectiveness of the halfway house has been a subject of considerable public controversy. The criminal, being what he is, continues the same patterns wherever he goes. In the second chapter of Volume 2, we discuss the halfway house and other programs that have been established for rehabilitating the criminal.

If the criminal is arrested again, the same set of tactics begins all over —except that now he can play on society's sympathy for the plight of the "ex-con." With the correctional system coming under attack everywhere, the criminal has even more to add to his presentation of himself as an unjustly treated victim. The authorities again and again hear the hard-luck stories of the "ex-con" who "couldn't make it" in society. Criminals who have recourse to the hospital have an "ace in the hole": A man gets admitted to the hospital, is declared "not guilty by reason of insanity," and receives a mental-illness diagnosis. Once discharged, if he is arrested again, particularly if it is within the same jurisdiction, he uses the mental-illness tactic again. This time, however, it is on the books that he has a record of mental illness. If he piles up a series of mental hospitalizations, as some do, he is in an even better position to beat the charge, because he is more likely to be regarded as chronic and incurable. Examiners speak of "relapses" and of "continuing mental illness." There are ways in which long proceedings can be avoided and the criminal assured of a speedy return to the hospital. If he remains on "convalescent status" or "conditional release" for a long time and is then apprehended, he avoids a sentence simply by being called in to the hospital, because he is still an active patient on the hospital rolls. This can go on for years, virtually assuring a criminal of a hospital bed, rather than a prison cell.

In any event, when the criminal is again arrested, the same chain of events is set in motion. The script is basically the same, although the specific crime and its location may be different. The scenario is played out many times, day after day, across the country.

SUMMARY

The material presented here is based on a dissection of the criminal's patterns of thought and action, and not on after-the-fact accountability justifications. We know that what the criminal tells others when he is held accountable and is looking for excuses is totally self-serving and at variance from what really occurred.

We have indicated that criminals come from a broad spectrum of homes, both disadvantaged and privileged. Within the same neighborhood, some are violators, and most are not. It is not the environment that turns a man into a criminal. Rather, it is a series of choices that he makes starting at a very early age. What is particularly striking is that siblings within the same home can turn out so differently. By his actions, the criminal child elicits responses from his parents that are different from those elicited by his responsible brothers and sisters. One might be tempted to surmise that this occurs because the parents initially treat each child differently. However, after spending thousands of hours with criminals and their families, we found that no single practice or set of practices can be causally connected with a criminal outcome. In fact, we have been far more impressed by how the criminal child affects his parents than by how his parents affect him. This finding is in line with reports by other investigators who have been reexamining long-accepted causal ideas about child-rearing. Among such studies are those by Chess et al. (1959, 1960), Schaffer and Emerson (1964), Birns (1965), Korner (1965, 1971), Bell (1968, 1971), Kagan (1971), Harper (1971), and Lewis and Rosenblum (1974). They cite individual differences in temperament that are present in children from early infancy. Our investigation indicates that the criminal youngster has a profound impact on his entire family early in life. Although the parent has an important role in raising the child, so too does the child bring up the parent.

In this chapter, we have pointed out that the criminal shows himself for what he is everywhere. There is a continuity in his thinking and action, regardless of setting. In his neighborhood, the young criminal goes against the tide of most children, which is in the direction of growth within the social structure. He scorns that direction and sets out in quest of excitement, which for him means violation. Crime does not come to him; he goes to it, often traveling far outside his neighborhood to do so. He seeks out other delinquent youngsters and wants to be like them and accepted by them. He wants to be older and "bigger," in the sense of more important, than the "straight" youngsters of his age, whom he considers stupid and sissies. Community activities, social organizations, and recreational programs have little impact on the crime problem, because they do not offer the criminal child what he wants.

We have traced the patterns in school. The criminal's tactics and basic attitudes toward school are similar whether he is a grade-school dropout or a college graduate. He exploits school for his own purposes, as he has exploited his family. The criminal's lack of commitment to school itself cannot be remedied by extra time, extra effort, or a change in curriculum, because school does not give him the particular kind of excitement that he wants.

Work is basically the same as school. The criminal has pretensions of being a hero and an overnight success. Starting at the bottom and acquiring skills and education is not for him. Some criminals do not work at all. Others work only to present a facade of respectability and thereby make crime easier. If they work, they expect to step into a slot immediately and have a tremendous impact on others. Those who hold positions of authority are rarely content where they are. They often jockey for more and more power for its own sake, or they violate on the job. Wherever they go, they have little sense of obligation and place their own self-serving objectives ahead of anything else. In all arenas of life, they take the most and give the least, stepping on others and inflicting financial, emotional, and sometimes physical harm.

We have pointed out that the "first offender" notion is a mistaken one. The criminal gets away with far more than is ever known by anyone else. By the time he is apprehended, he has more than likely committed hundreds, if not thousands, of offenses. The criminal has far more thoughts about violation than he can ever put into action. To classify the criminal as a "check-writer" or "rapist" is inaccurate. Most criminals have committed violations in all three categories—property, sex, and assault—but have not been arrested. A few who have not been active in a particular category still have the desires to violate in it. Sometimes, a criminal operates in only one category for a while. But it is likely that he will be active in more than one. Thus, for example, a man may be arrested for robbery, but no one knows that he has also raped. Not all criminals have committed all offenses or even desired to, owing to deterring factors that are discussed in Chapter 6.

We have stated that the criminal's appetite for excitement grows and that patterns expand. The proceeds are not what is important, but rather the excitement of the scheming, the execution of the act itself, the getaway, making fools of others, and so forth. Men with plenty of money in their pockets steal things that they can well afford to buy and often for which they have no use. The excitement involved is what is important.

In short, the criminal expresses himself for what he is wherever he goes, whatever he does. We have indicated how changeable the criminal is and perhaps have puzzled and intrigued the reader by revealing what appear to be paradoxes of the criminal personality. For example, we stated that a man who prays at 9 o'clock may be out stealing at 10 o'clock. A criminal who writes love poems may exploit the object of his "love." A man who opposes war and killing may assault people. These apparent paradoxes will be unraveled as the reader becomes familiar with the material of the following chapters, which deal with criminal characteristics and thinking processes.

Perhaps most important is that the material in this chapter has demonstrated that the criminal is not a victim of circumstances. He makes choices early in life, regardless of his socioeconomic status, race, or parents' child-rearing practices. A large segment of society has continued to believe that a person becomes a criminal because of environmental influences. Several factors account for the persistence of this conclusion. Parents who have criminal offspring deny that there is something inherent in the individual that surfaces as criminality. They desperately look for a cause and, in the effort to explain, they latch on to some event or series of events in a person's life for which he is not responsible. Many social scientists have promulgated a deterministic view of man and for years have been explaining criminality largely in terms of environmental influences. Government programs have operated on this basis. The media have espoused this attitude. In efforts to eradicate crime, society has tried to do something, rather than nothing. Attacking environmental sources has been considered one positive step. However, these efforts have met with failure for reasons that the reader will understand as he reads this volume. Changing the environment does not change the man. Finally, the criminal is ever ready to present himself as a victim once he is apprehended. He feeds society what he at best only half believes himself. In discussions with others, he agrees with them that the cause of his criminality resides in life's circumstances, rather than within himself. Actually, he knows that circumstances have nothing to do with his violations, but he uses that rhetoric if he thinks it will lead others to view him more sympathetically.

BIBLIOGRAPHY

Bell, Richard Q. "A Reinterpretation of the Direction of Effects in Studies of Socialization," *Psychological Review*, 1968, 75, 81-95.

Bell, Richard Q. "Stimulus Control of Parent or Caretaker Behavior by Offspring," *Developmental Psychology*, 1971, 4, 63-72.

Birns, Beverly. "Individual Differences in Human Neonates' Responses to Stimulation," *Child Development*, 1965, 36, 249-256.

"Blood in the Streets: Subculture of Violence," *Time*, April 24, 1972, pp. 44ff.

Buckley, William F., Jr. "Sen. McGovern Discovers Crime," *The Evening Star and The Washington Daily News*, October 12, 1972, p. A17.

Chess, Stella et al. "Characteristics of the Individual Child's Behavioral Responses to the Environment," *American Journal of Orthopsychiatry*, 1959, 29, 791-802.

Chess, Stella et al. "Implications of a Longitudinal Study of Child Development for Child Psychiatry," *American Journal of Psychiatry*, 1960, 117, 434-441.

"Crimes by Children Growing in Number and Severity," *The Washington Post*, July 2, 1972, p. B1.

"GI Crime, Violence Climb Overseas," *The Washington Post*, September 13, 1971, p. A1.

"Guards Ask Jackson for Equal Time," *The Washington Star-News*, August 16, 1973.

Harper, Lawrence V. "The Young as a Source of Stimuli Controlling Caretaker Behavior," *Developmental Psychology*, 1971, 4, 73-88.

Henderson, David. "Psychopathic States," *British Journal of Delinquency*, 1951, 2, 84-87.

"Inmates at Mercy of Crime Leaders," *The Evening Star and The Washington Daily News*, December 14, 1972, p. E4.

Kagan, Jerome. *Change and Continuity in Infancy*. New York: Wiley, 1971.

Korner, Anneliese. "Individual Differences at Birth: Implications for Early Experience and Later Development," *American Journal of Orthopsychiatry*, 1971, 41, 608-619.

Korner, Anneliese. "Mother-Child Interaction: One- Or Two-Way Street," *Social Work*, 1965, 10, 47-51.

Lewis, Michael, and Rosenblum, Leonard A. (Eds.). *The Effect of the Infant on Its Caregiver*. New York: Wiley, 1974.

"More Workers Steal From Their Employers and Get Away With It," *Wall Street Journal*, February 5, 1970, p. 1.

President's Commission on Law Enforcement and the Administration of Justice. *The Challenge of Crime in a Free Society*. Washington, D. C.: Government Printing Office, 1967.

Schafer, Roy. *The Clinical Application of Psychological Tests*. New York: International Universities Press, 1948.

Schaffer, H. R., and Emerson, Peggy E. "Patterns of Response to Physical Contact in Early Human Development," *Journal of Child Psychology and Psychiatry*, 1964, 5, 1-13.

"The Rise and Fall of Mike Sharp," *Parade* (*The Washington Post*), May 17, 1970, pp. 4ff.

Wechsler, David. *The Measurement and Appraisal of Adult Intelligence*. (4th edit.) Baltimore: Williams and Wilkins, 1958.

West, Damon. "The Games Convicts Play," *Resident and Staff Physician*, November 1971, 107-113.

"Youth Facility an Alternate to Jail Term," *The Evening Star*, December 29, 1970, p. B1.

Chapter 4

Thinking Errors Characteristic of the Criminal: I. Criminal Thinking Patterns

THIS CHAPTER AND THE NEXT TWO are designed to give the reader a conceptual understanding of the thinking processes of the criminal. All three chapters describe thinking errors that are present everywhere in his life. We regard them as "errors" solely from the perspective of responsibility; the criminal does not consider them "errors"—indeed, they constitute his very fabric. This chapter deals with general thinking patterns of the criminal. Chapter 5 discusses thinking errors that are on the one hand obvious, but on the other are often just labeled and then ignored. Chapter 6 presents thinking patterns that are manifested most prominently in the execution of criminal acts.

Some of the criminal's thinking patterns have been touched on by other investigators, who have usually identified them as characteristics or traits. We shall refer occasionally to what others have observed. However, we have gone beyond labeling or identifying characteristics. Our objective has been to develop a conceptual framework based on a dissection of thought processes. The concepts thus obtained will be made operational (as described in Volume 2) for effecting change.

We have derived our concepts through the phenomenologic approach referred to in Chapter 1. The criminal has revealed the workings of his mind to us over many thousands of hours.* Rather than try to fit these data into a preconceived explanatory framework or set of assumptions, we have built a conceptual framework from the raw data of experience furnished by the criminal. All the material here is derived from an examination of the criminal's

---

* In Chapter 3, we presented a breakdown of our sample and the number of hours spent.

251

thinking processes during twenty-four-hour periods of his regular daily living. This is in sharp contrast with the material that he presents when he is held accountable; as we have already pointed out, many current ideas about the criminal are based on his own self-serving statements, rather than on an understanding of his thinking *outside* the accountability situation.

For clarity in presentation, each criminal thinking pattern has been singled out from a constellation of patterns. Each individual pattern, as it is understood, acquires more meaning when related to all the others. No thinking pattern or group of patterns should be viewed as causal. The reader might be tempted to conclude, for example, that power and control thinking, being so pervasive, is what "makes" a person criminal. However, it is the direction of this pattern toward specific ends and in combination with other thought patterns that constitutes the very essence of the criminal mind. Every component must first be understood by itself and then be related to the others. In short, we fractionate the criminal's mind and then synthesize it.

As he proceeds with this chapter, the reader may think that he has encountered much of the same material in Chapter 3. There is, to be sure, a correspondence between the two chapters in terms of topics treated. One important difference does exist. Chapter 3 discussed the criminal's behavior, which is observable. However, what a criminal does is often not reflective of his thinking. Sometimes he acts in a particular manner, but his thinking does not correspond to that action. More important is the fact that a tremendous amount of thinking is never translated into behavior. For example, when the reader comes to the section in this chapter on sexuality, he will discover the wide spectrum of thinking behind the sexual activity described in Chapter 3. We have learned that the thinking that is not immediately expressed in behavior is frequently the precursor of later conduct that is injurious to others.

The focus of this and the next two chapters is *thinking patterns*. Anyone who desires to effect basic change in a criminal must be totally familiar with this material, for it is these thinking patterns to which correctives must be applied.

THE CONTINUUM OF CRIMINALITY

A continuum can be established in terms of something specific and easily measurable, such as height and hue; and less tangible entities, such as personality features, can also be conceived of as lying along a continuum, although they cannot be quantified. For example, it has been said that there is larceny in every soul. If this is true, we would say that a person with the feeblest desires to commit larceny is at one end of the continuum, and a person for whom larceny is virtually a way of life is at the other end.

The term "criminal" evokes stereotypes and strong emotional responses that confuse or mislead more than they inform. It is essential for the reader to understand that we do not use "criminal" in a legal sense. Our emphasis is on *thinking processes* that the irresponsible but nonarrestable person, the petty thief, and the "professional" criminal all manifest, but to different degrees and with different consequences. A person who lies frequently may be cut of the same mental fabric as the arrestable criminal. A responsible person may also lie, but infrequently. In his case, lying is not a way of life. Lying may be just a piece of ice floating in the sea, or it may be the tip of an iceberg that contains the entire spectrum of criminal patterns, untruthfulness being only one element. The criminal continuum allows a more precise description and analysis and guides us in our work to effect change.* We may diagram this continuum with the basically responsible person at one end and the extreme criminal at the other.

RESPONSIBLE		IRRESPONSIBLE	
	Nonarrestable	Arrestable Criminal	Extreme Criminal

The basically responsible person has a life-style of hard work, fulfillment of obligations, and consideration for others. He derives self-respect and the respect of others from his achievements. Desires to violate do occur, but they disappear, usually without the person's having to make a conscious choice. A thought about violating is discarded because it does not fit his view of life; no effort is needed to eliminate it.** When a deviation does happen, it does not become a way of life. For example, he has moments of extreme anger, but anger and vindictiveness are not automatic responses to things that do not go his way, as they are for the criminal. The basically responsible person has a pattern of being conscientious in occupational, domestic, and social affairs. He works productively and contributes toward the good of others while trying to advance himself. If he is a recluse and is unconcerned with other people, he does not infringe on their rights and property.

---

* Lindner (1946, p. 47) also described a "continuum concept of crime," beginning with "simple law-breaking" and extending to "real criminal acts." Each point on the continuum was viewed as the outcome of the degree to which certain "traits of character and temperament" played a role. The framework for the discussion was primarily psychoanalytic.

** It is the feeble desires that quickly enter one's mind but are almost always just as quickly eliminated which constitute the "larceny in every soul" that some people, including the criminal, talk about. This is quite different from the extreme criminal, who has dozens of these desires a day and acts on some of them.

In referring to people as "irresponsible," there is room for misunderstanding. Some people do not violate the law, but can be considered irresponsible. These are the defaulters, liars, excuse-offerers—people who are generally unreliable. They are chronically late, perform poorly at work, or fail to fulfill promises and obligations at home. They cannot be arrested for any of these shortcomings. They may show irresponsibility in some ways and be conscientious otherwise. We do not call such people "criminal." Their irresponsibility does not result in criminal acts.

People referred to on the continuum as "arrestable criminal" have all the thinking patterns of the extreme, or hard-core, criminal, but their crime patterns are less extensive and serious. They are minor violators who rarely get caught, such as employees who take items from their jobs that do not belong to them and people who may steal merchandise from a store whenever surveillance is not too tight. Many of these people are failures in life, as judged by societal standards. Some do advance, despite their violations, which go undetected. People in this group have recurrent strong desires to violate, but are deterred. Occasionally, someone in this group who had always seemed responsible surprises everyone by getting caught at something fairly serious. In a situation where restraints are not great, he might indeed implement the violations that he has previously only thought about. A criminal might move from a small rural community to a large city. In a small town, it is harder to get away with infractions; but when such a person moves to an area where he experiences greater freedom and anonymity, the criminal components emerge. His basic personality has not changed, but now the violation will occur, because external restraints are fewer.

At the opposite end of the continuum from those basically responsible are the "extreme criminals." The thinking processes described in this chapter are operative in this group from an early age. The outcome of such mental processes is inevitably crime. This is not to say that these people are in crime every moment. As we shall point out in Chapter 7, they have a succession of mental states that range from active criminality to an intense striving for purity. Although the extreme criminals constitute only a small fraction of the population, they pose the greatest problem because of the heavy injuries they inflict. When people use the term "criminal," it is usually with reference to the extreme criminal. It is primarily the extreme criminal who is the subject of our writing.

We want to avoid giving an impression that we are seeing things only in extremes—we do *not* divide the world into two groups, criminals and non-criminals. We acknowledge that even the use of the word "criminal" will draw objections. We could well have used the term "violator" to speak of a person who breaks the law, as well as a person who deviates from moral standards without being arrestable. Such a term might have been less offensive. However, in the process of change, we have a formidable task. We try to effect change in people who have been constantly in crime, but who do not view themselves as being at all criminal. To bring about change, we must counteract their conviction that they are good people. And to this end, we avoid euphemistic labels like "offender" or "violator" and use the word "criminal" to refer to them for what they are. (The importance of this procedurally will be developed in Volume 2.)

The reader should keep the continuum concept always in mind for the sake of perspective. Otherwise, he will think that we are indiscriminately calling everyone, including him, a criminal. It must be understood that our work is with a population that is at the extreme end of the continuum. Just as severe back-ward schizophrenics were often the subjects of early efforts to understand thinking processes of schizophrenia and to effect change, so we have chosen to work intensively with the severe criminal in an attempt to comprehend his mental processes and to develop procedures for change. Only by this method can one understand those who are less extreme on the criminal continuum so that they too can be changed.

A pitfall in presenting this material is that the reader might be offended or worried by finding that, to a degree, he has some of the characteristics attributed to the extreme criminal. The reader may think of times he has lied or misrepresented a situation. He may recall with some embarrassment an occasion when he has let temper get the best of him or an isolated instance of taking something that did not belong to him. Such behavior does not automatically place him on the criminal end of the continuum. We warn the reader against "medical student's disease," in which one wholeheartedly applies everything to himself. Every characteristic of the criminal is present to some degree in the noncriminal. But, for example, although everyone has fear, what is at issue is the nature of the fear and how one copes with it.

ENERGY

The criminal is tremendously energetic. According to reports of parents and teachers, as a child he shows more intense motor activity than the average youngster. All young children have short attention spans, but the criminal youngster's is even shorter. There is also a faster, more intense quality to his play. Criminal children are often so unmanageable that they have to be physically restrained, for lack of any other way to control them. The energy is also present in the criminal child who for a time is good and hangs onto his mother's skirts. He is spontaneous, colorful, imaginative, and restless, but still hanging on to his mother. By the age of nine or ten, this child makes a turnabout and seeks another homeostasis, and his activity turns from the good to the forbidden.

The criminal shows a corresponding mental activity. His thinking is rapid, continuous, and intense. If one could measure a child's physical and mental activity, he would find a greater total in the criminal than in the noncriminal. We do not assert that every active, restless child is going to be a criminal, but rather that this combination of motor and mental hyperkinesia is always found in the criminal child.* As he grows older, it increases. The Gluecks (1950) observed this characteristic when they studied a group of 500 delinquents and a group of nondelinquent controls.

> A much higher proportion of the delinquents than of the non-delinquents are reported to have been extremely restless as young children in terms of energy output (p. 274).

> As a group [in school], they were less interested in academic tasks, less attentive in class, more often tardy, less reliable, more careless in their work, lazier, more restless (p. 277).

This hyperkinesia is different from that which occurs in organic states, such as after encephalitis, in which the activity is random. It is the intensity and extent of the mental activity guiding the physical activity that have been insufficiently recognized. Even when a criminal child is restricted by his parents or teachers to the point where physical activity is limited, his mind is enormously active. In daily assignments and in attacking new tasks, such as learning to read, he may be uninterested, not because of mental lethargy, but because his mind is on nonacademic things, of which some are approved and others cause trouble. He may be all over the classroom erasing blackboards, running errands for the teacher, pulling the girls' hair, and getting out of his seat. It is important to note that his activity is not random, but is the purposeful result of a flow of ideas as to what would make life more interesting and exciting. As he grows older, the flow is organized more into patterned fantasies and schemes, the modus operandi in crime becomes more elaborate, and the scope of crime increases.

---

* We are not calling the criminal child "hyperkinetic" or the hyperkinetic child a "criminal." The criminal does not show the following hyperkinetic symptoms described by Renshaw (1974, pp. 82, 83): ceaseless, purposeless activity, poor concentration due to an inability to screen out or discriminate stimuli, perceptual difficulties, irregular developmental milestones, poor motor coordination. In fact, quite the reverse is true of the criminal youngster. He acts purposefully and cleverly, with periods of intense concentration. There are at times lengthy periods of physical inactivity, but with a tremendous amount of mental activity. We have not worked with hyperkinetic children. However, we do wonder whether those who steal and violate in other ways might not fall more into the criminal category than the hyperactive.

The criminal's mental and physical energy is channeled in the direction of excitements that are necessary to the homeostasis that he desires. Some people—the Walter Mitties who are not criminals—have a fantasy life of one triumph after another and remain content with the fantasy, lacking the energy and resourcefulness and refusing to resort to violation to actualize it. The criminal has his fantasies of triumph, power, and control that he impatiently seeks to realize. He has both the fantasy of living in opulent splendor and the crime fantasy of the spectacular armed robbery. For him, the two are linked. In whatever he does, the criminal drives to be the top man and shows remarkable energy, at least initially, in this drive. However, no matter what he undertakes, his enthusiasm wanes as he has ideas of new and different excitements. He soon shelves the current enterprise and goes on to something else. The criminal is a sprinter, not a long-distance runner.

Even as the criminal grows older, his energy is astonishing.

> C, 36 years old, played singles tennis for 6 hours continuously, and then he wondered why he was tired.

> Mrs. F said of C, age 35: "He is so active he never tires. In fact, he tires me out. He goes on 2 or 3 hours a day walking, and he could do this all day long."

A state of average activity followed by reasonable fatigue is intolerable. If he is not full of vitality and energy and ready to go, he thinks that something is wrong with him. His idea of normal energy differs from that of most of the noncriminal population.

> C was complaining about his very demanding work routine. He had to get up at 6:30 A.M. and then work two jobs, finishing at about 9 P.M. and arriving home at 10:30. He constantly complained of fatigue. However, if there were something he wanted to do, such as attend a party, he could do this, be the life of the party, and stay out all night. There would be no difficulty in finding the energy for that.

Even with physical disabilities, the criminal is hardly slowed down. He does not sit around and feel sorry for himself when there is something he wants to do. We have encountered criminals who could move rapidly even with a physical handicap like muscle weakness, a withered leg, a broken bone, or a wound.

The criminal's energy is sometimes not so apparent. He may appear indolent or tired when he is in a situation that he regards as boring. One has to see the same man in the right place at the right time to realize that he is by no means lazy. He becomes bored easily unless he is where the "action" is.

The activity can occur alone or with others; but when he is with a non-criminal group, his boredom can become almost intolerable.

The criminal eschews the rest and relaxation that some people wish they could enjoy more often.

> On a beautiful day, C and Mary went to the country. C was generally irritable, although they were doing something that was away from the routine. The following day was also nice, and Mary wanted to lie down and sunbathe. Again, C was restless and irritable. He made up some kind of excuse that they ought to go home to do some things around the house. C once stated that a 2-week cruise was inconceivable, unless he had some project that he could work on throughout the cruise.

Even when he is watching a television show, the criminal's very busy thinking continues. If the program is boring, he pays no attention. If he is attentive to the program, his mind goes further than what is on the screen; being extremely imaginative, he elaborates on the content.

When we work with a criminal in a program for basic change, his energy must be taken into account. We may first encounter him in confinement, where he is spending hours lying on his bed, ignoring his environment. He seems to be without energy or interests. If he is asked what he is thinking, he says "nothing." But we have found that his mind actually is racing with criminal thinking; and he admits this, once we have established rapport with him. Although the criminal has tremendous mental and physical energy available, it is not apportioned to the many activities that responsible living requires. The criminal becomes fatigued when he is faced with having to do what he does not want to do. In efforts at change, the agent of change will hear many complaints of lack of energy. However, if the criminal were free to do as he wanted, his energy would suddenly be present and observable, even after exhausting work. The reserves of energy for excitement appear almost limitless.

FEAR

Fears in the criminal are widespread, persistent, and intense throughout his life. We use the term "fear," rather than "apprehension," "worry," "concern," "anxiety," or a number of others, which have fear as their common denominator. Some of the criminal's fears can be traced to a traumatic first experience or to specific teachings; if a child is taught that he will go to hell for doing something wrong, such a pronouncement may be a basis for fear. But most of the criminal's fears are not traceable to a prototypic experience. His fearfulness is so pervasive from an early age that it almost seems independent of experience. If one were to survey the criminal child's various fears in terms of "minutes of fear per day," the greatest number would be related to being apprehended for some infraction or violation.* Other than those, two basic types exist: the fear of bodily injury or death and the fear of a putdown.

FEAR OF INJURY AND DEATH

The fear of death is very strong, persistent, and pervasive in the criminal's mental life. He lives every day as though it were his last. Indeed, some criminals who believe that they will die at an early age write their own epitaphs. Fear of death assumes some terrifying forms, especially during childhood. The preoccupation with death is not a phenomenon only of childhood, but prevails throughout a lifetime.

> "One of the things I daydream a lot about is death, thinking about dying in different ways. The whole thing about life and death is pretty near to me. I can never figure out why I was born in the first place or why anybody is born in the first place. At times, I am terribly afraid that I will die before I get to be old, that I will die earlier than most people. Then I wish I were dead; death can be a very scary subject at times. In a lot of ways, I wish that I could be an angel or something like that, you know, and yet still be able to see everything that is going on and try to be an influence on people."

The criminal is so afraid of losing his life that he perceives threats emanating from many sources. He may be afraid of heights, water, lightning, insects, and closed spaces. Later in life, some are afraid to drive. These fears do not appear to be linked with an early traumatic experience.

> C was afraid of bodies of water long before he had experience with them. When he went to the beach, he remained in shallow water. He wanted to be a Navy man, mainly because of his image of their being heroic, but he feared that any ship that he might be on would sink.

> C was exceedingly fearful of heights. For a while, he worked on the 57th floor of an office building. He was so tense about being up so high that he had to go to the ground floor whenever he had to defecate. This fear reached panic proportions.

Closely related to the fear of death are fears of physical illness and pain. Criminals tend to stay away from doctors and dentists. They are far more fearful of experiencing a little discomfort at the hands of a doctor than they

---

* The major treatment of external deterrents (that promote fears of getting caught) and the fears of conscience (that also serve as deterrents) is presented in Chapter 6.

are of the pain that they might experience from a condition that will grow worse if unattended. Many criminals undergo painful extractions and have bridges and plates early in life, even in their twenties, because they avoided seeing a dentist until their teeth were too deteriorated to save. When he has something wrong with him physically, the criminal becomes frightened out of proportion to the actual seriousness of the malady, but still fails to do anything about it unless there is an advantage for him. Consequently, the condition worsens until others force him to see a doctor. The exception to these patterns is the criminal who may avail himself of free medical and dental services in confinement, but even then it is often with reluctance and deviousness. Once he sees the doctor, he rarely gives a straight story of his ailments, especially if they are crime-related.

Many a criminal believes that to be disabled or disfigured is worse than death. A not uncommon fantasy is that of a grand flourish in which the criminal shoots everyone in sight and is then killed himself. In such a fantasy, he always envisions himself killed, rather than maimed. This fear of injury is so strong in some that they are impeded in carrying out everyday acts. One man was so afraid of electric wires that he had someone else plug his radio in for him. Throughout their lives, these people have feared injury in a fight. Even the very toughest have been terrified of this.

Fear of the dark is especially common. As children, some are afraid of the supernatural—spooks, ghosts, goblins, and monsters that might haunt them at night.

> In C's community, there was talk among the townspeople about the return of the dead. C believed this to the extent that he feared that one day he would be snatched, mutilated, and killed. He believed that this could occur any day as he was walking along the street. If a person ran up to him and made a loud noise, he panicked. These fears bothered him greatly at night.

Some criminals, even as adults, sleep with a light on.

It is remarkable how many of their fears persist beyond childhood. Some criminals never go near water, always avoid heights, never drive, and so on. They may even rule out some crimes because of these fears.

FEAR OF A PUTDOWN

The type of fear that is tolerated least is of a different sort from those just described: fear of being put down by people or by events. The fear of a putdown is global in the criminal, because a putdown can reduce him to a zero. There is an enormous fear of being a zero forever, without redeeming qualities, and having it obvious to everyone. The zero state is discussed in the next section.

The criminal is hypersensitive when it comes to interpreting others' attitudes toward him. Wherever he goes, he is vulnerable, in that anything that is not in line with his inflated image of himself as a powerful person is viewed as a threat. To be told what to do by others is a putdown. To have to ask a question of someone is a putdown, because it reveals ignorance. Being seen riding a bus, rather than driving a sporty car, is a putdown for some. Having to wait for the bus is a putdown. If it rains while he is waiting, this is a putdown. The criminal is put down by any adverse event over which he does not have control. Indeed, almost anything that does not give him a buildup is a putdown.

The putdown must be distinguished from the "idea of reference." A putdown occurs in the mind of a criminal who misconstrues something that another person has said or done with respect to him. An idea of reference occurs when one interprets as referring to him an event that is not related to him at all. If a man gets on a train and believes that the other passengers are out to do him in, when in fact he has done nothing wrong and has never seen these people before, his belief is an idea of reference. If a man gets on a train and the luggage rack is too crowded for his bags, he considers himself the victim of a putdown—he is angry that the world is not meeting his needs, and he may curse, shove a few parcels around, and jam his case onto the rack. He does not perceive the other passengers as menacing to him, but any failure to get his way punctures his inflated conception of himself.

Like anyone else, the criminal may be on the receiving end of criticism or disparagement. A student may be criticized for a poorly written theme. If the essay does not meet established standards, then the criticism is a statement of fact and is merited. No personal affront is involved. However, the criminal perceives such criticism, even when deserved, as a total indictment of him as a person and reacts accordingly.

> C began sloughing off in his work at a department store. His immediate superior rebuked him for his increasing tendency to arrive late. C was enraged: "I almost wanted to go through the window. I was never patted on the back for being early. One time I might just belt the guy."

C indicated that he expected a buildup for doing the expected but no criticism for poor performance. He was put down by what was a statement of fact.

The putdown must also be distinguished from the deserved rejection. The criminal is rarely rejected without earning it. When a criminal pursues a woman, for example, he fails to recognize that, just as he has the right to reject her if she is not what he wants, so she has the right to reject him. Instead, when she does not act as he wants her to, he is put down.

In the face of undeserved criticism, insult, or rejection, a responsible person evaluates its source and reacts accordingly. The criminal makes no such assessment, but simply becomes angry and sometimes violent. Of course, not all people who are hypersensitive are criminals. Many responsible people find it difficult to accept criticism, whether constructive or not. In these people, criticism may tap self-doubts or what have been termed "inferiority feelings."

For the criminal, an ordinary day can be fraught with putdowns from beginning to end. Again, we underscore the self-deceptive quality. Putdowns would be far fewer if the criminal were not determined to control everyone and to insist on top priority for what he wants. For the criminal, a putdown occurs when someone else fails to meet his every desire, bend to his will, fulfill his every expectation. He believes that it is impossible for him to fail, with "failure" defined as being anything less than number one. A putdown can occur even with the anticipation of failure. The self-deceptive element plays a role, in that the criminal will experience a putdown due to failure, although he has not yet taken preparatory steps toward success. For example, a criminal wants to pass a vocational licensing examination. If he is not in confinement, he is likely to regard the preparation as too boring to bother with, because it requires mastering much detail. Naturally, he flunks the test.* Instead of regarding this as a consequence of not studying, he experiences a blow to his self-image and reacts as though it were someone else's fault. To his way of thinking, it should not be possible for him to fail at anything.

The criminal is put down when people disagree with him. His refractoriness to another's views is shown when someone questions a decision he has made. Instead of regarding the other person's ideas or questions as worthy of consideration, the criminal responds with exaggerated dogmatism and anger. Even acknowledging that the other party's view has merit threatens his view of himself. If the other person is clearly shown to be correct, the criminal is put down because his own ignorance is manifest to all. Then he seeks an opportunity to put down the other person. The transaction does not have to be verbal for the criminal to experience a putdown. If he comes home expecting to find dinner ready, and it is not, he is put down. The most ordinary experiences evoke a sense of putdown in the criminal.

A putdown occurs when a probability or a possibility does not pan out,

---

* If he is confined, he may study very hard for a test in order to impress others. This is especially likely to happen if a criminal knows that vocational preparation will facilitate getting out.

because if the criminal is counting on something to happen, in his mind it is a sure thing.

> C wanted to sound out his former wife, Ann, about a resumption of their relationship. He wrote to her, inquiring about a visit. C assumed that she would be amenable to this. Her slowness in responding was a putdown. Finally, a carefully worded letter arrived in which she held the door open if he could prove himself to be a responsible person. C had counted on a more affirmative and enthusiastic reply. He was put down, because he did not receive the response he expected. He figured that Ann was still his wife. It was his "right" to rejoin her. In C's thinking, he discounted the years when he abused her and the years of separation; only his current desires mattered. He interpreted Ann's cautious response as evidence that she had found someone else and was not interested in him.

The reader should bear in mind that the criminal usually does not think in terms of "putdown," although the word is common enough in daily usage for him to be familiar with it. This habitual reaction is our conceptualization based on the dissection of his mind. Putdowns occur frequently, and the criminal's responses are as automatic as the stance and strokes of a well-trained athlete. An experienced tennis player does not consciously decide how to meet his opponent's shot as it speeds over the net. The foot placement, body position, and racquet grip are coordinated automatically. The criminal's reaction to a putdown is similar. He does not "decide" how to handle the situation, but becomes angry, and his solution is inevitably illogical. To deal with the event so as to emerge in a position of advantage, the criminal runs, fights, cons, sneaks, or does something else irresponsible. If his ultimate objective is to be achieved by a con operation, he does not become angry, because this would be counter to his purposes. We shall say more about the criminal's response to the putdown in the section on anger.

ATTITUDES TOWARD FEAR

Although we are describing fearfulness as characteristic of the criminal, the criminal himself does not use the word *fear*. He does not want to admit that he is afraid. As one man said, "To admit my fear would be equivalent to death."

> "I don't even like to talk about fear. It gives me butterflies [an actual psychosomatic reaction]. [When confronted by fears,] I have to club somebody down; it is fearful to be fearful. I would be helpless. My balance is to convince myself that I have control. I have to pull the strings."

Sometimes the criminal does admit his fear by avoiding or running away from things that frighten him. If he fears getting beaten up, he might decide to stay away from altercations that could provoke physical retaliation. If he dreads the water, he may not go near a beach. More often, the criminal wants to conceal his fright, because he does not want to be regarded as "weak," "sissy," or "chicken." Even during a severe beating, he tries to keep a stiff upper lip and show that he can take it. A common pattern in the young criminal is to take a dare from other children even though he is terrified. Taking the offensive, negating his fears to others, and showing that he has "heart" by stealth or muscle are all ways in which the criminal shows the world that he is unafraid. This appearance of fearlessness is what writers characteristically describe when they discuss the psychopath or criminal.

> Those called psychopaths are sharply characterized by the lack of anxiety (remorse, uneasy anticipation, apprehensive scrupulousness, the sense of being under stress or strain) . . . (Cleckley, 1964, p. 271).

The criminal is very fearful, but does not tolerate fear. Most of his fears are within his control, so he can eliminate them long enough to do what he wants. Redl and Wineman (1951) have observed that the fears are eliminated so rapidly that the criminal is not aware of them. They described the delinquent child's ego as taking "drastic measures" to cope with fear:

> They have a tendency to react so fast by these extreme techniques [of avoidance or attack] that self-awareness of the very experience of insecurity, anxiety, or fear, has no time to develop, or, if it does, is totally repressed (p. 81).

This remarkable capacity to eliminate fear is discussed in terms of the processes of "corrosion" and "cutoff" in Chapter 6. In reality, the criminal never truly eliminates fear.

It should be pointed out that the criminal does admit to fear when it is in his interest to do so. He may say that he is afraid, if that will serve as a sufficient excuse for not doing something he dislikes. We have indicated that the criminal may go to the extreme of admitting to qualities that he does not have in order to establish a mental-illness defense. Once in the hospital, he may try to enlist sympathy by showing fear and then try to score points by showing insight into his fearfulness. In addition, he may urge that he be released before long, citing as a reason that the hospital is making him worse or that he will be "institutionalized."

Criminals are often said to show their fearfulness by their strongly suspicious nature. They are commonly described as "paranoid." The criminal is suspicious, but he is not paranoid. Paranoid operate on the basis of fixed beliefs that continue even when contradicted by social reality. These beliefs are called "delusions." The criminal's suspicions are founded on reality. The paranoid believes that others are "out to get him" or are in conspiracy when they are not. The criminal is on the lookout for others who might harm him because of his activities. Suspicion is necessary for crime, because, if a criminal is not suspicious, he will not take the proper precautions. If he has already committed a crime, he must be suspicious to protect himself from apprehension. Anyone could turn him in; he is always a fugitive from justice. The criminal believes that others think and act as he does. Thus, his reading of how others function is often distorted. However, he does not necessarily believe that others are out to harm him. It is a pattern of projection, but not paranoia in the technical sense.

Many criminals have incorporated the word *paranoid* into their language. For example, a man will say that he is "paranoid" about the police or, if he is in jail, about a fellow criminal. All this means is that he is on guard. He takes a term to which he has been exposed and uses it without understanding its technical meaning. We say more about this alleged "paranoia" in Chapter 6.

CRIMINAL VERSUS NEUROTIC

The reader may view many of the criminal's fears as being identical with those of the neurotic. This is a valid conclusion. Some fears persist from childhood and do not seem to be at all related to crime. The criminal has learned to live with these. He is not particularly bothered by them, so long as others outside the family do not know that they exist. All of us have fears. They differ in kind and intensity. Most of us learn to live with them or master them. Fears that are realistic guide us in our daily activities. Both the criminal and the neurotic noncriminal are especially beset with fears, but they deal with them differently. Neurotics admit that they are afraid, and they seek help. The criminal who is equally fearful does his best to conceal it and tries to convince the world that he is fearless. (The criminal's fear of fear is discussed further in Chapter 5.)

ZERO STATE

The criminal fears being reduced to a "nothing" more than he fears almost anything else. He is said to be in a "zero state" when his self-esteem is at rock bottom; this zero state paralyzes him in a way that other fears do not. It is difficult for the noncriminal to imagine how disabling (although transient) this sense of worthlessness, hopelessness, and futility is. It is truly a comprehensive phenomenon in which the criminal believes that he has failed in every way.

The term "zero state" is derived from what criminals have said in describing themselves: "I am a zero." In their thinking, there are no gradations between being "tops" and being "nothing"; criminals usually assess a situation in extremes, perceiving it as better or worse than it really is. In the zero state, things seem hopeless to the criminal, despite the fact that an objective observer would not come to the same conclusion. It should be noted that, when the criminal is in such a state, he is not presenting the classical picture of depression. Rather than appearing flat, inert, and despairing, he is blazing with anger (often unexpressed). We shall say more about this in describing anger patterns.

Lest the reader be confused, we distinguish between *being* nothing and *having* nothing. On the one hand, a man can be destitute, ill, without resources, and very much alone, but still value himself as a person who is doing the best with what he has. On the other hand, a person may enjoy the benefits of wealth and status, but still view himself as a worthless human being. The state of mind that we are describing is not necessarily contingent on what one has.

The zero state has three components: the basic view of oneself as a nothing, a self-deception in that it does not conform to the facts; "transparency," in which the criminal believes that everyone else shares his view that he is worthless; and permanence, in which the criminal believes that his state of being a nothing will last forever and will never change.

The criminal fears the zero state even when he is not in it. He has experienced it enough times to know its depths. He is afraid of all three components, not only of being a nothing. When he is actually in a zero state, his fear is extreme. At such a time, it appears to him that there is no way out; he cannot believe that tomorrow will bring a better day. He is a zero, others know he is a zero, and these conditions will last forever.

A prolonged difficulty in one area of life that the criminal considers important is more likely to lead to a zero state than is a single putdown. This is because a sizable problem in that one area activates unfavorable thoughts about his functioning in other areas.

> C had always been ill at ease with girls. Whenever he had to deal with them, he was awkward, clumsy, and scared. Any occasion on which he had to spend time with them spelled defeat. He thought not only that he was unacceptable to girls, but that he was totally worthless.

The term "transparency" refers to the criminal's belief that his worthlessness is so evident that everyone else must perceive it. Actually, when a criminal believes that he has triumphed, the responsible world is likely to view him as a failure; and when by his own estimation he has failed, society may think of him as having done well. The following example is typical: A criminal child goes to school and does well; but high grades in school do not provide him with lasting gratification; being a good student is meaningless; in his view, to be only a good student is to be a nothing, even if he is praised by others; he becomes "somebody" through other kinds of enterprises, which are often incompatible with maintaining his high academic standing; when his work falls off, he is regarded as a problem at school; he is now "somebody" in his own opinion, not because he is failing at school, but because he is doing things that most children are afraid to do; responsible people now regard him as a failure. It is the incidents that the *criminal* views as failures that trouble him. Then he thinks that everyone sees through him, and this makes him less than the powerful person that he wants to be.

The third component that makes a zero state so intolerable to the criminal is his belief that it will last permanently. He cannot see his situation ever changing. Rather, there is a finality and irreversibility to his present state. The zero state does not become a suicidal state unless the criminal regards himself as evil, in addition to being worthless. In a zero state, the criminal continues to view himself as basically a good person, even though he is a failure. An example of a zero state in which the zero thinking and permanence features were clearly visible is the following:

> C told us that when he left our office he went home and hung around the house. He talked to his mother, did little else, and went to sleep. Then he got up and went to work. C told us that he had no faith in things now, no faith in people and no faith in the future. He seriously questioned whether he could go through life this way—gloomy, pessimistic, with faith in nothing. As far as he could remember, life was "like a dose of castor oil."

> Working was a charade. He got nothing out of it. But he had gotten nothing out of crime either. Life should be fruitful, but there had been nothing fruitful in his life, despite successful crimes. Clothes, cars, and women were not the answer. He had had these. C said that, when he'd tried something, whether it be work or crime, there had been something missing and it was never fulfilling. He could see nothing to live for—"I feel like nothing." Then he reflected that maybe he was missing something, but just did not know what it was.

> In this state of emptiness, nothing mattered. His general pattern was to blame others. He realized that this too was a mistake. He recognized that he was out of touch with people, but was not sure he wanted to be in touch with them, because to be in touch with them was to live like them. He drew the analogy that life was not wanting to partake of a meal but hanging around the garbage can anyway to pick up the leftovers.

The pessimism about change is evident. Had we pressed C as to how he believed that others regarded him, he would have verbalized transparency in his own terms.

The reader may be unclear as to how we differentiate the zero state from the "inferiority feelings" that are common in the noncriminal. We emphasize a strong quantitative difference. The inferiority feelings of the noncriminal are usually not all-encompassing, as are those of the zero state. The noncriminal may believe that he is inferior in some ways, but worthy in others.

The noncriminal may be afraid that others will find out about what he considers his own shortcomings; the criminal is certain that others already know. The noncriminal may fear that his flaws are permanent, but he is likely to act to remedy them, rather than adopt an attitude of hopelessness. He can live and function constructively, despite feelings of inferiority. If they become overwhelming, he will probably seek help. The criminal is certain of permanent nothingness from which he sees no redemption; he seeks no help, because he knows that he would reject what a responsible person would offer.

The zero state differs from the depression of a responsible person. We have not observed psychomotor retardation or poverty of thought in the zero state—indeed, just the opposite, with plenty of physical and mental activity. In fact, it is rare to see a prolonged zero state in undiluted form, because the criminal is able to dispel it so rapidly. His control over the zero state is in sharp contrast to the helplessness experienced by the depressed noncriminal. As we discuss the criminal's anger reactions and the power thrust, it will become clear how the criminal copes with zero-state thinking, and this will set the zero state in starker contrast with neurotic and psychotic depression.

ANGER

Anger is a universal human emotion. The criminal experiences anger with such frequency and intensity that it has serious repercussions for himself and others. Anger, though pervasive in the criminal, is not always shown. The criminal is chronically angry—even as he walks down the street. Anger is a mental state that is sometimes expressed outwardly, but more often boils within. It is most dangerous when it is not on the surface. Anger is as basic to his personality as the iris is to the eye.

The danger of anger as it occurs in the criminal is that it has more harmful consequences than anger in the noncriminal. An anger reaction in the criminal "metastasizes." It begins with an isolated episode, but spreads and spreads until the criminal has lost all perspective. Eventually, he decides that everything is worthless. His thinking is illogical, and the door is open to criminal thinking. An example of an everyday situation with serious consequences for a criminal, but not for a noncriminal, may help to clarify this.

> C took his car in to have it repaired. He picked it up later in the day only to find on the way home that it still had problems that had not been attended to. He was furious. He drove recklessly and began to think about a variety of other things about which he was angry. Anger fed on anger. He developed a stomach ache, a headache, and then a loss of appetite. He arrived late at a meeting. His thinking was: Nothing in life is worthwhile. Why live in this world? and so on. Then began a torrent of criminal thinking along sexual lines—exhibitionist, voyeurism, and finally rape. This was deterred at the time, but only because he was in our program for change. However, on other occasions when he had been this angry, some of the criminal thinking had been translated into action.

The point here is that, although noncriminals also are infuriated by poor car-repair service, they do not undergo this "metastasis" of anger that results in criminality.

Fear is the most common basis for anger in the criminal. Fear gives rise to anger in the noncriminal as well, but the criminal is more thin-skinned than the noncriminal and thus can be reduced to a nothing by even a slight criticism, which he interprets as a putdown. His response is anger.

> "When anybody criticizes me on a detail, I am furious. I jump down their throats. I won't tolerate it."

Because putdowns occur many times a day, no day of his life passes without numerous anger reactions, overt or covert. The anger is not expressed if it is expedient for the criminal to contain it. There may be indirect indicators, such as facial expressions, posture, or gestures. Verbal expression may range from sarcasm to intense rage.

The criminal responds angrily to anything that he interprets as opposing what he wants for himself. If he is planning a particular enterprise, he tolerates no interference with any part of it. If someone introduces a deterrent, he becomes angry, although he may not show it. The criminal may even feign or simulate anger if it will help to achieve his objective. Others may be frightened and do his bidding without recognizing that he is not serious. But, if he is not taken seriously, then what began as contrived anger develops into a potentially dangerous state.

When the criminal is put down, he angrily injects considerations not pertinent to the issues at hand. This is rejected as grossly unfair by the other party, a kind of "hitting below the belt." A dispute may begin over money. If the criminal thinks he is not winning the argument, he may utter a racial slur, which is irrelevant, but which helps to deflect attention from the issue so that he can gain the upper hand—a necessary condition for his existence.

We have been talking about the criminal's reactions to a putdown by another person. However, he is put down and angry when he himself functions improperly. His reaction then is to take his frustration out on others. If a criminal has made an appointment to see an employment counselor and appears on the wrong day, he becomes angry with everyone whom he encounters. He vents his wrath on the receptionist, on the counselor (if he has a chance), and even on the parking attendant whom he has to pay. He overlooks the fact that he made the mistake.

The antidote to the putdown is to reestablish control over others. The failure to control is a major ingredient in the putdown. With the possibility of not being in control always present, the situations to which the criminal responds angrily are limitless.

> C described an incident in which he and his brother were about to drive to a shoe-repair shop. He wanted his brother to take him somewhere else. The brother said he did not have time. C's response to this consisted of angry words, a punch, pulling a knife, and slashing his brother's coat.

C was put down by his brother's not acceding to his demands. Anger was his response to his fear of losing control and thus an attempt to preserve his image of himself.

Anger to achieve control is a way of life. Even as a little child, the criminal lashes out at people to get his own way.

> At the age of 3, C chased a ball into a man's yard. He ran across the lawn, stepping on some plants and finally into the garden in pursuit of the ball. The owner of the property came out and offered to retrieve the ball. This would allow the plants to be spared more trampling. C was very angry and kicked the man in the shins.

The striking back and attempt to intimidate occur everywhere—at home, at school, with friends, and on the job. Two criminals rarely disagree without anger. Each seeks to manage the other; neither allows for a legitimate difference of opinion.

When anger is futile and the criminal does not get his way, he is vulnerable to the occurrence of a zero state. Because there is less opportunity to control others in confinement, this sequence is especially likely there. It is in this state that he appears depressed. "Depression" in the criminal is basically an angry state in which he blazes at the injustice of the world. If a criminal has requested a privilege in confinement but is turned down, he may say that he is "depressed." However, he is plotting a way to get what he wants. In fact, in this "depressed" state, he may seek retribution and violate. This is the antidote to the zero state; it is an attempt to reassert control.

There is often an interval between the occurrence of a putdown and the commission of a crime. The criminal takes time to cool off and deliberate, for he knows that when he is angry he is less effective and runs greater risks. Thus, when he does commit the crime, it is carefully schemed and anger is minimized.

C had lived a lifetime of committing just about every sort of crime, including some very violent ones. However, when he was put down, he usually held his anger in check. He allowed himself time to scheme and gather weapons. His way of dealing with others he expressed as, "Don't get mad. Get even."

Anger reactions are prominent when the criminal is bored. If he is prevented from seeking the excitement that gives his life meaning, this constitutes boredom and is basically a putdown, and he is likely to stir up some excitement.

For C to be home with his wife and children in the evening was boring. To relieve this state, he would deliberately prompt an argument. He would then have justification for going out later, slamming the door, and thus escaping the intolerable.

This stirring up of "action" is all too familiar to beleaguered parents and teachers who have to contend with children who provoke others in order to have some excitement. These youngsters incite arguments and fights and then innocently maintain, "He started it." The instigation of trouble relieves the bored, angry state of mind.

When life would appear to a noncriminal to be running comparatively smoothly, the criminal is bored. He is wholly dissatisfied with life. He wants excitement and proof of power. It is not that he lacks things to do. Rather, he is either restrained by others or is restraining himself from doing the forbidden, and he is angry with the restraints. At such a time, anyone crossing the criminal's path may be a target for the expression of anger. Actually, the criminal's desire for excitement is so much a part of him, that he becomes jaded and always has to reach new peaks. To live without this increasingly high pitch of excitement is a putdown.

"The thought of the rest of my life stretching out day after dry, dusty day with none of the secret thrills which light up my life is impossible.

> Sure, when I get out of here [confinement] this time, the very newness of holding my wife in my arms again, of breathing free air and eating good food will sustain me for a time—but what comes after that—what else is there? For me, there must be something else. Your nature [the noncriminal's] is such that you are willing to put up with the dryness, the pressures, the frustrations and failures while seeking to attain something. My nature is otherwise. I do not choose to put up with the dullness, the tensions and rejections for the sake of *any* good. Rather, I choose to seek my own secret thrills. . . . My need for excitement is so chronic and I've been accustomed to maintaining it at such a constant level that most of the time I'm unaware of its presence. I only notice its absence—that is, boredom."

When the criminal is experiencing what he calls "boredom," violation is likely to be an antidote. After the fact, he uses the monotony of his existence as a justification for what he did.

Writers often describe the criminal's angry ways of dealing with the world in terms of "rebellion." Some people believe that this is a primary and causative factor in criminal behavior. Indeed, it is implied that if the criminal were not so rebellious, he could be a responsible member of society. In conventional formulations, the "rebellion against authority" is traced to difficulties of early life that left the child disappointed and angry with his parents. Consequently, the child is seen as harboring resentment throughout life and transferring it to anyone whom he sees as representing and imposing "authority." Cameron (1963) described antisocial reactions in sociopathic personalities as often being due to a "deeply emotional rebellion against authority which owes its intensity and persistence to its origins in the childhood family life" (p. 659). "Betrayals and suffering in childhood" are seen as crucial etiologic factors in the "defiant" stance that the criminal child takes toward the world.

What constitutes rebellion by almost any definition is opposition to and defiance of the existing order. We submit that the criminal is not rebellious in this sense. He is angry with society only when it interferes with what he is doing.* The child's search for excitement inevitably brings him into conflict with some adult authority. It should be noted that he does not start by seeking a contest or battle. If anything, he tries to avoid it. However, confrontations occur as the criminal violates. If he is out at night without informing his parents where he is, the "authority" will hold him accountable

---

* Maurer (1974) observed of con men that they are not antagonistic to society. "Although they sometimes perform sensational crimes, they are not the supercriminals of fiction. They are neither violent, bloodthirsty, nor thieving in the ordinary sense of that word. They are not antisocial—whatever that term really means. They hold no especial hatred or antipathy toward the individuals they fleece, nor toward society as a whole" (p. 152).

and probably punish him. He then "feels rebellious." McCord (1956, p. 7) observed that "he does not purposefully attack society, but society too often blocks his way to fulfillment." Miller et al. (1961) conducted street-corner studies of a group of teenagers called the "Junior Outlaws" and found no evidence that the delinquent youngster is a rebel against authority.

> Aggression was predominantly a characteristic of interaction *within the corner group,* and only rarely with outside groups. Aggressive actions toward the adult world were not markedly antagonistic or rebellious, but rather entailed resentment of perceived injustices and impersonal treatment (p. 296). . . . Active malice toward adult groups was a negligible factor in the motivation of delinquent acts. . . . The picture of corner-gang members as angry, frustrated boys lashing out in rebellious fury against the adult world is not substantiated. . . . The behavioral content of Junior Outlaw delinquencies . . . indicates that the desire to gain prestige and achieve personal stature in the eyes of one's peers was far more important than the impulsive or uncontrolled venting of anger (p. 297).

These boys were jockeying for status in their own world. Rebellion was not an ingredient of their activities.

Anger is costly to both the criminal and the noncriminal. The toll of anger is defective thinking, reduced energy for the task at hand, poorer performance, internal distress, and alienation of others. However, the noncriminal does not react to events that do not go his way as though his entire existence were being threatened. The consequences of the criminal's anger are injurious on a broad scale. When he is angry, he attempts to reassert the worth of his entire being. Everything is at stake, and so there is likely to be damage to persons and property.

PRIDE

Pride in its nonpejorative aspect is a state of mind of one who has achieved something worthwhile by responsible means, usually hard work and perhaps some ingenuity. Pride may be visible, as in a housewife who shows her neighbor a flowering garden that she has cultivated. Then again, pride may be invisible, as when a person is pleased with his achievement and others do not know about it. One also experiences pride when he completes an obligatory task and has had to overcome obstructions. And pride may be attributed to a person by others, as when one man says to another, "You must be proud of your son for doing well." Pride may be an undesirable quality, synonymous with conceit, arrogance, vanity, and egotism, as in "Pride goeth before a fall."

"Criminal pride" corresponds to an extremely and inflexibly high evaluation of oneself. It is the idea that one is better than others, even when this is clearly not the case. Criminal pride is manifested in all aspects of the criminal's life. As a child he shows it at home when he considers himself "above" such chores as taking out the trash. At school, the criminal resents having to do what others ask and being evaluated by others. He believes that he is better than others and therefore need not be accountable to them. At work, the criminal has pretensions that are far out of line with his skills and training. He may be too proud to work at all, believing that jobs are only for "suckers" and "slaves." Or he may consider himself too good for specific types of employment.

> C had been working as a salesman in a department store. On the third day, he reported that a man whom he knew happened to pass by and see him there. He was embarrassed and said he wanted to sink under the floor. His response was to quit the job, which he had thought he was too good for in the first place.

Pride's major expression is in the criminal's ideas of manhood or manliness. The major index of manhood is sexual acquisitiveness. Criminals report that, if there is an attractive woman in the room, one is not a "man" unless he conquers her. It does not matter whether he or she is married. To see this as anything but a challenge is to be a "faggot." But masculinity is not limited to the sexual. For example, to avoid a fight by backing away or running away is evidence of no manhood. Criminal pride entails a criminal's taking what he wants, outwitting or overpowering others, and coming out on top. Any other stance toward a person makes one unmanly. The criminal regards his masculinity as being at stake if he submits to another person or a system. To surrender a belief that one has held is also experienced as a loss of manhood. To be a man means to accomplish objectives, but for the criminal these objectives are a never-ending series of attempts to assert his own power, invariably at the expense of others. Finally, to be responsible, to live without excitement, is to negate one's masculinity and thus to lose one's pride.

Pride is a factor in where the criminal lives, what he eats, how he gets from one place to another, and with whom he associates. Such decisions have nothing inherently illegal in them, but this unyielding pride is part of his criminality. The criminal will do anything he can to maintain the life-style to which he believes he is entitled. He must live in the swankiest apartment despite the facts that the rent is astronomic and that it will cost a great deal to furnish. Usually, one way or another, the criminal manages to live in line with his pretensions, rather than within his means. This is where illegality may play a role. His criminal activities, although engaged in for the excitement more than for the proceeds, permit him to live beyond his means. His appetite is insatiable; the more he has, the more he wants. Thus, there is more crime and even grander living. It is being a big shot that is important.

The criminal takes pride in his M.O. in crime, boasting of being the slickest or the strongest and pointing to the value of the proceeds as an index of the "success"of his crimes. His pride is expressed in his derogation of how other criminals operate. He may revel in being "smooth," while belittling a criminal who is violent. He may pride himself on being closemouthed; this earns him a reputation for being a slick operator and gives him something of a mystique in the eyes of other criminals.

In the discussion of sentimentality, we shall indicate that the criminal prides himself on being a good person on the basis of his appreciating the arts, having some talents, having participated in charitable causes, or having done some nice things for people, especially his family. We shall also explain how pride in his own decency in the long run only promotes one's criminality.

Criminal pride is often not visible. In fact, the criminal may seem remarkably modest. However, the inner state is far different; while adopting such an outward mien, he is deceiving someone. Although he is ostensibly humble, he is enjoying the triumph of a "con."

Criminal pride is rigid in that it preserves a self-created image of a powerful, totally self-detemining person. It is an unbending posture that is maintained toward the world, despite the unfavorable and even punitive attitudes of others. It is not modifiable by argument or persuasion. This rigidity is based on the fear and despair of the zero state. Pride is a perch that must be maintained, lest the criminal fall into the abyss of being a nothing. The criminal does not want to surrender to any system or anyone's program. One man reported that at the age of twelve he decided he would never submit to any individual, institution, or system—that to do so would make him a nonperson. Thus, there is a "standing on principle" by which the criminal inflexibly asserts that he is in the right. The attitude behind this intense pride was clearly expressed by a man who asserted, "If I bend, I break." That is, if the criminal yields to another person on one issue, his entire position in life is threatened. He must emerge on top in any contest. If a situation is not a contest to begin with, he will make it one. Achieving a victory is more important than any single issue itself.

The criminal may be guided by pride to such an extent that he appears ridiculous. He may appear to be courting punishment or engaging in self-defeating behavior deliberately. When backed against the wall, he takes a stand "on principle," even if it is detrimental in the long run.

C, confined to minimum security, was anticipating a job on the hospital grounds with increasing privileges. When he learned that he was assigned to the bakery, he protested vehemently. He insisted that he was not going to take such a menial job. He was given a choice between going ahead with the assigned position and being returned to maximum security. C objected to both alternatives. Finally, he asserted that he would return to maximum security before he would ever go to the bakery, and he was remanded to maximum security.

This display of pride resulted only in a penalty. But in C's eyes this was not a defeat. Indeed, because he had stood firm, he considered it a victory.

We have seen displays of pride that were obviously contrived. If a criminal believes that expressions of this sort will accomplish an objective, he may act accordingly, and his "standing on principle" will have an exaggerated quality. The show of pride will be to put others on the defensive and to get his way. He may even insist on something in which he no longer believes, although this occurs relatively rarely.

The criminal insists that he knows it all, that his way is right. He closes his ears to any contrary view. At every opportunity, he imposes his opinion on others and rejects what they offer, or he refuses to participate on the same level at all and adopts a smug, aloof, superior attitude, which may be transmitted by sullen silence. He hangs onto his position as though it were precious. He will not climb down from the castle in which he dwells to face the facts of life. Instead, he dons his armor and presents a proud front to the world. In this way, he can ward off further putdowns and respond to those which he believes have already been directed toward him. Maintaining and reinforcing this pride is a matter of psychic survival to him—were he to bend, he would break.

THE POWER THRUST

A criminal in the zero state believes that he is worthless and that everyone knows it. He will not live with this notion of himself, and so he engages in activities by which he will become "somebody." In his excitement-seeking, he moves from an undervalued conception of himself to an overvalued one. His greatest excitement is in doing the forbidden and getting away with it. In his thrusts for power, arrestable and nonarrestable, the criminal views himself as an extraordinary and prestigious figure. This is as unrealistic as the perception of nothingness of the zero state.

We are describing "control" and its resulting "power" from the viewpoint of the criminal, even though he does not use these words.* An observer and

---

* "Control" is our term used to signify management of another person. "Power" refers to the triumph the criminal experiences from managing others and achieving what to him is a victory at their expense.

a criminal may view the same act very differently with respect to who is doing the controlling and who is being controlled. A criminal youngster who is whipped views himself as triumphant because he does not cry. He has a sense of power, but his parents regard him quite differently. To them he is only a whipped boy who might have been taught a lesson. Another example is that of the criminal in confinement. Observers think of him as reduced in stature and tightly controlled by others. However, again the criminal has a very different view. He regards confinement as yet another arena in which to operate. He builds himself up on transactions with other criminals. He approaches the staff with scheming and tactical maneuvering, controlling others through either intimidation or conning. He uses the system as well as he knows how to achieve what he wants, the ultimate objective being release from confinement.

Some criminals are obvious in their power-thrusting—the big shots who try to impress others. But not every criminal disports himself in the flashy, expansive manner of "Mr. Big." Triumphs and conquests can also be achieved and enjoyed through a well-concealed sneakiness and slickness. People who get a kick out of being "operators" do not advertise their acts. For them, the inner triumph is sufficient; they do not need the outward show. In fact, they gain a tremendous sense of power through secrecy. These criminals view themselves as gaining more power through their silence than those who use flamboyant tactics. They view "Mr. Big" as the fool and the sucker who is most likely to give himself away. It is typical for each criminal to regard his own M.O. as the most effective.

The following sections show how the quest for power pervades the criminal's thought. Much of the behavior illustrated in Chapter 3 is related to the thinking patterns discussed here.

POWER THRUSTS IN DAILY LIVING

Hobbies and Interests

The search for power is shown in the criminal's interests and in what he aspires to be. The criminal child wants to be a powerful person—combat hero, fireman, law enforcement agent, clergyman. His hobbies and interests, although usually short-lived, attest to his fascination with power—fast cars, motorcycles, minibikes, chemistry sets.

> "I [mixed chemicals] trying to get the most powerful one without blowing up the container. I had no aim in mind; it was just pleasurable in itself."

The criminal child views himself as more powerful if he can manage the powerful. Powerful machines, powerful natural phenomena, and powerful people are objects of fascination. During his teenage years, these interests can be more easily expressed in behavior, because then he has access to motorcycles, automobiles, guns, and so forth.

Work

Criminals who want to work, as distinct from those who work to satisfy others, view occupations in terms of the power and influence that attend them.

> C said that he found it hard to entertain seriously the idea of working at McDonald's or even at a bank. He tended instead to think more of *owning* McDonald's or a bank.

Some college dropouts who could be deemed criminals made the following comments to characterize various occupations:

> On teaching: "There's no limit to the amount of influence you can have socially and politically."
>
> On economics: "High finance, manipulation . . . multimillionaire."
>
> On research: "Your own show where you make your own decisions."
>
> On medicine: "Love to be a doctor and have all sorts of people tell me, 'You're smart.' "

The power thrust is observable even when the criminal does the most menial work.

> C worked for a leading French restaurant at the rate of 75¢ per hour as a night dishwasher. Although his salary and status were low, he viewed himself as a most important person. The management asked him to report at 3:30 P.M. rather than the customary 6 P.M. C had nothing to conflict with the earlier time, but he insisted on coming in at 6, simply because he wanted to determine his own hours. C managed to stay close to the chef, so that he had top priority when it came to the most unusual and expensive items on the menu. Thus, he was eating better than most patrons of the restaurant. He then began to give orders to the other dishwashers. Although C had no objections to dishwashing, he much preferred to direct others. He took particular pleasure in managing a worker who had been there for 15 years as a dishwasher and who happened to be a very good friend of the owner.

Actually, the criminal is unlikely to hold such a job for long, because he believes that he is far too good and capable to be a flunky.

C believed that he could qualify to practice in some medical specialties without "going through all that training." He stated that he could learn to prescribe medicine in a day. Another criminal said that he could go to an underdeveloped country and be a competent doctor, because he had the brainpower and the wits to cope with any problem that might arise. Never did he believe that he would need any formal training. An eighth-grade dropout declared that he could be a better psychiatrist than anyone else if he put his mind to it.

Not only does the criminal believe that he can do anything, but sometimes he goes ahead and does it, qualified or not. Without training and licensing, criminals have offered their services as ordained ministers, psychotherapists, physicians, and social workers.

The power thrust is prominent in the way the criminal functions on the job. The case of one man who worked as a cook illustrates this point.

A customer sent his hamburger back to the kitchen, because it was too rare. The waitress told the criminal this, and he was put down by the idea that anyone would criticize his cooking. He thought he would really give the customer something to complain about by charring the hamburger so that it was inedible.

The idea was that the world was to function as the criminal desired. As he viewed it, the job should adapt to his demands, rather than his adapting to the demands of the job.

Appearance

The power theme plays a role even in the criminal's appearance. The criminal may select a style of dress or a way of grooming to set himself apart from some people and to give himself a badge of "belonging" to others. The criminal is well aware that appearance is an important component of first impressions. He adopts a habitual mode of dress and appearance that reflects his personality and is in line with his objective, whether it is swindling a bank or promoting himself with a woman.

A criminal who fancies himself as a great entrepreneur may spend $250 for a suit while he is thousands of dollars in debt. As one of our men commented, "I don't know. I just feel more comfortable in a suit." Such a person pays close attention to color, cut, and fit. His clothing is wrinkle-free and spotless. His wardrobe may contain suits that he never wears. But the knowledge that they are there, hanging in his closet, enhances his image of himself, and his being well-dressed conveys an image of affluence to others. The fashionably outfitted criminal, carrying an attaché case (which many do), is sure that he is ready to rub shoulders with anyone, although he himself has no credentials.

For some criminals, wearing stolen or deceptively procured clothing adds to the power thrust, even if what they have obtained by violating is not as good as what they could buy. However, most would rather shop at the best stores and pay for the merchandise.

Although some criminals compete with one another in dress and some criminal youngsters who cannot afford school supplies may sport $60 shoes, many criminals do not care about high style. They prefer to remain inconspicuous and dress like their contemporaries. Thus, depending on the circles in which they move, blue jeans and a denim jacket may be the epitome of style.

Some criminals want to make an impact with long hair, beards, moustaches, or tattoos. Responsible people also dress or groom themselves in styles designed to make particular impressions. They may be trying to advance themselves with a job interviewer, a girl, a new business client, or even their friends. Unlike the criminal's intentions, their intentions are usually not exploitative.

> "When I first wore my hair long, it was as a slug in the nose to people I didn't like. Cutting it is submitting to the pressure applied by society; it is submitting to some people I don't feel akin to. I went back to my [parochial] high school just a while ago and my hair was long and I had boots on. I walked into the school and really got stared at. I was undoubtedly the most unusual person that walked into school all day. I got a couple of comments from students, and I told them I was an alumnus; that sort of blew them."

Speech

The criminal may embellish his speech to make a particular impression. He may use large words for this purpose. We have encountered many a criminal who has an excellent vocabulary but who, in his attempt to prove that he is a big shot, misuses words inadvertently. While trying to demonstrate his erudition publicly, he fails to realize that he is making a fool of himself. If his usage is correct, it is often pretentious. The criminal may use flowery language to appear suave and debonair. Such a person can make a virtue out of even his worst vices. With his choice of words and his style of approaching others, he can talk his way into or out of many situations.

Sex

The criminal child always desires to be older, and this shows itself especially in sex, where power is the predominant driving force from a very early age.

The criminal child is in pursuit of sexual conquests, although very little, if any, sensual gratification is possible. Even when sensual gratification is possible, the power aspect transcends it. From puberty on, most criminals need a partner to control, or they regard themselves as failures. The objective is to conquer and possess. Once the conquest is achieved, interest wanes. Even in a relationship that continues for years between a criminal and his spouse, the power and control aspects are dominant. The criminal regards his partner as property. As long as he has his way, matters run smoothly. If the partner ever asserts herself (or himself) and claims rights, she will be pushed around or discarded. Every married criminal asserts his control in even the smallest decisions.

> C and Linda went to purchase a toaster. They narrowed it down to making a selection from among three models. Linda preferred the ———— brand toaster because of certain conveniences. C immediately became angry and walked away. As a result, Linda did not buy the toaster. She knew from experience that, had she done so, C would not have let the matter drop. He would always be trying to demonstrate that she had chosen the inferior model. This was because C tried to prove he was right in every situation.

If the partner seriously threatens the criminal's control, the putdown may be so severe that serious injury results, even to the point of homicide.

"NUMBER ONE" EVERYWHERE

> "I always wanted to feel like a king. I wanted to top the top. I wanted to be a man."

For the criminal, emerging from all situations on top is an overriding concern. Both in everyday situations and in fantasy, the criminal must be a winner every time.

> One of C's fantasies was that a hidden talent in sports might one day emerge. This could be in basketball, where he would never miss getting the ball into the basket; his percentage would be 100. In football, he would have some kind of shield around him that would prevent contact between him and an opposing player, so that he would score a touchdown every time he had the ball; again, he would score 100% of the times he gained possession.

What begins as a game rapidly becomes a serious contest. There is no interest in skill improvement, no enjoyment of companionship, and no satisfaction in having fun. A game is no longer a game. Targeting for victory, the criminal almost inevitably ruins the event for the other participants. In bridge, he bawls out his partner. If he has a bad frame in bowling, he either quits or remains angry, which usually results in his doing even worse. A playful touch football scrimmage becomes in his mind a tryout for the varsity. Win or lose, the criminal shows no sportsmanship. If he wins, he brags and scorns the loser. If he loses, he complains about the rules, the referees, the playing field, or the other players.

The criminal must also be number one in a discussion. Actually, the criminal does not know what a conversation is. No matter whom he talks to, issues are closed. He has prejudged everything. The criminal knows it all, and everyone must pay attention to him and recognize him as the authority. He does not listen to others either because he is so busy proving a point or because he is trying to outwit the other person as an end in itself. The issue at hand does not matter. As one man put it, he enjoyed "playing games with people's minds."

> *A statement by a 19-year-old:*
>
> "I have lived a lot of life for my years, and since I am middle-aged mentally, I have arrived at a lot of conclusions and ideas that many people never arrive at, many don't arrive at until they are advanced in years."

Others are wrong, and he is right. He tries to shape others' thinking so that it will conform to his, no matter who they are.

The criminal's requirement for a comfortable life are strongly colored by the theme of being number one. One criminal enumerated the following fantasies as to what it would take in life to make him "comfortable":

1. To be an archeologist who would cross the world to study great problems of civilization, making important discoveries, such as why men in the Himalayas do not get cancer.

2. To spend his life in a monastery and achieve a grand closeness to God.

3. To be a great actor who would actually research, act in, and write his own plays.

4. To be a topflight auto racing driver, breaking records with high-powered cars.

5. To be a top musician who would synthesize all musical patterns into one universal pattern.

6. To be a great flyer.

This was a set of ideas from one man, but we could list here hundreds more from other criminals, all expressing the same notions of being exceptional or doing some unusual deed. There is never more than lip service to what is required to accomplish any of these deeds.

> "I accept for myself the fact that given a year to do anything I wanted, I could do very well if I wanted to. I could be a good artist, or a good writer, a good musician, a noted one. This is in itself a reason for not doing anything because I don't have to prove [anything] to myself. I don't particularly want at this point to do anything. It means limiting yourself in many ways."

In other words, the criminal views himself as already tops in everything, and therefore there is no need to prove anything to anyone.

THE POWER THRUST IN CRIME

The power thrust is most prominent and of greatest consequence to society in violation. In crime, the criminal finds excitement, "kicks," a "charge," or whatever else one wants to call it. The conquest is the sine qua non for the crime. The proceeds play a secondary role. Both the poor and wealthy steal. Money is merely an instrument for accentuating self-importance. It is used to impress others and to gain influence. Almost invariably, the criminal lends this money, buys things for others with it, or gives it away, obligating others in the process. Offering unusually large tips, for example, accomplishes two objectives. First, it impresses others.

> "People would form around me at the racetrack, and I would feel like a big shot. This would give me a tremendously good feeling. I used to tip heavily, and I made sure people saw me tip. For instance, if I had a check at the racetrack for $4.25, I would always order a drink, although I never drink, so that the bill would be a little over $5. Then I would leave a $5 tip and appear to be a big shot to others."

Second, it leads the recipient to remember the criminal, so that next time he will receive special service and a good table in the clubhouse. This builds him up in his guest's eyes as a man who carries some weight. Even if he has no one with him on a return visit, the criminal will be gratified by the special treatment. In addition, he might exploit the waiter for other things, asking of him far more than good service. By such means does the criminal become "Mr. Big." "Mr. Big" thinks and lives on a grand scale, doing almost anything to satisfy insatiable tastes—that is, anything except hard work.

> "I want one thing and one thing only—to be successful. I would rather be dead than just a mail sorter. I want to have a large impact on the way things happen."

It is particularly on women that "Mr. Big" wants to make an impression. Making an impression is part of the scheming to conquer and exploit.

> C was embezzling money from his father's store. At that time, he was pursuing a woman who made many demands on him while she lived with another man. C spent $75 on dinner for two, purchased a stereo, and spent $200 in one weekend on the woman and her cousin. He wanted to buy her a $10,000 car and an emerald ring, but did not go quite this far. All this was part of his attempt to be number one with her.

Not every criminal steals primarily to establish a public image. Some are very quiet and seek no recognition. Knowing that they did what most others would not gives them a buildup.

> "There was some excitement involved [in shoplifting], [the uncertainty of] whether or not I could just pick it up and walk out with it. So that is what I did. I didn't know how expensive it was. It was just something that struck my fancy. . . . I got a great feeling of exhilaration. I was great at it, putting stuff over on people; it was a talent I had that others did not."

Some criminals take pleasure in knowing that they can make people suffer, be paralyzed by fear, or even die. In fantasy and in behavior, it is exciting to induce fear in others.

Arson: "I Made a Lot of People Scream"

> A kitchen helper at the cafeteria said the arsonist "sloshed [gasoline] all over the floor, looked around with a smile on his face and set a match to it" (*The Washington Post*, 2/4/73, p. A1).

In this tragic incident, which left at least fifteen people in critical condition, the arsonist demonstrated to himself that he had the power of life and death over others. The ultimate exercise of control over another person is to destroy him. Killing may occur for any of a number of alleged reasons or for no reason apparent to others. In recent cases of assassination or attempted assassination of public figures, the power and control elements are very evident and subsume political ideology. The case of Arthur Bremer, who attempted to kill Governor Wallace of Alabama in 1972, is illuminating in this respect. Bremer kept a diary in which, knowing what he was going to do, he predicted that "these pages [of the diary] will be closely read as the pages of the scrolls in those caves" (*The Evening Star and The Washington Daily News*, 8/3/72, p. A1). Bremer was not guided by ideology; he desired to assassinate figures at different ends of the political spectrum. Crimes become political after the fact, either because of the social repercussions or because the criminal uses political considerations to justify what he has done.

> We come to the term "political crime," which we don't have in this country, in my opinion. . . . We don't have crimes related to people's political beliefs or statements. We have protections in the Constitution, such as the First Amendment, that protect those adequately. It's hard for me to see the difference between the bombing of a bank for the purpose of obtaining the money or the bombing of a bank for the purpose of protest against the establishment.—Guy L. Goodwin, Chief of Internal Security Division's Special Litigation Section of Dept. of Justice [in *The Washington Post*, 2/11/73, p. D4].

To one who understands how the criminal mind works, this statement appears reasonable. It takes a particular type of person, a particular type of thinking to bomb a bank or to commit any other crime. Many citizens have grievances against society. However, only a tiny number exploit a social issue and use it as a vehicle for their own criminality.

The control element is very pronounced in suicide. Every criminal with whom we have dealt who has committed murder has at one time or another thought seriously of destroying himself. At least half our people have scars from suicide attempts or have institutional records of such attempts. In the mental state in which suicide is contemplated, the criminal is put down and angry about his loss of control of external situations. To destroy himself would be to relieve himself of a control problem.

> C believed that it was better "to be under the sod than not to be God." After trying to control and manage everyone around him at Saint Elizabeths for more than 10 years, he was released, despite ongoing violations. On returning to his small home town, he tried to dominate family and friends there, but did not succeed. This man, who had murdered his wife over a decade before, was still trying to control others, and he failed. We soon got word of his suicide.

Many a criminal has had the fantasy of going down in a blaze of glory if cornered. In such a case, he obviously would not be in control, but there would be a final power thrust so that he could at least achieve some notoriety posthumously. In the words of a frustrated hijacker and presidential assassin, "I'd rather live one day as a lion than 100 years as a sheep" (*The Washington Post*, 2/28/74, p. A10). This statement emphasizes the point we are making relative to the criminal's power aspirations.

The power thrust clearly plays a role in sexual crimes. The conquest feature is readily apparent in rape, whereas the sexual indulgence is brief and minimal, with ejaculation before entry common. However, this feature may not be so easily discernible in exhibitionism, voyeurism, or child molestation. The exhibitionist selects the person whom he is targeting and then performs a series of very calculated acts.

> C, who has exhibited himself perhaps thousands of times, tries to gain control over his victim. He believes that, if he turns his back, if he bends over, if he shows his penis at a particular angle, or if he walks a particular distance, the female onlooker will follow him so as to view him as well as she can. C expects that while he is doing this, she will function according to how he behaves. If he turns in a certain way, she will turn. If he walks a certain distance, she will follow suit.

The criminal's excitement is based on this "control" of the other person, as well as on his own concomitant fantasies. Of course, sometimes the victim turns away and shows no interest whatsoever. The power thrust of the voyeur shows itself, in that he has dominion over the other person's lack of privacy. In other words, the criminal's advantage lies in the mere fact that the person being watched does not know that the criminal is there. This advantage is what constitutes the triumph. The voyeur can fantasy anything he wishes, and in that sense he runs the show. The child-molester can be rather well assured of a successful sexual performance with an inexperienced minor. He usually is "number one" literally, in that he is the one and only person in the child's sexual experience.

We emphasize that the power thrust plays a role in every aspect of crime, whether it be a crime of property, assault, or sex. The criminal never fights fairly. He loads things in his favor, so that there is little, if any, competition. The following example indicates how a criminal victimized a sixty-eight-year-old man.

> Mr. R had achieved a position of some distinction and wealth in public life. He was well read in psychiatry and took it upon himself to sponsor people who had been in trouble, usually criminals. His desire was to give them a new start in life.

> C was one of the people whom Mr. R took in. Here was a young man who had been in serious crime all his life, but Mr. R saw C as a young person with charm who was worth taking under his wing. C lived with at his benefactor's home and was given money. Although he liked and was appreciative of Mr. R, C was only too ready to exploit him. "Being kept" by this distinguished gentleman had an element of challenge. No ordinary person could wangle money and extract whatever he wanted from Mr. R. It took wits and perseverance to get this shrewd millionaire to part with his money. C played on the man's humanitarian sentiments by using the threat of getting in trouble or hurting himself. When he was in maximum security, he threatened to elope unless Mr. R gave him money and other items he wanted. C also persuaded Mr. R to use

his "influence" with hospital personnel so as to make his stay at the hospital more comfortable.

It was the matching of wits and the opportunity to control a public figure that were gratifying to the criminal.

THE CRIMINAL'S REJECTION OF LEGITIMATE POWER

"If there were a national contest to reward the greatest exploiters, with people who were willing to be exploited participating, I think I should soon tire of the sport. It would be like getting a free lunch; it wouldn't taste as good as one obtained by conning."

When a criminal derives considerable power from his station in life, it is insufficient. The legitimate power that a lawyer, a doctor, or a businessman might have is not enough. Many of our criminals have held positions of legitimate power and authority. As a lawyer, one of them had the power of influencing decisions regarding freedom or imprisonment. This power did not satisfy him. He neglected his work for other, more exciting illegitimate activities. A criminal may have a sexually responsive wife who is uninhibited and amenable to anything he wants. But legitimate sexual power does not fulfill his appetite. He prefers to reject the situation in which he can "get it free" and seek a conquest elsewhere. And so it goes throughout the criminal's life. He always wants something more, and so he violates to get excitement.

POWER IN THE CRIMINAL VERSUS POWER IN THE NONCRIMINAL

It has been observed (e.g., Stafford-Clark, 1964, p. 59) that the criminal is "omnipotent," much as a young child is in his interactional patterns with the world. Both are very demanding. Neither is a social creature with respect to sharing and interdependent behavior. The normal omnipotence of childhood is described by Brenner (1957):

The child's attitude toward the first objects of which it is aware is naturally an exclusively self-centered one. The child is at first concerned only with the gratifications which the object affords, that is, with what we might call the need-satisfying aspect of the object (p. 111).

Some children respond to the socializing influences of the outside world; others do not. The infant lacks the awareness of what is forbidden. He may do what is not permitted because he is ignorant of the limits of tolerable behavior. But once he learns these limits, he usually abides by them. In contrast, the criminal child rejects the socializing influences and makes doing the forbidden a way of life, even when he knows what is considered out of bounds.

Five kinds of power are enumerated by Rollo May (1972, pp. 105-112):

"Exploitative": "Always presupposes violence or the threat of violence"

"Manipulative": "Power *over* another person" (the "con man" rather than the gunman)

"Competitive": "Negative form" ("one person going *up* . . . because his opponent goes *down*")
"Positive form" ("rivalry that is stimulating and constructive")

"Nutrient": Such as a "normal parent's care for his or her children"

"Integrative": "Cooperative" on a voluntary basis

The criminal exercises mainly "exploitative" and "manipulative" power and perhaps also the negative form of "competitive" power. The noncriminal does compete for positions of power in both the positive and the negative senses. The criminal knows little of the "stimulating and constructive" rivalry that occurs as people work hard and achieve a degree of success based on merit.* It is doubtful that the parent or the member of a team thinks of himself as exercising "power." Thus, the descriptive labels "nutrient" and "integrative" do not reflect how a person views what he is doing.

The responsible person spends his life learning limits in addition to those imposed by parents and society, increasing his understanding of man's finitude. One of the continuing lessons of life is the recognition of one's own individual limitations, as well as those of others, and learning to deal with them constructively. The responsible person discovers that attempts to control the world are usually frustrated, and he comes to gain satisfaction from exerting control over his own life and destiny. Most responsible people wish to be important in at least some small way, even if it be only within their own family circle, but oblige no one to be their servant. Responsible individuals learn that legitimate power and control usually have to be earned by hard work and responsible thinking and action.

We have referred to the continuum of personality features in our discussion of the meaning of the word "criminal." We must also keep the continuum in mind is discussing any individual thought process. We reemphasize this concept here, in discussing the power thrust. At one extreme is the hardwork-

---

* Alfred Adler (1961, p. 70) described people with a "pathological power drive" as seeking "to secure their position in life with extraordinary efforts, with greater haste and impatience, with more violent impulses, and without consideration of anyone else." Adler (see Ansbacher and Ansbacher, 1956) was a determinist probing a person's life before the age of five to explain his current condition—a psychoanalytic effort at explanation, but not a process for changing a criminal, which requires free choice to build a responsible base in life.

ing person who makes no calculated attempts at self-aggrandizement. Many of the impoverished parents of ghetto criminals could be characterized in this manner. They plod along relatively uncomplainingly day after day, making both physical and emotional sacrifices in the interest of improving themselves and facilitating the welfare and development of their children. They ask little of life, and they give far more than they receive. Somewhere in the middle of the continuum are the businessmen and politicians who actively seek to promote themselves. Some are unscrupulous and are willing to compromise principle and integrity to achieve power. At the other extreme of the continuum is the criminal, who views most undertakings in terms of winning a personal victory. Relentlessly, he pursues power for its own sake, with no moral concern as to means. He seeks control over not merely his own destiny, but the destinies of others. The responsible person who has a position of authority exercises the power to benefit others and thereby adds meaning to his life. The criminal's beneficiary is only himself.

Criminals recognize no limits to their personal power and control. Their thinking has a quality that may be termed "mind-expanding": there are no limits to what they believe they can do, the world is theirs to do with as they please, their avarice is without restraint, and they live without regard to law and custom. Noncriminals have aspirations and dreams, but they do not believe that wishing for something guarantees it; they work for what they want. To criminals, possibility is fact.

The search for power is global in criminals—it is present in thinking, conversation, and action. To avoid being "zeroes," they must be powerful. We have said that criminals seek excitement as an antidote to the zero state. Everyone has his excitements, but the noncriminal's excitements do not include pursuing power for its own sake and then exploiting others. Criminals spend their lives proving their power; noncriminals spend their lives improving themselves.*

SENTIMENTALITY

The "soft side" of the "cold-blooded" criminal has been capitalized on by writers to add human interest to fiction, television shows, and films about the

---

* Throughout this section, we have stressed the difference between power used responsibly and irresponsibly. This distinction is widely recognized. The emphasis on the responsible use of power is reflected in a leaflet (1974) of the National Training Laboratories (NTL). NTL was offering "Programs in Power" during 1975.

One-week residential programs focusing on the development of heightened sensitivity to power dynamics, increased self-awareness regarding one's strengths and limitations in working with power, and insights regarding *more effective and responsible uses of power* in organizational, family, and community life [italics ours].

criminal. In his novel *In Cold Blood,* Truman Capote (1966) graphically described Perry's compassion for human beings that emerged just before the murder of the Clutter family:

1. Perry took a chair into the bathroom so that Mrs. Clutter could sit down because she was weak and had recently been ill.

2. In tying up Mr. Clutter, he did not want him to lie on the cold floor, so he had him lie on a piece of cardboard from an old mattress box.

3. The young boy in the family began coughing after Perry had bound him, so Perry returned and placed a pillow under his head to relieve the coughing.

4. After Perry had bound each of the Clutter family members, he asked them if they were comfortable and managed to put them on couches or in chairs. The girl was tucked into bed.

The sentimentality of the criminal sometimes gets him into trouble. Fictional accounts of the criminal have him coming back to the girl he loved and getting caught in a stakeout in the process. News features on criminals sometimes describe their talents and aesthetic sensitivities, as in the following sketch of an armed robber who killed a policeman during a bank holdup.

"He Just Wanted to Get Away from People"

Eros ———, named by his parents 22 years ago after the Greek mythological god of love, is a dreamer. . . . [His friends] talked about the way he loved cats and classical music; his fine craftsmanship in making and repairing furniture; his desire to play piano. . . . In the group was the mother of one of the young people [who said] "Eros always came over here and offered to do errands for me. He even laid the tile in the kitchen. He did a beautiful job. Such a craftsman. I offered to pay him but he told me he wouldn't accept any money. He said, 'I do things like this only if I like people' " (*The Washington Daily News,* 5/28/71, p. 5).

Observations like those just cited attract attention because they so sharply contrast with the brutality exhibited by the subject. It astonishes one to read, for example, about a man who kills his mother to save her the embarrassment of learning that her son had killed nine people (*The New York Times,* 10/21/73).

We have found from the beginnings of our work that such sentimentality is common to every criminal with whom we have dealt. Both clinical descriptions (e.g., DeRiver, 1950; Eissler, 1949) and popular stories about criminals mention the sentimentality, but do not explain it. People cannot understand how the same person can be vicious and kind. We shall try to show how sentimentality is related to the criminal pattern.

Nearly all criminals are intensely sentimental toward their mothers. The criminal virtually enshrines his mother as though she were a holy figure. It has been observed that the most common tattoos of criminals are those which say "Mom" or bear some other reference to mother. If one asks a criminal who the most significant person in his life has been, he is most likely to reply, "Mother." However, the criminal's "love" for his mother does not deter him from a way of life that causes her worry and grief. The criminal's crimes may affect his mother directly.

> C broke into the home of people that his mother worked for. This family had had great confidence in her. The woman of the house was confined to a wheelchair and had complete faith in C's mother, on whom she was very dependent. When C was arrested, the woman did not trust his mother as much, and a strong bond was weakened.

This criminal cut off all sentiment for his mother and used information that he got from her for breaking and entering. What appears incongruous to laymen is that the criminal reveres his mother one moment and wants to attack her verbally or physically the next. The latter comes to mind when he does not get his way and when his mother interferes with his plans.

The parent who in life was injured by a sentimental but criminal son is honored after death. One criminal worked for money to buy flowers for his mother's grave, because he did not want to pay for them with the ample proceeds of his crime. We have seen a criminal of the Jewish faith who had never observed the rituals of his religion say Kaddish (the mourner's prayer) in temple on the anniversary of his father's death.

The criminal may be especially sentimental toward his children. He may abuse and even desert his family, but his ties to his children usually remain strong. It is striking that the criminal expresses deep concern with signs of irresponsibility in his children. Most want them to grow up to be moral, law-abiding citizens. He brags about a son or daughter who is doing well in school. However, although the criminal may say that he will do anything for his children and may in fact be a good provider, he eventually hurts them through his own irresponsibility.

> C said that one of the saddest events of his life was being in jail on Christmas eve. His children came to visit and begged him to come home. The memory of this stayed with him, and the following Christmas, when he was no longer in prison, C spent $500 on gifts for them.

Many criminals are very attached to animals—perhaps to the extent of refusing even to kill a roach. On the other hand, some criminals brutalize animals merely to show others how tough they are (by displaying control and power). However, the criminal who hurts a cat in the neighborhood may be extremely devoted to a pet of his own. The following was written by a criminal in confinement.

"I had a dog once, a real dog. To me that dog was everything. I loved that dog more than any other thing in the world, and now she is gone. I wish I was in the ground with her. I wish I was in the ground to keep her warm. Please, if there is a God somewhere, look out for her. Love her as I loved her. Hold her, she has to be held and loved. I wish I could do it, but I cannot. I am going to keep her in my mind, and then she will still be alive with me, and we can go on loving each other as we did then. Whenever I saw the need for warmth, I could get it from her."

These were the sentiments of a nineteen-year-old who had done some $20 million worth of damage in arson, theft, and vandalism. One confined criminal became so upset about not being allowed to care for a stray kitten that he threatened an attendant with a hammer. The criminal's fondness for animals was tapped at the California Institute for Men at Chino in what was called "one of America's most unusual prison rehabilitation programs" (*The Washington Post*, 11/19/72, p. E8). It was called "animal psychology," and it consisted of grooming and training animals.

The criminal usually is sentimental toward the helpless, whether they be babies, children, old people, or the physically infirm. We have seen numerous incidents of criminals helping those who cannot help themselves. At the Lorton prison near Washington, D.C., some prisoners established a "trust fund" for a sixteen-month-old infant abandoned on a doorstep in freezing weather (*The Evening Star and The Washington Daily News*, 1/29/73). It is not unusual for a criminal to stop on his way to a crime to help an old lady across the street, put money in a beggar's cup, or give away something valuable (which he does not value) to someone he pities.

The criminal may show unusual consideration for a disabled person. But he rarely maintains a relationship with such a person, because, as he sees it, there is little for him to gain.

While in daily active crime, which he termed his "work," C befriended a girl with muscular dystrophy. He often spent time with her, playing cards or taking her to the movies. In time, they became well acquainted, and she invited him home for meals. He treated this girl differently, in that he did not make any sexual advances. He did his best to assist her in every possible way.

We have described in detail the criminal's exploitation of women. There are some instances in which the criminal idealizes a woman's qualities and treats her with consideration, rather than setting her up for future use.

> Pat was a "breath of innocence and freshness," a girl of absolute integrity. C knew that she was married and a faithful, devoted wife. This he respected, as well as revering her for her candor and honesty. He was amazed when she had to be talked into taking a few hours of leave to make preparations for moving to another state, so intense was her loyalty to her job. On her birthday, C presented Pat with an ode he had written. He indicated that he was very careful never to overstep his bounds with her. He did not push himself on Pat or try to monopolize her time. C realized that she was totally different from the women with whom he had usually associated.

A criminal, although very active in sexual and nonsexual crime, may respect a decent woman and may even be envious of her decency. He may place her on a pedestal and endow her with characteristics that she does not have. Such treatment allows him to think well of himself. The criminal may also describe an irresponsible or frankly criminal woman in glowing terms, building her up as responsible. He does this to impress others. It is also part of his attempt to build himself up in his own mind. The fact that he thinks he has a "cool chick" overshadows her untruthfulness and unreliability.

The criminal's sense of justice and honesty emerges sporadically in a variety of situations. He may steal hundreds of dollars worth of property, but run back two blocks to a store to return a few cents of excess change. He may cheat an unwitting victim, but be indignant when he sees someone else being cheated by an unscrupulous merchant. He may squire a woman around town on the proceeds of a crime, but work hard at a legitimate job for the money to buy his sister a birthday gift. Examples of criminality and transient decency within the same person are numerous.

Part of what we call the criminal's sentimentality is his artistic sensitivity expressed in talents and interests. Some criminals are fine artists, having turned out sketches, artifacts, or paintings since childhood. One criminal skipped school as a young boy to spend time in art galleries and museums. Another, known as the "gorilla," had produced murals that were displayed in local commercial establishments. Still another became a consultant to a leading art gallery and established a school in which he instructed others in the arts. Some of these men are musically gifted, playing instruments by ear with no formal training. Many who are not musical themselves have a passion for music. The whole spectrum of music, from country to classics, is included among the criminal's tastes. We have encountered criminals who have murdered who love Brahms. The talents of the criminal have been gaining attention in the community. Talent shows, concerts, and art fairs are becoming more widespread in prisons and other institutions. Some criminals are skilled writers; many are self-taught. Prison publications are full of poetry of good quality and high sentimentality. The work of some criminals is recognized and published.

> C has had writings published in several leading magazines. He achieved some distinction in the literary world with both poetry and prose. However, he stated that he did not want to make writing his career because the work involved was so laborious and "it takes time."

The messages conveyed in their artistic productions may be idealistic and humanitarian. These men manifest compassion for the underprivileged and the underdog. They decry political and social injustice and express their despair at the inhumanity of man. The following essay condemning hatred and violence was written by a criminal in the 1960s while he was in jail.

OBJECTIVE INDICTMENT

America the beautiful, the land of milk and honey. The milk has soured and the honey turned to venom. "Black Power" shout some, "Get Whitey" yell others. "Kill those Niggers," scream the Ku Klux Klan. The Catholic hates the Jew, the Protestant hates the Catholic, the Jew hates the Arab, the Black hates the White, the Left hates the Right, the North hates the South, people who wear black shoes hate those who wear brown.

HATE—HATE—HATE—all of the self-righteous hate. Why? Because they like to hate. It bolsters their sagging ego, makes them feel good to downgrade others. They say, "I'm Superior"; "I'm Better"; and this self-assurance that they are better than someone else covers up for those twisted feelings of inferiority that keep nagging at them.

(A White red-neck waits in the bushes, beside the highway in Hernando, Miss. His twisted little mind schemes to blast James Meredith on his unsuspecting march.) (A gang of Negro youths beat 3 newsmen in Watts with 2x4's because they are white and because this is Watts '66). Are either of these people justified in what they are doing? No, they are not! All they are doing is letting their hate and frustration control them. "Hate is a useless emotion. There is no profit in hate."

How much time and energy do people waste in hating something? How many lives are twisted by the self-consuming poison of hate? "Hate is a negative device. There is no constructive facet to hate. It is totally destructive to everything it comes in contact with."

People or Society today are supposed to be advanced and sophisticated. It is ridiculous and pitiful indeed to see so many people spend so much time and accomplish so little simply because they are hung-up in the frustration that goes hand in hand with HATE.

This man, who described violence, was himself a violent and exceedingly dangerous criminal who later continued his violence.

The reading habits of these men also indicate sensitivity and sentimentality. A seventh-grade dropout ferreted out quotations from Chaucer, a gunman read Montaigne, and a non-Jewish rapist expressed interest in the Talmud. Many criminals read widely, especially in periods of reflection and self-disgust. We have seen them in confinement reading Kipling, Baudelaire, existential philosophy, and religious works. If one quizzes them on what they have read, he sees that they have missed a lot because of their failure to think conceptually and because of their lack of knowledge about the responsible world. They do pick up a few stimulating ideas, and then think that they have mastered the entire content. A common pattern is for them to focus on the idealism expressed.

Most criminals conceal their sentimentality. To acknowledge it is in their view an admission of being weak or "sissy," which would be at odds with the image that they wish to convey to others.

> C was ashamed when a probation officer saw him at a Leonard Bernstein concert. He negated his artistic interest, because he thought it would make him seem weak. He would not let others know of his interest in plays and opera.

The criminal can wall off this sentimentality even from his own awareness, because it is incompatible with his self-concept. He readily boasts of his toughness, but he hides his sensitivity. For the criminal to cry or feel sorry for someone and reveal it to others is rare.

> When C was in the service, a heroic pilot was wounded fatally. Some men reacted by crying, some by cursing the enemy. C's comment was terse: "Nobody lives forever." The commanding officer responded to him by asking whether he had ice water in his veins. Actually, C was very upset and afraid, and in a secluded area he cried by himself.

> C wept on hearing of his wife's death. He could not recall the last time he had cried. Then he remembered that it was in the seventh grade. He had given his mother a pair of earrings, and they had had a fight that resulted in her telling him that she did not want the earrings and in his crying. He regarded sentimentality as weak then, when he was 12, and as even weaker when he was a grown man.

Secrecy is one pattern, but some criminals are not embarrassed to show their knowledge of the arts. In fact, the criminal may learn about art, music, and literature not out of a deep interest in the arts per se, but to use them for self-serving purposes. Familiarity with the arts may be an entrée in the exploitation of others, especially women. Or he can build himself up as a source of knowledge and teach others. However, in most cases the interest and sentimentality are genuine.

Sentimentality, whether genuine or contrived, can be used to score points. If the criminal knows that others will be impressed, he displays his sentimentality. He may even try to convince others that he has interests that he does not have. He may turn on classical music, but not listen to it. He may be seen with a particular book, but never read it. If he is confined, he may claim to be fond of his children and plead to see them, even if he neglected them for years and never bothered to write to them while he was in prison. The criminal often succeeds in these ploys with corrections officials, therapists, and teachers who are watchful for some "redeeming" qualities.

Sentimentality may also be used as a weapon.

> C's dog was lost. This had upset him for a long time. In fact, he referred to it whenever he did not get his way at home. When he became angry, whatever the issue, he threw in the idea that the loss of the dog was the family's fault.

In such cases, the criminal resorts to an "old chestnut" that was valid enough at one time, but is not currently stirring up deep sentiment.

The reader may be confused by what basically is an issue of semantics. When one says that a person is "sentimental," one usually implies that sentimentality is an enduring quality that guides the person's conduct over time. However, sentimentality in a criminal, even if it endures, is not functional. Its operational effectiveness depends on the criminal's state of mind at a given moment. A striking example can help to clarify this. In one of his autobiographic writings, a criminal described his compassion for an unhappy woman:

> "I just went up the hall and I saw a woman crying. When I saw this it hurts me. I know a little about this woman and I understand she has had a hard time most of her life. She is very easy to be hurt, when you think of all of the people in the world who have been treated this way it is really shocking. Then you wonder what the world is coming to. On the other hand it has been this way for a long time and I feel this way, if people don't care what happens to other people, then the world is going to be in one hell of a mess. There is one thing I don't like to see and that is a woman crying, or anybody for that matter. I am sure there are a lot of people who think I am a bitter guy, but I am not as bitter and cold as other people think I am."

This man, who could not stand to see a woman cry, murdered a young woman because she rejected him as a lover in favor of another.

How can such diametrically opposing attitudes reside within the same person? The criminal is a fragmented person, with shifting states of mind. (This is discussed later in some detail.) Whatever the criminal wants to do at a given moment is "right" for him. Sentimentality gives way to overriding desires. *From the criminal's point of view,* there is nothing antithetical in helping and exploiting the same unfortunate person. In one instance, a criminal helped a blind man and later stole $100 from him. One cannot assume that the assistance rendered initially was a "con job." Many such acts are sincere at the time, and only later does the exploitive element play a role.

In summary, we have found sentimentality in even the most cold-blooded criminals. Sentimentality sometimes acts as a deterrent to a specific crime, but rarely. During the execution of a crime, sentiment may be expressed, but still does not prevent the crime itself. Sentimentality never eliminates *patterns* of criminal thought and action. In fact, it contributes to their continuation. The criminal's kindness, charity, and aesthetic interests and talents enhance his opinion of himself and add to his belief that he is a good person. We shall say more about this view of the self in Chapters 6 and 8. For now, the reader should remember that the apparently positive qualities described here are really not so positive. Ultimately, they give the criminal greater license for crime, they do not contribute to making him responsible, and they do not form a basis for rehabilitation to a responding way of life.

RELIGION

All but one of the criminals with whom we have dealt were exposed to religious ideas and training. Elements of religious belief and interest remained as permanent facets of each of them, to be evoked at various times in their lives. In Chapter 3, we described the criminal's religious practices. Here, we shall discuss the mental processes that accompany those practices—first, the genuine religious sentimentality that appears in the criminal's life, and then how he uses religion for self-serving purposes.

GENUINE RELIGIOUS BELIEF AND SENTIMENT

Perhaps the most striking early difference between criminal and noncriminal is that the former takes the basic religious teachings extremely literally and is inordinately frightened. He regards God as an all-powerful, all-knowing being who sees everything all the time. He believes that, to remain in God's favor, one must be virtually a saint. Many a criminal child has vivid images of hell and lives in fear of immediate punishment for wrongdoing.

Because of their religious exposure, some people have a fear of hell. The criminal reacts strongly. He dwells on sinfulness and gives it such emphasis that it is hard for him to function in the world. To him, almost everything is tainted with sin. He perceives an extreme duality in life—good and evil, God and devil. We described in Chapter 3 the extreme pattern of trying to be good and the fears of making the least little slip. This might involve crossing oneself after uttering a curse word or having an "impure" thought. Criminal children strive to achieve a state of absolute purity. They fear that they may be consigned to eternal damnation in the fiery pit for the slightest transgression. Many of these children embrace the strictest possible form of religion, in the hope that this will help them to remain pure. As we noted earlier, several among our group converted to Catholicism at a very early age.

It is important to note that the religious ideas of adult criminals have not evolved beyond their childhood forms. As we shall point out in the next section, the criminal fails to develop conceptual thinking. He lacks the concept of religion as a way of life or as an ethical or moral system. He believes that a few concrete acts, such as going to church and saying a prayer, make him a religious person. The criminal's use of religion and his view of God are ever changing in line with his wants. A criminal may attend services at church Sunday morning and rob a church bingo game later in the week. He may pray for forgiveness of sins at bedtime while contemplating the next day's crime.

To understand these patterns, we need to have a knowledge of the functions that religion serves for the criminal. We get some insight into how the criminal's desire for power finds an outlet in religion when we consider that many criminals of all faiths aspire to be clergymen.

> C was extremely impressed by the tremendous power and authority of the minister of a "Holy Roller" Baptist Church. The minister said things that induced his congregants to shout and moan. C wished that he too could have such power. He tried to get himself involved religiously, but gave up at the age of 16. At 19, he began teaching Sunday school. The impact he got out of this did not compare with the excitement of crime. After teaching for 8 months, he dropped the activity. In jail, he returned more seriously to religion, reading a variety of books, especially about the Muslim movement. He was always the minister to those who knew less.

Some criminals embark seriously on a course of religious devotion and training.

> C entered a Jesuit order and was a novice for 2 years, taking the vows of poverty, chastity, and obedience. He liked the clerical life, but did not comply with the restrictions. C resented the regulations and often disobeyed them. His first crimes there were stealing a forbidden magazine and not turning in some money. The violating patterns expanded.

Such careers in the service of God usually do not materialize or are short-lived as the criminal moves to other arenas in which to seek power. If the criminal child perseveres during the training period (which few do), religion becomes an arena for self-aggrandizement in later life.

> "I had power over the congregation in the pulpit like a stickup artist had. Instead of representing God, I was supplanting him."

Criminals of all ages have periods of self-doubt and may go to church to cleanse themselves. This state of mind sometimes lasts no longer than the church service itself and is concurrent with criminality. Church-going serves as a palliative measure for the criminal's conscience. Confession eradicates fears of God and conscience: "I could always go to confession in order to get to heaven." Asking forgiveness in church or elsewhere requires little effort. There may even be a genuine resolution to sin no more, but it is temporary, the criminal having no real conviction about working out his salvation "in fear and trembling."

The criminal uses religion as a desperate last resort. He goes to church and reads the Bible most often when his fears are the greatest. He may give stolen money to the needy and believe that God will forgive him because he is doing "good." This goodness does not emanate from his adherence to a consistent set of moral principles.

Religion serves still another function: it is of sentimental value to some. The criminal may cling to the religion of his childhood. Walking into a church, hearing the music, reading psalms, and participating in the ritual may evoke a strong nostalgia. This sentimentality may be a factor in frequent church attendance.

Criminals often choose stricter religions and religious movements so that, by following the explicit practices, they can convince themselves that they are truly religious people. The obligations spelled out in Catholicism make its church appealing to many. During a monastic phase, a criminal may find a group or cause that appeals to his idealism. He may participate in a religious movement with the same energy and zeal that he brought to crime.

Even within religion, the power thrust may take precedence over ideals. Thus, the criminal may act as a fervent missionary to others. He may become a leader in the group to the extent that he is largely running a branch of a particular religious order.

As a child, the criminal who is religious finds that trying to be very good, or perfect, is too burdensome. His fears of slipping are too strong to tolerate for long. When he realizes that he cannot be perfect, he begins to question why he should even bother to try to be good, especially because there are things he would rather do. Eventually, competing excitements predominate, and the criminal decides to abandon religion altogether. When he is a youngster, it may be difficult for him to break away. He may therefore continue to attend church because his family requires it, but he will be there only in body, not in spirit. Most criminals, however, do not eliminate religion permanently from their lives. Instead, they swing back and forth from one extreme to another, either being very observant or eschewing religion altogether.

> C began having sex when he was 13. He then became very frightened, regarding the devil as close at hand. The fear of going to hell bothered him incessantly. He was preoccupied with it as he sat in school and then later at night. So he began saying extra prayers alone in his room or in the bathroom. He tried to refrain from "sinning." But between 14 and 17, he abandoned such efforts altogether. At 17, he returned to the church, seeking God's forgiveness. At 18, he again abandoned religion.

The criminal may go through a period in which he considers himself "unworthy" of going to church. He then stays away, not because of any dislike of church itself, but because of an unfavorable view of himself. As we have said, the criminal tends to think in extremes. If he is not perfect, he may think that he ought not to set foot in a church at all.

> C took his daughters to Sunday school and church, but could not bring himself to enter. He thought that he was totally unworthy and that he should go to church only if he were perfect. In his view, church was for those who were already saved, but was not to be used for the process of "saving."

When we say that the criminal regards himself as "unworthy" of being in church, we do not mean that he considers himself a "sinful" person. It is not his stealing or check-passing that he condemns in himself. Rather, it is the liquor on his breath or the profane word he utters. That is, his "sins" consist of the offenses that are readily apparent to others. When they are pointed out, he does not deny that they are sins. He does not consider himself a sinner at all until his activities are known to others.

SELF-SERVING ASPECTS OF RELIGIOUS BELIEF AND OBSERVANCE

Since childhood, the criminal has viewed God as potentially a grantor of wishes. The wishes might be for material things or for the welfare of someone dear to him. He often asks God to help him get away with something or get out of a jam. He may pray to God before a crime, asking forgiveness for the act he is about to commit; but this is very rare, because the criminal usually believes that whatever he does is for a worthy purpose and that he is in the right. The criminal may invoke God's blessing as he plans a crime.

C made a deal with God: he would kill his wife and then confess. As C reasoned it, he would be convicted and executed, he and his wife would meet in heaven, and they would live a better life there than they had on earth. He asked for God's blessing in this enterprise and believed that God would protect him. After the homicide, when he saw that he would be treated as a mental patient, C lied about everything and continued with old violating patterns.

The religious element was transient. Usually the criminal prays to God for assistance during a crime, asking that he not be apprehended. God is to serve as the "getaway car" for his crime. After a crime, a criminal will occasionally pray not for forgiveness, but to forget the crime. This is a prayer to prevent his conscience from bothering him. If he is caught, he is likely to call on God to help him out of the situation, promising that he will no longer act as he has.

A criminal who is apprehended in crime might revert to saying, "God willed it." In doing this, he refuses to acknowledge his own ineptitude or foolishness. Putting the burden on God is a way of disowning responsibility. He believes that he was in the right, but that, for some reason, God intervened. The buck is thus passed to someone else. In jail, he begs God for a good lawyer, a merciful judge, and, of course, a speedy release. The criminal asks God to do his work for him. Depending on how things work out, God may be protector or scapegoat. A chaplain who worked with juvenile offenders observed the "pragmatic" aspect of the delinquent's religious faith:

The existence of a pragmatic religious faith is a near universal characteristic. . . . It may take a crisis to summon the basic belief in God as a personal resource and to initiate the practice of prayer. Placement in an institution constitutes a crisis for young people and leads them to seek the presence of God. God is believed to have more coercive power than the State and he becomes the court of final appeal (Miller, 1965, p. 53).

This chaplain observed further that, when God "fails to come through," the delinquent dismisses God. We have found this to be true of the people we have worked with.

Religion allows the criminal to cloak himself in a mantle of respectability. He shows others that he is a good person by observing some of the formalities of religion. He can, for example, impress others by quoting the Bible, writing spiritual essays, and participating in church functions. In addition, all this enhances his own self-image. Religious observance and sentiment reinforce his idea that he is basically decent, and this gives him further license for crime.

> C—gang leader, thief, and child molester—prominently wore a large silver cross on his chest. C explained the significance of this cross: the cross was his guarantee that he was a good person, despite his crime; because he wore it, he was decent. After he had violated a number of times within a short period, he temporarily returned to the observance of his religion, which was symbolized by the cross.

The cross did not serve as a deterrent to crime. Rather, it legitimized crime, in that it contributed to C's having a good opinion of himself.

When there are competing sets of desires, it is usually religion that is discarded, not the violating patterns.

> C came from a very observant Catholic family. He considered himself to be a religious man, despite his having committed thousands of crimes. When he was challenged about the propriety of a sexual relationship with a particular lady, he decided that he should give up Catholicism if such an act were incompatible with Catholic teaching.

Recognizing the religious attributes of the criminal, the clergy has made attempts to reform inmates of various penal institutions. Religious activities and instruction are organized with the purpose of helping to "bring out the good" in the criminal. The criminal may respond to these appeals solely to make a good impression. Often, however, he is sincere, but the sincerity is transient. In the Washington, D.C., area, prisoners were transported to nearby churches to perform a series of dramatic worship services. A few inmates used this opportunity to escape (*The Washington Post*, 8/9/71, p. C1).

Efforts by responsible people to capitalize on the criminal's religious sentiment only provide the criminal with more of a license for crime. The clergy is likely to tell the criminal that he is basically a good person, even though he has "gone astray." This is like saying that a devastating hurricane is basically good because it watered parched lawns. Such a point of view emphasizes the fragmentary "good" and ignores the lack of a solid structure of mental processes that is conducive to living responsibly. Like the devastation of the hurricane, the damage done by the criminal far outweighs his isolated good acts. But the few good deeds nevertheless contribute to his building himself up further, so that he is ready for more crime.

CONCRETE THINKING

Mental processes in man evolve from the concrete to the conceptual. In a discussion of primitive man's cognition, Werner (1948) pointed out that early man lacked concepts of necessity and causality; his thinking was in terms of isolated events. Werner also observed that primitive mentality is "paralleled" by the structure of the child's thought. Young children are concrete in their "operations of thought and interpersonal relations" (Piaget and Inhelder, 1969, p. 92). It has also been noted that concrete thinking predominates in some mental disorders.

> The schizophrenic's abstract level is lost or completely replaced by the concrete form (Arieti, 1967, p. 272).

Werner and others identified concrete thinking in the mentally retarded, the organically brain-damaged, and those with toxic mental conditions.

The criminal, too, is a concrete thinker. Glueck (1952, p. 125) found that delinquents express themselves in a direct, concrete manner rather than through use of intermediate symbols or abstractions. Eissler (1950, p. 117) declared that concreteness is the most difficult "symptom" to cure in the treatment of delinquents. Their failure to recognize the similarity between situations is often characterized as a "failure to learn by experience."

> No matter how many times [the psychopath] comes to frustration or disaster, he does not learn by such experience to avoid the type of conduct responsible for his failures (Cleckley, 1959, p. 582).

The criminal's concreteness is not due to any known organic deficit or to mental illness. Unlike the mental defective, most criminals can do well on the "Similarities" subtest of the Wechsler Adult Intelligence Scale, which is supposed to assess concept formation. The criminal knows, for example, that a chair and a table are alike in that they are both furniture. The schizophrenic or person with an organic brain syndrome might give a concrete response, saying that each has four legs. If the criminal says this, it is likely to be due to a lack of formal education or a lack of reflection in answering, rather than to a disease process. As we discuss this aspect of the criminal's thinking patterns, we are referring not to the "concreteness" that may show up on an intelligence scale, but to a conceptual deficiency with respect to responsibility that is, for the most part, independent of IQ. A person with below-average intelligence knows what obligation, trust, and loyalty are; even if he cannot satisfactorily verbalize them, his responsible actions reflect this knowledge. The criminal lacks such concepts.

The noncriminal acquires a concept of "family" as he adapts to the stresses and strains that occur within every family. He is a member of a team that functions constructively to make life together as fulfilling as possible. His emerging concept of education embraces the idea that it is preparation for life, whether it involves broadening one's knowledge about the world or acquiring skills for a specific trade or profession. Similarly, he develops a concept of work. At the least, the noncriminal has the rudimentary idea that work is a means to pay the rent and put food on the table. For those who think of a "career," rather than a job, work is an opportunity to learn, develop oneself, and contribute to others, as well as to make money. The noncriminal develops concepts of right and wrong, good and evil. Beginning with the child's interpretation of his parents' behavior, these concepts come to embrace written laws, the mores of society, and perhaps religious precepts. Concepts of what is right are based in part on a sense of justice and consideration of others' needs. Even where the parental example is irresponsible, the noncriminal child is likely to form his own, independent concepts of right and wrong that are responsible.

The criminal is exposed to all these concepts, but does not internalize them. He, too, has a family, goes to school, holds a job, and is taught the difference between right and wrong. However, he does not develop concepts of responsible living, because such concepts would preclude his criminal life style. It is almost tautological, for example, to say that a person would not be in crime if he implemented religious teachings so that they became a way of life.

> Throughout life, C had believed that his calling was to preach the word of God. He had an incomplete and erratic theologic education, having dropped into and out of various seminaries, none of which seemed to suit him. Despite all his ministerial training and nightly scripture readings, his religious background did not deter him from lying, trying to control others, and finally murdering his wife.

The criminal lacks a concept of a home or family. The function of a parent is to give him what he wants or else to interfere and make things hard for him. The criminal does not regard a parent as a human being with thoughts, wishes, and fears of his or her own. There is no concept of a reciprocal relationship; it is all take and no give. The criminal child exploits the parent that he claims to love, in order to have his own way. He tries to gain the favor of the parent who is a "soft touch."

> C and his mother left the family and moved to a different state. The mother was an irresponsible woman who indulged her son by giving him a .22 rifle, a gas-powered model plane, and just about anything else he wanted. C stated that he would return to his father, who was awarded custody, only if his father agreed to specific conditions. C then laid down a series of demands. This playoff of one parent against the other continued, with C extracting from each what he wanted with the threat of running to the other if he were thwarted in achieving his objectives.

There was no concept of a "mother" and a "father," other than that each existed to serve C. He required that they be responsive to his ever-changing desires.

Most noteworthy in the criminal's growing up is his failure in what social scientists term the process of "identification." The criminal does not maintain a balanced view of a person over time. He does not abstract anything that has to do with human qualities, temperament, abilities, and dispositions. There may be some limited copying behavior, but it is never sustained, because to be like another person is demeaning. The criminal is an island unto himself and will not even use another criminal as a model for long, if at all.

The criminal has a knowledge of what is right and what is wrong. As a child, he is perfectly aware of what parents, teachers, and others forbid. He also learns what is against the law. However, what others forbid is not considered at the time a criminal decides he wants to do something. That is, when he has his mind set on violation, considerations of right and wrong are not pertinent; only whether he will get away with it matters. An action is "wrong" if it is distasteful to him (something he would not do) or if he stands a strong chance of getting caught doing it. He, not others, is the arbiter of what is right and wrong for him at the time. There is no abstract concept or set of principles deterring him. The mental processes by which a criminal eliminates considerations of right and wrong are discussed in Chapter 6.

In school, some criminals do learn to conceptualize in academic fields of interest to them. A criminal may successfully complete college and even graduate school, and thus there are criminals in all professions—law, medicine, pastorates, teaching, etc. Many of the criminals with whom we have worked have been well informed in particular academic fields. In some cases, their interests have been in esoteric subjects that allow them to impress others easily. Several have read deeply in religion and philosophy. In quoting ethical principles, they appear to be conceptualizing. Actually, if one listens carefully, it becomes apparent that the criminal does not really grasp the meaning on a conceptual basis. He often distorts what he quotes and uses it to serve his own ends. The broad idea of becoming an "educated man" has no meaning for him; it is defined in purely literal terms.

C, who had some college education, stated that an educated man is "someone who has gone beyond four years of college in the area of their choosing." He perceived the schooling before high school graduation as providing the "generalizations" one needed in life. He viewed college as going beyond book-learning to provide social contacts.

C had defined an "intellectual" as someone removed from the world— very mild, if not meek. An intellectual was also someone who assumed a rather effeminate physical posture. When C wanted to impress others that he was an intellectual, he assumed a cross-legged position and tried to appear meek and very learned.

Although both these men had spent some time at college, they had not utilized that experience to prepare for the future or to expand their knowledge about the world. They used the information they acquired to impress others and thus to build themselves up.

The fact that most criminals do not conceptualize in the academic realm is not due to a lack of ability, but to a dearth of interest. The high incidence of reading disabilities among criminals has often been noted. Some say that the criminal is in crime partly because he cannot read. Indeed, the task of learning to read is experienced by many criminal youngsters as a dull, tiring process—an onerous requirement that the school imposes. If he is not interested, he does not bother with it. If the criminal does read, he often does not complete what he begins, but instead looks for exciting parts and dashes from one section to another. Even if he is a college graduate, he may be a poor reader, in that he becomes absorbed with details of particular interest to him and misses leading ideas. The momentarily intriguing or exciting passage captures his attention. He does not read for broad concepts or for enrichment for its own sake.

The criminal lacks a concept of integrity. He tells others that he is honest and reliable. This is often done indirectly through criticism of others in which there is an implied contrast of their lack of integrity with his honesty. At times, the criminal demonstrates his integrity to others in some small matter to obtain their confidence, but this is not a consistent honesty grounded in a moral view of life. In practice, integrity is foreign to his way of life. He views the consistently honest, reliable person as a "sucker."

As we mentioned earlier, the criminal's religiosity is a conglomeration of concrete practices and isolated ideas, rather than of convictions about how to live. The criminal may regard himself as a religious person merely because he attends church. He might be able to quote church doctrine and be familiar with the Bible, but he has no concept of the relevance of religious teachings to life itself.

> C was brought up as a Catholic and attended Catholic schools. For years, he was exposed to religious teachings and writings. When asked what the Catholic Church sees as living a good life, he responded rather blankly, "Are you talking about going to church on Sunday or the Ten Commandments?"

There is little conceptualization regarding social institutions besides the church. For example, although some people believe that all criminals hate the police, this is not the case. Criminals recognize the need for law enforcement, and many criminal youngsters aspire to be members of the police force. Whether a policeman is good or bad depends on the criminal's personal need for him. In a neighborhood where a criminal youth gang is operating, the gang members may be friendly with a patrolman on the beat. To the youths' way of thinking, if a police officer overlooks what they are doing and is pleasant, they like him. If he poses any interference, he is scorned. The criminal may even offer to assist the police force; it gives him some excitement and a buildup. At times, he may exhort the police to clamp down on crime, but, obviously, this attitude changes when applied to him.

> C wrote the police force a letter, stating that he hoped that its members would take a hard line and prosecute offenders to the fullest extent of the law. He offered his assistance and full cooperation. Of course, when he himself was on his daily tour of housebreakings, he had no use for the police.

Parents, siblings, neighbors, teachers, employers, and others are evaluated as good or bad in the same manner by which the criminal assesses the policeman.

The criminal often speaks in such a manner as to appear to conceptualize more than he actually does. One may be misled by viewing the criminal's generalizations as concepts. For example, a criminal being tested may use language to lead others to think that he knows more than he does. Rather than refuse to admit that he does not know an answer, the criminal may respond anyway. If the examiner is not alert, he might interpret the criminal's pretentiousness, coupled with his concreteness, as indicative of a thought disorder or mental defect.

> C offered definitions to words that were not in his vocabulary. He came close enough at times to get partial credit. In scoring the test, the examiner was sometimes unsure of how to evaluate the responses. For example:
>
> CONSUME: To keep back. (Examiner: Use it in a sentence.) I have consumed these papers in my desk so nobody would find out about them.
>
> OBSTRUCT: To disobey a law or break something. (Sentence?) A man obstructed the glass window.

This quality of answering, by being off the track and yet sometimes close to the correct solution, can confuse a diagnostician.

The criminal is intellectually capable of developing conceptual thinking. There is no inherent mental defect. In fact, just as he does in school, the criminal conceptualizes within a restricted range when something interests him. He may become interested in electrical work and be able to repair a variety of appliances. The same may occur with regard to other interests, such as photography or furniture-finishing. He may also conceptualize with respect to sentimental interests, such as music or art. The ability to conceptualize is present, but fixing a radio has little in common with the mental processes of responsibility that he lacks.

Some concept formation is evident in criminal activities. The criminal uses specific M.O.'s and skills. When he has learned how to pick one kind of lock, he approaches a different kind with the same "principles" of lock-picking in mind. Basically, however, the criminal is concrete with respect to the criminal world. His crimes are a series of unrelated acts, each of which is perpetrated to achieve a triumph. He does not conceptualize a criminal lifestyle. Life for him is a ceaseless search for excitement, a continuing pursuit of conquests—always on to new things, looking for a higher and higher pitch of excitement. His restricted vision allows him to focus on one situation at a time, to the exclusion of all others. This movement from one isolated event to another was graphically described by a criminal:

> "Picture an automatic searchlight revolving from a lonely turret somewhere—the only part of the universe that exists for it is that which falls immediately within its cone of light. All the rest of the world is automatically blotted out."

FRAGMENTATION

Inconsistencies in the criminal's behavior are readily apparent. Cleckley (1964) observed of the psychopath that there is "not even a consistency in inconsistency, but an inconsistency in inconsistency" (p. 369). We shall show that contradictoriness is a standard component of the thinking processes of criminals. There are consistent and predictable aspects to this element of the criminal mind.

"Fragmentation" refers to fluctuations in mental state that occur within relatively short periods. Although the term is descriptive of the mental activity and resulting behavior of the criminal, there is a continuum of fragmentation that includes the noncriminal irresponsible person and (sporadically) the responsible person. The inconsistencies in attitude and behavior are apparent in every part of the criminal's life. The criminal may revere his mother, but cause her untold anguish. At school, he may be helpful and hateful toward the same teacher. He may have a strong sentimental bond with his own children, but take money from their piggy banks to visit a drug pusher. He may pledge fidelity to a friend, but abscond with his money. In confinement, he writes an antiviolence essay, but stabs a fellow prisoner. These and other contradictory actions have been described in Chapter 3.

It is hard for an observer to understand this phenomenon of fragmentation. It is as though a criminal is several people rolled into one. The most obvious manifestation of fragmentation in behavior is the social and vocational instability of criminals. Their lives reveal a pattern of starting something and then changing their minds. "If I like it, O.K. If not, to hell with it" has been their way of responding to most situations. Whether they "like" something depends on their mental state at the time. Basically, they move from one activity to another to generate excitement. It is when they are bored and not in control that interest wanes and a new thrust for power ensues. "I didn't like it, so I quit" has characterized this group's way of life from childhood, whether it be job, school, church, social groups, or individual friendships.

The most common characterization of the criminal is that he is unreliable and a liar. When he fails to keep his word, it is usually deliberate, but it might be the result of fragmentation. To make this clearer, we differentiate between sincere, momentary intentions and convictions. An intention is what one has in mind to do. The criminal may go to church with every intention of being responsible. He says his prayers and listens to the sermon. However, if he truly had religious conviction, he would make the principles and teachings of his religion part of his life. Conviction applies to an enduring, habituated state of mind carried over into action. A judgment about whether an intention will become a conviction should not be made at the moment the criminal expresses it. Only time will tell. Because sincere intentions are usually not sustained, an observer is often led to conclude that the criminal was conning to begin with. That is not necessarily the case. The intentions may have been crowded out by other thoughts and actions more immediately exciting.

A criminal's intentions often go by the board when he is tense. That is, his sincerity is short-lived owing to a competing set of desires. A man may intend to meet a vocational counselor at one o'clock. As he sets out to keep that appointment, he is diverted by a fellow criminal, who suggests that they go to a bar. This generates excitement, but the criminal is still aware of his previous obligation. Once he shelves the original intention and becomes involved in the new activity, the tension dissipates. The pattern of intention giving way to the excitement of the moment is evident in the following narrative:

> "I was coming home from my office where I had just made a number of telephone calls (obscene, of course) and as I looked into my apartment this warm summer's evening, I thought, 'Look, you've got all this, and the phone calls are threatening to destroy it.' And I automatically made

one of my thousand and one resolutions to quit (this one lasted a few days longer than usual) but it was as if the phone calls had never happened or as if they existed in another world. This was my world now, this wonderful home, this loving, adoring wife. Then, when I'm in front of a phone alone, that's my world and the other is misty, cloudy, irrelevant. . . . For me life without some form of deviation becomes unutterably and intolerably boring."

The intentions to be conscientious and a good husband were clearly short-lived in the face of competing desires for excitement. The desire for what this criminal here called "deviation" was overriding. It is erroneously construed by some psychiatrists as "compulsion."

If we adopt a definition of conviction that entails not only the holding of a belief over time, but also a sustained implementation of the belief, then we must say that it is impossible for a criminal to have a conviction. This is not our subjective definition; in common usage, people talk about "living up to a conviction." A criminal may espouse a responsible point of view, but, because of his fragmentation, it never becomes part of his life. In this sense, we maintain that, *constructed as he is,* the criminal does not hold a conviction even in his criminality.

Concrete thinking as it occurs in the criminal is related to fragmentation. For example, the criminal thinks that responsible living entails a set of concrete, isolated acts—going to church, giving money to a charity, visiting his mother, and so forth. Responsibility for him is not based on concepts of ethical and moral standards. As one man put it, "When I'm in church, I think 'church.' When I'm in crime, I think 'crime.'" He never stopped to think about the relationship between the two.

The criminal has no solid plan of operation in his daily life. From an early age, he has sought to prove himself over and over through an endless series of conquests and triumphs. He does not even sustain an interest in a particular kind of crime. Very often, fresh possibilities make the current situation seem dull by contrast. What was once exciting no longer is, and so the crime pattern expands. In the absence of newer arenas, however, he returns to earlier patterns, which then no longer appear drab. Such a life precludes maintaining a consistent stance toward other people, because the criminal is appraising others in the light of his concrete objectives. It is what he wants at the moment and whether others are in accord that determine his view of them. Thus, he is both sentimental and injurious to a person that he says he loves. Not only is the criminal fragmented with respect to his view of others, but he also lacks a consistent view of himself. We have described how he plunges from the heights of pride to the depths of the zero state. He is at one moment all-powerful and better than others and at the next moment a "nothing" and obvious to everyone. The criminal is a "many-splintered thing." We have heard men talk of not being their "real selves." This is not depersonalization or some other severe mental disorder, but a reflection of their own fleeting consternation at the contradictions within themselves.

> "I am seventy-five people in one. My natural inclinations are not to be violent (although he had often been very violent). I am deathly afraid of people. I am bitter and hateful, but I don't mean these things. I love and care about people though my actions deny this."

An outstanding characteristic of the fragmented mind of the criminal is the speed with which it changes. However, unlike a person with a severe mental illness, the criminal has conscious control over both his thinking and his action. The following account illustrates how fragmentation shows itself in a series of transactions with a therapist or other agent of change.

FROM DICTATED NOTES ON THE CASE OF C

12/17

[C was awaiting word as to whether the court would have any objections to his returning home for Christmas.] Today, he said he wanted to talk about what he would do in the near future. He was thinking vocationally. . . . He emphasized that he wants to be of service to people. . . . He emphasized that, as he views himself, there is not a thing he said or a word he has uttered, a movement he has made or a thought he has had which was not criminal. . . . How do we characterize this state? It is a state in the process of change. It is a statement of intention to function noncriminally. Now these statements of intention do not indicate in any way certainty of the future. But they are necessary beginnings. . . . I have learned a great deal in these nine years and will no longer go through the phase of believing that we have accomplished something permanent.

[C left for home with statements of intention to act responsibly and change old patterns.]

12/29-1/4

C stated that he was less than delighted with the week at home. The areas of irresponsibility while he was there were as follows:

1. Looking up certain criminals who suggested major crimes, which C rejected
2. Association with irresponsible women, resulting in his pulling a knife on one of their boyfriends
3. Alcohol and marijuana

I am fully in accord with his statement, "My will to control myself diminished day by day." This is a matter of will. Behind [his activities] was an itch for excitement, for power, for control, for conquest, and to do the forbidden.

1/12

On Sunday, he slept late, called me, did laundry, wrote, and read. Yesterday morning, he shopped. Then he went to work. The situation at work is very smooth. The direction of the effort to deal with the violence in him has taken this form. [He stopped eating meat.]

1/25

On Sunday, he wrote a very good piece, which is a well-written basic presentation of the struggle for change. There are three options: crime, suicide, and suffering and change. It can be seen from this that he elected the last.

2/2

He stated that he is tired of Washington, and with clear anger he was profane about the responsible life. It was a void. It was empty. It would reduce one to an automaton. He doesn't want the miserable empty existence of responsible living.

2/3

He wants the job at [a store]. He wants the best relations there. What he does is set his mind to control that anger to such an extent that he has not shown it at all. In fact, there is, if anything, perhaps an exaggerated affability to deal with it. From one extreme to another.

[Things go on like this with their ups and downs until May, when once again the itch for excitement is strong and C takes off for home.]

5/18

He called me today and stated he would like to return.

6/11

[He said he would return but did not.] C called. He says he is in everything now. He went out to get some kicks. The other night, he borrowed a gun. Last night, he bought a sawed-off shotgun.

6/24

[C returns.] He admitted that everything he had done was a free choice. Every time there is crime, there is the desire for more and bigger crime.

6/29

C was very self-condemnatory. He called himself "scum." This is a state of self-disgust.

[Within a week, C had decided to go his own way and become a "hippy." He dropped out of the program.]

The changes occurred not only from week to week, but day to day, within a single day, and even within a few minutes. Each statement of intention was sincere with respect to a desire to live a decent life. All C's actions were products of choice among mutually incompatible desires.

Fragmentation is necessary for criminality. If the criminal sustained his desires to be decent, if he had convictions, if he developed and implemented concepts of responsible living, there would be no crime.

> C stated that hurting somebody is wrong, no matter what the circumstances. When asked whether he would harm another person, he said he would not. He did not like to think of himself as a killer.

That shows a temporary state of mind of a criminal who was being interviewed in confinement. At the time, he could not foresee himself harming another person. Not long after that, he was involved in an assault.

"Fragmentation" is our descriptive term for one of the criminal's mental processes—it is not his own formulation. He assumes that everyone experiences these changes of mind, but that some conceal them better than others. It does not occur to the criminal that a responsible person may change his mind after much thought. The criminal believes that everyone operates as capriciously as he. When anyone takes him to task about his own frequent changes of mind, he replies that he has a right to change his mind just like anyone else.

It would be well to differentiate here between fragmentation and other mental processes. The criminal's inconsistencies are not always due to fragmentation. For example, point-scoring tactics that are not even initially sincere can account for inconsistencies. A criminal may befriend a person and then betray him. This could be the outcome of a well-laid scheme, rather than of fragmentation.

Fragmentation is also distinct from, although coexistent with, ambivalence. Ambivalence, as defined by even the most elementary textbook of psychology (e.g., Hilgard, 1962, p. 613), has to do with simultaneous, opposing attitudes toward a given object. The criminal, like the rest of us, has true ambivalent attitudes. For example, he may want to see his mother and at the same time not want to. This is different from changes in points of view based primarily on a self-serving objective usually determined by the desire for control and power.

Fragmentation must be distinguished from the concept of "weak ego." Redl and Wineman (1951) were puzzled by their observation that the same ego could be "so poorly reality related" in some situations and so "reality-sharp" in others. They then realized that the delinquent's ego serves him very well for whatever he wants to achieve.

> Far from being helpless, the ego in these children is suddenly a rather
> shrewd appraiser of that part of reality which might be dangerous to
> their impulsive exploits and becomes an efficient manipulator of the world
> around them as well as an energetic protector of the delinquent fun
> against the voice of their own conscience. . . . The task of their ego is
> primarily to make it possible to "get away with things" and to defend
> their delinquency against the threat of the world around them (p. 144).

The delinquent ego is "healthy." Ego functions of memory, concentration,
attention, and so forth are highly developed along specific lines that are out
of tune with what society wants. Certainly, the ego functions well in crime as
it schemes and appraises risk.

It is not uncommon for therapists and others to explain what we call
"fragmentation" in terms of the unconscious. For example, if a criminal is
suicidal one day and reckless the next, these two are linked. That is, it is
assumed that he was reckless because of unconscious suicidal tendencies. The
concept of the unconscious is invoked to connect events to make a neat
psychodynamic formulation. A phenomenologic study of the mind will show
that, although such dynamic explanations are clever, they are rarely correct
when applied to the criminal.

Fragmentation can also be distinguished from psychotic disorganization.
A psychotic person's thinking is fragmented, in the sense that thoughts are
disorganized and irrational.

> It is extraordinarily difficult to follow the thought-processes of a schizo-
> phrenic patient. . . . Their thinking falls to pieces, it defies logic, it
> contains weird constructions (White and Watt, 1973, p. 449). . . . The
> patient has almost entirely deserted the level of realistic thinking. . . .
> Infantile, preverbal conceptions are pushing their way forcibly into the
> fabric of adult logic and rationality (p. 453).

The criminal does not function like that. He knows what he is doing. The
fragmentation is based on what a man decides he wants at a given moment.
The criminal shifts in his wants in line with his desire for excitement and
a buildup. Also, there is not the confusion in ideation that is typical of the
psychotic.

We have encountered criminals who are fragmented and who also show
signs of transient psychosis. The following are two notes that we made at
different times after interviewing a criminal who experienced transient
psychosis.

Criminal in a Psychotic State

"All I can say is that the behavior is quite inappropriate. The mental
processes are more scrambled than in fragmentation. It is difficult to

have a consecutive conversation. I think basically he has a nonhallucinatory psychotic tail end of a very intense and clearly defined psychotic reaction of spirituality."

Fragmented, but Nonpsychotic

"The discussion was the most coherent we have had. He was very calm; he did not jump from one subject to another, but there were conflicting attitudes in his own thinking. . . . As he talked about an armed robbery, one could see the fragmentation with the excitement and desire. Then, after a period of time, he would quiet down and talk about going straight."

In Chapter 7, we shall distinguish between fragmentation and longer-lasting shifts in patterns of thought and action, such as psychosis.

Throughout this chapter, we describe prevailing patterns of the criminal. In each feature discussed there are transient, fragmented exceptions. For example, we discuss the criminal's specious friendliness when he utilizes others for his own objectives. Nevertheless, there are brief periods in which he is genuinely friendly, an expression of his sentimentality. These, however, pass quickly.

UNIQUENESS

If one compares human beings on the basis of the important issues that they must face in their lifetimes, one finds that most of the issues are faced in common, rather than being peculiar to individuals. All humans have generally similar physical needs and are generally alike in their bodily functions. Everyone has to cope with problems that are intrinsic to the life cycle. We all pass through the same stages of physical and mental development, although at different rates and with different degrees of success. Although we may emphasize our differences from others, we relate to each other more on the basis of our commonness. We marry people who share our goals and values. We work with colleagues whose interests are much like ours. We choose neighborhoods to live in and a circle of friends mostly on the basis of common means and tastes.

The criminal, however, emphasizes his total difference from other people. Although he pays lip service to what he has in common with others, a pervasive sense of uniqueness constitutes the cornerstone of his self-image. We may draw an analogy with a set of fingerprints, which have a particular configuration that is unique, but also common components, such as whorls and tents. There is something a little different about each fingerprint that renders it one of a kind. The criminal emphasizes this type of difference in his view of himself. Although aware of a multitude of common characteristics, he operates on the basis of being one of a kind, different from everyone else. We do not deny that there are individual differences among criminals any more than we would deny their existence among noncriminals. Criminals have their tastes and preferences in women, crime, the arts, and so forth. But the common patterns in their thinking processes and their approaches to life are far more significant. The characteristic thinking errors presented in this volume apply in every case. Without exception, one criminal is like another with respect to mental processes described in this volume.

Each criminal's belief in his personal uniqueness is manifested early. As a child, the criminal considers himself different from other members of his family and from his more conforming peers. He thinks he is so different from others that no one can truly understand him.

> "I always felt that I was one way, and my brothers and sisters were another way. I often used to fantasy that I was not one of my brothers or sisters, that I was adopted perhaps, and therefore I was not responsible to them or my family for anything I did. It was my life, and I could live it differently since I was different. I have always tried to find the person just like me that I could be with. I have always looked around for this. I just refuse to get involved with people because I don't want them 'diggin' me. I don't think they could 'dig' me anyway because I was so different."

The criminal believes that no one can have the thoughts that he has. His belief in his uniqueness is an outgrowth of the way the criminal shuts others out of his life. He is very secretive, even with other criminals, and he does not solicit the ideas of others, except when it suits a self-serving purpose. Thus, he is not likely to know whether others share "the same ideas and feelings." Having set himself apart by closing the channels for communication, the criminal claims that no one understands him. This eventually becomes true, because, as a result of his self-imposed isolation, he becomes a mystery to others.

The criminal's sense of uniqueness is expressed everywhere. At school, he scorns his classmates as being nothing but a "herd of cattle." He believes that he is the answer to every woman's desires. In the job world, he thinks that, although others need training, he is equipped to step right in and do the job better than those already there. The criminal generally tends to see himself as more knowledgeable than anyone else. For a criminal to accept advice is for him to lose his uniqueness, his identity. Sound and mature advice is counter to what he wants. Advice in line with his objectives is likely to be repudiated simply because he considers advice of any kind demeaning. He does not need it; he knows it all. When it comes to issues of right and wrong, legal and illegal, he makes his own rules. In crime, he may refer to "we," but he regards other criminals as part of a common pack. He has contempt for those who commit crimes in which he would not engage and those who are afraid to do what he does. In addition, he regards his M.O. in crime as special. A great sense of power is derived from thinking this way. If one believes that he is the only person constituted as he is, then he believes that he has powers that others do not.

A belief in his superiority over others is an important component of the criminal's uniqueness. It is a sense of being better than others at anything he wants to undertake. As one man mused, "How many supermen can there be? I am it." He admits that others are capable, but he regards himself as singular.

> "In a way I feel I'm good at everything. . . . I'd say that I could do things better than most people. I believe that I can handle any problem."

We have said many times that the criminal wants to be number one in everything. It goes beyond that: he wants to be a unique number one.

> C was taking a mathematics course. One night, he stayed up 6½ hours to work on one problem. He was determined to achieve a solution in order not to be outdone by any other student. In fact, he thought about how he would show up the others. C was averaging 4-5 hours of sleep per night as he held a job and was striving to be number one in his class. For him, a score of 100 on a test was insufficient if anyone else got 100. Then, he needed 101 to be satisfied. If he received a grade of 80, he might as well have failed. He had no sense of proportion. His achieving a unique number one status was costly. The cost was defaulting in other responsibilities.

This aspect of the criminal has broader implications. The importance of being number one leads the criminal to refuse to submit to any person, program, or system. To do so is to lose his identity.

> C said that he resented being classified or designated in any way. Whenever this happened, he said, he rebelled. Thus, when he was an "A" student and known to others as a superior student, he started failing, and vice versa. Being known in a particular way, he thought, was "categorizing" him and depriving him of his uniqueness.

When he is dispirited, he believes that no one else can experience or understand what he is going through. Thus, even in a "zero state," he is unique —no one is as unfortunate as he. Furthermore, he believes that he does not deserve to suffer, so there is angry, righteous indignation. The most serious consequence of the sense of uniqueness is that the criminal believes that he is not bound by the restraints of society. There is nothing "wrong" with doing the irresponsible or violating, inasmuch as the rules that apply to others do not apply to him.

> "I'm not really bound or governed by certain laws, by laws or regulations by authorities . . . they have no control over me because I live a life unto my own. . . . I could escape if the police were coming, if the draft was coming. I could survive doing what I wanted to do. . . . I now look at what I do naturally, independent and uncluttered by thoughts of social or legal consequences . . . put on you by people who don't agree with you."

One man declared that he did not have to obey the laws, because they were made before his birth, and he therefore had had no say in them.

Although the sense of uniqueness is closely tied in with power and control, we treat it separately here, because it presents a formidable obstacle in the process of change. As we described in Chapter 1, we were often frustrated in working with groups of criminals, because each man saw what applied to others, but did not apply it to himself. Some wrote essays on the topics we introduced and instructed others, without ever thinking about the application of the concepts to themselves. In the estimation of each, he was unique, and what was descriptive of others was not true of him. Every criminal views himself as unique; there is no other like him. This, like the zero state, is one of the criminal's misconceptions of himself and shows how far removed are his perceptions from the more realistic perceptions of responsible people.

PERFECTIONISM

Not every perfectionist is a criminal. But every criminal is a perfectionist. Perfectionism has traditionally been viewed as an idiosyncrasy or, if it impeded a person's functioning, as part of a neurotic "obsessive-compulsive" syndrome. The criminal's perfectionism may appear neurotic, but its consequences in him are very different from those in the noncriminal. The criminal does not suffer the psychosomatic distress, depression, anxiety, and guilt from his perfectionism that the neurotic does, because the criminal is perfectionistic only in the things he chooses; it is not a global characteristic. His perfectionism depends on what he values. For example, he may dress immaculately, or he may be a slob. If it is important to him, he gives attention to every detail. This perfectionism is particularly evident in crime itself.

Like other characteristics of the criminal, perfectionism does not appear consistently, even with respect to one type of activity. The criminal may clean a floor on a given day, rendering it spotless. His standard of "clean" is so high that, if he maintained it, he could do little else but clean his room. The same person on a different day neglects the floor entirely, because he prefers to do other things. Merely to sweep it is unsatisfactory to him; he adheres to the standard, "When I clean a floor, you can eat off it." Thus, he goes from one extreme to the other—from an immaculate floor to a filthy floor. With respect to matters that are more important to him, however, the perfectionism may be expressed more consistently. Many a criminal is fastidious about his personal appearance and spends a great deal of time in front of a mirror. A tiny spot or hanging thread would not escape such a person, who does not evaluate realistically the expenditure of time, money, and energy that this degree of meticulousness consumes.

> C was very particular about his clothes. Whatever he wore had to match perfectly and be wrinklefree. Every night, he prepared his clothes for the next day. It was not unusual for him to spend an hour each night ironing one or two items. He would examine a pair of slacks to be sure that every wrinkle was removed. What he failed to realize was that after 15 minutes of wear, some wrinkling would inevitably occur. This evening ritual was often at the expense of more important duties.

Perfectionism with respect to appearance can also be seen in the young criminal. It is often manifested in his denigration of others who are not so well attired.

The criminal child may show perfectionism in his schoolwork. When he decides to comply with an assignment or undertake a project, he plans for it to be a flawless masterpiece.

> C would not hand in work, because it did not meet his own standards. At other times, he would not even attempt the work, because he viewed himself as incapable of fulfilling the standards he had set for himself.

> C worked diligently in the school woodshop. If a project he completed were not of the highest quality of workmanship, he destroyed it. If a lamp had one nick in it, he would break it to pieces, because it was not perfect.

Some criminal children are painstakingly orderly in how they keep their notebooks and supplies. They insist on having the best equipment.

> C complained whenever he could not obtain a particular type of pencil and the highest-quality paper. Standard pencils and the oatmeal paper that was usual for the times were unsuitable for him.

Criminals who take jobs often turn out to be superb workers, partly because of their perfectionism. For a time, a criminal may function even better than is required, producing a perfect result. However, the criminal may well be indiscriminate as to where perfection is required and perform elaborately the most routine detail. Doing a competent job gives him no satisfaction; he must do the best and outshine others. Perfectionism in an irrelevant aspect of a task may interfere with the final result.

> C always neatly arranged the stock of clothing tossed aside by customers trying on garments. When the store was busy, the other salesmen left the stock lying around while they attended to customers, and replaced the stock afterward. C was so meticulous that he would put the clothing back first, piece by piece; as a result, he gave less attention to the customers. This decreased his total sales for the day.

In crime, perfectionism is related to the criminal's having in mind the idea of the "big score" that is the "perfect" crime. In the scheming and execution of the crime, the criminal believes that he has it all planned down to the last detail, with every contingency taken into account. Even in confinement, perfectionism shows itself, when the criminal is assigned to a work detail or in the upkeep of his own quarters.

This characteristic thinking pattern appears early and manifests itself everywhere. The criminal applies his high standards to others and is hypercritical of those who are not as perfectionistic as he. He may berate them for poor housekeeping, a lack of personal cleanliness, and dress that is not up to his standards. He is perfectionistic in the standards he sets for others, even in activities in which he himself defaults. He expresses his contempt for anyone who falls short of perfection in anything that he deems important.

> C had the greatest scorn for people who were poor record-keepers. But he himself went 2 years without filing an income-tax return. When he finally started to complete the forms, he had almost no records of his financial transactions.

As in other sectors of life, the criminal is extreme in matters of morality, always ready to accuse others of wrongdoing. If a person keeps a penny too much change, he is a "criminal." A man who breaks the speed limit is as serious a violator as one who holds up a bank. If a person is not 100 percent virtuous, he has no virtues at all. In the criminal's view, a man is a saint or a hoodlum; there is no gradation of evil, and one negative feature can obliterate a person's assets.

> C's mother was very devoted and sacrificed for her children. She tried to pay her bills on time, was a churchgoing woman, and never stole anything. C said his mother was a criminal: she spent 20¢ a day playing the numbers, and she once did not answer the door when she lacked the

money to pay a bill. In C's mind, there were only two categories of behavior—larceny and saintliness.

The hypermoralism may be genuine or contrived. Whichever it is, it surprises and often impresses others when it is expressed.

The criminal's perfectionism bolsters his belief that he is number one—the best. It is an antidote to being a nothing, a zero. Doing the top job enhances his idea of himself as a worthy person. If he *does* the best, then in his mind he *is* the best. He then views himself as immune to criticism. When he wins the confidence of others, this is a further enhancement of his idea that he is unique in his abilities and talents.

Perfectionism in one activity rarely lasts, owing to desires to do other things. When working, the criminal may initially perform extraordinarily well, setting up the expectation in others that he will continue to function this way. However, he sloughs off as the work seems more and more routine. If he becomes bored, he then becomes angry and produces less, and interpersonal relationships suffer. In time, he is likely to quit or be fired.

The criminal sometimes completes an assignment, but fails to present his work, lest it not be awarded the recognition to which he thinks it is entitled. The fear that others will judge his work as less than perfect may prevent him from doing anything constructive with it. Again, a reasonably competent performance is insufficient in his estimation; it must be topflight, second to none.

> C was skilled in cabinetry. But if a single flaw appeared, he would drop a project. A man gave him a chair to repair, and he duplicated exactly the leg that was broken. But, because he could not get the exact kind of wood and the grain was different, C refused to fasten the leg to the chair. He also decided not to charge the man, because the grain was imperfect. Had he known from the outset that he could not match the grain exactly, he probably would not have undertaken the job at all, despite the fact that the customer did not care about the grain.

Another pattern involves not making the effort at all. In other words, better not to try at all than to try and risk failure, failure being viewed as anything less than a top performance.

The noncriminal, not so easily thwarted by threats to his self-esteem, does not operate with the same pretensions, but renews his efforts under stress and when there are diversions. The criminal, however, is vulnerable to the zero state; in whatever he undertakes, his entire worth as a person is at stake. Thus, he moves from one enterprise to another, and his perfectionism surfaces from time to time for various periods.

SUGGESTIBILITY

Those who have tried to influence the criminal to be responsible have found him impervious to suggestions. Correctional and rehabilitation workers run into a stone wall when they try to help the criminal move in the direction of change.

> The psychopath . . . is wholly unsuggestible . . . he does not feel himself dependent, and will not yield to others except on his own terms (Karpman, 1961, p. 622).

The criminal is described as "rigid," because he steadfastly persists in his former patterns. Even when threatened with additional confinement or loss of privileges, he can be exceedingly recalcitrant. He sometimes heeds a suggestion for the purpose of scoring points, but the response is not genuine. People who repeatedly encounter this rigidity or contrasuggestibility become discouraged in their personal and professional transactions with the criminal. Accordingly, they try to motivate the criminal toward programs of education, job training, and other "rehabilitative" activities, in the hope that the learning of new skills will generate new ways of thinking.

But there are also those who point to the opposite behavior—the criminal's apparent extreme inclination to follow the lead of others. Sociologists and some other observers have long considered "contagion" and "peer pressure" to be causative factors in a man's becoming a criminal. They see the criminal as entering the world as a "tabula rasa." On this clean slate fall the malevolent suggestions of others, which are viewed as corruptive.

A third group has recognized both extreme suggestibility and extreme contrasuggestibility. The discrepancy leaves them puzzled. They wonder how a man who is easily influenced at some times can be totally resistant at others.

All these observations are accurate, depending on the circumstances. When it comes to responsibility, the criminal is indeed contrasuggestible with respect to people who want to change him. He appears indifferent, does not listen, argues, scores points, and even flies in the face of what others urge. The criminal is suggestible, however, when he is already looking for action.

In Chapter 3, we described how the criminal searches for excitement, even if he has to travel miles out of his neighborhood. The youth to whom crime "comes" goes along eagerly if he is already in search of action. The teenager who values friends, family, and school and who thinks of his future is unlikely to participate in delinquent acts, even if the opportunity is at his doorstep. As we shall discuss in Volume 3, the teenager does not have to experiment with drugs to gain acceptance. But, if he is already in search of a new thrill and is among excitement-seekers, he is very suggestible when someone offers him a drug. There is no being led astray by associations and no need for persuasion. A person is influenced only if what is suggested is what he already wants. The criminal chooses to associate with those who will offer him what he desires. Thus, he spurns "squares" for criminal cohorts.

In a classroom, it does not take long for delinquents to get together. Criminal youngsters become well versed in picking up cues. Speech, dress, topics of conversation, and attitudes are all indicators of a person's characteristics and interests. A youth does not have to be talking about anything frankly "criminal" for another to size him up as "one of us."

The criminal plays on the suggestibility of others when he cons and deceives them, but he insists that *he* is "nobody's sucker." To admit that he can be influenced would be to destroy his image of himself. He is suggestible though. When an exciting enterprise is in the offing, he is usually reluctant to say no. These hard-nosed, skeptical, suspicious, and intelligent people are often extremely gullible and imprudent when there is an opportunity for excitement. They are likely to exercise poor judgment and wind up the worse for it. Such people are taken in by flattery, particularly from a woman who will give them a buildup, but they are suggestible to almost anything, arrestable or not, that promises some kind of personal triumph.

In short, the criminal is amenable to almost anything that he thinks will prove his importance. He may give away his last dollar to another criminal who promises to repay him. Whether he sees the money again is not as important as his show of generosity. He may risk plenty in these efforts at power-thrusting. The careful judgment that the criminal sometimes exercises seems to vanish at other times.

> C had been in the hospital for many years and, though in active crime, was close to getting out. He had occasionally received calls and letters from a girl who was previously a patient. She told him of her love for him, and he in turn had been attracted to her. After a histrionic phone call, during which the girl said that she was "taking pills," C eloped from the ward in a missionary effort to help her. It was discovered that he was missing from the ward; on his return he was restricted. He had endangered his current status and had imperiled a long-standing relationship with a woman whom he had planned to marry.

C was suggestible to the girl's appeal and acted at considerable risk to himself. He saw a chance to be a rescuer, and to him this had the same impact as a crime.

Just as many noncriminals are suggestible to the newest in fashion, so is the criminal suggestible to the newest style in crime. This has been demonstrated time and again by a spectacular event's being followed by a rash of similar incidents. Airplane hijackings and kidnappings are two examples. This is not to say that hearing about a particular type of crime turns a man into a criminal. But, having seen that someone has successfully executed a particularly unusual or exciting crime, a person already disposed to such an act may want to try and do even better. If the earlier attempt was a failure, this makes the challenge even greater. The pattern does not apply as much to movie or fictional plots, possibly because they seem contrived and less feasible.

The point here is that the criminal is geared for action: he has an idea in mind, but it may take someone else's urging or example to give impetus to the fantasy or scheme. He may get into trouble if, in his restless state and in his eagerness for excitement, he swallows an entire scheme uncritically; he may get a "hot tip" about a place to burglarize and then be off and running without checking the reliability of the source.

The criminal is suggestible with respect to *any* behavior, arrestable or nonarrestable, if it will achieve what he wants. He may fall for get-rich-quick schemes and sink money into a shady enterprise. He fails to check facts and ascertain details. He is prey to advertising campaigns that stress affluence or "status symbols," assuming that having the symbol grants him the status. Thus, he may spend a lot of money on a particular car, clothes, or some other status symbol without comparing prices or checking quality. Costliness is a sufficient recommendation for purchase. Possession and display are the overriding considerations.

Suggestibility rarely operates when a person's attitude is relatively neutral. The key is the activation of what is already riding within the man. If a criminal is approached by a cohort and is for some reason not interested in a suggested scheme, he rejects it. However, the criminal later may adopt and improve on the idea that he formerly considered unsound. In other words, when a criminal says no to another criminal, it is by no means final.

If one tries to influence a criminal to function as most responsible people do, he is likely to be frustrated. The criminal resists efforts to get him to save money, to plan, to consider others' feelings, and so forth. Over the years, the criminal remains impervious to the urgings and pleas of parents, teachers, and scores of other people to "straighten out." It is not totally accurate to say that the criminal rejects all suggestions along noncriminal lines. When he has to make a decision about some matter in which he has little interest, he may allow others to tell him what to do. That is the quick, easy, and compliant way out.

In conclusion, we can say that, as long as man has been concerned with crime and its causes, he has believed that a person can be corrupted by the company he keeps. We have found that people *choose* their company, whether good or bad. A person's suggestibility depends on what he wants. This applies to criminal and noncriminal alike. An honest businessman is cautious and contrasuggestible to anything that suggests fraud. A dishonest businessman is suggestible to fraud when the opportunity arises, but he is not suggestible to propositions based on ethical principles.

THE LONER

The criminal may appear to be something of a recluse because he shuns responsible people and their activities. However, with other criminals, he is active and gregarious. Our characterization of the criminal as a loner does not depend on either of these patterns, which anyone might readily observe. We base our description not on his outward behavior but on his thinking—his view of himself and other people. The criminal regards himself as one of a kind, and this sense of uniqueness sets him apart from others. He approaches life thrusting for power, trying to control others as though they were pawns. Living a private, secretive life, the criminal functions as one in the world and one against the world, including fellow criminals. One of our people put it this way as he described himself:

> "Here we have a guy who is secretive—a sneaky, manipulative cheat with a broad yellow streak who, while mixing freely and pleasantly, keeps most of himself hidden from others so that he can achieve his ends by using them. At the same time, he needs the people he's using and hiding from."

At an early age, the criminal decides to "go it alone," isolating himself from the responsible world. The criminal child does not have a trusting, open relationship with his parents. At school, he remains secretive and aloof, at least from the learning process, and is puzzling to his teachers, who find themselves thwarted in their efforts to reach him. Even when he appears to be sociable, his participation is somehow unlike that of most of the responsible youngsters. If one examines his role in clubs and other groups, it becomes clear that he is not playing or working cooperatively with others; rather, he often tells others what to do and sets himself up as the authority. He wants to prevail over others, whether it be in a street gang or on the student council.

As an adult, the criminal is an outsider to organized groups even when he is a member. He is no joiner unless he has a criminal objective, whether it be frank criminality or power-thrusting for its own sake. A criminal joins groups to use women, set up relationships for later exploitation, and establish a power base where he can manage others and step into the limelight. There is little *genuine* interest in advancing the causes and programs of the organization; he further's the group's objectives when he can use them as a vehicle for achieving power within the organization, for exploiting the entire organization for criminal purposes, or for building up his opinion of himself.

One of the most important aspects of being a loner is the criminal's unwillingness to reveal much about himself. Few people know what kind of person he really is. He is calculatingly vague, deceptive, and flagrantly untruthful. He does not inform others as to what he is going to do, because this might constitute an opportunity for them to interpose their objections or in some way interfere. Furthermore, he believes that being open leaves him exposed and in a position to be taken advantage of. The criminal is secretive even when there is no ostensible need. It keeps him apart from others and enhances his sense of uniqueness.

> "I'm often secret about things I need not even hide. Since I'm uncomfortable with myself, people are uncomfortable with me. Since I don't open up, people are closed to me. It is this which sets me apart."

Secrecy is essential for survival. Apart from the necessity for secrecy in crime, if the criminal did not have his secrets, he would in his view be less of a person.

> "If anyone knew [my] secrets, I would be a pawn. I would then be nothing at all. If I were to tell my secrets, I would be like a prostitute being run by a pimp."

The fear that others will know about his private life is strong. One criminal expressed the belief that, if even one person knew his secrets, everyone would know everything about him.

Whether with other criminals or with noncriminals, the criminal's relationships are one-sided. They are also fragile, owing to his insensitivity to the other person's wants and needs. The criminal does not know what a conversation is. He usually is uninterested in exchanging ideas. Instead, he either seeks to promote himself or gathers information for later use in crime. He discounts others' opinions and experiences and sets himself up as an authority on almost any subject.

> C said that he had enjoyed his conversation with a Mrs. W. He said that they had had a discussion about houses. Because of a lack of funds, the W's had a house with plasterboard, rather than plaster. C lectured her about the superiority of plaster. He talked about the house that he would own one day and all the excellent features it would have, including plaster walls.

This turned out not to be a conversation at all. To view himself as an equal in a transaction would be intolerable—in his opinion, no one is his equal. To be ordinary is a putdown: "If I blend in, I get lost." He must emerge on top, or he is a nothing. Thus, the criminal criticizes others, sets himself apart, and regards himself as better than others. In so doing, he antagonizes people who could be helpful and whom he could help.

The criminal rarely shows warmth or tenderness. He believes that expression of affection and concern would put him in a vulnerable position in which others could exploit him. One criminal said that if people knew they were tapping a sentimental spot in him, it would be as though he were bleeding and seemed weak enough to need a wheelchair. According to the criminal's view, *kindness is weakness.* If he were kind to others, he would be seen as a sucker. And that is how he perceives those who are kind to him.

Believing that others function as he does, the criminal remains guarded. He perceives transactions between people as "deals," with each one giving as little as possible and extracting as much as he can from the other. He does not consider the possibility that one man might do a favor for another without expecting anything in return. A failure to trust others is understandable, in that the criminal thinks that others operate as he does. One man stated that the only creature he trusted was his dog, because it could not double-cross him. We shall show in Chapter 5 that the criminal lacks all trust in others, just as he himself is untrustworthy.

The criminal divides the world into those who are for him and those who are against him. Those "for" the criminal include noncriminals who have helped him even though they know him for who he is. Also "for" the criminal are the responsible people who are favorably disposed toward him because they do not know him well and have no reason to distrust him. Many of these are exploited in time. Those "against" the criminal are people who interfere with or stand in the way of his objectives. The same person may be viewed at different times as "for" and "against" him. If his mother, whom he regards with near-reverence, interposes obstacles to his activities, his affection turns to anger.

The criminal may have numerous associates or acquaintances, but no friends. He lacks relationships with sustained bonds of affection or esteem.

"I can't be sure I have any friends."

"The only thing you have is yourself."

"It's a rare thing to have a real friendship. It's like having another person that's like yourself or another person who can really help you and let you see yourself. I really don't know what it is. I just know that I haven't found it."

The criminal's idea of a friend is one with whom to share criminal thought, talk, and action. When criminals get together, each is looking for his own action. The power and control motif determines what a criminal is looking for in a transaction. A friend is a friend only as long as he does what the criminal wants.

> C said that he had only one friend in his life—a boy whom he could control completely. This boy did not have the "heart" to commit crimes on his own, but he did as C wanted without betraying him.

The criminal may speak of affection in a long-standing relationship with another criminal. To be sure, they may have some common noncriminal interest. Two criminals may share an enthusiasm for photography. However, their association, if there is one, is based primarily on criminality. Each criminal may think that he knows the other well, but the lines of communication are never truly open; each reserves a large portion of his thinking and action to himself. We have worked with bosom "friends," each of whom says that the other knows all about him. What we find out is that more about each is unknown to the other than is known. Inevitably, exploitation characterizes these relationships that the criminal calls "friendship."

> C developed a relationship with another criminal, Tom; the two of them were inseparable. In dealing with the administration at the hospital where they were confined, the two presented a "united front." By various maneuvers, they arranged things so that they could live on the same ward. C said that he objected to 99.9% of all homosexuals, but Tom appealed to him. C stated that he knew Tom better than anyone else and could advise him about his therapy and his plans for the future. Gradually, he exercised more and more control, trying to dissolve Tom's relationships with others. Eventually, the two eloped and traveled together, still in crime. C continued to view Tom as totally dependable and honest with him. When an agent of change was working with C after the two were apprehended, he pointed out to C the ways in which Tom was using him. At first, C rejected the idea. One day, finally, he approached Tom and asked him about what the agent of change had said. Tom's response was, "Of course, you sucker, I'm using you," at which point C cracked Tom's skull.

When a criminal likes another person, it usually means he is deriving something from the relationship that serves his own ends. There are brief periods in which the criminal is genuinely friendly. Usually, however, the criminal "likes" a person who will do what he wants and provide him with the build-up he desires. He "likes" those who recognize his brightness, his talents, and his knowledge or who admire his criminality. He also "likes" someone whom he can associate with in a crime.

C, a black, stated that he liked Frank, a ruthless white bigot. The liking was based on their similar interests in crime. Both enjoyed talking about the slickness of their operations with women. Together they violated hospital rules and left the grounds to go drinking.

The "liking" continues as long as the other party does not try to use or obstruct the criminal. The liking can change to anger within a matter of seconds if one puts the other down either deliberately or inadvertently. Because criminals so often associate with others like themselves, they are usually disappointed in their relationships and find that they are being used.

"I'm tired of some of the types of relationships I've gotten into with some people. . . . It seems that they were sponging off me in various and sundry ways, borrowing money from me or borrowing my car or asking to borrow something and not bringing it back in nearly as good shape as they took it."

The criminal does not seek companionship for its own sake. A relationship with another person is not based on mutual give and take. Occasionally, association may be based on common interests. The criminal may find another person who is a jazz fan or is interested in Far Eastern religions. In confinement, he may "rap" with others about this or even engage in a joint project. This may be for purposes of point-scoring with the authorities, who consider it a sign of progress for a criminal to "socialize"; or it may be sincere, but usually short-lived, owing to interpersonal frictions. Interest in the arts, or some other avenue of expressions, is often used as an entrée to a situation in which exploitation occurs later.

Although the criminal scorns conventional living, there are always some noncriminals whom he likes. Most people do not know the criminal for the kind of person he is, so they may respond favorably to his phony presentation or accept him for what they see as the "good" or "potential" in him. Usually, the criminal likes a person who lets him do as he wants. For example, the criminal child is fond of the teacher who tells jokes, allows the pupils to talk, and assigns little work. When such a teacher likes him, this raises his opinion of himself. However, if the teacher starts to pressure him to study or interferes with the "fun" he is having, his fondness disappears. Becoming enthusiastic about and then disenchanted with a person is a pattern in the criminal's life. Both the criminal's fragmentation and his untruthfulness preclude loyalty in a relationship. There are extreme reversals in the criminal's attitude toward parents, spouses, teachers, employers, and other criminals. He may appear loyal when he wants to ingratiate himself or do something that enhances his opinion of himself.

> C was loyal to a boy with whom he often played in childhood. This boy had taken a fall that resulted in the amputation of a limb. C was faithful to the youngster, coming around daily for a visit. He had nothing to gain, because the boy was disabled and thus was not in a position to join with C in any exciting adventures.

There is no loyalty—only the idea that carrying out some *concrete act* of kindness *makes* him loyal.

There is no loyalty even to other criminals. As we pointed out in Chapter 3, despite popular lore, the "criminal code" of "no snitching" is not maintained. Loyalty is a short-lived commodity if a criminal can save his own skin. The criminal will inform to cut down a possible sentence, to retaliate against another criminal, to prevent the loss of something valued, or to gain any other kind of advantage. Even the closest buddies will betray one another. It is in this lack of loyalty, even to one of their own, that the loner quality is perhaps the most striking.* Again, it is a matter of being simultaneously one in the world and one against the world.

Without friendship, loyalty, or trust, the criminal is ill-equipped for a love relationship. He is often viewed as loving people because he has some sentimentality toward them. However, accompanying this sentimentality there is often cold-blooded *use*. This is not "love" by most definitions.

> "When I say, 'I love you,' what I mean—really—is, 'I *need* your love.' When I say, 'I really love you or I love you very much,' what I mean is, 'I am going to do anything to manipulate you into giving me that love I need so badly.' Because my words do not mean the true intent of my mind, any love exchange becomes exploitative and hence criminal. To see this operating day by day, has been more than scary. I could see—after a while—that [my] relationship [with Thelma] was anything but love between a man and a woman."

In this statement, the "love" that the criminal says he needs is in terms of possessing someone. The criminal's brand of "love" was to enter into a series of relationships in which he exploited women for sex and money. The equation of love with sex by the criminal has, of course, been noted by others:

> Their positive activities are consistently and parsimoniously limited to literal physical contact and relatively free of the enormous emotional concomitants and the complex potentialities that make adult love rela-

---

* Maurer (1974) has noted this lack of loyalty among con men who are partners in crime. "In spite of evidence of a well-developed sense of professional honor among con men, there are equally impressive indications that they sometimes step over the line—dangerous as that may be—and tear off their partners for a part of the score" (p. 167).

tions an experience so thrilling and indescribable. . . . What is felt for prostitute, sweetheart, casual pickup, mistress, or wife is not anything that can bring out loyalty or influence activities into a remedial or constructive plan (Cleckley, 1964, pp. 396, 397).

A relationship with a woman invariably includes using her, usually in a sexual sense. We have not encountered one case in thirteen years where this did not hold true. It is inconceivable for a criminal to associate with a woman on any other basis.

The word *love* has other uses for the criminal, as when he berates his mother or wife for not "loving" him, which means that she is not doing everything that he wants or that she is resisting his efforts to exploit her.

> To C, mother's love meant a total acceptance of him—with no prohibitions. If he had to come in from the playground at 6 P.M., he could not be truly loved by her. If, after 6 months of her cajoling him to be prompt for dinner, his mother whipped him, then she must have hated him. If he wanted to stray away to a beach miles from home and were told that he was too young to go, he also would think that he was not loved enough.

If a criminal continually upsets his parents and they finally decide not to bail him out when he gets into trouble for the fifteenth time, then he claims that they do not love him. Proof that they still love him would have to take the form of covering up for him or offering him assistance.

The criminal child responds to the love of a parent in extremes. He may hang onto his mother's skirts and demand so much love and attention that he allows his mother hardly any other activity—an early manifestation of control. Or he may totally reject her affection and love. We have pointed out that many criminal children disappoint and bewilder their parents by turning away. Whether they demand love excessively or reject it, they reach the same view: to verbalize a need for love or make a show of it is weak or "sissy." Rather than the child's being deprived of love, he deprives his parent of a chance to be loving. To seek it or even accept it invites being controlled, he believes.

The criminal may express a great deal of affection toward nonthreatening figures. This is not so much love as sentimentality toward babies, old people, animals, and so forth—figures that cannot control him.

Some clinicians, observing what we call the "loner" quality, have said that the delinquent and the psychopath make a "schizoid adjustment." The schizoid has been described as aloof and unsociable (Cameron, 1963). He is a "colorless person" who retreats into fantasy and is a "prototype of the ivory tower, detached and abstract thinker" (p. 64). The criminal, in contrast, may appear very sociable and involved with others. He is in no way an "ivory tower" thinker, but is extremely concrete. To be sure, he does have an active fantasy life, but the fantasy content is different from that of the schizoid. What the two share on the surface is a "distrust" of others. However, as we have said, the criminal has good reason to be distrustful, owing to the nature of his activities. Cleckley (1964) has contrasted the "typical psychopath" with the "schizoid personality":

> The typical psychopath contrasts sharply with the schizoid personality or the patient with masked schizophrenia. No matter how free from delusions and other overt signs of psychosis the schizoid person may be, he is likely to show specific peculiarities in his outer aspect. Usually there are signs of tension, withdrawal and subtle oddities of manner and reaction. These may appear to be indications of unrevealed brilliance, perhaps even eccentricities of genius, but they are likely to complicate and cool easy social relations and to promote restraint. Although the psychopath's inner emotional deviations and deficiencies may be comparable with the inner status of the masked schizophrenic, he outwardly shows nothing brittle or strange. Everything about him is likely to suggest desirable and superior human qualities, a robust ·mental health (pp. 364-365).

Cleckley then went on to describe the criminal's affability, congeniality, and sense of humor, which are not characteristic of the schizoid.

We should emphasize that we do not equate loneliness with being a loner. As a subjective experience, the criminal does not suffer the pangs of loneliness in which a person is starved for the warmth of human contact and companionship. A noncriminal can be very much alone and lonely without being a loner in the sense described here. He is yearning for things that are not even within the criminal's experience. The criminal is a loner by choice. Indeed, the interest of another person may be regarded as intrusive. When the criminal desires to be with people, he finds those who will satisfy his immediate wants. The criminal lives his life without truly knowing another person. He is a wanderer, always seeking conquest, rarely satisfied except in short-lived flashes of triumph. When a criminal says that he is "lonely," he means he is bored and wants action. This is quite different from missing the warmth and enjoyment of companionship for its own sake.

Helping criminals to be more sociable is an objective in many efforts at treating them. Therapists believe that the more gregarious criminals do not need this so much, but that the asocial ones do. Actually, from the standpoint of the concepts presented here, both types are equally loners. What some professionals do not realize is that mere socializing does not represent or produce a change in basic patterns of thinking and action. No matter how much socializing they do, criminals remain loners who set themselves apart by secrecy, by a belief in their uniqueness, and by the other mental processes we are describing.

SEXUALITY

Sexuality deserves separate treatment in this chapter, because it is a significant arena for the expression of thinking patterns already presented and for others still to be discussed. Most accounts of human development describe a period between the ages of seven and twelve in which youngsters' sexual interests recede. This sexual "latency" occurs in most children, in great part because of the many important life adjustments being made at this time. The latency stage is missing from the development of the criminal child. His search for excitement, which begins at an early age, persists, and sexual patterns of thinking or action expand. In Chapter 3, we cited the criminal child's unusual amount of sexual curiosity and play within the home, especially with siblings. Activity between brother and sister, for example, includes breast play, vaginal inspection, and other kinds of sex play, often with attempts at intercourse. Such play extends to other children in the neighborhood. The adult nature of the accompanying fantasies is what is remarkable—clearly, the attempt to be older involves more than playing house.

> C's fantasies of playing doctor included having an office with bedroom, bathroom, and all the equipment a doctor would have. His sister or a girl friend would come into his office. They would undress by degrees; if her breasts were well developed, so much the better. When they were nude, there would be touching of the body in the course of "examination," but no intercourse. The important thing was that the "cure" was the penis. Perhaps the girl would masturbate him, and later he would insert his penis. There was even the introduction of fellatio in later years of his fantasy. This occurred for about a 5-year period beginning at the age of 10 or 11.

The criminal as a child has fantasies of being bigger and more well developed. His fantasy of himself as sexually more mature is in line with his ideas of being older and doing the things that older people do. The noncriminal may also wish to be older and may have similar sexual fantasies. However, unlike the criminal, he does not come close to implementation.

> As C experienced it, he was a nothing if he was just an ordinary 9-year-old. He could be "somebody" only if he lived the life of someone at least a half-dozen years older. He was determined to have a sexual experience with a female. His first experience was with a prostitute

whom he asked for intercourse. He did get an erection, but he had no ejaculation. However, he felt great after this; now he was big, bold, and competent, and no longer a 9-year-old. He then went on a spree, combining his sexual search with force. He sought out girls his age or a year or two older and started to play house or doctor. However, C went far beyond games, threatening and punching the girls until he got his way, which was to attempt intercourse. This was a troublesome procedure mechanically, and he got no sexual satisfaction out of it. Despite this, he continued to search for girls whom he could persuade or force to have sex with him.

In the attempt to be older, criminal children seek out older children or go to peers who are more experienced. They scorn the unsophisticated and the cowards. In all this early behavior, there is great emphasis on proof of self. Concurrently, however, the fears of genital inadequacy and sexual incompetence persist. Sexual contact is a badge of being older. Criminal youngsters engage in group masturbation and various other sexual gang activities. They compete to see who has the largest genitals or who can get an erection the quickest and engage in numerous other sexual contests.

All this is not to say that the criminal is the only child who does this type of thing. Noncriminal children also engage in some of this behavior. However, in the criminal's life, these are fairly regular events, which could be called "patterns"; he engages in them often and with little evidence of psychic conflict or guilt. If the noncriminal child participates in such activities at all, he does so fearfully. Sometimes, conscience factors preclude even thinking about such behavior. Another distinction between criminal and noncriminal is in the importance attached to sexuality early in life. As opposed to what happens in the noncriminal, the criminal's total sense of self-worth may rise or fall, depending on his sexual success.

The criminal is usually indiscriminate in choosing his sexual partner. His youthful sexual behavior may occur within the circle of his immediate family. But whether it is family, neighbors, other children, or animals is of no importance to him. He seeks out the most readily available. He may have his tastes and preferences, but he will do almost anything that is exciting.

> At the age of 15, C was hunting with his dog. C had to defecate and did so in the woods. The dog sniffed his feces, and he allowed it to lick his rectum. This excited C and gave him an erection. The dog then licked his penis. Thereafter, he continued this pattern with the dog about every 2 weeks for a year. The dog would spontaneously go to his penis and perform fellatio. It is important to note that, when the dog was not inclined spontaneously to do this, C engineered him into a position and manner to get him to.

C got a charge out of doing this, primarily because it was something that he knew very few others would do.

In some areas and socioeconomic classes, there are greater sanctions against sexual activity and fewer opportunities. Even when this is the case, there is a tremendous amount of untutored sexual thinking. No matter how surprising a criminal's sexual behavior may appear, there is far more in his thinking that he does *not* do. Some draw the line when it comes to particular acts, as they do in crime. Just as a sneak thief may scorn a mugger, so may a rapist have contempt for a child molester and vice versa. Although there is a great amount of bisexuality, some criminals may consider it "weak" to indulge in homosexual contact. However, the idea of "have gun, will travel," as one criminal termed his sexual behavior, is pervasive. The excitement and the taking advantage of a particular opportunity are far more important than the personality of the partner with whom one participates. When it comes to the choice of a partner, the criminal does not see a whole person. When he encounters a woman, he perceives only breasts, thighs, buttocks, or some feature idiosyncratically attractive to him, such as long hair. As one man put it, he would prefer his partner to be "deaf, dumb, and blind. I just want her torso for sex."

As noted by others, the criminal has plenty of sexual experience, but very little in the way of sensual satisfaction or competence in performance.

> The male psychopath, despite his usual ability to complete the physical act successfully with a woman, never seems to find anything meaningful or personal in his relations or to enjoy significant pleasure beyond the localized and temporary sensations. . . . Even these sensations seem to wither precociously and leave the subject a somewhat desiccated response to local stimuli (Cleckley, 1964, p. 397).

The experiences themselves are very shallow. One man described having intercourse with a woman as "like getting a drink of water and going back to work." At most, the criminal has a "localized, temporary" set of pleasurable sensations; for some, intercourse is not even pleasurable, but disgusting.

The gratification in sex lies mainly in the thrill of conquest. Sex is a control operation, with the criminal possessing full rights of ownership. It must occur at the time and place and in the manner ordained by the criminal; the woman has no rights.

> C's conception of a woman is that she is to furnish a "piece of ass." If necessary, she is to be pushed and kicked around. He never lets women know whether he cares for them and certainly does not recognize their needs or desires. He never permits a woman to put him down. When one woman observed that another man had better sex techniques, he

punched her around. When she summoned a nearby girl friend for help, C broke the friend's nose. His way of operating was to knock around anyone who resisted, subdue her, have sex, and leave—in short, rape. He believed that the proper pressure would lead any woman to "come through." He considered all women to be basically the same; even a "high-class" woman must have a secret sexual life and really want him. No matter how conventional or unconventional the woman seemed, she was still only a "piece of ass."

The element of conquest is also present in the homosexual criminal.

> "Homosexuals are insatiable. The conquest is wonderful. They want to make the world. The homosexual continually has a roving eye. If he is with someone, he is always on the lookout for someone a little better. I can see it in myself. A compulsion to be loved by the world, an insatiable quality about me."

Inasmuch as the conquest is the overriding element, the criminal often does not know or care what satisfies his partner. As a result, he may have some humiliating experiences when he fails to satisfy her (or him). He is put down and angry when he thinks he has performed inadequately, and he may get violent if his partner comments on it verbally or physically.

Each criminal has his own set of criteria of "manhood"—e.g., producing multiple orgasms in his partner or the duration in his partner's vagina.

> C would count the number of orgasms that he produced in his women. He counted 9 in one, 20 in another. Eventually, after permitting himself to ejaculate, he required testimony by the woman that he was indeed the best sex partner.

> C's idea of a man is that he should have his penis in the woman's vagina for 45 minutes—anything less than that meant that he was less of a man. To prolong his erection he had to conjure up a fantasy of mutilating the woman. He had considered himself mostly a sexual failure, because he could never last more than 30 minutes without resorting to these fantasies.

The criminal wants to accomplish what no one else has before with his partner of the moment.

> "I literally built her into the greatest sex partner I ever had. She had been frigid for the 10 years of her marriage, then learnt to have mentally induced orgasms with a lover she had before me. With me, she felt for the first time—a woman! I felt it. It made me very happy.... Now [I] was sexually better than all the men [she] had gone to bed [with]. Performance in bed became an obsession with me. She loved it and so did I, until [she] started speaking of marriage."

If the criminal achieves the desired "results," it provides him with a buildup. One criminal was so eager to have others know that he was regarded as proficient that he had a sex partner tape-record her testimonial. For many, the most important criterion of their performance is the period during which they can sustain an erection. In Volume 3, we shall discuss some criminals' resorting to drugs to produce erections that last up to twelve hours.

Degrees of impotence and other forms of sexual incompetence are common among criminals. Their difficulties run the gamut from not being able to achieve or sustain an erection to extreme prematurity. Even with erection, many fail to achieve ejaculation. The few who are sexually competent regard themselves as incompetent, because their potency is not in line with their conception of themselves as sexual giants. Some criminals find that they can perform adequately only when there is a major conquest to be made. In a consenting situation, they have problems maintaining an erection.

One criminal who had been sexually active since childhood said, "I don't think I ever had sex with a woman." What he meant was that he had not experienced the mutual pleasure and satisfaction that he had heard were supposed to characterize most sexual relationships. The criminal has sex on his mind a great deal of the time, in the sense that every female is a potential target (or every male, in the case of the homosexual). The idea is to conquer a body rather than to have a relationship with a person. The criminal, who is so often thinking about sexual conquest, gets erections as a conditioned reflex. The mere sight of a potential target is enough to arouse him. It is not a result of sexual "need," but the excitement of a chance to acquire a partner whom he finds desirable. The presence of the potential partner is not even necessary; simply thinking about the acquisition is sufficient to produce an erection. The occurrence of erection is not derived from an unconscious process, but is a habituated response to this kind of thinking. Once it occurs, it is experienced as a "need" to be fulfilled. If the thinking is diverted, the erection subsides. The criminal will attribute his sexual marauding to this "sex drive," making it an issue of "manhood." He does not face up to the way in which he uses sex primarily to achieve control of another person. The charge is derived from the pursuit, or even the idea of pursuit. To "make" a woman is a challenge; to fail is a put-down. There is little satisfaction in a sexual experience with someone who is a "sure thing." A wife attested to her husband's great sexual activity with other women, but to the minimal amount he had with her. She found this to be true of him and of her former husband, also a criminal.

> "Both he and [C] are not very sexual. They use their energy for outside interests. I hate them for this. [C] brags about his ability to have sex two or three times a night with other women and he knows this hurts

me. I guess I hate him because he is not very sexual. I am so different from him. When I love someone as I once did him I want them over and over but he does not have much interest in that. He would prefer a different woman all the time I think. Our sex has been a once every two weeks sort of thing."

In his approach to potential sexual partners, the criminal regards himself as "irresistible me." He believes that he is admired, loved, and sexually desired by all. He thinks that any person who looks at him will be attracted instantly. A friendly smile confirms in his mind that he is desired and that he can go ahead and take possession. In fact, the criminal considers it as a favor to a woman to make a pass and pursue her; he thinks someone who fails to do this is a "faggot." This thinking occurs even with total strangers, whom the criminal quickly regards as his property. He always seeks confirmation that he is indeed irresistible.

C liked to go to the bus station and pick up women who satisfied his physical criteria. He preferred large, muscular women. Such women did not attract many partners. They built C up as a physical specimen and in terms of his sexual performance. They were satisfied with him and built him up, no matter how incompetent he was sexually.

Although the choice of partner is usually indiscriminate, the personal qualities and the setting in which the partner is found may be important. If the criminal can conquer a "high-class" woman or one who appears to have status and money, this is a greater triumph.

C left the grounds of the hospital to go to the apartment of a head nurse who lived on a grand scale far beyond her means. She was supported in part by prostitution. He described her apartment as exceedingly plush with a thick carpet and a large hi-fi system, which resounded with "music which sounded like it was coming from everywhere." She had quite an array of liquor, to which C helped himself. From here on, there was flattery: every queen should live in a palace like this, and she was indeed a queen. He complimented her on her beauty and then kissed her. There was a good deal of bantering and flattery back and forth; the excitement of sex talk was followed by their going to bed. His ego was built up by her admiration of the size of his penis and his performance. It was not long before he once again returned to what he called "the gates of paradise."

C enjoyed the surroundings, but even more he took pleasure in the fact that his partner was confirming that he was irresistible.

The criminal expects to be number one with his woman. The woman who is criminal knows this and is likely to play one man against the other. This may be at considerable peril to herself, but she too wants her collection of admirers.

> Brenda was involved with a number of men at once. She lived with Bill, a man of some means, in New York. But when she was in Washington, she lived with C and still continued her liaison with him. When C stopped by the apartment in New York, she tried to rush him out for no apparent reason. Finally, she admitted that Bill was coming. C left angrily, with ideas of a torture-murder of both Brenda and Bill. But Brenda managed for months to live off both of them.

When the criminal finds out that he is not the top man, he is tremendously deflated. Anger, assault, and retribution, even in the form of homicide, may follow, as he seeks to reassert control.

> C had been engaging in a one-sided relationship with an attractive, young woman. He tried on a number of occasions to date Barbara and be seen with her. Even though she never even agreed to a date, he told all his friends that he had been intimate and were contemplating marriage. Barbara, however, was more interested in another man. In describing what happened, C said:

> "She told me that she was going to call the relationship off, that her mother was against it. I could feel this thing coming, but I just didn't want to face it. I pleaded and begged her not to call it off. . . . Like a kid who panics, I started screaming in a phone booth. . . . The only thing I could think about was dying. I was a complete disgrace. I thought,, 'What will my friends and family think when they hear that Barbara has called the relationship off?'"

> C related that earlier that day he had no intentions of harming Barbara. After further thinking and a bit of drinking, he began saying to himself, "I'm going to kill her." The next day he had a large butcher knife sharpened at the grocer's. Looking at the knife, he decided that this was not the way to kill her. Three days later, C shot and killed Barbara and seriously wounded her boy friend.

What we have said of the male criminal applies also to his female counterpart.* She too regards herself as irresistible. She regards her man as a possession, and she attempts to manage him in line with her own objectives. Her control tactics may be obvious or devious. She demands fidelity and accountability from her partner and yet expects to come and go as she chooses without questions. The female criminal believes that, when she walks

---

* We have not systematically studied female criminals. However, as we pointed out in Chapter 1, we have had prolonged contact with many of them, owing to the fact that the criminals in our study have, in many instances, gravitated to them and in many cases married them.

into a room, others will drop what they are doing and flock to her. She expects confirmation of her irresistibility. She does not exchange views, but issues directives and ultimatums. Like the male, she is intent on conquest. Sex is a vehicle for achieving control. She likes to keep men on a string and may make sex contingent on her partner's fulfilling her desires for other things. Sometimes, these women are so intent on retaining control that they deliberately become pregnant or claim to be pregnant when they are not.

The criminal often prefers older women, although he by no means limits himself to them. In fact, he also may be having sexual contact with very young women. Early in life, seeking out older females is part of the attempt to be older himself. Later, if this pattern continues, it may appear to others that he is searching for a "substitute mother" to take care of him. That is not the case; such a choice is in line with the criminal's concept of a woman who will provide him with what he wants. He may not have to invest the time and money in an older woman that he would in a younger one. The older woman may be so eager for sex that she may overlook the criminal's shortcomings, including sexual incompetence. In addition, he may have the convenience of a ready-made situation, if he forms a liason with a woman who is well established in life and can provide him with material comforts. If he finds a woman who is insecure, lonely, and desirous of companionship, he may virtually have a slave at his command.

When the criminal "wins over" a virgin, he has acquired a "pure" person. By deflowering her, he literally achieves something that no one else has. He has given her her first sexual experience and has received her approval, regardless of his performance. Usually, the relationship corrodes thereafter. The criminal often leads the girl to expect marriage, but is apt to lose interest once she has sex with him. In some cases, the criminal is so enamored of a girl who has remained undefiled that he does not have sex with her until after marriage, although all the while he is having sex with others. As one man said of his virgin wife, her virginity was a "token" of a woman's belonging totally to him. In time, the exploitative element emerges, and he treats her like anyone else.

When a criminal who molests children is put on the psychiatric couch, it is easy to obtain material about his fear of the adult vagina. He considers it a stinking, oozing, infectious structure. Thus, he prefers the younger vagina, which lacks the unattractive physical attributes of the older woman. It can be said that the criminal rejects the dangerous and impure for the safe and pure. But the important feature, which commonly is not considered, is the aspect of total control over an inexperienced person. As we have pointed out, the criminal doubts his sexual ability and endowment. With a child, he is in a position of total mastery and is not likely to be criticized for any incompetence. An inexperienced child has little or nothing with which to compare performance. Thus, it is almost guaranteed that the criminal will not be put down, that he will be viewed as sexually competent. It has been noted (e.g., McGeorge, 1964) that some of the children are willing and cooperative, and thus not victims.

> At the age of 18, C was staying at his aunt's home. She had a 10-year-old daughter, Mary, whom C became very fond of. He became her counselor, and she would go to him for guidance, rather than to her own parents. While at the aunt's, he became Mary's teacher in sexual matters. This led to their sleeping together and engaging in a great variety of sexual activities. C was in the role of teaching a heretofore inexperienced girl. In this capacity, he was not subject to criticism.

A child like Mary may actually welcome such excitement, as did the criminal when he was younger, and thus go along willingly, if not eagerly, with whatever the criminal proposes. In addition to approaching children, the criminal may engage a retarded or psychotic partner whose emotional status is much like that of a child.

Both heterosexual and homosexual relationships among criminals are basically exploitative, as are the dealings between a pimp and a prostitute. In fact, it is accurate to characterize all the criminal's sexual liaisons with other criminals as "pimp-prostitute relationships." Each party gets what he values and gives away what is worthless to him. In Chapter 3, we described such a relationship, that of Bob and Paula. Bob got a place to live, sex when he wanted it, and an attractive woman to be seen with. Paula had sex when she wanted it, a man around to do things for her, and the satisfaction of having taken Bob away from his family. In situations like this, each partner thinks that he is calling the shots and controlling the other. Neither believes that he is prostituting himself. Eventually, the friction reaches a point where the couple separates.

Very few of our criminals are exclusively homosexual, although they do engage in homosexual activity. The criminal will usually deny that he has a homosexual component. The "active" partner maintains that his partner is the "faggot," not he. The "passive" partner views himself not as a homosexual, but as an extractor of favors, money, or possibly prestige. Neither considers the sexual act paramount, because sex is easily available. Rather, it is what they are getting out of a "pimp-prostitute relationship." We are not stating that every homosexual is a criminal. Obviously, there are homosexual relationship between consenting *responsible* people. We are addressing ourselves here to the way in which homosexuality is used to provide an arena for criminality. As is true of heterosexuality in criminals, homosexual behavior in criminals has to be regarded as an avenue to the achievement of criminal excitement. It is the criminal component, not the sexual preference, that we are emphasizing.

Homosexuality for gain may begin early, perhaps first when a criminal boy who is already adventurous is approached by an older man. Although he may be scared, the boy wants the excitement and so consents to a sexual act. If held accountable, he may claim that he was coerced. The youth learns that from such acts he may get money, praise, and other things he wants. Homosexual prostitution may become a way of life.

Homosexual prostitution is a way of life for some, but for many others it is a series of isolated acts that may be concurrent with heterosexual interests and activities. The homosexual activity is usually part of a criminal operation. Homosexual prostitution may become an M.O. for theft, blackmail, drug-dealing, or entrée into other avenues of criminal activity.

> C earned $100,000 in 3 months through homosexual prostitution. But it was not the prostitution itself that netted him that sum. Rather, through this activity he gained entrance to some of the most affluent homes in various parts of the country. The prostitution was part of an elaborate burglary and safecracking ring.

Here, the criminality was more important than the homosexuality. The same criminal was having sex with women during the same period. The homosexual pattern can take some violent forms.

> C used to "roll" drunk homosexuals in alleys, taking their money and clothes and leaving them nude.

> C began looking for new patterns of operation. He joined with 3 other fellows. They would all congregate where the homosexuals were. At the signal of one's blowing his nose, one fellow would pick out a man and lure him into an alley. Then all would pounce on him, restrain his arms and gag him, and roll him for money and jewelry. This was a stealing process without sex, but using the promise of sexual activity as bait.

Homosexual acts themselves are relatively insignificant, as demonstrated by the fact that most criminals do not seek out consenting relationships. One man reported being at a resort where it was easy to procure partners. But he had no interest; instead, he preferred a setting where there was less availability and thus more search and pursuit.

In discussing power and control, we indicated that voyeurism and exhibitionism are activities in which the criminal achieves triumph. In voyeuristic activity, excitement comes from invading another person's privacy without his knowing it. Gazing or staring openly—e.g., at a beach—provides no thrill: girl-watching is permitted. But stealing a look and peeking into an apartment window produces kicks. The criminal has the experience of control, both in terms of secret watching and in terms of the fantasies that elaborate on the scene. The theme of fantasies is usually the mastering, perhaps even the forceful domination, of the woman in question.

The exhibitionist selects his victim carefully, hoping to entice someone who he figures will be curious enough to follow him. By his movements, he tries to lure the other person, and thus it is a control operation. He seeks an admiring gaze and then directs that gaze. Most psychiatrists emphasize the compensation aspects of this behavior. That is, the man exhibits himself to "reassure himself of his own intactness" (Cameron, 1963, p. 666). However, the triumph of getting others to watch and follow is given little attention. Some criminals are not exhibitionists on the streets, but display themselves and parade back and forth with their partners. They may walk around nude, strut before mirrors, and bask in the partner's admiring gaze. Voyeurism always accompanies exhibitionism and invariably precedes it.

> C prowled the streets sometimes until 4 A.M. Night and day, he searched out situations in which to view women; he made himself known to them by exposing himself.

> In Palm Beach, C hired a girl to pose in partial and then total nudity. He paid her for this and then recalled her the next day. He repeated the experience, but this time he had himself photographed exposed. At this time, he was also doing a lot of looking at himself in mirrors.

The fantasies of the voyeur and the exhibitionist often extend to rape. Those who do not in fact go on to this activity are deterred by the thought that they might get caught or by inner attitudes against it. If one has the techniques to probe the mind of the voyeur or exhibitionist, he is almost certain to find rape thinking present, even if there have been no actual rape offenses.

> C, known to the police as an exhibitionist, woke up one morning at 3 A.M. There was a flood of sexual thinking. First, it went along voyeuristic lines. He thought about a woman whom he had known for years. He thought of her masturbating and his watching. He then thought about another woman parading nude in front of a mirror before his eyes. There then came to mind an elderly woman whose body appealed to him. Finally, he thought of abducting a girl and telling her that, inasmuch as she was going to be raped, she may as well relax and enjoy it.

We have found exhibitionistic and voyeuristic characteristics in every rapist. Using a somewhat different form of expression and emphasis, Cameron (1963) hinted at this phenomenon:

> Within recent years there has been an increased interest in the aggressive, sadistic components of sex deviations. Thus, for example, the intrusive attacking characteristics of both exhibitionism and voyeurism are worth considering in any attempt to evaluate exhibitionists and voyeurs (p. 667).

In this statement, Cameron emphasized the "attacking" features of the voyeur and the exhibitionist. Of course, the attack or power thrust is most obvious in the act of rape itself. In the act of rape, the criminal forcibly takes possession. To be able to understand the thinking processes that lead to rape, the reader must eliminate from his mind the idea that rape is based on sexual need. Men who have an active and varied sexual life at home still go out and rape. Many acts of rape reported in the newspaper appear "senseless," and indeed they are when considered as a result of sexual "motives." Physical attraction plays some role. But even more critical are the time and place at which the opportunity presents itself and the criminal's state of mind at the time. Thus, it has happened that eighty-year-old women have been raped (*The Washington Post*, 10/28/71, p. A3), although such a victim is not ordinarily a first preference.

As in any other crime, the criminal does not expect interference. Yet, depending on circumstances, he may welcome a bit of a struggle on the part of the rape victim. This heightens his excitement. If the woman resists his advances, he figures that she is merely putting on a show, and he becomes even more intense about vanquishing her. He may brandish a weapon to subdue her. His charge comes from the final domination—getting her to submit and do his bidding. The sexual act in a rape is usually hastily and poorly executed, with a minimum of sensual pleasure. Often, the criminal is completely impotent and forces the woman to perform fellatio.

> Having problems in maintaining erection, C preferred fellatio in rape. Then it would be impossible to prove rape by looking for semen in the victim's vagina. He intimidated the woman into performing fellatio, at times becoming assaultive if she rejected it. His orgasm was unimportant; the sensuality lasted only briefly.

Again, what mattered was the triumph. The woman was his victim, and he was the man of power. This is graphically illustrated in one man's fantasy about rape. When we first asked him to write down how his mind worked, he stated that the fantasy would be so exciting that he would not be calm enough to write it. In talking about it, he reported the following:

> He would think about a beautiful, talented girl in New York who was a dancer. He had had sex with this girl with her total enthusiasm and compliance. The fantasy involved spending a lot of time and money on her—bicycle rides in Central Park and so forth. Instead of repeating the many varieties of sexuality that he had enjoyed with her, his fantasy was of her refusing sex and then his raping her. He imagined her fighting, his being scared, and in fact little actual sex.

The criminal preferred this rape fantasy, which gave him greater power and less sex, to a fantasy recapitulating consenting sexual practices of many forms over hours. It is characteristic of the criminal that, in both fantasy and action, he prefers sex with someone whom he has to conquer. Criminals have reported to us that, while having conventional sex with their wives or girl friends, they got greater "voltage" by thinking about more exciting sex with someone else.

One might speculate that the criminal who attacks women actually hates the victim or women in general. The people that we have worked with, however, harbor no ill will toward women. In fact, they have described a fondness for them. The power thrust is central and has occasionally been recognized by other investigators.

> Again we must reiterate that the will-to-power element undoubtedly plays a great role in man's nature, as well as the desire for mastery and possession. The sadistic rapist is a jealous, vain, selfish and egotistical creature, a potential thief, with complete disregard for the rights of others, who violates the laws of man and nature, and who looks longingly and greedily at every female, whether it be the child, the adolescent, or womankind in general, as a possible victim. His very glance in the direction of a female strips her to nudity (De River, 1950, p. 42).

By now, the reader should understand that a criminal is not a rapist *or* a voyeur *or* an exhibitionist *or* a child molester. The combinations are many, and both fantasy and behavior involve all the components.

> C was visited by two 13-year-old girls who came to the door taking up some kind of collection. Quickly, the idea of sex occurred. That night, he followed them, hoping to find out where they lived. But in the course of their money-collecting, he lost them. He later encountered one of the girls, who asked about the possibility of earning some money working for him. He grabbed the opportunity, giving her some money there on the spot. In the meanwhile, he was building up a fantasy of seduction. It was one in which he would get the girl up to his room

and give her something to drink that contained an aphrodisiac. He would be in his undershorts, whereupon he would stand up and she could easily view his genitals. As the fantasy went along, the girl would become excited, and eventually he would use her sexually—there would be cunnilingus and eventually intercourse. He would then recruit the other girl, so that there could be activity on his part with one girl cunnilingually and the other vaginally.

The obscene phone call is another arena in which the criminal seeks control. As he thinks about the woman on the other end of the line, the criminal may contemplate raping, beating, and various other acts, including mutilation and homicide.

> C found one or two receptive women out of every 500 calls. He never attempted to contact a woman in person because he feared that a trap might be set and he would be arrested. He masturbated as he talked with the receptive party. Talking with a living being, exciting another person stimulated more exciting fantasies, which extended to rape and homicide. It was a triumph to locate a person who would respond to his request for obscene talk.

> "The phone gives me a wide scope for power. I initiate the contact. I arouse the passions of the woman; her melting compliance and response give me a fantastic thrill, and I can break off the contact whenever I wish."

C was not sex-starved. He was making obscene calls during a period when he was having sex with his fiancée. He continued with the calls at the time of his wedding and thereafter. Whatever sex he proposed to others over the telephone, he could have had at home with his wife, but he would not experience the same high pitch of excitement as he did in the forbidden activity.*

Sexual crimes are often coupled with another type of criminal act. One man reported that rape for him was an "incomplete experience" unless he also stole something. When he was peeping at a woman, he was also mapping out a plan for breaking and entering. A criminal's involvement in one crime does not preclude another. In the extreme criminal, there is a steadily mounting crescendo of excitement. The more sex he has, the more he wants and the more likely he is to engage in other criminal activities. These criminals (called "players") maintain steady crime patterns in all three cate-

---

* A psychiatric report by Kentsmith and Bastani (1974) noted that an exhibitionist in group therapy changed "in symptom" from exhibitionism to making obscene phone calls. Although they considered this noteworthy, we have consistently found that criminals who think about one kind of sexual deviation also entertain ideas about others and, in some instances, act on them.

gories—property, sex, and assault. Some criminals are so active in other kinds of crime that sex does not matter.

"As far as I'm concerned, the hell with sex. Really I don't need sex at all because I'm busy 24 hours a day scheming and in the action. So who bothers with that?"

There is no indication that, if such a person were to have sex more often, sexual release would lead in the long run to a reduction in crime.

We have left masturbation until last, because it often provides the initial thinking for the acts just described. Some criminals refrain from masturbation, because they regard it as a sign of weakness. To masturbate is a putdown; it means that they have been unsuccessful in procuring a partner. To admit to others that they masturbate is almost unthinkable. In their bragging to fellow criminals, they flaunt all the "action" they have been getting, even if they have to make it up. For those who do masturbate, masturbatory fantasies form the premeditation for later criminal activities. More than physical release, the accompanying criminal fantasy is the great tension-reliever. In fantasy, there are no limits. For many, the repetitive fantasies are not sexual. The criminal may imagine himself committing a crime, such as a theft or bank holdup. He gets a charge out of fantasying successful efforts at this. To complete the masturbation, he may imagine seeking out a sex partner. Some criminals avidly read pornographic material. Such reading does not *cause* sex-crimes. Pornographic material appeals to people who already think along particular lines.

C, a rapist, selected books in which women were humiliated and placed at the mercy of rather savage men. He concentrated specifically on the violent parts of these writings.

C was reading a book about a very frightened young man who was a voyeur. For every 10 pages of talk about the man's sexual incompetence, there was one page of exciting material about peeping. This is the part that engaged C.

In no way could the material read be said to cause rape or voyeurism in these men. The patterns of thought and action were well entrenched before they read the particular books.

In this section, we have tried to demonstrate that the criminal is indeed very active sexually. Sexual sophistication and a wide variety of sexual acts begin very early and increase rapidly without a latency period. The sensual aspect is subordinate to the power, the conquest, the buildup, and the triumph of a man who regards himself as irresistible. The sexual activity is part of the power thrust, an antidote to the zero state, a search for a satisfactory homeostasis. This is why he makes such statements as, "I could not live without the touch of female skin." It is not the female skin but the other elements that are parts of the power thrust that he "could not live without."

There is no such person as a criminal who is *only* a "sex offender." We have described the panoply of sexual violations that may be committed by the same individual. However, such a violator does not limit himself to sex crimes. Invariably, he has engaged in thefts, assaults, con operations, and many other types of crimes, often in combination.

LYING

Both the criminal and the noncriminal lie, and each knows when he is doing it. For the criminal, however, lying is a way of life. Without exception, lying is incorporated into every criminal's basic makeup and is a nutrient of criminal patterns.* To choose to be in crime necessitates lying for self-preservation. Therefore, to the criminal, lying is essential and justified. He may even go to the extent of practicing and developing lies. But more common than premeditated lying is habitual lying, which becomes automatic. Lying is one of the most often cited characteristics of the criminal. We shall quote from only one of the many descriptions of this aspect of his behavior.

> The psychopath shows a remarkable disregard for truth.... During the most solemn perjuries he has no difficulty at all in looking anyone tranquilly in the eyes. Although he will lie about any matter, under any circumstances, and often for no good reason, he may, on the contrary, sometimes own up to his errors (usually when detection is certain) ... After being caught in shameful and gross falsehoods, after repeatedly violating his most earnest pledges, he finds it easy, when another occasion arises, to speak of his *word of honor*, his *honor as a gentleman*, and he shows surprise and vexation when commitments on such a basis do not immediately settle the issue (Cleckley, 1964, pp. 370, 371).

We could cite many statements of the criminal's facility for lying. In fact, he has often been declared "unable" to tell the truth—a statement with which we disagree. In this section, we shall go beyond the obvious fact that

---

* Healy and Healy, in 1915, noted that lying is "not the only delinquency" of what they called the "pathological liar." They alluded to the idea that lying feeds into other criminal patterns:

> The tendencies soon carry the person over to the production of other delinquencies, and if those do not come in the category of punishable offenses, at least, through the trouble and suffering caused others, they are to be regarded essentially as misconduct (p. 11).

the criminal lies. Our purpose here is to study the structure and function of a mind to show how the criminal views what we call "lying," the circumstances under which he lies, and the specific forms that his lying takes.

HABITUALNESS OF LYING

It is not difficult to extract from the criminal the fact that, as far as his memory reaches, lying was a standard way of dealing with the world. At first, he deliberately lied, experiencing fear in so doing. In time, lying became a way of life. Lying is a necessary part of the criminal's thinking processes. Untruthfulness is mandatory if he is to live the kind of existence that he has chosen. Lying is so intimate a part of daily living that it sometimes requires effort to tell the truth. One lie breeds another, and so lies are told to cover other lies. As a consequence, the criminal sometimes slips and forgets what lies he has told. This pattern of telling lie after lie is often perceived as "compulsive lying." There is actually no element of compulsion in it. Lying is habitual and it achieves what the criminal wants in life. But it is still totally under the criminal's control, not random and indiscriminate. The criminal examines others and anticipates how they will react. A drawback of the premeditated lie is that it is often based on a prejudgment. The criminal is usually better off if he does not plan his lies in advance. He is so practiced in lying that spontaneity is more effective than contrivance.

The criminal gets away with many more lies than those for which he is held accountable. At an early age, he becomes skilled at thinking fast. In time, he develops a repertoire of lies that can be modified to fit particular situations. That is, the pattern of lying is habitual; only the details need be changed.

> C eloped from the hospital in December 1963 and, while walking along a highway, was seen by a state trooper. The officer stopped C and asked whether he could help him. C's response was that he was taking a 50-mile hike in memory of President Kennedy. The trooper apologized for interrupting him, and C continued on his way unimpeded.

Habitual lying is self-preservative for the criminal, in that it enables him to achieve objectives. However, the criminal also lies to build himself up, either for future criminal enterprises or for the buildup itself.

LIES FOR A BUILDUP

Those who have contact with criminal children know that they appear to lie for no reason. The criminal youngster lies about his age, about where he was born, or about a variety of inconsequential things. He enjoys the mere telling of a lie, because he can fool others. This builds him up—he has put one over. The telling of a multitude of lies is unrelated to whether he has done anything wrong. He says, for example, he is going to one store when he is actually going to another. The criminal is very much an actor, and the world is his stage. He plays for the effect on others. He does not derive excitement from every lie, inasmuch as lying is habitual. The excitement is visible mainly when there is a lull in active criminality. One can see more easily at such times that the criminal is taking pleasure in making fools of others.

Even when the pattern of lying for a buildup is not tied to crime, it may lead to trouble for the criminal. When he is caught in an obvious lie, his general credibility is diminished, and people begin to regard him with suspicion.

Building himself up as a criminal may be a form of excitement, depending on where he is. Many a criminal swaggers and boasts, taking "credit" for crimes that he had nothing to do with or exaggerating the details of those in which he did participate. This boasting takes place with his cronies on the street and in confinement, each attempting to outdo the other. He even builds himself up to the authorities if he knows that no penalty is involved. Where there is merit in confession, he may list the most nefarious exploits in which he was never involved.

> C reported a number of activities for which he had been arrested. This, of course, could be verified by police records. He then enumerated the crimes for which he had not been apprehended: robberies, drugs, jewel thefts, check-forging, "enforcement" procedures for bookies and loan sharks, "favors" for the underworld, such as pistol whipping, making someone eat a pound of dry rice and a gallon of water, throwing bombs for teamsters, sending undertakers to homes to measure bodies, and so on. A few days later, when questioned further, he said he enjoyed "bullshitting everybody." He stated, "You wanted me to talk like a gangster; it seems like that is what you wanted to hear."

> C stated that he had killed five or six people. He emphasized that he had hanged one. He had also shot a couple, but did not know whether they were dead. C added that he looked in the papers for reports of the acts. Later, when skepticism was expressed about all this, C hung his head, smiled faintly, and said that he did not kill even one person.

An aspect of this lying for a buildup is the misrepresentation of one's station in life. There is a tremendous triumph in having others swallow one's stories and be taken in.

C posed as a divinity student at a local college. Arriving in the city where the college was, he looked up a minister he had been referred to, who told him, "When the Lord called John and Peter to preach, they didn't go to school, so why are you?" The minister got C a place to stay with a married couple; C was soon having an affair with the wife. Everyone he met referred to him as "Reverend." C was called to preach in a church.

"When I got out in the sanctuary, it was full of people. There were two other preachers sitting with Bishop ———— and I. I was the youngest one of them all. As I looked over the crowd of people they all had their eyes on me. . . . Bishop ———— said, 'I am very proud to have a young man here from ———— and I have been hearing a lot about this fine young preacher.'. . . When the sermon was over Bishop ———— got up and told the people how wonderful he felt the sermon was, needless to say this made me feel good, and then he told the people I was a young man trying to make something out of my life and he told the people in the church to give with an open heart and then he reached in his pocket and pulled out $5 and put it in the offering plate. . . . When the people got through pulling out the money, the amount was $60.76 and that made me feel real good."

In this situation, there was both a buildup and a criminal objective. C used his ministry to acquire money and exploit women.

The criminal continually finds it necessary to build himself up, because he does not want to come face to face with his fears. To do so would reduce him to a zero. And so the lies continue, compounding the situation and often puzzling others, who see no purpose in them.

LIES TO ACHIEVE AN OBJECTIVE

Lying to achieve specific aims occurs very early in the criminal's life. The criminal child lies to escape punishment or deprivation of privilege. When held accountable, the criminal lies everywhere—at home, in the community, at school, to friends. There are more lies of omission than lies of commission. The prevailing attitude is that what others do not know will not hurt them and will help him. Some criminals consider it a putdown to resort to lies of commission at all and scorn those who brazenly do so. They view themselves as truthful, because they do not engage in lies of commission. Their pattern is to resort almost exclusively to leaving things unsaid. The fellow who is silent gets himself into less hot water, because he does not commit himself to particular lies and then have to remember which ones he has told. Being silent forces others to do the guessing and draw the inferences. There is a great sense of power in remaining mysterious.

A device that may be more effective than omission or total silence is to tell a small part of the truth. People may become suspicious of a man who reveals nothing of himself. So the criminal says just enough to satisfy others. This is a standard tactic, especially when he is held accountable by the authorities. Having confessed to one percent of the truth, he is regarded by them as having been one hundred percent truthful. It is a diversionary tactic preventing more significant violations or pieces of information from coming to light.

Besides the deliberate withholding of material by not talking or by telling only part of the truth, the criminal restricts emotional expression. He may be sweating, trembling, and having palpitations, but he presents a calm, expressionless, or even smiling facade. It must be kept in mind that the criminal has developed the habit of remaining outwardly composed. He has trained himself not to show any emotion, even when a brutal or shocking incident is recounted to him or he tells of one. He views any display of his inner reaction as a sign of weakness. Inside, he may be terribly tense; outwardly, the most he might show is some laughter, which relieves a bit of strain. A psychiatrist might consider the criminal to be showing "dull" or "inappropriate affect"—inappropriate because, under such tension, the noncriminal would react quite differently.

The criminal is a master at calculated ambiguity. The following letter was carefully worded so that, if it fell into the hands of anyone but the addressee, it would appear innocuous and possibly be interpreted as a statement of appreciation. Actually, it contains a veiled threat against a woman's life.

Dear Cindy,

By the time you get this I will most likely be out of Saint Elizabeths. In fact, you may have already seen me before you read this, but I thought I would write just the same.

I feel I owe you a great deal and will do my best to find some means of repaying you. But I can assure you, whatever I do, I always do a good job. You can think about this and perhaps it will give you some comfort. At least I hope so.

Well, I just wanted to let you know that I will be seeing you soon. So with that thought I close.

Yours,

C boasted to us that the letter was a statement of retaliation against Cindy, who had put him down. He believed that death was too good for her, and he intended to make her suffer. "Owe you a great deal" and "find some means of repaying you" express the desire for revenge. His statement that

"I always do a good job" is designed to intimidate her by implying that his treatment of her will be pretty rough. Of course, only Cindy could fathom all this from the letter itself.

Another aspect of lying is outward agreement with something despite inner disagreement or indifference. We term this "assent." It is commonly used when the criminal has his own ideas but goes along with someone else to score points. He generally understands what is being said and may engage in dialogue regarding it. His agreement terminates the conversation about the current issue. His plans remain unhindered, while the other individual believes that he has had some influence. The criminal may also agree simply to avoid alienating another person. He may have no definite scheme in mind at the time, but he does not want to lose a contact that might be of use later. We include assent as an important part of the lying pattern, because it is clearly misleading and so often used. More often than not, it is a successful tactic in concealing ongoing violation and further criminal thinking.

The criminal has been referred to as a "con man" or "con artist." These are terms that he himself does not use, except when speaking with those who already view him this way. The conning efforts of the criminal may involve both lies of commission and lies of omission. The term "conning" is derived from "confidence." The criminal makes an effort to put himself across, so that others will have confidence in him. Because conning entails persuasion, the criminal views all attempts at persuasion, legitimate or not, as deceptive. As one man put it, "Jesus was a con man in that he was so persuasive and evoked so much confidence that others revered him." The criminal's view is that everyone "cons," but he fails to differentiate between exploitative and nonexploitative objectives of persuasion. When he is attempting to be persuasive, he is pursuing what he believes is rightfully his, regardless of what anyone else says. "Conning" is simply a way of getting all that one can and giving as little as possible. The criminal's view of his place in the scheme of things is articulated in the statement, "There's a sucker born every minute and a con artist born every hour to take care of the sixty suckers." Conning is a way of life that takes many forms: misrepresentation or impersonation, as in confidence games, use of false identification, and check-cashing.* However, telling the truth may be the most persuasive ploy or the greatest con of all.

---

*Maurer (1974) described in detail how confidence men operate. He maintained that they are not criminals "in the usual sense of the word," that they are "set apart from those who employ the machine gun, the blackjack, or the acetylene torch" (p. 4). We have found that confidence men are "set apart" only by M.O. They have the criminal thinking patterns that all other criminals have, whether they operate by muscle or stealth.

"I've lied since I could talk. When a lie will serve my purpose better than the truth, I'll tell a lie. The only reason that my lying has become rarer these days is that I've learned that the truth, when properly presented, can be the biggest con of all."

To gain sexual access to a woman, a criminal may be very honest, frankly informing her that he is not ready for marriage or a deep involvement. Such apparent candor may disarm her to the extent that she believes that, given time, a worthwhile relationship will develop. The criminal has thus set her up for exploitation.

A criminal may say that he was "conning" as an excuse for not following through on an avowed intention. That is, he attributes his fragmentation to conning, because it would be a putdown to admit that he changes his mind so often that he does not follow through and keep his word.

C assured Diane that he cared about saving their marriage. Then he proceeded to be unfaithful and treated her abusively. When she would ask him what he had meant when he said he "cared," he would reply that he had really been conning her.

In this case, C used conning as an excuse for not sustaining his intentions to contribute constructively to the marriage. Inasmuch as the criminal is already known as a con man, it is easier for him to attribute his behavior to conning than to a lack of fortitude to implement an intention. Of course, to say that he was conning when he was not is in itself a lie.

Point-scoring is a form of conning that entails saying and doing things to gain others' approval, but with a deceptive purpose. A criminal who wants to ingratiate himself is skilled in this. He can pretend to be something he is not, currying favor with others by putting on a show of manners or excessive politeness or performing some kind and generous acts. He may set up a relationship that he can exploit immediately, or it may be done with an eye to the future. Anyone whom the criminal can influence positively toward him is a possible target for exploitation. As we pointed out in Chapter 3, point-scoring behavior is especially prevalent in confinement. There, the criminal attempts to feed the staff what he thinks it wants to hear and complies with the regulations. His ulterior motive is to expedite his release.

The criminal who prides himself on his slickness may say he conned even when his conduct has been aboveboard, thus trying to add to his stature as a conning expert. If there is no basis for triumph, he attempts to establish one.

C was very interested in a philosophy course in college. He diligently reorganized his notes and typed them meticulously. One day, he went to the professor with a question about some of the material. As he thumbed through the notebook to find the particular point, the professor asked, "Did I say that much?" From that point on, C got straight A's in the course. He presented this incident as his conning the teacher into giving him an A.

C referred to this as "uncontrived" or "unplanned" conning. The facts are that he worked very hard, had a legitimate question, and was working to understand the course content. It was proper for the professor to regard him as a good student. However, to obtain something in a routine way is not gratifying; there is no charge. The criminal would prefer to believe that he got something through conning, rather than merit.

> "There seems to be a fundamental premise in my thinking. Another person can only act favorably to my cause if I con or pretend. It is as if I were totally blind to the possibility that someone can act in my favor by my being completely honest. This is a habit I have had since childhood."

A person who has been a victim of the criminal's conning may claim that he was "manipulated." Manipulation is a word used by everyone except the criminal himself, unless he is being held accountable. The word explains more about the criminal's effect on others than about what the criminal is thinking. The criminal does not view himself as a manipulator. He is merely trying to achieve an objective that he considers legitimate. What others see as a willful, deliberate, and insidious attempt to mislead, the criminal views as part of a day's work. If he considered it insidious at the time, he would not do it. He simply lacks a moral base for evaluating what is harmful to others. Of course, if it will get him off the spot, he will tell the authorities that he was "manipulating," feeding back what he thinks someone else wants to hear. This is often perceived as evidence of "insight," for which the criminal is praised.

The criminal tells some lies so often that he actually comes almost to believe them himself.

> C told everyone that he fought in Israel during the very years that he was confined. He was never in Israel. However, in his rapid-fire way of accounting for his time, he said, even to those who knew where he was, "when I fought in Israel." This was a fabrication that had become so habitual that it rolled off his tongue with no hesitation whatever.

Here, there was no intent to deceive. Half-beliefs of this sort can be broken down very easily. When C was reminded that he was not in Israel, he quickly acknowledged it. The criminal may incorporate into his thinking some ideas that will serve him well in the future but that he knows do not correspond to the facts. Many of these beliefs are consonant with positions taken by society. Over time, he is exposed to views as to what causes crime from the press, politicians, mental health workers, and others. Having heard their opinions many times, the criminal incorporates them into his thinking, and they become half-beliefs. He may say that he could not help when he did, and he is a criminal because he grew up in a ghetto, and go on offering a list of psychologic and sociologic excuses. The accounts that he gives reinforce the current ideas of society. If the criminal is pressed on these half-beliefs by a knowledgeable person with a different position—and if he does not have too much to lose—he will admit to their inaccuracy.

THE CRIMINAL'S VIEW OF LYING

The criminal knows what is right and wrong in terms of laws and mores. On the street, however, he goes by what is right for him at the time. He knows the difference between the truth and a lie, but what is expedient for him at the moment is what is important. Just as he does not consider himself a criminal even though he commits crimes, so he does not regard himself as a liar even though he lies in his day-to-day activities. In both cases, crime and lying are part of life. As we shall explain in Chapter 8, if the criminal viewed himself as anything but a good person, he would choose not to go on living. By lying, he merely does what he needs to do to promote himself and achieve his objectives. Furthermore, he believes that everyone except fools acts as he does, given similar circumstances.

Only when he is personally affected by someone else's lying does the criminal on the street even think in terms of lie versus truth. Even if another criminal double-crosses him, he is likely to call him something other than a liar. It is only when held accountable and when it is to his advantage to do so that he admits that he is lying. If someone confronts him in a lie, he may say he was "rounding," "gaming," or "jiving," but he still is unlikely to use the term "lying."* In confinement, the criminal may atttempt to justify his behavior by saying that everyone lies. In group therapy or in encounters with staff members, the criminal is very quick to point out the smallest lie told by another person. But, as on the street, if anyone calls him a liar, he flares up, taking it as a flagrant insult and a putdown. That is because he regards himself as basically a good person. The exception to this denial of lying occurs when it benefits him to admit that he has perjured himself.

---

* The criminal quoted a few paragraphs earlier did call himself a liar. However, he did this after being in our program for a number of months. It was not a term that he used on the street to describe himself.

SUMMARY

We have tried to dissect "lying," a pattern of thought and action that is a universally recognized and obvious characteristic of the criminal. We have tried to indicate in detail how the mind of a liar operates. The criminal's existence entails living a lie. He tries to appear respectable to others while violating. To him, the "truth" is relative. There is no concept of truthfulness as an integral part of a moral way of life.

"You don't tell the truth if it does not give you what you want. You say whatever must be said in order to get what you want. It is as simple as that."

BIBLIOGRAPHY

Adler, Alfred. *Understanding Human Nature*. Greenwich, Conn.: Fawcett Publications, 1961.

"Animal Training Pays Off for Men Long Imprisoned," *The Washington Post*, November 19, 1972, p. E8.

Ansbacher, Heinz, and Ansbacher, Rowena R. *The Individual Psychology of Alfred Adler*. New York: Basic Books, 1956.

Arieti, Silvano. *The Intrapsychic Self*. New York: Basic Books, 1967.

"Arson: 'I Made a Lot of People Scream,'" *The Washington Post*, February 4, 1973, p. A1.

"Bremer Diary Details Stalking of President," *The Evening Star and The Washington Daily News*, August 3, 1972, p A1.

Brenner, Charles. *An Elementary Textbook of Psychoanalysis*. Garden City, N. Y.: Anchor Books, 1957.

Cameron, Norman. *Personality Development and Psychopathology*. Boston: Houghton-Mifflin, 1963.

Capote, Truman. *In Cold Blood*. New York: Random House, 1966.

Cleckley, Hervey. "Psychopathic States," in Arieti, S. (Ed.), *American Handbook of Psychiatry*. Vol. 1. New York: Basic Books, 1959, 567-588.

Cleckley, Hervey. *The Mask of Sanity*. (4th edit.) Saint Louis: C. V. Mosby, 1964.

De River, J. Paul. *The Sexual Criminal: A Psychoanalytical Study*. Springfield, Ill.: Charles C Thomas, 1950.

"Doorstep Baby Fund," *The Evening Star and The Washington Daily News*, January 29, 1973.

"8 Murders Laid to a Californian," *The New York Times*, October 21, 1973, p. 44.

Eissler, K. R. "Ego-Psychological Implications of the Psychoanalytic Treatment of Delinquents," *The Psychoanalytic Study of the Child*. Vol. 5. New York: International Universities Press, 1950, 97-121.

Eissler, K. R. "Some Problems of Delinquency," in Eissler, K. R. (Ed.), *Searchlights on Delinquency*. New York: International Universities Press, 1949, 3-25.

Glueck, Sheldon, and Glueck, Eleanor. *Delinquents in the Making*. New York: Harper and Brothers, 1952.

Glueck, Sheldon, and Glueck, Eleanor. *Unraveling Juvenile Delinquency*. New York: The Commonwealth Fund, 1950.

"Have Jury, Will Travel," *The Washington Post*, February 11, 1973, p. D4.

" 'He Just Wanted to Get Away from People,' " *The Washington Daily News*, May 28, 1971, p. 5.

Healy, William, and Healy, Mary T. *Pathological Lying, Accusation, and Swindling.* Boston: Little, Brown, 1915.

Hilgard, Ernest R. *Introduction to Psychology.* (3rd edit.) New York: Harcourt, Brace & World, 1962.

Karpman, Ben. "The Structure of Neuroses: With Special Differentials between Neuroses, Psychosis, Homosexuality, Alcoholism, Psychopathy and Criminality," *Archives of Criminal Psychodynamics*, 1961, *4*, 599-646.

Kentsmith, David K., and Bastani, Jehangir. "Obscene Telephoning by an Exhibitionist During Therapy: A Case Report," *International Journal of Group Psychotherapy*, 1974, *24*, 352-357.

Lindner, Robert M. *Stone Walls and Men.* New York: Odyssey Press, 1946.

Maurer, David W. *The American Confidence Man.* Springfield, Ill.: Charles C Thomas, 1974.

May, Rollo. *Power and Innocence.* New York: Norton, 1972.

McCord, William, and McCord, Joan. *Psychopathy and Delinquency.* New York: Grune and Stratton, 1956.

McGeorge, John. "Sexual Assaults on Children," *Medicine, Science and the Law*, 1964, *4*, 245-253.

Miller, Marshall E. "The Place of Religion in the Lives of Juvenile Offenders," *Federal Probation*, March 1965, 50-53.

Miller, Walter B. et al. "Aggression in a Boys' Street-Corner Group," *Psychiatry*, 1961, *24*, 283-298.

"National Training Laboratories," *Programs in Power*, Boston, 1974 (leaflet).

Piaget, Jean, and Inhelder, Barbel. *The Psychology of the Child.* New York: Basic Books, 1969.

"Posthumous Fame Sought by Hijacker," *The Washington Post*, February 28, 1974, p. A1.

Redl, Fritz, and Wineman, David. *Children Who Hate.* Glencoe, Ill.: Free Press, 1951.

Renshaw, Domeena C., *The Hyperactive Child.* Chicago: Nelson-Hall, 1974.

Stafford-Clark, David. *Psychiatry for Students.* New York: Grune and Stratton, 1964.

"2 Inmates Worship, Escape," *The Washington Post*, August 9, 1971, p. C1.

Werner, Heinz. *Comparative Psychology of Mental Development.* New York: Follett Publishing Co., 1948.

White, Robert W., and Watt, Norman F. *The Abnormal Personality.* (4th edit.) New York: Ronald Press, 1973.

"Woman, 82, Raped, Found Dead," *The Washington Post*, October 28, 1971, p. A3.

Chapter 5

Thinking Errors Characteristic of
the Criminal: II. Automatic
Errors of Thinking

BY "THINKING ERRORS," we mean mental processes required by the criminal to live his kind of life. They are "errors" solely from the standpoint of society, and not from that of the criminal. For him these thinking patterns are indispensable to achieve his objectives. This chapter is devoted to the thinking errors that are habitual and, in a way, are the most obvious. Most people know that criminals disregard injury to others, do not trust others, default on obligations, and so forth. But merely identifying these patterns has no operational value. To facilitate change, we have dissected them into their component parts. At no point did we have to infer the existence of these errors. There was no need to re-create the past to identify them. They were and are patently obvious in day-to-day transactions with criminals.

Throughout this volume, we use the words *irresponsible* and *responsible*. In our program for change, responsibility is defined as the outcome of implementing thinking patterns that are corrective of all the patterns described in Chapters 3 through 8. The specific correctives and their applications will be discussed in detail in Volume 2. At this point, the reader needs to be clear about the fact that "responsibility," as we use it, is operationally defined to extend beyond legal accountability or a state of crimelessness to an entire way of life that is the outcome of eliminating criminal thinking patterns and learning new ones.

The reader will recognize in this discussion some of the errors that responsible people make. For example, we sometimes act precipitately and find out later that we are at a disadvantage for not having planned. We occasionally say or do something without thinking of the possible repercussions and find, to our consternation, that we have hurt someone. However, these occasional errors of the noncriminal are not part of a criminal

359

pattern. They may be gaps in foresight, sensitivity, and judgment, but they are not derivatives of criminal thinking.

Every error of thinking expressed by the criminal could be discussed by us in terms of a "feeling," rather than as a thought process or decision. For example, the *closed channel* (no disclosure) could be articulated by the criminal as, "I don't feel like talking about it"; the *failure to assume initiative* as, "I don't feel like doing it now"; *"I can't"* as, "I don't feel that I can do that." We are writing here in terms that are operational in the change process, where we correct thinking errors directly and feelings indirectly. For an agent of change to talk in terms of "feelings" is to introduce an obstacle, because the criminal uses his feelings to justify anything.

The reader will note that one error merges into another and that there is overlap among errors and thinking patterns already described. For example, that the criminal operates as though he owns the world makes his failure to put himself in another's place more comprehensible. "Ownership" is an elaboration of an aspect of the control function. Only for purposes of presentation do we isolate the components of mental events. Each error contains an aspect of thinking not developed in any of the preceding material.

CLOSED CHANNEL

In psychiatric literature, the criminal is said to fail to establish a positive transference. He does not enter into a relationship with a therapist in which the two conduct transactions that are based on valid data to achieve a common objective. We speak of a "channel" of communication, because a clear two-way passage is mandatory. An open channel has three components: disclosure, receptivity, and self-criticism. For a channel to be open, *both* parties must be open and receptive. In addition, a constructive self-critical attitude enhances each person's functioning. As we shall point out, the criminal operates on the basis of a closed channel. He is secretive, has a closed mind, and is self-righteous. These patterns present formidable barriers in the change process. It is as though a patient who desires a physical examination refuses to get undressed—the doctor has no access to the information he needs. A wide-open channel is fundamental to the change process. Without it, change is impossible.

DISCLOSURE

Failure to disclose extends far beyond the lies that the criminal tells. His dealings with people are filled with omission, assent, diversion, circumlocution, exaggeration, distortion, and point-scoring. Given the life he has chosen, it could not be otherwise. The criminal avoids disclosure, because revealing his thinking and action would place him in jeopardy for crimes past, present, and future. He chooses not to dig his own grave by revealing himself. Concealment is as necessary as breathing.

People are tempted to say that the criminal's refusal to disclose is symptomatic of his "paranoia." However, as we pointed out earlier, the criminal is not paranoid, but, from his standpoint, logically suspicious. Without secrecy and guardedness, he would fail as a criminal.

Concealment allows the criminal to build himself up and to maintain his self-esteem. If he exposed his thinking to the critical eye of others, his inflated self-image would be ruptured. Telling the truth might invite others to try to dissuade him from doing as he wants. In addition, he might very well incriminate himself in the process. If others do not know much about him, they are more likely to give him the benefit of the doubt and think well of him. If he opened the channel, others would see behind the facade that he presents. He does not want others to learn about his fears and vulnerabilities, nor does he want to face them himself. Consequently, his thoughts and actions are directed toward maintaining a powerful, unique self-image. A trusting, mutual relationship with full disclosure would demand an acknowledgment of faults and weaknesses and leave the criminal naked and defenseless. He would just as soon not live at all, and suicide is a possible alternative to full disclosure. There must always be a secret part of him unavailable to anyone. Once he has decided that something is his business and no one else's, the criminal responds to the person who properly should know (parent, teacher, employer, etc.) with a variety of diversionary and misleading tactics.

The criminal does open the channel when it suits his purposes. If, for example, he believes that a lie would get him into trouble, then the truth comes out. This is the expedient tactic of telling the truth to save oneself. In addition, as we pointed out in Chapter 4, telling a portion of the truth may be the biggest "con" of all. Confession or telling a part of the truth may lead others to think that the criminal is far more honest than he is. He may appear to have told the entire truth when he has told only a fraction. Such tactics are used when he is in a jam and wants to extricate himself. Then he does almost anything that serves his purpose, including admitting to things that he did not do, in order to convince others of his sincerity and honesty.

In confinement, the criminal carefully studies others around him and tries to determine which tactics to use. In short, he opens and closes the channel to suit his purposes. Openness is not a way of life. In Chapter 8, we shall discuss more precisely the many ways in which the closed channel manifests itself.

From childhood on, the criminal develops a habit of selective listening. He is very attentive, in the sense of being alert to what goes on around him; he is not off in another world. But he decides what to heed. As one criminal said, "We all hear, but we don't listen." The criminal decides what is important to him and quickly rejects the rest. Parents of criminal children experience this lack of receptivity to the point of excruciating frustration. They give their offspring instructions to do something, and it is as though they had not spoken. Whatever the youngster does not want to do, he ignores, even though he hears his parents telling him what should be done. This starts in early childhood. People are always telling the criminal what he should do—go to school, study hard, get a job, save money. But all this is irrelevant to what he wants to do. If someone describes a prospective setup for a bank robbery, he listens attentively. If anyone states a position opposed to his plans, however, he is unreceptive. He does not entertain ideas of others that are incompatible with what he already has in mind.

The criminal also closes his mind to anything that is counter to his image of himself. He is a poor listener, for example, when he is likely to be stirred up sentimentally. Because he considers sentiment a form of weakness, he eliminates from his mind stimuli that evoke sentiment within him. Often, he is so busy building himself up, playing the big shot, that he does not even acknowledge that others have ideas, much less consider what they are saying. If he is focusing totally on achieving an objective, he disregards anything not in line with his designated purpose. Simply listening to another's point of view means admitting that he does not know everything there is to know. He rarely acknowledges that anyone has greater knowledge and wisdom than he. He does not seek clarification if something he does not understand is said, because criminal pride stands in the way. In light of all these patterns, it can accurately be said that the criminal does not know how to participate in a conversation. He does not disclose, and he does not receive, unless he determines the direction and the tenor of the interaction.

The criminal is often preoccupied. As someone talks to him, his mind entertains a scheme for another crime, conjures a woman, or considers ways of bailing himself out of trouble. He simply is not paying attention.

Receptivity is also low when the criminal argues his "case." That is, if he is trying to convince someone else of his point of view and approaches a situation with his mind made up, attempts to influence him are futile. This, of course, proves a formidable obstacle for parents, teachers, employers, and agents of change who are trying to convince the criminal to act responsibly. The basic position of the criminal is: "I have made up my mind; don't bother me with the facts. I have set my course in life. Don't try to dissuade me." He goes to great lengths to avoid anyone who conceivably might try to persuade him to take a path different from the one he has chosen.

When the criminal chooses to disregard what someone is saying, he may be subtle about it, so as not to alienate people with an obvious brush-off. He may assent, which is his way of leading others to think that he is listening and agreeing when, in reality, he is not.

SELF-CRITICISM

Taking stock of oneself is an asset in progressing in the responsible world. The criminal is self-critical to improve his criminality, as is evident in his evaluations of M.O.'s and schemes. But a self-critical attitude with reference to responsibility is clearly incompatible with criminality.

The criminal criticizes others, but angrily rejects any criticisms from them. However, he responds to others' criticisms of him if it helps to maintain a facade of responsible functioning, keeps others off his back, and generally makes it easier to conceal his criminality. As one sees the criminal in the family, at school, and at work, it is obvious that he seldom examines his own functioning, unless he thinks that it will ultimately enhance attainment of a criminal objective. Rarely does he look at his own performance, assess his shortcomings, and initiate remedial procedures. The criminal appears to be self-critical when a point-scoring objective will be served. If he is in a jam, it may be expedient to criticize himself to others to find a way out. Here, the self-criticism is deliberately misleading; the criminal is feeding others what he thinks they want to hear, and not necessarily what is true. Listening to the criminal when he is confessing wrongdoing, one might think that he is truly coming to terms with himself. This may be a fraudulent attempt to convince others that he is at last on the road to achieving insight.

Bona fide self-criticism may appear during fragments of self-disgust. This differs from a man's genuinely taking stock of himself or doing what Alcoholics Anonymous calls making a "searching moral inventory." The life the criminal has chosen to lead precludes self-criticism with respect to responsible functioning. He lacks the appropriate frame of reference, because he has never learned what responsible living entails. Rather than adapt to the world around him and fulfill obligations, he demands that others adapt to him and cater to his desires. Criminal pride, a sense of uniqueness, and other characteristic thinking patterns are antithetical to a self-critical attitude. The criminal does not engage in a process that can destroy his self-image. From his point of view, however, he is self-critical, his aim being to increase his capacity in crime. From our point of view, he is not self-critical. To be self-critical in a responsible way would be to destroy his whole way of life.

Genuine self-criticism is absolutely essential to the change process. Without it, any effort at change is condemned to an early failure. As we shall indicate in Volume 2, self-criticism is a practice that can be taught.

SUMMARY

We have presented the three components of the closed channel—failure to disclose, lack of receptivity, and lack of self-criticism. These are not three independent elements. If the channel is closed because one component is out of order, then the others are also malfunctioning. For example, when a man is not self-critical, he rejects criticisms from others, thus being unreceptive. In turn, he will not disclose fully, because he does not want to provide information for others to use in substantiating their criticisms. In other words, a defect in one element of the channel results in the channel's being defective, thus rendering any transaction with him futile.

"I CAN'T"

The criminal's basic attitude toward life is: "There is nothing I can't do that I want to do." For the criminal to say that he "can't" do something is opposed to his self-concept as a powerful person. If someone else asserts that the criminal is limited in some way, he finds it degrading; it is a putdown. Even when the criminal is afraid, he manages to rid himself of his fear or to find some way out other than saying, "I can't." For example, if someone approaches him with a criminal enterprise that he deems too risky, he maintains his sense of control. Rather than acknowledge his fears, he downgrades the scheme.

However, the criminal does say "I can't" to express his refusal to act responsibly. Occasionally, the noncriminal does this to avoid something unpleasant. The criminal does it constantly. In his childhood, "I can't" starts at home as a response to requests to do various chores or to parental restraints. The youngster says, "I can't do the dishes" or "I can't stay home tonight." With respect to school days, "I can't do math" or "I can't learn French." Regarding work, he claims, "I can't do that kind of work" or "I can't stand my boss." With the least bit of pressure, out pops "I can't": "I can't stand drudgery," "I can't be truthful," "I can't write my family," "I can't resist it," "I can't be there on time," "I can't save money." In all these examples, "can't" is equivalent to "don't want to" or "won't." "I won't" indicates his refusal to perform on someone else's terms. He dismisses effort and hard work. The criminal does not think about "I can't" when he says it. Verbalizing it is habitual, to the extent that it sometimes rolls off his tongue before he even gives the matter at hand any thought. "I can't" is not a rationalization, but rather a dismissal of requirements that are outside the domain of his own desires and interests.

What reinforces his saying "I can't" is its effectiveness. People tend to excuse the criminal, because they think he lacks the capability to do some things. He says "I can't" so often and with such success that it becomes a half-belief. What is a half-belief for him continues to be used and accepted by others as fact, reinforcing the view that the criminal truly *cannot* fulfill specific responsibilities.

"I can't" is extremely useful when the criminal is held accountable and pressure is applied. If others say that he can do something, he debates the point, offering a variety of excuses to reinforce his position. When therapists try to work with the criminal in confinement, they encounter a plethora of "I can'ts." It may be couched in psychologic terms. "Impulses," "compulsions," "feelings"—almost any state of mind can be expressed in terms of "I can't." The criminal may come to an interview with bottled-up physical tensions and say, "I can't talk." The compassionate therapist may say, "If you can't now, maybe later." This occurs even when the session is being held in part to relieve the tension through talking and catharsis. When the therapist hears "I can't," he may interpret it literally as a statement of incapacity and then elect to explore the past with the criminal to find out why he "can't" do something. As we have explained, such an exercise provides the criminal with more excuses. As one man later admitted, "My depression is an out; my bleak outlook is an out."

There is one sense in which the "I can't" theme accurately applies. If a person is committed to a particular path, he cannot at the same time implement a contradictory course of action. If we are devoted to our families and someone tries to persuade us to do something that will place our families in jeopardy, we will not do it, because the two are incompatible. We might then say, "I can't do that." Similarly, the criminal cannot abide by the mandates of responsible living and at the same time obtain his criminal gratification.

When approached by a therapist or another agent of change about living responsibly, the criminal makes statements couched as "I can't." In part, this is because the task appears overwhelming—too formidable even to try. If he continues with "I can't," this amounts to an affirmation that he wants something else and is not willing to give up his excitement to be a "slave" or a "square." The self-deception occurs when the criminal repeats "I can't" so often that he half-persuades himself that he cannot be different. We encounter this phenomenon in our meetings with the criminal as we try to achieve change—a half-belief in a self-constructed myth of inherent unchangeability. The criminal then makes a half-hearted "rehabilitative" effort, only to fail. His failure in turn gives him license for more crime, inasmuch as he always has recourse to the argument that he tried but "could not" make it. He has shown himself and the world that he "can't" change.

THE VICTIM STANCE

When the criminal is held accountable for a crime, he portrays himself as a victim. The excuses are offered only when he is interrogated; they are not part of his thinking in daily crime. In the next chapter, we shall describe the criminal's thinking processes in accountability situations. Here, however, we are extending the concept of "victim" to include the criminal's refusal *everywhere* to take genuine responsibility for his role and for situations largely of his own making. His assumption of the victim stance is the opposite of self-criticism. Instead of taking stock of himself, the criminal blames others, on the grounds that he is a victim.

A person can indeed be a victim. There are situations in life in which people have no control over a predicament in which they find themselves. Passengers imprisoned in a hijacked plane through no fault of their own are indeed victims. A miner injured in an underground blast is also a victim. People are victims of physical and mental illnesses that incapacitate them. Whether a person is a victim is at times a matter of how he views life's misfortunes. As we indicated in Chapter 2, most observers have regarded the criminal as in some way a victim of the circumstances of his early life. Often, it is because they have confused environmental conditions with the human response to the conditions. From an outsider's perspective, perhaps the mere fact of being born in a ghetto makes a person a victim. But such a fact of life does not determine one's destiny. Instead of viewing themselves as victims, many ghetto-dwellers have recognized that they had more obstacles to overcome than other people and have succeeded in rising on the socioeconomic scale.

Criminals view society as unfit for them, rather than regarding themselves as unfit for society. The world does not give them what they think they are entitled to, so they view themselves as poorly treated and thus victims. They constantly cry "victim" when things do not go as they want. It is always something that is wrong with others—e.g., "My parents are acting up again."

Although C's father was not in the home, the family was a stable unit. His mother was a parole officer, his aunt a teacher, and his uncle a steady worker. They all lived together and tried to use modern psychology and good judgment in rearing C. Despite a stable home and many opportunities, C was constantly violating. Finally, in exasperation, his mother whipped him once. From then on, he went around telling others that he was beaten at home. Later in life, he told a psychiatrist that he had been cruelly treated as a child.

Criminals assume the victim stance in innumerable daily transactions around the home.

C, at age 14, balked at doing chores and telling his parents where he was going when he went out. When they reprimanded him, he claimed that he was being treated unfairly: "They keep bugging me. They are trying to make me mad." He became sullen, uncooperative, and uncommunicative, and continued to neglect his household duties. His parents then restricted him in some way as a punishment. C's response was to cry "victim" louder. No matter what approach his mother and father used—whether discussion, reasoning, yelling, punishment—nothing would move him. He saw the situation totally in terms of his being treated unfairly.

This kind of thing occurs repeatedly in school. The child picks a fight with others and blames another party—"He started it." He brings home a report card and has a variety of excuses predicated on the notion that he has gotten a bad deal.

C brought home failing and below-average grades. He complained that the teachers were poor, that they would not help him, and that all they did was discipline. He went on to say how hard it was to learn in a school with racial problems. C had not gone to see the counselor because "she is black."

C had not gone to the teacher and asked for assistance. He had taken no steps at all to remedy a steadily deteriorating situation, mainly because school had little meaning for him. The things that the criminal dismisses, such as school, are precisely those in which he is sooner or later held accountable and wherein he cries "victim."

On the job, a criminal may be totally bored and unproductive. He becomes indignant about being treated unfairly when he is reprimanded. When he enters a new situation—whether it be a job, a neighborhood group, or a club —he expects to assume a position requiring more skills than he has and then from there to rise very quickly. If that does not happen, he blames "the system" and views himself as its victim. The examples are countless.

As the criminal relates his story, he tailors it to a particular person. He determines how to assume the victim stance so that it will be most acceptable —shall it be presented in terms of feeling or thinking? In a psychiatric setting, it sounds authentic if he talks in terms of feelings, because thinking is often considered "intellectualizing." Therefore, he says that he was bored, angry, scared, or depressed; this is the acceptable currency in most transactions at many mental health centers. Mental health personnel may help to divest the criminal of responsibility further by labeling his behavior or feelings as "sick," much as we did when we began. We have already discussed the devious tactics of the criminal who tries to establish mental illness as a defense.

The victim posture is expressed by the criminal and accepted by others so often that he starts to incorporate it into his own thinking. In a state of self-pity, the criminal may tell *himself* that, if only it had not been for some particular event, things would have turned out differently. If the criminal can half-believe that what he did was attrabutable to forces outside himself, this can help him to hang on to the idea that he is basically good. The criminal may tell himself that he would not have done as he did had his girl not left him, or had his mother not died recently. He may cite something recent or factors of long standing, such as being born in the ghetto. A criminal with a background of affluence may attribute his criminality to the "sterility" of the suburbs or to having had things too easy. When the criminal's conscience bothers him, he latches on to these things, which he has used in a self-serving way before, but which he has now come to half-believe, owing to frequent and successful repetition. In addition, the victim position is part of the common parlance of prison talk. To get along with other criminals, especially in jail, one repeats the same line over and over, complaining about the injustices of society. The criminal's pitch of indignation rises even higher when he adds to this his complaints about prison conditions. When a person rehearses the same argument and hears it from others, it eventually becomes a part of him. It is not a firm conviction, however, and can be broken down with the proper techniques of interviewing.

When the criminal actually does encounter circumstances that by almost any standards are adverse, he creates a vicious circle by responding in a nonconstructive manner. Rather than adopt an approach of enduring the situation or trying to improve it, he responds with irresponsibility, which makes things worse. Then, he can always turn around and blame the original unfavorable circumstances.

C came from a home in which the parents had separated, leaving a loving but somewhat inadequate mother with three children. C exploited his mother's weaknesses until he became so unmanageable that she sought outside help. C, at the age of 13, told the mental health clinic staff that he was there because his parents were divorced, owing to his father's drinking problem.

It came to light that C had been a problem long before the separation. He took advantage of the separation by wearing his mother down. Then he blamed his delinquency on his father's drinking, despite the fact that his siblings, who had lived with the same problems, had reacted very differently.

As we have indicated throughout, the criminal seeks to be the victor in every situation. To admit that there are things over which he lacks control is a putdown. Thus, the criminal says that he is a victim *only* when he is trying to extricate himself from a self-created dilemma or when the world does not treat him as he thinks it should. When the criminal sets out to victimize someone else and things do not go according to his plan, then he becomes a victim of injustice. He refuses to own up to the fact that the many disagreeable situations in which he finds himself are of his own making.

LACK OF TIME PERSPECTIVE

People who work with the criminal in correctional programs are perplexed as to why a person with intelligence and in complete possession of his faculties does not learn from experience and plan for the long term. In fact, some experts have concluded that there is some incapacity in the criminal for this kind of learning.

> The *sociopathic personality* seems unable to learn, that is, to profit by his experiences, in certain areas of interpersonal relationships. He may be of average or superior intelligence. Yet he repeatedly acts out in such a way as to invite social ostracism and often legal prosecution, without being able to change his impulsive behavior (Cameron, 1963, p. 652).

Eissler (1950) has a somewhat different view, although he also used the word *incapacity*.

> In most studies on the psychopathic personality it is claimed that the psychopath is unable to learn from his life experiences. As far as the delinquent is concerned, I think the claim is exaggerated. Delinquents learn very well, only they do it in fields where society—and their environment—would prefer their not learning anything new. The psychopath, or delinquent respectively, appears incapable of learning in some sectors of his life. This incapacity is restricted to certain fields (p. 113).

A statement of "incapacity" amounts to the notion that the criminal does not learn from the experience that society wants him to learn from or that society assumes he should learn from. Instead, he learns from the experience that advances him in his objectives. To an extent, experience guides him in planning new crimes. He even chides himself for not learning from experience if he gets caught. The criminal's utilization of experience is indeed as habitual and automatic as that of the responsible person, but in directions vital to his own interests.

When held accountable, the criminal refers to his past. He also draws on experience in boasting about accomplishment in crime. In street talk and in confinement, criminals congregate to recount and embellish past triumphs. In addition, the criminal dwells on the past during periods of self-disgust in confinement or when he has contact with a person toward whom he is sentimental. However, self-disgust is transient, and thinking about the past in such a state of mind does not serve as a guide to the future.

It has been said that the criminal's time frame is mostly in the present.

> He is a man for whom the moment is a segment of time detached from all others (McCord, 1956, p. 14).

> If we tried to point out "future consequences" of anything [the delinquents] were about to do, we might as well have saved our breath. For what is trouble that may be brewing for tomorrow, no matter how fatal, compared with even mild fun right now (Redl and Wineman, 1951, p. 120)?

Instancy pervades the criminal's thinking and his attempts to achieve a homeostasis. The criminal refuses to defer gratification. We all *want* what we want when we want it. The criminal *demands* triumph now. He must be the best now. He must have the best now. Instancy colors even the smallest objectives.

> C wanted to lose 15 pounds. To accomplish this, he said he would do morning exercises. Then he added that he would do this "to the extent that it is possible." He then laughingly admitted that he wanted to be in good shape immediately and lacked the commitment to exercise daily.

Instancy also characterizes the criminal's thinking about more important considerations. As he grows up, the criminal expects to be on a par immediately wth people who have worked a lifetime for what they have. He wants the achievement without the work: "I wanted to be in a position of responsibility without being responsible." He balks at acquiring skills and experience, building step by step. For the noncriminal, a goal involves persisting toward a responsible objective and weathering setbacks. The responsible person attains a degree of self-respect and satisfaction, even if he does not reach the absolute pinnacle of success. "Goal" means something very different to the criminal: it entails an instant triumph achieved via criminal thinking and action. Instant triumph is a delivery from the fear of permanent nothingness (the zero state). He wants to hit the jackpot fast and succeed overnight.

Almost everyone who writes about the criminal emphasizes the latter's disregard for the future. He does consider the future, but not in the way a noncriminal does. The criminal has no enduring concept of the length of a life, or even of a "lifetime." His idea of how long he will live is based largely on the "occupational hazards" of crime. Considerations of the future enter into his thinking mainly because he is so fearful of dying tomorrow. That is not to say that he plans for the future, only that he is aware of it. Eissler (1950, p. 108) saw among delinquents "a pathological attitude towards death." Street criminals have told us that when they were youths, they estimated that they would die around the age of thirty. They foresaw that at that age they would be less agile, less able to get around, and thus more vulnerable to mortality.

Another way in which the criminal thinks of the future is in terms of getting caught. If a man wants to minimize the risk of apprehension, he forgoes some enterprises, even though they are attractive. A criminal may decide to become a "fence" for stolen goods, rather than perform the burglary himself. He may be the power behind the scenes—setting up the crime, but not actually executing it. When it comes to getting out of confinement, the criminal clearly has the future in mind. He gives considerable thought to tactics for achieving his release.

> C spent a decade at Saint Elizabeths Hospital. He had many opportunities to join our program. He made a number of sincere beginnings, but eventually getting out *his* way took priority over basic change. He exerted more energy in his criminal schemes on the grounds and his conniving to get out than in trying to change, which might have allowed him to be released years sooner. And so finally, after spending his youth, from 18 to 28, he was released—the same person as when he was admitted. We know that he is arrestable, although not yet arrested.

In his shortsighted way, C rejected our program because it did not guarantee his release. The reader might conclude that C did not consider his future. He did think of the future, but in criminal terms, plotting and originating schemes to get out of the institution. Like other criminals, C was, as Karpman (1961, p. 639) put it, "the perfect opportunist, but one without foresight."

It is usually within a criminal context that delay of gratification occurs. The criminal postpones gratification when he plans to achieve a "big score," i.e., when he contemplates the "ultimate crime." Sometimes a criminal thinks of a crime and spends years scheming and waiting for the perfect opportunity to commit it.

> At the age of 12, C schemed to rob the rent collector who came to his family's home. For years, he fantasied how to accomplish this. Eventually, his parents permitted him to take the money to the landlord's office. This gave him numerous occasions to case the premises. At 18, C broke into the office and stole a large sum of money, a crime for which he never was suspected.

This crime incubated for six years. But there was no hiatus of other criminal activity between twelve and eighteen. Thus, only in a very limited sense could it be said that C delayed gratification. In short, the criminal does consider the future, but in terms that are in line with his objectives.

The criminal has the capacity to develop a responsible time perspective. This capacity is obvious from the fact that he does take the past and future into account to serve his own purposes. However, he is totally inept in utilizing the past and future responsibly. He does not develop a responsible time perspective because it is not necessary for his criminal way of life.

FAILURE TO PUT ONESELF IN ANOTHER'S POSITION

From early in childhood, youngsters are taught to put themselves in the shoes of others. Most people learn to do this in a responsible way, but not the criminal. He demands every consideration and every break for himself, but rarely stops to think about what other people think, feel, and expect. The criminal has little but a transient sentimentality to induce him to consider what other people are experiencing. It is mainly in crime that he puts himself in another's place: imagining how the potential victim will react helps him to carry out a criminal act. Along with his lack of consideration of others, he has little regard for rules, customs, and laws.

> "My thinking would never extend as far as a consideration of what might be the reason for a rule and how it might be helpful to others. Not only that, but the circuit of my thinking is far shorter. All I think is, 'There's a rule. How do I get around it?' In my equation, rule equals how to avoid. . . . I never look at the reason for a rule because it would usually involve some consideration for others, some interaction, and when I want something, that's foreign to my nature."

This thinking error is understandable: it allows the criminal to preserve his self-image. His mind is closed, and he views people as favorably disposed to him, even when they are not. To examine an alternative position could damp his plans. That is, if he is really sensitive to others and listens to them, he runs the risk that he will hear ideas opposed to his position. It can be truly said that, for this very reason, the criminal rarely holds a discussion with anyone. He wants to be the one who prevails. Thus, he does not "discuss" a topic with his parents, teachers, or associates; he imposes his view. An interchange of ideas would become a power contest; so, rather than seriously consider the merits of another's position, he demands that his ideas be accepted.

The criminal has little, if any, basis for understanding a noncriminal's perspective on most things. If a responsible person is trying to persuade him to be economical, the criminal is unresponsive. He does not see the merit of long-range planning and saving or of responsible management of money in general. Even if thrift is mandated by the requirement to support his own children, the criminal still may refuse to consider others' needs. In this and a multitude of other instances, the criminal is deaf and blind to responsible viewpoints. His entire existence is patterned along altogether different lines. Many issues remain outside the realm of his comprehension, not because he is stupid, but because he has chosen a way of life resulting in total ignorance of responsible thinking.

The criminal's failure to see himself in another's position has been described by Freyhan (1955) as related to "dysfunctions in empathy."

> Much of the symptomatology of cold egoism, emotional callousness, and aggressive violence of the rights of others, characteristic of psychopathic personalities, arises in relation to dysfunctions in empathy (p. 24). . . . One is tempted to declare that lack of capacity for empathic experiencing puts the psychopath in the position of a stranger who does not speak or understand the language. No matter how well he observes, imitates, or pretends, he does not understand the language of the tender mind (p. 25).

Freyhan referred to a "lack of capacity for empathic experiencing." This lack is not an innate characteristic of the criminal; it is developed. If the criminal put himself in the position of responsible people, antisocial acts would be more difficult. We have avoided the word *empathy* in our discussion of this error of thinking, because it relates mostly to one person's trying to "feel" what another person is feeling, and our focus in the change process is on thinking processes, not feelings. When we teach the criminal a corrective for this thinking error, we replace it with a new pattern of thought. For some criminals, this turns out to be the most important corrective of all.

FAILURE TO CONSIDER INJURY TO OTHERS

"The psychopath sails under his own flag like a pirate; he does not care about ship or crew except as they contribute to his own goal." This particular aspect of psychopathic behavior is perhaps the most universally recognized criterion. It represents the most disturbing element since it always involves or hurts another person if not society generally (Freyhan, 1955, quoting Kahn, pp. 24-25).

To society, the "most disturbing element" of the criminal's way of life is his injuring other people. This aspect of his life is an outcome of his failure to put himself in another's position. The criminal's view of injury is extremely limited; it usually refers to bodily harm as a consequence of violence—muggings, beatings, and other forms of assault. As we use the term here, "injury" extends far beyond physical harm. The criminal does indeed injure people and property physically. However, there is a "ripple" effect that only begins with the immediate victim. In the wake of every crime, there is emotional damage, fear, and inconvenience both to the immediate victim and to others not directly involved.

As we pointed out in Chapter 3, the injury to others begins very early in life, and the pattern grows. The criminal child puts his parents through untold anguish with his lies, evasion of responsibility, and delinquent activities; he steals from them and exploits them in every way possible. In school, he injures other children by interfering with their learning opportunities. It takes only one or two criminal children to throw a classroom into chaos. Teachers and school administrators spend countless hours trying to teach, evaluate, counsel, and discipline these youngsters. School property is destroyed and stolen. Innocent children are bullied. In the neighborhood, the criminal child intimidates and fights with others, and steals and vandalizes property. Citizens are afraid to walk the streets at night and in some places during the day.*

As adults, criminals inflict enormous injury on the business community. Because of thefts, customers pay more. Merchants in high-crime areas are often threatened and sometimes maimed or killed. Some have to shut down their businesses. Considerable emotional damage is inflicted on those who employ or work with criminals.

The criminal's failure to consider injury to others is an outcome of all his other thinking errors. He does not view himself as injuring anyone. When held accountable, he regards himself as the injured party. After all, he was the one interfered with; he is the one now under restraints. Even when

---

* A particularly graphic account of youthful crime is rendered by Stevens (1971), who wrote about the "teen-aged rat packs" of New York City.

he is confronted with the harm he has inflicted, he blames others or minimizes the harm done. Others started it, he claims—he had to defend himself. Or it is the other person's fault—he had it coming. The criminal may claim that there should have been better security where he broke in. To justify a theft, he may stridently proclaim that it is the profit-gouging merchant who injures, not he. In other words, there is no injury inflicted by him—there are only unjust laws.

The criminal's sentimentality constitutes a temporary deterrent to injuring others, but, like other deterrents, it gives way to competing excitements. Thus, he will injure even those whom he professes to love. He rarely injures them by direct attack. Instead, he causes them anguish by his whole way of life, or he exploits them without their knowledge.

> C said that he was very indebted to his mother for all she had done for him. She was a hard-working woman who held two jobs and made many personal sacrifices for the family. While his mother was at work, C used her home as a house of prostitution. He also kept guns hidden there.

C did not consider how upset his mother would be with what he was doing, even though he was not personally threatening her with injury. There are times when the criminal wants to make amends for what he has done. However, he generally does not follow through on good intentions. Merely having thought of restitution reinforces his idea of himself as a good person.

> C wanted to retrieve an expensive ring that he had stolen and given to his girl friend. Several times, he said that he would write to her and expedite this matter, so that the ring could be returned to the rightful owner. He never did. Another party finally intervened and obtained the ring.

> During a holdup at a bank, C took $1,500 from a woman. The woman pleaded with him not to take it, because she had a sick husband and unpaid bills. C's accomplice was impatient, and so they made off with the money. This act bothered C for a long time. A couple of weeks later, he started to look for her to return her money and give her even more. However, he quickly gave up the search, because he could not locate her immediately.

In these examples, it might appear that the criminal desires to make amends from a sense of guilt. However, this was merely a fragment of self-disgust that did not last. Accountability to conscience and the prospect of experiencing guilt after wrongdoing are not lasting deterrents to injuring others.

FAILURE TO ASSUME OBLIGATION

The concept of "obligation" is foreign to the criminal's thinking. He seldom, if ever, even uses the word. To be obligated is to lose his status as a powerful person. Obligation is a position of weakness and vulnerability to others' control. In part, the criminal regards himself as above the ordinary person because he does not consider himself bound by obligations.

The criminal views obligations as interfering with what he wants to do. If he is married, having to be with his wife, doing household chores, and fulfilling other family responsibilities are often incompatible with his search for excitement; thus, they are often left undone. Punctuality and the keeping of appointments also are not appropriate to his way of life. When the criminal says, "I'll see you tomorrow at three o'clock," he means that he will keep the appointment if nothing better comes up; unless there is a criminal objective in mind, he will not be there. There is no moral imperative to keep the appointment or to give notice that he will not keep it.

Day after day, even in the smallest actions, the criminal defers and defaults on obligations. The criminal child leaves chores undone, goes out of the house without telling his parents where he is heading, and fails to return on time. Promises are made and easily broken. They are kept only if they are part of a larger self-serving operation. In any case, the criminal does not view his words as "promises," but rather as statements of convenience. At school, the criminal youngster does not do his share of a group project, or he "forgets" to bring something from home. On the job, the criminal is late to work, is sloppy or neglectful about details that do not interest him, and does not follow through on work assigned. With girl friends, his word is more often broken than kept. In every sector of responsible living, the criminal disregards obligation. One man remarked that his existence in this world did not require him to do anything for anyone else, especially in view of his not even having had any say in whether to be born and when.

Not only does the criminal disregard obligations; he also avoids situations in which he might incur new obligations.

> As a boy, C lived in a home in which there was very little food. He would not go to his neighbor's for supper when invited, because he thought that, if he went, the neighbors would have some kind of claim on him.

A similar pattern occurs in school when the criminal child refuses to volunteer for a task, because he knows that it would mean having to do things he dislikes. Furthermore, he may want to avoid putting himself into a situation in which others will constantly pressure him if he does not do his share.

What might appear to be the fulfillment of obligation usually has a more directly self-serving purpose. A criminal visited his ex-wife after committing a homicide. His "mission" was to give her several hundred dollars to help her and their children. He did this out of a transient sentimentality for the family. Actually, he had no sense of obligation—he had not seen them for years. Giving stolen money to his family allowed him to think well of himself. The criminal may fulfill an obligation to win others' recognition and esteem. The criminal child may volunteer for a class project with the thought that he will show the others "how to do it." That is, he will be the big man with all the answers. He makes an enthusiastic start, but does not consider himself obliged to follow through; when an activity bores him, he quits.

When it appears that the criminal recognizes obligations to a fellow criminal, this is not actually the case. A criminal's ulterior motive is to have others obligated to him. Fulfilling an obligation may be part of a con job. He may be setting up another party, so that he can claim later that he is owed a favor. When it comes to standing by one another, one criminal is ready to stab another in the back, if that is what best serves his own ends.

When the criminal is held accountable for failing to honor obligations, he responds with a variety of excuses. One of the most common is, "I didn't have a chance to get around to it." What is left unsaid is that he never had any intention of doing what was required. Another ploy is to say that circumstances beyond his control arose, so that a task was left undone. This is a variation of the "victim" theme. Other tactics may include saying that he forgot or did not feel well. He may plead ignorance and say that he was not even aware that he was expected to do something—"I didn't hear" or "I guess I didn't understand." He might well acknowledge his defaulting and say he is sorry. The admission implies that he will be more conscientious in the future, but, in the criminal's own thinking, the admission by itself clears him and rectifies the situation. Thus, the same thing is likely to recur.

We have pointed out four ways in which the criminal responds to what the responsible world considers an obligation: by blatantly disregarding obligations, avoiding new obligations, fulfilling obligations out of transient sentimentality, and fulfilling obligations to advance an exploitative scheme. Whenever he upholds an obligation, the criminal builds himself up in the process. In contrast, the noncriminal views obligation in moral or ethical terms. Obligation is a way of life that includes consideration of others and fulfillment of expectations that are required for social living. We speak of an "inner sense" of obligation. We routinely live up to obligations without much deliberation as to whether they are obligations or not. An obligation is a "must" of life. It is a discharging of duties to others that a person has built into the way he functions. The criminal may do things for others to advance his own interests, but he never experiences a genuine inner sense of obligation. Obligation is not a functional concept in the criminal's life, because it is incompatible with how he chooses to live. Yet he is tyrannical in requiring others to fulfill what he considers their obligations to him.

FAILURE TO ASSUME RESPONSIBLE INITIATIVES

The criminal generates tremendous energy and plenty of initiative, but not in the direction of what is socially acceptable. Throughout life, he refuses to take responsible initiatives, because they do not provide the power thrust that he seeks. Only violation provides this, and he is tremendously resourceful in doing the forbidden. The criminal also assumes initiative in activities that appear to be responsible, but that he utilizes for point-scoring purposes. For example, the criminal child may volunteer to help clean the house. Having pleased his family by such an act, he is freer to violate. Similarly, a criminal may go out of his way to help a neighbor, only to violate the neighbor's trust later. For the criminal to show initiative regularly in responsible matters would be absurd on the face of it; to do so would be to show initiative in activities that he scorns.

In crime, the criminal may be extremely energetic and resourceful.

> Each day, C took his wife to work, returned to his apartment, and got dressed for his "job." At 10 A.M., he set out on his "tour of duty." First, he met the pusher at 11 A.M. After a day of shoplifting and breaking and entering, he met the "fence" at 3 P.M. Having completed his day's "work," he picked up his wife at 4 P.M.

Such a pattern shows much initiative. He did what he believed was necessary to "play both sides of the street." He met his wife at the agreed time and spent a few hours with her. In fact, he occasionally gave her gifts, such as a dress that he had stolen. The initiatives were assumed both in crime and in whatever it took to maintain a facade of respectability.

The criminal also shows initiative in nonarrestable activities that provide arenas for power.* He makes contact and works his way into organizations in which he can be a "big man." When it comes to promoting himself and thrusting for power, he is active and effective, at least for a while. When he tires of one activity, he moves on to another and assumes new initiatives in it.

Some observers have designated the criminal "passive-aggressive." The

---

* The criminal's power striving in nonarrestable activities is discussed in detail in Chapter 7.

American Psychiatric Association diagnostic manual (1968) characterized the "passive-aggressive personality" as follows:

> This behavior pattern is characterized by both passivity and aggressiveness. The aggressiveness may be expressed passively, for example, by obstructionism, pouting, procrastination, intentional inefficiency, or stubbornness. This behavior commonly reflects hostility which the individual feels he dare not express openly. Often the behavior is one expression of the patient's resentment at failing to find gratification in a relationship with an individual or institution upon which he is overdependent (pp. 43-44).

Because the criminal defaults on obligations and fails to assume responsible initiatives, he may be termed "passive." He is given this label because of his outward demeanor when it is bland and nonreactive. The criminal's passive behavior is often seen as an indirect expression of anger.

> To many adults, C, an active teenager, appeared inert, silent, and sullen. When his parents asked him to do something, he was unresponsive. He often did not argue with them, but simply shrugged off their requests and demands. At school, he behaved somewhat similarly when asked to do something he did not want to do. When he was brought by his family to a community clinic for his delinquent behavior and difficulties at home, C sat like a lump of clay. He responded in monosyllables and usually in the negative—"I don't know," "I don't remember." But in the neighborhood, with his friends, C was assertive, talkative, and enthusiastic.

The assumption that parents, teachers, and clinic workers made was that C's passive behavior was his way of expressing anger. In reality, C was not angry at all. He was nonverbal because he did not want to reveal himself. Anger reactions occurred only when others tried to force him to do what he did not want to do. Although he was unresponsive to chores, homework, and counseling, he was very assertive in activities in which he was interested. The terms "passive" and "aggressive" are nonspecific and depend mainly on the frame of reference adopted. The criminal is "passive" to what society expects of him; he is "aggressive" when it comes to taking initiatives in crime or criminal equivalents (see Chapter 7). The noncriminal may be "passive" with respect to crime, but "aggressive" about earning a livelihood and advancing himself. C was not angry at his parents or teachers for living as they did; he grew angry when they interfered with his living as he wanted.

Some have called the criminal "lazy." As Freyhan (1955, p. 21) pointed out, however, "psychopaths are, at least in principle, not 'guilty' of negligence, laziness, or lack of will power." Ordinary social incentives simply have little meaning to the criminal. The adjective "lazy" is applied to the criminal because of the effect he has on people who see him as a nonperformer. He does not fulfill the expectations of society, so he is called "lazy." He is probably more active physically and mentally in crime than the noncriminal is in any activity.

Criminals are not "do-nothing" people; they are doers! Even in confinement, they are energetic in thought, talk, and action. They show responsible initiatives to score points and thus mislead others. It is not unusual to see a locked-up criminal complaining about how confinement blocks his taking initiatives to straighten out and adjust to the responsible world. When he is granted his freedom, he does almost nothing in this direction.

> As soon as C had his freedom to go into the city, he sought out a girl with a reputation as a "swinger." He did nothing about seeking a job. He was "too busy" to go to weekly meetings at the Catholic church to which he had been invited. He missed Sunday Masses repeatedly and did not talk to the priest. Nor did he do anything about trying to establish friendships with more responsible people. His oft-stated intentions made in confinement were never translated into action.

When held accountable, the criminal has a variety of excuses as to why he has not assumed initiatives in responsible activities. He may tell others that something more pressing came up or that he did not "get around to it." He resorts to motivational arguments, such as not being interested. One man said, "I don't like to look for a job. I am used to getting turned on, to a job." This meant that he left it to others to get him a job, which he really did not care about, anyway. He told others, however, that he was not motivated or "interested" enough to look for himself. If the criminal is having contact with mental health personnel, he talks about feelings.

> C knew that the outpatient department would question him as to why he was not working. From experience, he knew what would get him off the hook. So he talked about feeling nervous, depressed, or afraid.

Even doing this was taking a criminal initiative. The tactic permitted the criminal to continue to hide behind "mental illness" and kept him on the hospital rolls. This entitled him to free medical services and made him eligible for financial assistance.

The criminal may also respond in terms of "can't" when others ask him to assume a responsible initiative. "I can't" may refer to a lack of knowledge or skill, but it more commonly refers to a lack of determination.

An important element in the refusal to take responsible initiatives is that the criminal has no guarantee that there is anything in it for him. He may not phrase it in terms of wanting a guarantee, but this is an important element in many of his excuses. A guarantee of *opportunity* to progress is never enough. The criminal wants absolute assurance that he will be an instant success in whatever he does.

There is still one more factor in this thinking error: the criminal often declines to take initiatives because he does not want to appear ignorant. He tries to avoid situations in which his lack of knowledge and his ineptness are visible. This presents a great obstacle in the change process, as we shall describe in Volume 2.

OWNERSHIP

"Ownership" is the process of thinking whereby, if a criminal wants something, the item is his or the person will do as he desires. Ownership is the extreme form of control and is so pervasive in the criminal's thinking and action that it warrants separate treatment. When a criminal wants something that belongs to someone else, it is as good as his. He knows that the object or person does not actually belong to him. But "belonging" is established in his mind, in the sense that he is perfectly justified in getting his way. It is a minor task to acquire the item or to make the event come to pass—"minor" because of the criminal's certainty that things will work out as he expects.

As it applies to objects, "ownership" is meant to imply a transient state of affairs. The criminal quickly tires of his latest acquisition and moves on to something more exciting. There is not a sense of permanence and lasting gratification in acquiring something, using it, and appreciating it for its beauty and utility. Actually, the process of acquisition is usually valued more than the object itself.

Ownership with respect to people reflects a relatively sustained attitude of control. The criminal views people as "pawns or checkers waiting for me to deal with them as I wish." Whatever he encounters, he controls; whatever he thinks about, he controls. One man commented that, when he walked down the street and saw a jewelry store, he thought, "I hope they guard the jewelry well so that it is there when I want it." We have said that, in the criminal's thinking, his rights transcend those of others. He does not view himself as obligated to others, but instead sees others as owing him. This thinking is habitual and without malice. The criminal continues to regard himself as a good person. It is a short step to ownership when a man considers himself a decent person with the right to do whatever suits his purposes and views the world as his oyster. We can bring this concept more sharply into focus by describing some of the manifestations of the ownership pattern.

The criminal child functions as though his family is his property. He makes his own rules and follows them. If the requirements of the home do not interfere, he abides by them. His parents tell him what is expected, but he decides whether to comply. In addition, the criminal youngster appropriates whatever he wants for himself. As one criminal said about his "right" to his brother's money, "I just saw his money as being mine. I was just reveling in what I would do with *my* money." He then was able to con his brother out of the money.

The criminal youngster asserts the priority of his rights over those of others in the neighborhood, as well as in the home. If he wants something, he thinks he is automatically entitled to it.

> As a young boy, C would approach another child and demand money. If the boy protested, he would get a beating. C did not think that the boy owed him a dollar. Rather, C wanted to be rich, and this desire entitled him to anyone else's dollar.

The criminal knows that the money or property is owned by someone else, but he believes that wanting is synonymous with having. He can define what is right or wrong for others, but, in his own case, it is his prerogative to take it. We emphasize that ownership is *implied* in his thinking and action. No criminal child, if asked, would say outright that he owned another person or another person's property.

At school, the pattern is the same. He owns others and their belongings. Accordingly, he determines how to deal with school requirements. He does not see it as incumbent on him to perform on anyone else's terms. He takes it on himself to determine whether and when he reports for school. He virtually takes possession of the classroom through conning or coercion —disrupting classes, cheating, intimidating other children and teachers, extorting property on the playground.

On the job, the criminal functions as though he owns his employer and therefore owes him nothing. His view is that the boss is fortunate to have his services. The criminal uses time as he pleases, setting his own schedule and pace whenever possible. He pushes others around and tries to run things. Some regard the job as a base for criminal operations.

To provide a complete picture, we should note that the ownership ideas are often present, but usually are not acted on as blatantly as described here. The criminal is more likely to manage others calmly and with a facade of cooperation. He ingratiates himself with others, so that he can "take possession" later. Ownership is also expressed through conning and point-scoring.

In his sexual forays, the criminal functions as though he owns the person desired. Anyone he eyes is his "territory," to invade as he wishes. He functions as though he possesses the person's body, soul, and material goods. He approaches a potential partner with the belief that he is irresistible. Then he cons or coerces to get what he believes is rightfully his.

> When C spotted a woman, she was as good as his. He went through the process of getting to know her. He courted her by treating her nicely and by spending money on her. But his thinking throughout was that whatever she had was already his; he was simply moving in and taking possession.

As we have pointed out, there are various tactics that the criminal uses, whether it be in a homosexual or heterosexual conquest. In Chapter 4, we noted that the criminal shows little consideration and tenderness toward a sexual partner. It is as though the partner has already been mortgaged to him. In the commission of rape, as soon as the criminal enters the premises, he assumes that the woman is his. If she resists, this suggests to him that she is "playing hard to get." Whatever the specifics of the sexual situation, the criminal treats the other party as being totally without rights.

The tyranny of ownership is expressed in many ways with women.

> C had built up a relationship with Monica, an older woman. This had taken a long time to solidify, because of Monica's fears about C's returning to crime. Monica was finally convinced that C was changing and becoming responsible. A wedding was planned for some time in the near future. Then a series of events occurred in which C used a car purchased for Monica's son and escaped from confinement. C did not consult her or inform her of his whereabouts. In time, Monica learned from others that C had been betraying her in many ways. Disillusioned, she dropped her interest in him. While in flight, C called Monica just as though nothing had happened and asked her to set a date to marry him in a nearby state.

As far as C was concerned, he owned Monica. He expected her, even after all his betrayal, to dance to his tune. He had complete confidence that she would still want to marry him.

The married criminal treats his wife like a vassal who is there to serve him. If he comes home for dinner and wants a special dish, his wife should have anticipated this, although he never mentioned it. If he wants to wear a particular shirt, it must be ironed and ready when he wants it. The criminal dictates to his wife whom she may talk to. He scrutinizes her household expenditures and interrogates her critically if he thinks she is spending unwisely. He operates the same way with his children, trying to arrange their lives to suit his convenience.

The ownership concept extends everywhere. The criminal recognizes no social boundaries, even in nonarrestable activities. Although he invades the privacy of others at will, he insists on his own right to privacy. He is secretive about his own life, but he thinks that he is entitled to know everything about everyone else. Basically, the criminal believes that no one has the right to do anything that he, the criminal, does not like.

> When C saw a Christmas tree in the lobby of our building, he became very angry. He had wanted to go home for Christmas, but it was not feasible. He was furious that anyone would have the enjoyment of Christmas and a tree when he could not see his family.

According to C's thinking, what he could not have, others should not have. Jealousy is an inevitable consequence of "ownership." If someone makes a move toward a person or an object that the criminal wants for himself, it threatens his sense of ownership. If, in his own mind, one owns something, he controls it totally.

The criminal expects others to gravitate toward him and hold him in high esteem. In fact, when a criminal, male or female, joins a group of people, he may do so with the expectation that everyone will find him fascinating. He believes that he will command the attention of the group, that the people will be attracted to him as pins are drawn to a magnet. By dominating a gathering, he functions as though he owns the people there. When others do not find him so fascinating, this is a putdown. The criminal then concludes that the group is a bunch of boors anyway. People who think this way are vulnerable to many a putdown, because whenever they do not receive the anticipated response, they are offended.

> C was indignant because Dr. S did not greet him effusively. Dr. S was preoccupied with some work at his desk; although he had said "hello" politely, C perceived him as being rude and responding sarcastically.

Because C did not receive the anticipated response, he was put down. The ownership idea was operative, in that C had ordained in his own mind how the other party should reply. The presumptuousness of ownership in this and other situations is obvious. But the criminal, with his "private map of the world" (Thorne, 1959), does not see the presumptuousness at all.

If the criminal does something for others, he believes that he has a great claim on them. If he goes to the store for his wife, he believes he then can ask anything of her for the next week. If he shows some special consideration toward his mother, he expects her to rally to his support in whatever he decides to undertake. Perhaps this phenomenon is illustrated most sharply when the criminal borrows money and decides to repay it. He does not regard the lender as having done the favor. Rather, *he* is doing the favor in electing to repay the debt. It is not a matter of simply paying back a debt and making everything equal. Instead, the borrower is doing the lender a favor. In fact, the criminal views it as though he has made a gift to the lender by repaying the money. What was originally a favor is now a continuing obligation on the part of the lender. The criminal expects a loan at any time—"Didn't I repay you?" is his grounds for demanding a new loan.

As we stated at the beginning of this section, it was in the realm of crime that the sense of ownership initially became apparent to us. The criminal knows the difference between right and wrong. He also is well aware of what is his and what is not his. But, as many a housebreaker has told us, when he opened that door, he became entitled to whatever was in the room. There is a sense of ownership on mere inspection. His task is to remove what he "owns." The mental process by which the criminal decides how he will actually take possession is scheming. The earning of ownership is the execution of the crime. Having completed what one criminal called "my work," he reaps the proceeds to which he believes he is entitled.

The sense of ownership appears in its most brazen form when the criminal's power and control are seriously challenged, as occurs in confinement. There, he often disregards completely the reality of the situation—others' control over his life. He is certain that others will fall into line with his wishes. In a mental hospital, he has gained admission on his terms, lying to beat a charge. Once admitted, he thinks that the hospital owes him the quickest possible release. The same applies in prison, where he is nearly certain that he will be granted parole. In either case, if release or parole is denied, it is an injustice, a rebuke of ownership.

We have attempted to point out the pervasiveness of this error of thinking. Ownership is part of the criminal's view that his rights are unlimited. He insists that society defer to his desires to follow his own pursuits, whatever they might be. Basically, this makes the criminal an anarchist, in that he recognizes no authority other than himself. When others fail to fall into line with his requirements, the criminal's sense of ownership is threatened, and he is confronted with the prospect of being a nothing. Ownership is an antidote to being a zero. Instead of being nothing and having nothing, the criminal functions as though he is "somebody" and owns everything.

FEAR OF FEAR

We have already developed fear as a characteristic thinking pattern. Our emphasis here is on one important error of thinking with respect to fear: the criminal does not allow fear to guide his behavior along responsible lines. *Fear* is a dirty word to the criminal when it is applied to him. He reacts to it as he might to leprosy. When a fear reaction occurs in him, it is a put-down, destroying his self-esteem. When fear is discernible in others, he points it out, scorns it, and exploits it. In short, he is both fearful of fear and contemptuous of fear. This applies also to the many states that denote degrees of fear—doubt, concern, apprehension, anxiety, dread.

The criminal's view of the undesirability of fear is similar to current attitudes in some other segments of society. In the military, the virtue of bravery and the elimination of fear are stressed. In the mental health professions, fear is also regarded as undesirable, largely because practitioners work with patients who are disabled by fear. The severely neurotic person is at the mercy of fears that may be irrationally carried out from childhood to the point where he has trouble functioning in adulthood. When mental health personnel begin to deal with the criminal, many usually take the same approach as they do with the neurotic, that fear is undesirable and should be eliminated.

Although he scorns fear, the criminal admits being afraid if it serves his purpose. In a psychiatric setting, he offers his fears as excuses for infractions or violations. For example, a man escapes from the hospital. On his return, he states that he left because he was afraid that he could not control himself in a threatening situation on the ward. He reminds the staff that he had previously "acted out" his feelings and gotten into fights. The staff, which is oriented to freedom from fear, praises him for his insight and reacts less punitively.

In a transient state of self-disgust and in a zero state, the criminal is fearful. He sees the present as bleak and the future as frightening. Unfortunately, this is not an incentive for lasting change. The fears corrode and are eliminated, rather than being used as guides for responsible living. The discussion of the process of "cutoff" in the next chapter will enable the reader to understand how the criminal rids himself of fear.

What the criminal does not know, and the mental health practitioners all too often fail to stress, is that fear serves many constructive purposes. There is no responsible living without fear. The most important fears are not visceral; they do not evoke sweating, trembling, and palpitations. Rather, they are the fears that we live with all the time. We automatically internalize and incorporate them into daily living. When a person has a physical examination, he does so out of fear for his health. When a husband subscribes to a life insurance policy, it is because he fears for his family's future. The criminal, living as he does, spurns fears of this sort.

> C stated that he would cash in his life insurance, which he had acquired owing to some earlier circumstances of life. The reason that he gave was that, because he was unmarried, the money would be of no benefit if he died. He gave no consideration to the possibility of marriage in the future or any thought to the future at all.

> C avoided trips to the dentist for years. As a result, his teeth were in such poor condition that in late adolescence he required massive treatment, including the making of a plate. Rather than take preventive measures, he had allowed his teeth to rot.

Of course, matters like dental care and insurance are so routinely handled by most noncriminals that the element of fear does not stop them.

The fears that are necessary for harmonious interpersonal relations are absent from the criminal's life. For example, a criminal may threaten and abuse his wife until he is in danger of losing her. He then becomes afraid that this will happen. For a while, he shows contrition and some signs of reform. Soon, however, the fear corrodes, and he returns to treating his wife as badly as ever. The fear of losing her does not guide him. Instead, he becomes certain that she will forgive him for all that he does and that she will never leave him. When she decides that she has had enough, he is surprised and either entreats her to stay or explodes in indignation. The criminal follows the same pattern with others—using and abusing them, trying to hold onto them in any way possible, and eventually losing their friendship, trust, and esteem.

In short, fear is not a guide to responsible living for the criminal. In fact, fear is not even a reliable guide in crime, where it is eliminated and replaced by what we call "superoptimism" (see Chapter 6). Thus, even when the criminal should be guided by fear for his own safety, he is not. One of our criminals, returning home from a night job, was mugged by a gang of youths. Instead of being careful when he got off the bus the next evening, he armed himself with a razor and searched for his assailants of the previous night. Fear was eliminated and homicidal thinking replaced it. Clearly, the absence of fear can result in a variety of injuries to society.

LACK OF TRUST

The criminal rarely trusts another person. To him, trusting in someone is a weakness. It makes him dependent and personally jeopardizes him. He does not even trust others who have proved themselves worthy of it. He knows that a personal friend is a potential enemy. Even when he is in collusion with another criminal, he is vigilant in protecting his own interests, because criminals steal from, lie to, con, and in other ways betray each other. Although the criminal does not trust others, he demands that others trust him. In the few cases in which he earns someone's trust, he later exploits that trust.

The criminal has been termed "paranoid," because his distrust is so all-encompassing. Observers cite the fact that the criminal is always looking over his shoulder, expecting some kind of harm to befall him. He continually assesses people to determine whether they are "police," this term referring to anyone who can get him into trouble. A parent, neighbor, teacher, virtually anyone is viewed as "police" and often so named. The criminal is wary of a rap on the door, a phone call, or an inquiring look. This is not paranoia but suspicion mandated by the criminal's requirements for existence. As one criminal commented, "You have to live by your wits twenty-four hours a day or else you fall prey."

The criminal does not use the word *trust* in the way the noncriminal does. Fragmented as he is, the criminal does not often trust a person long. His notion of trust is tied in with the element of control. He may say that he trusts another person as long as that person does what he wants, does not obstruct the criminal, and basically agrees with him. In the criminal's language, trust refers to no "snitching" or informing. When a criminal states that he has placed his trust in someone, it often means that he believes that the person will not betray him.

Because he is so fragmented, there are periods when the criminal genuinely appears to trust another person. He does so when there is not likely to be any interference with his plans. He may display this quality in a sentimental state or in a period of monasticism. At such times, those who care about the criminal are heartened, because he appears to be trusting others and willing to listen. Pessimism lifts, and everyone takes heart because the criminal is finally changing for the better. This encouraging state of affairs is short-lived. The state of mind does not last, and the criminal thrusts for power in a new enterprise. Those who have begun to have some faith in the criminal then believe that their trust has been betrayed. But they do not realize that the criminal was no more trusting or trustworthy than he had ever been. His trust of others was sincere, but it was only one of many fragments of his personality.

The criminal contrives a relationship of trust when actually he is setting up an exploitative situation. Trusting others so that they will trust him may be part of a confidence operation. One criminal bragged about how he established what would appear to be a series of relationships in which responsible people trusted him while he remained active in crime.

> "I know that it is ten thousand times as good to be walking down the streets . . . walk into a store and have the manager say to someone, 'My God, Mr. [C], sure, I know him, nice fellow, sure he has a business—a service company—and owns a few enterprises here. . . What do I know about him? Well, he is a promoter, a bull-shitter, but I tell you one thing about him. His word is good and he pays his bills.' This is a good reputation. The only thing that makes my word good to people is when I tell somebody something, I stick to it."

At the time, C maintained that he was restricting himself to the "legal larceny" of conning people through misrepresentation. In reality, he had gone far beyond this and was eventually arrested and convicted on several charges and confined. His attempt to convey an image of trustworthiness was a thoroughly criminal operation.

The criminal may profess a trust in God. He does not use the word *trust*, but is more likely to say that he "believes" in God. This too has its exploitative quality: he asks God, much like a partner in crime, to help him out. He calls on God to assure his success, to bail him out of trouble, or to get him out of confinement. If trusting in God is in any way incompatible with what he wants to do, the criminal simply cuts off this "belief." This is another example of control; the criminal is striving to manage God in line with his own wishes.

When others ask him about his objection to trusting others, the criminal quickly points out relationships in which his trust in others has been betrayed. It is true that the criminal is often let down by others, because he associates with people who are not worthy of trust. The company he chooses is composed largely of unreliable people like himself. He often counts on others who are fragmented and whose promises therefore are not worth much, and he is inevitably disappointed. When it comes to trusting responsible people, the criminal's outlook and objectives are so different that he cannot very well depend on them to assist him.

There is a kind of trust that is essential in social existence: the trust that we place in people we do not know. When we eat in a restaurant, we trust the proprietor and his staff to serve quality food. When we pick up a prescription at the drugstore, we trust that the pharmacist has given us the correct dosage from a fresh supply and charged a fair price. The criminal is doubtful even in this sense. With an attitude of "ownership," he expects others to do as he wants. Securing what he believes to be rightfully his does not require trust.

The criminal wants to be seen as a trustworthy person, even though he does not trust others. He believes that he is a good person, deserving of others' trust. When held accountable, the criminal says that everyone is dishonest, but, because he admits his dishonesty, he is being honest and therefore worthy of trust. In this way, he tries to make a virtue out of his criminality. He often argues that he cannot progress unless others trust him. Then he deploys tactics to try to win others' favor. His basic argument is that others must give him a try and be willing to put some faith in him. This argument is compatible with the view of many people who believe that the criminal must first be trusted by others if he is to learn to trust others. We ourselves insisted on this when we began our work. We said in 1963, "The doctor who trusts the patients and lives through all betrayals of trust, ultimately gets the patient's trust." Believing this, we were easy marks for the criminal. We trusted him, but then were lied to and witnessed a rising tide of violation. We concluded that a criminal does not learn trust and trustworthiness simply by being trusted. Accordingly, we changed our approach, making our trust conditional on the criminal's *sustained* implementation of new patterns of thought and action.

REFUSAL TO BE DEPENDENT

Like anyone else, the criminal depends on other people for some things in life. However, he does not see himself this way. He fails to believe that a degree of interdependence is a necessary part of existence. To him, dependence is a weakness; it would render him vulnerable.

From a psychodynamic standpoint, the criminal has been characterized as a dependent person who has reacted to frustrated dependence needs with anger and delinquent behavior (Bandura and Walters, 1959). He is viewed as still suffering from those early unmet needs.

> The most important clue to a possible psychogenic factor . . . would appear to lie in the weakness of feeling toward other people. The emotional blunting, the lack of affectional ties, the mimicry of love without evidence of real feeling all point to a possible disturbance in the child's early human relations. . . . We can make the hypothesis of a very early injury to affectionate relations, a serious deficit of gratifying love and care perhaps even in the first year (White and Watt, 1973, p. 329).

As we pointed out in Chapter 3, most of our criminals did not lack affection or support when young. In fact, instead of seeking and accepting affection, they rejected it, pushing their parents away. The criminal child desires other forms of gratification, namely, power, control, and excitement.

As a young child, he desires to be older and to associate with older children. He wants to be "big" very early and consequently goes his own way, quite independent of family requirements and expectations. Even the criminal child who tries to be the "very good boy" is not really dependent. He is a very active youngster who is not looking to mother to take care of him. In his moralism and perfectionism, he tries to outdo all the other youngsters. At the age of about ten, this stage ends, and he seeks a power thrust by doing the forbidden. An observer might regard as "dependent" an adult criminal who lives with his mother and is supported by her. However, a knowledge of how the criminal functions in such a situation points to a different conclusion. The criminal exploits his parents by expecting them to provide the comforts of home while he contributes little to family life. He may use the house as a base of operations for sex, drugs, or other activities when his parents are not around. If he gets into trouble, he is in fact "dependent" on his family to bail him out, but, as he sees it, he is entitled to this. His relationship with his family is one-sided: he does what he wants and expects the family to adapt to him. This pattern is pure exploitation, not dependence.

The criminal child scorns the children who maintain close relations with home and who, in fact, are dependent on their parents, teachers, and other adults. To him, this is "sissy," "lame," "weak," and a sign of incompetence. The differences between the criminal and the noncriminal child with respect to dependent behavior are readily observable. They are particularly obvious in play, even to the casual observer. Hadfield (1962) pointed out that the noncriminal child plays at activities that train him for roles that he will have to assume later in life. In a sense, play is training in appropriate forms of social dependence.

> *Imaginative play*... The child plays at being the grocer, the milkman, and the sweep. All this is a valuable preparation for life, for children are imagining the kind of situations they will meet with later, and this will of course help them to cope with these situations when they occur (p. 173).

> Games are... of more value than play in teaching boys and girls *to keep to rules and to respect the rights of others.* They are a good training in citizenship (p. 175).

These are perhaps somewhat idealistic views of play. However, they are at least conceptually accurate in describing the responsible child. Criminal children have little respect for rules and rights of others. In Chapter 3, we described the lack of a sense of fair play and the way in which rules are either ignored or else utilized to suit one's convenience. The criminal is not a team player. Even when he is a member of what is ostensibly a team, he has to be top man. If a group is working on a project in school, the others must do things his way. In an athletic contest, he tries to function as the team captain, whether entitled to or not. If one observes a group of criminals playing football, he will see that there are eleven quarterbacks, each telling the others what to do. The players do not function as an interdependent, harmonious unit.

When the criminal is asked to assume a responsible initiative, he may shift the initiative to someone else and thus appear "dependent." Some people find it astonishing that the criminal asks for help in carrying out some of the easiest tasks. Actually, he is very good at asking for assistance and then letting someone else take over and do the job while he stands by. If one judges by appearances, the criminal looks truly helpless, whereas he has been shrewd enough to arrange things so that someone else does his work for him.

Another instance of what might appear to be dependent behavior is the criminal's relationship with older women. We described earlier the tendency of many criminals to seek out older women as sexual partners and then exploit them. It might appear to the observer that the criminal is dependent on a woman who provides him with shelter, food, money, and virtually anything else he wants. But it is really exploitation.

The criminal may appear to be dependent on other criminals, but he is not. One criminal may need another for a specific activity. However, their relationship is founded more on expediency and mutual exploitation than on enduring trust and interdependence. The criminal knows that he would be foolish to rely totally on another criminal; from his own experience, he realizes that each puts his own self-interest and immediate gain first.

In most situations, the criminal passes off as ridiculous any description of him as dependent. Dependence is the antithesis of control. What is viewed by others as dependence is the criminal's maneuvering, scheming, lying, and exploiting to get what he wants. This is a deliberate process. The criminal is dependent only in the sense that the mugger is dependent on having an available victim to mug. Of course, when it is expedient, he can play the role of being dependent and may even talk about his "dependence needs," if this will advance him toward achieving his objectives.

The task of people who function as agents of change for the criminal is to understand how the criminal views life. A change agent who focuses on dependence conflicts is dealing with something that is irrelevant to how the criminal thinks and functions. As we shall point out in Volume 2, the objective is not to reduce the criminal's dependence, but to teach him to be appropriately dependent and to live interdependently in the responsible world.

LACK OF INTEREST IN RESPONSIBLE PERFORMANCE

The criminal is not interested in the many possibilities for developing himself within a framework of responsibility. He rejects, on the basis of lack of interest, much of what others have to offer, but then wants the benefits of the very things he rejects. He desires a particular status with its attendant benefits, but is not "interested" enough to achieve that status responsibly. Parents, educators, and other members of the community commonly find themselves exasperated and in despair over the unrealized potential of many a delinquent youngster. We have pointed out that these are children of promise. They are energetic, generally of average or above average intelligence, and in many cases talented and creative. Unfortunately, at least from the standpoint of society, the promise is never fulfilled. Owing to competing interests, the criminal child does not acquire the skills and knowledge needed to progress in the responsible world, nor does he cultivate his talents in any disciplined manner so that he can utilize them. When the criminal child is taken to task about his failure to perform, he makes it clear one way or another that this does not matter to him.

In the competition of interests, excitement is transcendent. A criminal youngster in school may show flashes of interest in particular subjects, but his enthusiasm eventually wanes. The fact that he receives high grades in some subjects is not a valid index of interest. As we pointed out in Chapter 3, some of these children are bright enough to get high grades without doing much work. Of course, doing well is to the youngster's advantage. He receives the approval of adults and then is free to pursue his own interests. Another pattern in school is for the child to perform adequately to please a particular teacher of whom he is enamored; here, the attraction is not the subject matter, but the instructor, who for one reason or another is exciting to him. Most criminal youngsters are not interested in school, because it has little, if anything, to offer that they value. Thus, there is the refusal to do what is required and the consequent high incidence of reading disabilities and dearth of general information. These children are offered special help and individually tailored programs, but to little avail. The programs fail, because the criminal youngsters do not want them. Even if some interest is aroused, the programs still have no impact on the criminality of the individual.

A guidance counselor chose to teach Latin in order to deal with students on an "experiential" basis. In his attempt to do this, he showed special interest in potential dropouts. He tried to establish rapport by informality, which entailed talking their street language. Rapport was established, and the boys learned Latin. Although they were becoming proficient in Latin, they also were continuing their delinquent activities. After the course was over, two of the three were arrested on serious charges.

The net result was that three criminals learned Latin, mainly because they liked the teacher. The criminal personality itself was untouched.

The criminal is not totally without interest in responsible activities. He may join the Boy Scouts, go to Sunday School, or belong to school clubs. His interest is likely to be short-lived, unless he can make himself highly visible. He remains in the Boy Scouts if he becomes a troop leader, or he stays active in student government if he assumes a position of prominence. We have indicated earlier that even the things that he once liked to do and did well, such as painting or finishing furniture, are dropped in favor of forbidden and therefore more exciting activities and then resumed again temporarily later on.

This pattern of not being interested appears again and again as the criminal is asked to participate in society on a responsible basis. An experience common to probably all corrections workers is the criminal's expression of lack of interest as he is approached about working. No matter what seems to be available, the criminal says that he is not interested (unless he is trying to score points).

> From childhood, C had wanted to combine medicine and religion to help others. As he viewed it, if he were a preacher, he would be in the most unchallengeable position of any possible vocation. He was absolutely convinced of the superiority of this line of work. C made two abortive attempts at seminary study. Each time, he quit, claiming that the faculty did not know how to teach. The real problem was that he would not do the work. Decades later, he still regarded the ministry as the only occupation that would satisfy him.

C refused to settle for anything less than a particular position of power and influence, but he would not do the work required to achieve it. The rejection of activities or jobs on the basis of lack of interest is not always a contrived excuse to get out of them; it is usually a genuine statement reflecting the criminal's tastes, preferences, and priorities.

In confinement, some of the criminal's interests surface, and new ones are developed. Some of these interests have a specious quality to them; that is, they may be for point-scoring purposes. Others have a power-thrust component, for example, the establishment of inmate councils or the assumption of the chairmanship of some activity. Sometimes, a criminal may engage in an activity for a power thrust or for point-scoring and then find the activity itself stimulating.

C, 18 years old, was illiterate. While in confinement, he received individual reading and writing lessons for an hour a day. He diligently did his homework and came promptly to all classes. Initially, it was clear that he was doing this to curry favor with the staff and because he liked the young, attractive reading teacher. During his confinement, C escaped several times. On his return, he was eager to resume lessons. He eventually became more and more involved and eager to learn to read. However, the desire to improve himself in this way did not affect the major path in life that he had chosen. He once again escaped and remained unapprehended. The last we heard from C was a request that we write a government office supporting his request for welfare status (a request to which we did not accede).

A genuine interest was established, but it was temporary, and in a minimum-security setting it was totally subsumed by a desire to be free. There are many striking instances of criminals generating some interest within themselves and pursuing projects and courses of study.

C dropped out of school in the fifth grade. The time he spent in school was a total waste, in terms of academic learning. He established a reputation as a troublemaker rather than student. Active in crime, C was finally apprehended for rape and given a life sentence. Instead of being a "dumb" prisoner, C wanted to be educated, indeed smarter than all the other inmates. He studied diligently and achieved extraordinary knowledge in a wide variety of fields. C also received two years of intensive psychoanalytic treatment while in prison. To the institution's staff, C appeared to be doing so well that he was granted parole after 15 years of confinement. He was the first "lifer" to receive such a parole from that particular institution. Within 6 months of his release from prison C was apprehended at his third armed robbery.

Initially, C believed that acquiring some skills and information would put him on a par with or above the most educated criminals. The emphasis shifted to an interest in education for its own sake. However, all the academic knowledge C gained was insufficient to produce a change in the inner man, with respect to his criminal patterns. It enabled him to be an educated criminal, rather than an illiterate criminal.

The criminal does have his own "interests" along the lines of irresponsibility and crime.

C pointed out that by accident he associated with a man who turned out to be an expert at locks. He acquired quite a store of information about locks. Recognizing that this would be "useful" later on, he became "interested" and learned about various types of locks.

The end in sight appealed to C—namely, greater proficiency in crime—and so he became interested. What interests the criminal is a high-voltage activity yielding excitement. Nothing in the responsible world can provide this for him on any lasting basis. There may be some momentary enjoyments, some things he likes to do. He may look forward to watching a football game and appreciate many of the finer points of tactics and strategies. He may enjoy a concerto, a painting, or a poem. But these interests do not effect a change in life-style; they do not extend beyond the momentary pleasure.

Society listens seriously to the criminal's complaints of not being interested. A great deal is done to try to interest these often talented, energetic people. Consequently, special programs and incentive systems are established. Sometimes a parent, teacher, or other person in authority is heartened by what appears to be the development of a "healthy interest" in a criminal, only to be disillusioned when it is learned that ulterior motives were operating or that the criminal was simultaneously continuing his irresponsible behavior. Depending on his sophistication and, in particular, on what he picks up from the communication media and in confinement, a criminal may couch his lack of interest in motivational terms. This often gets back to the matter of "feelings." Such a tactic works to the criminal's advantage with mental health personnel who are disposed to making allowances for him if he can report the feelings that "underlie" his lack of interest in doing what is required and necessary to progress in the responsible world.

The noncriminal is also uninterested in many things that are required of him. As a child, he may complain about boring courses at school or chores at home. A difference between him and the criminal youngster is that the former meets the requirements, whether he is interested or not. He may do it in a complaining, slow, inefficient manner. But he usually fulfills what is obligatory. After this, he has a wide range of options to choose from, and he can elect what interests him. Sometimes, in doing what is required, he becomes interested. For example, he may have to build and present a science project in which he is initially uninterested. As he does the research and constructs the project, he may find that he is becoming increasingly fascinated. In contrast, the criminal takes the attitude, "If I like it, O.K. If not, to hell with it." He may take this attitude even before he knows anything about an activity. If he begins work on something and it does not offer him the excitement that he desires, he cuts corners or dispenses with it entirely. His degree of "interest" governs whether he will do anything at all and it determines the quality of his performance.

PRETENTIOUSNESS

Pretentiousness is a component of power and control, but is of sufficient importance to warrant separate discussion. The criminal thinks of himself as superior to those around him. Despite his unwillingness to do what is required, he thinks that he can be anything. In this sense, accomplishments are not necessary; by fiat he thinks he can do what he wants.

The pretensions are present in all parts of life. Criminals as schoolchildren do little to achieve, but carry tremendously inflated ideas about their capacities. Their notion is that they either are or will be the best, not that they will *do* the best they can. They disparage doing what is necessary to achieve. They scoff at students who take their work seriously and who spend hours in study.

Employment is another example. Many criminals who aspire to fame or fortune believe that they are born to attain it. Some go so far as to rehearse for the day of public acclaim, although they do nothing toward meriting it.

In our discussion of the "big shot," we described the pretensions with respect to money, notably flashing large amounts of it and giving it away. Some criminals present a show of material wealth to the world in the way they dress. A man may say, "I don't have anything to wear," after he has worn something fashionable and different every day for two weeks. Behind what appears to be a pretentious manner of dressing is a calculation as to what the "executive look" will do for him. The pretensions are not matched by the development of skills or achievement. We commonly encounter criminals wearing expensive suits who are seeking to make contacts without having any business experience.

The criminal frequently makes outlandish statements claiming that he could be something for which he has no education, training, or information.

> C stated that he had certain virtues and was a very important person. He declared that he could have been a doctor if he had wanted to, that he was a born analyst and teacher. He maintained that in general he was quite a gifted person.

C did not believe that he actually was a doctor, but he was totally certain that he should be. However, he denigrated the requirements for earning a medical degree.

The criminal regards himself as more important, more knowledgeable, and more experienced than others. He believes that he is always right and that it is others who must change and come to see things his way.

> "When I know something is right and somebody tells me it's wrong, I usually get mad. . . . If I hear somebody say anything wrong, I usually try to set them right."

As the criminal moves about in the world, he views things differently from the responsible person. Adverse things that happen to other people should never happen to him. The reaction that "This can't happen to me" occurs many times every day.

> C went to a religious meeting. En route, several hoodlums accosted him and wanted to buy the medal he was wearing. He said it was not for sale, but then one fellow grabbed at it. C cursed him, punched him, and went on his way. After the meeting, he reported to work still angry about the earlier incident. This anger mounted as he found himself doing more than what he considered his fair share. As the work shift ended, he found out that a telegram with some money was await-ing him at Western Union. He asked permission to leave a little early, because there was nothing to do. As he was about to leave, the boss criticized him for leaving early, saying that he had done this once before. C explained that one of the supervisors had told him he could leave. Inside, the sense of righteous indignation rose.

C spent the entire day in anger, because things did not go as he thought they should. He was particularly indignant at the impudence of the hood-lums who had beset him. This should not happen to him, he complained, especially because at that time he was not harming anyone.

This is how the criminal spends his day—in putdowns and anger reac-tions due to his pretensions regarding how the world should treat him. Every wish of his should be someone else's command. Even if he works at a job where the unexpected happens all the time, he gets angry whenever his schedule is interrupted. If someone offers to do him a favor, it must be done at a time dictated by him (the criminal), not at the other party's convenience. It should be noted that these pretensions are not "fantasies." They are *lived;* they constitute part of the criminal's view of himself. Thus, he does not have a fantasy of being a business magnate; he *is,* in his think-ing and action, a business magnate.

There are also fantasies that are elaborations of pretensions. These may not be acted upon simply because they are not feasible. For example, one criminal fantasized that he was a priest delivering a message before a huge throng in Rome. This could not happen, because the criminal was not a clergyman. But the fantasy reflected a basic view of himself. It was an elaboration of his pretensions of being a great leader who had wisdom to impart to others.

When the criminal is confined, the pretensions are still in evidence. Al-though he is not invited to a prison or hospital, he acts as though he is a special guest in a hotel suite. He regards himself as more knowledgeable than the staff and seizes every opportunity to teach others.

The criminal does not have to justify his pretensions to himself, but he is often called to account by others when he does not live up to his proclaimed intentions or extravagant boasts. Only then does he offer his innumerable excuses, most of which involve blaming others and making himself a victim.

From society's vantage point, the criminal's pretensions are unrealistic, because his expectations and demands are out of line with his accomplishments. The criminal puts on a show of knowing everything when he is lacking basic information. His pretensions far outstrip his successes. He sports the trappings of success without having earned them. He does not want to perform on society's terms, but he expects society to award him accolades for accomplishment.

The criminal is in solid contact with reality, but he is unrealistic. This is sometimes hard to discern solely by observation. One criminal illegally practiced medicine and wrote prescriptions. He knew that he was not a doctor, and at no time did he confuse fact and fantasy. Therein lies a major difference between the criminal and the psychotic. The psychotic is out of touch with reality. He thinks he is what he represents himself to be. The criminal, with his scheming and deliberation, is very much in contact with reality. He knows fully who he is and what he is doing.

Both criminals and noncriminals have pretensions. In the noncriminal, these are either stimulants for responsible action or else merely idle fantasies. However, in the criminal, pretensions are an integral part of criminal thinking and action.

FAILURE TO MAKE AN EFFORT OR ENDURE ADVERSITY

In popular usage, the words *effort* and *energy* are commonly used interchangeably. After a homeowner has been out in the broiling summer sun trimming hedges, mowing the lawn, and pulling weeds, a passing neighbor might say, "That must have taken a lot of *energy* on a day like this." The neighbor could have said, "That must have required a lot of *effort* on a day like this." For all practical purposes, the words are synonymous. The question is how the homeowner experiences the task. It may be a labor of love; because he takes pride in his yard, he does not think of what he is doing as involving much effort even though it does require a lot of energy. Another person might devote himself to a day of lawn care only because he wants to avoid disapproval on the part of his neighbors; there are many other things he would prefer to do, and yard work is an onerous task that requires both energy and effort. "Effort" thus used refers to doing things that go "against the grain" or are contrary to what one prefers.

The criminal does what he wants to do. His "daily grind" in crime requires energy. He may have to meet his drug connection, go on a round of housebreakings, meet the "fence," and then rush to pick up his wife at a designated place and time. But all this is what he elects to do. For a criminal to be a criminal is relatively easy, even though the way of life requires tremendous energy in the scheming, execution, and getaway. However, as we have pointed out, the criminal has a superabundance of physical and mental energy to achieve what he wants.

The criminal is sometimes forced to make an effort or to do what he does not want to do. A delinquent youth's parents may warn him that, unless he raises his grades, he will have to remain in the house every night. Characteristically, when the criminal is pressured to do something that he dislikes, he either looks for a way out or plunges into it only to quit shortly thereafter. When something does not go smoothly and the criminal has to expend effort, he usually says, "To hell with it," and quits or does it any old way just to get through with it. He is unlikely to say that a task is too difficult, because nothing is too difficult for him. Rather, he dismisses the entire enterprise, calling it a waste of time and energy. Or he blames the person who assigned the task: "The teacher didn't explain it clearly." The criminal leaves whatever he finds disagreeable—school, job, clubs, marriage, friends. He accomplishes little in the responsible world, because he makes few efforts to deter criminal thinking patterns.

The criminal endures hardship and overcomes obstacles in crime, but he refuses to endure the adversities of responsible living. The criminal's definition of "adversity" is different from the noncriminal's. Adversity is failure to control, failure to be a big shot. Adversity is anything that is not going his way. When something unexpected occurs, the criminal is easily frustrated and angered because he is not prepared to endure life as it is and constantly runs into things that he has not anticipated. Frustration with "adversity" results in anger, quitting, and ultimately criminal excitement.

"Adversity" is something disagreeable, and, throughout his life, the criminal has avoided the disagreeable. If a task, an idea, or a memory of the past is distasteful to him, the criminal does not tolerate it. If it is a disagreeable task, he refuses to do it, unless he wants to create a favorable impression and later exploit the situation. If it is an idea or memory, he pushes it out of his mind.* Instead of dealing with what is disagreeable, the criminal's mind goes to something that he prefers to do. He does not escape *from* something without going *to* something else. The "something else" inevitably is criminal thought and action, which is exciting. He does not have to encounter the disagreeable act criminally, but being faced with a

---

* This is accomplished through the process of "cutoff" (to be described in Chapter 6), by which an idea can be abruptly and totally eliminated from mind.

disagreeable task, idea, or memory may precipitate ongoing criminal thinking into action. Noncriminals may meet the disagreeable for what it is or shirk it. When they try to avoid what is disagreeable, they may simply turn to something else or become inefficient at what they are doing, their minds being on other things. Because a disagreeable idea or memory or the knowledge that a task remains undone continues to tug at them, they find it not so easy to flee from the disagreeable. Consequently, they may develop anxiety, depression, or psychosomatic symptoms in their attempts at avoidance. Whether the noncriminal meets the disagreeable or shirks it, a criminal solution is not the outcome.

The criminal refuses to endure pain—physical or mental. Suffering, as the responsible person knows it, is foreign to the criminal. The criminal "suffers" only when his inflated self-concept is punctured and he is reduced to a zero. But even this kind of suffering is something that he does not endure for long. It is resolved by an elimination of fear and suffering, followed by crime. As one man in our program said, "A crime a day keeps the zero state away."

All his life, people have begged and pleaded with the criminal to make the effort to change. However, he has put the burden on others to give him reasons why he should. Society has made the effort, through motivational incentives, to interest the criminal in school or work. Criminals have even been paid to learn skills that are considered to have social value. The outcome is always the same. Society makes the effort, but the criminal does not (although, when he makes a token gesture at something responsible, he calls it "effort"). For the criminal to make efforts in the directions urged by society is for him to work at something that he scorns and rejects.

POOR DECISION-MAKING FOR RESPONSIBLE LIVING

The responsible person and the criminal approach making major decisions very differently. Inasmuch as one views life's goals differently from the other, areas requiring such decisions by the former have little or no significance for the latter. The criminal works if it is expedient, using work to give himself an aura of respectability, to make engaging in crime easier, or for the power thrust of the job itself. He marries as a matter of convenience, out of momentary desire, or out of transient sentimentality. He neither saves nor budgets money.

However, the criminal makes decisions that the noncriminal never has to make. He decides on a particular criminal enterprise, chooses an appropriate modus operandi, and evaluates the risks. As a decision-maker in crime, the criminal does reasonably well, as proved by the infrequency with which he is apprehended.

In most of the criminal's decision-making there is no weighing pros and cons, no careful evaluation of a course of action.

> C planned to move into a home in an expensive area. He was going to share the cost with an old friend, who he knew was also irresponsible. C had not seen the property and did not know lease conditions, utility costs, the price of insurance, how much it would take to furnish the place, or whether the area was safe. All he knew was that the rent would be $400 a month. He had not figured out whether he could afford this. But he was eager to move.

It is characteristic that the criminal has constantly failed to figure things out for himself when it comes to a personal decision like this. There is no sound reasoning, fact-finding, or consideration of budget and options. The criminal simply does whatever is compatible with his state of mind at the time. Decisions are guided by unrealistic expectations, pretension, and often the desire for excitement. In the example above, living with his friend would offer C the opportunity for additional criminal talk and action. Fragmentation, lying, failure to plan for the long term, and all the other thinking errors that we have described can result only in unsatisfactory decisions with respect to responsibility.

Even when the criminal goes to the supermarket, he is not equipped with the thinking processes or information to make wise purchases. Ignorant of quality, brands, and unit pricing, he nevertheless acts as though he knows it all. He does not ask questions to learn. However, if he is planning to rob the supermarket, he finds out what it takes to circumvent security operations.

The criminal's decison-making is poor even when he wants to do something responsible, such as looking after his children. Decision with respect to their welfare are faulty.

> C had been in nearly every type of crime, including armed robbery, but he was very sentimental about his children, wanting them to grow up to be law-abiding citizens. His idea was that, on release from confinement, he would be a "lower-level" criminal. He decided that he could run gambling parties, sell liquor, and write numbers. He thought that if he were arrested he would be sentenced to no more than 2 years, owing to the nature of the charge, and he could get out even sooner with good behavior. C stated that his children would benefit financially from these lower-level crimes. If he were arrested, his children would not view him as a big-time criminal, so he would not lose their esteem completely. In addition, if he were apprehended for a petty crime, he would not be in confinement and away from home for very long.

This is indicative of the kind of thinking that occurs. The faulty premises and assumptions are many. There is no realistic long-range planning, no consideration of injury to others, and no putting himself in the place of others.

The responsible person may err in making decisions, but his errors are not as global as the criminal's. A man may buy a home that he has fallen in love with, without careful calculation of monthly payments, taxes, insurance, and maintenance costs. The outcome of such a faulty decision is that he is a slave to his house and must make sacrifices that he might have avoided if he had been more prudent. So he struggles to do the best he can, meeting the problem with effort and endurance, rather than criminal thinking and action. If there is a loss, the noncriminal suffers it—something the criminal does not do.

In deciding on a course of action, the criminal is reluctant to ask a question about noncriminal activities, because he views it as a putdown to reveal his ignorance. He does not even like to admit to himself that he is without an answer. As one criminal said of himself as a student, "The majority of the time I would ask a stupid question and would feel like a worm." In his mind, it was the asking of the question that was the most painful. Furthermore, the criminal thinks that he might not get the answer he wants if he does ask a question. If his pretensions and expectations are controverted by the facts, he does not want to hear them. The criminal also figures that, if he asks questions, he might be obligated to answer someone else's. If he lacked the answers, he would again be put down. There are some exceptions to the criminal's aversion to asking questions. He asks a question to put down someone else and obtain an advantage. For example, the criminal child may try to embarrass his teacher by asking an obscure or irrelevant question. Putting another on the spot and making him look foolish provides the criminal with a sense of triumph. When the criminal needs facts in order to further a criminal enterprise, however, he does not hesitate to ask questions. He will be a bloodhound in seeking facts when planning a crime. When he wants to score points, he also does a thorough job of investigating.

We are describing a general pattern of the criminal: failure to ascertain the facts. The criminal is not a fact-finder, except when it comes to crime. He gets an idea, forms an opinion based on it, and then believes it as an established fact. Facts are not sought, because the criminal thinks that he already has the information he needs. As one scholarly criminal put it, his style of thinking is "Cogito, ergo est"—"I think; therefore, it is."

With his "cogito, ergo est" thinking, the criminal prejudges people. The prejudgments are usually erroneous, being based on many other thinking errors. Innumerable situations are misconstrued in a single day.

> A group of criminals called on an office secretary to gain her assistance in planning a party. Because she was a secretary to an administrator, they figured that she must be "bitchy." Expecting to be rebuffed, they approached her with a chip-on-the-shoulder attitude. To their surprise, she was responsive and helpful.

For the criminal to suspend judgment and live in uncertainty is a put-down. His way of operating demands immediate conclusions. Prejudgment is in line with ownership and control. A group of criminals may size up a woman as "an easy make." What might be a game of idle speculation to someone else becomes a statement of fact to these people. If a criminal thinks it, it must be so. Very often, he is correct; he *is* astute at picking up cues of availability from women. But he does misjudge. If a criminal knows one thing about a person, he believes that he knows everything about him. For example, he may judge a woman as a potential target, because she is wearing a short dress. He may then make his approach, only to be rejected. Then he is put down, and anger results.

Prejudgments by the criminal are usually in the direction of down-grading a person, so that the criminal can build himself up. One man quickly concluded that his co-worker was a "dummy," only to find out later that he was working to support himself while he was a candidate for a Ph.D. at a university. The criminal may also do the opposite and over-estimate a person. He may build up the qualities of a woman whom he has just met and then view himself as one who associates with high-class women.

The criminal makes fewer prejudgments in crime. The success of his enterprise requires fact-finding. He schemes, deliberates, and considers possible outcomes. But "superoptimism" can lead to acting on prejudgments and result in recklessness. When this occurs, apprehension is more likely, as we shall explain in the next chapter. In short, prejudgments in crime may lead to arrest, so the criminal is somewhat more disposed to collect information.

Another feature of the criminal's poor decision-making for responsible living is his "tubular vision." The failure to establish and consider different options severely restricts him. This is a consequence of never having learned enough about responsible living to know that there *are* alternative courses of action. Almost everything he does, from choosing a job to buying a pair of pants, is on the basis of assumptions and immediate desires. He alights on one solution to a problem and acts, mainly because he does not care about alternatives when engaged in something that does not matter to him to begin with. In crime, he is fully aware of his options and selects among them cautiously. The criminal's tubular vision leads him to make decisions in line with how things look to him at the time. Long-range prospects and possibilities are not taken into account. Owing to his fragmentation, there is no conceptual thinking about the present or about his ultimate objectives. In addition, he lacks facts about both the present and the future. The range of his considerations is very narrow, and his attitude shifts as a result of transient conditions or moods.

When the criminal attempts to function in a manner that is routine for the noncriminal, he is incompetent, because he lacks both the basic information and the thinking processes required. Even a relatively simple undertaking is marked by a failure to acquire facts and consider options.

> C and Debbie planned to visit Lancaster, Pennsylvania, to view the Amish market. The plan was to leave at 10, but C did not pick her up until 11. He arrived unshaven and with the car needing gas. Debbie was talking unnecessarily on the phone. After getting into the car, she wanted to eat. There was then the problem of finding a place that she considered suitable. Not long thereafter, she wanted to eat again. The result was that C was irritated by the delays, and they arrived at dusk, when there was nothing to see and shopping was limited because the stores closed at 5. Then came the problem of locating a friend of Debbie's, who was not at the address Debbie thought. They found her name in the phone book, called, and were invited to visit. They left at 8 P.M. It had been an afternoon of irritation, with nothing accomplished except visiting the friend. There had been no fact-finding as to when the Amish market was closed. There was no attempt to find Debbie's friend by phone and inform her that they were coming. The car was not ready, and no schedule had been set up. The two of them failed to consider options for the use of time and thus wasted hours.

Within a short period, error compounded error, resulting in the waste of a day, frustration, and anger. The criminal lacked the foresight to have the car ready so that they could leave promptly. His failure to plan and to consider the need for food along the way further delayed the trip. Poor fact-finding resulted in their late arrival, so shopping was not feasible. In fact, many errors of thinking played a role in a series of poor decisions, making for an unpleasant day.

The criminal has little comprehension of how responsible people think. Thus, he habitually forms erroneous conclusions and makes faulty decisions. Even if he attempts to accomplish a responsible objective, he is likely to fail. Society's error is to believe that a man totally unfamiliar with the thinking patterns that are necessary for responsible living can become responsible simply by schooling, work, or a change in environment. This is similar to expecting an automobile to fly. It just is not equipped for that.

BIBLIOGRAPHY

American Psychiatric Association. *Diagnostic and Statistical Manual of Mental Disorders.* Washington, D.C.: American Psychiatric Association, 1968.

Bandura, Albert, and Walters, Richard H. *Adolescent Aggression: A Study of Child-Training Practices and Family Interrelationships.* New York: Ronald Press, 1959.

Cameron, Norman. *Personality Development and Psychopathology.* Boston: Houghton Mifflin, 1963.

Eissler, K. R. "Ego-Psychological Implications of the Psychoanalytic Treatment of Delinquents," *The Psychoanalytic Study of the Child.* Vol. 5. New New York: Oxford University Press, 1955, 239-256.

Freyhan, Fritz A. "Psychopathic Personalities," *Oxford Loose Leaf Medicine.* New York: Oxford University Press, 1955, 239-256.

Hadfield, J. A. *Childhood and Adolescence.* Baltimore: Penguin, 1962.

Karpman, Ben. "The Structure of Neuroses: With Special Differentials between Neurosis, Psychosis, Homosexuality, Alcoholism, Psychopathy and Criminality," *Archives of Criminal Psychodynamics,* 1961, *4,* 599-646.

McCord, William, and McCord, Joan. *Psychopathy and Delinquency.* New York: Grune and Stratton, 1956.

Redl, Fritz, and Wineman, David. *Children Who Hate.* Glencoe, Ill.: Free Press, 1951.

Stevens, Shane. "The 'Rat Packs' of New York," *The New York Times Magazine,* November 28, 1971, pp. 29ff.

Thorne, Frederick C. "The Etiology of Sociopathic Reactions," *American Journal of Psychotherapy,* 1959, *13,* 319-330.

White, Robert W., and Watt, Norman F. *The Abnormal Personality.* (4th edit.) New York: Ronald Press, 1973.

Chapter 6

Thinking Errors Characteristic of the Criminal: III. From Idea Through Execution

EVALUATIONS OF HOW the criminal's mind works before, during, and after a crime usually are undertaken to determine his mental status for legal purposes. The issues of "impulse," "compulsion," "premeditation," "substantial control of self," "diminished responsibility," "crime of passion," "irresistible impulse," and "temporary insanity" all have been prominent in both legal proceedings and psychiatric treatment. Such concepts have been formulated on the basis of what criminals have said when held accountable after crimes. As a result, instead of a psychology of the criminal, there is now a "criminal psychology" unwittingly derived from what criminals have told the authorities. Society's understanding of the criminal is based on information supplied by criminals when they were in jeopardy or pressing to be released from confinement. Those accounts are always self-serving and made up of distortions, justifications, and lies. From the criminal's point of view, this is understandable; he does whatever will best satisfy his objectives.

In the early phases of our study, we too relied on retrospective accounts. In spite of a guarantee of privileged communication and our lack of involvement in administrative decisions, we were given self-serving accounts. Consequently, we had to develop new techniques. Over more than a dozen years, we have had the opportunity to study the minds of people who were participating actively in crime. In our investigation of the criminal mind, we have obtained an authentic picture of thinking processes *as they were occurring*. An important source of information has been the group of changed criminals, who are neither in jeopardy nor concerned about getting out of confinement. These men, now responsible citizens, have been of great assistance in elaborating and clarifying the concepts to be presented here. Instead of relating self-serving stories, they have told us what mental processes are operative specifically with respect to crimes, including the period before they are committed, the period during the commission of a crime, and the aftermath—from idea through execution.

EXTENSIVENESS OF CRIMINAL THINKING

Street criminals have a steady diet of criminal activity; they regard crime as their "work."* Some are called "players," because they are known to engage in almost any crime, whereas others reject specific types of crimes. The criminal has hundreds of ideas, but can implement only one at a time. Like the street criminal, the nonextreme criminal is a habitual violator. However, his violations are usually less serious, so he is less subject to arrest. He may lie, cut corners, and show irresponsibility in innumerable ways without placing himself in legal jeopardy. Although his mind is not full of criminal ideas, it is not unusual for him to think repeatedly about and deter particular crimes.

Sometimes a criminal is evaluated in light of the details of a single crime that are brought out by an investigation. But one crime for which a criminal is apprehended does not tell the whole story. He has usually committed many undetected crimes, and there is invariably a tremendous amount of criminal thinking that he has never acted on; therefore, others never know of it. The story does not start with the idea of a single specific crime, but rather with an ever-growing multitude of ideas. As we have pointed out, the criminal is very energetic, both physically and mentally. Criminal thoughts pass through his mind in a steady stream, with some dropping out simply because of the limit on the mind's capacity to process them.

The criminal, with his energetic and imaginative mind, is the originator of many of these ideas. He also picks up ideas from other criminals on the street and in confinement. Criminal talk itself provides a charge, and, although exposure to other criminals does not make him any worse an of-

---

* Letkemann (1973) wrote a book, *Crime as Work*, in which he discussed the criminal's "work habits" and spoke in terms of "work satisfaction." Maurer (1974) noted that conmen think of their daily routine in crime as their "work."

> Although they do not contribute anything useful to society, they have a tradition of hard and consistent work. They think of a working day as six to eight hours of concentrated work, though by the nature of their occupation, they can pursue it almost any time of the day or night. Ironically, many of them work hard every day, observing certain hours which they have found most productive, and then like any working man, spend their leisure hours loafing around a tavern or hangout. They grind away at their little racket day in and day out (p. 249).

fender, it may offer some new ideas for a modus operandi or a particular opportunity. The same is true with respect to the influence of the entertainment and communication media. Exposure to books, newspapers, television, and movies does not cause criminality. Only occasionally does one whose criminality is already well-established get an idea for an M.O. from television or the movies. Because their plots are usually presented in contrived situations, the criminal rarely utilizes anything he sees there. Far more often, it is the accounts of actual crimes that may have some influence. Clearly, there are periods when particular M.O.'s and types of crimes are fashionable. Most of our older criminals did not use guns when they were younger, but armed crimes are more frequent among the present group of youthful criminals. When the criminal observes that a particular type of crime has been successfully executed, he may consider doing the same thing. In 1971 and 1972, a rash of airplane hijackings occurred. One man bailed out with a parachute and was undetected, and the same M.O. was repeated soon after. From 1973 to 1976, there were numerous attempts to seize hostages and bargain for release from prison. The important fact is that publicity of a crime by the news media and fictional episodes in the movies or television *do not make someone a criminal.* The critical variable is how the mind deals with what it has been exposed to, rather than the nature of the material itself.

Restraints on criminal thinking are few, and the criminal spends many hours wrapped up in this kind of thinking. Whatever their source, far more ideas occur than are realistic to implement. When a criminal enters a store merely to purchase cigarettes, possible crimes immediately begin to run through his mind. He views the merchandise, the customers, the salesmen, the cash register, purses, and credit cards all in terms of crimes that he could commit. This kind of thinking occurs repeatedly, wherever he goes. An indeterminate number of ideas pop into his mind, necessitating selectivity. The criminal weighs options and deters most ideas, for reasons to be discussed later. Some criminal thoughts are too "fantastic" ever to be implemented. *Thinking* about a crime, even if it is not to be executed, is itself exciting. Some crimes are not immediately feasible, owing to such practical limitations as confinement, lack of an accomplice, lack of connections, and lack of adequate equipment, but these may be possible later.

We differentiate between two types of criminal thinking—fantasy and scheming. A fantasy deals with the execution of a crime, but does not include mapping it out in terms of an M.O. or pinpointing specific circumstances under with the crime would occur. A man may have fantasies about a "big score" in a bank robbery, but he has not worked out the details in his mind. In scheming, he carefully and deliberately thinks out the logistics of a specific crime. Scheming occurs in relation to many nonarrestable activities, as when a person plans a deception for his own gain. Scheming is an habitual feature of the criminal's thinking, but here we are focusing on scheming related to the planning of a crime. In a scheme, the criminal takes into account such elements as the time, the place, the date, how others will function, how he will get away, and even how he will spend the proceeds. A scheme can be formulated over hours, days, weeks, months, or even years as the M.O. is carefully worked out.

In the spectrum of thinking, there are thoughts of violations in all three categories—property, assault, and sex. Thinking in each is present in all extreme criminals, although much of it is not implemented. For example, the criminal who is not violent in his actions nonetheless thinks of violence; and when a criminal who has never been violent commits an assault, others are astonished because they did not think he had it in him.

> C was mainly a "sneak thief" who was active in burglary and drugs. In his 30 years of crime, he had rarely used physical force. C had put a deposit on a bicycle. After 3 months, there had been no delivery. He consequently bought a different bike and phoned the store, requesting a refund of the deposit. He was informed that deposits were not refundable. Over the phone, he warned them that they did not know whom they were dealing with. He threatened them with trouble. His thinking was that, with knife in hand, he would barge into the store, smash it up, and beat up the personnel. In another incident, someone gestured toward him while he was riding his bicycle, as though to push him against some parked cars. He tried to grab the fellow; he was wishing that he had his knife handy.

Those who did not know C very well would have regarded this behavior, if implemented, as out of character. Inasmuch as deterrents corrode under the appropriate circumstances, we maintain that every hard-core criminal is capable of any kind of crime. Here is a sample of the stream of criminal thoughts that occurred to one man in a period of only a few hours:

1. When passing a jewelry store, thought of writing fraudulent checks to make a purchase
2. When passing a bank, thought of armed robbery
3. When looking at a National Geographic exhibit, thought of stealing a skull
4. When seeing an alley, thought of "dragging a broad," or pulling her in and having sex (rape)
5. When seeing a woman with a valuable piece of jewelry, thought about how to acquire it by con or force
6. A stream of thoughts about holdups, assaults, and homicide possibly followed by suicide

This is only a sample of the criminal thinking that occurred day after day in one man. The criminal mind has a reservoir of criminal ideas. One of these ideas may be activated solely as a consequence of a desire to stir up excitement. But the valves of the idea reservoir may also be opened by a triggering external stimulus. Certainly, when the criminal thinks that he has been put down, the increase in criminal thinking is enormous. Instead of thinking only about retaliating against one individual, many other criminal thoughts may be unleashed and implemented.

DETERRENTS

It is not humanly possible for the criminal to implement every criminal idea that occurs to him, and most of the crimes considered are not committed. Some are not committed, however, because the criminal fears that he will get caught. We refer to fears of this nature as "external deterrents." There are also restraints that we designate "internal deterrents"—conscience components of the criminal's makeup that oppose particular crimes. Neither external nor internal deterrents operate consistently. The criminal's fragmentation makes it impossible for an outsider to predict when the deterrents will emerge in the criminal's thinking and be effective. Internal deterrents are the less predictable of the two.

EXTERNAL DETERRENTS

The criminal must always contend with external deterrents. The basic question is, "Will I get caught?" He fears detection not only by the police. Family members, teacher, employer, or anyone else may be viewed as "police," because the criminal, if found out, will have to answer to one or more of them. The criminal child may fear detection and punishment by his parents. He may stop trying to get away with so much if he knows that his parents are suspicious and ready to move in with strong disciplinary measures. Similarly, the adult criminal may fear apprehension by the police and a stiff sentence by the courts. If the penalty for a particular crime is very severe and the risk of detection seems great, the criminal may decide not to act. For example, if security at a bank is tight, and if the courts have imposed long sentences for armed robbery, the criminal may decide not to participate in a holdup. The "occupational hazard" of being maimed or killed in such an activity might also serve as a deterrent. Some criminals reject crimes in which violence is likely, because they fear serious injury. We might also add that a criminal who has recently served a sentence might be more cautious, at least for a while, because the memory of the penitentiary is vivid. This deterrent is underrated in its effect on the nonextreme criminal, for whom serving some time is a restraining factor when it comes to committing crime later. The hard-core criminal, however, is likely to be deterred only temporarily from the more serious crimes by the memory of prison.

INTERNAL DETERRENTS

"Internal deterrents" are conscience fears. Some writers have said that the criminal lacks a conscience.

> [The psychopath] has no conscience or guilt feelings. In his moral or ethical obtuseness he reminds one at times of the organically demented, notably the general paretic in whom destruction of the frontal lobe affects foremost the mental functions that are phylogenetically latest to develop (Karpman, 1961, p. 623).

And others have said that the criminal has "too much" conscience.

> Far from the popular belief of no conscience, no regard for the rights of others, he more often than not has too much of it. . . . He has to act bad because it is the only way he knows of subduing a recurrent, guilty voice which keeps saying over and over "you've been bad from the beginning, and you will have to suffer the consequences of being bad" (Uehling, 1962, p. 45).

Neither of these points of view is accurate. We indicated both in Chapter 3 and in the discussion of sentimentality in Chapter 4 that the criminal does have a conscience. However, it usually is not operational. Committing some types of crimes constitutes a putdown, in that the criminal has "standards" of what is personally offensive to him. An armed robber may express loathing for a child molester, characterizing him as "sick" or a "pervert." In his view, a man who molests a child should be locked up for life. Similarly, the child molester may abhor the armed robber because of his readiness to take a human life. Each criminal strengthens his opinion of himself as a good person by emphasizing the things that he would not do. There is an internal prohibition against particular kinds of criminal activity in which others engage, but not against the acts that he commits, which are also harmful to society.

Sentimental, religious, and humanitarian features, brought out in our discussion of sentimentality, all may serve as deterrents. Some criminals have reported their irritation at having a conscience, because it sometimes stands in opposition to what they want. However, this usually does not last; the criminal has a way of eliminating internal deterrents from his awareness.

CORROSION AND CUTOFF

The most important factor in the criminal's response to deterrents is that he has to decide whether or not to heed them. It is a matter of his choice. An idea that arises may be pushed aside by deterrents or competing desires. The idea may recur dozens of times, even hundreds of times, over a period of weeks or months. Eventually either the idea is eliminated by choice in favor of something else or the deterrents are removed by the process of corrosion and cutoff.

"Corrosion" is our designation for a mental process in which external or internal deterrents are slowly eliminated until the desire to commit an act outweighs the fears to the point where the desire is implemented. This is not a process of rationalizing; the criminal does not believe that he has to justify anything to himself.* With more and more scheming, the deterrents are reduced, because, as the criminal perfects his scheme, he considers himself more immune from apprehension, and thus a successful crime seems ensured. As we pointed out in Chapter 5, the future is not considered, except for the vague notion that he could get caught; but the criminal believes that that will not occur "this time."

Internal deterrents corrode as the criminal's sentiments and ideals give way to the desire for excitement, which is an antidote to both the zero state and boredom. The gradual process of corrosion occurs up to a point, and then a mental process that we call "cutoff" comes into play. Cutoff allows the criminal instantly to dispose of deterrents, both internal and external, freeing him to act. With mounting excitement, the internal deterrents are more easily eliminated than are the more pragmatic external deterrents—i.e., the clear and present danger. It is not conscience that restrains him from violation as much as it is the fear of apprehension. It could be said that corrosion is a gradual cutoff, giving way to an abrupt final cutoff before violation. Sometimes, the cutoff occurs almost immediately and so quickly that the act is viewed as the result of a sudden "impulse."

Cutoff differs from suppression and repression. Suppression is the conscious decision to exclude specific ideas and considerations from present thinking. It occurs when we want to rid ourselves of anxiety and we resolve, "Well, I just won't think about that." Suppression is often unsuccessful, because things that are bothersome do not go away, but instead recur and preoccupy us. Repression is the relegation of painful thoughts, memories, and images

---

* Rationalizing comes later, however, when he is held accountable. Then the criminal may attribute causation to an event before the crime, although the thought of the crime occurred many times before. So he blames wife, employer, mother, etc.

to the unconscious. In contrast with both these processes, in which there is no urgency for action, cutoff permits a criminal to think about action that he wants to take without interference by thoughts opposing it. Cutoff is a rapid eradication of fears from the mind. We call it "cutoff" because it is sharp, complete, and instantaneous, much like a surgical incision.* This rarely, if ever, occurs in the noncriminal, but the criminal accomplishes cutoff rapidly and deliberately. Cutoff is a learned mental process; it is discipline to eliminate fear, and the criminal child begins to practice it early in life.

The criminal makes the cutoff of fear a cornerstone of his life. It allows him to do as he wants. In search of triumph and conquest, he cuts off deterrents, including experience. (People say that the criminal is "unable" to learn from experience, but we have already indicated that the criminal chooses to learn from experience that which is significant to him.) Cutoff is always available for situations that require it. It is so much a part of the criminal's life that it is invoked automatically.

Even though cutoff is so rapid and automatic, it is still a mental process that is under the criminal's control. Whether he invokes the cutoff is his choice. The more sophisticated criminal learns from experience that too rapid a cutoff is hazardous. An abrupt, instant cutoff can eliminate deterrent considerations so rapidly that the criminal is not as cautious as he might be. Thus, the control that he exercises over his mental phenomenon is very important to him.

The criminal does not think about cutoff as a phenomenon or give it a name. But he does regard it as an achievement to be able to change from a trembling man into a cool, dispassionate thief; as one man put it, "I can change from tears to ice." Cutoff enables him to dispel even strong sentiment.

> C was in the process of robbing a bank when he saw that one of the people in the bank very much resembled his mother. He paused, but then became determined to go through with it. After the commission of the act, a return of a degree of sentiment nagged at him, causing some regret.

---

* The only other usage of this phrase that we encountered was in Salzman (1961):

> It is not true that they do not experience guilt or anxiety. They simply *cut off* every interpersonal relationship of significance at the root and thus avoid the development of anxiety or guilt (p. 183, italics ours).

Salzman was not describing at any length a process, as we do here, but his use of the phrase approximates the sense in which we use "cutoff."

Here, the deliberate choice to cut off sentimentality is clear. One criminal described the cutoff process without using the term, which is, of course, ours. The italics highlight the way he dealt with fear.

"It is exciting, very exciting. You know that you can get killed at any time if any number of things were to happen, and you know that if the police catch you it is going to be extremely severe punishment, *but this just doesn't seem to enter into the picture. It is like you are in another world altogether.* It is a dangerous world, an exciting world even though you are bound to get killed if you keep doing this type of thing. . . . It is just like being in a world all your own. You know that you are doing something that nobody is supposed to do and that you are putting everybody else's life in danger, but *you just shrug off these things.* It is a sort of feeling of being happy and being scared at the same time *but the happiness always comes out on top.* After you get finished playing a game like this, you are all ready to want to play it some more. I never get tired of it. It was just exciting, just very exciting. It was the same thing when you were in trouble with the police. You were *scared to death* that you were going to get caught and put into prison, *but this didn't matter.*"

This remarkable capacity to eliminate a state of mind allowed this basically fearful young man to change from being "scared to death" to being what he called a "real terror to others," no longer bothered by fear. Only *he* knows the intensity and extent of the fears that he has had to eliminate to achieve his objective. The cutoff itself is a triumph for the criminal, the final product being that he is not afraid.

C spoke of his paralyzing fear of punishment: "When you talk to me about punishment, it is like an atom bomb dropped on my body." If sustained, this fear would have made it impossible for him to be in active crime. But it rarely served as a deterrent, in that he could readily cut it off.

Cutoff is a mental process that produces fragmentation. When the criminal chooses to employ the cutoff, much that he appears to value is eliminated. It is a mental process that operates with surgical precision in getting rid of internal deterrents. Thus, a criminal may serve Mass at nine o'clock in the morning and steal at ten. A striking example of this phenomenon is the man, referred to in Chapter 4, who wore a cross around his neck and was a child molester and thief. All that the cross stood for was eliminated through cutoff, leaving him unimpeded to commit crimes. As we have stated, conscience must be eliminated for the implementation of a criminal scheme. One man stated, "When I have a conscience, I am fucked up." He did have a conscience, but he was so fragmented that it was not very functional.

Another way of stating the criminal's attitude toward his conscience is, "I don't want to hear what I already know." In other words, when he is geared for "action," he wants no reminders or appeals to have conscience reinstated. Conscience is a fragment of his mind that serves him best at such a time by not serving him at all.

We must emphasize repeatedly that, although cutoff becomes habitual, the invoking of cutoff is still an act of choice. The criminal always has control over his own thinking. When he chooses to be guided by his fears, cutoff is not invoked; he deters cutoff for his own gain. Another way of saying this is that he can cut off the cutoff when it is to his advantage. Thus, if an enterprise underway suddenly appears too risky, he may abandon it. He may also refrain from a criminal act to accomplish a criminal objective of higher priority.

> C's automatic response to provocations in confinement (as elsewhere) was to haul off and hit someone. When he came to Saint Elizabeths Hospital, he refrained from doing this, even though he had a rock in his pocket and was often very angry. Instead, he put on the charm to achieve his ultimate objective, which was to be found competent to stand trial.

C was afraid that striking someone would imperil the favorable staff evaluation for which he was hoping. His overriding objective was to beat the system and be released. Thus he kept alive fear of the consequences of an assault. This control over the cutoff process runs counter to the idea of "lack of control" or operating on "impulse."

Most of this discussion has referred to the habitual criminal. However, the same concepts apply to the less extreme criminal. In the man who commits a single extraordinary act, there is the same requirement that, for the act to occur, deterrents must be mentally eliminated. The thought occurs over and over, but is deterred. With continuing scheming, corrosion of deterrents progresses. Then there is a final cutoff, and the crime is committed. This is what others then call a "crime of passion," "psychotic behavior," "impulsive," "senseless," and so forth. They are unaware of the offender's antecedent thinking.

BUILDING UP THE OPINION OF ONESELF AS GOOD

The criminal's belief that he is basically a good person is a powerful factor in the corrosion of deterrents. As he plans a crime, he still maintains the notion that he is decent. If he thought of himself as "evil," he would not do the things he does. The criminal has no need to rationalize or justify himself before or during his activities, for he is "not a criminal," but a decent person. The action contemplated is desirable and acceptable to him, and others are fools not to do it; so what is there to justify?

> C stated that, if a criminal works at his "trade" and is successful, he is no different from those in affluent neighborhoods who also work hard. Both have put in the effort and achieve success.

In the discussion of sentimentality, we described the kind and generous acts that the criminal occasionally performs when he is not in crime. He also does these things when he is on his way to commit a crime. We know of numerous instances in which a criminal en route to a crime deposited money in a blind man's cup or offered some coins to a beggar. He may assist an elderly lady crossing the street. If it does not throw his timing off too much, he may stop to comfort a crying child or assist a hurt animal. Even at the scene of the crime, he may engage in what appears to be a kindness.

> C was in a bank, waiting for the proper time to hold it up. He saw an elderly blind woman led by a dog moving in the direction of a door, but not the correct door. C, in telling about this event, said, "I was a knight in shining armor when I opened the door and sent her out." Then he proceeded with the robbery.

The criminal may act as a protector of another person to the extent that he finds himself "out of a job."

> C spotted a pocketbook and targeted it as an item for him to steal. However, he then saw someone else eyeing it, at which point he stopped the other would-be thief and informed the potential victim.

In this case, he got more satisfaction out of being a hero than he would have from a petty theft.

Performing kind acts enhances the criminal's view of himself and reinforces his idea of his basic goodness. The image of himself as a good person gives him a license for more crime. When the stock of "goodness" runs out, he is in a zero state and not in crime.

DEFERMENT

We speak of deferment in three different contexts. The first is the postponement of the ultimate crime, the "big score." A related pattern of deferment is the criminal's putting off self-reform, "going straight"; he has the idea that one day he will quit crime and settle down, but that day never seems to arrive. Finally, there is the deferment of responsibilities that are incompatible with crime. We shall discuss each of these patterns of deferment separately.

The "big score" idea has often been dramatized in fiction as the ultimate, perfect crime. The most well-known type of "big score" is the supercrime, such as the holdup of an armored truck in broad daylight. Actually, there is no "ultimate crime," in that the criminal's idea of what constitutes it constantly changes. Furthermore, in reality the criminal does not function with the idea of the ultimate crime ever-present in his thinking. A "big score" to the criminal is a relative matter; it is a bigger crime than that to which he has been accustomed. If his thefts have been yielding several hundred dollars and a breaking and entering yields more than $1,000, this to him is a "big score."

The second type of deferment is the criminal's intention to establish himself in the world as a citizen in good standing, not subject to arrest. This may be after a "big score" or without it. We mentioned earlier that in fragmented states the criminal does think about "going straight." This occurs more intensely in monasticism (see Chapter 7). The desire to change does not last, and change becomes something always to be realized in the future.

The criminal defers the responsible, because it is outside his range of interest and does not give him the control and power that he seeks. In addition, he views responsibilities and obligations as herculean tasks. They appear this way because he resents having to fulfill them; they take him away from more exciting things. When he is a child, the criminal's parents and teachers implore him to do his homework. Their entreaties are often brushed aside in favor of other, usually forbidden activities. In daily life when he is an adult, this pattern of deferment continues, often to the point of total default. The noncriminal also puts off things, such as writing a letter, paying a bill, and filing a tax return, but not because his interests and energy are absorbed by competing criminal thinking and action. Furthermore, when he experiences the consequent stresses, embarrassment, and penalties of excessive deferment, the noncriminal does not react with righteous indignation and vengeance. In contrast, the criminal finds mundane responsibilities and obligations antithetical to the course that he wants to pursue; they are boring. Rather than pay bills, he discards them. He postpones visiting his hospitalized mother for something more exciting. Such activities offer no "voltage," and so he shoves them aside, sometimes with a faintly stated intention to get to them someday. It is noteworthy that the criminal fails to do even what is in his own interest if more exciting things are available. He may delay doing his laundry until he runs out of clean clothes. He may postpone writing a letter even if it will assist him in retrieving money. This type of deferment is due to the lack of immediate excitement or to the priority of criminal ideas and action.

With every deferment of responsible activity, the criminal progressively gets himself into more trouble. The following is a prototype of what happens in case after case.

C came to us in jeopardy of arrest for passing bad checks and disgusted with himself for the way he was living. We presented what was involved in our program, and he agreed to allow us to help him help himself. However, he continually delayed taking the steps necessary to begin to get his financial affairs and personal life in order:

Looking for a job: "I can always go tomorrow. It will be there."

Writing a letter to promise payment on a bad check: C deferred for months; only when threatened with legal action did he beg the money from a relative.

Independent study: C was going to study for a professional license, but did so only sporadically.

Handling marital problems: C compounded a bad situation by suddenly leaving his wife and two children and going to live with another woman.

C finally obtained two part-time jobs. He quit one after several months, which left him still unable to meet outstanding financial obligations.

In short, over a period of a few months, C managed to dig himself into more holes. He became "bored" with doing things slowly and responsibly. His mind became filled with schemes and "big shot" fantasies. Deferment of the responsible increased, and "big score" thinking emerged. He had an entrée to a real estate deal that involved compromising others in a conflict of interest and misrepresentation. He was certain that he could clear $150,000 for himself quickly, pay off his debts, and then open his own firm and live as he wished. After a "big score" of this sort, he could wine and dine women, jet around the country, and try to "make contacts." However, default piled upon default as C was increasingly dissatisfied with what he considered living responsibly, which he referred to as "prison." The itch for excitement overrode the mundane tasks of starting from the bottom and working up.

This is how the criminal lives. He looks for the short cut, puts off what does not offer excitement, and looks toward the time when a "big score" will put him on "easy street." As he sets out to commit a crime, he is in the position of having deferred the responsible. In effect, he has also again deferred the "big score," inasmuch as what he now views as a "big score" will seem insignificant as bigger schemes evolve.

The criminal may be prompt when it is to his advantage in a criminal enterprise. In fact, as part of a "con," he may attend promptly to something and even do a bit extra. The criminal will also stop deferring if there is a threat that another person will move in and assume control. The criminal just referred to began to pay his debts only after a collection agency threatened to take him to court. He said, "I would rather be in control of the situation as much as possible." Not all criminals fit the deferment pattern described here. Some commit crimes and attend to other matters promptly in an effort to keep up appearances of responsibility. The less they default, the less others take them to task and the easier it is for them to pursue criminal objectives. In all cases, even when they are active in crime, criminals regard themselves as responsible simply because they have the *intention* of one day doing that which they are putting off.

SUPEROPTIMISM

We have been describing events that take place from the initial occurrence of a criminal idea to the time when the criminal is en route to the crime. The closer he gets to committing the crime, the more sure he becomes that all will go as planned. The money will be in the safe, the night shift will have fewer personnel, police surveillance of the area will be minimal. But most important is his rising certainty that he will not get caught.* This "superoptimism" increases with the cutoff of deterrents."

The superoptimism present during a crime is an extreme form of optimism. It goes beyond the criminal's certainty regarding day-to-day matters. This extreme certainty is absolutely necessary for a crime; if he lacks it, the criminal backs away. He works up to it through scheming or through a rapid, habitual pattern of thinking to be described later. It is not a consistent state of mind.† The superoptimism is likely to be viewed by others as present when it is not. A criminal may brag about his talents, abilities, and "accomplishments" either in crime or out. But this bragging is not superoptimism. The criminal may, indeed, consider himself vulnerable, but appear

---

* Claster (1967, pp. 84, 85) made one of the few references to this. He found that delinquents have a "greater belief in ability to evade arrest" than do nondelinquents. Claster's questionnaire study provided quantitative evidence of what he called "the 'magical immunity' mechanism posited in psychoanalytic ego psychology." The perception of immunity from arrest was found even among boys who were repeatedly apprehended and confined. Commenting on Claster's study, Jensen (1969, p. 200) stated that, because of the delinquent's idea of "immunity," changing enforcement patterns might have little deterrent effect.

† The use of drugs to achieve and maintain a superoptimistic state is discussed in Volume 3.

superoptimistic solely for effect. Again, external appearance is not a valid index of mental state.

In a superoptimistic state, the criminal views the crime as a fait accompli. He has already spent the proceeds in his thinking. Indicative of this is the criminal who, contemplating the robbery of a particular bank, thought, "I hope they keep my money safe." It was as though the money in that bank already belonged to him. Another set out to hold up a bank, but found when he got there that someone else had already robbed it. He thought, "They got my money."

The criminal's personal experience supports this certainty. He knows that his chances of arrest are extremely low. This is borne out by his experience, not only in major crimes, but in numerous smaller offenses.

> C owed money to many car-rental companies. He would obtain a car by paying an initial deposit. Then he would drive it for hundreds and sometimes thousands of miles. When he returned the car, he would convince the clerk that he was a good credit risk and request that the company mail him the invoice. Then he would ignore bill after bill. None of these companies went to the trouble and expense of tracking him down to collect payment.

Every "success" reinforces superoptimistic thinking.

The criminal is, however, aware that he could slip. He may even acknowledge that he will eventually be caught, but it is never "this time."

> C stated that, if he were ever caught, punishment would be intolerable, and that would be enough to end his crime. But in no case was the crime that he was about to commit regarded as the one for which he would get caught. He would say that maybe this would happen "next year." But during the next year, he still regarded each crime as safe. "Next year" never arrived.

> C had committed thousands of thefts in some 30 years of crime. In discussions, he would readily acknowledge that he might get caught. Even though he had never been arrested for stealing, he knew the risks of his daily crime. Yet, on the street, as he approached each crime, once he made up his mind to steal, all doubt was eliminated, and he regarded himself as 100 percent safe for that particular situation.

The criminal knows that, even if he is apprehended, there will be a long series of proceedings before he is convicted and sentenced, and he usually believes that he will either beat the charge or receive a light sentence. When the criminal seriously questions the wisdom of committing a particular crime, it is because the risks are indeed considerable, and if he fails to arrive at a state of superoptimism, he does not go through with it.

Superoptimism, an intrinsic part of the criminal's thinking processes, can turn out to be his worst enemy. A criminal may not evaluate realistically or even consider the consequences of what he is about to do. Although he knows that he is likely to get caught some time, the excitement of the enterprise overrides such considerations. His appetite for more excitement grows, and crime patterns become more extensive. Eventually, the "one day I might get caught" arrives.

> C exploited a number of women. At the time, his partner was D. However, during this period, he had sex with a young girl in a hotel room. He figured that D would never find out and that, even if she did, she would be angry only for a moment. C miscalculated on both counts. D turned him in on a charge of "carnal knowledge of a minor."

> C stated that he would not take minor risks, but would play only for large stakes. One week after saying this, he was arrested for driving without a license. This occurred near his apartment. He had been certain that the police would not be around that area, much less spot him.

In both these examples, the criminal was sure that he was in the clear. In examining such situations, one criminal in our program stated that "superoptimism kills a criminal more than anything else."

Generally, superoptimism grows with scheming. As the criminal perfects his scheme and cuts off deterrents, superoptimism develops. A few criminals are recklessly superoptimistic from the start. They eliminate consideration of deterrents almost immediately, believing that it would take a most unusual set of circumstances for them to get caught and that, even hen, apprehension or conviction would be unlikely. This is the type who gets caught most frequently because their superoptimism leads to increasing carelessness. Thus, a criminal may go on a round of bank holdups, being careful to wear a different disguise each time. As he has a few successes, he throws this degree of caution to the winds and stops altering his appearance. Then he is detected. The important fact is that every step before, during, *and after* a crime is an opportunity for another criminal scheme and triumph. Encountering the law is no deterrent if the criminal can bask in publicity, glory in the turmoil that he creates in court and later in confinement, and finally be the center of publicity when he is released.

> Having committed crimes of many types, C had "beaten the system" countless times through a string of insanity defenses. Instead of serving a sentence in prison, he had spent much of his life in mental hospitals. However, every time he beat a charge on the basis of mental illness, this gave him more license for crime. C viewed himself as invulnerable and was extreme in what he did. Even when he was apprehended, this afforded further arenas for excitement. He enjoyed engaging in sensa-

tional acts in courtrooms, in hospitals, and before news cameras. He acquired such a reputation as a "maniac" that he was virtually certain that he could avoid jail at any time. At one point, after he had been released from confinement, he still had several serious charges pending. At that time, he claimed immunity from a prison sentence: "There is no way in the U.S.A. in 1970 that they can put me in prison. I'm not going to jail."

C could easily say such a thing on the basis of his previous avoidance of jail. It reflected "superoptimism." The possibility always existed that he would not be declared mentally ill on the latest charges and would be sent to prison. He had spent some time there, and it could happen again. But the threat of prison was not an effective deterrent because of the tremendous excitement that C generated during legal procedures and even in confinement itself.

From childhood on, the criminal's mind works in such a way that a possibility or an assumption is an accomplished fact; an idea is a reality. If someone tells him "maybe," he regards it as a promise. Anything that he decides to do is as good as done. The criminal uses cutoff to eliminate fear and doubt. The near certainty that is evident in crime appears elsewhere. It is tied in closely with control and ownership, in that the criminal exercises a mental tyranny over others. He has the near certainty that everyone will function as he, the criminal, sees fit in every situation.

C said that he planned to "call a family council" to make some decisions about his future living and financial arrangements. He declared, "I expect everyone to agree with me." He did not even know whether his parents were able to meet with him, and he had never sounded them out as to their views. He assumed that they would fall in line, agreeing with whatever he proposed. As matters turned out, his mother was out of town, and so the meeting was not held. When she did return, it was clear that she had quite a different view of what would be best for C and the family.

In this example, the assumption was that everyone would automatically fall in line with the criminal's plans. C had ordained before the meeting how everyone would act. In his mind, the issues were resolved and were not open to question.

Superoptimism permits the criminal to function according to what he wants, rather than who he is. A criminal may decide that he wants to be responsible. To his way of thinking, the decision is a guarantee of accomplishment. One criminal, about to be released from confinement, proclaimed, "When I get out of here, it is a new chapter. I am an entirely different person." He did not mention "becoming" a new person; instead, the change had already occurred. A criminal is likely to believe that the job of becoming responsible has been completed, simply because he has deterred a few ideas and stayed out of active violation for a time.

Superoptimism differs from the confidence experienced by the noncriminal. Confidence, like superoptimism, is based on anticipation of success. The noncriminal expects success only after he has appraised what is needed to achieve it in a responsible endeavor. His confidence is warranted by responsible considerations, rather than pretensions and unrealistic expectations. Thus, the layman is often astonished at the chances that the criminal takes. In fact, observers have concluded that the criminal must *want* to get caught, or he would not assume such risks. The noncriminal views everything as loaded against the criminal, whereas the criminal sees everything stacked in his favor. The superoptimism may appear "crazy" or "stupid" from the noncriminal's perspective, but it is warranted by the criminal's ability to cut off deterrents, by his past successes, and by his present carefully thought out scheme.*

Clearly, superoptimism is mandatory for a criminal enterprise. The criminal is fully cognizant of the hazards of his "work." He knows that his "luck may run out" some day. He is aware that a simple miscalculation could prove costly, if not fatal. With success in prior enterprises and the scheming of new ones, deterrents corrode and are cut off, giving rise to the superoptimism that permits him to get on with the "job."

EMERGENCE OF NONPSYCHOTIC HALLUCINATORY DETERRENTS

Early in our investigation, we learned that some criminals hear a voice speaking to them at critical times. We since have found this to be the case in more than half the criminals we see. Extreme care was taken to distinguish an actual voice from a corresponding thought. The voice generally appears later in life, as crime becomes more frequent, but it may go back as far as the age of five. This voice does not distress the criminal; it is a part of his life, and he assumes that others have the same experience. The voice emerges for only a moment when the criminal is about to violate but is still hesitant. With increasing violation, many criminals hear the voice more frequently and intensely, but only with respect to violation—occasionally during the scheming, but mostly just before and during a crime, not afterward.

---

* Actually the criminal objects to being considered either crazy or stupid. He may have committed a stupid act, but *he* is not stupid; it was what he did that was stupid. Criminals have often said, "You may think I'm crazy, but I'm not stupid." However, the criminal does not consider himself "crazy" either.

The voice is not a manifestation of psychosis. The criminal remains firmly in touch with reality, a necessity for the successful execution of the crime. The voice urges him to *refrain from commiting the crime.* In almost all cases, the criminal listens to the voice and heeds it so as to avoid apprehension.

The voice may take different forms. It may be that of a parent: one criminal said that, as he was about to commit a crime, a voice would come through that he identified as "Mother" telling him, "Don't do it"; another heard the voice of his dead father saying, "Don't," when he was about to commit a crime. Or it may appear to be that of a supernatural being: one criminal stated that the voice that urged him to do good was the voice of God; another heard the voice of Christ telling him not to commit a crime; still another would hear a quiet male voice (he was a Muslim, so he called the voice "Allah") talking to him from the back of his head, telling him not to commit a crime. The criminal may experience the voice as coming from outside himself, as emanating from within, or both.

The voice usually operates as a deterrent, because it is a return of an internal deterrent or conscience that has been cut off. Less often, the criminal hears a voice that reminds him of an external deterrent, e.g., that he will get caught.

> C said that the presence of a voice made it hard to steal. A soft voice, somewhere between those of a child and a woman, would say, "Don't do it. It's wrong. You'll be caught."

In discussing this, C was unsure whether this was a warning of the likelihood of apprehension or a deterrent emanating from his conscience.

Each criminal experiencing a voice has reported that it is always the same. He can identify and describe it according to pitch, loudness, and timbre. It is brief, transient, and limited to a short message. In fact, the criminal gives the voice a name, because it is recognizably the same. Criminals have called this nonpsychotic hallucinatory deterrent "my friend," "Jiminy Cricket," "guardian angel," "God," "Boy Scouts," "Mother," "Father," "that guy," and simply "something." The criminal regards the voice as friendly, because it offers warnings to help him avoid apprehension. He admits to us that generally he would hate to lose the voice, because it is a form of protection. Occasionally, a criminal says that he would like to rid himself of the voice, because it stands in the way of what he wants to do at the time. His evaluation of the helpfulness of the voice depends on whether he believes that he missed out on something or thinks that he was spared trouble. We have found that a criminal may experience these voices as unbearably tormenting when they repeatedly condemn him for his "evil ways." One man tried to rid himself of the voices by smashing furniture, but not because the voices instructed him to do so. Rather, this was an external attempt to eliminate inner turmoil.

We have emphasized the occurrence of nonpsychotic hallucinatory deterrents just before a crime. They may also occur during a crime. Criminals have told us that hearing a voice during the execution of a crime tends to slow them up. One man described it in terms of hearing the voice and then "freezing" in the midst of the act. He would cut off the anticrime message and finish the crime.

As we have indicated, the voice is perfectly natural to some criminals. It is part of their mental life, and they are not frightened by hearing it. We have found that they believe that everyone, including their parents, hears such a voice. They consider the voice as ordinary as having eyes and ears and are astonished to discover that most people do not hear one. Despite the fact that the criminal regards the voice as part of himself, he does not talk about it spontaneously. It would be a sign of weakness for him to tell others that hearing a voice sometimes prevents him from committing a crime. The criminal is frightened by hearing the voice only if he is told that it is unusual. Being in a mental hospital, some criminals had heard that people who hear voices are crazy. Thus, they asked us whether it meant that they too were insane. It was ironic that criminals who had deceptively convinced others that they were mentally ill were now asking us whether in fact they might be.

As an accountability defense to establish mental illness, the criminal may say that voices told him to commit the crime, whereas in fact they had said the opposite. One criminal, for example, told examiners that a voice said, "Kill"; he later admitted to us that it had said, "Don't kill." In addition, criminals have claimed that voices have compelled them to act in specific ways, although they really were in total control of themselves and had a choice as to whether to heed the voices. Some claim to have heard a voice instructing them, whereas no voice was heard at all.

Although the criminal does not usually admit to mental health personnel that he is hearing voices, he is likely to be prescribed medication at a hospital or clinic, especially if he has been diagnosed as psychotic. The criminal who experiences the nonpsychotic hallucinatory deterrents, but who wants to rid himself of them because they oppose crime, welcomes the medication, unless the dosage is so strong as to disable him. The medicine tones down the castigating voices, and thus removes a deterrent to action.

> C stated that without medication, "I get wild." By this he meant that he became very irritable and was inwardly tormented. His distress was due to the voices' telling him over and over how evil he was. When he

received medication, he left the hospital grounds and committed crimes. Without drugs, there were far fewer crimes.

The medicine does not affect whether the person wants to commit crimes. Underlying thinking processes are not affected. A criminal like C does not have to have medication to commit a crime. He is able to overcome the voices on his own. As C said, "I rebel against them." Contrary to what their doctors expect, criminal with nonpsychotic hallucinatory deterrents find that medication makes the "rebellion" that much easier.

Very few criminals experiencing nonpsychotic hallucinatory deterrents actually become psychotic. We have had three cases of prolonged reactions of a psychotic nature that were accompanied by these same hallucinatory deterrents. In each of these cases, the voices were on the side of not commiting crimes. When the psychosis was cleared up by medication, the nonpsychotic hallucinatory deterrents remained.

The voice that the criminal hears is different from the noncriminal psychotic hallucination, in that every criminal who has heard it has acknowledged that he had the choice of whether to obey it. The criminal does not have control over whether the voice makes its presence known. But he can decide whther to heed its message. If he is opposed to what the voice says, he cuts it off and proceeds with the crime.

> While considering whether to molest a child sexually, C heard the voice of his deceased father saying, "Don't." When he wanted to proceed with the crime, he could break the communication with his father and simply ignore the voice.
> Whenever C heard a voice opposed to crime, he thought he should disregard it, because it was "chicken" to do otherwise.

Usually, the criminal heeds the voice, regarding it as protective. In only two cases have we had reason to believe (after exhaustive probing) that a criminal heard a voice actually urging him to commit a crime. In both instances, the voice came in sporadically, but was repeatedly deterred. In neither case did a crime result. This is because the criminal made the choice not to listen to it.*

---

* We have not invesigated whether noncriminals also have experienced nonpsychotic hallucinatory deterrents that operate in the same fashion. Unexpectedly, a criminal cited a reference in Plato's dialogues that describes this phenomenon.

> You have heard me speak at sundry times and in divers places of an oracle or sign which comes to me, and is the divinity which Meletus ridicules in the indictment. This sign, which is a kind of voice, first began to come to me when I was a child; it always forbids but never commands me to do anything which I am going to do. This is what deters me from being a politician (Plato, 1959, p. 26).

REEMERGENCE OF FEAR DURING THE EXECUTION
OF THE CRIME

We have described how fear is reduced by the corrosion and cutoff of deterrents. However, even what appears to be "airtight" scheming does not totally eradicate fear for the duration of the criminal enterprise. Just before the crime, the criminal is in a state that perhaps can best be termed "hyperactive and excited." Part of this can be attributed to the excitement from the power thrust that accompanies the commission of any crime. But another aspect is a rise in the fear that he might get caught. We have described how, in some cases, a nonpsychotic hallucinatory deterrent emerges when there is residual fear in the form of a conflict as to whether to act. But it is far more common, just before the crime, for the criminal to experience a return of fear and consequently a slight decrease in superoptimism. For example, at some point before the criminal enters the house that he intends to burglarize, he becomes frightened. He can deal with this fear again through his remarkable capacity to cut it off "surgically." He is then composed, and superoptimism again rides high.

> C related that, just before an armed robbery, as he was about to make his way into the place, he would be highly charged with excitement and a return of fear. But in a very short time, he said, he could "get like ice." He pinpointed this as occurring when "I get that gun in my hands."

The cutoff is so precise that the criminal may be almost trembling one moment and not be bothered by fear at all the next. Not only is he calm, but he is absolutely certain that he cannot fail.

Superoptimism is usually not so great that it eliminates prudence with respect to a safe getaway. If things do not go according to schedule, the fear of detection once again emerges, and appropriate steps must be taken.

> C had timed the holdup of a savings and loan association to take 3 minutes. He held a gun on a woman who was to open the safe. However, she was so flustered that she could not open it. Five minutes had elapsed, and C's superoptimism was waning. He was on the verge of leaving when the manager passed by and opened the safe, owing to the woman's pleading. Otherwise, C would have left.

If there is a clear and present danger of arrest, the fear may be so great that the criminal will not even attempt to execute the crime or, if he is in the midst of it, he might try to clear out.

> C broke into a house and threatened to harm a woman and her two children unless she submitted to a sexual act. He had begun the act but

had not completed it when he heard an automobile drive up. He ran away and was never identified. He later discovered that the car had entered the driveway next door, and he regretted not having stayed to finish what he was doing.

In some cases, the emergence of fear is exciting in itself. It creates a double challenge to meet: the fear and the authorities.

C broke into a place, stole a television set, and then hailed a cab. He achieved a double triumph: he eluded security at the site of the theft, and he entered a cab with a policeman standing right there.

A small proportion of criminals experience the persistence of slight fear throughout the crime. This is advantageous for them, in that it makes them more cautious.

The most tragic consequences of the return of fear is injury to a victim beyond what had been planned. The criminal's mind is so programed that, if he is faced with the unexpected—being reported or in any way opposed at the time of the crime—a homicide or serious injury may result.

WHEN THE CRIMINAL REMAINS UNAPPREHENDED

Most criminals experience a return of the fear of apprehension after a crime—not panic, but fear that is sometimes as intense as that experienced just before the crime. The fear may last several minutes or several days. The criminal may worry about having left a telltale sign, that witnesses will be able to identify him, or that somehow the police will trace him. At this time, the criminal who knows that he is being hunted will appear "paranoid" to others. He may even call himself "paranoid." He regards with alarm every passerby and every knock at the door. He is hyperalert to the possibility that any stranger constitutes a danger to him. This is not true paranoia at all, but a necessary suspiciousness justified by the fact that people are indeed looking for someone and he knows that he is the "someone." However, unless there is an immediate danger, this fear gives way to a tremendous sense of triumph in having succeeded.

There are occasions when something "goes wrong" and the criminal believes either that he was seen or that he left some clue. Consequently, he fears that the authorities have a good chance of catching up with him. Some are able to cut off this worry and, occupying themselves with new enterprises, avoid being bothered. Sometimes, the criminal knows that he has been identified and that it will be only a matter of time until he is apprehended. He will do his best to elude the authorities, and he may go into hiding, often leaving the area to do so.

C killed a man in a western city. He went to Nevada and was picked up and returned. He changed his appearance so as not to be recognized in a lineup. He was not identified. He received permission to go to another city for "necessary" business, at which point he took off. He went to Mexico and decided to lie low, because he did not want to get mixed up with the Mexican authorities. Meanwhile, he kept in touch with people in the city of the crime until he learned that the "heat was off." He returned briefly to the city of the crime and then went to other cities. Within a matter of months, he was involved in extensive crime in nearly a dozen cities, including Phoenix, Cleveland, and Fargo, North Dakota.

C's pattern was to jump from one geographic location to another. Many criminals think of leaving home, but do not.

Most criminals remain in the geographic area where the crime has been committed. They regard running as demeaning. Furthermore, they do not want to leave their friends and connections. Their whole setup is there, and they have other crimes in mind. Remaining and walking unapprehended in that area adds a dimension to the excitement. From our observations, it appears that the black criminal is less likely to move around than the white. The main reason for the black's remaining close to home is the same as that for the white: his associations and connections are there, and planning for other crimes is going on; but the black criminal's reluctance to leave is due to the fact that he believes it is harder for him to gain acceptance in a new criminal group.

In some cases, the criminal remains at the exact location of the crime and even aids the authorities.

The family four doors away from C was away on vacation. C knew the contents of the house and figured that he could burglarize the place successfully, because the family regarded him as a friend and would never suspect him. Under these conditions, this 9-year-old stole cameras, radios, piggy banks, and a diamond ring. When the family returned, the police were called. C made himself available to the police, who went through the list of what was missing and what was left untouched. Doing this gave him ideas for future thefts. But C went even further and offered the police the names of fellows who he indicated might have participated.

C enjoyed pulling the wool over everyone's eyes and succeeded in directing their attention elsewhere, virtually ensuring his safety, inasmuch as he had never been suspected in the first place. One man burned down a three-story building next to a fire station and then got a charge out of helping the fire department extinguish the blaze. Some criminals enjoy merely staying in the area and taking in the confusion and excitement after the crime has been committed.

> After holding up a bank, C went around the block and disposed of his coat, hat, and dark glasses. He then returned to the bank and stood in line, all the while laughing to himself at the description being given to the police. The criminal, who must have appeared tall as he stood there with gun in hand, was described as being over 6 feet and as wearing a black suit, an overcoat, a hat, and dark glasses. C was considerably under 6 feet and wore a blue suit. As he stood in line listening to all this, he was not likely to be recognized.

In short, very few flee from the area. Certainly, they do not leave because of a burglary or something else that they regard as relatively small. In the case of a big crime that has attracted a lot of publicity, and where evidence is known to have been collected, the criminal may leave town for a while and return when he hears that things have "cooled off."

The crime is not necessarily completed in a single act. There are often several stages. A criminal may steal some credit cards. There is, to be sure, excitement in such a theft. But this is only the beginning. Later, he will have to contend with someone who has received notification not to allow one of the stolen cards to be used. There is the victory to be won in persuading an authorizing agent that he, the criminal, is the person named on the card. And there is the excitement of using the stolen card to get other identification and engage in further criminality. In other words, it is not a matter of a solitary act; rather, a specific crime may be only the first link in a chain of crimes.

Some criminals enjoy the publicity of a crime they have committed. They rush to buy a copy of the paper and watch the evening news or switch the dial back and forth on their car radios. Some compile scrapbooks of clippings reporting their activities. Cases have been reported in which the criminal kept a diary of his offenses. One man, in a journal he kept, provided full descriptions of twenty-nine sexual assaults that he committed during a sixteen-month period (*The Washington Post*, 7/13/71, p. C1). For those criminals who follow the news, there are two benefits. One, of course, is the self-buildup. The other is that they have a better idea of how close on their trail the authorities are. However, some criminals react in an opposite manner, in that the fear that emerges after a crime is so intense that they do not look at a newspaper or television, lest it increase their agitation.

The criminal who is in a daily grind of crime goes through the thinking described in this chapter with great speed—indeed with automaticity. The same questions, doubts, and fears are aroused in him as in the sporadic criminal, but the crime pattern is so habituated that it all occurs in a more rapid, routine, and subdued manner. In other words, if a man is breaking and entering a half-dozen times a day, he does not devise elaborate schemes and go through a prolonged debate of deterrents before every act. His behavior is analogous to that of a secretary who is composing a series of a hundred letters with basically the same format, but tailored to individual recipients. The first half-dozen require more attention with respect to phrasing than the remaining ninety-four. So does the criminal go through all the steps of thinking that we have described, and with great deliberation until he establishes an M.O. that is successful. He then proceeds from one crime to the next with relative efficiency and speed.

> C was in a daily grind of larceny. This entailed the theft of some 30–50 items a day with a yield of $300 once he had sold them to a "fence." Averaging 40 thefts a day, C ran up a total of about 15,000 thefts a year. He was not arrested for any of them.

C had developed a successful M.O., which was as automatic as driving a car. A criminal like C does go through the mental processes described here, although very quickly. He still must deal with internal and external deterrents. For every theft, there is the possibility that he will get caught, but he becomes so proficient in his operation that he usually can make the necessary determinations almost instantly. Internal deterrents plague him comparatively little in the course of his routine, but they do surface from time to time. In other words, if one were to dissect C's thinking, one would eventually get to the scheming, corrosion and cutoff of deterrents, building up the good opinion of oneself, deferment, and superoptimism. But because these processes are so automatic, they require greater probing to isolate them than in the case of a man who is not in a "daily grind," whose crimes are fewer, and who is thus less habituated in these mental patterns.

CELEBRATION AFTER THE CRIME

After the commission of a crime, the criminal is still psychologically "amphetamized." His energy output remains high. There is no letdown after the big event; instead, he goes on to more activity, some of which is arrestable but a great deal of which affords him a power thrust as the "big shot" in legitimate activities.

The criminal "celebrates" after a crime (or, in the case of a criminal in a "daily grind," moves from one crime to another and celebrates after his "tour of duty," often at night). These celebrations occur more among drug-users than among nonusers. They drink or use drugs, or both, to eliminate fears and to seek new excitements, often sexual, after a crime. If the crime was risky and rather out of the ordinary, celebration is more likely.

In the fictional treatment of the criminal, we see him entering a bar, taking a seat with his buddies, flashing his money around, treating others to drinks, and all the while bragging about his exploits. There is some accuracy in this. Of course, he is careful about where he does this and to whom he talks. The more gregarious criminal plays the big shot in this style. The focus of conversation may be his M.O., and he may brag about his slickness or strength. The talk itself is very exciting. He may also flash a roll of money and try to impress others with the size of his "haul." With each narration, the criminal embellishes the story so as to appear even slicker and stronger. By the time the story has been retold a few times, the yield may have increased substantially

As we have indicated, the conquest and triumph are far more important than the proceeds. In an assault, success in overpowering the victim and escaping outweighs in importance what the criminal took from him. In a sexual crime, the conquest is far more exciting than the sexual act. In fact, it is not sex that the criminal is after; he often rejects consenting sexual relationships because they are not exciting and there is no challenge. In a theft, the monetary value of objects that he has taken is secondary to the manner of acquisition. The critical factor is how difficult the enterprise was. As noted earlier, the criminal often steals what he does not need or even value. A man with $184 in his pocket who stole three steaks from a grocery store hardly needed to steal to eat; he gave the steaks to friends. An eighteen-year-old made off with a huge iron cross for which he had no use; indeed, he had trouble carrying it and even more trouble hiding it. We know of countless instances that confirm the statement that the proceeds are far less important than the excitement of the crime. That is the underlying reason for the many "crimes without reason" that one reads about in the newspapers (e.g., Arnold, 1971; Cromley, 1972). Incidents in which the criminal gives away or throws away what he gains through a crime are so numerous as to be the rule, rather than the exception.

The same applies to money. Far more money passes through the hands of many criminals than they ever use. Money is the vehicle or instrument by which the criminal extends his criminality. The need for money is part of the desire for more criminal activity. It helps to put him at the right place at the right time. He knows that "money talks." With dollars in his pocket, he is in a better position to control people and have them do as he wants. But he places little value on money itself; its value lies in what it will accomplish in terms of further power thrusts for criminal ends.* The more

---

* This view is consistent with the drug-user's attitude toward the value of money. A discussion will follow in Volume 3.

money the criminal has, the quicker he spends it. Some go on spending sprees and live in an opulent manner. They rent luxury apartments and furnish them lavishly. Having such a place to live and filling it with expensive items is another boost to the big-shot image. Almost legendary is the criminal who drives the deluxe automobile with all the extras. Some deck themselves out in the latest styles, buying $300 suits or the latest in fashions. Many criminals who are clothes-conscious acquire such extensive wardrobes that they never wear half the items they purchase. But having a closet filled with expensive apparel gives them a buildup. The criminal often goes to even greater lengths, actually giving away the proceeds. This pattern also begins very early.

> As a youngster, C stole a purse containing $12. He did not know what to do with it, except to go to the movies and spend money for candy. So he left a couple of dollars on some seats in the theaters he attended.

As he gets older, he throws his money around to impress others. He gives money to his friends, buys expensive gifts for his women, and builds himself up by bestowing money on objects of sentimentality, such as church, charity, and family, sometimes with special attention to his children. Occasionally, he even returns some of the proceeds to the victim.

> C altered the date on some bonds to render them negotiable. On the basis of $30,000 worth of these bonds, he obtained a $24,000 loan. He later heard that this private, uninsured bank was going broke and that the depositors, all relatively poor people, would suffer. On learning this, he repaid $22,000.

Sometimes, the money is literally discarded, as in the case of one criminal who enjoyed shocking everyone by going to nightclubs and lighting cigars with dollar or five-dollar bills and by giving twenty-dollar tips. As a result of the way he handles money, the criminal is invariably broke, no matter how much he acquires.

It is not demeaning to be broke. For many criminals, being without money is standard operating procedure. The criminal never looks at himself as broke; it is only a temporary state, correctable tomorrow. This is because of his knowledge that more crimes are to come. He does not worry, because more is easily procured. He is contemptuous of those who save. His idea is to "live it up" now. If he must get his hands on some funds, short of a crime, he can always turn to other sources, such as family and friends, to help him out.

In short, money is of no importance, except for the kick that the criminal gets out of acquiring it illicitly and then getting rid of it. It is not valued for day-to-day subsistence or for what it will buy, but rather to promote the criminal's image with others and his own image of himself.

Perhaps the aspect of the celebration of a crime that brings most of these patterns together and is in itself a criminal pattern is the criminal's gravitation toward a sexual partner after a crime.* During the scheming of a crime and its execution, the criminal has little time or use for women, because his mind is zeroed in on the activity at hand. But after the commission of the crime, the female is what one criminal called his "psychological Rolls Royce." He does not consider himself a "man" unless at least one woman is readily available to him. He either already has one or seeks out a woman who is eager for "some action." From there on, the patterns differ among criminals. All regard themselves as irresistible, but some make more of a show than others. "Mr. Big" is nattily attired, sports a big car, and has a bulging wallet. One man even went so far as to borrow additional money, so that he could flash it in front of his women. With cash in hand, the criminal can go to the best restaurants and order the most expensive items on the menu. This wining and dining is in itself part of a criminal operation, in that the criminal is after more than a good meal and pleasant company. To his way of thinking, to have a woman with him is to own her. It may be her money that he is after, but almost always it is for a buildup, so that he can be "Mr. Big" sexually. Picking the kind of woman he does, the criminal usually succeeds in getting her into bed. There may then be hours of sexual activity (especially in the case of the criminal who uses drugs, some of which lengthen the duration of erectility for hours). But the criminal is rarely satisfied with merely a sexual conquest. The woman becomes his, body and soul. As one man referred to himself, "I am a collector of souls." The sex may be only a one-night stand, with the criminal committing an arrestable offense against his partner.

C won a lot of money in a crooked dice game. In the course of this activity, he picked out an elegantly dressed woman and offered to buy her a drink. C then took her to a hotel where he had had other women. She had been drinking so much that, after they had sex, she passed out. C then stole her jewelry and money. The next morning, he left; she was still unconscious and lying nude on the bed. He spread her legs apart and left the room door open. He brought the hotel clerk back to exhibit this woman whom he claimed he had just found, but did not know. He got quite a charge from the sexual conquest, then the theft, and finally the humiliation of the woman.

---

* We speak here of the male criminal who seeks out a female, but the same concepts apply with respect to homosexuals.

In this case, a single contact was followed immediately by the next act of conquest. With others, it may be what we have termed a continuing "pimp-prostitute relationship," in which the two partners exploit each other over a longer period. The excitement in these relationships runs particularly high after a crime.

No matter what form the celebration takes or how exciting it is, the criminal's appetite for further excitement, power, and triumph is still hearty. Thus, one crime begets another.

THE CRIMINAL APPREHENDED

When the criminal is arrested, he protests the arrest if there are grounds. Otherwise, he knows enough not to talk. Some are silent, and others talk, but they say very little.* The criminal's idea of "justice" is not being caught; "injustice" is interference with his plans. There may be other, relatively minor, injustices, such as being informed on or being handled roughly by the authorities. Any environmental factor that contributes to his being apprehended is considered unfair. But the *inherent* injustice is getting caught, never what responsible people would consider the injustice of the crime. In fact, he has no shame about what he has done, no thought about people whom he has harmed, and little concern about his own family. He may express a sense of remorse about it when he is held accountable later, but it does not cross his mind at the time of the crime.

Having been apprehended, he asks himself, "Why did I do it?" This does not mean that he doubts the morality or desirability of doing what he did, but that he questions why he got caught. He was so certain that he was in the clear, but he got caught; what went wrong? Broadly speaking, the injustice lies in the offender's belief that he is a good person, helpful to society, not a criminal; now, here he is, in the hands of the law; what greater injustice could there be!

He begins immediately to think about getting out. He approaches the question of bonding with absolute certainty. A criminal may be certain that a bondsman with whom he has done business before will bail him out and put up bond money for him. Failing this, he is sure that a fellow criminal or his wife or his parents will bail him out. In his thinking, they are obligated to do this. In the last ten years, it has become increasingly common for a criminal to plead indigence and be released on his own recognizance. As we have pointed out, the reason for his indigence is that he has let

---

* A delinquent youngster with no record or a record of only a minor previous offense may admit to a crime, if he is told that confession will result in his release.

thousands of dollars go through his hands and currently happens to be broke. Once broke, some cannot turn to their families, which truly are indigent. As a consequence of recent trends, the criminal counts on being released on his own recognizance. To have to put up bond is a defeat—a further injustice. With the jails overcrowded, if the criminal does not have a long record and the present offense is not serious, he is especially likely to be released in this manner. At times it seems as though even the length of the record appears not to matter.

While the criminal is being held for arraignment, the prevailing theme in his mind still is the injustice of getting caught. He does not believe that he should have to be accountable to anyone. This belief may be obscured by a barrage of other issues that the criminal raises, which have to do with his present circumstances and life history. That is, he goes through a list of other injustices—"others do it," he was led into it, he associated with the wrong people, he was born in the ghetto, he never had a chance in life, he needed the money, and so forth. The sociologic and psychologic excuses may camouflage what to him is the basic injustice—being apprehended and confined. A small number of criminals voice their indignation less and instead experience transient depression, with some suicidal thinking that comes and goes. In a few, there may be first a panic state that then subsides. And, in a tiny fraction, there is a postconfinement psychosis (about which more will be said in Chapter 7). Except in the event of psychosis, the scheming to get out persists.

Once the criminal is bailed out or released on personal recognizance, he is not worried. He knows that it will be a long time between the arraignment and the trial. His mental state is as though the crime never happened. He has to be reminded when to appear in court. He quickly raises money, usually through more crimes, to pay off whoever bailed him out. In a rare instance, the criminal tries to exonerate himself from the charges, doing whatever seems necessary.

> C and his partner were arrested for the sale of counterfeit stock certificates. Both had actually participated in the crime. Once C was released on $5,000 bond, he was able to recover two of the valid certificates. He arranged with his partner to tear up the phony documents. He then had the corporation that issued the stock certify the validity of the certificates. After this, C went to the police to show that they had no case. He even maintained that they were open to charges of false arrest.

As the time for the criminal to defend himself in court draws near, he gets his defense counsel primed and enlists anyone else who he thinks will be sympathetic. He manages to convince these people that he has been dealt with unjustly.

The immediate challenge is to rectify the injustice done to him. Although he has broken the law, the law now must be inviolate when invoked in his behalf. The breaker of laws becomes a constitutionalist. There is *no inconsistency* in this, from the criminal's viewpoint. In breaking the law, he exercised the freedom to do as he wanted. He will now use the law to achieve the same freedom, which is being denied him. In other words, he both breaks and uses the law to get what he wants. He has an array of tactics to deploy in his own defense.

He may try to have the hearing or trial postponed. He knows that evidence has a tendency to fade with the passage of time, because people move, forget, or lose interest in the case. He may threaten a countersuit, but he rarely takes action. One man said that he would sue a chain of stores for $100,000 for injuries sustained when a security guard tackled him as he was making off with twenty-seven pairs of pantyhose. When a criminal can tinker with the system and beat it at every turn, this provides a series of triumphs. Not only does he insist on his rights, but he gets added satisfaction out of playing games with the courts. One man charged with a felony admitted his guilt to a detective. In court, he denied having committed the crime and denied what the detective testified that the criminal told him. Thus, the hearsay evidence from the detective was nullified. This criminal was acquitted for lack of evidence. He then returned to the judge, admitted in open court that he was guilty, and dared the judge to do anything to him. The criminal in this case was the subject of extensive publicity and had enforcement officials and the victims of the crime trading charges with one another. In another situation, a relative of a criminal, C, was arrested. C bailed him out and offered, for a few thousand dollars, to go to the authorities and claim that he, C, was really the offender. C had beaten many charges before and was sure that he could do it once again. The relative declined the offer. It is in the gamesmanship, the making of fools out of others, that the excitement lies.

Knowing that he is on the way to prison constitutes the greatest injustice for the criminal. It does not matter how well treated he is. That he is confined is unjust, and everything that follows is also unjust. Some of the younger criminals who have been confined in training schools view going to the penitentiary as something of a "graduation." They turn adversity into triumph. Some of these men reported how important they thought they were when they were led away in handcuffs. One nineteen-year-old who was quite frightened nevertheless thought that he was the biggest criminal since Al Capone. Once a sentence has been handed out, the more notorious the penal institution and the greater its security, the bigger the buildup for this group of criminals. One of our men spoke with pride about how he had made the "big house" as a youth, a reference to one of the large penitentiaries. Once inside, some of the criminals flaunt their superiority over other criminals who committed what they regard as comparatively petty offenses.

Whatever front the criminal puts on, at no time is there resignation to being in prison. The thinking about getting out persists. This used to be a greater challenge than it is now. It is easier to accomplish this than it was ten years ago, because of social attitudes about the ineffectiveness of penal institutions. Today, even the criminal who has committed homicide and has a long sentence is more optimistic about being released. He thinks that, with a forty-year sentence, he should make it out in five to eight years. To sustain the criminal, there is not only the expectation of getting out relatively soon, but also the excitement in the way he goes about it. Most criminals have means other than escape, which carries tremendous risk. Using law libraries and drawing on their own experience and the help of lawyers, some criminals act as "jailhouse lawyers" for themselves and, at times, for others. The preparation of writs and other legal maneuvering may be done openly or more discretely, depending on the setting and the staff's attitude. Some criminals charge others for their services, particularly if a person requests help because he is not educated enough to do the work himself. The criminal is constantly looking for loopholes, before and during confinement. In his mind, a loophole is a legal protection intended to assist him. He approaches the legal process with superoptimism. He is absolutely certain that he will find an "out." Not granting him the use of a loophole is an injustice, inasmuch as it is there for his personal benefit.

In Chapter 3, we described how the criminal may try to avoid going to prison by pleading insanity. He may do this before the final disposition of the case in court or try later to get moved from one kind of institution to another. Once he achieves his purpose and is admitted to the hospital, he has to work his way out. Both in prisons and in hospitals, most criminals "go along with the program" and score points. In Chapter 8, we shall go into detail in describing the tactics that characterize the criminal's relationships with change agents.

A minority do engineer escape attempts. Of course, if the security is less tight, as in a hospital, more will avail themselves of opportunities to escape. If we examine the psychology of escape thinking, we see at work processes that are now familiar to the reader.* An escape attempt is a power thrust

---

* We have been privy to escape thinking. In one instance, we knew the details of a plan that was successfully executed. The criminal later entered our program after a voluntary return to the institution.

with enormous excitement and an effort to control. The criminal schemes the escape, deterrents corrode, and superoptimism rises. As far as he is concerned, it is his "right" to leave. If he is caught, it is a blatant injustice for anyone to punish him for the attempt; after all, he reasons, one should not be punished when one tries to avail himself of the freedom that is rightfully his, and so such punishment becomes another occasion for accumulating grievances.

In Chapter 3, we also described the criminal's behavior in confinement. Confinement is a continuation of the criminal life-style, except that the criminal is under tighter surveillance and his opportunities for excitement are more restricted. Prison is an arena in which to exercise his criminality and enhance his "education" about crime. There, he commits some crimes and incubates ideas for others to be committed once he is released. Many opportunities exist for power-thrusting: group meetings, leadership experiences, participation in activity programs, earning special privileges, boasting to fellow criminals and to staff members. Some criminals create excitement even in their method of leaving a penal institution. Those who have achieved considerable notoriety derive excitement from the publicity attending their release. One man even went so far as to phone a television station to announce that a dangerous criminal was about to be released, referring to himself in the third person.

Criminals differ in how fast they return to "action." Some set up crimes before leaving the penal institution. Others are deterred for a while, because their desire to remain unconfined exceeds their desire for crime. Being on parole or probation does not necessarily deter the hardened criminal.

> When C was released from jail, he was supposed to report to the probation officer in 1½ hours. Twenty minutes out on probation and on his way to the probation officer's quarters, he stole a coat. He had been warned that any crime anywhere at any time within 5 years would lead to an indeterminate stntence. Despite the warning, he committed this crime and got away with it.

Probation or parole is regarded as merely another obstacle to surmount, and not a particularly formidable one, owing to the infrequency of contact and the usually superficial nature of the reporting. The criminal does with the authorities what he has done all along with people to whom he is accountable. He sizes up the person with whom he is dealing and anticipates what it will take to satisfy him. Some criminals violate the conditions set by the parole board or the court by failing even to show up for appointments. Those who do report are adept at restricting their accounts to what the officer is interested in. This is part of the pattern of feeding others what the criminal thinks they want to hear. If the parole officer wants to see a bankbook as proof of money saved, the criminal presents one. If the officer wants him to report for urine tests as a check on drug usage, the criminal complies. He will satisfy his interrogator on whatever score is necessary, and that usually puts an end to the questioning.

Once the criminal is released, his old patterns continue. For the criminals who are not successful as criminals, the prison or mental hospital is a revolving door. But most continue to live as they did, perhaps even being a bit more cautious, and rarely, if ever, being apprehended again.

THE PSYCHOLOGY OF ACCOUNTABILITY

Why are so many of the concepts presented in this volume at variance with most current views? The major reason is that much contemporary thinking about the criminal is based on what the criminal himself says when held accountable. His explanations are accepted not only during interrogation after an arrest, but in many other situations. The child who begins a fight at school must answer to the teacher who catches him. The delinquent teenager who fails to come home one night must contend with his parents. The criminal who is absent from work and fails to call in must account to an employer for his whereabouts. In each of these situations, the criminal blames others. His excuses have come to constitute a network of explanations that a large segment of society has believed and then elaborated according to particular biases and theoretical persuasions.

What the criminal thinks before and during a violation does not correspond to the story that he tells to people who might penalize him. To them he relates self-serving stories that he concocts. Such accounts then become the basis for current views of crime causation. The criminal learns what experts commonly believe and feeds his interrogators more of it, in a circular process.

As we pointed out in Chapter 1, we initially received the same treatment that the criminal gives everyone else. We were led to believe that many of the rationalizations offered after crimes reflected the thinking that occurred during the crimes. As we studied the criminal more penetratingly, a totally different picture emerged. The evidence was compelling that the criminal was using for his own benefit an array of sociologic and psychologic explanations that he had picked up. Under conditions of privileged communication, we were able to elicit from the criminal his objectives and how he had intended to achieve them. Our work was furthered by the contributions of criminals who had progressed considerably in the change process.

They helped us to clarify and formulate concepts about how the criminal mind works before and during a crime.

None of the official records that we have reviewed indicate that the examiner truly understood what occurred in the mind of the criminal involved. All the examiners' reports have contained, instead, some version of the criminals' after-the-fact, self-serving accounts. We offer the following case to demonstrate the various discrepancies between hospital records and our information. The first statement, describing a psychiatric condition, attests to the subject's lack of competence to stand trial. The second, written while the subject was in a mental hospital, describes his condition as being "in remission." In contrast with both these statements, our findings indicate that there never was a "condition" of the type described.

Excerpt of a psychiatric examination conducted for legal determination of competence

At times he appeared rambling and vague, and in general his emotional reactions were flat and detached. . . . He states that there is some nervousness in the family, and that an aunt was a patient in a mental hospital. . . . His present trouble is the latest in a long series of problem behavior going back to childhood, after his father's death. [A partial list of some of his activities follows.] He broke into [a hospital] carrying weapons. His reason was his belief that two doctors were Communists and he was going to expose them. . . . Examination brings out underlying paranoid attitudes. From time to time he has experienced hallucinations and delusional ideas. There have been episodes of detachment from reality. . . . At times he has been suspicious of his lawyers, has experienced grandiose ideas and feelings of persecution. . . . It is my opinion that he is suffering from a major mental illness, i.e., schizophrenia, and that he lacks substantial capacity to tell right from wrong, to appreciate the wrongfulness of his conduct, and of conforming his conduct to the requirements of the law.

This criminal had fed the examiner a story that had worked for him many times before. He was careful to tie in everything, including an aunt's mental illness. As the patient spent time at the hospital, his condition appeared to improve, according to the following report:

Excerpt from his hospital record

During several interviews with the patient, I have found him to be the most cooperative and congenial individual who at times, however, becomes most stubborn. He stated that he was sent here to get treatment and has little realization of his actual legal status. He will, however, state that he is incompetent to stand trial when he is pressed on this point. He is invariably neatly dressed, and is able to converse rationally and coherently about his problems. He shows no current signs of any thought disorder ... and relates no recent history of hallucinations, delusions, or obsessive behavior. He does relate that in the past he has been troubled with hearing voices.... In his past examinations [he] has presented physicians with the picture of depression, schizophrenia, and sociopathic personality. From the history, it seems to be a case of paranoid schizophrenia which is currently in remission. There is no doubt that [he] has very poor behavioral controls and that the long-term prognosis is rather poor. However, our current problem is to evaluate his competency to stand trial and I feel that at present he is competent to stand trial.

The following is a summary of our contact with this patient, in which we address ourselves particularly to the points raised in the two statements above:

This man in a deliberate and calculating way had built up a steady backlog of mental-illness defenses since the age of 14. In fact, he stated that being found "mentally ill" gave him a license for crime. Were he to be caught, he would go to a hospital, instead of serving a long sentence in prison. One doctor who recognized some of his malingering stated that the man was "crazy like a fox."

He had been a hellion even before his father's death. This man indicated that he never had desired for any period to live the "dull" life of an "ordinary" person. Every crime he committed was an act of choice. In fact, there were many crimes that he chose not to commit because of circumstances at the time that made them infeasible. The breaking into the hospital described in the first report above was a calculated act. At the time, he knew that the police were looking for him for other crimes and that it was only a matter of a very short time before he might be picked up. He then chose a bizarre crime that would establish to others beyond a doubt that he was "crazy." This criminal indicated to us that he had done a lot of reading about schizophrenia and knew well how to fake it behaviorally and on psychologic tests.

We obviously obtained a very different story from this criminal, who finally sought our assistance because he was fed up with his way of life. At no time during our 750 hours with him did we see any sign of mental illness—not even a transient psychotic state (of the type to be described in Chapter 7).

Almost every man we have interviewed has stated emphatically that he does not view himself as mentally ill. Each has acknowledged the role of choice in what he does. Only when he is held accountable and wishes to divest himself of responsibility does he resort to mental illness.*

---

* Once a criminal is convinced that we hold no decision-making power or administrative authority with respect to him, he is willing to speak more candidly to us than he does to hospital staff members.

For a criminal to be mentally ill he must lack the self-control that is so necessary in crime. It is true that, owing to his superoptimism, he may commit an act so brazenly and with such poor judgment that he appears to invite apprehension. Reflecting on it later, he calls himself stupid for getting caught, but not mentally ill. Illness is tantamount to lack of control, and the criminal predicates his life on the control of his own destiny and that of others. He uses the word *sick* or *crazy* to apply to another criminal whom he does not understand or approve of. He calls a criminal "crazy" for being reckless and taking unnecessary risks. "Crazy" sometimes is applied by one criminal to another, because the other is trying to stay away from crime; he is then crazy for staying "out of the action." In addition, one criminal calls another "sick" if the other is in a transient psychosis (although the criminal usually suspects that the psychosis is malingering). It is when he is in personal jeopardy that a criminal calls himself whatever is necessary to excuse what he has done. Being considered mentally ill by others is then acceptable, indeed desirable. In fact, the criminal does his best to convince others of his insanity. Once he accomplishes this and is admitted to a mental hospital, he tries to show others that he is no longer sick. His new objective is to demonstrate a rapid recovery from an illness that he never had.

In a minority of cases, a criminal may have become half-convinced that he is mentally ill (a "half-belief"). That is, he comes to believe an excuse that has "worked" for him. Furthermore, he may have been told so many times that he is "sick" that he comes to think that there may be some truth in it. In the relatively few cases of true psychotic episodes, after the psychosis is over the criminal knows that he has experienced something unusual. If a doctor ties this to his crime, the criminal is pleased, even though he knows that he has not been in crime *during* a psychotic phase. The half-belief in mental illness can be shaken by asking the right questions in the appropriate circumstances. We have encountered no strong opposition by the criminal to disposing of the mental illness concept and emphasizing will and free choice instead. But, of course, the criminal has nothing to gain from us by contending that he is mentally ill. We are not his jailers. He has no points to score with us. In his pretense of mental illness, the criminal actually exercises free choice and in so doing shows how much in control of himself and of others he is.

The criminal chooses to take the accountability situation and make it work for him. Thus, he offers excuses for what he has done, voices his grievances about how others have treated him, and does his best to establish a defense. From the criminal's point of view, it certainly makes sense for him to tell any story that will reduce personal jeopardy. When held accountable, he tries to avoid incrimination. Misrepresentation, vagueness, distortion, and calculated lying are among the means to accomplish this end. He knows that these tactics are *necessary* for him and may even save his life.

The criminal's accountability story follows society's expectations for an excuse or understandable motive. Excuses are abundant and satisfy the criminal's desire to be absolved of responsibility. Enforcement officials seek to establish an acceptable motive for the crime in order to hold the criminal responsible. They prefer to avoid calling a crime "senseless," because this immediately puts the criminal into some mental-illness category. Thus, such motives as jealousy, revenge, money, sexual lust, or some other objective are attributed to the criminal. Superficially, it may appear that there is such a motive—e.g., money in a holdup. We have found that this is not the case. Crimes in which motives are established and "senseless" crimes are identical in being the criminal's means of asserting power and enjoying the attendant excitement. For example, if a criminal youth goes around smashing windows or if he sneakily steals money, the excitement is the same. Broadly speaking, all crimes have a motive—the thrust for power. However, when held accountable, the criminal pleads his victim excuses, and enforcement authorities strive to establish a motive acceptable to the layman.

It could be argued that the criminal distorts or forgets, owing to a normal lapse of memory between the time of apprehension and the time of recounting. In no case in which this was claimed did it turn out to be fact; memories were clear, and details were recalled.

Even before the criminal meets his interrogator, he tries to find out what he is like. In a mental hospital, where the doctor is a known figure, this is relatively easy. In a precinct station or jail, it is usually not possible to gather such information in advance. When the criminal comes face to face with the authority, he makes as careful an examination of the authority as the authority does of him (see Chapter 8). No matter to whom he talks, the criminal's story is colored by "victim" themes. There are two main lines of presentation: being the victim of forces outside himself and being the victim of feelings and various aspects of his personality. If the criminal perceives that blaming others will go against him, he refrains from doing it.

One of the myths that the criminal helps to perpetuate in accountability is that he "wants to get caught." The criminal will go along with this if he thinks it will satisfy the authorities (usually mental health workers). The theoretical background for this formulation is Freud's "Criminality from a Sense of Guilt" (1915) Freud was speaking of children who violated, but grew into adults who were "upright" citizens. His central explanatory concept was that, in addition to these youngsters, some adults do the forbidden to seek punishment, thereby obtaining relief from inescapable, unconscious oedipal guilt. Freud granted that this formulation might not pertain to all criminals, especially those "who transgress without any sense of guilt" (p. 343). The professional literature contains conflicting opinions as to how accurately "unconscious guilt" explains the motivation of a person who leads a criminal life.

> *Unconscious guilt,* or as it is more accurately expressed, the *unconscious need for punishment* . . . surely is the key to all problems of delinquency (Glover, 1960, p. 302).

> I have not been able . . . to discover such a sense of guilt or remorse (conscious or unconscious) in any of the psychopaths I have studied. . . . It strikes me as a quaint fantasy to assume without real evidence that they unconsciously go to such pains to obtain punishment and win redemption for unknown sins when they plainly and glibly ignore responsibility for every known misdemeanor and felony and pride themselves in evading penalties and in flouting the basic principles of justice (Cleckley, 1964, pp. 249, 250).

Our findings support Cleckley. The criminal does everything possible in his scheming to ensure the success of his enterprise. This is what scheming is all about. He may run into trouble through his superoptimism, in which he has cut off fear and is absolutely certain that he will not be apprehended. Superoptimistic thinking is basically unsound, in that it takes the form of "thinking makes it so." But even considering that possibilities are viewed as facts, most criminals are still very cautious in the actual commission of their crimes and take precautions to ensure their safety.

> C told the hospital authorities that he must have wanted to get caught for a rape-homicide. What really happened was a calculated crime in which he bludgeoned his victim only when she screamed. The killing was to avoid apprehension. If he had wanted to get caught, he would not have stifled her scream. He had been very careful in planning this crime to find out about access to the apartment, the safety lock setup, and the means of exit.

Only when he knew that the psychiatric staff believed this "insight" did C say that he wanted to get caught.

In the interest of being a "big man" and establishing a reputation, the criminal may be brazen and reckless in a crime. He may appear to be inviting punishment,* but this does not correspond with his thinking at the time. The criminal may want to make a spectacular impact. For some criminals, it is good "protection" to commit a "wild" act, because, if he is being sought

---

* Salzman (1961, p. 183) pointed out that punishment is not a "goal," but rather an "unexpected and unsought for consequence."

anyway, doing something that seems "crazy" may help him ultimately to beat a charge on the basis of insanity.

Another view is that the criminal wants to get caught to satisfy needs that are not being met elsewhere and can be met only in confinement.

> If a man manages his affairs in such a way that he spends over three-quarters of his life locked up, it is surely not frivolous to suggest that he has found some quality in prison life that is necessary to his psychic security. Freedom can be a desperately threatening condition, and I suspect this may be the untold message of Carasov's book—Review by Kenneth Lamott (1971) of Victor Carasov's *Two Gentlemen to See You, Sir: The Autobiography of a Villain.*

Actually, a man who spends three-fourths of his life in prison has been an unsuccessful criminal. The leap to the conclusion that he wanted to fail, especially in order to seek security in confinement, is an analytic principle that some criminals have also learned. Some people believe that, because a criminal has been hard to manage and therefore in confinement a long time, he must want to remain there. A common next step is to conclude that a criminal is becoming too dependent—that he is "institutionalized"† and should be released as soon as possible. These "insights" also are not accurate. Like other criminals, long-term inmates maneuver to get released. Some tell the staff that they are becoming "institutionalized" if they think it will spur the staff to think about letting them out.

Some observers hold the view that crimes may serve as a "cry for help" or a plea for an authority to provide "structure" and "set limits." These formulations are applied especially to delinquent youths whose behavior is perceived as unconsciously seeking the guidance of adult authority. This conclusion is sometimes reached when a youngster does something so obvious that he can hardly help but be noticed. An example of such superoptimistic carelessness is a teenager's leaving in plain sight a sum of money that his parents know is not properly his. When confronted, the youngster is likely to lie and claim either that the money is not his or that he won, earned, or temporarily borrowed it—anything to try to throw his parents off the track. If a greater advantage is to be gained by telling a part of the truth, he will do so.

> C recalled that one day as a child he had stayed home with his grandmother. He went out and returned with two sodas. He told his grandmother that he bought them with the money he borrowed. However,

---

† "Institutionalization" is used here, as it is frequently in psychiatric parlance, to refer to a patient's remaining in an institution too long for his own good.

she knew that he had been in the house all day and had had no contact with anyone but her. She said, "Tell me the truth and it will be all right." C admitted stealing the sodas, and his grandmother gave him the money to pay the storekeeper.

The central point in all this is that the criminal held accountable responds in whatever way will best serve his advantage. He is quick to discern what others want to hear, and he responds according to how he thinks he can benefit.

PREMEDITATION VS. IMPULSE-COMPULSION

We have indicated that the mind of the criminal who makes crime his "work" is loaded with criminal ideas—far more ideas than he can possibly implement. He weighs the feasibility, practicality, and appeal of these ideas and rejects most of them in a kind of selection process. Some acts are rejected because of external or internal deterrents. With more scheming, deterrents corrode and are finally cut off, leaving the criminal ready and eager to commit a crime. The reader may raise the question as to whether all crimes are so deliberate and premeditated. Newspapers often carry accounts of "impulsive" crime and "crimes of passion," which do not seem based on such scheming and deliberation. We must address this issue.

If we were to speak of a crime as having been committed "impulsively," we would mean that the act was sudden, that hardly any time elapsed between thought and act; and we would be referring to an act that was not deliberate or premeditated.

> [Impulses] betray a characteristic irresistibility, which is different from that of a normal instinctual drive.... "Irresistibility" means that the patients in question are intolerant of tensions. Whatever they need, they must attain immediately (Fenichel, 1945, p. 367).

Similarly, if a crime was the result of a "compulsion," it means that, try as he might, the person could not have acted other than as he did. The action would be forcing itself on the person; it would be something that he "had to do."

> Compulsion: An insistent, repetitive, intrusive and unwanted urge to perform an act which is contrary to the person's ordinary conscious wishes or standards. A defensive substitute for hidden and still more unacceptable ideas and wishes (APA Committee on Public Information. *A Psychiatric Glossary*, 1964, p. 20).

We maintain that the concepts of impulse and compulsion are not applicable to the criminal. Although most writers characterize psychopaths, delinquents, and criminals as impulsive, there are some exceptions.

> The popular hypothesis that delinquents are more impulsive than non-delinquents is not supported by empirical evidence based on standard tests of impulsivity (Saunders et al., 1972, p. 7).

> Paradoxical as it may seem, the true psychopath is the least impulsive of all. Apparent impulsiveness results from the fact that conscience does not stand in the way of action, since conscience is minimal or non-existent. Rather than being hasty, the psychopath often coolly plans his actions as seen in the case of professional criminals; there is none of the hot-headedness that is seen in neurotics and psychotics (Karpman, 1961, p. 619).

Throughout his life, the criminal has considered it a putdown not to be in total command of himself, as well as in control of others. When our criminals use the term "compulsion," what they are talking about is something they want and a state of great inner tension. It is a state of mind in which the criminal experiences what he wants as virtually preying on his mind, with or without attendant psychosomatic manifestations. "Compulsion" (as the criminal speaks of it) is a clash between his *choice* of what he wants to do and his *choice* of restraint. If the risks are too great, the criminal does not act. Compulsion (again, as the criminal uses the term) amounts to a choice of a desire that overcomes a choice of deterrents. We have described how this occurs through corrosion and cutoff. To use the term "compulsion" properly, one would *not* apply it to a strong, persistent desire that is under conscious control.

The dictionary definition of premeditation that is basic and widely agreed on is "the act of speculating, arranging, or plotting in advance" (*The American Heritage Dictionary*, 1969, p. 1034). Premeditation involves awareness and evaluation of an idea. The criminal may plan the act down to the last detail, specifying person, location, time, and contingency plans. However, the act may not be so totally calculated. The criminal may consider and deter an idea over and over until conditions are favorable. Thinking about an act and discarding the idea, only to have it pop up again, may recur hundreds of times before it is implemented.

Crimes are often described as "impulsive," owing to the speed with which they occurred. However, what appears to be an instant and therefore impulsive act has a history of premeditation behind it. The more we know of the criminal mind, the more we understand that a man may plot and scheme for a very long time. There is nothing "irresistible" about what he does, no pressing *need* to commit the crime immediately if there are *good reasons* to delay. The criminal may consider engaging in a crime, but simply wait for the best occasion to do so. The idea does not die by a choice of deterrence alone. Although he may have chosen to deter it many times, it is still alive. The crime is the outcome of a habitual pattern of thinking that is eventually put into instant operation, just as an electric light responds to the touch of a switch. The actual occurrence of the crime may be lightning-fast, but the idea has had a period of incubation. In our experience, no criminal has ever suddenly done something that he has not *repeatedly* considered before.

The criminal is mentally ready to commit crimes of one or more types. He may not have chosen a particular time and place, but he is ready for any occasion.

> At the store, C often had thoughts about killing two men who came in and caused a commotion. Whenever he thought about them, it was in terms of killing.

In such a situation, the criminal is geared mentally to the idea of killing. The idea may have occurred hundreds of times. That is, there is a pattern of thinking as to how to deal with people who put him down by thwarting his objectives. The thinking remains alive and is subject to expression at an undetermined time. A variety of circumstances determine the commission. A "crime of circumstance" occurs when a person who has fantasied a crime (but not the details of its execution) one day encounters a suitable opportunity and implements it. The crime itself appears to be impulsive, because of its suddenness, but the fantasy pattern has occurred repeatedly. As one man said, "What do you expect me to do with [the fantasy] in the middle of the night?" To the observer, the crime may be totally out of character for a person who has not been a "criminal." But in every case that we have studied, we have established that the crime at issue was preceded by long-standing violating patterns in thought and action. We were able to ascertain this only after developing new techniques (which we shall describe in Volume 2). Using these procedures in long interviews, we have determined the thinking before criminal acts that happened so quickly as to appear "impulsive."

What we are calling "crimes of circumstance" have also been called "crimes of passion." In the following case, a homicide occurred suddenly. The exact time and place had not been determined in advance, but it was not impulsive. Rather, the criminal had had thoughts of harming the victim, and several incidents of violence preceded the homicide.

> C's wife, Carol, began asking him for more and more money and then denied him sex to get it. Around payday, she would cooperate with him

sexually. The money would go fast, as Carol began drinking more heavily. The two separated. On at least three occasions, their arguments were intense enough for C to slap her. Once, when she was out, C came to the house and slashed her clothes with a knife. She never knew who had done this. One Saturday, Carol did not come home until 5 A.M. On her return, C, who was waiting for her, found a picture of a boyfriend in her purse. She gave excuses, and he slapped her again. This pattern went on for some time, with both drinking heavily. At times, Carol would disappear for days. One afternoon, she made it clear to C that she wanted nothing more to do with him. He pleaded with her to stay. She angrily called him a "black one-eyed bastard," at which point he threw her to the floor and stabbed her with a knife that he had been carrying. He then calmly left the house, leaving her to die, and went to visit his parents in another state. His father, a local preacher, was mortified at what had happened and advised his son to return and to say that he had done what he did because of his drinking. At the precinct station, C stated that he had been drinking and had amnesia for what had happened, although he confessed to having committed the crime. In the hospital, he also claimed amnesia and was diagnosed "schizophrenic." He was told that until the amnesia cleared, he could not get out. Soon, he reported that he remembered what had happened. He was declared competent to stand trial and then found not guilty by reason of insanity. On the hospital grounds, he continued his criminality, although not to the point of homicide.

There was no carefully planned scheme to stab his wife on that particular day. However, by our methods, we learned that C had repeatedly thought of killing his wife. He had already slapped her around and had used a knife on her property. In response to the putdown of "black one-eyed bastard," he murdered her. This was the last straw, the culmination of months of criminal thinking and action with respect to her. (There was, of course, no amnesia.) Such acts are not uncommon. Indeed, it is often said that most homicides are family affairs.* To many observers and psychiatrists, the criminal's behavior appears to be impulsive because of its suddenness. We have found that the so-called impulsive crime occurs many times in the criminal's mind before it is committed.

Another kind of seemingly impulsive crime depends on an established M.O. For example, if a housebreaker has mapped out where he is going on his "daily tour," but sees an unattended loaded car en route, he may decide not to pass it up. He takes advantage of the ready-made situation, assuming all the necessary precautions, as he does in his other break-ins. There is nothing "impulsive" in this; the man is supplementing his daily routine; his M.O. is well ingrained, and this is just one more "job." (It is

---

* See, e.g., *The New York Times*, 9/3/67, p. 40.

analogous to setting out on a Sunday to look at two houses advertised in the newspaper, seeing another "Open: For Sale" sign on the way home, and stopping to look at the third house.) We call a crime committed in this manner an "opportunistic crime." It differs from the "crime of circumstance" or "passion" in which antecedent thinking about a particular crime is ultimately implemented when circumstances allow.

The criminal resorts to whatever he deems necessary to deal with a threat to his control of a situation. Many follow the basic pattern shown in the following specific instance.

> C held up a public official and his wife as they were getting into their car. When the man came around the side of the car, C saw him as "going to play the superman hero" and shot him in the stomach.

C did not plan to shoot the victim. But he perceived the man as putting him into jeopardy and responded with a well-patterned contingency. An even more explicit example is the following, in which the criminal verbally warned the victims of what might occur.

> C indicated that he not only gives his victim a choice in his own mind, but announces it to them. He tells them that he will not shoot if they will not stir up any trouble. But he warns them that, if they do, he will have no compunction about firing.

Every criminal has his way of dealing with the question of what to do if someone interferes. Not all announce it.

"Impulse" and "compulsion" are applied with great frequency to sexual crimes.

> C was found not guilty of rape and robbery by reason of insanity. His hospital records stated: "The patient does seem to have poor control of his sexual and aggressive impulses. . . . He is certainly obsessed in his thinking of sexual matters. . . . There is also some compulsively connected with his antisocial acts. He indicates considerable tension and excitement and a very strong drive to commit these antisocial acts and says that he has been unable to resist committing them at any time. Diagnosis: Obsessive-Compulsive Reaction"

The idea of irresistible impulse is that a "drive" is so urgent that the criminal cannot control himself. C's rape and robbery patterns contained not only the element of premeditation, but also a frequently implemented decision to delay or forgo the action altogether if there was any thought that apprehension was likely to occur. C admitted that in one situation he had followed a woman to her apartment, but that on that night the circumstances were not favorable to commit the rape. The next night, he returned, assessed the situation, and found conditions more suitable. He entered the apartment and raped her. This scheme was executed after a twenty-four-hour delay. No irresistible impulse had propelled him into immediate action.

Classifying criminals according to type of crime is pointless. Any of them can do almost anything at any time, owing to the violating patterns that have been present in their thinking. When a "Madison Avenue" executive cracks someone's skull, it is no surprise to us, because we know that, even if he has never been violent before, violence has been present in his thoughts as a way in which he would like to deal with the world.

The criminal even goes so far as to scheme or premeditate about what might happen if he is apprehended. Chapter 3 contains a description of some of the maneuvers of criminals who knew in advance the tactics that they would use if they were apprehended. This does not mean that any of these people planned to get caught, but rather that they recognized that it was likely to happen one day and therefore had contingency plans. This was especially obvious in cases in which the criminal planned a mental-illness defense.

In summary, all specific criminal acts are programmed in the thinking of the criminal. Impulse and compulsion imply loss of control. But all his life, the criminal has been calculating, scheming, and controlling. His behavior may *appear* to be impulsive or compulsive, because it is sudden to the observer. In no case has impulse or compulsion held up. No crimes have occurred when they were thought of for the first time. No criminal is foolish enough to act so rashly. Incipient criminal thinking has preceded the crime in question. The idea has been considered, but rejected, many times before. The crime occurs after deterrents have corroded and been cut off. When a specific crime, such as an assault, has not been planned in advance, it is a matter of the criminal's responding in a habitual manner. He still maintains control of his behavior. All of us are habituated to doing some things in a specific way, such as driving an automobile; but we maintain control over what we do. To say that a pattern is ingrained or habitual does not diminish personal responsibility or decision-making capacity. To avoid a penalty, the criminal may try to convince others that he acted impulsively. What has been so striking and consistent is that, to a man, our criminals have eventually revealed to us that what they did was an exercise of choice, and that all crimes were products of prior thinking.

THE EFFECTIVENESS OF DETERRENTS

For a long time, society practiced retribution: if a man were convicted of a violation, he was to be punished. The old idea was that the punishment should fit the crime: "An eye for an eye, and a tooth for a tooth." Later, the concept was advanced that punishment should have more of a deterrent function. It was to serve as a lesson to the lawbreaker, so that he would learn that "crime doesn't pay" and would not repeat his offenses. But penalties also were imposed to demonstrate to others that they too would suffer undesirable consequences, most notably a loss of freedom, if they broke the law.

Society's views have changed. Many now think that punishment as a deterrent does not work. They point to the high rate of recidivism to support that contention. Judge David Bazelon of the United States Court of Appeals (1961) maintained that deterrence that relies on punishment is not effective. Furthermore, he stated that punishing one person to deter another is immoral and not in keeping with the ethos of a democracy. A similar view was voiced strongly by Karl Menninger (1968) in *The Crime of Punishment:*

> To renounce vengeance as a motive for punishing offenders leaves us with the equivocal justification of deterrence. This is a weak and vulnerable argument indeed, for the effects of punishment in this direction cannot be demonstrated by sound evidence or research. Furthermore, to make an example of an offender so as to discourage others from criminal acts is to make him suffer not for what he has done alone but because of *other* people's tendencies. Nevertheless the deterrence theory is used widely as a cloak for vengeance (p. 206).

Many workers in a variety of disciplines have been sympathetic to this point of view. In the literature review of Volume 2, we shall present a brief history of the changing social attitudes and practices on this issue. For the moment, we offer some facts based on a dissection of the criminal's thinking, without entering into moral or political aspects of deterrence.

To understand the impact of punishment, some investigators have gone back to childhood experiences. Excessive punitiveness and permissiveness in child-rearing have both been viewed as having unfavorable results.

> While too much punishment for aggression may lead to heightened aggressive motives, too much permissiveness of the child's aggression may act as a reward and lead to an increase in the frequency of overt aggression (Mussen, Paul H. et al., 1963, p. 285).

In Chapter 3, we noted that the criminals in our study come from homes that displayed the whole spectrum of disciplinary practices. Some are from families that were explicit in their expectations and swift and severe in the administration of punishment when these expectations were not fulfilled.

Others had parents who constantly made allowances for their behavior and rarely punished them. There was an intermediate group in which the child was neither indulged nor punished severely, but encouraged by his parents to participate in family decisions in what might be called a "democratic parent-child relationship." Regardless of the pattern of the parents in rearing their young, these criminal children violated early in life and continued to do so with increasing frequency and severity as they grew older.

Some people have called for stiffer penalties, in the hope that, if a criminal knows that execution or a long sentence is in store for him, he will be less likely to commit a crime. When severe penalties are discussed, criminals agree that they do have a deterrent effect. The trouble is that there is a difference between academic discussion or accountability reasoning and what actually occurs in the criminal's mind as he thinks about and commits a crime. Whatever deterrents there are get cut off, and the criminal becomes superoptimistic. The issue in his mind is not the severity of the penalty, but the possibility of apprehension. When he is superoptimistic about this, the penalty is of no significance whatsoever. It is not even a consideration in his thinking. At most, it prolongs the inner debate about the likelihood of apprehension. That is, if the penalties are known to be great, the criminal may take greater precautions. But he eventually goes ahead with the crime. There are several additional reasons that the prospect of a stiff sentence or execution does not deter the brash criminal. He believes that he will not get caught; if caught, that he will not be convicted; if convicted, that he will not be executed or confined for long. These beliefs have considerable basis in fact. The criminal knows from experience that the odds are with him; he has been caught very few times, despite many violations. He also knows that the death penalty is rarely meted out.

The threat of a long sentence may serve as a temporary deterrent for the criminal who has already served a long term in confinement. Some criminals who have just been released from the penitentiary say that they have recurrent thoughts and even dreams about being behind bars and that this is a potent deterrent—moreso than any law. Others have reported while in confinement, or shortly thereafter, that, if they violate in the future, they will be "misdemeanor criminals" and not risk long sentences. However, these criminals do not remain satisfied with petty crimes. As they get away with small offenses, they again move on to more serious crimes. In most cases, external deterrents do not hold. They are more effective for the aging hard-core criminal, who is not as agile as he used to be and who has had enough of confinement.

Strong external deterrents occasionally have an effect opposite to that intended. The increasing possibility of apprehension can incite the criminal to be that much more calculating and adroit. He may then learn enough to be able to outwit the authorities if he is confronted by them. Even a pending sentence may fail to interfere with the execution of a crime.

> Some bank robbers were to be sentenced on a Wednesday morning, having been convicted of a bank robbery. They were out on bond. Their lawyer requested a 24-hour delay in the sentencing. Actually, these criminals had arranged a setup for yet another bank robbery. Fortunately, the judge refused the delay, and the holdup did not occur.

The more society tightens its security and surveillance, the more ingenious the criminal must be. A double triumph is possible: the commission of the forbidden act and success in overcoming the more watchful authorities. In other words, the criminal may respond to considerably increased personal jeopardy as a challenge to prove his mettle as a criminal.

Scheming is the process of eliminating external deterrents. Actually, the fear generated by external deterrents is necessary for a criminal to be successful. One man commented to us, "When I'm not afraid, I'm finished." That is, the fear of being caught contributed to his perfecting his scheme and taking more precautions in the execution of the act.

A few criminals claim to find a crime more exciting *because* it is serious enough to warrant a long sentence. However, this is usually an observation that a criminal makes after a crime, when he is boasting. In confinement, he can build himself into something of a celebrity by talking, for example, about the odds that he had to overcome with the squad car in the neighborhood. He may well have had no idea that the car was there and was surprised in the act. But this is not the way he relates it to others.

The effectiveness of deterrents cannot be assessed unless one probes the minds of people who occupy different points on the criminal continuum. Recidivism statistics present only numbers and do not tell how the criminal's mind works. Society does not know how many crimes were prevented by existing laws and enforcement procedures. We have found that external deterrents do prevent many crimes, or at least diminish the seriousness of some crimes. Clearly, the extreme hard-core criminal is deterred the least. But even he decides against a crime when the odds of getting caught are very high. From our experience with less extreme criminals, we know that strong external deterrents reduce their involvement in criminal activities. For example, a security guard reported to us that fewer prostitutes hung around a downtown Washington hotel during the Brezhnev visit in 1973, and no thefts were reported in the area. This was because security generally was much tighter. After the Russian party left, crime on the hotel's premises rose to its former incidence. Conversely, we were informed that during the Presidential inauguration of 1969 there were more than the usual number of reports of robberies, because police concentration was heavy around the Capitol and Pennsylvania Avenue, the scene of the inaugural parade, diluting coverage in other areas. Security officials in stores have attributed a decrease in shoplifting in some establishments to the increased presence of detectives and a public awareness of the merchants' rigid prosecution policies, plus the tendency of judges to mete out stiffer sentences (see, e.g., *The Washington Post*, 12/22/72, p. A1). The housewife who engages in shoplifting and gets caught may be deterred for life by the consequences, and publicity about the incident may deter others contemplating the same type of activity.

Mrs. Jones Goes to Jail

She wouldn't head anybody's list of criminal types. She's 41 years old. Her husband owns a small business. She has three children and is an active member of a PTA.

But Mrs. Jones (not her real name) is an ex-con. Last week Fairfax County Judge Martin E. Morris ordered her jailed two days for shoplifting. . . .

She adds retrospectively, "I learned enough in one night in jail to last lifetime." . . . She has one word of advice for prospective shoplifters: "Don't" (*Northern Virginia Sentinel*, 2/15/73, p. A1).

In short, with less extreme criminals like Mrs. Jones, external deterrents are effective, and internal deterrents are also effective because they are not easily cut off. For extreme criminals, external and internal deterrents are brief and quickly cut off.

BIBLIOGRAPHY

American Heritage Dictionary. Boston: Houghton Mifflin, 1969.

American Psychiatric Association Committee on Public Information. *A Psychiatric Glossary*. Washington, D.C.: American Psychiatric Association, 1964.

Arnold, Mark R. "The Silent Murders," *National Observer*, September 6, 1971, p. 1.

Bazelon, David. *Equal Justice for the Unequal*. Isaac Ray Lectureship Award Series of the American Psychiatric Assocation. Lecture #3, 1961.

Claster, Daniel. "Comparison of Risk Perception between Delinquents and Non-Delinquents," *Journal of Criminal Law, Criminology and Police Science*, 1967, *58*, 80-86.

Cleckley, Hervey. *The Mask of Sanity*. (4th edit.) St. Louis: C. V. Mosby, 1964.

Cromley, Ray. "New Criminal," *The Washington Daily News*, June 8, 1972.

Fenichel, Otto. *The Psychoanalytic Theory of Neurosis*. New York: Norton, 1945.

Freud, S. "Some Character-Types Met with in Psycho-analytic Work," (1915), in *Collected Papers*. Vol. 4. London: Hogarth, 1946, 318-344.

"Get-Tough Methods Crimp Shoplifter Style," *The Washington Post*, December 22, 1972, p. A1.

Glover , Edward. *The Roots of Crime*. New York: International Universities Press, 1960.

Jensen, Gary F. " 'Crime Doesn't Pay': Correlates of a Shared Misunderstanding," *Social Problems*, 1969, *17*, 189-201.

Kaplan, J. D. (Ed.) *Dialogues of Plato*. New York: Pocket Books, 1959.

Karpman, Ben. "The Structure of Neuroses: With Special Differentials between Neurosis, Psychosis, Homosexuality, Alcoholism, Psychopathy and Criminality," *Archives of Criminal Psychodynamics*, 1961, *4*, 599-646.

Lamott, Kenneth. "The Prison Pattern," *Book World* (in *The Washington Post*), November 21, 1971.

Letkemann, Peter. *Crime as Work*. Englewood Cliffs, N.J.: Prentice-Hall, 1973.

Maurer, David W. *The American Confidence Man*. Springfield, Ill.: Charles C Thomas, 1974.

Menninger, Karl. *The Crime of Punishment*. New York: Viking Press, 1968.

"Most Murders Found Committed in Families or Among Friends," *The New York Times*, September 3, 1967, p. 40.

"Mrs. Jones Goes to Jail," *Northern Virginia Sentinel*, February 15, 1973, p. A1.

Mussen, Paul H., et al. *Child Development and Personality*. (2nd edit.) New York: Harper and Row, 1963.

Salzman, Leon. "Guilt, Responsibility and the Unconscious," *Comprehensive Psychiatry*, 1961, *2*, 179-187.

Saunders, J. T., et al. "An Examination of Impulsivity as a Trait Characterizing Delinquent Youth." Paper presented at the 80th annual convention of the American Psychological Association, Honolulu, Hawaii, September, 1972 (reprint).

"Slain Suspect Kept Diary of 29 Assaults," *The Washington Post*, July 13, 1971, p. C1.

Uehling, Harold F. "Group Therapy Turns Repression into Expression for Prison Inmates," *Federal Probation*, *26*:1, March 1962, 43-49.

Chapter 7

Nonarrestable Phases in the Criminal

WE HAVE SAID that the criminal is fragmented. This means that his thinking and the resulting behavior shift frequently in accordance with what he wants, often changing many times within a single hour. However, he goes through phases of thinking that last for a relatively longer time. They may be concurrent or successive, triggered by external events or independent of them. They are all the results of choice, except for psychosis, which has elements of choice in terms of how the criminal deals with it.

The phases of thinking discussed here we have designated criminal equivalents, limbo, monasticism, suicide, and psychosis. We speak of nonarrestable phases, but the reader should know that, when the criminal is in criminal equivalent and limbo phases, he remains active in crime, although sometimes on a reduced level. These mental states are alternatives to crime. In each state, criminal thinking processes are evident, but they are expressed differently. The reader must keep in mind the concept of the continuum of criminality and should understand that, when we describe criminal equivalents in police work, politics, or the arts, we are *not* saying that all policemen, politicians, or artists are criminals, but that a small group of people in these professions share some mental processes with the criminal. To retain perspective, the reader should be aware that this section, like all the others, has as its focus the person who is at the extreme end of the criminal continuum.

CRIMINAL EQUIVALENTS

A criminal who is not thrusting for power through crime may be doing it in other ways. He may be simultaneously involved in arrestable crime and be thrusting for power in a nonarrestable activity. We have pointed out that the noncriminal achieves power through responsible conduct and generally uses it for constructive purposes. Not all power-seekers are criminal. Many people hold power legitimately and steadfastly resist the abuse of it. When we speak of a "criminal equivalent," we are referring to an action or series of actions in which a criminal seeks *power for its own sake.* Wherever the criminal is—at home, at school, at work, on the street—he seeks to promote himself, usually at the expense of others. His doing something for someone else is a criminal equivalent, because his purposes are self-serving; he thinks of it in terms that enhance his image of himself as a good person. His reason for doing a favor is not that he believes in helping others as a way of life. Everywhere a criminal goes, even in confinement, he tries to run things. Criminal equivalents may be expressed hundreds of times a day as continuing expressions of what a man is. Criminal equivalents are expressed in the speed and recklessness with which criminals drive cars and motorcycles, in the clothes they wear, by the way they boast, lie, and take over conversations. Equivalents are present in even the smallest transactions.

Criminal equivalents may involve individual acts like the ones just described, or they may characterize a criminal's long-range performance. One can find criminals in any field; no profession or trade is immune. However, power-wielding is part of the job in some occupations, thus making it easier for the criminal to seek excitement along legitimate lines. But the criminal eventually abuses power within these arenas or seeks further conquests outside and returns to crime.

Some schools and communities have found that one way to divert youngsters from delinquency is to appeal to their interest in law enforcement and to invite them to function on security patrols (*Parade*, 4/18/71, p. 18). Hardened criminals have shown an interest in enforcement, inventing antitheft devices (*The Evening Star and the Washington Daily News*, 4/15/73, p. B1) and becoming crimefighters in confinement settings (Kiger, 1967). Some of our criminals have entered law enforcement work as policemen or security guards. They have been able to do this either because they lacked criminal records* or because their employers failed to conduct complete background checks.

> C was neatly dressed in a security guard uniform with the handcuffs sticking out prominently from his belt. He spoke of the apartment complex at which he worked. C launched into a severe criticism of the manager, who he said had a "chip on his shoulder." He stated that he arrested two people in the apartment, one in the numbers racket and

---

* Criminals found NGBRI (not guilty by reason of insanity) do not have the crimes for which they were arrested recorded on official police records. Of course, the records are inaccurate to begin with, because criminals commit many crimes, but are rarely apprehended.

the other in narcotics. He accused the manager of being involved with the numbers man; as a consequence, the manager was fined $500. C and the manager argued so intensely that on one occasion C called the police, who refused to take action. One reason that C wanted to be a security guard was to get a gun. Although he could not legitimately use it on the outside, he could keep it at home.

As things turned out, C's regular confrontations with the manager ultimately became intolerable and he was fired. It was clear from his description of his work that for a while he enjoyed being a guard. Having the authority to detain people, working with the police, playing detective, and eventually having a gun were all appealing aspects of the job. In another case, a criminal worked as a security officer at a large hotel. He experienced all the excitement of conducting security checks, evicting "undesirables," teaming up with the police to crack some cases, and testifying in court. On this job, he sought out for sex the very prostitute against whom he had testified in an earlier hearing. In a previous security position, he had stolen valuables from the very hotel rooms that he was supposed to be protecting.

Recognizing that police work attracts some people who are fascinated by crime and who have criminal "tendencies," behavioral scientists are beginning to help police departments refine their selection procedures. Mills (1972), a psychologist, viewed excitement-seeking as an unfavorable motive for police work. An Illinois consulting firm evaluated candidates for the police and fire departments and found that 10-15 percent of the applicants were criminals (*Time,* 8/28/72). The leading reasons for disqualifying applicants for positions on the Fairfax County, Va., police force were falsification of applications, "basic dishonesty," disregarding moral values, and extensive use of illegal drugs (*Virginia Sentinel,* 1/4/73). Wide-scale corruption in police forces around the country has been publicized in the media. In the course of our work, it has become evident that being a policeman allows a criminal to exercise the same mental processes and M.O.'s that he uses in crime. Another pertinent aspect of law enforcement and related fields is that the criminal experiences vicarious pleasure in his contact with other criminals. We have found this to be true of lawyers who worked in criminal law, but were themselves criminals: "Shortly before my arrest, I tried and won an armed-robbery case. It was the most exciting thing I've done." The preparation for the trial was so time-consuming and absorbing that arrestable activities were not necessary to achieve a state of excitement. Shortly after the trial, with his excitement ended, the lawyer resumed criminal activities for which he eventually was arrested.

Some criminals utilize fire fighting as a criminal equivalent, rather than engaging in it for a social service. Speeding through traffic in the large trucks, making dramatic rescues, and controlling crowds and the fire itself all offer excitement. For some criminals, volunteer fire fighting does not suffice. A few set fires and then help extinguish the blaze. (We know of cases in which they have been indicted.) One of our criminals had a thorough knowledge of the various types of firefighting equipment and spent hours in listening to radio calls for police and firemen.

> While listening to the fire calls on his short-wave radio, C visualized the operation. He had elaborate lists of the fire departments in the area and their equipment. As he listened to the radio, he thought of the expert direction he would give if he were present. C viewed himself as managing the entire operation, deciding the most efficient way to put out the fire.

C set fires, sounded the alarm, and then appeared at the scene as a volunteer fire fighter. Helping to put out the blaze was a criminal equivalent that added to the original arson.

Politics is another field that by its very nature lends itself to the abuse of power. There is little need to offer documentation here, other than to refer to the many newspaper accounts of corruption on national, state, and local levels.

Some criminals are adept at gaining a forum and attracting listeners. Owing to their energy and ability, they work their way into organizations and reach positions of leadership. When one criminal went to look for a job as a hotel clerk, the impression he created was so favorable that he was told that he belonged on Capitol Hill. Accepting the idea, he joined, through family contacts, a civic commission and went on the lecture circuit to speak on local issues. This man—without a college education, without a career, and without a job—was welcomed by people eager to hear what he had to say. The propulsion into the limelight was as exciting to him as many of the arrestable things that he had done. He could listen to the proceedings of a presidential nominating convention and easily see himself on the podium in the near future.

Another of our criminals, whose repertoire included almost every kind of arrestable crime we have come across, wrote to us that he had decided to "go straight." He had established a new corporation, which he named, after himself, "[C] Enterprises." C told us that he was accomplishing what he had always wanted, but was staying within the law. The criminal equivalents in what he called "honest living" will be apparent to the reader:

> "The ease with which I have made a success of honest living, if that is what it is called, and that is what everyone else calls it, so I will do the same, has been unbelievable. In fact it is so simple that as I told

you I am very much ashamed of the stupidity that went into the years I wasted being a crook. Today I am a man with a little brains, some experience in life and the ability to talk, to do anything he wants to and when I say 'do anything he wants to,' I mean he can set himself up a business and can make himself well liked and respected and very successful in a short period of time. All he has to do is give them what they want or what they think they want.

"[C] Enterprises has many clients. [C] Enterprises is handling the refinancing of a local hospital.... I am raising the money that is necessary.... The way [financial consultants] figure it, I should raise $15 million, of which I will receive 12½%. Do you think I will raise $15 million? Hell no, I have no thought of raising that much money. But, I know damn well I could raise $2 to $3 million and naturally that's a nice piece of money in anybody's language.... I am dickering with three publishers [to do some publishing to raise money] but so far they are not quite ready to meet my terms. You wonder what terms they are? They are my moral terms. (Laugh) You see, nobody but nobody is going to do anything, even in the name of a good charity like ——— Hospital, that is going to be high pressure, off color, illegal, or fattening. Ha... You would be surprised at the nice, honest people out there who want a piece of some action, but want to do it their way with the corners cut here and there.... Me—I don't mess with crooks.... I am known as one of the most scrupulously honest promoters in the city."

With no capital and no experience in running a business, C bragged and misrepresented himself to others. He created an organization solely by printing stationery and presenting himself as a successful entrepreneur. His objective was ultimately to become a financial "big shot," with arrestable crime unnecessary. He argued that such power (a criminal equivalent) would provide sufficient excitement. He would operate legally, not write bad checks, forge documents, or swindle people as he had been doing with great frequency. However, C's intentions were not sustained, because he still wanted other excitements. It was not long thereafter that he returned to crime not involving "[C] Enterprises," was apprehended, and went to prison.

Another man organized a church in which, by simple designation, he became a minister, although he had no ministerial training. In this capacity, he was paid living expenses, travel and clothing allowances, maintenance, and a salary. All this and the community's recognition did not give him what he wanted. He too returned to crime.

A criminal may become an activist in social movements. He may appear to have a sense of social justice, through decrying social injustice. However, on examination it becomes evident that he is merely building himself up by frequent, glib, superficial rhetoric. Although he may forcefully present himself as a spokesman for the oppressed, he is using his cause as a vehicle for self-aggrandizement. Some prefer to be the "brains" behind a movement.

> "People have got to pay attenton to me. I mean you're not being very effective if people don't pay attention.... I presuppose I'm going to have something valid to say to people and they're going to benefit by having heard it.... I doubt that I'd throw my body in to stop the machine.... I would be frightened by a lot of shouting. I could never be a good revolutionary.... I'm the theoretician [who] stays in the background and runs the show."

For those who take direct action, the excitement of the event outweighs the merit of the cause. One criminal emphasized this point in describing his participation in a civil rights march.

> "It was a completely new thing, very exciting, kind of dangerous and immensely rewarding. I got some first hand experience with a sheriff's posse. They broke up a march with their horses and billy clubs. I was prodded a couple of times.... Eight people were hospitalized. They trapped people into situations where they could inflict as much violence as they could.... There were all kinds of things for us to do when we got back. There was a reporter with us, giving massive publicity and we had meetings and talks and things. We were kind of campus heroes...."

Political extremism can be a criminal equivalent and may in some cases involve outright criminal acts. Extremists on both the right and the left have been known to engage in assault, burglary, kidnapping, hijacking, bombing, torture, killing, and various other forms of criminality, all of which they justify with the rhetoric of the cause.

Many of our criminals have held positions in the "helping" professions. Here, the criminal equivalents are enormous, as the person becomes reformer, adviser, and source of knowledge. Some function in such a capacity with bona fide credentials, whereas others operate wholly on the basis of misrepresentation and pretense. In Chapter 3, we mentioned criminals who acted as physicians, although they had no medical training. One criminal—without a college degree, untrained, and unlicensed—worked as a director of treatment in a center for delinquents.

> "We established [my] version of a psychotherapeutic community.... I had never seen a therapeutic community. Yet I took upon my shoulders a whole program and the lives and future of five kids.... I was doing so well with this that I became bolder. [He went on to direct psychodrama.] My success was such that overnight I became a 'psychodramatist.' I was interviewed by [a radio station] and was called to give a lecture on psychodrama to the nurses in [a] mental health service and

I was hired as a consultant at $25 an hour at [a] school for delinquent children. I started actually believing my own myth."

This man's criminal outlet for a while was in being guru, therapist, and teacher. Later, he utilized his "therapeutic skills" in activities other than therapy. At one point, he was an insurance salesman and won clients and friends on first contact.

"Oh I was smooth and savvy! She was captivated. I sold her a $10 a month 'savings plan.' Soon, she told me the story of her life. In retrospect, I can see now how I used my 'therapeutic techniques' during my 'selling interview.' At the moment of the 'close,' they were doing what their 'therapist' advised them, not what a salesman was peddling."

Whether he was therapist, con man, or salesman, what was important was achieving influence over the patient and clients, some of whom he later seduced and exploited. Social trends have made it possible and even desirable for criminals to become counselors, therapists, and administrators of entire programs. In Volume 2, we shall direct attention to both the arrestable and nonarrestable criminality in "ex-con" counselors and indicate why the term "ex-con" itself is a misnomer. In every instance in our experience, the criminals who served as counselors or therapists have themselves reverted to patterns of irresponsible and arrestable behavior.

We have referred (see Chapter 3) to the appeal of careers in the clergy for some criminals. Several of our people had religious training. It would be accurate to say that they were far more interested in getting out of the seminary than in getting anything out of their education. They had ideas of being among the greatest preachers of all time or of being important missionaries. One of the appealing aspects of the ministry for the criminal is that he is the head man. He is considered by some of his congregants as the "closest to God" and enjoys great prestige in his position as spiritual leader. In addition, he has considerable influence in running the activities and setting the policies of the church. The ministry does not satisfy the desire for excitement in the clergyman who is at the extreme criminal end of the criminal continuum, and so we have found ministers who do the immoral and the frankly illegal.

C was a minister of an important southern congregation. He enjoyed his preaching and commented in an interview with us that one reason for this was that [his congregants] can't talk back." He described religion as a "Linus blanket"—a kind of protective mantle by which he built up an image of himself as a righteous man. However, he violated his own church's teachings about smoking and drinking. He lied without hesitation when it was a matter of protecting his reputation. C stated that, if he were sure he could get away with it, he would not be beyond taking money out of the church's till. Actually, he was rather circumspect about taking chances, until, in what turned out to be a highly publicized case, he was arrested for interstate transportation of pornographic materials.

Father C was partial to criminals who had artistic talents. One criminal who was an accomplished sculptor decided to create a life-size statue of Christ. Father C was so enamored of the statue that, when it was completed, he had a truck remove the statue to the chapel without the permission of the sculptor. In the haste of moving, it was damaged. To mollify the artist, the priest promised him favors and concessions. Father C wanted the statue painted. The sculptor objected; he thought it should be left in its natural state. Over his objections, Father C hired someone to paint the statue. It happened that the artist was later put into solitary confinement. At that time, Father C credited the person who painted the statue with the entire creation, omitting the name of the sculptor. Eventually, the sculptor committed suicide. It is not known what role, if any, this series of events had in the suicide.

Father C had been involved in countless deceptive practices like this. He was known to the inmates as "a great guy," one who would bring in contraband, deliver unauthorized messages, and do various other favors. What we have observed over many years is a shocking revelation to the public when similar incidents occasionally come to light in the news.

The Evening Star, 3-12-71
[Reverend] Arrested on Assault Count

The Washington Post, 10-17-71
Four Rabbis Charged in Bilking Case

The Washington Post, 3-11-73
Minister in District Charged in Sex Case

Criminal thinking patterns occur in *some* artists, and these were poignantly described to us by an architect who frankly discussed criminal features of his own personality, although he was not at the extreme criminal end of the continuum.

Mr. M stated that some artists do not abide what is repetitious and routine. They seek to "anoint themselves with pleasure" and do anything to get pleasure. However, they do not run "too far afoul" of society. Such an artist is hypocritical, in that he makes his living through the "trappings of deceit" and yet calls for authenticity. Mr. M described some well-known painters as being "Pied Pipers" whom people blindly follow when all the artists are doing is "putting them on." He described such artists as masters of "oneupmanship" who may resort to mechanical tricks to achieve their effects and let this substitute for real talent. He pointed out that these artists do a "flimflam job," in that they take a painting, stick a price tag on it, tell the consumer how much blood and sweat went into it, and then state that they really do not want to sell it. This only makes the customer more eager to have it. Mr. M believed that such artists get their kicks out of "drawing things out," making people pay and think they are really getting something. He regarded the criminal and some artists as similar, because both get their kicks at the expense of innocent victims.

Mr. M pointed to the criminality in himself. He wants beauty and pleasure with no strings attached and will violate principle in this pursuit. He stated that to live a normal life, as most people do, would be intolerable. Early in life, he had done some stealing. He wanted to be a fighter, but was a coward. He admitted with some embarrassment that on one occasion he had so enjoyed beating his son with a belt that it produced an erection. His wife said about him, "You use so much force and break things when you are angry." Mr. M would kick the door, slam it, and break objects, such as a stove or a TV knob. His wife described him as a Jekyll and Hyde with respect to his angry and more placid states. Mr. M chose to live beyond his means. His home, which he designed himself, was more expensive than the others in the neighborhood. The home was built against his wife's wishes and out of personal vanity—he wanted the most expensive and the most different. The construction was shoddy, and much rebuilding was needed. For him, "good taste" meant having the very best. This applied to everything, including such items as cameras. In 25 years, he had gone through 12 cameras, the last of which cost more than $500.

This is one man's self-analysis of his character, in response to our questions. Among our group, several men have utilized their artistic talents for a power thrust. For example, one formed a locally recognized rock-and-roll band. Performing before others was a criminal equivalent—"a trip," as he called it. The interactions among the musicians involved a series of power plays. There was frequent dissension, as one person tried to impose his will on others. When interpersonal relationships were relatively harmonious and the band had bookings, the organizer had "enough of a trip" so that he was less involved in crime. Another reason was that he had less time available. For short periods, the band was all he needed.

In this section, we have tried to highlight some of the fields that may lend themselves to the expression of criminal characteristics. When engaged in by the extreme criminal, these activities afford many opportunities for power-thrusting and self-aggrandizement, usually at the expense of the activity and of the other people involved. An agent of change may think that a criminal is doing well, because he has found a job that seems to engross him. Those who know the criminal's record will be pleased at his application to a job. "At least," they will say, "he is not out robbing banks." However, all the hard-core criminals in our investigation have gone beyond criminal equivalents in their search for excitement. In time, they break out into more violations, which may be arrestable.

THE LIMBO PHASE

Some people appear to go through a stage of criminality as youngsters and then "outgrow" it. For the most part, they were not at the extreme end of the continuum of criminality in the first place. These people have changed from being "hellions" as youths to being "straight" as adults, owing to a combination of external and internal deterrents. They want excitement, but deterrents are keeping them from engaging in criminal activity. There may still be plenty of criminal thinking and talk, but little implementation, if any.

In contrast with the nonextreme criminal who straightens out is the full-fledged extreme criminal who is in the "limbo phase." This phase is found in criminals as young as thirty, but occurs more often among criminals who are considerably older and have lost their agility. We call it a "limbo phase," because the criminal is less active in crime. There are a number of reasons for the inactivity. For a while, all criminal activity may be held in check because of an intense fear of getting caught. For a criminal who has been in and out of confinement, the fear of jail may temporarily act as a strong deterrent. However, irresponsibility and much criminal thinking are still present, and it usually does not take long for some moderate criminality to begin, in the form of gambling, playing numbers, petty larceny, or drug use. Often, the criminality shows itself in the exploitative relationships that the criminal sets up with others.

During the limbo phase, the hard-core criminal does not constitute a serious threat to the community. This mental state is characterized more by inertia than by apathy. The criminal does little for himself and functions in an aimless, drifting manner. He may refuse to work, or he may wander from job to job. Whatever the case, he has an income. Although he has contributed nothing to society, the criminal demands what he thinks is his rightful share. He may establish himself as eligible for welfare or social security, live on a military pension, or find another person or agency to support him. If he qualifies for government support, he may refuse to work, for fear of losing this source of funds. In contrast with noncriminals who might be in a similar position, he *prefers* not to work. The more he is given, the more he demands. He criticizes others, claims injustice, and blames others when he does not get what he wants. Accompanying this is considerable self-pity, inasmuch as the criminal is no longer enjoying the high excitement that was part of his former life. For a while, he may find some satisfaction in an activity that provides him with criminal equivalents. For example, there is some triumph and smugness in getting one or more institutions or programs to support him. But the satisfaction is brief, and he remains a malcontent. Now in "retirement" from massive crime, he is no longer a big shot in crime, and he is far from being a success in the responsible world. He is in limbo.

The extreme criminal may be in a limbo phase for months at a time, but he eventually demands greater excitement. Criminals who are physically impaired by age, illness, or injury may remain in limbo out of necessity, but they still show increased initiative in petty crimes.

> After release from Saint Elizabeths 50-year-old C worked as a busboy, until he was fired for gossiping at such length with customers that he neglected his job. Unemployed, he received money from social security and from welfare. He virtually had a "license" not to work because of his history of "mental illness." Sporadically, he found jobs, but he failed to report the earnings, in order that he could keep collecting welfare and social security money. C regularly visited places where criminals congregated and enjoyed talking about former exploits, as well as current happenings. He did a lot of girl-watching and tried to advance himself sexually with girls much younger than he. This was a major activity in which he spent $10 once or twice a week for unsatisfactory sexual experiences with young prostitutes. If anyone approached C with a stolen item, he bought it or passed it along. His drinking was substantial, and it drew heavily on his finances. C also engaged in petty thievery and in small conning operations.

C was almost incapable of major crimes because of his physical condition. Furthermore, he was tired of jails and hospitals, and this played a role in his resolution to stay out of major crime. However, crime still appealed to him, as evidenced by his association with criminals and in his dreams and fantasies, in which he was using drugs and brandishing firearms in criminal acts. Age and health may be the major determinants in a resolution to stay out of crime.

> At 58, C decided to commit no more crimes because he was getting old and he had been warned by relatives that he would one day die in prison. Still, he drank heavily, associated with criminals, and became a skid-row bum. When he was 61, the deaths of 3 people whom he knew frightened him. One was a buddy who died as a result of drinking. C began to worry about himself, because he had a gastrointestinal

problem due to drinking. He went to live with a relative who was responsible and very evangelical. C promptly stopped drinking. He said that he was trying to change his life. However, the desires for crime were still present in this man, who had been in crime for 50 years. The fears of jail and death were deterring him. In addition, there were some internal deterrents of a religious nature. Because C was not in massive crime, he was considered a "success," despite the fact that he was living off others and was making no effort to find work.

Those who are around a criminal in a limbo state might view him as being in a depression, because, in contrast with the supercharged person that he was, he is less active and relatively unenthusiastic about life. Clinically, there is no depression. As soon as an opportunity for excitement arises, his inertia vanishes. If he meets some old buddies and they start talking—or, as one man put it, "making crime shine"—he is lifted out of his "depression." A minor theft is sure to remedy even more quickly what he calls "depression."

Society may view the criminal in a limbo phase as inadequate, dependent, or parasitic, but this is not the criminal's view of himself. As we have said, he never views himself as dependent or inadequate—quite the reverse. What is significant is that there is a great deal of criminal excitement in this "parasitism." Rather than "depending" on others for income, he regards it as a conquest and triumph that he can fool the system. He gets what he wants on his terms and does not comply with the terms of society. Meanwhile, others are viewing him as inadequate, helpless, and easily victimized. The criminal in limbo may be the one who appears to be "institutionalized" by his experience in confinement. The institutionalized criminal derives whatever benefits he can from his status as a prisoner or patient.

C, 35 years old, was afraid of becoming involved in major crime, because he had already served 15 years in confinement. After release from Saint Elizabeths on "convalescent status" (C.S.), he lived at his mother's house. He had taken a job at a restaurant to meet the hospital's requirement for a C.S.; then, a day before actually getting the C.S., he quit without informing the hospital. When he reported to the outpatient department on a monthly basis, he said that he was working part-time, because full-time work was not available. The fact was that he was totally against working and had not even looked for work. C was informed that, if he worked 2 months, he would be released unconditionally, but not until then. This did not have any effect on C, in that maintaining a C.S. offered him such benefits as free medical and dental examinations and treatment. He availed himself of this, including the fitting and ordering of $30 orthopedic shoes at no cost to him. Furthermore, C figured that, if the hospital recalled him, he would still have a place to sleep, 3 meals a day, no expenses, and in time the run of the grounds and access to the city, because he would not be placed in maximum security. Living outside and retaining his active status as a patient on hospital rolls could only be to his advantage, as he figured it. In fact, his diagnosis as a "chronic undifferentiated schizophrenic" eventually enabled him to go permanently on welfare.

What appears to some as "institutionalization" is a form of exploitation. Sometimes, the criminal continues to reside in the hospital. The institution cannot get rid of him, because release requires solid proof of employment and he refuses to work. Institutional life satisfies most of his desires. He poaches, panhandles, drinks, and has sex on the grounds. A small number of criminals in limbo are "burned out," in the sense that they do not want to return to the daily grind and are afraid to get into bigger crimes. Thus, they stay for "three hots and a cot" and whatever excitement they can find.

The criminal in limbo is usually successful in avoiding arrest, unless he becomes careless. He does things that annoy others, but he is rarely prosecuted. A criminal may be disorderly when drunk and become known as a local nuisance, but his noticeable infractions may remain at this level. The limbo criminal does commit petty thefts and con people, but the powerful fear of getting caught and his recognition that he is not as adept as he used to be restrain him from major crimes.

In the criminal who is not incapacitated by age or physical condition, the state of limbo does not last for long. The itch for more excitement erodes deterrents. The scope and frequency of violation progressively increase, until old patterns are in full operation.

MONASTICISM

In a state of "monasticism," the criminal desires to eradicate his past, purify himself, and become good. In contrast with the fragments of decency and religiosity described earlier, monasticism is a sincere state that may last for months. The sincerity during this period distinguishes it from point-scoring or any other contrived effort to impress people. The first expression of monasticism may be a religious conversation. We use the term "monastic" to describe this state of mind, because it connotes the intensity and sincerity of the criminal at the time. However, as we shall point out, the components of criminal thinking are still evident. Instead of being a "humble sinner," he derives a sense of power from being "pure."

Monasticism is not a psychotic state. The criminal has decided for a time how he wants to live. Clearly, conscience plays a strong role. (A criminal retrospectively described this phase as one in which he was subjected to the "tyranny of conscience.") He is in touch with reality, although his all-or-nothing thinking is not very realistic.

A criminal may be "monastic" without invoking God; he may be oriented toward self-reform and restrain his activities. An arsonist, for example, spent months in fire prevention work. He went to the fire department and helped to polish every piece of metal on the engines, and he was crime-free during this period. Most criminals, however, have some religious faith to which they profess devotion when they become monastic. Often, the criminal returns to the religion of his childhood. Or he may embrace a new religion, commonly one that is stricter than that of his youth. The criminal latches onto specific teachings and restrictions that are concrete and can be implemented. He may forswear meat and become a vegetarian; he may abstain from a variety of things, such as tobacco, alcohol, and pork. He believes that these practices will help him to achieve salvation.

Hypermoralism and perfectionism are characteristic of monasticism; the criminal tries to avoid the slightest infraction. His moral standards are absolute, and he views others' behavior without any gradation of goodness or evil. A minor infraction is regarded as though it were a felony.

In Chapter 3, we mentioned that some criminals are monastic as young children. We described their religious observances, conversions, aspirations to be clergymen, and exaggerated efforts to be good. This phase can occur at any age, although characteristically it is seen most often in adolescence, in both the criminal and the noncriminal. Monastic phases occur both in confinement and outside it. Monasticism in confinement appears to last longer, because there the criminal is faced with his failure in life and conditions restrict his field of operation.

In the monastic phase, there is often great missionary zeal. As the criminal tries to convert others, there is a thrust for power and self-buildup. Some criminals, during a period of extreme monasticism, have preached on street corners. One man cleared some land in a rural area and held revival meetings that were attended by several dozen people. The missionary criminal often promotes himself more than he does the religious message. None of this discussion should be construed as disparaging the noncriminal missionary, who has a set of principles and tries to educate others. Indeed, some missionaries fulfill the highest ideals at considerable self-sacrifice. But they are not made of the same fabric as the criminal. The missionary theme as it appears in the criminal must be viewed for what it is and not mistaken for any true conversion or change in him. Being a missionary allows him to build himself up as a superior person. Ultimately, the criminal's missionary zeal vanishes, and he violates the very ideals and principles that he has been espousing.

When a parent, spouse, teacher, corrections officer, therapist, or chaplain sees a criminal in a monastic state, he is likely to be encouraged and think that perhaps the criminal finally is changing. Disillusionment and disappointment set in when the criminal returns to old patterns, which he almost inevitably does. Many who see their hopes shattered by this course of behavior conclude erroneously that the talk and action of the monastic state were a hoax. What was a sincere state of mind while it lasted is then viewed simply as more conning and "manipulating."

An important outcome of the monastic phase is that it actually facilitates crime. The criminal considers himself to be purified. In his mind, the slate is wiped clean. As the criminal views it, when a man gains absolution, it is God's wish that he not even think of evil anymore. The objective is to blot out the past, not to bring it up—the past is off limits. This inner cleansing adds to the reservoir of "good" that he has always believed is part of him. Fortified with this point of view, he has even greater license (as the monastic state begins to corrode) to do as he pleases, needing no justification and offering no apologies.

SUICIDE

The criminal is not a happy person, as to either external appearance or internal mental state. He has no peace of mind and is chronically dissatisfied with the world around him. His life is spent in digging himself into holes and then digging himself out. Occasionally, the criminal reaches a point where he sees himself as a zero and life as not worth living. Sporadic suicidal thinking has occurred in the life of every criminal whom we have encountered. The seriousness of this thinking is documented in institutional records of substances that they have ingested and in the multiple scars that they bear. Our discussion of suicide here bears only on cases of genuine intent as opposed to phony suicidal gestures to recruit sympathy or be considered mentally ill.

Suicidal thinking is conceptually related to the mental phenomena of the zero state, although the two are not identical. We have described the zero state as being a living death. The criminal sees himself as a nothing, believes that others see him this way, and expects it to last forever. He thinks of ending his life when this view is *coupled with a collapse of his opinion of himself as a good person.*

> "The sky was a bleak ominous gray with no hope of sunlight bursting forth, only the silent threat of drizzling rain covering the horizon in all directions...

"My life drags at my soul like a leaden weight—the past, the present, the future, all combine to depress and ensnare me. If I go under, I will surely stifle and smother. . . .

"I am like the poor immigrant in the Bob Dylan verse, who 'hates his life, and likewise fears his death.' . . .

"How is it that I now sit and ponder dark, beckoning suicide who grins at me now and smiles that false smile of a whore?"

These were thoughts expressed vividly in writing by a man who at the time regarded himself as having nothing good in him. He was disgusted with his criminal past and wanted to be decent. But living without excitement in a bleak room, having few companions, going to and from a menial job—this in itself was a living death to him. He could not foresee any improvement, but rather saw the intolerability of the moment as lasting a lifetime, his current state as final and irreversible. True suicidal thinking is a prolonged state that goes beyond a mere fragment of "I might as well be dead" or being reduced to a zero by a single incident from which one quickly rebounds.

The suicidal phase is not simply a depression with anger turned inward. In all cases, we have found that, whether he expresses it or not, the criminal is angry because the world is not catering to him. Furthermore, he has always regarded suffering as unacceptable. This is especially true during a suicidal phase, in which he sees the suffering as never ending. This frame of mind is accompanied by righteous indignation, which may or may not be expressed outwardly.

The criminal has always had the idea that he is destined to be number one. Now this seems to be forever out of reach. He is "too good" to suffer in that he is deprived of reaching his deserved station in life. He blames much of his failure on circumstances of life and concludes that he was not made for this miserable world. It is the "born to lose" idea, which many criminals have thought at times and some have even had tattooed on themselves. It is as though they were misfits from the beginning, people not suited for life on this earth. It is sometimes expressed as being a victim of "fate." One man declared that he was born on the wrong day, at the wrong place, and at the wrong time. The criminal is angry at what "fate" has allotted him.

C's concept of himself as a "god" among men determined all states of mind. When others did not react in accord with this image, despair and anger resulted. It must be emphasized that this was not a psychotic condition. He did not claim to be God. Rather, he acted as though others' opinions and wishes did not count or did not exist. What he wanted was primary and was all that mattered. For C, not to function in a position of total control was not to exist at all. When he was confined for the homicide of his wife, things failed more than ever before to go his way. C's pattern was to swing from power thrust to suicidal thinking. In the hospital, he was successful for a while in virtually running the ward, pushing doctors and attendants around, as well as other patients. C was bright and educated and had well-practiced tactics for getting his way. Despair came when he was not reelected Ward Chairman. His opinion of himself dropped, his anger at others boiled, and he regarded life as not worth living.

C was almost constantly at war with the hospital. When things did not go as he planned, he erupted in anger, reciting a list of grievances. He always made it an issue of how the hospital functioned, rather than of how he functioned in the hospital. It was always others who were in error, rarely he.

With the many disappointments that came in confinement, there were considerable periods of suicidal thinking, elopements, and returns to the hospital. He continually tried to set the conditions of his life in the hospital. "I've been able to work any time I wanted to, but I'll be damned if I'll work as long as I'm a patient in this hospital."

Actually, C could have been released long before the 10 years or so that passed, had he not insisted on being the sole authority in what he would do. For example, if the court did not grant what he wanted, he took matters into his own hands and violated.

As things worked out, C was eventually released unconditionally, an unchanged man. He returned to his home and tried unsuccessfully to push people around. Failing to manage others there, he finally ended his life.

It had always been C against the world. He demanded more from life than life could possibly offer him. To that extent, he considered himself a victim and consequently was indignant. He was not for the world, and the world was not for him. In a final gesture of contempt and despair, C separated himself from the world once and for all.

Suicidal thinking and actual suicidal efforts are greatest in number when the criminal is in confinement. But even there, suicides are rare. The mere fact of incarceration forces a criminal at some point to take stock of himself.

After return from elopement, C thought about his life—his many crimes and his continual misrepresentation and deception. He had caused much difficulty for anyone who had had anything to do with him. No one in the legal system seemed to see much hope for his release. He called himself a perpetual loser who had failed in every venture. Thinking in religious terms, he stated that his present suffering was so severe that hell could be no worse. He saw his current personality as like a cancer that was refractory to any corrective procedure. His death would relieve other people. As he thought about this, he began to consider writing a will.

At the same time, C was angry about injustices on the part of the hospital, the courts, and the people with whom he had to live in confinement. He did not kill himself. Instead, he began legal maneuverings, eloped from the hospital, and returned to crime.

Thinking about self-destruction is, of course, far more common than the actual efforts made. There are various deterrents, not the least of which is the criminal's fear of death. Another deterrent is the criminal's thinking of the effects on a parent, child, or wife. However, the major reason the criminal does not commit suicide is that he eliminates suicidal ideas from his mind through a renewal of criminal thinking and a subsequent breakout into crime. If the criminal is in confinement, he may instead become monastic or psychotic. Suicidal thoughts may be potentiated by the use of alcohol or drugs (to be discussed in Volume 3). Criminals who are violent tend to commit violent acts of self-destruction. This observation has been made by others. West (1965) studied seventy-eight incidents in which murder was followed by suicide; in this group, there was a history of violence even among those with no previous criminal record. Roth (1972) found that 23 percent of the violent patients he studied had actually attempted suicide. Suicidal thinking has been present in every one of our criminals, but it has been most pronounced in the more violent ones. These are the criminals who show the sequelae of suicidal attempts, whether they be scars or the results of ingestion of various substances.

Suicide is a resolution of a lack of self-esteem and a resolution of the anger that rages against the outer world. We include it among the longer-lasting nonarrestable phases, because suicidal thinking may occur for days or even weeks at a time. However, the overwhelming majority of criminals resolve the suicidal phase by a resumption of criminal thinking and action. The criminal takes his own life only when there is a total collapse of his opinion of himself as good and he sees no way out of his situation.

PSYCHOSIS

In the confinement section of Chapter 3, we described the criminal's attempts to fake mental illness in order to be admitted to a mental hospital, rather than serving a sentence in jail. The criminal may be exceedingly resourceful in his malingering, and some are quite sophisticated about psychiatric symptoms and syndromes. Thus, one situation in which the diagnosis of psychosis is made occurs when the criminal has successfully defrauded the examining authorities. The failure of the examiners to comprehend the criminal's behavioral inconsistencies (fragmentation) and unrealistic thinking also may result in his being labeled "psychotic." An examiner who is favorably impressed by a criminal might stretch the diagnosis to psychosis in order to save a criminal from prison.

Less than 3 percent of the criminals with whom we have worked have had bona fide psychotic phases. (Our criteria of psychosis are independent of whether a crime has been committed.) Other authors have acknowledged a low incidence of psychosis in the criminal population (Guze et al., 1962; Gulevich and Bourne in Daniels, 1970). In perhaps the most extensive study of mental disorder among criminals, Bromberg (1961) stated that the incidence of psychosis among 60,000 convicted criminals varied from 2 to 2.5 percent. Approximately 80 percent were considered "normal." It is possible that the 2-2.5 percent is high, if some who malingered were not detected and excluded.

None of the 3 percent experiencing psychosis in our sample were psychotic at the time they committed crimes. We had the opportunity of interviewing these criminals at length daily and evaluating their mental states while they were psychotic. At such times, they were too preoccupied with their noncriminal, often religious ideas to scheme and successfully execute elaborate schemes. Only in a toxic psychosis did confusion occur. Psychosis absorbs a great amount of energy, which then is not available for other activities. To succeed in a bank robbery, a criminal must be energetic, alert, observant, and completely in control of himself. In short, he must be very much in touch with reality. We have yet to encounter a case in which a crime is a "product" of psychosis.

The content of the psychosis in the criminal is strongly and consistently anticrime. Psychosis appears to be a severe backlash of conscience, to which some criminals are more vulnerable than others. We have found that a criminal who experiences psychotic phases has fewer of them once he begins to deal responsibly with the world as he progresses in our program for change. In the psychotic phase itself, many criminals are preoccupied with religious concerns. Unlike his functioning in monasticism, the criminal during psychosis loses touch with reality. Monasticism involves a self-imposed restraint and a concerted effort at what may become a truly ascetic life. In psychosis, the criminal goes beyond seeking an inner condition of purity via self-restraint and other rational means. If he is religiously inclined, he becomes a personal messenger of God, instead of merely seeking God. Mental hospital personnel have observed these obvious religious features of psychosis.

From two hospital charts:

> [C] has remained agitated and has responded to auditory hallucina-
> tons. He has exhibited excessive motor activity while on the ward,
> signing the cross and raising his right arm, calling out, "Peace."

> The report of psychiatric examination made at this institution diag-
> noses [C] as "schizophrenic reaction, paranoid type" in partial remis-
> sion manifested by ideas of grandeur and omnipotence, of the feeling
> that he is the Lord and the ability to control the state of others.

We have observed in detail the mental processes operating at various times
in such psychoses.

> C's psychosis began with his hearing voices telling him that the people
> around him were going to kill him. He prayed to God for help. Then,
> he began hearing organ music, which he associated with God. Later,
> C developed the idea that he had a superior I.Q. and could be a great
> mathematician or a gifted composer. He believed that he was granted
> superior endowments by God. Fortified with this idea, he laughed at
> his earlier ideas that others could injure him—he had achieved an im-
> munity as one of God's chosen. In the next phase of the psychosis,
> he decided that he had been appointed as God's agent to fight the
> battle of good and evil here on earth. At this time, he began to hear
> female voices admiring his power and soliciting him sexually. He iden-
> tified these voices as devils that were trying to "torture" him. C prayed
> frantically and even swallowed a rosary with a crucifix attached. His
> first two initials were J. C., and he believed that he represented the
> second coming of Christ, sent by God to wage the war against evil per-
> sonally. Somehow, he won the battle, believing that God was behind
> him and protecting him so that he would not succumb to temptation.

That this psychosis was indeed a backlash of conscience was attested to by
C's later stating that God had ordained the psychosis because He wanted
C to turn from his evil ways to being good. As it turned out, C was completely anticrime during the psychosis, but once the psychosis lifted, he
returned to active crime.

Although there is no criminal activity in psychosis, power themes are
prevalent. The criminal is the purest of the pure, God's chosen agent. When
the religious aspect is absent, the theme may be that of special talents or
powers. One criminal believed that he had electricity in his eyes with which
he could deal with those who posed a threat to him. Another, believing
that he was a great photographer, rushed out to spend $1,200 on photo-
graphic equipment. However, this was money that he had saved, and no
violation was involved.

Drugs and psychosis will be discussed in detail in Volume 3, but we note in passing that the disorganization and confusion in a toxic psychosis induced by drugs or alcohol are such that the criminal is in no condition to scheme and execute a criminal act. In such psychoses, we have seen the criminal act in bizarre fashion, for example, climbing up the outside of a tower nude or eating grass on a lawn. Religious features may play a role during a toxic psychosis. One criminal was seen walking around the ward holding a Bible in one hand and his scrotum in the other. He was reading the scripture and asking God to amputate his penis.

The time of onset of a psychosis is of critical importance for legal determinations. If a criminal is psychotic at some point after the crime, it is likely to be assumed that he was psychotic when he committed the crime. That is, an examiner who encounters a criminal in a state of psychic disorganization after his arrest may assume that psychosis has been the prevailing and preexisting mental state. A transient psychosis may quickly follow arrest, when the criminal is in a panic about what will happen to him, but even this occurs seldom. We have seen cases in which a man became psychotic in confinement after his arrest and then was declared "not guilty by reason of insanity" at the time of his crime. Later, with privileged communication assured, he revealed his thinking processes, which made it clear that he was totally rational when he committed the offense.

A remarkable feature of the criminal's psychosis is the degree of control that he has over it. He is aware of the onset. As he is sliding into psychosis, he is coherent about some things, but not others. He realizes that he is living in "two worlds"—reality and unreality. Some criminals continue to hold a job with little decrement in performance, despite a psychotic condition.

> C reported that, even though he knew that a co-worker had just died, he found himself thinking that he was alive. Then he reported that he was getting careless with his money, having contributed $40 to donations in this man's memory. He found himself engaged in "mental conversations" that he knew were "not for real." These apparently had the quality of brief hallucinations. C referred to feeling detached—"as if I were on an island far removed." At home, he played music for hours and felt as though he were drifting in space. Because the experience of "unrealness" was strong, C directed increasing energy and attention to the "real." He was especially apprehensive that others might detect what was going on with him, especially because something like dream states occurred at work. It was like waking from sleep and not being fully conscious, but being aware of everything around. At work, he tried to function with accuracy. But he found himself making mistakes, such as making too many copies of a report, although he could hide these errors. He tried extra hard to be conscientious and to please others. Owing to his feeling of detachment, C did a little more

chatting than usual, but did nothing considered inappropriate. He apparently was successful in concealing the psychosis from his fellow workers, with whom he spent 8 hours a day.

In another incident, a criminal chose to disguise his condition from the mental health staff on the ward where he was confined.

> In an interview with us, C was clearly disorganized in his thinking. Successive statements contradicted each other, and there was no coherence in theme. Furthermore, he blurted out absurd statements, which he would not allude to again. He talked about his special powers, being the "universal maker" and so forth. It was a jumble of thoughts covering a wide range, including mother, God, devil, Vietnam, guns, and morality. The interesting thing is that on the ward he was conforming perfectly and was no trouble to anyone. He never touched on these topics with others. This was a ward that was headquarters for a lot of contraband drugs. Yet, in this state, C would have no part of them. He was thoroughly anticrime when psychotic. All the psychotic processes, however, remained concealed from the doctor and ward personnel.

Another aspect of the control over psychosis is that sometimes the criminal can assist in bringing it on. He may actively desire it, because he has learned from previous psychotic episodes that he will not be criminal in such a state. One man feared that he might resume his violating patterns and consequently desired a return of the psychosis; he knew that, once he was again in touch with God, he would not be tempted to violate. Furthermore, he could then make God responsible for what he did, divesting himself of the burden to make decisions. We have encountered the criminal resorting to drugs to try to recapture a previous psychotic state.

Some criminals go through successive states of crime and psychosis. When treatment or even the passage of time clears up the psychosis, the criminality emerges. In fact, if an agent of change first meets a criminal in a psychotic phase, he may treat him like any other psychotic. When the psychosis is cleared up, he may see criminal or "sociopathic" features emerging. In our early work, we thought we had a treatment success, only to find that the psychosis had masked serious criminality.

> C was referred to us as one of the most depressed and psychotic young adult patients on the ward of a state hospital. The content of the psychosis as expressed was that she was being contaminated by semen whenever she passed a man and that she was a no-good prostitute. She asked repeatedly and poignantly, "How can I be a lady? I want to be a lady." She would rub her hands together, fearful of touching anything, lest she be contaminated by semen or a vaginal discharge. She

described dreamlike states and kept saying, "I can't find myself." With an approach that can best be described as structured and rational, the therapist experienced success with total remission of the psychosis. However, as treatment went on, it was possible to learn more about C's background. In fact, she had not been "a lady," but rather a sexually promiscuous girl. She had threatened a girl with a knife and had been in numerous fights as a teenager. As C emerged from her psychosis, she chose as her boy friends the most delinquent male patients. Moving into the community, she became increasingly unreliable and broke the rules of her family-care residence. Often, no one knew where she was. It appeared that she was well on her way to resuming old delinquent patterns.

We had "cured" a woman of psychosis, only to see other types of "disturbed" and disturbing behavior emerge.

In summary, only about 3 percent of our criminals have a history of genuine psychotic episodes. In a psychotic phase, they are preoccupied with thinking that is jumbled and anticrime in content. Crimes are committed only when they are in touch with reality.

PSYCHOSOMATIC SYMPTOMS

Some observers have viewed the criminal as being without emotional conflict. Lack of anxiety is a commonly cited hallmark of the psychopath. Thus, it has been concluded that the psychopath or criminal is not likely to develop psychosomatic symptoms, which are displacements of inner conflict.

The psychopath has no need to develop psychosomatic illness since he has no emotional conflicts to convert into physical symptoms. It would be impossible for the pure psychopath to develop psychosomatic symptoms (Karpman, 1961, pp. 608–609).

We have found, however, that psychosomatic symptoms are very prevalent in criminals. They may occur in all the phases we have described. The symptoms are the same as those experienced by the noncriminal—headaches, gastrointestinal distress, dizziness, neck tension, backaches. Although the criminal and noncriminal may experience identical symptoms, the circumstances that give rise to them are different. (We leave the discussion of psychosomatic symptoms in the drug-user for Volume 3.)

The criminal develops psychosomatic symptoms when he is deterred from doing what he wants. The absence of excitement gives rise to tension and other symptoms. When he says he is "depressed" or "bored," the recital of physical complaints begins. The criminal also may experience physical distress when he is pressured to do something that requires more effort than he is willing to exert. In short, psychosomatic symptoms occur when the criminal is not doing what he wants or is doing what he dislikes.

It is in confinement that the criminal is most likely to have the itch for excitement but encounter prolonged frustration and boredom. In prisons and mental hospitals, sick calls are well attended by criminals who suffer from psychosomatic ailments.

Tension is also produced by excitement before a violation. Thinking about holding up a bank may give rise to tightness in the chest and abdominal region. When the criminal actually carries out the robbery, the symptoms disappear. Then there are the symptoms that are evoked by fear during the commission of a crime. If a man spots a police car, internal tension may suddenly grip him. If he musters his "courage" and proceeds with the crime, the tension subsides. The psychosomatic symptoms that attend the excitement of criminal thinking and those concomitant with fear are dispelled with successful execution of the crime.

As we mentioned in Chapter 3, the criminal does not tolerate physical distress for long. He endures it better if it is not a consequence of external or internal restraints. For example, one criminal lost a shoe in a race, but persisted to the finish, coming in with blisters on one foot. The same man was holding himself in check with respect to some criminal patterns and consequently experienced psychosomatic distress at work. He came to his office fatigued and with headaches. Rather than endure these symptoms, he left work and had sex with a girl friend who shared her heroin with him. C's symptoms disappeared instantly, even before he had the heroin.

The criminal uses his psychosomatic symptoms to gain sympathy and to avoid responsible commitments. In Volume 2, we shall show that psychosomatic symptoms in the criminal can be controlled and reduced, if not eliminated, by alterations in thinking patterns—not in conditions of life.

SUMMARY

All criminals are involved in criminal equivalents and have psychosomatic reactions. There is suicidal thinking in all, but very few suicides, although many efforts are made. Monasticism is comparatively rare, and psychosis is the least often encountered of all the phases described. Some phases coexist. For example, criminals may simultaneously be in active crime, engage in criminal equivalents, and have psychosomatic symptoms. We saw no purpose in quantifying the occurrence of each phase, but instead have concentrated on describing the mental processes of each.

BIBLIOGRAPHY

" 'All Kids Want to Be the Good Guy,' " *Parade*, April 18, 1971, p. 18.

Bromberg, Walter. *The Mold of Murder*. New York: Grune and Stratton, 1961.

"Don't Set a Thief To...," *Time*, August 8, 1972, 32-33.

"Drugs, Dishonesty Disqualify Many County Police Applicants," *Virginia Sentinel*, January 4, 1973.

"Four Rabbis Charged in Bilking Case," *The Washington Post*, October 17, 1971.

Gulevich, George D., and Bourne, Peter G. "Mental Illness and Violence," in Daniels, David N., et al. *Violence and the Struggle for Existence*. Boston: Little, Brown, 1970, 309-326.

Guze, S. B., et al. "Psychiatric Illness and Crime with Particular Reference to Alcoholism: A Study of 223 Criminals," *Journal of Nervous and Mental Disease*, 1962, *134*, 512-521.

Karpman, Ben. "The Structure of Neuroses: With Special Differentials between Neurosis, Psychosis, Homosexuality, Alcoholism, Psychopathy and Criminality," *Archives of Criminal Psychodynamics*, 1961, *4*, 599-646.

Kiger, Roger S. "Treating the Psychopathic Patient in a Therapeutic Community," *Hospital and Community Psychiatry*, 1967, 18, 191-196.

Mills, Robert B. "New Directions in Police Selection," Paper presented at the 80th annual meeting of the American Psychological Association, Honolulu, September 1972 (reprint).

"Minister in District Charged in Sex Case," *The Washington Post*, March 11, 1973.

"[Reverend] Arrested on Assault Count," *The Evening Star*, March 12, 1971.

Roth, Loren H., et al. "Violent and Non-violent Prisoners, A Comparison," Paper presented at the 125th annual meeting of the American Psychiatric Association, Dallas, May 1972 (reprint).

"Va. Crime Fighters Are Prisoners," *The Evening Star and The Washington Daily News*, April 15. 1973 p. B1.

West, Donald J. *Murder Followed by Suicide*. Cambridge, Mass.: Harvard University Press, 1965.

Chapter 8

Tactics Obstructing Effective
Transactions

> Having regularly failed in my own efforts to help such patients alter
> their fundamental pattern of inadequacy and antisocial activity, I
> hoped for a while that treatment by others would be more successful....
> I have now, after more than two decades, had the opportunity to ob-
> serve a considerable number of patients who ... were kept under treat-
> ment not only for many months but for years. The therapeutic failure
> in all such patients observed leads me to feel that we do not at present
> have any kind of psychotherapy that can be relied upon to change the
> psychopath fundamentally (Cleckley, 1964, pp. 476-478).

IN 1964, AFTER more than twenty years of working with psychopaths,
Cleckley concluded that there was no available form of treatment that could
produce change in this group. Since then, others in the field have expressed
the same opinion about the criminal, as will be shown in detail in the literature review of Volume 2.* Like Cleckley, we have been through the mill
and experienced failure. Cleckley attributed his defeats mainly to the nature
of the psychopath. We started where he stopped; we studied why such
failures result. Our work has shown that it is possible to reach the criminal
and change him.

The first step in an evaluation or "rehabilitation" program is to deal with
the thinking patterns and behavior that obstruct effective transactions with
the criminal. We have described these thinking errors in earlier chapters.
In this chapter, we shall discuss specific manifestations of the thinking
errors as they arise when the criminal is held accountable. In fact, it is
accurate to say that the behavior described in this chapter constitutes the
criminal's M.O. in accountability.

---

* See Chapter 2 of the present volume for a discussion of the terms "psychopath" and "criminal."

When a criminal is confronted with an evaluation or is placed in a program for "rehabilitation," he manifests the characteristic patterns of thinking and action that he has shown everywhere else—these are all he knows. The evaluation or new program evokes from him nothing that has not been present and usually observable elsewhere. The criminal's tactics are habitual and every bit as "criminal" as breaking and entering. We are not referring here to arrestability, but rather to criminal thinking patterns of which these tactics and crime are both products.

The criminal's major objective is to avoid restriction and confinement —i.e., to continue his way of life. This, of course, is diametrically opposed to the objective of the examiner or agent of change. Therefore, the basic requirements of an effective transaction between the two are not even grasped by the criminal, much less fulfilled. Fundamental issues are not faced; there is no agreed-on purpose. The criminal's tactics are not for the purpose of setting the record straight or of changing. To achieve a common ground, an examiner or change agent must overcome the tactics of the criminal and alter his own approach, which the criminal seeks to exploit. Otherwise, he is certain to fall into the criminal's hands; his objective will be thwarted, and the criminal will eventually achieve his own objective.

In our work, we have been made painfully aware that examiners and change agents introduce additional obstacles to an already difficult task. Whoever makes a judgment or decision about a criminal without knowing his thinking patterns and without having techniques to deal with them offers the criminal a fertile field for the exercise of his tactics. Specific examiner orientations elicit specific tactics from the criminal. If the examiner or change agent adheres to a particular theoretical persuasion, he becomes easy bait for the criminal, who feeds him what he wants to hear. In addition, one's own personal approach in dealing with people may pose problems, so that a transaction turns into two people manipulating each other. When this occurs, the criminal perceives the contest and is encouraged in the use of his tactics, usually achieving success; the result that Cleckley speaks of is then ensured.

The first part of this chapter presents an obstacle that affects all transactions with criminals: the criminal's view of himself not as a criminal, but as a good person. This is followed by a description of the criminal's view of the examiner or change agent. We then treat in detail the specific tactics that the criminal uses when he is being examined to determine his mental competence or legal responsibility and the tactics encountered by a change agent once he begins to work with criminals in a program for change. The final section deals with semantics. Anyone who works with a criminal must know how the criminal uses language, if issues are to be discussed with anything approaching clarity. An awareness of semantic difficulties is mandatory when two people with radically different philosophies of life attempt to embark on a common enterprise.

We derived the material for this chapter primarily while working with hard-core criminals. Some of it was obtained from work with adolescent criminals at various points on the criminal continuum. The essential clarifications and refinements were obtained from changed criminals who later identified the specific tactics that they had used in trying to thwart us.

THE CRIMINAL'S VIEW OF HIMSELF

The apprehended criminal believes that, although he broke the law, he is inherently not criminal. He thinks that he is a good person who should not be punished. Although he was caught for an act that has a penalty attached, he believes that he should not be confined, which he views as being caged or "warehoused." He wants to fulfill his objective in life, which is to maneuver in the world as he has in the past. Considering his premises, this view is perfectly understandable. The criminal is satisfied with himself as a person, but he is dissatisfied with his lot when apprehended. Whether or not he expresses it, he regards the people who interview and judge him as naïve, uninformed "marks."

The criminal knows that a given act is illegal from society's point of view, but he deems it proper for him. He knows what the laws are; in fact, he has a more detailed knowledge of the law than many responsible people. He knows the difference between right and wrong, but the question of what is right or wrong *for him* is always subjective. Actually, the question does not come up at all, unless others raise it. The criminal thinks about right and wrong only when others introduce the issue. What follows its introduction is a transaction that may be called a "nondiscussion" for reasons that we are about to explain.

The criminal does what he believes is "right" for him, disregarding the fact that it is against the law. He applies the designation "criminal" not to himself, but to those who commit crimes that he disdains. The so-called white-collar criminal may have contempt for the violent criminal, but the violent criminal may scorn the white-collar criminal for being afraid of a fight.

> C identified slickness with being "feminine." This applied to operations like embezzling and confidence games. To him, a crime should be more "manly," and this in essence involved "more direct methods"—namely, physical violence.

Nothing said about a criminal's criminality from a responsible point of view applies to him, as he sees it. This is in keeping with his "uniqueness" (discussed in Chapter 4). We, as change agents, have often heard a criminal self-righteously declare, while he is lying, that he hates liars. His own lying is "justified," because it achieves his objective. A criminal may object to a "sneak," and at the same time talk about his own sneakiness.

> "Always I've been a sneak, looking over my shoulder while I did some rotten thing. The irony is I hate a sneak, and I have nothing but contempt for a coward. And the louse...who betrays the one who loves him and then covers it up with a smile, merits my special loathing."

There is no connection between what he regards as wrong for others and right for himself. There are always circumstances in which he must lie and sneak, but these circumstances do not apply to others. The "right" course of action is the expedient one, and the "wrong" course is the one that will result in being apprehended. At any given time, the criminal will not do what he considers wrong; i.e., he will not do anything that does not serve his objective.

> "I have never done anything wrong in my life. The things I have done aren't wrong. I do believe there is a right and wrong. When I do something, I don't feel it's wrong. If I did, I wouldn't do it. I wouldn't do anything that I thought or felt was wrong."

His idea of "right" is "what I want to do."

> "My thinking conforms to the elements of my nature: lying, stealing, rape, anything is allright. So long as the thoughts conform to the pattern of my personality, I don't even question them. They must be right. After all, I'm perfectly allright. This thought pattern is so automatic... I literally don't know how to think any other way."

In short, he knows the difference between right and wrong, but the application of this knowledge is based on what is expedient for him at the time.

What society calls his "criminal activity" the criminal regards as his "work." As we have pointed out, he may have a "daily grind," just as responsible people do. His "job" is a necessity, and one does not have to justify necessity. Because he has lived this way so long, it has become habitual, and he does not view what he does every day as in any way "criminal." In short, the unapprehended criminal never has to justify a crime. That he fears being caught does not imply that he thinks that his act requires justification. The impropriety is not in the act itself, but in the getting caught. When he is held accountable, the criminal believes that he has been wronged, that he has been obstructed in the exercise of his rights and privileges. He is offended by the very idea that he has to defend himself. He does not relate being apprehended to the idea that he has committed a "crime." It is a matter of the authorities' disapproving what he did and having the power to punish him. His getting caught sets up another contest in which the criminal tries to avoid or minimize a penalty.

The criminal may acknowledge that he is a "criminal," even exaggerating the extent of his criminality, if it will score points. He knows that he has committed what society calls "crimes." Similarly, if he has been confined and released, he may even accept the designation "ex-convict." This is a fact of his life. But acknowledging such things does not make him a criminal as he regards his own character. He is still a good person.

> "Whenever I have said that I was guilty, all I meant was that the jury found me guilty. I still have the right to appeal."

As a criminal defends himself, he seeks to demonstrate that others are wrong and he is right. The person to whom he is accountable hears various justifications: "there's larceny in every soul," "others get away with it," "society is rotten," and all the other excuses covered earlier. This set of attitudes is truly formidable when an interviewer is confronted with a man who has committed thousands of crimes and yet sincerely maintains that he is no criminal.

It is futile to become embroiled in a discussion of right and wrong with the criminal. Even when there seems to be basic agreement, such a discussion is inconsequential. The same words may be used by both parties, but the two are still poles apart in their frames of reference. Even if the examiner (or change agent) and criminal reach some agreement on the wrongfulness of a specific act, the criminal regards himself as having done the right thing (except for getting caught). To try at the beginning to debate or teach him broad concepts of right and wrong, criminal and noncriminal, only provides an arena for a power struggle in which the criminal tries to convince the other party of the correctness of his own view. If he agrees with the interviewer and admits that he is a criminal, the interviewer may incorrectly conclude that the criminal understands the implications of his criminality, when really he does not believe a bit of what he is saying. It is as though criminality is no longer an issue, once the criminal admits that he is a criminal. This is tantamount to saying, "We have agreed that I am a criminal, and now that this is clear, let us go on to something else."

The examiner or agent of change should realize what is behind the criminal's tremendous resistance to seeing himself as he is. These men make it very clear why they continue to refute our unfavorable view of them.

> "How could you live with yourself if you thought of yourself as a cruddy, nasty person? You have to be able to live with yourself. Suicide or insanity would be my only recourse if I thought of myself as evil."

> "It is degrading to consider a 'larceny pattern.' These words spell doom and punishment. You have your own personal opinion of yourself."

In short, not only is the criminal who is being evaluated, rehabilitated, or changed not a criminal, but he is indeed a very good, worthwhile person. (This theme was developed in Chapters 4 and 6.) If challenged on the issue, the criminal enumerates his virtues. This view of himself is an integral part of the personality of every criminal we have dealt with.*

THE CRIMINAL'S EVALUATION OF THE EXAMINER, AGENT OF CHANGE, OR OTHER INTERVIEWER

The criminal approaches an examiner or any other person in a position of authority over him as he does a criminal enterprise. The examiner, in the criminal's view, is a gullible person to be defeated by a series of tactics. Thus, the criminal functions toward him as he does in planning a crime. He begins by "casing out" his interviewer. In other words, it is the examiner who is to be examined. This process is an important first step in a criminal enterprise in which the criminal diverts others' efforts to learn about him into having them assist him in the achievement of his objective.

Every criminal we have dealt with acquired as much information as possible before meeting with an examiner, judge, or anyone else to whom he might have to answer. This practice enables him to load the encounter in his favor. He asks other criminals, staff members of the institution, or other appropriate people what kind of person the interviewer is, what his interests are, and what kinds of questions he asks. Most important, the criminal

---

* Cudrin (1970) is the only person we have found who has written about this. In a study of the self-concept of prison inmates, he found that 33 of 42 denied that they were criminals and 37 of the 42 said that they were not bad people. Cudrin observed:

> The large number of men in this sample consisting of people who continuously and severely violated social restrictions had no lasting sense of badness or evil about themselves (p. 65).

> In our own group we find the majority of men strongly committed to belief in their own self-worth (p. 69).

Cudrin fitted these observations into a psychoanalytic theoretical framework.

wants to find out whether the person is a "hard-liner" or someone on whose sympathies he can play. He tailors his line of defense to the situation. If it is a policeman or attorney, the criminal is legalistic, invoking his rights, looking for loopholes. If he finds out that conveying an impression of remorse will help, he does this. If he talks with a psychiatrist, he relates his past problems, traumas, and emotional states.

> C stated that he was in crime because as a young child he saw his parents having intercourse and from then on had a need to be punished.

If the interviewer is sociologically oriented, the criminal may establish a causal relationship between his crime and a broken home, neglect and mistreatment as a child, poverty, lack of opportunity, and so on.

> C stated that he was in crime partly because he had never acquired an education. Because he could not read the laws, he declared he could not understand them. Consequently, he did not know the difference between right and wrong.

In all cases, he takes his cue from the examiner. If the position of the interrogator is not known, the criminal plays cat and mouse. He may remain totally silent or be vague until the examiner reveals more of himself. For clues, the criminal looks to things other than the examiner's profession or theoretical bias. He learns from the kinds of questions asked. If the interviewer focuses on the details of the crime and appears interested in them, the criminal may regard him as being naïve and thus a subject for teaching. Or he may think that the examiner is a criminal like himself who gets a charge out of talking about crime and who wants to learn some new tricks. Sometimes an examiner focuses on the criminal's mental state during the crime, instead of assessing the whole person; the criminal may conclude that the examiner is interested in the crime itself. Once a transaction of any of the types just described occurs, the criminal is in control. He either functions as the "teacher" or enjoys the excitement of criminal talk.

Talk about crime opens channels irrelevant to the examination. When the criminal thinks that the interviewer is interested in crime and wants to learn more, he feeds the interviewer more details, many of which are not true. In other words, instead of providing solid information, the criminal builds himself up. During the course of his descriptions of crime, the criminal uses slang or street talk. If the examiner uses the criminal's language, this puts him at a disadvantage. It creates an arena for a contest that the interviewer cannot possibly win. What often occurs then is a digression into a discussion of the criminal's terminology. Some professionals advocate using the criminal's language in order to enhance communication with him.

> Usually, it is effective for the therapist to communicate with the sociopath in his own jargon, thus establishing further evidence in the mind of the sociopath that he is understood. Such handling often earns a grudging admiration from the sociopath who accepts that he is confronted by someone who is "on to him" (Thorne, 1959, p. 329)

We have found the opposite to be true. To use the criminal's slang and street expressions arouses his suspicion that the interviewer is cut of the same cloth as he. Then there is always the risk that the examiner will misuse a street expression and lead the criminal to think that he is dealing with someone who is stupid or uninformed. In such a situation, the professional's skill and stature are devalued even further. Perhaps the worst effect of using the criminal's language is that the criminal sees it as an attempt to court his favor, and this immediately gives him the upper hand.

Those who deal with the criminal should recognize that he puts great stock in physical appearance, as well as in style of speech. He may focus on one aspect of the interviewer, such as hair length, and view him totally from that perspective.

> In 1971, many of the new physicians at Saint Elizabeths had long hair, beards, or moustaches and "mod" dress. Many of the criminal patients perceived these men as effeminate and their exaggerated styles in dress as indicators of a discomfort with their roles as part of the establishment.

This is not to say that these doctors were in fact effeminate, weak, or antiestablishment. What is important is what the criminals thought; it was part of the sizeup, and they conducted themselves according to their perceptions. A criminal would believe that he had a "soft touch" to deal with when a doctor showed up with long unkempt hair, shirttail sticking out, and avant garde dress. If a staff member dressed this way and also used the criminal's language, the criminal would tend to assume that the person was easily susceptible to influence, because he was basically like himself.

The criminal views the examiner's attempts to gain rapport as a sign of weakness. Anyone who tries to court favor when working with the criminal is finished before he starts, because he is beholden to the criminal for approval. The criminal exploits the examiner or any other worker if he perceives the person as overly concerned about being liked. Whenever a criminal sees that an interviewer has a particular interest in anything—crime, mechanics, clothes, sex, etc.—he initiates a discussion on that subject to sidetrack the examination. Seeing a common ground for discussion, the interviewer thinks that rapport is being established. Rapport is of course essential, but it must be achieved properly. Showing an interest in crime, speaking criminal street language, or dressing flamboyantly only creates more obstacles. (We shall say more about this in Volume 2 when we discuss our initial approach to the criminal and the characteristics necessary in the agent of change.)

The criminal does not always approach an examiner in this way. If he is in a state of self-disgust, he may be sincere in his desire to cooperate and even to change. But he still withholds information, because of his overriding wish to convince the other party of his sincerity. If he revealed "everything," he might regret it in the future. First, he might endanger himself with respect to incurring a penalty of restriction. Second, others would think less of him as a person. Occasionally, a criminal refuses to talk at all, and the examiner may then ask him to produce a written statement. This occurs in mental health settings, where criminals may be asked to write autobiographies. The result of such a practice is a collection of self-serving statements. Because he is writing, rather than speaking, the criminal has more time to tailor what he says to serve his purpose.

No matter how the transaction with an examiner is structured, the criminal brings to it the thinking processes of a lifetime. He could not realistically be expected to approach the situation in any way but criminally.

THE CRIMINAL'S TACTICS DURING EXAMINATION

The criminal awaiting determination of legal status, placement in a program, or some other decision will do whatever he can to improve his situation. He views the evaluation interview as a struggle for "survival," and he schemes and calculates to do anything that is expedient. "Survival" to him means regaining a maximum of freedom to live as he chooses. Given this orientation, the examiner finds that the criminal is not likely to reveal any more than he must, and even what he reveals is not true. The criminal has at his command a wide array of tactics with which he seeks to gain advantages for himself while revealing the least information. He has used most of these tactics so many times that they are automatic and require little thought. In fact, the more automatic they are, the more effective they usually are. When the criminal enters a situation, he has his array of tactics at hand. However, it is to his advantage to be spontaneous about which particular tactic he uses at a given time. If the criminal fails to disengage himself from prejudgments sufficiently, he may not perceive the situation at hand as it truly is.

The criminal's overall strategy is to reverse the roles. He does not view himself as being on the defensive for very long. Instead, he seizes the first opportunity to go on the offensive. Even when he is silent or is assenting to what the interviewer says, he thinks of himself as being on top in the transaction.

We shall describe the tactics that examiners encounter as they attempt a discussion with the criminal intended to help them to arrive at sound conclusions and decisions. There is considerable overlap, because the tactics have a common objective. The tactics are numbered to simplify reference to them.

1. BUILDING HIMSELF UP BY PUTTING THE EXAMINER DOWN

At nearly every turn of a transaction, the criminal strives to gain the advantage over his examiner. He begins by regarding the examiner as an adversary who is to be overcome. Whether expressed or not, there is contempt for that person. If the examiner is in an important decision-making position, this scorn is muted and perhaps not expressed at all, because the criminal does not want to antagonize him.

The criminal takes the offensive by trying to put others down and thereby avoid a putdown himself. He often does this in so subtle a manner that the examiner is unaware that he is being made a fool of. The criminal may use veiled sarcasm in his choice of words—e.g., "You might not realize it, but . . ." and "I guess you wouldn't happen to know that . . ."—to indicate that he views the examiner as ignorant, whereas he, the criminal, is an expert. There are occasions when the criminal is not at all subtle in his attempts to put down the other person. For example, he may take what is supposed to be a fault of his and attack the interviewer for having that same fault. Sometimes he is correct in his observation. At other times, he stretches a point to put the other party on the defensive. If the interviewer is intense, the criminal calls him "angry." If he is persuasive, the criminal says that he is conning. If he contrasts how he has had to function in life with how the criminal has operated, the criminal says that he is "boasting." The criminal may take the offensive in such a way as to try to embarrass the examiner.

> C decided to humiliate the examining psychologist. On the blank card of the Thematic Apperception Test, he told this story: "The psychologist was a voyeur. He was peeping into the internal life of another person. This is sanctioned by society. So he gives a test. He is practicing. His objective is to make $30,000 a year as soon as possible."

C got a sense of triumph out of embarrassing others. Here, he was clearly attempting to put the psychologist on the defensive.

2. Feeding the Examiner What the Criminal Thinks He Wants to Hear

Examiners, program directors, agents of change, and laymen have their own beliefs about why a man commits a criminal act. The criminal is quick to discern what these ideas are. The process of sizing up the authority begins before the first meeting whenever possible and continues, so that the criminal can feed the person what he desires to hear. As one criminal admitted to us, "You know, I'm always examining you, appraising you, trying to find out what makes you tick." This is point-scoring, which is a criminal operation that uses a variety of deceptive tactics. It is an exercise of power and control in defrauding others to gain personal advantage.

The criminal tries to convince the examiner of his sincerity and good intentions. He appears agreeable and amenable to open discussion. For example, he appears to respond thoughtfully and sincerely to make the examiner think that he is having some impact. All the while, the criminal is figuring out the examiner's orientation. As one criminal put it, "Telling a criminal what you're looking for is as good as programming him to come up with it." Previously, we described the criminal's resourcefulness in presenting his case to others for an insanity defense. Once he is hospitalized, the criminal decides, "I will play their game and use my rules." Although he does not use psychologic jargon on the street, he learns it and rapidly incorporates it into his speech to demonstrate "insight" to a hospital staff and examining psychiatrist. He uses the proper terms even if he is not sure of their meaning.

> C told us that he had "flat affect." He said that a psychiatrist had told him this and that he had not known what it was until it was explained. Knowing that this was considered a sign of "illness," he could then use it to his advantage.

In either a prison or a hospital, the criminal scores points through deed and word. He tries to impress others by following the rules and participating in programs. Although a few refuse to cooperate, most put up a facade of commitment, even if they are simultaneously and secretly violating. When observers see an improvement in behavior, they conclude that the criminal is changing. A favorable report to a parole board helps the criminal to achieve privileges and eventually release.

> C, who had a 10-year sentence, was permitted to attend junior college outside the prison. He did so well that some members of the faculty spontaneously sent a letter to corrections officials praising his conduct and academic performance. As a consequence, he was released 2 years ahead of his scheduled parole date.

3. Feeding the Examiner What the Criminal Thinks He Ought to Know

Not only does the criminal specifically tailor answers to an examiner's questions, but he also decides how advantageous it is to volunteer other information. He believes that he has the sole prerogative to decide what is important. If he regards a matter as insignificant, the interviewer is likely never to hear about it. It is typical, for example, for an interviewer to ask a criminal what he has been doing during a specific period and to get the response, "Nothing much." If the examiner probes more deeply, the criminal nevertheless reserves a lot. If the examiner pushes him, the criminal may respond, "It's personal," "Let's drop it," "I'd rather not go into it," or "I can't talk about it now." When something is initially concealed and later revealed and the criminal is asked why he had not reported it, he replies, "I didn't think it was important at the time" or "I forgot."

What the criminal considers "important" enough to remember is anything that puts him in a favorable light. He automatically omits anything to the contrary. As one criminal exclaimed, "How can I be blunt without exposing myself too much?"—a kind of Fifth Amendment remark.

4. Lying

In Chapter 4, we pointed out that lying is a way of life for the criminal, largely because it is necessary if he is to live as a criminal. Consequently, an examiner or other worker usually approaches a criminal with skepticism bordering on outright cynicism. No matter what the criminal says, the examiner probably considers it a lie and discredits it. This raises the question of what kind of relationship is feasible when truth is scarce and appears only when it is self-serving.

The criminal enters reluctantly and warily into all transactions in which he is held accountable. As he tries to avoid a penalty, receive a privilege, or get released, he knows that the truth will usually work against his best interests. As one man put it, "If they don't know, they can't use it against me."

> "Why should I tell the truth when it will keep me here? Talking keeps me here longer. The more I talk, the longer I stay."

It is standard operating procedure for the criminal to maintain his innocence and simply refute charges placed against him. When pressed for details, he often maintains that he does not remember. He may go so far as to claim amnesia. He may offer false alibis and mitigating circumstances. An automatic tactic is to blame others and thereby attempt to clear himself.

Lies of omission are more common than lies of commission. The criminal discloses only what benefits him and omits the more vital information. He knows that telling a part of the truth may be the best "con" of all, so he tells a bit of it and conceals the rest. When the criminal uses the phrases, "to tell the truth" and "to be honest," the examiner's antennae should be extended. We have found that a criminal who prefaces a statement wih these words is usually leaving a lot unsaid.

> C would return from his work and report how tired he was. He complained incessantly of fatigue and declared that he had a lot of sleep to catch up on. What he did not disclose was that part of the fatigue resulted from a daily pattern of taking drugs and stealing. When this information came to light, he insisted that he had been truthful in that he had stated how tired he was. For this he wanted credit.

This kind of reporting is typical. The criminal tells the truth once or tells part of the truth and gives the impression that he has provided the entire story.

If an interviewer is encouraged by hearing what the criminal terms "the truth," he may be satisfied enough not to inquire further. The criminal has then achieved another triumph: he has successfully diverted the probe for additional material that might jeopardize him legally or reveal him for the kind of person he is. Later, when more facts emerge, the criminal says, "You didn't ask me about that," although he has been asked for all pertinent information and sometimes has been interrogated specifically about the matter in question.

When the criminal is caught lying, he takes the offensive and asks the examiner, "Wouldn't you lie under these circumstances?" In this way, he tries to achieve equality. The criminal insists, if the examiner denies that he would lie under the same circumstances, that such a denial is itself a lie.

The criminal may be cooperative and not attempt to conceal the truth. But even a genuine "opening up" can later be used in a devious way. That is, the criminal denies what he said earlier, claiming that what appeared to be telling the truth was really a con. He prefers saying this to facing the consequences of whatever it was that he revealed. Furthermore, by saying that he was conning, he conveys the impression that he is now being truthful (which he of course is not, because he was not conning in the first place.)

Distortion is a form of lying in which the criminal twists facts to his advantage. He distorts his report of what occurred by shifting the emphasis, omitting part of what happened. Distortion is also achieved by vagueness, minimization, and other tactics, as will be seen.

5. VAGUENESS

The criminal is indefinite to avoid being pinned down. In a variety of ways, he qualifies what he says: "You might say," "It could be put this way," "It might be," "Perhaps," "Sometimes," "In a way," "I guess," "In a sense," "Not necessarily," "To a degree," and so on. Everyone uses these phrases when he is unsure about something. But the criminal uses them to skirt issues in an effort to conceal wrongdoing.

The criminal is also vague when he gives words idiosyncratic meanings and leaves it to others to figure out what he is saying. Unless the examiner asks him exactly what he means, the message is lost.

> One criminal, to conceal his boredom, said, "My head was ragged." This could have meant a dozen different things. We learned that he had had a lot of criminal thinking: he was bored and wanted to stir up excitement.

Had we not pursued the meaning of this vague expression, we would have missed an important statement about the criminal's frame of mind. Also, if the interviewer fails to ferret out the meanings of such phrases, he is later put in the position the criminal wanted—he must admit that he did not know what the criminal meant initially. Thus, he has erred as the criminal himself often does, failing to ask questions in the absence of knowledge. When both parties are vague, they get further and further from the facts, which is the criminal's objective.

The criminal is a master at circumvention. When asked a question, he avoids giving a direct answer. Even as a child, the criminal is adept at this.

> C had told his mother and therapist that things were "fine" at school. As report-card time grew close, C started to fudge when pressed as to how "fine" his grades would be. He said he didn't know what his grades would be. Then, he admitted that there "might" be "a few" unsatisfactory grades. When asked about grades on conduct or behavior, C said that he did not know what that meant. After 2 months of this elusive responding, the moment of truth came. C received the lowest grades possible in 2 academic subjects and in 7 aspects of deportment.

Vagueness may take the form of superficial wordy presentations loaded with generalization and empty phrases—"We're getting along O.K.," "We talked about this and that." The criminal's talk may be filled with verbiage really unrelated to the issue at hand. Another form of circumvention is circumlocution or what the criminal calls "rounding off the top." Using this tactic, he talks about an event that actually occurred, but he edits the story in such a way that his role is misrepresented. He misleads the examiner by a shift in emphasis. He tells enough of what happened to make his account seem plausible, but leaves himself out or makes himself a victim.

Any examiner who is himself vague in his transactions with criminals furthers the lack of communication. The word *maybe*, for example, used by the examiner, introduces an unnecessary obstacle, in that the criminal interprets it as promissory. No matter what the issue, the examiner or agent of change must not subject himself, by his behavior, to charges of obliqueness or "coming from the side," as the criminal calls it. He must express his own thinking directly and precisely, just as he asks the criminal to do. If the examiner does not know the answer to a question, he must say so. The criminal is both a "know-it-all" and a master at equivocation. The examiner must be sure that he does not act as the criminal does.

6. Attempting to Confuse

If the criminal succeeds in confusing the examiner, he believes that he has gained the upper hand. All the tactics that we are describing confuse, but there are some more deliberate methods that the criminal employs specifically to confuse issues. He offers inconsistent versions of a given event. He shades, qualifies, distorts, and shifts emphasis with each telling. If questioned about a discrepancy, he says that the interviewer was confused or misunderstood, thus shifting the burden to the other party. The criminal might accuse the examiner of being the one who distorted, misrepresented, and misinterpreted. Even if the examiner has a verbatim record of the transaction, the criminal attempts to becloud issues by further elaboration, qualification, and reinterpretation.

In another tactic for baffling an examiner or agent of change, the criminal makes a point seriously but, when effectively challenged later, says that originally he had only been joking. Furthermore, he accuses the interviewer of lacking a sense of humor.

> C was unemployed and in tight financial straits. He met his minimal living expenses by collecting a monthly check from the Veterans' Administration. One day, C phoned us and reported that he was putting in a bid of $50 for a used car. We questioned the wisdom of his doing this, particularly because he could not afford insurance, license plates, and upkeep of an automobile. However, we left him to make his own decision. When we asked him to continue to keep in touch with us daily, he responded, "I don't know that I can afford to use all those dimes." Our response was that, if C were bidding on a car, he most certainly could afford a dime a day to phone, inasmuch as he had elected to participate in our program for change. He answered with, "I was just joking about the dime. You always take me so seriously."

In this case, we knew that we had to take C seriously. Spending money on a car that he could not afford was very much in line with his past patterns.

The criminal may attempt to confuse an examiner by speaking so rapidly that it is hard to follow him. Or he may do the opposite and speak slowly and listlessly and deviate from the point. He may alter his speech by using a dialect that is difficult to understand; this is most common among black criminals who ordinarily speak clearly, but, when they want to conceal things, slur words and speak in a manner that is nearly incomprehensible to others.

Another device of the criminal is to begin to describe something that he did, then stop in the middle, admit that he is lying, and announce that he is now going to tell the whole truth. The criminal thinks that his acknowledgment of lying will lead the examiner to give him credit for honesty and to believe anything that he says later. This well-practiced tactic throws a very perceptive, but uninformed, examiner off the track.

7. Minimization

When it is known that the criminal has violated and he is called to account for what he has done, rather than deny it altogether, the criminal minimizes it. This need not be part of the lying pattern. Because the criminal thinks as he does, he tends to view an offense as less serious than others do; thus, he minimizes it in his own thinking. However, when he is confronted with what he has done and its consequences, the attempt to minimize is clearly to save his own skin. He may refer to even the most flagrant violation as a "prank," "mischief," or "just a mistake." It is not unusual to hear a criminal say that he "borrowed" something, as a euphemism for a theft. These phrases are intended to convey that he meant no harm by what he did.

In talking about his behavior, the criminal tries to conceal the harm that he is doing by deliberate understatement.

> C was discussing his school behavior. He said that he did not disrupt "continually" and was not difficult "all the time." Although he acted up in class, C maintained that it was "no big deal."

> C was talking about his relationship with his parents. He stated, "I see my parents." He meant literally: he caught sight of them, and that was the extent of it. This boy did not spend any time at home other than to sleep. So he would "see" his parents when he came into the house at 10 p.m.

In the first example, a disruptive adolescent criminal was minimizing the trouble he caused. In the second, C was trying to play down the *lack* of contact between him and his parents.

Another characteristic strategy is for the criminal to make light of some of his criminal ideas and maintain that, because he did not act on them, they were unimportant. In discussion with others, he dismisses the things that he thinks about and insists that only what he does counts. This kind of minimization is of crucial significance. As we indicated in Chapter 6, criminal acts always have an incubation period in antecedent thinking.

8. DIVERSION

The criminal is a master at diversion. Perhaps the kind of diversion that is best known to anyone who has worked with criminals is their bringing in irrelevant material. They try to interest the interviewer or agent of change in sports, chess, photography, theater, current events, or anything else other than their own criminal acts. They are not interested in the interviewer's experience. They do not want to learn, but to teach, thereby reducing the interviewer to a student. Before the examiner knows it, the time allotted for the interview has elapsed. Sometimes the topics appear relevant, and the examiner, giving the criminal the benefit of the doubt, continues the discussion; actually, the criminal intends this to be only a tangential time-filler designed to distract the interviewer. This is particularly useful in settings in which verbal participation is encouraged and discussion about almost anything is valued as a sign of cooperation, interest, and improvement. The interviewer or change agent must recognize diversion when he encounters it. Otherwise, the criminal achieves his objective; important information remains concealed, and the criminal controls the interview.

In a tough, "stick-to-the-point" examination, the criminal is more subtle. He dwells on something about himself that the examiner seems interested in, exaggerates its importance, and spends a disproportionate amount of time on it. He may label something a "problem" and describe it at length, thus distracting the interviewer from more important issues. For example, he may try to interest an examiner in his drinking, which is really no "problem" to him. In this way, he shifts the focus away from other issues that could put him in jeopardy.

Another diversion is to recount his qualities and good deeds. In some programs, the staff attempts to increase the criminal's "self-esteem" by emphasizing the good in him. If the examiner takes this approach, he contributes to building up the criminal's opinion of himself, which gives him further license to continue his old patterns.

Invoking the racial issue is another way of diverting. Clearly, there has been racial bigotry and discrimination by both whites and blacks, but racism is irrelevant to the issue at hand. The criminal knows that race is a sensitive issue, and that is why he raises it; he takes the offensive with charges of racism after he has failed to gain agreement on some point. In our work, we have dealt with more blacks than whites. The racism charge is especially impressive when used with us, because our work with blacks has been widely complimented by the criminals themselves, as they regard us as "color-blind." Although criminals say that we are not bigoted, they charge us with racism—but only when they are in disagreement with us.

> C, who was black, eloped to see a white woman about whom he worried because she was on drugs. He had been torn between a liaison with this woman and a very responsible black woman, who had stood by him loyally over the years. In talking with the agent of change about the violation, C maintained that the doctor disapproved of his "feelings" for the white woman because he, the doctor, wanted to keep the white race "uncontaminated."

This criminal had chosen an irresponsible white woman in preference to a responsible black woman, who many times had demonstrated her love for him. Only when he was accountable to the change agent did he introduce race. The racial issue is brought up usually after other tactics have been exhausted. Of course, an examiner seriously complicates the transaction if he fails to reveal that he perceives it to be a smokescreen. We do not deny that an examiner may encounter more resistance initially with a criminal who is suffused with racial antagonism. However, some specialists in the corrections and mental health fields have said that treatment is doomed if a black is treated by a white. All too frequently, this is basing a standard operating procedure on a principle that is a derivative of a tactic.

Racism and Mental Health: Pursuing Truths

> Dr. Comer and Dr. Claudewell S. Thomas of the National Institute of Mental Health declared that white psychotherapists could not successfully treat blacks because they subscribed to the philosophy of assigning individual responsibility for misfortune, rather than societal responsibility (*The Washington Post, 5/20/71*, p. H1).

We have met the racism charge directly when it was raised, informing the criminal how he was using it and then pointing out what we saw as the real issue. Proper handling dispelled the criminal's charge that we were racists.

In trying to evade accountability, the criminal may divert by talking about what other people do. He focuses on someone else's integrity, making that the issue, rather than his own. He talks about his co-workers' stealing or reports that personnel at the institution where he is confined are stealing. When an unchanged criminal complains of others' wrongdoing, he is usually doing it to divert the focus from his known violating patterns. Often when the criminal sees himself as cornered, he resorts to ideological argument, launching into a tirade on social injustice. He expresses his outrage over others' violations, evaluating himself as quite decent. Then, again, he may hold forth on a current issue and its social significance for him.

In a permissive setting, such as a psychotherapeutic or counseling session, the array and intensity of diversions introduced are likely to prevent any effective transactions. Knowing that he will not be penalized for his behavior in such situations, the criminal converts relative freedom into license. This is especially true with youths.

> "I don't act this way everywhere. I would get my ears knocked off if I acted this way at school or at home."

A worker is a ready target for flagrant diversion if he fails to take a tough, uncompromising stand at the beginning. The following is only a partial list of behaviors that we encountered in one of our early naïve sessions with a group of teenagers with whom we did not regard ourselves as being "permissive": shooting rubber bands, throwing objects into wastebaskets from a distance, note-writing, kicking one another, moving chairs around, opening windows, playing with objects brought in, passing around gum and candy, and asking to leave the room for water. No sooner did we clamp down and draw the line on one kind of behavior, than others arose. It was clearly an untenable situation. The obstacles were too great to permit any progress. These youngsters were not participating by their own choice, nor were there any unfavorable consequences to their unconstructive use of time. The group members operated as a gang and were there to create as much excitement as possible while "serving their time."

> "I don't mind coming here. What I get out of this is laughing. If I don't get anything out of it, I shouldn't come. I like to laugh a lot."

Statements like this might be considered rationalizations or a form of denial. Actually, they are only diversionary; the criminal does not have to rationalize. The group meeting referred to was simply one more arena for criminal expression. Had we seen the members of the group separately for several months and eventually met with them all together, a productive discussion might have been feasible. Groups of adult criminals usually do not use these particular tactics, but they also operate as a "gang" and continually introduce diversions.

9. Assent

The examiner may be fooled by a tactic in which the criminal appears to agree with him but is only momentarily acquiescing. This "assent" serves two functions. First, by not offering opposition, the criminal succeeds in cutting short the discussion (as one man said, "When I say 'yes,' it means 'drop it!' "); and second, he does not alienate the examiner. Both criminal and examiner go away satisfied. The examiner is pleased, because he thinks he has made some headway with the criminal. The criminal is pleased, because he thinks that the examiner is more positively disposed toward him.

> A doctor accused C of gambling on the ward. C, who on this occasion was not gambling, denied it. However, when he was badgered about it, he decided to confess. The doctor went away believing that he had accomplished something by having C admit that he had gambled.

In this situation, the doctor was satisfied by the confession, and the criminal was satisfied, because he had not antagonized the doctor nor incurred any penalty. In fact, he had advanced his cause by being so "honest."

By assenting, the criminal can mislead others into believing that progress has been made. Many a rehabilitation worker and therapist has observed groups of criminals enthusiastically embracing and verbalizing ideas and concepts, trying to impress each other and the worker with their apparent agreement on these issues. They do not apply the concepts to themselves nor implement them in their daily living.

Assent is expressed in a variety of ways, verbal and nonverbal. Intense concentration, a nod of the head, and good eye contact are nonverbal approaches. Verbal expression may include these phrases: "I guess so," "You're right," "I never thought of it that way," "You win on this one," and "It sure seems to make sense." These are not always words of assent. Although the criminal may be point-scoring or trying to terminate a discussion, he might be sincerely agreeing with the ideas of the other party. Saying, "It seems to make sense," may be a genuine expression of his evaluation of what the examiner or agent of change has said. One often cannot tell at the time whether the criminal is assenting for its own sake or being sincere. A criminal may think that an idea presented to him is valid. He may discuss it and expand on it, which he does not do when he is assenting because of its tactical value. However, agreeing with a point being made and being guided by it in daily living are not the same. He agrees that the idea has merit, but not necessarily that it applies to him. The agreement is transient and in time gives way to patterns of irresponsibility. The only way to differentiate genuine from tactical agreement is to observe the criminal over time. If he is assenting in a deliberate tactic to score points, this will eventually become evident.

10. SILENCE

The obvious purpose of silence is to maintain secrecy. Silence is an extremely potent form of control, because no examination or interview can proceed if one party refuses to talk. A man's impassively staring at someone while remaining silent has the effect of rendering the other party helpless, at least with respect to effective transactions. Many a worker in the field has encountered the criminal attempting to control a meeting through silence.

Note from a daily session:

Recently, when I picked the patient up in my car, he would say, "Hello, how are you?" This day, he said nothing. I remarked about the day, and got no answer. He sat down in the chair, and my first question was, "What decision have you come to regarding my presentation yesterday?" He said, "I didn't think about it." I reminded him that, after my presentation of the problem, he had stated that he would think about it and decide what approach to take. He would not comment. When I asked whether he understood what I was talking about, he stated that he understood everything very well and nodded his head knowingly. I did not quiz him on what he understood. I asked why he hadn't thought about it, and his answer was, "No reason at all."

This occurred repeatedly in our early work with criminals when we asked questions and awaited responses, or when we waited for criminals to raise issues, which they would not do, unless they wanted us to help them out of a jam. In our earlier work with noncriminals, we had dealt with neurotic patients who came seeking help with paralyzing fears. These patients offered resistance as we probed repressed memories of painful experiences. But, despite this resistance, the patients welcomed the probing, because they were eager to change. This was far different from the resistance of the criminal, who tried to prevent us from reaching the inner man. The criminal does not want others intruding into his psyche. Silence is often a manifestation of his anger when others attempt to do this.

There are many ways of being silent. The criminal rarely sits totally mute for an entire session. The tactics in the following list, which is by no means all-inclusive, are probably familiar to anyone who has dealt with criminals; all are ways in which the criminal says he is not talking: "I don't know," "I don't care," "My mind's a blank," "No comment," "I forgot," "Nothing happened," "I can't explain it," sighing, shrugging. The criminal may turn the question back on the examiner: "I didn't understand the question" or

"What do you mean by that?" If the examiner cajoles, begs, or pleads with the criminal to talk, in effect he places himself at the criminal's mercy. If the examiner resorts to threatening the criminal wih dire consequences for remaining silent, the session becomes a power contest.

The examiner must be sure to indicate that he functions differently from the criminal. The criminal uses silence both to control and to avoid disclosure, and when he sees others doing this, he perceives them as using his devices. Unless the examiner's opinions are openly expressed, the criminal views him as acting just as he does—communicating one thing while believing something else. Once this occurs, the interviewer or change agent loses respect and credibility. The criminal may also interpret the examiner's silence as evidence of timidity. Whether or not this perception is accurate, the criminal thinks it gives him a better chance of controlling the interview.

Silence on the part of the examiner is often interpreted as a sign of ignorance. The criminal initially sizes up anyone in authority as either knowing nothing or knowing everything. If he has the idea that the person who is examining him is not knowledgeable, he interprets silence as confirmation of it. However, if he believes that the examiner knows it all but is not revealing what he knows, then the criminal views the examiner's failure to respond as approval of him. Unless the interviewer responds to the criminal point for point, failure to comment is taken as endorsement of his thinking and action. This is true in any dealing with the criminal.

> C eloped and wrote to the administrative doctor, setting the terms under which he would return. The doctor was silent and did not bother to answer. This silence was interpreted by C as agreement with his terms. Nothing could have been further from the truth; the doctor had actually tried to arrange for C to be picked up by the authorities.

It should be clear by now that silence is not golden in the examiner's office, whether it be on the part of the criminal or on the par of the interviewer. If either party sits silently in an office, nothing productive can occur.

THE CRIMINAL'S TACTICS DURING THE CHANGE PROCESS

In this chapter, we are using the term "agent of change" very broadly to include almost anyone who works with the criminal over some period in a "rehabilitative" or change effort. This includes therapists, members of a rehabilitation team, and others who are offering the criminal a program for change, whether in a prison, a hospital, a school, or a counseling center or elsewhere.

A criminal agrees to participate in a program for change usually at the insistence of someone else. There may be some initial enthusiasm and even a sense of excitement in embarking on this new task, inasmuch as the criminal looks for excitement in everything. The man who is sincere at the time about wanting to change believes that he will accomplish it instantly. He begins with the notion that there is something magical about merely coming in for help. He believes that nothing will be required of him, but that the agent of change will miraculously turn him into a success overnight.

The relationship with the agent of change is usually harmonious at the outset, with the criminal adhering strictly to the program's requirements. But he soon becomes restless. A couple of months go by, and change has not been accomplished. He is not, in fact, an instant success. He begins thinking that he has had enough, that he can handle himself and be on his own. It is particularly at such a time that the tactics just described begin to be deployed, with additional ones that may not have emerged previously because the criminal was afraid of imperiling his status. The tactic of confession is one of the latter. The criminal tries to avoid self-incrimination with the examiner. He reveals as little as he can and tries to present himself in as good a light as possible. However, when he deals with an agent of change in a therapeutic context, where there is relatively little personal jeopardy, he may be open about his past and be praised for his disclosures. A constellation of tactics that inevitably emerges with an agent of change is the set of "attacking behaviors" to be described. The criminal is not as likely to use these with an examiner who is involved in a determination of his legal status.

The presentation of the tactics here in two separate sections does not limit the extent of their employment by the criminal. Tactics 1-10 are also used in dealing with change agents, and tactics 11-19 may appear in many situations other than programs for change (e.g., with parents, teachers, employers).

11. Selective Attention and Perception

It has long been recognized that a person's mental set determines his perception of a situation. Psychologic literature, experimental and clinical, contains numerous reports of controlled studies demonstrating this phenomenon (e.g., Dember, 1963 pp. 271–305). For the criminal, selective attention and perception form a well-practiced tactic in which he ignores everything unrelated to his objective. He prejudges and is subjective in his approach to people. With a closed mind, he hears only what agrees with his thinking. We have had conversations with criminals that were later reported to us by others (not criminals) in such a way as to make us wonder when and where such discussions were ever held. The criminal attends to that which supports his prejudgments and opinions and ignores all the rest. Often, the part of the conversation that he excludes is what we consider to be the central point.

> C listened to his therapist's dictation of a note in which the doctor developed at some length the exploitative nature of the relationship between C and a Mrs. E. In the course of dictation, the therapist alluded to the possibility that Mrs. E was in love with C. C ignored the central theme—the mutually exploitative relationship. He concluded only that his doctor agreed that Mrs. E was in love with him. That was the point that C carried away from the session.

The criminal may automatically construe a statement as being in agreement with his position when actually the opposite has been said. Again, the overriding tendency is to assume that others think as he does. An agent of change may belabor a point, or think that he has, only to find out that the criminal has gone away with an opposite view.

The agent of change compounds the problem if he is limited by preconceived notions. He must listen patiently and with an open mind. And he must not assume that the criminal is receiving the intended message. He must ask for feedback to determine how the criminal is construing what is being said. Otherwise, it is a selective "nondiscussion," which is more misleading than illuminating.

12. TOTAL INATTENTION

The agent of change often thinks that the criminal is listening when his mind is miles away. If the criminal is uninterested in what is being said, he allows his physical presence and a few nods of his head to serve as indicators that he is receptive. Meanwhile, he turns his attention to more exciting ideas and simply serves his time in the office. If the agent of change asks him a question to determine how much he is absorbing, the criminal tries to conceal his inattention. He may shift the burden to the agent—"You didn't make that clear." When the agent repeats what he said, the criminal responds, "Well, I knew that from the beginning." In other words, he is not at fault. He blames his lack of attention on the other party, accusing him of being unclear or boringly repetitious. A variant of this is to pretend that he heard. If he is pushed for a comment, he mutters something vague, e.g.,"I was not in touch with what you were saying." He might add that what was said did not apply to him, anyway.

13. TARDINESS AND MISSING APPOINTMENTS

As he begins to participate in a program for change, the criminal often goes through a "honeymoon" period. He appears for each interview and participates eagerly. As the newness of the experience wears off, competing desires arise, and he begins to pursue objectives that are incompatible with change. Then, if he comes at all, he arrives late and leaves early, usually offering phony excuses. Even when he plans to meet with us, he forgoes the session if something more exciting arises. As one criminal, stated, "I will see you tomorrow at three if nothing else comes up." In our experience, after the first few meetings, some criminals promise to return at a given time and simply do not appear again, unless there is a strong legal deterrent binding them to the program. The criminal may phrase it in terms of not wanting a program "at this time" or promising to call "in a few weeks." Such statements indicate that he wants to continue his criminality and does not want outside interference. Change is incompatible with his desires at the time.

When a criminal misses an appointment and does not call to offer an explanation, the agent of change can be fairly certain that the criminal is doing something irresponsible *beyond* missing the appointment.

> C was supposed to have deposited some money with us, so that we could help him with his budgeting and parcel it out as needed. As soon as it was evident that he had no intention of leaving the money with us, we surmised that he had left town and would soon return to crime. That is what occurred. He missed his appointment, left the area, and within a matter of weeks had committed many crimes, some major, such as several bank robberies.

These men also stay away because they know that, if they disclose their thinking, although it will not put them in legal jeopardy, they will have to subject it to critical examination. They want to avoid the change agent's challenging questions. Having chosen their course in life, they do not want to be deterred.

14. Feeding the Agent of Change What the Criminal Thinks He Wants to Hear

We have described the criminal's approach to an examiner as a criminal enterprise. Similarly, the criminal sizes up the agent of change and the staff of the institution in an effort to achieve his objectives. A few criminals consider it a putdown to cater to or court the staff. But even they will try to score points when they ultimately see that it is to their advantage to do so. In this section, we shall describe additional tactics for "feeding" the other party that are more likely to emerge in a program for change than earlier.

The criminal "feeds" the agent of change for several reasons. Just as he does with so many others, the criminal wants to convey a favorable image and be well regarded. He may have this as an objective in itself, but more likely he has a specific purpose in mind, such as avoiding confinement or gaining greater freedom. "Feeding" others serves another very important function. It conceals ongoing violations, in that people are thrown off the track because they conclude that the criminal is doing well.

CONFESSION

One error that the agent of change might make is to equate confession with insight; sometimes, the more sordid the act described, the more impressed the staff is. Confession by a criminal is often simply a tactic to score points.* Confession is interpreted as indicating an intention to be responsible. Nothing could be further from the truth. Acknowledgment of wrongdoing does not result in a man's changing. In fact, it may be used to avoid change. A criminal may think that reporting his violations makes them acceptable. In other words, to confess is to impress. If the agent of change values confession as an indicator of change, he will be falsely encouraged and inevitably disappointed. More often than not, although the listener thinks that he is hearing the entire story, the confession is only a small part of the truth. Admitting small infractions often helps the criminal to conceal major violations.

The criminal sometimes confesses to things that he did not do, if he wants to maximize the effect. Thus, confession becomes even more of a con job to impress the agent of change and the staff.

SHOWING "INSIGHT"

The criminal does not use psychologic jargon on the street, but only in the institution or in the office. We have often heard criminals flamboyantly spouting this jargon. These men, eager to display their psychologic sophistication, throw the terms around, albeit not always with the greatest of precision.

> As he came into our program, C continually spoke in terms of "reinforcement," "negative defense mechanisms," "introjection," "projection," "rationalization," and so forth. All this emanated from a man of little formal education, but schooled in mental hospital jargon. He admitted that using such terminology made him feel important. It set him apart from some of the more "common" criminals. He also used

---

* Confession may be part of a sincere but brief attempt at change. Here we are discussing confession only as a tactic. In order to determine whether confession is a tactical maneuver or is sincerely intended, the change agent often must await later developments.

the terms to explain "why" he did what he did, mainly to present himself as a victim of psychologic processes.

The criminal latches onto whatever is the most valuable currency for psychiatric transactions. We have described the process by which the criminal attributes his violations to feelings, is complimented for his insight, and, as a consequence, is spared a penalty or restriction. The idea is to feed the staff members a steady diet of material that satisfies their theories. For instance, he may tell the agent of change that he violated because unconsciously he wanted to be caught or punished. He tries to convey the belief that he has learned his lesson, that in fact he does "learn from experience." He chooses his words calculatingly. If he indicates that he feels "guilty," the staff may believe that at long last he is acquiring a conscience.

The criminal tries to score points by showing that he has put his insight to work through deeds, as well as words. He tells the agent of change how he has gone out of his way to help others, or he relates the violations that he has considered, but refrained from committing. Thoughtful actions and abstention from violation may be parts of a sincere, but transient, interest in change. However, the criminal is likely to capitalize on such behavior later to build himself up and impress a change agent. He may also boast about good deeds that he never performed.

Of course, the criminal tries to feed us our material, just as he does with any other practitioner. Once he understands what we mean by "fragmentation," he refers to this to demonstrate insight, usually within the context of an excuse. That is, after straying from intentions to be responsible, he accounts to us by saying, "Well, it was due to fragmentation." A criminal may tell us that he violated because he was in a "zero state." He expects us to be pleased with the insight and therefore to overlook the violation.

SOCIALIZING AND LEADERSHIP

Showing leadership is a tactic by which the criminal demonstrates to others that he is changing. Our experience has been that many criminals who show leadership do so to score points, but continue to violate on the side. For criminals not active in crime, leadership provides a criminal equivalent; it is not a valid index of change. We have seen unchanged criminals edit newspapers, organize activities, preside over meetings, and become active in many other functions. As leaders, they enjoy the buildup, the excitement, and the personal power in running such events.

It is generally believed that an important part of "rehabilitation" is the "socializing" of criminals. In prisons and hospitals, criminals are referred to programs where they are encouraged to take an interest in others and learn "social skills." Socializing at these activities is both a point-scoring tactic and a source of excitement, in that it provides additional opportunities for criminal talk, bragging, and building oneself up (a criminal equivalent). Many criminals eagerly attend such activities and enjoy trying to impress one another, as well as the staff.

TAILORING THE APPROACH

Part of the criminal's attempt to feed others what they want to hear involves the tailoring of his approach to his "audience." Broadly speaking, this is a tactic applied to his demeanor rather than to the substance of what he has to say. The tactic is basically an M.O. that he works out in dealing with people, just as he has his M.O.'s for particular crimes. The criminal's approach is designed to dovetail with the personality and views of the person with whom he is having contact. In doing this, he seeks information beforehand as to how to dress, what kind of language to use, whether to give lengthy answers to questions, and so forth. Usually the criminal tries to ingratiate himself and shows an exaggerated politeness.

15. MISUNDERSTANDING

When the criminal says, "He understands me," or "We had an understanding," he means, "He agrees with me," or "We reached an agreement." When he is confronted by his failure to perform responsibly, the criminal often claims that there was a "misunderstanding" between him and the agent of change. A simple example may illustrate what occurs again and again.

> C agreed on a Wednesday to see his therapist at 1 P.M. the next day (Thursday). At 1 P.M. Thursday, C did not show up. At 2 P.M., the therapist found out that C was reported to have been seen leaving the grounds (unauthorized to do so) with a woman earlier that afternoon. On Friday, when the therapist did see him, C attributed their not meeting to a "misunderstanding."

The two parties had clearly agreed on the time, date, place, and feasibility of the appointment. Despite this arrangement and a later unsolicited confirmation by the criminal, he claimed a misunderstanding. The criminal had simply found something else more exciting. When held accountable, he shifted the blame. Here is another example:

> C informed the agent of change that he had discussed plans involving a violation with his mother, and that she had approved. The agent could not conceive of this, because a violation of the sort proposed

would be anathema to C's very responsible mother. When the agent of
change asked C about this again the next day, C replied that the agent
had misunderstood. It was his sister who was collaborating with him
and with whom he had discussed his plans, not his mother.

"Misunderstandings" occur concerning meeting times, who said what, and
innumerable other details. No matter what the issue, if the agent of change
calls the criminal to task for not living up to an agreement, the criminal
turns the tables and claims that it was the agent who did not understand.

If the agent of change is unaware of the semantics of the word "misunderstanding," he may start to believe that he did misunderstand. With a
large caseload, he is particularly vulnerable to this tactic. We have seen
a criminal convince a probation officer who had many cases that he (the
officer) was totally confused about what the criminal had said and done
earlier. The probation officer, knowing that he sometimes had difficulty
keeping the details straight for so many cases, accepted responsibility for
the misunderstanding and apologized to the criminal.

16. Generalizing a Point to Absurdity

The agent of change strives to teach the criminal what is necessary to cope
responsibly with life's adversities. In doing this, he indicates to the criminal
that new ways of thinking and acting are necessary. On hearing specific
requirements that are not in line with what he wants, the criminal may
distort a "virtue" and turn it into a "vice."

> The change agent was making the point that, to live responsibly, C
> would have to refrain from doing some of the things he wanted to do
> and do some things he did not want to do. In the beginning, this would
> entail a degree of "suffering," in that he would be deprived of the
> excitements that his criminal life-style afforded. Furthermore, he would
> be obligated to do many things that were disagreeable. To this C re-
> plied, "You mean that I'm supposed to suffer *all the time!*" C ridiculed
> the agent of change's position, on the grounds that it was absurd to
> think that he would spend the rest of his life not doing what he wanted.

A point that was made, but ignored, was that one experiences less "suffering" as new patterns are habituated and one begins to find fulfillment in responsible living.

> The agent of change was describing the criminal's building up a good
> opinion of himself as a totally criminal process—one that gives him
> greater license for crime. C maintained that this meant that anyone
> who has a high opinion of himself is a criminal.

This was not a belief of his, but a tactical statement made to belittle a point the change agent was making.

An agent of change may tell a criminal that, because he lacks education and skills, he must consider taking a job in which he has to start at the bottom. The criminal then accuses the agent of change of asking him to be a flunky for the rest of his life. He may contend that there is no room in responsible living for a person to enjoy life. Such a statement has to be probed, because the criminal's use of the word *enjoyment* implies criminal excitement. To that extent, he is correct: there is no room for that kind of enjoyment. But life as a responsible person is not devoid of pleasurable moments and "excitement" of a different variety.

The criminal often takes the concept of an open channel of communication and generalizes it in a distorted manner. If he is angry at someone, he tells that person off and then comes to us and says that we told him to disclose fully. He maintains that he was being honest in expressing his anger. If he had bottled it up, he claims he would not have conformed to our requirement of disclosure. Of course, this is a perversion of the "open-channel" corrective (to be explained in Volume 2). The *reductio ad absurdum* would be that, if anyone wanted to kill a person, it would be honest to do so.

Another way of generalizing a point to the ridiculous is to twist it so as to render it meaningless. For example, an agent of change may tell the criminal that the words he utters in the office are worth very little; actions speak louder than words. The criminal turns this around and asks why he should bother to talk at all if his words are not believed.

The criminal often takes an objective of a program and turns it into an absurdity.

> C took issue with us, because we emphasized building from scratch and acquiring things for oneself on the basis of achievement. C accused us of stressing materialism and claimed that this would inevitably drive him back into crime. He failed to differentiate between simple ownership and the mode of acquisition. All his life, he had taken what he had wanted. He was now accusing us of emphasizing ownership of things, rather than responsible activity as a route to obtaining material possessions.

A common misrepresentation of a program's objective occurs in the criminal's charge that we want him to be a copy of us. He complains, "I can't be exactly as you are." The agent asks the criminal to be as responsible as he is; the criminal interprets this as meaning that they must be identical in all respects, including even aesthetic tastes and preferences. The criminal responds to stringent requirements for becoming responsible by calling the change agent a "puritan," an "extinguisher of the flame of life," "a robot," and so on. This does reflect the criminal's view of what responsibility entails, but such statements are sometimes calculated tactics to generalize a program's philosophy to absurdity and thereby discredit it.

We might also note that the more literate criminal does the opposite of expanding on a point. He may take a word out of context, give it an extraordinarily literal meaning (even though he knows better), and then use it to object to a new idea. He takes words that the change agent uses broadly, such as *education, democracy, religion, bigotry, conservative, liberal,* and so on, and uses them in a narrow way. He limits the meaning of the word to suit his purposes and then quarrels with the change agent about it.

> Dr. Yochelson was discussing what constitutes good health with several criminals. He was pointing out how their fears operated so that they did not take care of themselves. The criminals attacked Dr. Yochelson for smoking a pipe, despite their knowledge of his many other health-care practices, such as a severely disciplined diet and regimen of exercise. The criminals were narrowing the discussion of health to pipe-smoking.

17. DELIBERATE POSTPONEMENT

We have pointed out that deferment of the responsible is characteristic of the criminal. It is part of a thinking error, not a tactic. However, there are occasions when the criminal has little intention of doing what is required and deliberately postpones things indefinitely, which means an ultimate default. In these situations, there is no intention of initiating the responsible activity. When he talks with the agent of change, however, he does not acknowledge this. Instead, he offers excuses related to his lack of readiness to do certain things: "I wasn't ready yet." Or he puts the agent of change on the defensive by implying that the agent is too demanding: "I can't do it overnight," "I have to do things one at a time, not all at once," and "What more do you want, blood?" He diverts the focus from his lack of effort and charges that it is the other party who is to be faulted for expecting too much too soon. He uses this tactic, even though the tasks that he puts off are easy to complete quickly.

Behind this alleged lack of readiness is the criminal's doubt that he truly wants a different kind of life. When he makes such statements as, "I need time to think," it is merely another means of postponing what is necessary for change. He may carry this a step further and, after much delay on his part, chastise the agent of change for not accomplishing the job of change: "I gave you a year to have this work done, and now I'm ready to go."

A related move is to use the estimate of duration of the program as a reason for not changing more rapidly. For example, a criminal may be informed that he is expected to participate in sessions regularly for a year. After two months have elapsed and little change is evident, the criminal defends himself by saying, "I have a whole year." He uses the estimate as a license for deferment. Then, as time elapses, he reminds the agent of change that his habits are so ingrained that it will still take a long time to break them.

18. CLAIMING THAT HE HAS CHANGED ENOUGH TO LEAVE THE PROGRAM

When the criminal is bored, restless, and seeking excitement, he says that he is ready to leave the program for change and stand on his own feet. At such a time, he wants to overcome any restraints and get into the "action." He has decided to be the judge of what is best for him. The argument for setting forth on his own course may emerge in different forms. He may justify his declaration of independence in terms of not wanting to become "too dependent," or "institutionalized."

> "I have to do things for myself. If I make mistakes, I make them. I *have* to make them."

> "Let me go and knock my head against the wall if I need to. I can't sit back. The only way you do it is to go out and fail. This is not the kind of thing I have been doing. Books can't tell you how hard it is."

There is some truth in those statements. Books and sitting in an office do not do the job. A man learns from life's experiences. However, when one knows the mind of a criminal, one sees that this argument is used as a screen for a decision to continue violating patterns. The trap for the agent of change is that he may subscribe to the idea of "too dependent" or "institutionalized," because he knows that one tries to avoid this in treating the noncriminal. We have pointed out that one of the criminal's thinking errors is his refusal to be dependent. When closely examined, what others see as dependence is actually exploitation.

19. PUTTING THE AGENT OF CHANGE ON THE DEFENSIVE: THE TACTICS OF ATTACK

Although the criminal is participating in a program to learn, he tries to assume the role of teacher and wants to convert others to his point of view. Consequently, struggles and contests occur, during which he insists on prov-

ing a point. As he asserts the correctness of his views, the criminal may become combative and directly attack the agent of change in a variety of ways.
Some of the criticisms have merit. If so, the agent of change should acknowledge these, even though the criminal is using the tactic of trying to make
someone other than himself the target of discussion. If an agent of change
considers his own self-esteem to be at stake, he is likely to compound the
problem by responding to the criminal's control tactics with power tactics
of his own.

The criminal may take the direct tack of degrading the agent of change,
as in the following case.

> In the initial series of interviews with C, we promised that he could
> read the dictated notes. The notes were duplicated and given to him
> to look at. He became angry, claiming that it would take hours to cor-
> rect all the mistakes. Raising his voice, he berated the interviewer, the
> typist, and Dr. Yochelson. C then decided to go through the material
> page by page. He did so, pointing out every typographic error and
> misspelling, but never took issue with the content. In doing this, he
> was exceedingly derisive.

This criminal was hypercritical, sarcastic, and derogatory. He took every
opportunity to build himself up, by pointing to our smallest errors and
attempting to put us on the defensive.

The criminal may also attempt to degrade the agent of change by criticizing his appearance. He may refer to a person dressed in "mod" clothing as
a "faggot." A conservatively dressed change agent may be faulted for being
"old fashioned," for having a spot on his clothes, or for assuming a particular posture. For example, one criminal asserted that a doctor was a
homosexual, solely on the grounds that he sat with his legs crossed.

The criminal fights about a point that he later acknowledges as being of
no significance to him. He quibbles over words, turns meanings around, and
argues. He may try to embarrass the agent of change or pressure him by
invoking the opinion of an outside authority: "I talked it over with Mr.
———— and he said" or "I read that in...." In the attempt to control, the
criminal becomes dogmatic. He is struggling to maintain his good opinion
of himself and is fighting efforts to expose him for what he is. In such situations, it is more essential to win a point than to be logical, more important
to demonstrate his knowledge than to learn. In contests, the criminal departs
from the issue at hand and thrusts at the agent of change in more personal
ways: engaging in sarcasm, scapegoating, shouting, cursing, and other verbal
abuse. Such sessions may culminate in physical threats against an agent
of change (or other members of a group, if it is a group meeting). Another

tactic is threatening to ruin the reputation of the agent or to embarrass him by violation.

Although almost anything may initiate these ordeals, at their very base is the criminal tenaciously holding on to the view he has of himself. The criminal can become exceedingly belligerent and angry as he tries to defend his very being and to show he is "something," rather than "nothing." These episodes are always exercises in futility, with no winner. No new learning or useful communication occurs. They only indicate that the criminal has rejected the idea of making sweeping changes to live responsibly.

Anger is the habitual way in which the criminal attempts to achieve control. Anger is the weapon he uses to prevent probing of his mind. In one way or another, he tries to silence the other party. He may do it by simply shouting louder and drowning out the change agent. He may flatly and openly declare, "I don't care what you think," and refuse to listen further. In other words, he uses and abuses the agent of change, as he has everyone else in his life. When a criminal comes to the office in a state of anger, the session cannot be productive unless the anger is subjected to evaluation. However, it is very difficult to talk to an angry person about being angry. The agent of change can compound the difficulties if he is threatened by these control tactics. Even though the criminal is on the attack, the agent of change must not yield to the tendency to go on the attack himself. Otherwise, he will be using the very tactics of the person who needs to change. The criminal may charge the agent of change with almost anything—using the criminal as a guinea pig, being a racist, and so forth. If the agent is pulled into a debate over these charges, he is failing to keep his eye on the target—namely, the processes of mind that are operating, not the specific content of the accusations.

When a criminal has been irresponsible and it is discovered, one of his tactics is to cite angrily and self-righteously something that the agent has done wrong and to use it as an excuse for what he has done. Such a tactic is often a diversion from a still more significant violation that has not yet come to light.

> Dr. —— was a few minutes late for his session with C. During the interview, C asked whether he could go to the canteen to purchase some cigarettes. Forty-five minutes elapsed before C returned. Then, he came into the office very much on the defensive. He angrily maintained that Dr. —— had made him wait earlier, so there should be no issue now. Later, it came out that C had used the occasion to make a phone call to arrange an elopement from the hospital.

C used the tardiness of the agent of change as justification for his own staying away. His response was, in effect, "You made me wait, so I made you wait." But, by focusing on the issue of lateness, the criminal succeeded in concealing the planned violation for which arrangements had been made. He had attempted to put the agent of change on the defensive, thus taking the spotlight off himself.

Another ploy that the criminal uses to attack when a violation has come to light is to put the agent of change on the defensive by saying that he was "not clear." The criminal takes the position that, had he "understood" or had things been made more explicit, he would have acted differently. There are times when the criminal is so effective in shifting the focus that the agent of change begins to doubt whether in fact he had been clear; he may go so far as to shoulder some of the blame for the criminal's irresponsibility. For example, the criminal brings out what his thinking has been on an issue; the agent of change dissects it and questions his premises; the criminal responds that, by attacking his position, the agent of change is making it impossible for him to keep an open channel—that is, how can he disclose if he is going to be attacked. He then asserts that he should not have spoken out in the first place. A change agent, if he is not alert to what is going on, may then back off. Instead, he needs to remind the criminal that the channel has to be open, so that mental processes can be dissected. Such dissection is not an attack, even though the criminal perceives it to be one. Thus, the agent of change makes two points: the two people are there for constructive work, and the criminal needs to reexamine what puts him down.

The agent of change is especially liable to being pushed into a defensive position when the criminal wants to return to his old patterns and is looking for a way to rid himself of the constraints of the program. The criminal then may launch a strong offensive.

C had been considering violating during the Christmas season. One December day, as the agent of change was dictating the notes of the day's meeting, C muttered, "I don't believe that shit." There then ensued an attack that proceeded with a bunch of charges. C claimed that the doctor called everyone a "criminal." He said that the change agent was prejudging others and that his ideas were those of a racist. Then the climax came. Knowing that the doctor was a supporter of Israel, C called all Israelis criminals, because they are "criminal" toward the Arabs. The agent of change, seeing that there was little time remaining and little productive that could occur, drew the session to a close. The following day, C repeated the charges, demanded some money that was being kept for him, and stated that he was through with the program.

C was anticipating some "action." Going on the offensive was his method of trying to eliminate the agent of change as a deterrent, to free himself to violate. C later confirmed this.

A term that comes up often between agent of change and criminal is "testing." Criminals sometimes do "test" other people by deliberate maneuvers, to see how far they can push them. There are times when they do not test, but say that they do. When a criminal is held accountable for trying to get away with something, he may say, "I was testing you," purely as an excuse. In fact, he often turns the tables and blames the agent of change for doing something to "cause" him to do what he did; he claims that the agent was the provocateur who was testing him. Some change agents test criminals solely to see how they will react; in short order, this becomes a game of mutual testing, and the transaction is a charade. Usually, when the agent of change is accusing the criminal of testing, he is describing the effect of the criminal's behavior on him. That is, he thinks he is being tested, but that may not be at all what the criminal intended.

A favorite tactic when the criminal finally wants to back away from one of these ordeals is to deny that he had any serious difference of opinion. Instead, he maintains, he was playing "games," or he was "testing." This permits him to save face, if he sees that his position is untenable in the face of pressure from a change agent or a group.

Change agents are often pleased at the prospect of working with criminals who are educated, verbal, and intellectually inclined. However, we have found that these criminals are in some ways the most difficult of all. They go on the offensive in their own style. They speak in philosophic language, often downgrading the program; they quote Plato, Camus, Sartre, Zen Buddhist tracts, with which they are more familiar than the agent of change. These criminals view themselves as operating on a higher plane. They regard the change agent as a dull person who deals in the trivial and mundane issues of responsibility, never reaching the grander heights of philosophy and spirituality that they have attained. They criticize others for being intellectual inferiors. Their intellectual offensive consists of throwing up various smokescreens to put themselves into a position of authority and divert the focus from considerations of implementing the program.

> C stated, "I want spiritual guidance for stability." This meant that he did not want to work for anything. By sidetracking discussions to "loftier" considerations than the issues of responsibility, C tried to avoid seeing himself as he really was; in addition, he took the offensive and tried to make the change agent conform to his ideas as to what the program should be.

An Example of the Use of Tactics in the Change Process

To show the reader more graphically what a change agent encounters, we now present material from a session in which a number of tactics and obstacles were blatantly apparent. This interview occurred shortly after a criminal decided to rejoin our program. He was permitted to do so as a condition of probation on a larceny charge, rather than go to jail. The criminal had earlier been in the program for a long time, but he had never sustained a commitment for change. Now, with the alternative of prison or suicide staring him in the face, he was prepared to work more seriously toward his only other option—becoming a responsible person. However, it became clear once again that he had serious reservations about embracing a responsible life-style that he had always deplored. During this particular session, he was not even conforming to the requirement of reporting the day's thinking and action. We shall note here the main tactics and the thinking errors that posed obstacles to an effective transaction.

When C left here, he did not deposit the money for safekeeping. I learned on that day that he was sleeping in the park. He did not call me over the weekend as we had arranged, and he did not appear for our meeting yesterday.

CLOSED CHANNEL

TACTIC 13
MISSING
APPOINTMENTS)

I called him at work, and he spoke indignantly. He stated that I rejected him from the program, which is clearly not so, although I did say that his present pattern was "futile." He stated over the phone that, when I said that the present pattern was futile, he took that as meaning that I had thrown him out of the program. He attempted to debate the point over the phone, and I refused to do so. I told him to be here at 8:30 in the morning.

RIGHTEOUS INDIGNATION

TACTIC 16
(GENERALIZING A
POINT TO ABSURDITY)

TACTIC 15
(MISUNDERSTANDING)

In the course of this discussion, it came out that he believed that this program, which is "external to himself," could not get at a "program of the inner man," by which he meant drive or motivation. He had none of that. Then it came out that his behavior here produced the futility. It was clear that his ambling in at 9 most of the time in the last 2 weeks (a half-

TACTIC 8
(DIVERSION)

TACTIC 10
(SILENCE)

hour late) was an indication of no zest. Of course, the silence is even more important than the tardiness.

Dr. Yochelson: Well, C, what do you have to say?

Criminal: First, I want to say that I want to leave at 9:30. [No reason given.] I have to do things for myself. If I make a mistake, I make it. I have to make them. That is the way I'm living. [3 minutes of silence.]

TACTIC 18
(CONSIDERING THE WORK TO BE FINISHED)

Y: Anything more to report?
C: Not of any importance.

CLOSED CHANNEL

Y: Do you know the primary requirement of this program?
C: Yes.

TACTIC 9 (ASSENT)

Y: What is it?
C: A wide-open channel.
Y: If you know the term, what are its requirements?
C: To report all significant thinking and action.

CLOSED CHANNEL

Y: Is that all?
C: Yes.
Y: Anything else?
C: Nothing remarkable about work.

TACTIC 5 (VAGUENESS)

Y: Where are you living?
C: Sleeping in the park.
Y: Why do you live as a vagrant?
C: I am not a vagrant. I choose to sleep in the park.

TACTIC 7
(MINIMIZATION)

C stated that this program could not produce the zest, drive, or motivation that must come from within himself. I then asked him what he was doing about this. He said that he didn't know how he was achieving it. He went on to say that he needed what might be 100 or 200 "experiments" within himself. I persisted in asking what experiments he had tried, and he said none. He said that he had to just live and indulge. At this point I made the statement, "It is futile." Then I made the point of his tactics in coming here, which had the purpose of putting the onus on me to be the one to reject him.

NO INITIATIVE

TACTIC 6
(ATTEMPTING TO CONFUSE)

I then asked him what the "mistakes" were that he referred to. His
answer was the epitome of absurdity:
he said that the mistake he had made
was to keep his food in his bag while
he slept in the park, and it drew ants.
It was clear that his concept of "mistake" was limited to a concrete little
episode. I raised the question of
whether he was using me to stay out
of the penitentiary. After all, his decision to return to this program was
predicated on cooperation [with us],
but he was not so doing. He stated
that he was not using me. I saw no
point in arguing this statement. Basically, there was a clash of wills, as
evidenced by his statement, "I have
to do things for myself." He would
not go our way and was going his. He
certainly was not fulfilling the requirements of probation, as judged
by drug use, sleeping in the park, and
lack of cooperation with me.

OWNERSHIP AND
CONTROL

CRIMINAL PRIDE

The tactics and obstacles in this interview are not peculiar to this one man.
Any agent of change encounters similar situations as he works with the criminal. In fact, any person in the criminal's environment who holds him accountable has to contend with the same things.

SEMANTICS

Many disagreements arise because one party does not understand the terms
that the other is using. The different sides of a dialogue may be at cross-pur-
poses simply because the participants have different frames of reference. For
example, two people may use the same words but attach very different meanings to them. Such words as *religion, education, democracy* are cases in point.
The way a person uses words can be a key to his personality. But even to be
aware of differences in word usage, one must have some knowledge of the
type of person with whom he is dealing. When a noncriminal converses with
a criminal, their frames of reference are totally different, and therefore it is
as though they are conversing in different languages. As we shall point out,
the criminal's use of some words is so different from other people's that he is
only articulating familiar words, and that is where the similarity ends. An

agent of change misses a great deal if he fails to recognize that he and the criminal attach almost opposite meanings to some words.

When a person works in any capacity with the criminal, he is at a disadvantage with respect to language in still another way. As we have said, most people approach the criminal from the frame of reference of the noncriminal. By the nature of his formal training, a professional worker often views the criminal in terms of the mental processes of a noncriminal. We have already discussed the tendency to view the criminal as "dependent." A change agent may also say that the criminal has an "authority problem." The noncriminal might have difficulties in achieving personal autonomy, being either too submissive or counterdependent toward authority. The only authority with whom the criminal has problems is a person who seeks to deter him or interfere with him. He has no difficulty with people who do not oppose him. When terms that are useful in describing the noncriminal are used to describe the criminal, it is like applying terms descriptive of apples to cabbages. The terminology is rendered meaningless. Different premises of life are operative, and the thinking processes differ accordingly.

It is tempting to apply familiar theories and concepts in unfamiliar areas. For example, almost every thinking error of the criminal could be called a "defense mechanism." Criminal pride, anger, control, and so forth could be called "defense mechanisms" against a zero state. This would render the term "defense mechanism" impotent, because it would be so general that it could characterize virtually everything the criminal said, thought, or did. It would also erroneously ascribe a primary causal attribute to the zero state.

The criminal picks up terms that the agent of change is fond of, like "dependence," "authority problem," "defense mechanism," and others. He then incorporates them into his vocabulary and feeds them back to impress the agent. A word or phrase aptly used may become an explanation in itself. For example, if a criminal says, "I did it because I was paranoid," the "paranoia" may be seen by an interviewer as indicative of an underlying disorder that is pervasive and as causing the act in question. Another example is, "I hit the attendant because I was depressed over the way things were going." "Depression" is then seen as the explanation. The danger is that the criminal and the agent of change may think they are getting somewhere, when all they are doing is agreeing to use the same word to label a behavioral phenomenon.

The agent of change must have a thorough knowledge of how the criminal's mind operates, so that he can cut through the semantic thicket. Even though he does not use language as the criminal does, the agent of change must know what the criminal means, if their dialogue is to be of any value. We now present a compendium of words (excluding street language) to which the criminal attaches meanings in line with his own frame of reference. These meanings depart significantly from common usage.

The criminal is impressed by knowledgeability on the part of the agent of change. He has fooled people for so long that he has some respect for a person who can competently assert, "What you really mean is. . . ." When we tell the criminal that we know what he means by the use of a particular word and show how it differs from what is conventionally meant, he may think that we know more about him than we actually do.

PHRASE OR TERM	COMMON USAGE	CRIMINAL'S USAGE
ABSTRACT	Opposite of "concrete" —i.e., theoretical or conceptual	"Crazy," "off the wall"
BOREDOM	Ennui or weariness due to tedium	Angry, restless state of criminal who is deterred from doing the forbidden or is not power-thrusting
BORROW	Receive something that belongs to someone else with an intention to return or repay	Receive something that belongs to someone else with no intention to return or repay or with unsustained intention to return or repay
"CAN'T"	Refers to inability to do something	Refers to refusal to do something; equivalent to "won't"
CATER (to another person)	To supply what someone else wants or asks for	To abdicate control, as to listen to and abide by what someone else says without angry objection, fuming, or making things more difficult
CLEVER	Resourceful, ingenious	Holding or stating a position foreign to that of the criminal and contradictory to his thinking
CLOSENESS (with another person)	A degree of familiarity and intimacy	Refers to a person who does everything the criminal wants and does not question or criticize him; he is "close" to his girl friend on the basis that she is unquestioning and obedient

PHRASE OR TERM	COMMON USAGE	CRIMINAL'S USAGE
COMPANIONSHIP	Fellowship, comradeship	Refers to a conquest, person to exploit; frequently a sexual conquest
CON	A conscious deception for the purpose of attaining something; a swindle	Persuasion (including nondeceptive) and eventual control of another person
CONFIDENCE	Faith in oneself and one's powers based on prior achievement; a product of hard work and knowledge	Superoptimism with fear cut off and no humility; a shallow, cocky state of certainty; may also refer to playing the expert in the absence of expertise
CONFUSION (as a mental state)	Jumbled thoughts, lack of clarity in thinking	Shifts in what the criminal wants; changes of mind or fragmentation
EXCITEMENT	A "charge" from something out of the routine, a new experience; an extraordinary performance	A "charge," usually from pursuit and conquest, exercise of power or control, doing the forbidden, quick triumph, or conquest
FAILURE	Lack of success, falling short, proving inadequate	Not tops, not number one—thus, a "zero"
FRIEND	A person for whom one has affection and regard; a person with whom one shares	Used in several ways: (1) A person who will do as the criminal wants (2) Someone who will not jeopardize him (3) An acquaintance with whom the criminal has had a brief, casual contact
FRUSTRATED	Thwarted, baffled, foiled	Put down, reduced to a nothing because of failure to achieve an objective
GETTING INVOLVED	Implies emotional attachment	Conquering a partner sexually; implies no serious emotional commitment

Phrase or Term	Common Usage	Criminal's Usage
"HANGUP"	Refers to a problem, usually a psychologic conflict within oneself	Refers to something restraining the criminal from what he wants to do; an external deterrent, rather than internal (although a conscience factor may temporarily deter him)
HAPPY	Pleased, glad, with a sense of well-being	In a position of being top man, a powerful person, in control of others
INDEPENDENT	Not relying on someone else; able to make one's own way or do something without assistance	Not subject to the needs or requirements of anyone else; amounts to being free to violate and not be accountable to anyone
INSIGHT	Understanding of the true nature of something	Refers to tips, methods, or conning devices
LONELY	Without human companionship	Without someone to control, mainly a sex partner
LOVE	Warm attachment, affection, unselfish concern; may be a sexual attraction	Usually a sexual reference; sometimes refers to a transient sentimentality
MANHOOD	Refers to such qualities as bravery, courage, independence; also to sexual potency	Refers to conquering, outwitting, overpowering—usually with respect to sex or fighting
OBJECTIVELY	Implies expression of facts without distortion or bias, personal feeling, etc.	Implies viewing things from the criminal's point of view
ORDINARY	Average, common, unexceptional	Being a "slave," a "sucker," "lame," "weak," a "sissy"—in short, a "zero"
PARANOID	Refers to irrational suspicion of others	Refers to suspicion based on something that warrants suspicion; not a reference to an abnormal mental state

PHRASE OR TERM	COMMON USAGE	CRIMINAL'S USAGE
PERFECT (said of another person)	Refers to a person who shows the quality of excellence	Refers to a person who does everything for the criminal, who caters to him, whom he can control
PLEASURE	Satisfaction, gratification, joy	High-voltage excitement, usually through doing the forbidden
POLICE	A law-enforcement officer	Any person who checks up on the criminal and holds him accountable; could be teacher, parent, etc.
PRIDE	Positive sense: justifiable pleasure in accomplishment, self-respect. Negative sense: conceit	Notion of being better than others; refusing to yield to another person; the idea that, if one does not maintain his superior position, he is nothing
PROBLEM	An unsettled issue; an unresolved dilemma in living emanating from either external or internal forces	A jam in which the criminal has been apprehended and held accountable or a situation in which he is barred from a criminal objective
RESPECT	To hold in high esteem	To believe (a person)
RIGHT OR WRONG	According or not according to a moral standard	"Right for me at the time"; no reference to moral standard, but according to what serves the criminal's interest best at the time
SELF-PRESERVATION	Staying out of harm's way and alive	Often refers to preservation of criminal's chosen way of life
SQUARE (with reference to a person)	Someone who is conventional, conforming	Someone who is stupid; refers to the stupidity of living responsibly
STUPID	Dull-witted; lacking in intelligence; sometimes synonymous with "foolish"	Refers to failure of plans to work out, so that the criminal was caught and held accountable

PHRASE OR TERM	COMMON USAGE	CRIMINAL'S USAGE
SUCCEED	To turn out well, to achieve an objective, however modest	Refers to conquest; making a big splash, having a huge impact
TASTE	Sample or small amount	Refers to imbibing, which may be a large amount—e.g., up to a fifth of liquor
TRUST	Reliance on ability, character, or strength	Refers to control; criminal "trusts" whomever he can control, a person who will not oppose him and who will not "snitch" or inform
TRUTH	Veracity, full presentation of facts	Relating of enough of what happened to satisfy another person while leaving a lot or most unsaid
(TO BE) VIOLATED	To be harmed, to have one's rights interfered with	To have one's criminal way of life interfered with
WEAK	Feeble, frail, fragile, infirm	"Sissy," "lame," lacking guts to do the forbidden

BIBLIOGRAPHY

Cleckley, Hervey. *The Mask of Sanity*. (4th edit.) St. Louis: C. V. Mosby, 1964.

Cudrin, Jay M. "Self-Concepts of Prison Inmates," *Journal of Religion and Health*, 1970, *9*, 60-70.

Dember, William N. *Psychology of Perception*. New York: Holt, Rinehart and Winston, 1963.

Goldfarb, Ronald L. "Voices from Inside the Prisons," *The Washington Post (Potomac)*, November 21, 1971, pp. 16ff.

"Racism and Mental Health: Pursuing Truths," *The Washington Post*, May 20, 1971, p. H1.

Thorne, Frederick C. "The Etiology of Sociopathic Reactions," *American Journal of Psychotherapy*, 1959, *13*, 319-330.

Chapter 9

The Work in Perspective

WHEN THIS STUDY began fourteen years ago, we were aware that whatever knowledge society had about the criminal had not been applied successfully to changing him. Our objective has been to learn about the criminal's thinking and action patterns and to utilize that knowledge effectively in the change process. We have had the advantage of retaining privileged communication in a hospital setting, being well-versed in eclectic approaches, and not being bound by a diagnosis.

We began with criminals found not guilty by reason of insanity at Saint Elizabeths Hospital, but gradually expanded the population to study (just as intensively) criminals not confined at that institution. Criminals do not willingly give themselves up to an invasion of their thinking processes. However, questionnaires, statistical studies, and routine examinations have proved futile in acquiring valid information. To study the criminal in depth, we had to offer him the opportunity for "therapy," which he wanted because he thought that it might be conducive to an earlier release from confinement or from the court's jurisdiction. Thus we began our study of criminals, realizing that they were not interested in change, that they scorned what we thought and did, and that they looked on us as people whom they could take in hand to achieve their purpose. During this time, we were acquiring an enormous amount of information about the thinking processes of criminals. By persistence we were able to interest some criminals in the substance of the material that we were gathering. But our efforts at treatment were failing, despite the expenditure of much energy and time.

Our period of "re-search" ended when we realized that criminal thinking and action patterns were not explained by the sociologic or psychologic molds into which the material was being forced. We saw that providing the criminal with an opportunity to present excuses diverted him and us further and further from change. In fact, the criminal is far more skillful at elaborating sociologic and psychologic material than many experts.

529

A period of "search" began when we dropped these excuses and bowed to the overwhelming evidence that the criminals were not mentally ill. The application of a mental illness diagnosis to this population was a consequence of the tortuous extension of psychologic concepts by mental health professionals. Most diagnoses of mental illness resulted from the criminal's fabrications. By his accountability statements, he misled many examiners into believing that he was mentally ill. In addition, many diagnoses of mental illness were made by examiners who simply did not understand the situation.

We also had to deal with the emotional aspects of the criminal's experience. Neither emotional insight nor catharsis helped in the change process, because the criminal resorted to feelings to justify any heinous crime or irresponsibility. We studied the thinking processes concurrent with feelings, as well as those operative when there was no noteworthy emotional state. For the criminal, a crime or any other act is the consequence of thinking processes. The more we understood what those processes were, the clearer it became that crimes do not occur out of impulse, compulsion, or passion.

This volume has presented a detailed description of the criminal's thinking patterns from the point of view of their being erroneous. Of course, the criminal does not regard them as erroneous, but society does with respect to responsible living.

Procedural alterations were made as we learned more about the criminal's thinking processes. The data, derived phenomenologically, reflected the importance of choice and will. The enterprise of altering thinking processes, when successful, invariably led to the criminal's leading a moral life. To describe this process of change is the major objective of Volume 2. In addition, we shall present a critique of one of the better-regarded institutions for treating the criminal and offer a proposal for a way of achieving successful results that is more effective than current methods. We have achieved such results in criminals whom we followed for more than ten years. To have written Volume 1 without Volume 2 would have been only to engage in an academic enterprise for the classroom. The concepts in Volume 1 are validated by the results achieved in the change process described in Volume 2.

We have reserved discussing the drug-using criminal until Volume 3, where the focus is not on drugs, but on his personality. However, Volume 1's description of the structural components of the criminal personality also applies to the criminal drug-user. The procedures for change described in Volume 2 are also applied to him, with some minor modifications.

Index